Religion in Sociological Perspective

The Dorsey Series in Sociology

Consulting Editor
Charles M. Bonjean
The University of Texas at Austin

Religion in Sociological Perspective

Keith A. Roberts
Bowling Green State University,
Firelands College

Department of Religious Studies
Moore Reading Room
University of Kansas

1984

THE DORSEY PRESS
Homewood, Illinois 60430

RELIGION AND SOCIOLOGY

ISBN 0-256-03127-4

Library of Congress Catalog Card No. 83–71605

Printed in the United States of America

1 2 3 4 5 6 7 8 9 0 K 1 0 9 8 7 6 5 4

Dedication:

To my mother, Elizabeth W. Roberts, who first gave me a sense of the importance of religion in life and who encouraged a rigorous application of reason and empiricism to religion; and to my wife, Judy, whose constant support, advice, and understanding has made this book possible.

Preface

This book is designed as a concise introduction to the sociology of religion. My intent has been to present and illustrate the basic theories sociologists use to understand the social dimensions of religion. I seek first and foremost to help students understand the *perspective* from which sociologists view religion. By the time students have finished this book, they should understand the central theories and methods of research in the sociology of religion, and they should have an idea of how to apply these analytical tools to new groups they encounter. The goal of this text is to be *illustrative* rather than all-encompassing.

I have written this volume so that it will be comprehensible to the general public, but I have assumed that the primary audience will be students in courses on "Religion and Society" or "The Sociology of Religion." Insofar as it is adopted as a text, I have assumed that it will be complemented with monographs or anthologies that explore the specific groups or specific processes the instructor chooses to emphasize. That is one reason I have worked to keep the text relatively short. I have also anticipated that my primary audience will be seminary students and undergraduates—especially at colleges and universities that emphasize the liberal arts "general education" function. I have asked open-ended questions which challenge students to think about their own values and perspectives, as well as requiring them to think about sociological methods and theories. I have also student-tested each chapter for readability and clarity among nonsociologists and added diagrams to aid in comprehension. In short, I have assumed that readers have no sociology background beyond perhaps an introductory course. (Having co-taught a "Religion and Society" course at a seminary, I am aware that some students take sociology of religion courses with no sociology background.)

The theoretical perspective of this book is eclectic. I seek to help students recognize the contributions of various theoretical perspectives and the blindspots of each. Conflict and functional theories are used throughout the text, but discussion of specific processes includes a wide range of other theories. These range from phenomenology and cognitive structuralism to symbolic interactionism. I have also tried to provide students with an understanding of the relationship between research methods and findings. (Often as sociologists we don't deal with methodological issues until the "methods course" for majors.) Without belaboring the issue of methods, I have attempted to make students aware of these issues and have purposefully reported studies which use each type of research methodology.

In writing this text I have been careful to use sex-inclusive language. However, an author faces a dilemma when quoting those who wrote at a time when this was not a consideration. In most cases, I have modified the language of those I cited so that the text is consistent and avoids nouns and pronouns that seem to exclude women. However, in a few cases, such changes would have involved such convoluted sentence structure and such awkward phrasing that I left the passages intact.

The opening chapter of this text introduces the sociological perspective including its assumptions, its methods of investigation, and its limitations. The second chapter explores the definition of religion and suggests ways in which sociologists have sought to measure "religiosity." Chapter 3 involves a rather detailed introduction to functional and conflict perspectives and discusses the relationships between religion and the larger society. Chapter 4 sets forth an internal analysis of elements of religion (rituals, beliefs, symbols, mystical experiences, and world-views). This includes a discussion of the integration of these elements and the conflict between them. The fifth chapter investigates the processes of conversion and commitment, focusing rather substantially on recent studies of religious cults and the commitment of their devotees. Several models for understanding conversion and commitment are set forth. Although most students view religion as a set of values or beliefs, religion is also a set of ordered social relationships—an institution. It is to this issue that we turn in Chapter 6 as we discuss the routinization of charisma, the dilemmas of institutionalization, and the mobilization of resources. In the seventh chapter, students are provided with tools for the analysis of specific religious groups. Rather than providing a simple definition of such controversial terms as *sect* or *cult,* I have provided background on the development of these concepts and have demonstrated the various ways they have been used. I have found in my own teaching that this calls for careful discussion so that confusion does not reign, but the dividends can be rewarding. When students recognize that a single term has more than one meaning among sociologists, they learn to read monographs and other reports more discriminatingly. Chapters 8 and 9 demonstrate the complexity of the relationship between religion and society. The explicit focus of Chapter 8 is "religion and stratification," but the underlying theme is that religion can be both cause and effect of secular social processes. The topic of Chapter 9 is religion and prejudice (racial and sexual), but the underlying issue is a demonstration of the fact that religion may affect social processes in a multiplicity of ways. In fact, religion may simultaneously contribute to *and* combat a particular attitude or social process. For example, while some religious beliefs may combat prejudice, religious institutional structures and religious reference groups may contribute to it. Chapter 10 is devoted to a discussion of contemporary religious trends, including substantial discussion of "invisible" forms of religion and civil religiosity.

There is substantial value to texts which have interchangeable chapters, for they allow the instructor flexibility in designing the course. What a text gains in flexibility, however, it often loses in cumulative application of theory. While it is possible to vary the order of the chapters in this text, the text is designed to be cumulative. Each chapter is more complex in its analysis than the one before, and each succeeding chapter attempts to stretch students to greater levels of analytical sophistication. If an instructor does choose to use these chapters in a different sequence, I recommend that the first three chapters be covered first as a foundation, with other chapters altered as one wishes. In any case, the section on structuralism in Chapter 5 should be covered prior to reading Chapter 9. Instructors might also be alert to the fact that Chapters 4 and 5 utilize somewhat more functional theory, while Chapters 8 and 9 expose students to relatively more conflict theory.

While only one name goes on the book cover, a project of this nature is enriched by the labors and support of many people. I would like to thank the Bowling Green Faculty Research Committee for support in researching Chapter 9. I am deeply appreciative of the assistance offered by librarians of Bowling Green State University and especially that provided by Will Currie, Sherry Gray, and June Coughlin. I am also indebted to Katy Heyman for assistance in the library. Earlier drafts of this work have benefitted from the critical reading of Elizabeth Roberts, Linda Luck, and a number of students in my sociology of religion classes who have read selected chapters and offered specific feedback on readability and clarity. My reviewers deserve special comment for their incisive analysis, their helpful criticism, and their encouragement in this project. These reviewers were Richard Malchalek, Edgar W. Mills, Jr., Perry McWilliams, James D. Davidson, John S. Staley, and Chuck Bonjean. While all of these persons have contributed to the finished product, they are certainly not responsible for its flaws.

Finally, I must express my appreciation to my wife Judy and to my family. Judy has been enormously supportive, has typed several drafts of the manuscript, and has offered helpful comment and criticism. My three children have contributed in two ways: through their ability to provide delightful interludes away from the intensity of the project and through their patience on all those occasions when Daddy was at the typewriter rather than at the beach or playing ball.

Keith A. Roberts

Contents

A Scientific Perspective on Religion

At social affairs where a congenial atmosphere is desired, the social norm demands that two topics be avoided: religion and politics. These are topics about which many people have strong feelings and on which they are often not open to alternative views. In fact, a highly respected sociologist once said of religion: "There are few major subjects about which people know so little, yet feel so certain" (Yinger 1970:2). This seems to be true of both those who are sympathetic to religion and those who are hostile toward it. Yet, it is precisely this topic which we will be exploring in this book. Hence, at the outset of this study I would suggest two characteristics or attitudes which will be particularly helpful in approaching our topic of investigation: a healthy dose of humility and a corresponding openness to new ideas. No one has all the answers on religious behavior, but by listening to one another, we can each broaden our understandings.

In this text, I will be presenting the sociological perspective on religion and explaining some of that discipline's findings and theories. Sociology does not offer the whole truth any more than any other discipline or perspective, but it does offer insights that can be helpful to those interested in religion—whether they be believers or skeptics. My point is that we seek understanding here; a posture of defensiveness—with each person seeking only to preserve his or her own preconceived notions—is counterproductive. We seek neither to dissuade believers from their faith nor to convince skeptics of the efficacy of religion. Our goal is to gain a new perspective on religious behavior and thereby to expand our comprehension of religion.

Sociology offers only one of many possible vantage points from which to view religion. Perhaps an analogy would be helpful in clarifying the point.

Many people may interact with the same child and yet have quite different perspectives and understandings of that child. An artist may try to encapsulate the child's charm by focusing on his or her unique physical properties, such as facial features, body proportions, and shades of coloration in the eyes, skin, and hair. A doctor is interested in the physiological needs of the child and the requirements for good health—concentrating on such characteristics as height and weight, immunizations, and the family's history of congenital diseases. A developmental psychologist may study the child not because of an interest in the characteristics of this child but as part of a broader investigation of childhood development. This child is one case out of which a general theory of childhood maturation is sought.

Parents, of course, are interested in the uniqueness and specialness of this *particular* child. Their concern is not one of detached analysis, for the emotional attachment to the child changes the perception. As the persons responsible for the child's social and emotional development, they try to be concerned about the child's overall welfare. But because they are so close to the child, some important patterns of behavior may go unnoticed. The findings of each of the previous observers may be of interest to the parents as they come to a fuller appreciation of their child and a better understanding of their parental responsibilities. Of course, too, the child is a unique self-experiencing individual with his or her own self-understanding.

It would be foolish to ask which of these persons has the "true" understanding of the child. No one perspective is total and complete. In fact, the insights of the psychologist may influence the socialization practices of the parent, or the prescription of the doctor (for example, that the child needs to wear a back brace) may affect the child's behavior and experiences. In each case, the "objective" view of an outsider may differ from that of the parent or of the child, and it may lead to changes. But in the long run, those changes may be a good thing.

Just as people from many fields may have unique perspectives on a child—none of which contains the whole truth about that child—so also can religion be understood from many angles. The psychologist analyzes religious experience as a mental and emotional experience of the individual. The concern is not with religion as ideas or beliefs which may hold eternal truth but with the effect of religion on the human psyche. The philosopher of religion approaches the subject by comparing, contrasting, and analyzing beliefs of various faiths, focusing on the ideas of life, death, suffering, and injustice among the many religions of the world. The systematic theologian formulates doctrines about God and about God's relationship to the universe and to humanity to place what is believed about God (in a particular tradition) into a logically comprehensive and coherent framework. The religious ethicist attempts to define moral responsibility of religious persons, or at least to clarify moral discourse and identify moral dilemmas for members of a faith. The faithful follower understands his or her religion through yet another lens—that of personal commitment. The person's faith is viewed as a source of ultimate truth and personal fulfillment. Members of the clergy also view religion from a vantage point as committed followers, but they are also leaders who constantly seek understanding of religious processes so they can be more effective in guiding others. Hence, they may use the insights of the social scientist, the philosopher, the theologian, and the ethicist in order to understand more fully both their faith and their leadership responsibilities. The sociologist, as we shall see, offers a unique perspective which differs from these others and which can contribute to a holistic understanding of this multidimensional phenomenon we call religion.

The Sociological Perspective

The sociological approach focuses on religious groups and institutions (their formation, maintenance, and demise), on the behavior of individuals within those groups (social processes which affect conversion, ritual behavior), and on conflicts between religious groups (Catholic versus Protestant, Christian versus Moslem, mainline denomination versus cult). For the sociologist, beliefs are only one small part of religion.

In modern industrial society, religion is both a set of ideas (values, beliefs) and an institution (a set of social relationships). We will be looking at both in order to understand how they affect human behavior. We will investigate differences in beliefs not because we expect to prove their truth or falsehood, but because beliefs—regardless of their ultimate veracity—can influence how people behave and how they understand the world. Religious institutions, however, can also affect behavior quite independently of beliefs. In fact, religious institutions sometimes entice people to behave contrary to the official belief system of that religion.

Later in this book we will discuss the fact that religious organizations may contribute to racism and combat it at the same time. While the *belief systems* of most mainline denominations proclaim prejudice to be wrong, the institutional *structures* of the church unwittingly permit it—and sometimes even foster it. Furthermore, religious beliefs themselves can have contradictory effects. While some Christian teachings have maintained that antipathy against others is always wrong, certain other beliefs have contributed—often unconsciously and unintentionally—to racial prejudice, sex bias, and anti-Semitism. Many readers probably did not know, for example, that some 1st-century Christians believed that women were incapable of being saved—unless they were first transformed into men. These Gnostic Christians reinforced the accepted cultural view of that time that women are defective human beings. We will also find in this book that between A.D. 1400 and 1700, the Christian churches (both Protestant and Catholic) were involved in burning between 500,000 and 1 million women as witches. In fact, two towns in Europe in the late 1500s were left with only one female inhabitant each (discussed in Chapter 9). But this massive gynocide[1] was due much less to religious beliefs than to changing sex roles in the society. Secular conflicts (over the proper role of men and women) were expressed in "religious" activities (burning witches as infidels). Religious behavior can be either a cause or an effect of other social processes.

In short, there are many ways in which religious groups, religious values, and secular social processes can be interrelated. Beliefs are not always at the heart of religious behavior. Social scientists have found that persons sometimes become committed to new religious groups with little knowledge of the group's beliefs. They become committed through group pressures and social processes (to be discussed in Chapter 5). Sociologists are convinced that knowing what a group believes provides insights only into one small part of this complex phenomenon we call religion. For a fuller understanding, one must comprehend the social processes as well.

Most Americans believe that the central differences between religious groups have to do with their beliefs, but there are many interesting and important variations in style of worship, authority structures, and psychological appeal of religious groups. The short descriptions in Exhibit 1–1 of three religious services illustrate some of the range of diversity.

Sociology, then, focuses on the *social* dimensions of religion—and on those aspects of religion affecting social behavior. Like the developmental psychologist who studies the child to discover the stages of personality development in all children, we will be looking for the common patterns—the general rules—rather than for unique characteristics of each religion. When we do look at unique characteristics, it is to find how those characteristics affect behavior in special ways.

This sociological perspective is characterized by two fundamental principles: reliance on empirical data and objectivity. By reliance on empirical data, the sociologist considers only data that are observable through the

---

[1] Genocide is the annihilation or attempted annihilation of an entire people (such as the Nazi holocaust in Germany). Gynocide (*gyno* meaning women) is the attempted annihilation of the female sex.

Exhibit 1–1

Religion in America Varies in Content, in Style, and in Appeal

Religion is a diverse and multifaceted phenomenon. We can gain some insight into the diversity of American religion simply by observing the religious services of various religious groups. Religion can be big business, or it can be a small group experience. It can appeal to emotions, to intellect, or to tradition. It may be geared to an authority figure, may encourage individual autonomy and independence, or may stress corporate responsibility and social action. The worship experience may be designed to create a mood of awe and of quiet meditation, or it may be devised to stimulate critical thinking and motivation to join a protest movement.

The following descriptions by William Martin allow us to vicariously attend three very different worship services in the heart of Texas. The first is that of a growing, evangelical Baptist church where thousands take the leap of faith. The second is a liberal Unitarian congregation where members look (and analyze) before they leap. The third description is of Yom Kippur services in a Reformed Jewish temple, where tradition and social responsibility are blended. These glimpses into American religiosity suggest considerable variation, yet these include only a small segment of the entire range. They represent only the more conventional expressions of religiosity in the United States.

Readers may find it instructive to list the various ways in which these religious groups differ in content, style, appeal, and source of authority.

First Baptist [Appeal to the Heart]

"This place in the eye of God is more favored than any other. It is from here, from our dear church, that we are all going to heaven." He knows his words are hyperbolic. He also knows he can get away with them, because he is Wallie Amos Criswell, pastor for 35 years of the First Baptist Church in Dallas, largest in its denomination and the apotheosis of Texas religion.

First Baptist has over 20,000 members, a weekly budget of approximately $135,000, buildings and parking lots that sprawl over five city blocks, a staff of 256, a library of 30,000 volumes, and recreation facilities that include two gymnasia, a skating rink, bowling lanes, racquetball courts, Nautilus equipment, and a sauna. Among its dozens of programs are 21 choirs, 11 mission centers, an academy with a kindergarten-through-12th-grade enrollment of over 600, the Criswell Center for Biblical Studies with over 275 students pursuing two degrees of religious certitude, an FM radio station, and a Fellowship of Christian Truckers whose members minister at truck stops and terminals in Dallas County. First Baptist also produces one of the more notable worship services this side of the 19th century.

I knew the church had a 70-piece orchestra and a 175-voice choir, but I was not prepared for the processional. In a maneuver that is repeated each week, the musicians strolled casually to their places, picking up the strains of "On Jordan's Stormy Banks" as they settled in. Then, as I wondered why they hadn't coordinated things more smoothly, the orchestra was suddenly in place and a steady stream of tan-robed singers poured through four doors and the tympani pounded the cadence and the volume and intensity mounted so that when they reached the refrain—"I'm bound for the promised land"—I felt a tingle and an urge to shout, "Wait for me! I'm coming, too!"

Exhibit 1–1 *(continued)*

Our spirits thus lifted and charged, we prayed and sang awhile ourselves before hearing Diane Daniels, a stunning young woman with a beautiful voice and professional stage manner, sing "Come, Ye Sinners."

In the fullness of time, the announcements ended, and W. A. Criswell loomed into the pulpit. . . . Resplendent in a ceremonial white suit, with his deep-set eyes sparkling out of a broad face crowned with wavy white hair, Criswell looked like Nelson Rockefeller playing William Jennings Bryan in a fundamentalist pageant. . . . The world is groping for answers, he said; the politicians, the economists, the great literary men have failed to provide them, but there is an Answer and He's coming soon, "to take us in triumph and victory back to heaven [where] there'll be no more funeral processions down those golden streets. . . . Criswell speaks in a compelling measured rhythm, bobbing slightly on key words and punctuating his declarations by drawing down his hand in a controlled tremble, . . . He expands words like "God" and "glory" and "maaarvelous" and fills them with a sonorous vibrato that makes them more than they might have been if left to themselves, and he rolls out phrases like "through the centuries and the ages and the eons" just to revel in their rhetorical rumble. . . . Criswell made no effort to argue the truth of his sermon, but rested content simply to preach it with authority.

*   *   *   *   *

There is, no doubt, some lukewarmness in the veins of First Baptist's body, but it is unquestionably a thriving, vital enterprise, "a going church for a coming Lord.". . . Churches that proclaim, without apology or hesitation, that "*this* is the way, the truth and the life" are growing. . . . Sheep seek direction, not a philosophical discussion of alternative paths, and Pastor Criswell stands ever ready to point the way.

Emerson Unitarian [Appeal to the Mind]

In sharp contrast to the weathered stone or freshly painted white clapboard of the picturesque old Unitarian churches in New England, Emerson Unitarian in Houston is a new adobe-colored box that reminded me of a pueblo with a pipe organ. Large side windows, however, let in a great deal of morning light and produce a much airier quality than seems possible from the outside. The small, functional foyer contains a needlepoint sampler of Emersonian scripture—"Nothing is at last sacred but the integrity of your own mind"—and a framed scrap of inconsequential correspondence that serves as a relic from the Concord saint's own hand. On the morning I visited, the foyer also contained the church's minister, Dr. J. Frank Schulman, who not only greeted me warmly but took time to ask if I had ever been to a Unitarian church before and to offer to respond to any questions I might have about Unitarianism. A few days later, he followed this up with a cordial letter that touched on points in our conversation and reaffirmed his offer of assistance. As I entered the sanctuary, I was met by Jack Leatherman, a large, garrulous man who has been lavishly anointed with the spiritual gift of ushering. He commented on what a lovely Sunday morning it was, generously offered me a wide range of seats, suggested one that was "very quiet and peaceful," and encouraged me to attend the soup-and-sandwich luncheon immediately after the service.

Since Unitarianism is nothing if not ecumenical, I was not surprised to see a

Exhibit 1-1 *(continued)*

pulpit cloth bearing the symbols of the world's great religions clustered above a single flame that symbolized their essential unity . . . In good Unitarian fashion, the readings included a passage from the apocryphal book of Ecclesiasticus and a reflection on primitive religion by anthropologist Sir James Frazer. Overall, the service was well conceived and well integrated, with a skillful and pleasing interweaving not only of major components but of the internal segments of prayers and choral responses as well. When Schulman mentioned in the course of his sermon that he did not like a sloppy worship service, the knowing chuckles in the congregation led me to believe that the order and precision of the liturgy probably bore his strong imprint.

Schulman spoke on "Religion as an Intellectual Process." His education at the Harvard and University of Chicago divinity schools shone through in a presentation solidly grounded in history, philosophy, and theology and characterized by notable literary style and grace. He chastised fundamentalists for their inattention to the intellectual dimension of religion and affirmed that nothing is so cherished by Unitarians as the search for truth. Religion, he said, is a reaching for something beyond ourselves—"Call it God, call it the Spirit of the Universe, call it the Oversoul." It is not enough simply to do good; we must also *understand* and know what we want to accomplish if we are not to drift aimlessly. . . . [T]heologians have prepared us well to seek new answers to the enduring problems of religion, and if we will build upon rather than discard their traditions, we can erect theological constructs that will be adequate to our needs and times. The task, he insisted, is imperative: "We must not let the ranks of society close about us so that religion is shut outside."

Schulman's message, of course, was designed for people who have surrendered or never possessed the "blessed assurance" claimed by evangelical Christians. The modest crowd may indicate that such an appeal is limited in a city and state dominated by true believers. But for those who no longer find traditional theology plausible, [Emerson Unitarian provides a context] for pursuing religious questions in an intellectually responsible and systematic fashion . . .

Temple Emanu-El [Appeal to Conscience and to Tradition]

The Day of Atonement—Yom Kippur—has long seemed to me the most intriging of Jewish ceremonials. In biblical times it was the . . . day on which the sins of the Israelites were symbolically transferred onto the head of a scapegoat, which was then led into the wilderness. In October, at Temple Emanu-El in Dallas, [an] enormous crowd flocked to duplicate services, arriving an hour early to get good seats. No goat was set loose on Hillcrest Road, but the High Holy Day still provides ample opportunity to contemplate both commission and release of one's sins. . . .

Yom Kippur is a solemn occasion observed by 24 hours of fasting and several separate services.

* * * * *

Again and again, we read and were reminded by the rabbi and the choir that a multitude of sins separate us from God and His law and from one another. We confessed sins committed under stress or through choice, openly or in secret, in stubbornness or in error. We acknowledged that we had abused power, profaned God's name, shown disrespect toward parents and teachers, exploited and dealt

Exhibit 1–1 (concluded)

treacherously with our neighbors, been selfish when we should have been self-sacrificing, harsh when we should have been gentle, hard when we should have been kind, thoughtless when we should have been considerate, heedless of our better natures, and open to inclinations to swerve from the paths of purity and right. I soon began to wish we would come to the part about not making graven images, since that is one I have absolutely never committed, even in my heart. It was reassuring to be reminded, also repeatedly, that "the gates of repentance are always open" and that reconciliation with God is always a possibility.

In his sermon for the evening service, Rabbi Jack Bemporad inaugurated the season of repentance by focusing on Big Sin: nuclear war. . . . Buttressed with quotations from the Dalai Lama and Pope John XXIII, Bemporad cited the prophet Hosea, who warned that trust in weaponry is a false hope, a form of idolatry that places ultimate trust in that which is inherently limited and partial, and thus it violates the first of the great commandments. The impulse to power, long the basic sin of humanity, separates us from wisdom, love, compassion, and understanding, and lies at the heart of war. We have survived its evil in the past, he said, because we lacked the capacity to do the worst; now, with nuclear weapons. . . .

Peace is no longer a luxury, the rabbi insisted, but a necessity. We must recognize that the people on the other side are as human as we, are also made in God's image. . . . We must recognize, too, that God does not desire the death of His children but wills that all should repent and live, beating their swords into plowshares and studying war no more. . . .

The services on the following day maintained the serious tone of the first, with many similar or identical readings and extensive musical responses by an excellent choir and soloists, who sang in both Hebrew and English. . . . An afternoon service memorialized departed members and relatives of members of the congregation. . . . A concluding late-afternoon service extended assurance to worshipers that the forgiveness they sought had been granted. The Shema ("Hear, O Israel! The Lord our God, the Lord is One!") was proclaimed, the shofar (ram's horn) was sounded, and we were told that God had made our sins to vanish like a cloud and our transgressions to disappear like a mist. . . .

I was a bit hungry, a bit tired, and a bit sorry I had sat in a folding chair. I was also more than a little reflective over having been reminded of my shortcomings for the better part of a day. . . . Though fully aware I would inevitably fall short, I truly resolved to do better, not only that what remains of life might be fuller and richer but that from my grave, as the prayer book says, "may spread not the barren thistle but the fragrant myrtle, a blessed memory redounding to God's honor and glory."

Source: William Martin, Texas Monthly, September 1979, pp. 260–266, December 1981, pp. 218–224. Used by permission.

five senses. This limits sociological insight since sociology does not utilize reports of supernatural influence—except to investigate how such reports influence the subsequent behavior of informants. But the limitation of data to only empirical data is also a strength. The sociologist deals in facts that can be measured, observed, and tested. If a sociologist claims that belief *x* causes behavior *y*, empirical studies can be set up and data gathered to support or refute the hypothesis. If politicians and members of the public believe that devotees of religious cults are more likely than nondevotees to be mentally unstable, that hypothesis can be substantiated or disproven through empirical investigation. If members of certain religious groups or persons with particular religious beliefs are thought to be more racially prejudiced than others, only empirical investigation can establish the veracity of that claim. The sociologist is not satisfied with general impressions but seeks concrete, verifiable data to prove or disprove any generalization.

The sociologist also tries to be objective. Objectivity does not mean that the sociologist claims to be above error or to have the whole truth; we have already pointed out that no discipline can claim omniscience. Objectivity means that the sociologist tries to prevent personal beliefs about religion from entering the study. The social scientist is committed to the search for truth wherever that search leads. Although sociologists as private citizens have preferences and commitments, they seek to be open to the data and to avoid prejudgment of any particular group or any particular religious process. A sociologist may not agree with the views of a group being studied but makes every effort to understand the group on its own terms and to avoid bias in interpreting the processes of the group. For example, the charge by many people that religious cults engage in brainwashing is primarily an attempt to discredit those groups. The charge is based on hostility toward the groups and preconceived notions about what they do to recruit members. Sociologists—even if they do not agree with the activities of the group in question—try to base their judgments only on the data in front of them.

Sociologists seek objectivity as a rule of behavior in exercising their discipline. But this objectivity is not always easy to achieve. A sociologist who is active in a church or is otherwise a "believer" is perhaps more likely to be sympathetic to "believers" than is a sociologist who is a committed atheist. The difference is subtle, but the researcher who is personally active or is a believer is less likely to view religious behavior as irrational. In this case your author is an active church member[2] but one who is sometimes skeptical of religious claims and who remains open to persons with perspectives quite different from his own. Along with Andrew Greeley (1972:3), I am convinced that being an insider has provided me with insights into religious behavior and religious organizations which I would not otherwise

---

[2] I have a theological education (Boston University School of Theology) and was ordained in the United Methodist Church. However, my denominational affiliation has varied depending upon the theology, style of liturgy, church programming, and social involvements of the local congregations where I have lived. I have been active in United Methodist and United Church of Christ congregations in the past, and I am currently an elder in the United Presbyterian Church.

have gained. However, like any other set of experiences, this personal commitment may unconsciously affect my perspectives on religion. Readers may want to keep in mind that the author has sympathy for religion. However, my unabashed commitment to the scientific method also requires that I report the data accurately—even when it is an acute embarrassment to those of us who are believers.[3] The important point here is that the first step toward objectivity is to identify as clearly and thoroughly as possible any feelings and biases one might have about the object of inquiry. This is not a simple matter of declaring one's group memberships. It involves an ongoing soul-searching into previously unrecognized feelings and biases and a constant effort to understand each group on its own terms.

Resistance to the Scientific Study of Religion

Many religious people are highly suspicious of any scientific study of religion. The attitude of constant critical thinking and seeking empirical evidence of causality seems contrary to the utter trust faith requires. Hence, sociological analysis of religion is viewed as a threat to pure faith. Indeed, the sociological method does discover patterns that are sometimes unsettling to the faithful, and sociological theories sometimes offer interpretations of causality that challenge the believer's concept of "revelation." Although the ability to combine the posture of scientist and worshiper is sometimes difficult to maintain, it is possible. I have personally found that the scientific study of religion can be beneficial in that it forces one to be rigorous in the search for truth and demands logical coherence in the articulation of faith.[4] Of course, it cannot be proven that the scientific study of religion is always beneficial, but I would contend that the maintenance of ignorance about the social characteristics of one's religion—and the continuance of unconscious social patterns that are undesirable—is harmful in the long run. Knowledge is sometimes threatening, but ignorance is even more dangerous. For this reason, I am convinced that believers as well as nonbelievers can benefit from a scientific investigation of religion.

On the other side of things, some nonbelievers (especially in the scientific community) insist that religion is not worth studying because it is of so little consequence. They maintain that religion has little effect on human behavior. Social class is usually identified as the most important influence on social attitudes and behavior. However, Gerhard Lenski (1963:326) found in a Detroit study that of 35 variables studied, socioreligious group was slightly more important in affecting social attitudes than was social

---

[3] Not only am I an active church member; I am a white, middle-class male. While I shall strive to avoid any ethnic, sexual, or class bias, those who are sensitive to unconscious sources of bias may want to be cognizant of this background.

[4] These are qualities which I value in science or in faith.

class—both in potency and in range of influence. Religion was the most important single variable in predicting the social attitudes of respondents. Of course, religion was in some cases a cause, in some an effect, and in still others a noncausal correlate.[5] However, when other variables were controlled, religion still proved to be a significant factor in shaping the attitudes of people on a large number of issues.

Other studies have also shown religion to be an important determiner of social values and perspectives, but it is not always the same elements of religiosity which are significant. In some cases there are significant differences between members of different denominations. In other cases denominational affiliation is relatively insignificant, but social behaviors are correlated with theological orientation (fundamental, conservative, or liberal) or with level of devotionalism (frequency of personal prayer). In still other cases the extent of participation in the life of the church is the critical variable (including attendance at worship services and/or involvement in informal church friendship networks). Various dimensions of religiosity have been found to be significantly related to such diverse factors as racism and anti-Semitism, attitudes toward divorce and birth control, likelihood of completing a college education, inclination to support the idea of a welfare state, enjoyment of one's occupation, engagement in installment buying, tendency to vote Republican or Democratic, conviction that alcohol consumption is immoral, and likelihood of supporting traditional sex roles in society. Religion is related to larger social attitudes and values, but sometimes in rather complex ways. In this study, we will explore both external social effects of religion and internal social processes of religious groups which allow some to survive while others die. It is my conviction that the social processes of religion *are* important—or else I would not be writing this book. Furthermore, it is my assumption that readers find the social dimensions of religion worth investigating—or else they would not be reading this book.

Sociological Methods of Studying Religion

The sociologist of religion claims to use scientific methods. It is appropriate, therefore, to discuss the methods by which sociologists gather their data. Essentially, the methods they use to study religion are the same as those employed in investigating other social processes—historical material, cross-cultural comparative analysis, controlled experimentation, observational studies, sample surveys, and content analysis. The methods used in any

---

[5] A correlation is a regular, recurrent association between variables. Such recurrent associations may be due to a causal relationship (one variable causes the other), but not all correlations are causal ones. Noncausal correlations may be due to pure coincidence or to the fact that both variables are related to a third variable which has caused them both.

given situation are determined by the nature of the topic under investigation and by the predilection of the researcher. However, religion as a topic of study occasionally presents special problems.

Historical Analysis

Some sociologists have used historical data to look for patterns of interaction between religion and society. When sociologists use historical material, however, they tend to have a different emphasis than historians. Historians normally seek to offer a detailed description of historical situations and perhaps to elaborate the specific circumstances that seemed to have caused, or resulted from, a particular set of events. Sociologists are likely to be interested in whether a particular social situation is usually accompanied by or followed by some other "typical" situation or circumstances (Nottingham 1971). The sociologist is normally looking for a pattern—a general rule—in the relationship between social events and religious characteristics. The goal is to develop a generalization or theory that explains the relationship—not just in that particular circumstance but in most cases. This approach has led to the development of theories about the evolution of religion and to the development of typologies of religious groups (see discussion of Weber and Troeltsch's church/sect typology in Chapter 7). Historical analysis has been employed by Parsons (1964) and Bellah (1970c) in explaining the evolution of religion (discussed in Chapter 4), by Berger (1967) in describing the decline of religion in modern society (also discussed in Chapter 4), by Weber (1958) in suggesting that Protestant theology contributed to the rise of capitalism and to the affluence of Protestant Christians (see Chapter 8), and by Ruether (1974, 1975) and Nelson (1975) in exploring religious sexism (see Chapter 9). Historical analysis has been useful, but the danger is a tendency to impose one's own pattern on the data and thereby to distort history. The goal of this method is to recognize and uncover historical patterns that are relevant today, but a nonbiased execution of this method is far from simple to accomplish.

Cross-Cultural Analysis

Another method that can be extremely useful, but which is open to similar hazards of subjectivity, is cross-cultural analysis. By comparing socioreligious patterns in several cultures, sociologists can get some idea of whether a correlation is due to specific characteristics of one culture or holds for all sociocultural conditions. Weber tried to test his theory about the relationship between the Protestant ethic and the rise of capitalism by studying religion and economics in India and China. A pattern which supported his hypothesis would not prove its veracity, but contradictory evidence would serve to undermine it. He viewed the lack of negative evidence as support for his theory. Talmon used cross-cultural data to discover universal patterns among millenarian movements—religious movements in which the end of the world or a new era of existence is anticipated in the near future (see Chapter 8). Other scholars have used cross-cultural comparisons to demonstrate a correlation between religious beliefs in female sexual pollution and changing sex roles in the larger society. Furthermore, cross-cultural data have been used to support the thesis that religious witch-hunts correlate with changes in male/female relations in the larger society (see Chapter 9). One difficulty with conducting cross-cultural analyses of religion is that concepts of religiosity vary so widely from one culture to another that one can easily get caught in the trap of comparing noncomparable data. And, of course, the fact that a correlation between two variables is not universal does not negate the possibility of a causal relationship between those factors in a specific situation. Cross-cultural comparisons can be useful, but like historical analyses, they are sometimes difficult to employ with the precision that scientists prefer.

While historical analysis and cross-cultural analysis are empirical in the broadest sense of the word, the four methods which we shall discuss next are generally recognized as the primary empirical methods of sociology and allow the researcher to experience the data personally with his or her five senses.[6]

Experimentation

The most powerful tool of the social sciences in terms of ability to control variables is controlled experimentation. Experimental research in sociology has been undertaken primarily by social psychologists. But experimental research on religion—even by social psychologists—has been almost nonexistent. Obviously, one cannot use control groups and experimental groups to experiment on the factors operative in conversion to a new religious organization. (I cannot experiment on students with several techniques for converting people to the Hare Krishna.) In fact, most forms of experimentation regarding people's religiosity would be considered a gross violation of an unwritten social norm. The public would be outraged—and rightfully so. Religion is so intensely personal and so deeply felt by so many people that manipulating it for purposes of study would not be tolerated. Research ethics committees (which approve research projects) are unlikely to endorse such a study unless participants agreed to the experiment and were fully aware of its nature. But informing participants of the full nature of the research would bias the outcomes. And even if participants were to be

---

[6] Of course, anthropologists can personally experience several cultures and do cross-cultural analysis. However, most cross-cultural comparisons of religion—like historical comparisons—have been done by social scientists who use the written reports of other scientists who gathered the data.

informed, many ethics committees would balk at experimentation in this sensitive area. Thus, experimentation on religious behavior has been limited to only a few areas.

One area is with shamans and seers who claim powers of extrasensory perception (ESP) (Barnouw 1982). In this case, the individuals involved agreed to such experimentation. There are also a few other areas in which experimentation is possible—for example, in evaluating the differential effects of several different modes of religious education. In this case, many religious people are willing to have their children participate in an experiment in the hope that the findings will determine which methods are most effective for religious socialization. Other quasi-experimental designs may also be used if one allows a natural event to be the manipulator of variables. For example, Batson (1977) suggests that one could do pretests and posttests on psychological characteristics and values of people before and after a revival meeting. While such a procedure would not conform to all of the normal standards of an experiment, it could offer an important means for establishing the validity or inadequacy of certain theories regarding the effects of religious rituals and celebrations. Most people would probably not object to such tests, for the experimenter would not be attempting consciously to manipulate religion but only to measure the effectiveness of other "manipulations."

Darley and Batson (1973) also conducted a quasi experiment with seminary students in which they tried to measure effects of biblical stories on subsequent behavior. They staged a scene in which they placed a groaning, coughing sinister-looking man who was apparently in need of help in an alley through which the seminary students passed in route to where they were to deliver speeches. Some of the students had recently read the Good Samaritan story and were to speak on that parable. Others were assigned to speak on the role of theological education for nonpastoral occupations. The purpose was to see whether those who had recently read the Good Samaritan story and were to speak on it were more likely to stop and help. (They were not more likely to help—although other factors of religious orientation did affect the likelihood that the students would help.) In such experiments, the controls on variables are not as strong as in most experimental research, and that is why Batson insists they are only quasi-experimental.

Furthermore, the range of topics that can be explored with quasi-experimental methods is limited.[7] The fact remains that most research on religion must procede without this powerful tool of the social scientist. While the lack of much experimentation on religious behavior is fully understandable, it does limit the research tools available to the sociologist of religion.

---

[7] For discussion of the potential uses and limits of experimentation in the study of religion, see Batson, (1975, 1977, 1979); Darley and Batson (1973); Yeatts and Asher (1979); and Pahnke (1963).

Participant Observation

A frequently used method in studying new religious movements is participant observation. By participating in the group, a researcher can observe the behavior of people in a religious context. This can be done overtly (with subjects aware that the observer is studying them) or covertly (with subjects believing the observer is a new member). Participant observation has several advantages. First, it allows for observation of symbolic interactions between members of which the actors may be only partially aware. For this reason, observational studies are particularly popular with social psychologists who use symbolic interaction analysis.[8] Second, participant observation is useful when a researcher believes there may be a gap between what people say and what they do. Respondents may verbalize statements that express tolerance of others, yet they may unwittingly say things or behave in ways that reveal anti-Semitic attitudes. Or respondents may verbalize profound commitment to orthodox teachings of a major religion, but their everyday behavior may raise questions about how pervasive that commitment really is (see Chapter 10).

Several researchers studying religious cults have found that devotees present a front of profound commitment. But after several months, the researchers were able to get to know the devotees well and were interested to find them admit that they had serious reservations about the belief system of the cult (see the discussion in Chapter 5). This brings us to a third advantage of observational studies: they allow more authentic study of non-conformist groups that are very private and which maintain a front with the public. Obviously, no cult is going to admit to the use of brainwashing techniques in recruiting new devotees. Questionnaires and interviews with cult members will not satisfy the public that brainwashing is not occurring. Likewise, interviews only with those who leave the group will not satisfy scientists, for these persons do not represent a random sample of those who joined. It would represent only those who became dissatisfied. Moreover, apostates from any group have a tendency to "reconstruct" their experiences in ways that allow them to save face for having joined—an act they have come to view as foolish. Covert participant observation has been useful in the study of secretive cults to get accurate information about their internal social processes (see Chapter 5).

---

[8] Symbolic interactionism is one theoretical perspective of sociology—especially of social psychology. This perspective maintains that individuals do not respond to the world or to other people directly, but they place a symbolic meaning on objects and behaviors and respond to that meaning. Many times these symbolic meanings and rules of behavior are learned at a very early age and are so thoroughly assumed to be "the way things are" that they are taken for granted by the individuals involved. Clothing, eye contact, distance between people during a conversation, and gestures are examples of phenomena which are often symbolically significant in understanding a culture. These are the types of objects and behaviors which symbolic interactionists use as the basis for their analyses.

Participant observation allows the researcher to observe subtleties that would not be revealed through responses to a questionnaire or through a one-hour interview. Hence, observation is often referred to as a "qualitative" method of research. The quality of the data is rich, but it is also limited to the researcher's observations. This presents two problems with this research method. First, the data are normally limited to one case (one congregation, a single cult, clergy in one denomination). This limits the ability of the researcher to make generalizations. What is true in this one case may not be true in others. Case studies permit the researcher to go into great depth in gathering data, but breadth is thereby sacrificed. A large number of case studies is needed before generalized patterns can be identified, and then they are often specified by persons who did not have firsthand experience in each group.

A second problem is that the reported data are bound to be somewhat biased by the observer's own "filtering" system. First, not all observers are likely to notice or be interested in the same patterns. Hence, there is the issue of unconscious filtering of data. Second, what the observer chooses to write up cannot possibly include all those observations made. The researcher must consciously choose which data are relevant. This provides a second filtering of data. The same sort of filtering process occurs in all research, but in other sorts of research it is easier to identify the sources of possible bias by analyzing the nature of questions asked of informants or by checking other available data. Since it frequently happens that only one person is undertaking participant observation on a group at any one time, that observer's data are sometimes the only written record of that particular phase of a group's development. This subjective element in observational studies is a serious hazard. Nonetheless, the method has proven extremely valuable in the sociological study of religion. In fact, readers may find it enriching to do some participant observation of religious groups different from their own as they read this text. While you will not be trained in participant observation methods, you may find that your observations will provide illustrations and/or questions regarding concepts discussed in this book.

Survey Research and Statistical Analysis

Perhaps the most popular form of research design in sociology, especially in the past three decades, has been sample survey research and statistical analysis. The use of this method has also expanded recently in the sociological study of religion. The sociologist sends out questionnaires or conducts interviews with a random sample of a particular population. The more ambitious surveys undertake a sampling of the entire nation, but since such studies are very expensive, most surveys involve a smaller population base: a sampling of college students at a particular type of institution (such as state universities, private liberal arts colleges, or high prestige schools), a sampling of residents in a particular city or set of cities, or a sampling of members of a particular denomination. Respondents are asked about their religious affiliation, frequency of church attendance, frequency of personal prayer, knowledge of denominational doctrines, belief in specific religious concepts (such as life after death, existence of the Devil, infallibility of the pope on matters of faith and morals, or belief in a second coming of Jesus), and other measures of religiosity (this will be discussed more fully in Chapter 2 and demonstrated in Chapters 8 and 9). This procedure has been extraordinarily useful in demonstrating correlations of specific religious characteristics with particular social attitudes or attributes.

While historical or observational insights allow for subjectivity in interpretation of data and permit impressionistic guesses as to certain patterns and correlations,[9] survey data allow researchers to identify more precisely the correlations of religious characteristics with social attitudes and characteristics (fundamentalism with anti-Semitism, frequent church attendance with sex-role traditionalism, or denominational affiliation with social mobility and income level). In the absence of the experimental method, survey research and statistical analysis provide us with our best control of variables and most certain identification of correlations.

One difficulty is that while statistical analysis tells us on a large-scale basis which religious characteristics are correlated with which social attributes, it does not reveal very effectively which factor *causes* which. While there are ways to control for variables so that the sociologist can make educated guesses, a great deal of interpretation enters at the point of suggesting causality. The fact that the data are characterized by correlations of hundreds of answers to specific questions also means that the interpretations of the meaning of events for the respondents themselves is sometimes lost. Furthermore, the data do not demonstrate the process which an individual goes through; they are static or nonhistorical. They do not reveal, for example, the stages of progression in a conversion experience. Specifying causality requires that one determine which variable occurs first. Most survey data do not reveal this.[10]

A second difficulty is that sociologists sometimes assume that negative responses to certain questions mean that the respondent is "less religious" or "less orthodox" than other respondents. The questions frequently do not allow people to express alternative modes of religiosity and do not

---

[9] For example, impressions by church officials regarding the relative growth and decline of various denominations have been found to be in error by large-scale statistical analyses in which critical variables were controlled.

[10] Clearly, the problem of inferring causality is not unique to survey types of research. This is an issue in all research, but any static or nonhistorical method faces special problems—for the order in which variables occur is difficult to establish. Nonetheless, ingenius research designs and modes of analysis have helped to compensate for this potential problem.

account for the fact that what is orthodox in one denomination may be unorthodox in another. The presuppositions of the researcher (the filtering processes) are sometimes at work in formulating and interpreting the questions. The critical point in this type of research, then, is the objectivity of the questions and accuracy in interpreting the answers. A number of sociologists have shown great ingenuity in formulating questions (as we shall see in Chapters 8 and 9).

One final problem with survey studies is that sometimes what people say is quite different from what they do[11] (Deutscher 1966, 1973). Survey information does not involve a direct study of religious experience itself but focuses on reports of religious experience or, more frequently, on the consequences of religious experience. It is a truism in the social sciences that people often operate on assumptions and respond to symbols of which they are only partially conscious. Hence, the value of survey information is affected by how "hard" (how verifiable, objective, and unchangeable) the data are. Statements about the frequency of church attendance over the past two months are based on hard data. In such cases, the answers given to researchers are reliable. But in order to determine the relevance or the importance of religion to respondents, sociologists sometimes ask, "How significant is your religion to you?" or "How important is religion in your everyday life?"

The information gathered by such questions is much "softer" in nature than information about attendance. A person may say that his religion is very significant to him, and may want it to be so, but it may actually have little influence on the individual's everyday life. Another respondent may report that religion has very little influence, yet her childhood moral and religious training may significantly affect her daily decisions in unconscious ways. Moreover, a question on the "significance of religion"—as one question among two dozen—does not measure the saliency of any specific belief with accuracy. Individuals may say that they do believe in life after death or in the existence of the Devil and that they feel religion is very significant or definitely affects their everyday life. But this does not reveal the importance of those particular beliefs. A problem of validity of correlations exists unless the answers are interpreted with great care. Fortunately, any bias or questionable assumption by the researcher is made manifest in the questions and is accessible to other social scientists to recognize and correct. (In other methods of research the assumptions of the researcher are usually less explicit).

Surveys and statistical analyses are extremely useful tools for the social scientist and have provided us with a great deal of concrete data. While

---

[11] For example, in a study of why people switch denominations, Newport (1979) states that there is a strong basis for doubting the reasons people give for their own switching. He insists that the validity of such self-reports is problematic.

there are several pitfalls in the use of this method, the primary arguments usually occur over the validity of particular questions—whether they accurately measure those things they purport to measure. Readers might find it instructive to design a list of questions that would measure the religiosity of respondents. We will explore the problem of defining and measuring religiosity in the next chapter.

Content Analysis

A final method used by sociologists is that of content analysis. In this instance, the researcher tries to ferret out underlying religious themes or unarticulated assumptions by analyzing written materials. Attitudes toward women might be identified through analysis of sermons preached by popular evangelists in various decades (see Chapter 9), or differences in values and outlooks among denominations might be identified by exploring the themes in the most popular hymns sung by each group (see Chapter 8). One study of the popular religion of Americans involved an analysis of popular religious books (Schneider and Dornbusch 1958). This procedure allowed the researchers to get beyond the official doctrines of the denomination and permitted a study of the religious ideas that appeal to the common person. The assumption is that books that sell particularly well are those which express (or shape) the beliefs of common folks. Often these beliefs are quite different from those taught in the churches. Likewise, the civil religion of America (a kind of religion of the nation which will be discussed in Chapter 10) has been studied by one scholar through a content analysis of the religious references in the Declaration of Independence, the inaugural addresses of various presidents, and other official statements that articulate the goals and purposes of the nation. Content analysis has been useful, but one difficulty is its assumption that the written statements accurately represent the views of the people. Presidential inaugural addresses may or may not reflect the American people's attitudes and values. Best-selling religious books are worth studying, but we do not always know which population within the United States buys which books or which persons fully agree with the authors.

To some extent, the weaknesses of each research design can be compensated for and overcome. However, no one research design is entirely adequate in itself. The variety of approaches allows scientists to check the accuracy of their theories from a variety of data sources. Sociologists often quarrel over which research design is most adequate, and most researchers tend to prefer one approach over others. However, our ability to gather data in several ways provides checks on the weaknesses inherent in any one approach. Together these approaches allow social scientists to substantiate or dismiss various generalizations about religious behavior. Examples of each of these methods of research—except for the experimental method—will be incorporated in this text.[12]

Often the topic being investigated helps determine the research design. For this reason, the way of defining the object of research is very important. In the next chapter, we will turn to an issue of major controversy in the sociology of religion: a person's general definition of religion and the specific working assumptions regarding religiosity in any given study.

Summary

Sociology offers a unique vantage point for viewing religion and religious behavior. While sociology certainly does not claim to offer the whole truth about human behavior, it does provide insights which other approaches may fail to recognize. The sociological perspective focuses on religious groups and institutions or the behavior of individuals within those groups, and on conflict between groups. While religious beliefs are seen as important, they are not the exclusive focus of sociologists. In fact, beliefs are viewed as one variable of religion among many—and often beliefs are found to be the effect of other social behaviors rather than the cause. Sociology of religion does not attempt to prescribe how religion ought to work. Rather it attempts to describe accurately the social underpinnings of religious groups and to generalize about common patterns and apparent causal correlations.

Two fundamental principles characterize this sociological approach: reliance on empirical data and objectivity. The sociologist is not satisfied with general impressions, but seeks concrete, verifiable data to prove or disprove any empirical generalization about a group. And although sociologists have preferences and commitments of their own, they seek to be open to the data and to avoid prejudgment of any particular group or any particular religious process. Such objectivity is not easy to maintain and serves as an ongoing goal for each sociologist.

In order to gather empirical data, a number of different types of research methods have been employed. Each has its own advantages and disadvantages. Collectively, they can provide checks and corrections on errors which any single method might make. However, due to the nature of religion as a topic of study, some special problems arise. This is especially true in the case of experimentation. Ethical considerations prevent many aspects of religious behavior from being tested and analyzed through controlled experimentation. In any empirical study of religion an important issue is the method of defining and measuring religion or religiosity, and it is to this issue we turn in Chapter 2.

[12] Experimental studies of religion have been undertaken on only four or five occasions, and those have dealt with very specialized areas of theoretical interest—areas which we will not be investigating in this text.

What Do We Mean by the Term Religion?

Substantive Definitions
A Functional Definition
A Symbolic Definition
Implications of One's Definition for Research
The Concept of Religion as Employed in This
    Text
A Final Word about Definitions
Summary

To students who have never studied the sociology of religion, the definition of religion may not seem to be a problem. Certainly everyone knows what religion is! Let's get on with more important matters! But we dare not be so hasty. The way we define a subject provides boundaries for what is and is not legitimate grist for discussion. Some definitions are so narrow and specific as to exclude Buddhism as a religion. Other definitions are so broad and inclusive that many social phenomena may be considered forms of religion. There is no consensus regarding what religion is. Indeed, the definition is highly controversial.

    Max Weber (1963:1) and Clifford Geertz (1968:1) both have insisted that we define religion at the *end* of the study, if at all. That assumes we all know generally what religion is; let's just begin the investigation. However, I recall sitting in a graduate anthropology class on native American religions in which the professor spent considerable time discussing sword-swallowing. He obviously felt that this was a significant part of the religion of a group we were studying. My basic assumptions about what is fundamentally religious differed from his, and your assumptions may differ from mine. We must begin our analysis, then, by exploring the question of what

21

it is we intend to study. What, after all, is religion? The following discussion shows some of the ways in which social scientists have defined religion.

Substantive Definitions

Many sociologists employ what has been called a substantive definition. This approach hinges on identification of the "substance" or "essence" of religion. Edward B. Tylor used this approach back in 1873 when he defined religion as "belief in Spiritual Beings" (1958:8). For most of us a reference to God or gods does seem to be an essential element in religion. The reason Tylor used the term *spiritual beings* is that many nonindustrialized peoples worship and/or fear their deceased ancestors. They have little or no concern about gods, as such, but their world is peopled with many unseen beings. Hence, spiritual beings seemed to Tylor a more inclusive term than belief in gods. Some scholars have recently reaffirmed Tylor's insistance that religion involves a belief in a Being or beings which are not experienced by normal empirical processes (Spiro, 1966).

Trying to define the essence of religion is a difficult task, but it becomes more difficult if our definition is to be applied cross-culturally. In the Western world, we tend to feel that religion is essentially a matter of belief. In fact, some social scientists have attempted to measure the religiosity of people by determining how orthodox they are. (An orthodox person is one who believes the traditional doctrines of a church.) But as R. R. Marett (1914:xxxi) suggests, in many cultures religion is "not so much thought out as danced out." That is to say, ritual and emotion are primary to religion, and belief is only secondary. Other anthropologists have agreed that emphasis on belief is a Western bias which causes anthropologists to miss the underlying thrust of many non-Western religions (Kluckhohn, 1972). For example, several observers have insisted that any concepts of a deity or superhuman beings are peripheral to official Buddhism (Ernest Benz 1964; R. D. Zaechner 1967). On the other hand, most common folks in Burma who identify themselves as Buddhists do believe in superhuman beings (Spiro, 1978). So a definition that emphasizes a belief in superhuman beings leaves doubt about whether Buddhism is a religion. Strictly speaking, many Buddhist gurus (who are not concerned with superhuman beings) would not be considered to be practicing religion. Does religion refer only to those who hold a specific *kind* of belief?

Another definitional approach that tries to capture the essence of religion, but which avoids the requirement of a specific belief, was first suggested in 1915 by Emile Durkheim. Durkheim was fascinated with the cleansing exercises and the change of attitude which were necessary in many cultures before one could enter into religious ritual. He maintained that a recognition of the division of life into sacred and profane realms allows us to identify religion in any culture (1965:50–62). Peoples around the world seem to undergo a psychological shift when encountering holy objects or engaging in religious ritual. This shift involves a sense of awe, a feeling of fear and majesty. The attitude differs from anything one encounters in the everyday life of these people.

Durkheim recognized that not all experiences of awe or sacredness are religious in character. He observed tribal people engaging in rites of magic and suggested that the attitude is similar to that found in religious rites. However, he maintained that magic and religion are quite different. Religion is a communal activity. It involves a social group: "In all history we do not find a single religion without a Church" (1965:59). The sacred attitude must be fundamentally a group experience if it is to be identified as religion. Durkheim's formal definition, then, is: "A religion is a unified system of beliefs and practices relative to sacred things, that is to say, things set apart and forbidden—beliefs and practices which unite into a single moral community called a Church, all those who adhere to them" (1965:62). In the late 1950s, Mircea Eliade and his students reasserted the importance of the sacred/profane distinction in defining religion (Eliade 1959).

This approach is helpful in a great many cases, and it avoids the problem of deciding which specific belief is intrinsically or inherently religious. Social scientists who have used this approach have often implied (if not asserted) a dualistic world view. That is to say, life has a religious dimension and a nonreligious dimension. For example, Durkheim insists that

> the religious life and the profane life cannot coexist in the same unit of time. It is necessary to assign determined days or periods to the first, from which all profane occupations are excluded. . . . There is no religion, and consequently, no society which has not known and practiced this division of time into two distinct parts (1965:347).

Eliade concurs with this and writes regarding space:

> For religious [persons], space is not homogeneous; he [or she] experiences interruptions in it; some parts of space are qualitatively different from others (1959:20).

While it is true that many people organize their life experience into separate categories, not all do. The United Society of Believers in Christ's Second Appearing (the Shakers) attempted to sustain an attitude that all of life is sacred. More recently, a deeply religious utopian society called the Bruderhof (there are Bruderhof communes in New York, Pennsylvania, and Connecticut) has also attempted to make *all* life hallowed and has deemphasized sacraments and rituals. All one's life is to be lived in the spirit of worship, and the community works to sustain this attitude. Zablocki writes, "The Bruderhof is concerned with bearing witness in the simple, everyday acts of living . . . there are no activities, however trivial, that cannot be permeated by the divine spirit" (1971:31). This community even refuses to erect a church building lest religion be identified with a distinct time and place. Groups such as these do not seem to bifurcate life into sacred and profane realms.[1] In fact, Kingsley Davis has suggested that while this distinction is useful in studying nonindustrial societies, it erects a false dichotomy in contemporary society and religion (1949:520).

Andrew Greeley has employed this criterion of sacredness as a defining characteristic of religion, but has avoided the dualism of many writers. Greeley (1972:10–18) suggests that any being, social process, or value that gives meaning and purpose to life tends to become a source of reverence or profound respect. When Greeley refers to a sacred attitude, he suggests that it is not totally unlike a secular outlook, but is a matter of intensified respect. Hence, Greeley's reference to a sacred attitude does not entirely preclude the study of nationalism, worship of the free enterprise system, or any other example of profound loyalty as a form of religion. However, he does insist that not all experiences of transcendence or profound reverence are religious. He does not say how one distinguishes religious transcendence from nonreligious transcendence, but the distinction appears to pivot on the degree to which the object of awe is supernatural.

An underlying question in this whole debate, then, is whether religion by definition includes only that which has an otherworldly or supernatural dimension. What about the person whose ultimate values and deepest commitment is to America? He or she has a deep sense of loyalty to the flag of the United States and will even give his or her life to defend it. The American Way of Life and the American Dream provide a sense of meaning, purpose, and value in life. National holidays are celebrated with devotion, and a tear is shed when the national anthem is played. This individual may belong to several organizations for the preservation and promotion of patriotism and the glorification of America. The person loves this country above all else, according it highest value and deepest loyalty. Is this religious behavior? Can nationalism be a form of religion? It is not otherworldly, and it is not essentially supernatural (although the belief structure may include a God who overlooks, blesses, and judges the nation). Certainly the individual feels a sort of sacredness toward the nation and its primary symbol, the flag. But this sacredness does not involve the fear and trembling that Rudolf Otto (1923) and Emile Durkheim (1965) describe as part of the sacred attitude. How does the feeling of awe and reverence toward a nation differ from the awe and reverence toward a supernatural being or realm? Is this difference significant enough to call one experience religious and the other not? These are not easy questions to answer. Some scholars feel that nationalistic behavior as described above *is* religious in character, and that a broader definition of religion is appropriate.

---

[1] Anthropological studies of world views seem to support this view. Exclusive categories of thought are not universal. For example, see Jones (1972).

The major criticism of the substantive definitions is that they tend to focus the researcher's attention solely on traditional forms of religion. Some writers feel that people in complex and changing societies such as ours are religious in new ways. The substantive definitions are felt to be too narrow and too tradition bound, hence blinding researchers to these new modes of religiosity.

A Functional Definition

Milton Yinger (1970:1–23) has offered a more inclusive definition of religion. He suggests that we focus not on what religion essentially *is* but on what it *does.* He proposes that we define a social phenomenon as religious if it fulfills the manifest function of religion.[2] He follows Max Weber in asserting that meaning in life is a basic human need (although the nature and intensity of that need will vary among individuals). Theologian Paul Tillich (1957) has described religion as that which is one's "ultimate concern," and Yinger also draws on Tillich's treatment in developing his own definition. The underlying conviction is that a fundamental concern of human beings is to understand the purpose of life and the meaning of death, suffering, evil, and injustice. In line with this conviction, Yinger writes, "Religion, then, can be defined as a system of beliefs and practices by means of which a group of people struggles with these ultimate problems of human life" (1970:7). Religion helps individuals cope with these perplexities by offering an explanation and by providing a strategy to overcome despair, hopelessness, and futility. Using this type of definition, the range of phenomena which we consider under the heading religion is considerably expanded. Yinger insists that nontheistic and even nonsupernatural systems of belief and practice can be appropriate social patterns for the sociologist of religion. "It is not the nature of *belief,* but the nature of *believing* that requires our study" (1970:11). Wherever one sees a closing of the gap between fact and hope, wherever one sees a leap of faith that allows a person to assert that suffering and evil will somehow, someday be defeated, there one sees the manifestations of religion. Even a secular faith that science and technology will ultimately solve all our problems is, by this definition, a religious or quasi-religious phenomenon. Yinger writes, "A term that already includes, by common consent, the contemplations of a Buddhist monk and the ecstatic visions of a revivalist cult member, human sacrifice and ethical monotheism, may have room in it for science as *a way of life*" (1970:11–12). Intense faith in nationalism, in capitalism, and in many other objects of deep loyalty, may become grist for the student of religion if the object of loyalty and belief is expected eventually to solve the ultimate

---

[2] Manifest functions are the *conscious* and *intended* functions of a social pattern or institution. Latent functions are unconscious and unintended.

human perplexities over the purpose of life and the meaning of death, injustice, and suffering. Yinger argues that if a narrower definition is utilized, one may misunderstand and misidentify religion in a society, particularly in societies undergoing cultural change.

This definition assumes that, to some extent at least, all people are religious. Yinger writes: "To me, the evidence is decisive: human nature abhors a vacuum in systems of faith. This is not, then, a period of religious decline but is one of religious change" (1970:vii). The assumption underlying the functional definition of religion does not really invite the question of whether a society is becoming less religious, but rather asks what new forms religion is taking.

This assumption is similar to that adopted by some theologians. H. Richard Niebuhr, for example, writes:

> It is a curious and inescapable fact about our lives, of which I think we all become aware at some time or another, that we cannot live without a cause, without some object of devotion, some center of worth, something on which we rely for our meaning. . . . If we do not wish to call this faith religion, there is no need to contend about the word. Let us say then that our problem is the problem of faith rather than of religion.
>
> Now to have faith and to have a god is one and the same thing, as it is one and the same thing to have knowledge and an object of knowledge. When we believe that life is worth living by the same act we refer to some being which makes our life worth living. We never merely believe that life is worth living, but always think of it as made worth living by something on which we rely. And this being, whatever it be, is properly termed our god (Niebuhr 1960a:118–119).

Hence, Niebuhr agrees that nationalism and science and many other belief systems are religions; he differs from the social scientist in that he makes a moral judgment about those systems being inferior. According to Niebuhr (1960b) and Tillich (1957), the major threat to Christianity has always been idolatry (belief in a "false god," one that is not really ultimate) rather than atheism. Atheism was never a concern of biblical times; the challenge was the false gods of Baal (sex as ultimate fulfillment) and Mammon (worship of money). Yinger, without making judgments about the truth or falsity of belief, is also suggesting that all people have a god or gods which give meaning to life (although the intensity of the need for meaning and the relative consistency of belief patterns will vary widely among individuals). The task of the social scientist is to discover what it is that gives meaning to people's lives, for that is their religion. The majority of sociologists who study religion would probably agree that most humans are more or less religious. Some, like Geertz, think there has been too much emphasis on the more and not enough study of those who are less. Yinger and Geertz, then, differ in their judgments as to whether there is an innate religious drive in all humans.

One issue that emerges is whether private systems of belief are to be called religion. After all, many individuals have patterns of belief that solve the ultimate meaning issues for them, but which are not necessarily shared with others. Yinger insists, as do most sociologists of religion, that religion is a "social phenomenon: it is shared and takes on many of its most significant aspects only in the interaction of the group" (1970:10). Privately held patterns of meaning may have religious aspects, but they are not religion, per se. We might well use the vocabulary of Niebuhr here by referring to the individual belief as faith and the social manifestation as religion. Hence, religion is a community of people who have a shared faith.

One may question how many people must share a faith before one calls it a religion. Usually, a small cadre of individuals who solidify into a new faith group are referred to as a cult. Whether a cult is a full-fledged religion or not may be debatable, but certainly it is a form of religious behavior that interests students of religion.[3]

Perhaps more important issues are whether a supernatural dimension is necessary and how one identifies or measures ultimate concern or a primary loyalty. Religion often becomes concerned with less-than-ultimate issues, as in the case of faith healers who draw their congregations largely on the basis of a concern for physical health and well-being. Furthermore, ultimate concern is a difficult phenomenon to identify and is even more difficult to measure.[4] Nevertheless, Yinger is asserting that any system of belief and action which fails to address the fundamental questions of meaning in life is not a religion. Religion is not *limited* to questions of ultimate meaning, but addressing those questions is a defining characteristic of religion.

Some scholars have argued rather persuasively that a belief in the supernatural, or a supernatural dimension to the belief system, is a fundamental characteristic of religion (Stark and Bainbridge 1979). They argue that if religion is not limited to beliefs with a supernatural dimension, the term *religion* may become so inclusive that it is virtually meaningless. Yinger rejects the idea that a supernatural dimension is necessary.

Consider your own presuppositions: is a belief in the supernatural necessary when you use the term *religion?* Or is it the quality of one's convictions

---

[3] The faith of individuals, even if not celebrated in a group context, is also of interest to sociologists of religion. Such individualized faith systems are sometimes referred to as *invisible religions* (Luckmann 1967). These will be discussed in Chapter 10. However, individual meaning systems will be referred to henceforth as personal religiosity or as faith; religion will be defined as a social phenomenon.

[4] Paul Deats has suggested that we probably need to account for the difference between the ultimate concern and the primary concern of individuals, depending upon their circumstances. A person who lives on the raw edges of starvation in an impoverished country may be primarily concerned about a mundane issue: the source of his or her next meal. Philosophical issues of meaning of life or the nature of the universe may be of secondary concern at any given time. Since ultimate concern and primary concern may be different, how does one measure or identify the former?

and the depth of commitment that is essential? The "facts" about religion are not nearly as clear-cut as students often want them to be. Clifford Geertz pointed to the ambiguity involved in defining religion when he wrote that religion simply "cannot be delineated with Cartesian sharpness. . . . We are attempting to articulate a way of looking at the world, not to describe an unusual object" (1968:97).

Having discussed Yinger's approach to defining religion, it is appropriate to conclude with his full definition:

> Where one finds awareness of and interest in the continuing, recurrent, *permanent* problems of human existence—the human condition itself, as contrasted with specific problems; where one finds rites and shared beliefs relevant to that awareness, which define the strategy of an ultimate victory; and where one has groups organized to heighten that awareness and to teach and maintain those rites and beliefs—there one has religion (Yinger 1970:33).

A Symbolic Definition

Clifford Geertz has developed a symbolic definition of religion which is somewhat more detailed in describing what religion does. Symbols—things that represent or remind one of something else—are powerful forces in human behavior, and they are central to religion. Given the abstract nature of the focal point of religion, symbols become its indispensable medium. Symbols include objects (the cross, the Star of David), behaviors (genuflecting before the altar, baptizing a convert, touching the Mezuzza on the doorpost of a Jewish home before entering, or kneeling, facing Mecca and praying five times a day), and myths or stories (the creation story, the story of Jesus washing the disciples' feet, legends of ancestors).[5] Geertz is impressed with the way in which various levels of meaning can be communicated through symbols. Moreover, symbols are more accessible to observation than a subjective experience of ultimate concern. Hence, he uses symbols as the starting point for his definition of religion. Not all symbols are religious, of course. A handshake, a kiss, and a wave of the hand are all symbolic behaviors, but they do not normally have religious connotations.

Geertz treats religious symbols as distinct from others referring to the former as sacred. Hence, he seems to return us to the sacred/profane dichotomy. I believe a distinction between microsymbolic and macrosymbolic systems (which is implied in Geertz's discussion) would be more helpful in differentiating religious from nonreligious symbols. *Macrosymbolic* symbols are those that help one interpret the meaning of life itself and which involve a cosmology or world view. Many nonreligious symbols are *microsymbolic;* that is, symbols that affect everyday interaction with others and which en-

---

[5] Myths and rituals will be treated as symbols in Chapter 4.

hance daily communication and cooperation. Microsymbolic symbols do not claim to explain the purpose of life and do not suggest values and beliefs that claim highest priority in one's life. Geertz does not stress the macro and micro difference, but this distinction is implicit in his discussion and seems to me to be more helpful than distinguishing sacred symbols from nonsacred ones.

Geertz's definition is so fully and carefully developed that it deserves a close examination. He writes:

> Religion is (1) a system of symbols which acts to (2) establish powerful, pervasive, and long-lasting moods and motivations in [people] by (3) formulating conceptions of a general order of existence and (4) clothing these conceptions with such an aura of factuality that (5) the moods and motivations seem uniquely realistic (Geertz 1966:4).

Religion is a "system of symbols which *acts*" in that the symbols provide a blueprint for understanding the world. These symbols provide a model of the world by helping persons understand what the world and life really are. Many people believe, for example, that life is actually a testing ground in which God determines one's fitness to live in His kingdom. These individuals live their lives with reference to this understanding. Other religious perspectives offer alternative views of what life really is. But these symbols not only suggest a model *of* the world, they also propose a model *for* the world. Not only does the symbol system describe what life is, but it also prescribes what it ought to be. Not only do many Christians assert that life is a testing ground, but they claim access to the answers which will help them pass the test.

This system of symbols, Geertz continues, acts to "establish powerful, pervasive, and long-lasting moods and motivations" in people. In other words, acknowledgement of the symbols affects one's disposition. Religious activity influences two somewhat different types of dispositions: moods and motivations. Geertz suggests that *moods* are scalar, they involve *depth of feeling;* while *motivations* are vectorial, they suggest a *direction* for behavior. Moods vary in intensity, and they affect our total outlook on life, but they are not aimed at any particular goal. One simply experiences a mood; one does not gain a feeling of obligation about a specific goal to be attained from a mood. "If one is sad, everything and everybody seems dreary; if one is gay, everything and everybody seems splendid" (1966:11). Some born again Christian groups emphasize that to be a Christian is to be joyful, even in the face of adversity. The emphasis is on a pervasive mood that is to characterize the believer, regardless of the specific circumstances.

Some religions may emphasize moods as primary (in Buddhism the focus is on mystical experience) while other religions stress motivations and a system of ethics (the Unitarian-Universalist society illustrates this latter focus). Nonetheless, Geertz suggests that in all religions, the symbol system

produces moods that intensify commitment and motivations to act in specified ways. In another context, Geertz refers to this dispositional dimension
as the "ethos" of the religion (1958).

Not only do the symbol systems enhance a particular type of feeling or
disposition, they also act to "formulate conceptions of a general order of
existence." A distinguishing characteristic of religion is that it provides a
world view, a *cognitive ordering* of concepts of nature, of self, of society,
of the supernatural. Religion creates not only intense feelings, but it establishes a cosmology which satisfies one's intellectual need for reasonable
explanations. Geertz emphasizes that not all intense feelings of awe are
religious. One may be overwhelmed by powerful emotions (moods) in
viewing the Grand Canyon, but such feelings may be aesthetic rather than
religious. Moreover, one may be motivated to adopt a lifestyle of asceticism
(self-denial), but the goal may be either to reach Nirvana or to lose 25
pounds.

Geertz properly points out that religion involves an intellectual ordering.
In an interview a few years ago, a woman responded that she felt closest
to God when having sex with her husband. Certainly she felt some intense
feelings, but many theologians would question whether these feelings were
essentially religious. In commenting on this woman's response, one theology
professor remarked that she seemed to have an overly grand estimation
of her husband! Similarly, many people claim that their religious experience
comes from a walk in the woods rather than from going to church. Geertz
is suggesting that a religious sense of awe must include a reaffirmation
and commitment to a particular view of the world, a particular mode of
interpreting the meaning of suffering, pain, death, and injustice. A walk
in the woods may be refreshing and may involve an intense aesthetic feeling,
but in most instances it does not change the way one thinks about the
world.

> A man may indeed be said to be "religious" about golf, but not merely if
> he pursues it with passion and plays it on Sundays: he must also see it as
> symbolic of some transcendent truth. And the pubescent boy gazing soulfully
> into the eyes of the pubescent girl in a William Steig cartoon and murmuring,
> "there is something about you, Ethel, that gives me a kind of religious feeling"
> is, like most adolescents, confused (Geertz 1966:13).

There are three major challenges which seem to belie the meaningfulness
of life, and it is these that a religious world view must resolve. The term
world view refers to one's cognitive perspective on life. It includes one's
concept of the laws of nature or the laws of the universe; it explains why
the world is the way it is. Geertz points out, and much research in social
psychology confirms it, that most humans abhor an absence of explanations.
Many of Geertz's informants in his anthropological research have been
willing to admit that their current cosmology or metaphysical view was

inadequate. They were quite willing to accept a different world view. "What they were *not* ready to do was abandon [their current belief] for no hypothesis at all; to leave events to themselves" (Geertz 1966:16). Humans want to know why, to have some explanation, to be assured that life, after all, does make sense. Hence, the first task of a world view is to establish an explanation that offers intellectual coherence. The first challenge is to overcome bafflement.

Second, the world view must help the individuals discern some meaning from pain. Most religions do not attempt to deny the reality of pain; they try to make suffering sufferable. For the person who is grieving over the death of a loved one, there may be comfort in believing that God had some purpose in "taking" him or her. Comfort may also come from a conviction that there is life after death. In each case the world view helps to make pain bearable without attempting to ignore its existence. Often pain is interpreted as "God testing his servants," and how one endures hardship is a mark of one's holiness.

Finally, the problem of evil and injustice in the world threatens to obliterate any confidence that there is a moral order to the universe. The gap between things as they are and as they ought to be challenges the believer to explain why. Geertz's citation of the following quatrain is apt:

The rain falls on the just
And on the unjust fella
But mainly on the just
Because the unjust has the just's umbrella.
(1966:21)

The righteous experience the same evils as the unrighteous. Indeed, if anything the righteous sometimes seem to get the short end of things. Why should one bother to strive for righteousness? One's world view may or may not offer a specific answer to how righteousness will prevail; but the affirmation that virtue, goodness, and justice will ultimately win out must somehow be sustained.

Symbol systems, then, attempt to "account for, and even celebrate, the perceived ambiguities, puzzles, and paradoxes in human experience" (Geertz 1966:23). The world view represents an intellectual process by which people can affirm that life makes sense, that suffering is bearable, and that justice is not a mirage. If these generalizations seem terribly abstract, I suggest that you pick up some printed sermons or inspirational literature. It is startling to see how directly almost all religious literature addresses itself to at least one of these three concerns.

Geertz continues his definition by attempting to answer the question of how a particular world view or set of concepts comes to be believed. The symbols act to "cloth those conceptions in such an aura of factuality that the moods and motivations seem uniquely realistic." How is it, he asks, that in spite of common sense, in spite of everyday experience, in spite of empirical evidence, people will come to believe unrational and unsupportable things? What compels a Christian Scientist to deny that illness exists, even though the person experiences the symptoms of influenza? Why does a Mormon believe that a new revelation was written to Joseph Smith on golden plates, even though no one could read it but Smith? Why do members of the Unification Church assert that their leader, the Reverend Sun Myung Moon, is the Christ, even though other observers see him as a rather unexceptional man? Why do Christians continue to affirm that Jesus is the son of God who ushered in God's kingdom, even though he died in the manner of a criminal nearly two thousand years ago? Geertz points out that religious ritual often creates an aura in which a deeper reality is said to be reached. Truths are experienced or understood which are more profound than everyday experience provides. Indeed the New Testament boldly insists that the wisdom of this world is folly and that Christians must become fools in the eyes of the world (I Corinthians 1:18–25).

As we shall see, Geertz is pointing to a very important aspect of religion. We shall explore this issue in Chapter 6 when we discuss plausibility structures. However, underlying Geertz's treatment is an assumption that religion is inherently nonempirical in its search for truth:

> The major characteristic of religious beliefs as opposed to other sorts of beliefs, ideological, philosophical, scientific, or commonsensical, is that they are regarded as being not conclusions from experience . . . but as prior to it. For those who hold them, religious beliefs are not inductive, they are paradigmatic; the world . . . provides not evidences for their truth but illustrations of it. *They are a light cast upon human life from somewhere outside it* (1968:98, my emphasis).

While many religions are nonrational and reject empirical evidence which contradicts their world view, there are also many systematic theologians who constantly reformulate their views based upon recent scientific findings. Are we to exclude their efforts from the phenomena we call religion simply because they do utilize an inductive method? And what are we to make of the assertion by John Wesley, the founder of Methodism, that all religious truth must conform to four criteria, two of which are logical consistency and validation in personal experience? The problem of why some people believe in ideas that apparently defy reason and common sense is interesting. But this does not justify an assumption that all religious thinking and all religious knowledge are intuitional.

Many students have difficulty understanding Geertz's heavy emphasis on symbol systems (their importance will be discussed in more detail in Chapter 4). Let it suffice here to say that meaning is commonly "stored" or encapsulated in symbols. They are powerful factors in the lives of people. They are also more easily observed than ultimate concern. Certainly one is dealing with religious phenomena when one encounters symbols that "establish powerful, pervasive, and long-lasting moods and motivations in people by formulating conceptions of a general order of existence."

Geertz's definition is long, abstract, and quite elaborate. (His explanation of the definition runs 46 pages.) This makes it difficult to translate it into concrete research procedures. However, his definition does offer a contribution to the debate over what it is that distinguishes religion from other cultural phenomena. The central contributions are that religion must have a *macrosymbol system* which acts to reinforce both a *world view* and an *ethos*.

Researchers who like to employ the participant observation method of research find Geertz's definition useful, for it identifies the general properties of religion and helps the observer know what to observe. Yet, it does so without specifying the content of religious beliefs. Those researchers who engage in quantitative survey studies find Geertz's generalizations so broad and encompassing that his identification of religion is unhelpful. How does one quantitatively measure a world view or an ethos? The broadness and inclusiveness of Geertz's treatment is frustrating to those who seek unequivocal precision in categorizing types of behavior, but it is this same generality which attracts those who undertake cross-cultural investigations. (Geertz is an anthropologist.)

Geertz's analysis is really more than a definition. It is an essay on how religion "works" to reinforce itself and on what religion "does" in the society. Because of this focus on what religion does, the symbolic definition will be treated hereafter as one type of functional definition.

Implications of One's Definition for Research

One's definition of religion is often related to one's research strategy. To begin with, some definitions are more conducive than others to certain types of research designs (as we have seen in discussing Geertz's definition). More important, the definition one uses affects the types of questions one asks in doing research. Perhaps the importance of the difference in definitional approaches will become clear if we view the ways in which religiosity has been "operationalized." When we operationalize a concept, we simply translate abstractions into specific questions or statements which can be measured or observed. Let us turn to the issue of how religiosity is operationalized for research purposes.

Some survey research has attempted to study differences at the broadest levels of generalization. Large categories or groups have been compared and contrasted in terms of prevalent attitudes. Church members have been compared with nonmembers in terms of divorce rates, racial attitudes, and other factors. While some interesting differences have been discovered, the category "church member" is extremely broad, including Episcopalians and members of snake-handling churches in the same general category. Furthermore, it makes church membership the sole criterion of religiosity. It ignores those who may have an unconventional meaning system or faith and who do not affiliate with a traditional religious group.

A number of survey studies have taken a similar approach by asking people about their religious affiliation. Again, some interesting correlations have been discovered. For example, Gerhard Lenski found in his Detroit sample that 54 percent of white Protestants, 30 percent of white Catholics, 13 percent of black Protestants, and 3 percent of Jews were Republicans (1963:139). He also found that 11 percent of Jews, 34 percent of white Protestants, 38 percent of black Protestants, and 66 percent of white Catholics felt that divorce is always or usually wrong (1963:166). These figures are interesting and perhaps important. However, it must be remembered that such figures are crude. Such categories as Jew or Protestant include a broad range of theologies and religious organizations. Still other surveys have been more specific by assessing the differences between specific denominations. In these studies the extreme difference between Unitarians and Southern Baptists (both of which are Protestant groups) can be demonstrated. One may discover that Unitarians and Reform Jews are very similar in their views on certain questions, even though the national sample may show a wide difference on those issues between Protestants and Jews.

Identifying the denominational affiliation of people provides more specific information than the general categories of church member or Protestant. But knowing the denomination of a respondent still does not tell us much about that person's religious orientation. For one thing, there is a wide variation of theologies and world views within any denomination. Although the official position of the United Presbyterian Church, USA is that Jesus was both wholly God and wholly man, 8 percent of the United Presbyterians surveyed said that they do not believe that Jesus was any more the son of God than anyone else is a child of God. In fact, a small number of the Presbyterians admitted that they were not convinced that a person named Jesus ever existed! (Seventy-two percent had no doubt about the divinity of Jesus.) Furthermore, 7 percent acknowledged that a "higher power" exists but rejected the idea that this power is a personal God. (A small number doubted the existence of any higher power). The numbers of skeptics were even higher for the Congregationalists (now called the United Church of Christ), 29 percent of whom questioned or rejected the divinity of Jesus and 3 percent of whom questioned or rejected the existence of God. Another 16 percent accepted the idea of a higher power but rejected the idea of a personal God (Glock and Stark 1966:5–7). This leads us to the second limitation of studies that make comparisons simply on denominational lines: they measure only one's affiliation with traditional forms of religion. Other belief systems that may provide individuals with a system of ethics and a sense of meaning in life are not viewed as religious. The definition of religion is narrow and is operationalized in traditional terms.

The trend in survey research has been to develop more sophisticated instruments to assess individual variations in religiosity. The earliest of such measures were unidimensional, using a single criterion to determine one's religiosity. In some cases, it was frequency of attendance at religious rituals. The assumption was that people who attend services regularly are likely to be highly committed in other respects. Other surveys used a subjective measure; they simply asked respondents, "How important is your religion to you in everyday life?" Still others used a question about the frequency with which the individual prays ("frequent" being defined as daily). And finally, some surveys asked respondents about their beliefs in order to determine their orthodoxy. (In some surveys only literal interpretations of the Bible were assessed as religious responses.) The problem with this unidimensional approach was the assumption that a single index would be an accurate predictor of other religious behavior. This assumption has not been supported by more recent research. For one thing, different churches emphasize different behaviors as signs of faithfulness. The Catholic Church has traditionally insisted that salvation requires attendance at a certain number of celebrations of the Mass per year. Some Protestant denominations have stressed that a tithe of one's income to the church (a tithe is normally 10 percent) is a mark of the true Christian. Others stress prayer and personal devotions. Such liberal denominations as the United Church of Christ have asserted that participation in social action (working for racial and economic justice or in movements concerned about world hunger or international peace) is the mark of the Christian. But beyond group emphases, individuals within the same denomination may find different patterns most expressive of their faith. Hence, most survey instruments developed in the past decade have utilized several measures of religiosity (i.e., they are multidimensional).

The first major attempt to formulate and measure differences in religiosity was the work of Joseph Fichter in the early 1950s. He distinguished between Catholics based on frequency of attendance at Mass and on overall level of involvement in the life of the parish. He developed a fourfold typology which demonstrated differences between members within the same religious organization depending upon their level of commitment (Fichter 1954). Other measures have been developed since then that have shown even more complex variations within denominations. For example, Lenski studied the differences between "associational" and "communal" involvement. Associational involvement referred to frequency of attendance at church services and participation in the workings of the institution. Communal involvement was a measure of how many of one's close friends and relatives were members of the same religious group. Lenski found that these two indices were not highly correlated and that they tended to have different influences on church members. In fact, communal involvement was a more important influence than associational involvement in affecting everyday behavior and attitudes. Lenski also studied the difference between doctrinal orthodoxy and devotionalism as modes of religiosity. Doctrinal orthodoxy refers to agreement with the central beliefs set forth by that denomination. Devotionalism refers to a sense of personal contact with God. He measured this by asking about the frequency of prayer and by inquiring whether the respondents sought to determine God's will when they made important decisions. Lenski found that orthodoxy and devotionalism varied independently and that they influenced people differently in economic and political attitudes and in other arenas of everyday living (Lenski 1963). (These findings will be explored in more detail in Chapter 8.)

The most elaborate and influential multidimensional analysis is that developed by Charles Glock. His original formulation included four dimensions (1959), but he and Rodney Stark later published several revised versions, eventually specifying as many as eight dimensions (Glock and Stark 1965; Stark and Glock 1968). They sought to operationalize and assess experiential, ritualistic, devotional, belief, knowledge, consequential or ethical, communal, and particularistic dimensions.

The experiential dimension refers to a feeling of having communed with God, an experience one believes to have been a revelation from God, or a powerful experience that convinces one of his or her salvation. A report of some sort of personal experience one considers to be of divine origin or of supernatural dimension is an aspect of religiosity, but it may or may not be correlated with other dimensions. The ritualistic dimension involves frequency of participation in corporate worship services. The devotional involves faithfulness in private devotions and regularity in private prayer. The belief dimension refers to the degree to which the person agrees with the beliefs of the group. This is the same as Lenski's criterion of doctrinal orthodoxy, although Glock and Stark have used somewhat different questions to measure it. The knowledge dimension has to do with the extent to which members even know what the beliefs and doctrines of their group are. Several researchers have found that many church members are quite ignorant of the content of their religious scripture and of their church's official doctrines. Glock and Stark insist that people sometimes believe in doctrines which they do not understand. (For example, a substantial percentage of those who claimed to believe in the Ten Commandments did not know what they were. One wonders how central such a "belief" could possibly be to one's life.) The consequential dimension has to do with the extent to which explicitly religious commitments and behaviors affect attitudes and behavior in everyday life. The communal refers to the number of one's friends that are of the same denomination. Particularism is a measure of the extent to which one believes that one's own faith offers the *only* hope of salvation.

Multidimensional modes of analysis tend to measure religiosity in conventional terms. The way in which Glock and Stark operationalized the belief dimension will serve to illustrate. A person who is rated high in religiosity indicates most of the following:

1. Certainty of the existence of God.
2. Belief in the divinity of Jesus.
3. Belief that Jesus was born of a virgin, actually walked on water, and will someday return.
4. Belief in miracles as reported in the Bible.
5. Belief in life after death.
6. Belief in the actual existence of the devil.
7. Belief that "a child is born into the world already guilty of sin" (Glock and Stark 1968:22–44).

Each of the other dimensions were also measured with rather traditional conceptions of religion. Using these criteria for assessing religiosity, many people who believe strongly in astrology or in some other nontraditional cosmology would be considered nonreligious. The effect of such operational-ization is also to suggest that liberal denominations are less religious than conservative ones (McGuire, 1981). This is questionable. On what grounds can a sociologist insist that a devout Quaker is ideologically less religious than a Southern Baptist? When 94 percent of Congregationalists conform to the position of their church and reject a literal interpretation of original sin, how can a sociologist call them less religious than Catholics? Yet this set of questions would lead to such conclusions. Certainly the Congregation-alist and the Quaker do not think of themselves as less religious. Although Glock and Stark also discuss "ethicalism" as a possible alternative expression of religiosity, they assert: "Supernaturalism, in our judgment, is still the crucial variable in contemporary religious identity." (1968:70).[6]

James Davidson and Dean Knudsen (1977) have suggested an approach which overcomes many of the shortcomings of the Glock and Stark model. Davidson and Knudsen insist that since the content of religious beliefs varies significantly from one group to another, questions about orthodoxy are inappropriate for measuring religiosity. They suggest an important dis-tinction between "religious commitment" and "religious orientation." Spe-cific beliefs, tendencies to particularism, ethical application of beliefs in everyday life, communal involvement, and religious knowledge are elements of one's religious orientation. They vary among groups and indicate different *styles* of religiosity.

Religious commitment (or *extent* of religiosity) is measured in terms of two components: religious consciousness and religious participation. Reli-gious consciousness refers to a respondent's evaluation of the importance of religion in his or her life. That is, it is the extent to which religion is a

---

[6] This is in contrast to a national survey in which 86 percent of American respondents agreed with the statement, "The best mark of a person's religiousness is the degree of one's concern for others" (Hadden 1969:147). For a number of Americans, ethical behavior is the most important manifestation of religiosity.

Exhibit 2–1 _____

Measuring Religiosity

Readers may find it fruitful to design questions which they think would measure the level of religious commitment of respondents. What kinds of questions should be asked? What sort of beliefs or behaviors are indicative of religiosity? The following questions are among those which have been used by various sociologists to identify religious commitment. Which of these questions seem to you to best reflect religiosity? Some questions may seem unusual to you as measures of religion. Why do you suppose sociologists have felt that those questions measure religious commitment? Do you see any unwarranted assumptions about what is religious behavior in any of these questions? Would a highly religious person rank high on all of these, or is it possible to be highly religious and still have low scores in some areas? Are there some that a person *must* have a positive score on in order for you to consider them "highly religious"?

1. Which statement comes closest to expressing what you believe about God?
   I don't believe in God.
   I don't know whether there is a God and I don't believe there is any way to find out.
   I don't believe in a personal God, but I do believe in a higher power of some kind.
   I find myself believing in God some of the time, but not at other times.
   While I have doubts, I feel that I do believe in God.
   I know God really exists and I have no doubts about it.
   Don't know.
2. If you do believe in God, do you believe that God is like a heavenly father who watches over you, or do you have some other belief?
3. What about the belief that the Devil actually exists? Are you absolutely sure or are you pretty sure that the Devil exists or are you absolutely sure or pretty sure that the Devil does not exist?
4. The Bible tells of miracles, some credited to Christ and some to other prophets and apostles. Generally speaking, which of the following statements comes closest to what you believe about biblical miracles?
   —I believe miracles actually happened the way the Bible says they did.
   —I believe miracles happened, but can be explained by natural causes.
   —I tend to doubt that the miracles ever happened.
   —I do not believe that miracles ever happened.
5. How sure are you that there is a life beyond death? Are you absolutely sure or pretty sure there is a life beyond death or are you absolutely or pretty sure there is *no* life beyond death?
6. Have you ever had the feeling that you were somehow in the presence of God? Definitely; I think so; no, I have not; I am not sure.
7. All in all, how important would you say that religion is to you—extremely important, quite important, fairly important, not too important, or not important at all?
8. About how often do you attend worship services?
9. Do you believe that God answers people's prayers, or not?

Exhibit 2-1 *(concluded)*

10. How often do you pray—several times a day, once a day, several times a week, once or twice a month, less than once a month, or never?
11. How often do you read the Bible at home?
12. How often, if at all, are table prayers or grace said before or after meals in your home?
13. Do you ever make a point of listening to or watching religious services on radio or television? Regularly, sometimes, seldom, never?
14. How much, on average, does your family contribute to church each week?
15. When you have a decision to make in your everyday life, do you ask yourself what God would want you to do?—often, sometimes, seldom, never?
16. If you are married, are you married to someone of the same religion?
17. How many of your close friends belong to the same religion you belong to? All of them, most of them, about half of them, less than half of them, only a few of them or none of them?
18. On what church committees, boards, or organizations do you serve?
19. How frequently do you attend the meetings of these religious organizations? Frequently, occasionally, infrequently, never?
20. Are you, because of your religious commitment, a member of any service organizations, civic clubs, or benevolence societies? Please name them.
21. Do you believe that in order to be saved, a person must
    —be baptized?
    —participate regularly in Holy Communion?
    —be a member of your particular faith?
    —pray regularly?
    —tithe (give 10 percent of one's income to the church or the poor)?
    —do good works for others?
22. Do you believe that persons would be prevented from salvation if they
    —never heard of Jesus?
    —break the Sabbath?
    —take the name of the Lord in vain?
    —discriminate against other races?
    —are anti-Semitic?
23. Are you able to recite the Ten Commandments?
24. Please name the first book of the Bible.
25. Please name two major prophets mentioned in the Old Testament of the Bible.
26. Please name the person who delivered the Sermon on the Mount.
27. One person wrote most of the books of the New Testament. Can you name that person?

part of a person's sense of identity—intellectually, affectively, and behaviorally. It is operationalized through three questions:

Religious Consciousness

1. According to whatever standards are important to you personally, how religious would you say you are?

2. Overall, would you say religion is a positive or a negative force in making your life worthwhile?
3. To what extent would you say religious faith helps you in making daily decisions you have to make in life?

Religious participation refers to the respondent's involvement in explicitly religious behavior: ritual attendance, participation in other group-sponsored activities, and devotional behavior. Again, it is measured through responses to three questions:

Religious Participation

1. How many worship activities do you attend in a typical month?
2. How many church organizations or activities do you participate in regularly?
3. Do you ever do any of the following:
   a. Pray privately outside church?
   b. Say grace before meals?
   c. Read the Bible outside of church?

Pilot studies suggest that answers to religious consciousness and religious participation items are highly correlated. Together, Davidson and Knudsen suggest they measure the extent of a person's religiosity.

Differentiating between religious orientation and religious commitment could serve to clear up much of the muddiness in recent survey studies. Certainly there is an important difference between the *extent* and the *style* of one's religiosity. Davidson and Knudsen's approach avoids the fallacy of defining some theologies as inherently more religious than others. The authors found little correlation between the various elements of a person's religious orientation or between religious orientation and religious commitment. Hence, they conclude that people's religious orientations are inclined to be highly inconsistent and disparate and that they do not represent integrated wholes. This confirms earlier studies which found the elements of religiosity to vary independently.[7]

On the other hand, the lack of coherence between the elements of traditional religiosity may be evidence that traditional religion is inadequate to meet the meaning needs of modern people. Yinger (1969, 1977) has suggested that in rapidly changing societies, religion itself may be changing and may "look different." New forms of religion may be emerging—forms which are not measured by traditional questions. Rather than starting with traditional concepts of religiosity and trying to assess its effect on everyday life, functional definitions begin with the consequential dimension. They ask what it is that really provides meaning and purpose in the lives of people, for that is where one finds religion. If a traditional belief system

---

[7] Some interesting correlations between specific elements of religiosity and other social attitudes have been discovered. See Chapters 8 and 9 for specific applications.

does not affect a person's life, if it does not provide a coherent understanding of life's experiences, then it is not really that person's *faith.* If it is not one's real faith, then the question arises, what is? For those using a functional definition, it is inappropriate to try to assess levels of religiosity by asking only traditional questions.

Using such a functional definition of religion, Yinger operationalizes his research in a very different way. Rather than asking about one's *religion* (a term which brings to mind traditional concepts of ritual, prayer, and orthodoxy for most people), Yinger asks his questions in a nontraditional way. In attempting to assess a person's basic religiosity Yinger poses certain statements and asks respondents to indicate their level of agreement or disagreement. The following statements illustrate (1977:76):

> Suffering, injustice, and finally death are the lot of humanity; but they need not be negative experiences; their significance and effects can be shaped by our beliefs.
>
> Somehow, I cannot get very interested in the talk about "the basic human condition" and "humanity's ultimate problems."
>
> A person's most difficult and destructive experiences are often the source of increased understanding and powers of endurance.
>
> Despite the often chaotic conditions of human life, I believe that there is an order and pattern to existence that someday we will come to understand.

Depending upon how respondents answer these questions, Yinger feels one has an indication of the basic religiosity of the individual. He then seeks to determine what it is that serves as an ultimate concern for those religious persons by asking some open-ended questions:

> In your most reflective moments, when you are thinking beyond the immediate issues of the day—however important—beyond headlines, beyond the temporary, what do you consider the most important issue humanity has to face? Or, to put the question another way, what do you see as the basic, permanent question for humankind? (1969:93)

Since Yinger also believes that religion is essentially a group phenomenon, he also seeks to discover what groups the individual may be participating in which support the emphasis on this ultimate concern and which develop a strategy to address it. His follow-up question is this:

> Are you a participant in or member of some group, whether large or small, for which the "basic, permanent question" and the beliefs connected with it are the focus of attention and the most important reasons for its existence? If so, please characterize the group briefly (1969:93).

As one can readily see, Yinger does not presuppose what religion will look like or what sort of beliefs one might have. He uses an inductive method; he seeks to *discover* what concerns people ultimately and what provides people with a sense of meaning and hope. Clearly, such an approach does not make for neat correlations and computer-run multivariate analysis. At this point, at least, the method is too new to produce the sort of hard data that some sociologists prefer. The formulation of the questions will no doubt be modified and will undergo further sophistication as such research instruments are tested. One study has found that responses to Yinger's questions have elicited traditional religious answers (Roof et al. 1977). Persons who score high on traditional measures of religiosity are also the ones who score high on Yinger's measure. However, another study using Yinger's approach has reported that the procedure was helpful in discovering invisible or nonconventional religions in our midst (Nelson et al. 1976).

For researchers who define religion strictly in terms of a supernatural dimension, or for researchers interested in the effects of *traditional* religious beliefs and institutions, Yinger's operationalized questions are less fruitful than those of Glock and Stark or Davidson and Knudsen. For those interested in religion at the individual level or for those interested in religion as a cultural system, Yinger's approach can stimulate the development of a new area of investigation.

The discussion should make clear to readers that one's definition of religion is important to how one develops a research design. Furthermore, readers may have a clearer idea of how one's definition of religion can cause individuals to disagree on whether a particular social phenomenon is essentially religious. Of course, in both cases Methodism, Catholicism, Mormonism, Islam, and Krishna Consciousness are all considered forms of religion. Substantial and functional definitional approaches differ primarily on the questions "Where does one draw the line between religion and nonreligion?" and "How do you measure or discover religiosity?"

The Concept of Religion as Employed in This Text

My own underlying interest is in the way people generate and sustain new systems of meaning in the midst of social change. Moreover, I am interested in how individuals create their own systems of meaning. Usually, meaning systems involve a synthesis of official church doctrine with other cultural beliefs. Rather than dichotomizing religion from nonreligion, I seek to explore anything that provides meaning and purpose in the lives of people. I tend to ask *how* people are religious rather than *whether* they are religious. Hence, the perspective of this book will be most compatible with those of Yinger and Geertz, each of whom was interested in religion as a cultural system. While I will incorporate the research and the insights of those who use a more narrow definition of religion,[8] I will also address the broader issues of meaning in a changing culture.

---

[8] Actually, most of the book will be devoted to traditional expressions of religion.

Without attempting to offer a new definition, let me synthesize the debate over definitions by simply highlighting my own view of the distinguishing characteristics of religion. First, *religion is a social phenomenon* which involves the grouping of people around a faith perspective. *Faith* is an *individual phenomenon which involves trusting in some object, event, principle, or being as the center of worth and the source of meaning in life.* I sympathize with Yinger's insistence that the "nature of believing" is probably more indicative of religion than the "nature of belief" itself. Hence, a profound commitment to Marxism, intense nationalism, or faith in science and technology as the ultimate solution to our human predicament could be considered at least quasi-religious phenomena. For those who reserve the term *religion* for meaning systems that have a supernatural dimension (Stark and Bainbridge 1979), these outlooks are considered *functional alternatives to religion.* Regardless of whether we call them new forms of religion or functional alternatives, they are of interest to the sociologist of religion.[9] In any case, religion is viewed here as a *social* phenomenon—involving a group of people with a *shared faith* or a shared meaning system.

Beyond being just a social phenomenon, religion has to do with that assortment of phenomena which communicates, celebrates, internalizes, interprets, and extrapolates a faith. These phenomena include *beliefs* (myths[10]), *rites* (worship), an *ethos* (the moods and moral values of the group), a *world view* (the cognitive perspective by which the experiences of life are viewed as part of a larger and ultimately meaningful cosmology), and a *system of symbols* (which serve to encapsulate the deepest feelings and emotion-packed beliefs).

The criteria identified here should be specific enough to distinguish religion from many other cultural phenomena. For example, I have suggested that a world view and an ethical system are intrinsic aspects of religion. A feeling of awe or sacredness will not be considered religious in this text unless it includes a cognitive pattern which helps persons make sense out of life and which helps explain the meaning of suffering, death, and injustice.

On the other hand, it is hoped that the criteria for identifying religion are sufficiently broad so that we do not miss the religious significance of nontraditional groups. We are interested not only in Methodists, Baptists, Roman Catholics, and "Moonies"; we are also open to investigating scientific humanism, Transcendental Meditation, and American nationalism as religious or quasi-religious movements.

---

[9] While sociologists agree that nonsupernatural faiths are important, they differ in interpreting their meaning. For some they are signs of religious change; for others they represent religious decline. (This will be discussed in Chapters 4 and 10.)

[10] It should be mentioned here that the term *myth* does *not* refer to a belief that is untrue. Myth refers to any belief which helps people understand and interpret the events in their own lives. It is a macrosymbolic system of meaning.

A Final Word about Definitions

One's definition of religion is important, for it specifies what is and what is not appropriate data for study. The discussion in this chapter was designed to help the reader understand the differences in the way religion has been defined by scholars. I hope that the discussion has stimulated you to think through your own criteria for identifying religion. A consensus among us would be convenient, but a lack of agreement need not cause problems. The purpose of this text is not to convert readers to the author's theoretical persuasion, but to help them think more clearly about the relationship between religion, culture, and society. Before going further, it would be helpful for you to have clearly in mind (1) your own assumptions regarding the definition of religion, (2) the defining criteria used by the social scientists discussed in this chapter, and (3) the perspective of this author.[11] As Milton Yinger has written, "Definitions are tools; they are to some degree arbitrary. . . . They are abstract, which is to say they are oversimplifications. . . . We must relinquish the idea that there is any one definition that is correct and satisfactory for all" (Yinger 1970:4). The definition we each use will tend to "slice up life" a little differently and cause us to focus on slightly different phenomena as most important. Hence, we have begun by making our assumptions about religion conscious and explicit.

Although there is no consensus on the definition of religion, there is agreement among sociologists that any investigation of religion needs to explore the functions and dysfunctions of religion and to examine the role of religious conflict. We turn next to an investigation of the personal and societal needs which religion meets.

Summary

Definitions of religion are usually one of two types: *substantive* (which focus on the substance or essence of religion) and *functional* (which focus on what religion does). Substantive definitions usually emphasize a specific belief, such as a belief in spiritual beings or in a supernatural realm, or they stress the distinction between sacred and profane realms of experience. Substantive definitions delineate the traditional forms of religiosity. Functional definitions identify religion as that which provides a sense of ultimate meaning, a system of macrosymbols, and a set of core values for life. They

---

[11] As a suggested study tool, readers might (1) make a list of the factors they think are central to any definition of religion, (2) make a list of the defining characteristics specified by Tylor, Durkheim, Yinger, Geertz, Glock and Stark, Davidson and Knudsen, and Roberts respectively, and (3) develop specific questions by which they would operationalize their own definition of religion.

invite an investigation of any profound loyalty or ultimate meaning system as a form of religiosity.

One's definition tends to affect one's research design. Those who use substantive definitions can measure religiosity with questions about specific beliefs people hold, their religious affiliation and attendance, and their assessment of the importance of religion in their own lives. Multidimensional measures have usually offered the greatest insights. Those types of questions have generated significant insights into traditional types of religiosity and have usually provided more precision than is yet possible with functional definitions.

Those who favor the latter approach tend to ask open-ended questions which seek to *discover* one's ultimate meaning system—whether it be traditional religion, nationalism, astrology, or some other "invisible" religion. Social scientists who are interested in cultural change and the new forms of meaning which emerge in times of cultural transition tend to favor functional definitions. They view religion as changing rather than as declining.

This text will be based on a functional definition, but will include material from researchers using both approaches. The assumption is that religion is a social phenomenon that includes the following characteristics: beliefs, rites, an ethos, a world view, and a system of symbols.

3

The Role of Religion in Society

In the early stages of the sociological analysis of religion, the primary interest of social scientists was to find the origin of religion. It was believed that if we could discover an extremely primitive tribe, one which had never had contact with the outside world, we would be able to discover how religion got started in the first place. Early sociologists and anthropologists tried to understand social phenomena in terms of the same evolutionary schema that Darwin had used to explain the natural world. E. B. Tylor (1958), for example, maintained that religion began because people

47

dreamed about friends and family members who had died. A person would awaken and, believing that he had visited with someone who had died, conclude that humans have a soul which survives after death. These spirits or ghosts acted on the lives of the people; all things were believed to be animated by spirits. Tylor called this first stage of religion *animism*. According to Tylor's schema of evolution, people eventually came to believe in some independent spirits which had not lived on earth and which were more powerful: gods. As civilization emerged, people came to believe that the pantheon of gods was led by a single powerful god. The change from *diffused polytheism* (belief in many gods, all of whom are equal) to *hierarchial polytheism* (belief in many gods, each ranked within a hierarchial system) has been correlated with the emergence of the political state; the social structure of the gods seems to parallel the social structure of the people. Eventually, hierarchial polytheism gave way to *monotheism*. Of course, for those Christians who were not offended by such an evolutionary scheme in the first place, the idea that monotheistic Judaism next gave way to a higher stage of religion (Christianity) seemed only logical.[1] Tylor's evolutionary explanation of religion became quite popular among social scientists in the late 1800s.

Many other explanatory schemes have been employed, but anthropologists have given up the search for origins. In the first place, the unilinear concept of evolution has fallen into disrepute. Societies do not all evolve along one single line of development. Furthermore, there is no solid evidence to support the assumption that a simple tribal society which exists today is just like the societies of cavemen and women of yesteryear. The idea that we can discover the historical origins of religion is futile. Most unilinear evolutionary schema have been discarded. We will, however, explore a recently developed and more sophisticated evolutionary theory in Chapter 4.

Functional and Structural-Functional Analysis

The fact that religion is a cultural universal, found in some form in every culture in the world, has fascinated social scientists. The question that came to the fore was: Why is religion universal? Since giving up the search for origins, social scientists have focused on the function of religion. The term *function* refers to the human and societal needs that are satisfied by a particular social pattern or belief.

Although functionalism can be first attributed to Durkheim, it was popularized and developed as a systematic method of analysis by anthropologists Bronislaw Malinowski and A. R. Radcliffe-Brown. One principle of their

---

[1] The early evolutionary theories have often been criticized for being ethnocentric.

approach was that any social pattern or institution which does not serve a function will cease to exist. Furthermore, any pattern found among all peoples is believed to have its basis in innate human needs. Before focusing on the functions of religion, let us review the development and controversies within functional analysis itself, especially the divergences between these two theorists.

Bronislaw Malinowski maintained that all basic human needs or drives must be satisfied in a way that does not cause social chaos. The hunger drive, the sex drive, and the need to relieve oneself of body wastes are all satisfied in ways controlled by society. One cannot satisfy one's sex drive with just anyone and everyone. Certain norms specify which persons are or are not potential sexual partners. Lack of consent by the partner (rape) or close family relationship (incest) are only two of the more common prohibitions societies set down. Similarly, the society as a whole has a stake in controlling how one procures food and where one deposits body waste. Hence, all societies are made up of institutions—regularized patterns for the satisfaction of human need. Human needs or drives are satisfied without creating social conflict or chaos.

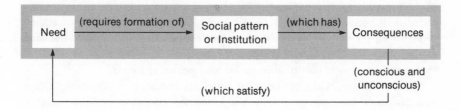

Rather than searching for historical origins of institutions, Malinowski believed that a search for functions would be more fruitful. If all institutions and regularized patterns of behavior fulfill some basic human need, then the task of the social scientist is to identify which needs, conscious or unconscious, each social pattern serves. (Malinowski 1944).

Malinowski states: "Religion is not born out of speculation or reflection, still less out of illusion or misapprehension, but rather out of the real tragedies of human life, out of the conflict between human plans and realities" (1931:641). Lack of control over one's life circumstances poses a predicament. Evil and misfortune cause persons to feel helpless. Religion allows one to feel that there is a source of power and hope which is greater than one's own resources. However, even more important is the need to cope with the anxiety and personal disorganization caused by the reality of death. According to Malinowski, "The existence of strong personal attachments and the fact of death, which of all human events is the most upsetting and disorganizing to man's calculations, are perhaps the main sources of religious belief" (1931:641). Although the various religions deal differently with death, all religions establish some belief and ritual that functions to reduce anxiety over death.

As Malinowski points out, the intended purpose of religion is not the same as its function. The purpose of religion is to worship God or the gods; the service of human need is a secondary consequence. It was Robert Merton who later introduced the terms *manifest function* (conscious and intended) and *latent function* (unconscious and unintended). At first, it seems that this is the distinction that Malinowski was making: worship of the gods or of God is the manifest function and meeting human needs is the latent function. However, reduction of personal anxiety for the bereaved is often a conscious goal of a funeral service. While addressing one's feeling of hopelessness may not be the primary purpose of conducting a religious ritual, such an outcome may nonetheless be conscious and intended. It would be a manifest function, but not necessarily the central purpose of the ritual as the people understand it. Hence, the *purpose* of religious belief and ritual as articulated by practitioners may be quite different from what the social scientist identifies as the *function* of religious belief and ritual. A social scientist may have a difficult time measuring whether the prayer for a safe fishing trip actually protects the natives from danger (the purpose of the prayer); but that prayer can be observed to provide a calming, anxiety-reducing function for those who pray. In studying other institutions in society (education, economics, politics), the manifest function is normally the same as the purpose. That is, the purpose of most social institutions is to satisfy empirically people's identifiable social and personal needs.

Malinowski traces the function of religion, and that of many institutions to individuals' basic needs, drives, and emotions. In this sense, functionalism a la Malinowski tends to be rather individualistic and psychological in character. The bottom line in understanding many social patterns is the needs of individuals (Malinowski 1944).[2]

A. R. Radcliffe-Brown developed a different approach to functionalism. According to him, the function of most social patterns is traceable not to individual needs, but to needs or requirements of the society as a whole. For example, according to Radcliffe-Brown (1939), fear of hell and damnation, and perhaps fear of death itself, would not exist if the teaching of religious groups did not instill such fear. Religion generally functions not to resolve anxiety but to create, foster, or heighten it. He maintains that in his own field studies, the subjects were more likely to experience anxiety if a ritual were improperly conducted than they were to turn to ritual procedures when they felt anxious.

Why would religion act to enhance anxiety? Structural-functionalists answer that social stability, especially in simple tribal societies, requires a

---

[2] Malinowski does, however, recognize that some needs are social needs and others are "derived needs"—needs created by the particular social structure. But his treatment of religion focuses much more on individual needs—such as that of coping with anxiety and fear.

rough consensus on values, beliefs, and norms. In most societies, formal legal sanctions are not the primary source of social control. In fact, in some societies they may be almost entirely absent. Hence, maintenance of a common world view and constant reinforcement of values and belief patterns are critical if the society is to continue as a stable system. Religious ritual acts to reinforce the belief structure, the values, and the norms of the larger society. Fear of hell, anxiety over offending one's gods, or fear of being bewitched by evil spirits tends to ensure social conformity. Radcliffe-Brown insists that by making one anxious about breaking cultural rules, religion functions to discourage deviant behavior. The function served is not an individual, but a societal, need. For Radcliffe-Brown the need for social integration and stability is a driving force behind most institutions.

While admitting that some taboos or rites may not have a structural function, he insists that structural or societal needs are usually primary. No society can exist unless individuals are willing to behave in ways that may not serve their own personal desires. For example, sex codes limit the range of persons with whom one can experience sexual satisfaction. Such codes may therefore contradict the desires of individuals; nonetheless many of those codes are necessary if the society is to continue.[3] Because his emphasis has been on the way social patterns meet societal or structural needs, Radcliffe-Brown's brand of functionalism has been called structural-functionalism. He does not deny that individual psychological needs may be met by any institution, but he believes that these psychological functions are secondary in importance.

Actually, Radcliffe-Brown's structural approach had been utilized earlier by Emile Durkheim. In 1915, Durkheim maintained that God stands in the same relationship to worshipers as does a society to its members. God transcends the individual in power and scope, is immanent within the individual, and occupies a world which is fundamentally different from the world of the individual. Furthermore, the divine has priority over the individual: human need must always give way to God's demands. Similarly, society transcends the individual in power, scope, and longevity. Society is contained within the individual in that each member of society has internalized the values and norms of his or her group. The demands and prerequisites of the society have moral priority over the desires of individuals (Durkheim 1958).

It is well to remember that one commonly quoted definition of socialization is "causing persons to *want* to do what they *must* do." A thoroughly socialized person is one who wants to do that which is necessary for the society to survive. Persons must be motivated to *want* to behave in ways that may contradict their own desires. An elderly Eskimo may take the

---

[3] This is not to suggest that every sex code is functional, but many sex codes do serve to enhance social stability. The point here is that a code which seems disadvantageous for the individual's gratification may be advantageous for the social structure.

"long walk" (suicide) because not enough food is available for all to survive. That course of action is not particularly functional for the individual in question, but he or she does it because of social necessity. Social morality in that culture specifies who is dispensable, and the individual voluntarily complies. In our own society, a man may feel sexual desire for a woman other than his wife, but if he has internalized the values of the society, he does not allow himself to act on those desires. This fidelity may function to preserve the stability of marriage, and hence the stability of the society. If the only argument presented to a person for not engaging in extramarital liasons was that social stability would be adversely affected, most persons would probably not suppress their desires. But when the prohibition is presented as a moral principle which is based on divine command, people will more likely internalize that norm. Similarly, people may not curb their desires if they are simply told that incest is wrong because it creates intra-family competition, undermines the socialization role of parents, and confuses the lines of inheritance and authority. These may be the functional reasons for the incest taboo, but many people honor the taboo because incest is an unthinkable sin. It is a moral absolute, the violation of which would seem to undermine the laws of the universe.

Durkheim's approach has been referred to as "metaphoric parallelism" (Winter 1977). He believed that the sacred world is a world that parallels the mundane world. Behavior patterns which would cause social chaos are prohibited by fear of sanction from the supernatural realm. That which is structurally dysfunctional is simply defined as taboo. According to Durkheim, the term *God* is a metaphor for *society;* worship of God is really worship of one's own society. People are not aware of this projection process, and taboos and moral codes become unquestioningly absolute and binding.

Functionalists do not always assume, as Durkheim did, that the belief in God is a mirage. For most functionalists, the existence or nonexistence of God is beyond the capacity of empiricism to prove or disprove. The question of the functionalists, regardless of the truth or falsity of a belief, has to do with how that belief or ritual operates in the society. What needs does it meet?

Durkheim and Radcliffe-Brown granted that religion may serve some individual function, but the most important functions of religion are structural. Do you find that you tend to identify with the functionalists or with the structural-functionalists? Does religion *alleviate* anxiety about death, or does it *create* anxiety about death in order to assure social conformity? Readers might find it instructive to attend funeral services in several different religious traditions. Notice comments made by the clergy who officiate, and listen carefully to the prayers. What emotions do they seem to create? During regular worship services, do prayers and sermons create anxiety about death? If so, how is this accomplished?

George Homans (1941) has offered a synthesis which attempts to avoid the either/or choice, pointing out instead that both processes may be at work. He uses the term *primary anxiety* to refer to the anxiety an individual may feel as a result of loss of a loved one. *Primary rituals* are rituals designed to alleviate this anxiety or grief; they serve an individual function, a la Malinowski. *Secondary rituals,* on the other hand, work to *create* anxiety, which ensures that society's members will conform to social norms. Hence, they serve a structural function, a la Radcliffe-Brown. In many cases, a specific religion will have some primary and some secondary rituals. It is also possible for a single ritual to relieve primary anxiety while creating *secondary anxiety.*

For example, a Protestant funeral service may emphasize that the departed loved one has gone on to the next world and is in the loving care of God. The virtues of the individual are emphasized. The minister may suggest that the bereaved family members will be united with "Grams" (as she was known) when they, too, pass on. "She is with us in spirit," they are assured, and "she wouldn't want us to stop and pine away. She would expect us to carry on. The best way to honor her is to remember the wisdom she offered, and to live our lives with faithfulness to the values she taught and lived." Comments that produce fond memories, assurance that the deceased is with us in spirit, affirmation that the bereaved will again see the deceased, and confidence that the deceased is dead only in physical form, are all reassuring to the survivors. They help to lessen primary anxiety: grief.

At the same time, persons attending the funeral may be reminded that their own lives have not been as noble or righteous as the deceased. The thought of meeting God and receiving one's just reward may heighten their anxiety. The challenge to remember Grams by living a righteous life like hers may increase the listener's sense of humility and inadequacy: "How could I ever be as generous and wise as Grams?" (One tends to recall primarily the most *positive* qualities of the deceased. Remembrance of faults often seems crass and creates guilt feelings. Hence, the positive qualities of old Grams may be magnified in the eyes of the mourners at that moment.) The funeral service, then, may remind one of his or her own finitude and may cause one to reflect on one's own life. This secondary anxiety may cause the person to reaffirm conformity to the mores of that religious group. Hence, the same ritual may *reduce* primary anxiety and *create* secondary anxiety. As Homans' synthesis illustrates, the analysis of the function of any institution may be a complex process. The diagram provided may illustrate the complexity of relationships between individual and structural functions, manifest and latent functions, and dysfunctions. (See Exhibit 3–1.)

A primary problem with functionalism as a social theory is that it is often based upon a *tautology.* In other words, it uses circular reasoning to posit and then prove a point. Certain basic human needs, whether biological, psychological, or social, are set forth as basic to human society. Any existing

Exhibit 3–1

Model of Functional Analysis

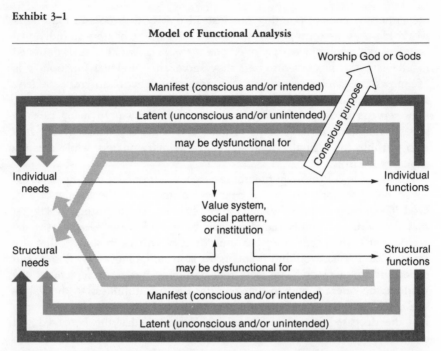

Those social patterns which are functional for the individual may be dysfunctional (harmful) for the structure, and social patterns which are functional for the structure may be dysfunctional for the individual. Since individual functions are more often conscious and intended and structural functions are more frequently unconscious, the heavy line illustrates the general pattern. However, either type of function may be conscious or unconscious, intended or unintended. Finally, the distinction between manifest function and manifest purpose may not exist in other institutions. The purpose of economic activity, for example, is to meet certain individual and societal needs. Religion as an institution is unique in having a purpose which is neither utilitarian nor expressive in its primary intent. Its purpose, as conceived by believers in many traditions, is to satisfy something outside the realm of human experience. This is represented by the "Conscious purpose" arrow.

social pattern is said to be *created* by certain basic human needs. The pattern or institution, in turn, has the *result* of satisfying that basic need (see diagram.) Hence, certain social institutions are viewed as necessary—even indispensable—for human society. This makes a neat theory, for it cannot be disproved. The answer is presupposed in the question; satisfaction of some posited basic need is both cause and effect! This sort of reasoning has caused many social scientists to reject functionalism altogether and to turn to the alternative paradigm: conflict theory. We will discuss this later in the chapter.

Classical functional theory also tended to explain almost all behavior in terms of a few basic needs which were assumed to be universal. The need for social integration or solidarity was perhaps the most commonly assumed. Furthermore, a social consensus regarding values and beliefs was believed to be absolutely essential to such solidarity. These needs were not empirically *proven*, but were amply *illustrated* and were incorporated into functional tautologies. Functionalism had become a social philosophy rather than a tool of empirical research. Most sociologists today do not accept many of the assumptions of the classical functionalists, although functionalism continues to provide an important methodology.[4] By this I mean that the basic questions of functional analysis continue to guide much sociological inquiry: What individual and social needs does a particular social pattern serve in a particular society at a particular time? In what ways and for whom is it positively functional and in what ways and for whom is it negatively functional? In other words, how does this social pattern or institution affect the lives of individuals and influence other social patterns and institutions? While there is no longer an assumption that a given institution, by virtue of its existence, is indispensable to the survival of the society, sociologists of religion continue to ask, "What does religion *do* in the society?" The answers usually address both individual and social functions. We will return later in this chapter to a discussion of problems in functional analysis. But let us turn now to some of the specific functions of religion and see how modern functionalism is applied.

The Functions of Religion

From our discussion thus far, it should be apparent that religion serves a variety of functions. Religious faith and religious organizations serve a number of needs of individuals and the social structure. However, it can be misleading to offer a general list of the functions of religion, for the way in which one functions will vary somewhat depending upon the social structure, the culture of the society, and the specific characteristics of the religion itself.[5] For a group that has immigrated to a new country, religion may take on increased significance as a source of identity. For a group experiencing great suffering, religion may offer a supraempirical explanation which makes the suffering bearable. In a society experiencing rapid social change, religion may provide a feeling of security and assurance, and the value-maintenance function is emphasized. For an individual who is geographically isolated from family members, a religious group may provide a sense of belonging. However, without overgeneralizing it is possible to point to three types of functions that religion typically serves: meaning functions, identity or belonging functions, and structural functions.

---

[4] For a more detailed treatment of the history, criticisms, and logical problems of functionalism, see Turner and Maryanski (1979). The authors also provide an excellent discussion of the difference between functionalism as an empirical methodology versus functionalism as a social philosophy.

[5] To assume that religion serves the same functions in all societies is to fall into a trap which Robert Merton refers to as the fallacy of assuming universal functionalism.

Before discussing these, I would again emphasize that the functions of religion (even the manifest ones) are frequently not the same as the purpose of religion. The purpose of religion is usually the worship or adoration of a being, an ideal, or a set of supernatural principles. Nonetheless, the practitioners of religion are usually conscious of many of the functions discussed below, and they may even be intended.

Finally, readers should be warned against the temptation to use functional analysis to "explain away" religion. Sometimes students new to the sociology of religion assume that functional explanations furnish a complete elucidation of religious behavior. This assumption limits rather than broadens our perception of religion. Functional analysis provides one lens for viewing religion. It furnishes important insights, but it does not establish the whole picture.

Individual Functions

Meaning Functions.   The function most frequently stressed by both believers and objective observers is that of providing meaning in life. Max Weber emphasized this as basic to all religions, and before him the theme was an undercurrent of Durkheim's writings. Religion provides a world view, or cosmos, by which injustice, suffering, and death can be seen as ultimately meaningful. As Geertz says, when suffering or death has meaning, it becomes sufferable. Nietzsche says the same thing when he insists that "He who has a *why* to live can bear almost any how."

In order to meet the meaning function, however, religion must include more than a set of ideas or notions about the world. Abstract philosophical systems of thought seldom satisfy this function for the masses. Meaning involves both concept (idea) and demand (imperative) (Kelley 1972:52). The world view must be presented to the prospective believer in such a way that the person seems to be held by the belief rather than voluntarily holding the beliefs. While religion affects patterns of thought, acceptance of a particular religious cosmology is seldom based on logical argument alone. Philosophical systems of thought may provide a cosmic world view, but they seldom address people's emotions and they are not presented in a way that makes people feel they are held by the belief system. There is nothing which emotionally impels them to believe: there is no demand. The communication of concepts through rituals and symbol systems incorporates both affective *and* cognitive dimensions.[6]

The desire to make sense out of the world seems to be nearly universal. People may be willing to admit that their own world view is less adequate than another, but they are not willing to give up their interpretation for none at all. They are simply not willing to say that human events are meaning-

---

[6] The affective dimension has to do with feelings; the cognitive dimension has to do with intellectual processes.

less. It seems that bafflement (lack of explanation) is an extremely anxiety-producing experience; religion acts to combat it. The religious response to the question, "Why?" is different from the answer provided by science. Science looks for empirical causality in answering the question. Religion answers it primarily in terms of values: What does a particular event *mean* in understanding the ultimate purpose or goal of one's life? Another way to say this is that religion locates a specific experience, event, or observation within a larger context of experiences, events, or observations. The larger context is attributed with ultimate meaning, and the specific event is viewed as having significance because of its relationship to the big picture (Wuthnow 1976b).

Belonging and Identity Functions. A less often recognized aspect of religion is its importance for the sense of identity of the believers. Andrew Greeley (1972:108–126) argues persuasively that the reason denomination-alism is so strong in the United States is because of the function religion has played in the lives of immigrants. Before coming to America, many Italians (for example) did not identify themselves primarily as Catholics. Placed in a new environment, however, with different norms and values, many Italian-Americans came to identify strongly with the Catholic Church. Many Italian Catholic congregations became community centers that helped members to preserve their sense of roots. Similarly, other immigrant groups have shown increased denominational loyalty and intensified religiosity after coming to America. The denomination, in effect, became a source of ethnic identity and a bastion of cultural stability for those facing culture shock. Church historian Martin Marty (1972) has similarly argued that religious denominations in the United States can be understood only in light of the ethnic issue.

But even beyond the issue of immigration, a sense of religious belonging often affects individuals' understanding of who and what they are. A teenager at a party may forgo alcohol or may refuse to participate in certain activities. The individual may identify herself strongly as a Christian and, according to her definition of what that means, certain activities are unacceptable. Or a young Mennonite fellow, faced with his draft papers for the U.S. Army, may conclude that his identity as a Christian conflicts with his identity as an American. As a Mennonite, he may accept the prohibition against war as categorical. His petition for status as a pacifist may be a profound statement of identity as a Christian. Similarly, many acts of individuals can be understood as responses to their identity as Jews, Moslems, or Buddhists.

The importance of the identity or belonging function will be emphasized in subsequent chapters. It is important to note here, however, that one of the reasons for the rise of religious cults in America seems to be related to a failure by mainline denominations to meet this need. Studies of the

Hare Krishna (Judah 1974), the Moonies (Lofland 1977), and of many communes and utopian groups (Kanter 1972) have documented the frequency with which converts cite their feeling of belonging. The original denomination or faith of the convert is often attacked for its lack of interpersonal ties. Lofland, Kanter, and Kelley have each identified emotional ties to group members as a primary element in the conversion of new members and in the continued commitment of established ones. Greeley emphasizes that while meaning functions may be *primary* (in the sense of being closer to the manifest *purpose* of religion), the belonging functions may actually be *prior to* meaning in terms of chronology. He writes:

> With some exaggeration we may say that instead of Americans belonging to churches because they believe in religion, there may be a strong tendency for them to believe in religion because they belong to churches (1972:115).

When I first read that statement by Greeley, I thought he was mistaken. After doing a good deal of research on the social psychology of religion, I have come to believe that he may be correct. As we will see in Lofland's study of conversional techniques in a doomsday cult, a sense of belonging is chronologically prior to a knowledge of or agreement with the belief system. There is evidence to suggest that the same can be said of the conversion techniques of the Children of God, the Hare Krishna, and many other conversion-seeking religious groups. The meaning functions may be primary, but the belonging function is usually prior.

The reason for this is that the community of believers comes to serve as one's reference group. As emotional ties with believers intensify and come to replace familial ties and old friendships, the novice wants to be accepted fully. He or she comes to want to believe and may be discouraged if the religious world view doesn't seem to make sense. The conversion process among most cults is not one of brainwashing, per se, but involves a transfer of reference groups. The important point here is that the research in social psychology overwhelmingly shows that one's reference group is among the most important variables of behavior and of self-identity. In a rapidly changing society, especially in a society with a high degree of geographic mobility, a sense of belonging is a critical need. If one's kin all live five hundred miles away, the need for emotional support during a time of crisis can be intense. Religious groups often serve to satisfy this need. This is true for mainline congregations as well as for cults (McGaw 1979; Roof 1978).

In some societies, religion serves another sort of identity need. As an individual progresses through life, he or she may undergo a variety of *rites of passage,* celebrations or rituals signifying changes of status in the community. Before such a rite, a youth may be considered a child; after the rite the individual is a man or woman. In many tribal societies, such rites of passage are important in defining one's role and the limits of appropriate behavior. This sort of function is deemphasized in American life, but it is part of the religious tradition in many cultures. Insofar as religion does recognize and celebrate role changes, it may contribute to the maturation process of individuals.

The maturation process may also be facilitated in other ways. The emphasis on a loving God who is in control of the universe may contribute to basic trust on the part of the individual, an outlook which Erik Erikson feels is essential to personal maturity. The importance of the religious group as a reference group may also enhance a positive and firm sense of identity. The stress on nurturing relationships in the religious community may facilitate a healthy sense of intimacy. The religious concept of mission may contribute to generativity, the feeling that one is making a significant contribution to one's community and to humankind. An affirmation of one's life *having been* meaningful is central to the final stage of development, ego-integrity. One's religious outlook may affect this ability to affirm the integrity and meaningfulness of one's existence.[7] As we will see in Chapter 5, religion may also have a retarding effect on healthy psychological development. Insofar as a religion contributes positively to these stages of development, however, it can be recognized as serving a positive function in personal maturation and mental health.

Another function of religion in some societies is to serve as a status symbol and as a sign of respectability. In American culture, to be an active member of a local church is such a sign. Church affiliation in itself is often considered an indicator of morally upright character, and one's specific denominational affiliation often has status implications. Obviously, this is not an intended function of religious leaders, but neither is it an unconscious one among the public. Note, for example, that politicians will frequently cite their church affiliation and activities. The assumption is that their ties to religion testify to their upright character. During the 1976 election, Jimmy Carter made a point of the fact that he was a born again Christian, and that may have won him votes among certain segments of the population. It is unlikely that the statement offended many citizens.

However, the tendency to identify religious affiliation as a symbol of respectability has created an odd sort of problem for some denominations. They find that although the membership roles are full, many members do not really believe the denominational doctrines. Joining a church may be for reasons other than conversion experience or an agreement on doctrine. Hence, the membership of many mainline congregations includes a broad spectrum of theologies and world views. Such members hardly share a common faith. The tendency for some people to join churches for status reasons also means that social scientists must be careful in making generaliza-

---

[7] See Erikson (1963) for a fuller discussion of psychological stages of development in the life span.

tions. Church involvement, or even active church attendance, is not necessarily a good index of a strong commitment to a faith.

Societal Functions

Emile Durkheim stressed the contribution of religion in defining not just individual identity, but in affirming the collective identity. Religion helps groups identify who they are: it offers an explanation of the significance of a group amidst the peoples of the world. Durkheim emphasized that religion served as a sort of glue to bond together people who otherwise had diverse self-interests; it helped them to define themselves as a moral community with common values and with a common mission in life. This unifying and self-defining function is especially true of religion in nonindustrialized, homogeneous societies. In the pluralistic society of America, no single traditional religion can claim that role. Some scholars insist that a sense of collective national identity and sense of purpose is critical, and that a new form of religion has emerged in the United States to fulfill that function. Referred to as civil religion, this new form of religiosity attempts to define the meaning and significance of America in relationship to some transcendent reference. (Civil religion will be discussed in Chapter 10.) In any case, religion often serves as a basis for collective identity.

Religion also enhances social stability by sacralizing (making sacred) the norms and values of the society. In fact, in simple societies which have no prisons or formal court systems, religious taboos may serve an extremely important function. Persons may hesitate to engage in deviant acts if they believe that someone may retaliate with witchcraft. Since a voodoo spell could cause death (Cannon, 1942), individuals avoid any activity that may cause someone to want to bewitch them. Furthermore, if certain behavior is taboo (so heinous and so dangerous that it is unthinkable), people may conform for fear of the consequences of breaking the taboo. Many Eskimos believe that Sedna, the goddess of the sea, determines one's success or failure in hunting seals. Such believers are not likely to risk offending her by violating one of her rules. Hence, no Eskimo kills more than is needed; waste is unthinkable. This conservation ethic is functional for Eskimo society; yet it is enforced by religious rather than legislative sanction. Of course, if a society has more than one religious group, religion may not be able to substitute for formal sanctions. Any two religions may disagree on basic prohibitions and taboos.

Taboos may also have the effect of reinforcing social stratification. Since many taboos or religious rules are applicable only for certain members of a community, they may emphasize one's social role. The Hebrews' insistence that women were unclean after each menstruation and must be purified tended to reinforce females' subordinate position. Similar ritual processes or behavioral rules may reinforce class or color lines. Mary Douglas writes:

> Not only may social intercourse be restricted, but sitting on the same chair, sharing the same latrine, or using the same cooking utensils, spoons, or combs may be prohibited, and negatively sanctioned by pollution beliefs. By such avoidances social definitions are clarified and maintained. Color bars and caste barriers are enforced by these means (1968:340).

Such taboos may enhance stability, but from the standpoint of the subjugated group, stability may not be a good thing! Hence, such taboos are positively functional for those in power, and dysfunctional for the disadvantaged group. Functional analysis must always explore whether a social pattern is functional for all members of the society or only for certain segments. Finally, it must be admitted that some taboos do not seem to serve any current function. Prohibitions against pork and many kosher laws regarding food preparation may have served an important function at one time. Given present-day standards of sanitation, these laws do not seem to serve a social function.[8]

Hence, religion establishes norms that benefit the social structure and creates an environment of moral obligation with reference to these norms. Since individuals do occasionally sin or violate the taboos, most religions have some method of regaining favored status. Guilt feelings can usually be relieved by some method of cleansing or repentence. The powerful norms which function for the *social structure* may be dysfunctional for *individuals;* shame and guilt can be debilitating. Hence, without lessening the importance of the norms, most religions incorporate a ritual procedure for purification. In such a case we see how the conflict between individual functions and societal functions can be lessened, if not resolved.

Although structural-functionalists have often emphasized religion's stability-enhancing characteristics, it can also be an instrument for change. This is referred to as the prophetic function of religion. The Old Testament prophets insisted that God required social justice, and they consistently pressed for change in the interests of a more just social system. They were early spokesmen for the poor. The Radical Reformation certainly played an important part in the Peasants' Revolt in Europe in the 16th century. Similarly, the religious faith of Martin Luther King, Jr., and of the black community in Montgomery, Alabama, was critical in the success of the nonviolent resistance strategy in the civil rights movement. In the 1970s Roman Catholic bishops in Latin America were demanding redistribution of wealth and a restructuring of the social systems in many countries. Numerous other examples in which religion has supported social change could be cited. In fact, one political scientist (Lipset 1960:107–108) claims that religion and radical political movements are sometimes functional alternatives and are often aligned with one another. It can be argued that change is not only functional for many subjugated individuals, but that it can also

---

[8] Douglas does suggest, however, that taboos often serve a psychological function of reinforcing a specific world view. This idea will be explained in Chapter 4.

benefit a social structure. While social stability offers many benefits to its members, stability is not an intrinsic and universal good. Functional analysis must evaluate the functions and the dysfunctions of both stability and change. Stability is necessary in that human society cannot exist without a fairly stable pattern of norms, roles, and values. Those patterns, however, may become inflexible and fail to meet human needs. Change can be positively functional for the social structure in such a case.

The Function of Religion in Social Morality

Is a system of social values and morality an inherent part of religion? The answer to this question will be affected to a large extent by how one defines religion. Which groups one considers to be practicing religion will vary, depending upon definition. Hence, the empirical evidence for making a generalization may vary from one social scientist to another.

The definitional criteria which I have set forth would suggest that religion is intimately bound with morality. With Geertz, I have suggested that an ethos (or set of moral moods and motivations) is by definition a part of any religion. After all, if religion focuses on that which gives meaning to all of life, then that being or object which one worships must be a significant value and perhaps a source of other values. In fact, the term *worship* itself suggests this emphasis. It actually means worth-ship, the state or quality of worth. During worship, that which is of central value is lifted up, praised, recognized. The worshiper reaffirms that this being or entity is the most exhalted of all values. In monotheistic religions, all other values are thought to emanate from this central value or being. In actual fact, monotheistic religion often does not affect everyday values as much as its theologians and more devout practitioners would like. Moreover, the relationship between ultimate value and everyday values may be seen as quite complex when we study polytheistic groups or ancestor-worshiping tribes.

The problem here is partially one of methodology. Who and what do we study when we study religion? If we study the religious belief systems and the most devout practitioners, the religious values or center of worth seem to affect everyday values directly. However, surveys of Americans, even of those Americans who say that religion is important to them, show that religion has little effect on their ideas of social morality. Two surveys conducted by the American Institute of Public Opinion demonstrate the trend. In 1955, interviewers asked, "Would you say your religious beliefs have any effect on your ideas of politics and business?" Of those Americans who said that religion is "very important" to them, 54 percent said no. In 1968, in response to a similar question, 53 percent of American respondents said churches should keep out of social and political matters (Yinger 1970:48).

Sociologists may respond in several ways to this discrepancy between what religion is supposed to do and what it really does. Some scholars simply assert that the role of the social scientist is to describe the reality, not the prescriptions of devout believers. This is the advantage of empirical research over purely philosophical investigations. The fact of the matter is that the religious affiliation of the average American does not significantly affect his or her everyday values.

Other social scientists may take a different tact: the problem may be in the definition of religious faith and in the use of traditional questions to measure the influence of one's religion. Faith has been defined in this text as that which gives meaning and purpose to life. For many Americans, Americanism may be their primary faith. However, faced with a questionnaire that asks for one's *religious affiliation,* an individual immediately thinks in terms of a denomination or religious organization. The person may be affiliated with the United Methodist Church, but is that organizational membership really indicative of his or her faith? Many people join churches because of the fellowship or the status or the respectability that such affiliation may provide. If an individual's faith or religion is actually the American Way of Life rather than Christianity, his or her verbal response may be misleading. These are complex issues. Does the sociologist accept an individual's self-definition of his or her faith, or does that social scientist probe more deeply into the social psychology of the individual's behavior for definitions? Do I have any right to suggest that your "real" religion is something other than what you claim it to be? On the other hand, do I have a responsibility as a social scientist not to accept statements simply at face value?

Many times people will respond to a question in terms of what they want to believe about themselves. Edward Stevens offers an example. Suppose we asked a man if he values reading. He may respond that reading is very worthwhile and is important to him. In a forced-choice questionnaire, he may rate reading more highly than television, and he may agree with the statement: "Daily reading should be a part of every adult's life." Yet we may find that this same fellow spends two or three hours per evening watching television, and that he has not read a book, magazine, or newspaper in the past year and a half. We might conclude, contrary to his verbal protestation, that he really values reading very little. His behavior suggests that television has priority on his time. Reading is not so much a *value* as a *velleity.* This fellow would like reading to be a value, but in the actual scheme of things, he does not act on his feeling of ought. Stevens concludes: "A velleity is something I would like, but I'm not prepared to act on it. A value is something I consistently act upon. Action is the acid test of value" (1974:13–14).

This example is simplistic. It is based on soft data (assessment of *opinion*) while a question regarding religion and everyday behavior often involves somewhat harder data (for example, assessment of one's own behavior).

There are ways in which surveys can be controlled for inaccuracies. The harder the data, the more reliable the information will be.[9] However, since surveys elicit information based on verbal responses, there always remains the possibility that a gap exists between verbal affirmation and actual behavior. When one claims that religion "is very important to me," does that always mean that religion is an intrinsic part of the person's everyday life? Or can the claim sometimes represent a velleity—what one would like to be the case? And when religion is said to be "very important," what part of religion is important: meaning? identity? belonging? The debate continues over which beliefs and which behaviors are the best indicators of religious commitment. The issue is complex, and I do not expect to resolve it here. But this example may illustrate the difficulty of making generalizations about the effect of religion on any aspect of society.

With full awareness that any generalization we make may be affected by the theoretical bias or by a limitation of our research method, let us return to the central question. Does religion directly influence our systems of social values and morality? Let us look first at how religious groups perceive this relationship.

Yinger (1970) points out that morality is often seen by a religious group as a *part,* a facet, of the domain of religion. The way one responds to one's neighbor is directly related to one's relationship to God. Others put the case more strongly and suggest that religion and ethics are one and the same thing. Bishop John Robinson of England, for example, has insisted that "Prayer and ethics are simply the inside and outside of the same thing" (1963:105). Similarly, one contemporary ecumenical group in the United States emphasizes the unity of religious and moral behavior. Members insist that a person is a hypocrite if he or she prays for God to feed the hungry, but does not give at least 1 percent of his or her income for that cause. Christians who emphasize the close relationship between religion and morality are able to find many supportive biblical passages. One of the most frequently cited is found in I John: "If anyone says, 'I love God,' and hates his brother, he is a liar" (I John 4:20). Another is Jesus' comment: "Whatever you do for the least of these my brothers, you do for me" (Matthew 25:40). Love of one's fellow human beings is viewed as one and the same as love for God. The Protestant hymn "O Brother Man" also stresses this theme. One refrain suggests: "To worship rightly is to love each other, each smile a hymn, each kindly deed a prayer." Other religious traditions could also be cited, for morality is often viewed as an integral part of religion.

However, Yinger goes on to suggest that some religions and some religious groups do not stress the unity of religion and morals. For example,

---

[9] Hard data is verifiable, is objective fact (rather than subjective impression), and is relatively unchangeable.

if the Greek mythology regarding a pantheon of gods really represented the religion (faith orientation) of that day, that religion certainly did not seem to sustain the conventional morality of the society. In fact, the stories of the gods often represented them as perpetrators of immoral acts. In this case, morality has more to do with habit, custom, or tradition than with a cosmology or religious world view. When I encounter such a disparity between the traditional religion and the moral system, my tendency is to question whether that traditional religion is really the predominant faith or religion of that culture. Institutionalized religion may continue to exist as a formal organization long after the faith perspective of the citizens has drifted to a different outlook. Religion is both a cultural system (a pattern of value-beliefs) and an institution in society. The world view of the citizens may be quite different from what the official, institutionalized religion sets forth.

Regardless, Yinger (1970:44) insists that "sin" is not the same thing as "wrong." Sin refers to a violation of suprasocial norms while wrong implies only evil social consequences. While a given act may be *both* sinful and wrong, not all condemned acts fall under both categories. Hence, some social values may be reinforced by supernatural injunction, while others may be the result of custom or of social law. In more complex societies, with elaborate political structures and legislative councils, social values and concepts of wrong may be more independent of concepts of sin. In simple tribal societies, concepts of social wrong and religious taboo (sin) are more likely to be indistinguishable.

The extent to which religion is concerned with everyday values and morals will vary between religions depending on their ideology. Furthermore, the way in which a moral code is related to religion will vary with the social structure of the society (Yinger 1970). Nonetheless, all religions seem to be concerned at least to some extent with personal morality. This may hold true even in the case of those people surveyed by the American Institute of Public Opinion regarding religion and politics. Their failure to apply religion to politics and business indicates that their concept of religion is not related to their social ethic.[10] But their concept of religiosity may be quite relevant for everyday *personal* behavior (personal sexual behavior, use of alcohol, individual kindness to others, and so on). Moreover, religions usually address at least some areas of social morality as well. The concern of the Roman Catholic church regarding legislation on abortion is only one of many examples of the concern of religious groups with social policy.

Generalizations about the relationship between religion and morality, or religion and everyday values, must be tentative. They are most accurately made with reference to a specific religion in a specific society. Nonetheless, I would concur with Geertz in asserting that for most individuals in most

---

[10] Social ethics refers to the morality of *social* policy.

religions in most societies, religion and everyday morality are closely linked. Geertz writes:

> The need for such a metaphysical grounding for values seems to vary quite widely in intensity from culture to culture and from individual to individual, but the tendency to desire some sort of factual basis for one's commitments seems practically universal; mere conventionalism satisfies few people in any culture. However its role may differ at various times, for various individuals, and in various cultures, religion, by fusing ethos and world view, gives to a set of social values what they perhaps most need to be coercive: an appearance of objectivity. In sacred rituals and myths values are portrayed not as subjective human preferences but as the imposed conditions for life implicit in a world with a particular structure (1958:426–427).

For most people, a moral code does not seem compelling if it is enforced by nothing more than social tradition. Would the great majority of people refrain from incest if the only argument against it was simply that incest would cause social instability? Possibly not. Incest is unthinkable because it is a sin which violates the will of God. Or, for the atheist, incest seems to violate the immutable principles of nature. This social wrong is reinforced by cosmology or world view; this cosmology suggests that the act is evil on some grand scale, that basic principles of the universe would be undermined if it were not so considered. In this way religion or a cosmic world view serves to reinforce social values and morality; there is nothing relative or arbitrary about them. The role of a cosmic world view is especially evident when one studies groups that challenge the values of the dominant society. Such challenges, as in the case of counterculture movements, nearly always involve an alternative cosmology or world view to support the alternative values. One of the important functions of most religions, then, is to provide a metaphysical basis for the moral order of the social group and to reinforce obedience to norms.[11] Despite my caution about generalizations, O'Dea's comment seems to be accurate for most cases: "By showing the norms and rules of society to be part of a larger supraempirical ethical order, ordained and sanctified by religious belief and practice, religion contributes to their enforcement" (1966:6).

Summary

Religion, then, serves a variety of functions. It provides a world view which reduces bafflement and attempts to interpret the meaning of injustice, suffering, and death. It establishes a cosmic grounding for one's values so that one's system of personal and social morality seems certain. It offers a source of identity and a feeling of belonging. It commemorates changes

---

[11] See Chapter 4 for elaboration of this issue.

in the lives of individuals and thereby offers formal sanction to role changes. And it functions for the social structure by providing a sense of collective identity and significance, and by enhancing change and/or stability. Keeping these general functions of religion in mind as a guideline, students of religion should approach any given religion or religious group to discover its specific functions in a particular society. The same religion (e.g., Catholicism) may serve somewhat different functions in different societies and in different cultural contexts.

Distinction between Religion and Magic

When studying religion, social scientists often find themselves immersed in a closely related phenomenon—magic. Erroneous generalizations about religion and spurious theories about religion and society have sometimes been set forth because religion and magic have been viewed as one and the same thing. In fact, the two are often found together, but because they serve rather different functions, students of religion should understand the distinction between them.

Many criteria have been used to discriminate between religion and magic. In the listing below, some of the differences are juxtaposed. Various scholars have emphasized one or more of these factors (Titiev 1972).

Religion	*Magic*
1. Sense of a "group" of common believers: a "church."	1. No "church" or "group consciousness" involved.
2. Moral ethos, or a system of ethics to guide behavior.	2. No moral ethos or systematic pattern of ethics.
3. Rites are meaningful; they reinforce patterns of belief.	3. Rites not necessarily meaningful; they are used to cast a spell or make something happen.
4. Rites occur calendrically (on regular basis each week, month, and/or year).	4. Rites occur at critical (crisis) times.
5. Functions for both the individual and the structure.	5. Functions only for individuals, not for social structure.
6. Participation is open; leader leads entire group in performance of ritual.	6. Leader is only one to know ritual and how to perform it; others present are passive.
7. Worship of transcendent Being or Power as intrinsically worthy of one's attention.	7. Manipulation of impersonal, transcendent power for utilitarian reasons.

These seven distinguishing factors make a nice, neat picture of magic and religion, but in reality the distinction is not so precise. There are many churches in which the members may not find the ritual meaningful. Many members may attend worship only at critical times in their lives (funerals, baptisms, marriages, or times of emotional stress for the individual), and the minister may emphasize utilitarian reasons for belonging (for example, God's blessing on one's business or promises of good health). Yet the phenomenon hardly seems to be magic rather than religion. Furthermore, the factors listed above do not show a high correlation with each other. The distinction between magic and religion remains somewhat foggy. Nonetheless, one factor seems worthy of our attention.

The primary difference between religion and magic has most commonly been defined in terms of the attitude toward the transcendent: Is it considered of intrinsic or utilitarian value? The religious perspective views the object of worship as being of inherent, categorical worth. It is not worshiped primarily because of favors to be returned for performance of the ritual. God is worshiped in the Christian tradition—or at least is supposed to be worshiped in that tradition—simply "because He is God." In religion the object of worship is the center of worth or the epitome of value.

In the case of magic, the world is believed to be controlled by supernatural forces that control one's destiny. The objective is to get those forces working for instead of against you. Magic involves manipulation of supernatural forces. In a discussion of magic in American culture, George Gmelch (1971) points out that many baseball players will often follow such patterns as rising at a specific time, eating only certain foods prior to a game, consistently taking the same route to the stadium, getting dressed according to a specific preset pattern (e.g., always putting on the right sock first), and always stepping on third base on the way to the outfield. The players who followed these rituals seemed to feel that they would be jinxed if they did not. Somehow, the unspoken forces of fate would betray them if the proper (nonrational) steps were not taken.

While this may be an unusual example, the world view of expecting supernatural and impersonal forces to control one's destiny is characteristic of what anthropologists have called magic. The supernatural forces are not personal beings to whom one prays or with whom one develops a relationship. Rather, they have no will of their own. They simply represent laws of the universe which must not be violated, and which might be used to one's own advantage. Hence, magic in tribal societies is a supraempirical means of controlling one's chances of success in any endeavor. Whenever the desire for success is high, but the chances of failure are great, people may look for any means possible to ensure success. Malinowski writes, "Magic is to be expected and generally to be found whenever man comes to an unbridgeable gap, a hiatus in his knowledge or in his powers of practical control, and yet has to continue in his pursuit (1931:638).

Some of the functions of magic are the same as those of religion. In a study of water witching (using a forked twig to locate a source of underground water), Evon Vogt (1952) found some important functions being served. In Homestead, New Mexico, the cost of drilling was high, the chance of failure great, and success in finding water critical. Hence, people turned to a dowser (water witch). The persons investing money in drilling were satisfied that they were doing *something* to increase the likelihood of success. Because the water witch had confidence, the anxiety of the people was reduced and they were willing to invest more in any given drilling site. They agreed to drill deeper because they were assured that water was there. Vogt insists that there is no scientific evidence to support the claim that dowsers can actually find water, and that mere chance is actually a more reliable means of hitting water than employing one. Nonetheless, farmers continue to use them because that lessens their anxiety. The world view of those farmers is magical in that they assume some supernatural force is at work in helping the witch to locate water. (Exhibit 3–2 offers another example of an appeal to magic.)

E. E. Evans-Prichard points to another kind of function of magic. For the Azande tribe in Africa, witchcraft helps its members explain why adverse events happen. They constantly want to know why? or why me? One of the incidents Evans-Prichard describes has to do with injury caused by the collapse of a shelter. The Azande understand that termites eat the supports, but why did it collapse when a specific person was seeking shelter from the sun?

> Now why should these particular people have been sitting under this particular granary at the particular moment when it collapsed? That it should collapse is easily intelligible, but why should it have collapsed at the particular moment when these particular people were sitting beneath it? Through years it might have collapsed, so why should it fall just when certain people sought its kindly shelter? We say that the granary collapsed because its supports were eaten by termites. That is the cause that explains the collapse of the granary. We also say that people were sitting under it at the time because it was in the heat of the day and they thought that it would be a comfortable place to talk and work. This is the cause of people being under the granary at the time it collapsed. To our minds the only relationship between these two independently caused facts is their coincidence in time and space. We have no explanation of why the two chains of causation intersected at a certain time and in a certain place, for there is no interdependence between them.
>
> Zande philosophy can supply the missing link. The Zande knows that the supports were undermined by termites and that people were sitting beneath the granary in order to escape the heat and glare of the sun. But he knows besides why these two events occurred at a precisely similar moment in time and space. It was due to the action of witchcraft (1937:69–70).

The Azande simply can't stand the "mental chaos" of thinking of events as meaningless or coincidental. Their response to misfortune is anger because

Exhibit 3–2 _____

Chain Letter Based on a Magical World View
_____

1. President of the largest steel company
2. President of the largest gas company
3. President of the New York Stock Exchange
4. Greatest wheat speculator
5. Great bear of Wall Street
6. Head of the world's largest monopoly
7. President of the Bank of International Settlement

These should certainly be considered the world's most successful men. At least they found the secret of making money. Now, some 50 years later, where are these men?????

1. The president of the largest steel company, Charles Schway, died a pauper.
2. The president of the largest gas company, Howard Hopson, is now insane.
3. The president of the New York Exchange, Richard Whitney, was released from a hospital, to die at home.
4. The greatest wheat speculator, Arthur Cooken, died abroad insolvent.
5. The greatest bear of Wall Street, Gosabee Rivermore, died by suicide.
6. The head of the world's largest monopoly, Ivan Krueger, the match king, died a suicide.
7. The president of the Bank of International Settlement shot himself.

The same year, 1923, the winner of the most important golf championship, Gene Sarazen, won the U.S. Open and the P.G.A. tournament. Today he is still playing an excellent game of golf and is solvent.

Conclusion: Stop Worrying about Business and Go Play Golf.

This letter originated in the Netherlands and has been passed around the world at least 20 times, bringing good luck to everyone we passed it on to. The one who breaks the chain *will have bad luck.*
Do not keep this letter. Do not send money. Just have your secretary make four copies and send it to five of your friends to whom you wish good. You will see that something good happens to you four days from now if you do not break the chain. This is no joke. You will receive good luck in four days' time.
Put your name at the bottom of the list, leaving the top name off, and mail the original and four copies to your five friends to whom you wish good luck.

(10 names followed)

About a year ago a friend of mine, a college instructor, sent me this chain letter. The letter lacks coherence and is absurd in its presumptions, yet my well-educated friend sent it in all seriousness. When I probed, I found that he had not been granted tenure in his department, his contract was running out, and he had had a job interview scheduled for the third day after he received this letter. With a sheepish grin he commented, "I just wasn't about to take any chances." The presumption of impersonal supernatural forces which may determine one's destiny is characteristic of the magic world view. My friend was afraid to take a chance of offending these forces by violating a ritual requirement: forwarding the letter. He would probably have destroyed the letter, except that he was faced with a task in which success was both important and uncertain. In American culture, a magical outlook tends to emerge at critical times rather than being continuously present. (Since my friend landed the job, his "superstition" is not likely to wane in future times of crises.)

someone has played a trick on them. Hence, the need to affirm that the world makes sense is satisfied by a belief in witchcraft. They do not have to face bafflement. Witchcraft provides an explanation of misfortune.

Notice that in both the water witching and Azande cases belief in magic not only serves certain individual needs, but it provides a concrete action to *control* adverse events. For the Azande, one has only to find a countermagic to successfully combat future misfortune. In actuality, magic serves as a form of primitive technology or as a complement to empirical techniques. If I want to control events, but I do not have at my disposal rational means to do so, then I may turn to supernatural methods. In the case of magic, I look for ways to manipulate supernatural forces for my own benefit. I do not have to confess sins or otherwise earn a right relationship with supernatural beings. The twig will work regardless of the moral righteousness of the dowser.

While it is true that religion is often concerned with mundane adversities, the method of resolving the problem calls for moral purification, confession, or some other transformation of the person involved. Faith healing, for example, is usually expected to be effective only after the person is in "right relationship with God." A person may be ill and may appeal to magic for a cure. In this case, healing will come if the words are said correctly and the ritual is properly performed. If healing is not forthcoming, the ritual was not performed correctly. However, if a person turns to a religious faith healer for help, and the ailment is not cured, the explanation usually is that the afflicted person *or* the healer is not in harmony (right relationship) with God.

When studying any one group, the question of whether one is encountering magic or religion may not be as clear and categorical as suggested here. Nevertheless, the primary appeal of magic is to manipulate the world. Science and technology are more rational means of controlling one's environment. As science and technology allow persons to have increasing control over their lives, magic tends to decline. The amount of magic in a society tends to be inversely correlated to the amount of science and technology.[12] As Malinowski says, we do not find magic wherever the pursuit is certain, reliable, and under the control of rational methods. This is not to say that magic and superstition will someday disappear, for it is highly unlikely that science will ever allow us *total* control over the events of our lives.

I have gone to some length to suggest a difference between magic and science. The purpose was to emphasize a difference in the primary functions of the two. In the 19th century, August Comte began a school of thought called positivism. Part of that system of thought was concerned with an evolution of human thinking. Comte believed that theology (which he considered based on mystical, nonrational patterns) would be replaced by philosophy (or metaphysics, as he called it). Philosophy is much more rational

---

[12] This does not mean that magic is the primitive substitute for science. Malinowski (1948:28–36) has shown that even the most simple society has some empirically validated knowledge, and technical skill is never replaced by magic. He writes: "Magic, therefore, far from being primitive science, is the outgrowth of clear recognition that science has its limits and that a human mind and skill are at times impotent" (1931:637). Only when technology can ensure success in a task does magic cease.

than theology, and is therefore superior; but philosophy is highly abstract and speculative. Hence, philosophy would ultimately give way to science, for science is based on positive, empirically based proof. The implication of this early positivism[13] is that science will eventually replace religion as we know it. Comte suggested a Religion of Humanity that he believed would predominate in this final Age of Positivism. A number of scholars continue to insist that religion is losing ground against secularism, and that the two cannot successfully coincide.

The challenge of secularism will be discussed in more detail in Chapter 4. By focusing on the functions of religion, however, I believe that Comte's prediction of the demise of religion can be found wanting. Magic, I would assert, will be replaced in large part by science, technology, and the modern secular world view. The primary functions of religion, however, are not to manipulate one's environment. There are other functions that are central to religion; explaining the meaning of life and preserving central values and ethical codes in the culture are among those. Technology may help us control our environment and can make life more comfortable, but it can never explain why life is meaningful in the first place. The function of science is to expand our knowledge; the function of religion is to offer people wisdom.

This is not a defense of religion. Often the "wisdom" offered by a given religion may be bizarre. But wisdom has to do with *values* rather than with *facts*. Science answers the question of why something happens in terms of causality; religion answers the question of why in terms of values and ultimate meanings. As we will see later, science and religion often come into conflict. Certainly, facts and values are closely related in any society. However, the central functions of religion are not likely to be replaced by science; for most people, science is not likely to be an adequate functional alternative to religion. Because I believe that religion addresses a common[14] human need (for meaning), I also believe that it is here to stay. With Yinger, I am convinced that the form of religion will change. Science will cause modifications and adaptations in religion, but religion is not likely to disappear.[15]

Dysfunctions and Variant Evaluations

A few years ago an agricultural agent from an international organization visited an impoverished country. The people were starving, and the agent

---

[13] The presuppositions and development of the logical positivism of the 20th century are somewhat different.

[14] Notice that I did not say universal. The need for meaning appears to be nearly universal, but at this time we cannot claim universality of the need.

[15] Readers may notice the importance of my definition of religion in making this assertion. Recall that my definition of religion has to do with systems of ultimate meaning and value. Those who use a substantive definition of religion are more inclined to view religion as being in decline. Traditional forms of religion are not indispensable.

hoped to teach them modern farming methods. He was certain that they could receive a better yield from their fields. He had several tractors flown in, and he began to teach them how to use a tractor to plow. The native people immediately protested and insisted that he stop at once. "The earth is our Mother," they began. "Would you take a knife and stab your mother in the breast? Neither would we so gouge the flesh of our mother, the Earth, who nourishes us. No, we barely scratch the surface of the ground with a stick and gently place the seed in the small furrow."

The religious world-view of these people may have provided them with certainty of values, may have reinforced their social structure, and may have helped them interpret the meaning of their suffering. However, their religion was quite dysfunctional in economic terms. Their religious outlook prevented the introduction of modern farming, and the result was continued starvation. Just so, religion may be serving both positive and negative functions at the same time. Development specialists from the United Nations and from the World Council of Churches have found that animism (the belief that trees, stones, animals, and other objects are inhabited by spirits), can be a serious obstacle to accepting scientific methods. (On the other hand, acceptance of a Western world view often plays havoc on the culture and the social structure of these people.) (Mead 1955)

In Western culture, religion has often opposed scientific advances. Copernicus's claim that the earth revolves around the sun was condemned as heresy, and Galileo was tried by the Inquisition for asserting that he had proved Copernicus correct. Much later, biblical literalists condemned Darwin's theories and insisted that such heresy not be taught in the public schools. The criterion of truth was the Bible, and alternative theories or ideas were to be suppressed. Such an attitude is certainly dysfunctional for scientific inquiry. More recently, the Roman Catholic Church has adopted official opposition to artificial methods of birth control. Many demographers who are concerned about the population explosion in predominantly Catholic Latin American countries see this stance as one contributor to world hunger. Our world population is increasing more rapidly than our food supply, they say. Religious opposition to contraception is therefore seen by many social scientists as dysfunctional.

Ogburn (1950) referred to this differential in the rate of change in technology and beliefs as "culture lag." This lag effect has often been evaluated as dysfunctional. More recently, scientists, social scientists, and many concerned citizens have wondered whether the rate of technological change has been too rapid and uncontrolled. The lag effect may be a good thing in some cases, they suggest. Here we come to the issue of variant evaluations. Are scientific advances and technological innovations the best criteria for defining progress? In terms of economic development, a profound reverence for the earth may be dysfunctional. On the other hand, viewed in terms of the ecologic system, such a conservational attitude may be functional. Hence, when one evaluates some social process as functional or dysfunctional, it is important to keep one's criteria in mind: functional *for whom* or *for what?* In terms of scientific inquiry, religious faith has often been dysfunctional, and religious doubt has been functional.

Another area in which disagreement occurs concerns the stabilizing function of religion as positive or negative. It is interesting that Karl Marx and Emile Durkheim basically agreed on the way in which religion functions in society. Religion tends to unite people around common values and beliefs. This occurs even when the self-interests of members are contrary. Durkheim admired the way religion functioned for social unity; Marx was appalled by it and referred to religion as the "opiate of the people." Marx claimed that religion unites people under a "false consciousness," a false sense of common interests. By interpreting injustice as meaningful and as being rectified in an afterlife, religion has served to keep oppressed people in bondage.

There are many instances in which the Marxian critique appears accurate. Religion's stabilizing function has often been economically dysfunctional for subjugated people. By consoling those who are frustrated and deprived, religion may inhibit protest and social change which would result in a more equitable society. "By postponing reforms, this effect of religion can contribute to the build-up of explosive resentments which eventually issue in revolution and in more costly and destructive changes" (O'Dea 1966:100).

The prophetic role of social criticism can also be functional and/or dysfunctional. Social change in the direction of greater economic equity may be functional for the poor and dysfunctional for the rich. Furthermore, insofar as the prophet sees himself or herself as an agent of God's will, he or she may employ an extremism and unwillingness to compromise which is not conducive to constructive and realistic change. A few years ago, 53 American hostages were held in Iran. The absolute certainty and self-righteousness of the Ayatollah Khomeini (the prophet and government leader who sought to restore Islamic righteousness to Iran) was a serious problem in the negotiations. The social changes which prophetic criticism enhances may or may not be functional for the society.

The identity function of religion is important in a heterogeneous and geographically mobile society. The sense of belonging a religious community provides can serve important psychological needs. However, this sense of belonging and this identity function may lead to extreme parochialism, bigotry, and ethnocentrism. As we will see in Chapter 9, surveys have shown church members to be more prejudiced against blacks and other minorities than are nonmembers. Religion often breeds narrow-mindedness and strong group boundaries. The conflict between Protestants and Catholics in Ireland has an economic component, but religious bigotry is certainly a significant part of it as well.

Finally, religion facilitates the process of role changes by celebrating the stages in the maturation process. But religion may also encourage immaturity and dependence in people. Many religious groups, including a wide variety of charismatic cults, insist that converts abdicate decision making. Members are simply to do what their leader tells them. The mass suicide of nearly one thousand people in Jonestown, Guiana, in 1978 caused many Americans to question whether religion is always a good thing. Jim Jones created in his converts an intense dependence upon himself. Unfortunately, the event has led to some outrageous and unsupportable generalizations about brainwashing among the Hare Krishna, the Moonies, and other cultic movements (see, for example, Conway and Siegelman 1978). The fact remains that religion, including many mainline denominations, does not always encourage independent and critical thinking. I would maintain that independent thinking is part of being a mature person and that religion is often dysfunctional in this respect.

The evaluation of functions and dysfunctions depends upon one's criteria of what is "positive." Hence, there are often differing evaluations of the relative positive or negative effects of religion. Moreover, religion may be positive in some respects and negative in others. The important point is that one must be clear about his or her criteria in using these terms. Furthermore, one must always be cautious about broad generalizations regarding religion. In order to be precise, we must discuss the functions and dysfunctions of a specific religion, for specific individuals, for a specific structure, in a specific society.

Problems with Functional Analysis

Functional analysis is but one lens through which any social process can be viewed and understood. There are, however, distortions in this lens. (1) Functionalism tends to err in the direction of overemphasizing social stability and underemphasizing conflict and change. In so doing, functionalists have often assumed that societies are quite well-integrated systems; the positive functions have been stressed more heavily than the dysfunctions. (2) Structural-functionalists have often evaluated social functions as being primary, while seeing individual dysfunctions as necessary evils. Hence, some functional theories have operated with a conservative bias. This need not be an intrinsic problem with this approach as a methodology, but it has been a tendency of functionalism as a social philosophy (Turner and Maryanski 1979). (3) In stressing functions, one also loses sight of the historical process by which any particular religion established its present character. The new emphasis on historical sociology (or diachronic analysis) in the study of religion is an important corrective to this oversight (Geertz 1968). (4) Functionalists have also been interested primarily in the factors influencing (and influenced by) faith. As O'Dea points out, more attention needs to be paid to the functions and dysfunctions of doubt (O'Dea 1966:17). (5) By emphasizing the critical needs that religion fulfills, one may assume that the traditional forms of religion are indispensable. Yinger has written of "secular alternatives" to religion (1957); Weber spoke of the role of "religion surrogates" in secularized societies; and much research in the past two decades has been devoted to discovering "new forms of religion." (Bellah, 1970b, 1975; Yinger, 1969, 1977; Luckmann, 1967; Wuthnow, 1976b). Hence, it is important to avoid the trap of thinking that traditional forms are indispensable. Whether all forms of religion can be dispensed with is highly controversial, but I believe that some form of ultimate meaning system is basic to human life. (6) Finally, the social scientist claims not to deny the existence of God, but simply suspends judgment. The existence of God is beyond the capacity of empirical method to prove or disprove. Yet the functionalist proceeds to offer naturalistic explanations, sociological or psychological, for every phase of religious activity. All behavior is believed to be causally related to a human or structural need. This assumption seems to belie the assertion that functional analysis suspends judgment. In fact, the functionalist often undertakes analysis "as if" there were no supernatural cause. This is a reasonable stance for someone dedicated to the empirical, scientific method. Nonetheless, it makes many believers uncomfortable with scientific investigation of religion.

Some of the shortcomings of functionalism have caused a number of sociologists to reject it altogether. Many of these have turned instead to one of the several forms of conflict theory.

Conflict Theory and Religious Conflict

Marx maintained that the fundamental reality of history and modern society is a conflict between the classes. The haves use every tool available, including coercion and ideology, to sustain their advantageous position over the have nots. Understanding modern industrial society does not necessitate an analysis of cultural values and beliefs. The basic issue is economic conflict. Hence, Marx is often identified as the father of modern conflict theory. He maintained that values and beliefs basically operate (after the fact) to justify the self-interests of various groups. Along this line, Marx viewed religion as an ideology that justified the current social arrangements. It served as a tool of the upper classes and helped to maintain stability. Marx, like Durkheim, viewed religion as a force for social integration. But for Marx, this had a tragic consequence; religion served to maintain an unjust status quo. Religion acts to unite persons of various classes when, according to Marx, all persons of the lower class should be uniting against all those in the upper class. In fact, the ideology which promised rewards in an afterlife for conformity in this world had as much of a pacifying effect as opium (hence, his comment about religion being the opiate of the masses).

Certainly there are many examples that would lend credence to the Marxian interpretation. The Hindu belief in reincarnation has led many low-caste Indians to conform to the laws of dharma. Only by conforming to dharma (which reinforces caste lines) can one expect to be reincarnated in a higher position. Those who violate these laws can expect to be reincarnated in some lower animal form. This sort of belief system tends to undermine any impetus to rebel against the social system. Christian beliefs in otherworldly salvation sometimes act in a similar way to pacify the poor and the disenfranchized (see Chapter 8).

Religion as a Source of Social Disruption

Not all conflict theorists emphasize the integrating and stabilizing function of religion. In fact, a number of them emphasize that society is not well integrated at all. Society is comprised of interest groups, each of which seeks the fulfillment of its own self-interests. They believe there is no consensus over values and beliefs which serves to unite the society; rather, modern society is characterized by conflict, coercion, and power-plays by various groups. When stability does occur in a society, it is due to a balance of power that exists when no one group can gain superior standing, or to the fact that one group gains enough power to control others. The stability lasts only so long as the distribution of power remains the same. Sometimes social stability is attributed to economic interdependence of groups—such that overt conflict would be dysfunctional to each. In any case, religious groups are viewed as simply one more set of interest groups in society. Common beliefs are viewed as relatively unimportant in social integration. Hence, Marx's principle—that self-interest is the key factor in shaping social relationships—is a central emphasis of all conflict theory.

Conflicts between Christians and Jews provide a vivid example. Christians and Jews have coexisted in the Western world for nearly two thousand years. Yet because Christianity has been the dominant religious force in Europe since late Roman times, Christian leaders have often determined the nature of the relationship. At some points in history, Jews have been enticed to come to predominantly Christian cities because they brought needed skills and services. For example, in A.D. 1084 the bishop of Speier attracted Jews to that city because of their professional skills and because they would provide loans, which Christians would not because they believed that usury (loaning money for interest) was immoral. Jews were quite willing to lend money, and so provided a needed service for the community. As part of the enticement, Jews were given their own section of the city, a section the Jews called a ghetto.[16] In fact, they willingly purchased a charter

---

[16] A ghetto is not necessarily a poor area of the city. A poor area is a slum; a ghetto is an ethnic enclave. While some ghettos in America are also slums, the terms are not synonymous.

and paid a lease for the privilege of having their own ethnic enclave. However, as Christian mores changed and usury became an acceptable Christian enterprise, and as Christians moved into the professions Jews had occupied, conflict between the groups began to intensify. By 1555, Pope Paul IV had made the Jewish ghetto compulsory rather than volitional, and Jews became objects of severe persecution (Berry and Tischler 1978:337–338).

The record of such conflict is long and consistent. The day before Columbus first set out for America, all Jews were ordered to leave Spain. The same thing had occurred in England in 1290 and in France in 1306 (Berry and Tischler 1978:94–95). Although we have not expelled the Jewish population, the pattern of discriminatory treatment continued in this country. Many Christians blame their victims for their plight, insisting that some characteristic of the Jews causes them to be persecuted. But the evidence is overwhelming that the primary cause of discrimination is the desire to gain an edge in a conflict over scarce resources (jobs, the best housing, the best educational opportunities). For many decades in this country, universities and professional schools had quotas for Jews. Only a limited percentage of Jews would be admitted each year, regardless of superior qualifications of Jewish applicants (Belth 1979). Christians have often used their power as the dominant group to place Jews at an economic disadvantage. Ironically, those same Christians have then labeled the Jews as devious, manipulative, and driven by economic interests.

But religioeconomic conflict has certainly not been limited to that between Christians and non-Christians. In the United States, Protestants have used their dominant numbers and established positions of power to oppress Catholic immigrants. Since they were here first, Protestants were well established before Catholic immigrants of Irish, Italian, or Hispanic background came to this country. The Know Nothing Party and the Ku Klux Klan are two examples of American movements which were intensely anti-Catholic and which limited membership to white, American-born, Protestants. Some analysts (e.g., Wilson 1978:313–314) insist that the temperance movement was also essentially an anti-Catholic phenomenon in which Protestants sought to force their own definitions of Christian morality on Catholics and Jews. The Anti-Saloon League, formed in 1896, specifically attacked the symbol of the urban, ethnic, Catholic, lower-class leisure lifestyle. For many Protestants, the saloon was a symbol of the Irish Catholics—who had come in large numbers, were taking jobs, were gaining political power in urban centers, and were beginning to upset the economic advantage Protestants had enjoyed. According to this analysis, Prohibition was largely an attempt to define ethnic Catholic lifestyles as illegal and thereby effectively to label such persons as deviants. Protestants continued to dominate the top positions in business and finance into the 1950s, with Catholics—regardless of competence or credentials—effectively shut out. For example, Anderson (1970: 143) reports that in that decade 93 percent of the top executives in manufacturing, mining, and finance were Protestant, and that Protestants held 85 percent of the highest positions in the 200 largest corporations. This was despite the fact that Catholics comprised approximately 25 percent of the American population (Stark and Glock 1968:8; Greeley 1974:42). Fortunately, since then levels of anti-Catholicity among Protestants and anti-Protestant sentiment among Catholics have declined.

Although some Protestants blame Catholics themselves for their so-called lack of success[17] (due to a supposed lack of a sufficient work ethic and an inadequate sense of delayed gratification), Wilson (1978:288–307) argues persuasively that the economic differential between Protestants and Catholics is due to discrimination against Catholics. In short, Protestants are an interest group which uses a position of power and influence to ensure an economic advantage.

The insistence by a group that its members have exclusive possession of truth, knowledge, and goodness is called *particularism*. Particularism tends to encourage a militance on behalf of one's beliefs, and this makes it easier for religious leaders to mobilize followers around the cause. Particularism thrives on opposition, for the in-group needs an out-group with which it can compare itself and against which it can define its membership. If no out-group exists, the tendency is to create one. Several studies have shown a high correlation between theological particularism and various forms of group prejudice. (Glock and Stark 1966; see the discussion of religion and prejudice in Chapter 9). Religious groups and individuals which do not manifest theological particularism do not reveal as high an incidence of out-group hostility. Hence, the specific theological orientation may affect the tendency of the group to establish high boundaries.

There is, however, a source of strong religious boundaries and exclusion that is even more important than theological particularism. Out-group hostility varies in large measure with the extent to which lines of religious affiliation are coextensive with ethnic and class lines. When ethnic ties and economic interests act to create social solidarity, religious differences may serve as one more symbol of differentiation. In fact, apparent religious conflicts may mask other underlying causes of intergroup conflict. The armed combat between Protestants and Catholics in Philadelphia in 1844 was an example of such conflict (Shannon 1963:43). Similarly, the conflict in Northern Ireland cannot be understood without reference to ethnic and class issues as well as religious ones (McGuire, 1981:166–179).

American society is increasingly characterized by many cross-pressures and countervailing forces. Persons may have group loyalties, friendships, and business partnerships which involve alliances with members of other

---

[17] A disproportionate percentage of the very highest paying and most prestigious jobs are still held by Protestants. But differentials in mean income between Protestants and Catholics are closing rapidly (Roof 1979; Greeley 1981). Exhibit 8–1 in Chapter 8 provides specific data on the mean income of the members of various denominations.

religious groups, social classes, and ethnic groups. Insofar as this is true, the multiplicity of crossed alliances provides the basis for integration and social stability. These countervailing forces tend to weaken the tendency to view members of other faiths as enemies. This is not to say that religious conflict is eliminated, however. For example, in one two-month period in 1960 there were 643 reported incidents of vandalism to Jewish property, beatings of Jews, and anti-Semitic paintings on synagogue walls (including Nazi swastikas) in the United States (Glock and Stark 1966:xi). Christians, especially conservative Protestants, continue to blame Jews for the death of Jesus, and they justify hostile and illegal acts on this ground. In the late 1970s there were also incidents of youths attacking Amish buggies, and at least one person was killed—an Amish infant whose skull was crushed by a rock. However, interreligious conflict is less severe in those settings where religious, ethnic, and class lines are not coextensive and where countervailing forces can afford structural integration to the society.[18]

Religion may prove divisive in another instance, that is, recognition of what constitutes proper authority. The central value system of a religion may come into conflict with the secular legal system. In this case, persons must choose which set of values and norms they will respect. Often this boils down to the issue of which value system is authoritative or which leader (religious or political) is attributed with proper authority. In the late 1960s and early 1970s a number of religiously motivated individuals violated federal laws in protest of the Vietnam War. For example, two Roman Catholic priests, Daniel and Phillip Berrigan, broke into draft board offices and poured blood on selective service files. They maintained that their Christian conscience would not permit them to remain idle while young men were being drafted for war. In this and other such cases, a person's theological understanding may generate norms which differ from those the civil laws uphold.

The Amish regulation that their children must not go to school beyond the eighth grade provides another example. When this norm conflicted with state law compelling all children to stay in school until graduation or age 16, some Amish parents in the 1950s and 1960s chose to go to jail rather than obey the law. The most severe conflicts were in Pennsylvania and Iowa. Eventually the issue was settled in a way that satisfied the Amish. In Pennsylvania, the governor arranged for the establishment of Amish vocational schools in place of ninth and tenth grades so that the letter of the law was satisfied. In Iowa, the legislature passed a law that allowed religious groups to petition for exemption from the mandatory school attendance law, but proof of competency in certain basic skills was still required.

---

[18] Note that in this case economic interests provide social integration and harmony. This, of course, contradicts the claim of some functionalists that social consensus regarding common values is necessary for social integration.

In still other instances, the courts made the final determination, usually in favor of the Amish (Hostetler, 1968:193–208).

The Mormons also encountered intense conflict with the federal government in the 19th century. In this case the issue was over which authority would decide how many wives a man may have, the church or the state. The Supreme Court ruled against the Mormons, and later church leaders revised their doctrine in conformity with federal law. However, conflict between the Mormon church and the government had nearly escalated to a small-scale war. Currently, some Roman Catholics and conservative Protestants are threatening to withhold tax money because of federal abortion policies. Given the intensity of feelings on this matter, the potential for strife is substantial.

In each of these cases, religious norms have conflicted with secular law. The result has been considerable disruption of social harmony and unity. Whether the disruption was good or bad is not our concern here; the point is that religious loyalties sometimes result in discord and conflict in the larger society. Religiously motivated people often march to the beat of a different drummer. Religion, then, may contribute to either consensus or dissension.

Conflict as a Source of Integration

While religious conflict may bring disruption to the larger society, it may also be a source of internal unity for the religious group. Some groups seem to cultivate conflict with the out-group because conflict is functional to the group's internal solidarity. As we will see in Chapter 5, groups with high boundaries usually sustain stronger member commitment and retention than those with low boundaries. Some Amish groups shun their deviant members, especially those who marry outside the group or who adopt the lifestyle of the outside. The shunning, or *Meidung*, involves a refusal to interact with persons so labeled. In some cases, Amish parents whose child marries outside the group have considered the child to be dead, have refused to speak the child's name, and have refused to acknowledge the child's presence when in the same room. Tevye, of course, does the same thing in *Fiddler on the Roof*. The interesting thing is that those groups which are very strict about practicing *Meidung* have greater retention of members than more liberal groups (Hostetler 1968).

Conflict produces internal cohesion for several reasons. First, repression and hostility by outsiders tends to create a feeling of common plight and common destiny. The more external animosity neighbors direct toward the Amish, the more inner unity is normally created within Amish communities. Second, a common rejection of something helps to articulate one's own beliefs. Actually, it is usually easier for a group to agree in the rejection of something than it is to formulate a constructive statement about what its members do believe. A shared disgust at the actions of a deviant member may provide unity for the conformists (K. Erikson, 1966). Likewise, rejection of worldliness or of some other specific group (e.g., Catholics, Jews) may be a significant source of group harmony. For this reason, social conflict and social integration must not be seen as opposites, but as different sides of the same coin. One can see the same phenomenon at work at the national level. When 53 American hostages were taken at the embassy in Iran, the sense of patriotism was greatly strengthened. Conflict at one level often creates integration and unity at another. Moreover, the most threatening conflict occurs within the context of a meaningful or important relationship with others. When conflict occurs, it is within a larger system of interrelatedness. Social harmony and social conflict must be understood together (Coser 1954:1967).

Conflict as a Pervasive Element within Religious Groups

Conflicts exist not only between religious groups, but within each group as well. Many times these internal processes can be analyzed as part of a struggle for power, privilege, and prestige. In other words, social behavior within the group is often a result of individuals protecting their self-interests.

For example, men have dominated the leadership roles in most denominations. In Orthodox Jewish groups, only male members were counted at congregational meetings. Until recently, most Protestant congregations excluded women from the ordained ministry or even from lay positions of leadership (such as offices of deacon or elder in Congregational or Presbyterian churches). Some feminist conflict theorists have viewed these practices as evidence that men are an interest group—whose members cling tenaciously to their positions of authority and power (see discussion in Chapter 9). Other examples can be cited of groups within a denomination perceiving themselves as "we" and others in the denomination as "they." The regulation in white churches which specified that black Christians must worship in the balcony (and not on the main floor) led to blacks forming their own independent churches (see Chapter 8).

There are other intrachurch conflicts as well, such as that between clergy and laity (especially when the clergy get involved in civil rights or antiwar movements), and that between theological liberals and conservatives. (These conflicts will be explored in Chapter 4.) Peter Berger (1981) suggests that clergy-laity and modernist-conservative conflicts are essentially part of a larger class conflict. The conflict is between two elites in American society that are struggling for power, privilege, and prestige. One is the business elite—a class of people managing industrial production and manipulating business enterprise. This group is more attuned to conservative theology, as is evidenced in the conservatism of most laity. Berger claims that conservative theology tends to justify the self-interests of the business elite. The new elite are those who manipulate symbols and words and who manage the production of ideas. This group includes intellectuals, educators, members of the helping professions, media people, and various social planners and bureaucrats.[19] Highly educated clergy of the mainline denominations are also part of this group, which advocates federal support of education, social welfare, minority rights, and environmental protection. This new class is highly represented in government-supported work, and its members argue for increased business regulation. Hence, this new elite really seeks its own self-interests. Berger insists that proclamations by the National Council of Churches normally reflect the current interests of this new class. Clergy and modernists are much more likely to support the National Council than are the laity in general and conservatives in particular. Producers of ideas and producers of material objects are viewed as two diverse social classes in a postindustrial society. The conflict between such groups as the Moral Majority and the National Council of Churches—a conflict that is manifested on a smaller scale between clergy and laity in local congregations—is interpreted as a conflict over self-interests (the struggle for power and privilege).

Even the conflict over creationism versus science can be viewed as being—in part—a conflict of self-interests. It is those who are well educated, whose professions are related to scientific investigation or whose business depends on scientific advances, who tend to dismiss creationism and claim that theology should be reformulated to be consistent with science. In other words, theological modernism can be self-serving. On the other hand, biblical literalism is adhered to largely by the lower- and working-class people—whose jobs are sometimes threatened by technological innovations. Furthermore, working-class Americans may be sensitive to the fact that many of the persons who occupy high-paying and high-prestige positions—doctors and scientists—are foreign born. Antiscientific views may be interpreted—through a conflict theory analysis—as veiled attacks on those who threaten the jobs and prestige of lower-class Protestants. Although such an analysis certainly does not tell the whole story, it does raise some interesting questions about the extent to which our behavior—including religious behavior and beliefs—is influenced by our self-interests.

Readers should be cautioned that because a particular position can be shown to be self-serving, it does not follow that the position is fraudulent. The analysis here does not seek to prove or disprove a position, but attempts only to show that people are inclined to believe something if it also fosters their own self-interests. This is the contribution of conflict theory to the sociology of thought (referred to by sociologists as the sociology of knowledge).

---

[19] Berger defends his position that this is a new class: "If a class is defined by a particular relation to the means of production (as Marx, for one, proposed) then indeed there is a new class here" (1981:197).

Readers may find it fruitful to reflect on their own assumptions about the role of self-interests in shaping beliefs.

Conflict as a Source of Change

Conflict is often a source of change, and as we have seen from our earlier discussion of the prophetic role of religion, change may be good for the society. Clearly, religion is capable of contributing to conflict and to social change. One aspect of religion that most interested Max Weber was the role of the charismatic leader. He found charisma to be fundamentally contrary to social stability and a major source of change. As a person who is attributed with divine authority, the charismatic religious leader is able to challenge social mores where there is otherwise little room for social and political dissent. (This will be treated further in Chapter 6.)

In the eyes of those who defend the status quo, such conflict is disruptive, and therefore dysfunctional. Such conflict is indeed disruptive, but disruption is not necessarily dysfunctional for everyone. Religiously motivated abolitionism was assessed as dysfunctional by slave owners. In terms of the interests of blacks, and in terms of contemporary American social values, abolitionism is viewed as having been a good disruption of the status quo. Religion is capable of disruption because religious values sometimes define social relationships differently from the way the encompassing culture does. If a religious ideology maintains that all people are equal before God, and if the society is rigidly stratified, a dissonance may be created for that small group which takes the religious ideology seriously. Christian churches in South Africa are among the most active opponents of that country's policy of apartheid (racial apartness). And as we shall see in Chapter 8, the black church in America has often served as a buffer for blacks and has reaffirmed their sense of innate worth, despite the negative definition of blacks by the larger white culture. By affirming the innate personal worth of black people, the church provided a foundation for many black Americans to assert their rights and to insist on social change. Whether the contribution is direct or indirect, religion can contribute to the modification of the larger society, for it can provide an alternative world view and an alternative set of values.

On the other hand, social conflict and change can also be a major source of religious change (see Chapters 8 and 9). Rapid social change is one factor in the rise of cults. Societies which are stable and highly integrated are not conducive to the emergence and expansion of religious cults, but loosely integrated, changing societies do experience such phenomena with great frequency (Stark and Roberts 1982). Social change may also mean a change in one's socioeconomic standing, and such changes are often accompanied by modifications in theology and world view. As we shall see in Chapter 8, declines in the socioeconomic standing of a group can significantly affect its theodicy (explanation of the meaning of suffering), and so can a rise in socioeconomic fortunes.

The broad sweep of social change in the direction of secularization has also brought modifications in religion. The advent of rational, scientific, empirically oriented culture has caused changes in the world views of many people. Scientific interpretations of such issues as the origins of humanity have induced liberal theologians to reformulate religious ideas so that they are compatible with scientific ones. This, of course, has involved conflicts between modernists and conservatives within religious bodies. Hence, the growth of science as a major institution in the modern world has led to changes and conflicts within religious groups. (The issue of secularism will be discussed in Chapter 4.)

Other cultural changes and social conflicts have also brought shifts in religious behavior. Some analysts have maintained that changes in sex roles in postmedieval Europe—including conflict between men and women over jobs—resulted in a rise of belief in witches and the development of institutionally sanctioned witch-hunts by the Christian churches (see Chapter 9). As will be amply illustrated throughout this text, changes and conflicts in the larger society often result in changes and conflicts within religious bodies.

Summary

One of the advantages of conflict theory is that it tends to focus attention on issues of change. (Functional theory tends to focus on stability.) Religious conflicts can contribute to social change, and social conflicts can cause religious change. Those changes may create social dissension and disruption, but depending on the nature and location of the conflict (external versus internal) they are also capable of contributing to the integration and cohesion of a group.

Conflict theory's tendency to use historical analysis lends it another strength. In so doing, it offers an important corrective to more static theories that ignore the *causes* of a particular social pattern by focusing only on current functions.

Most important, perhaps, conflict theory illuminates the many ways in which self-interests affect perceptions and behavior—including religious ideas and (supposedly) religiously motivated behavior.

Problems with Conflict Analysis

While conflict theory offers important insights and correctives to functional analysis, it is not without its problems. If functional theory often errs in overemphasizing consensus and harmony, conflict theorists often see only social stress, power-plays, and disharmony. While conflict theory is helpful in illuminating the causes of change, it is less complete in explaining social cohesion and cooperation.

Perhaps the most important criticism of conflict theory—especially by scholars within a religious tradition—is its tendency to view all behavior as motivated by self-interest. For those who believe that religious commitment may call a person to genuine unselfish action, the appeal to self-interests as the ultimate motivator of all behavior is unsatisfactory. The response among conflict theorists is that appeals to altruistic motives are simply ways of mystifying or hiding the true motives. However, the willingness of deeply religious persons to sacrifice even their lives for others or for their faith raises questions about this unicausal interpretation. Persons may be influenced by a wide range of motives. Conflict theory correctly points out that self-interests can be pervasive and can influence a wide range of behavior and attitudes. However, when it insists that *all* behavior is determined by self-interests, conflict theory commits the error of reductionism.

Another problem with this emphasis on self-interests is that interests are often interpreted only in economic terms. Although economic self-interests are more encompassing than we once realized, other sorts of self-interests can also profoundly affect behavior. For example, a calculation of one's spiritual self-interests—such as a desire to attain a heavenly afterlife and avoid hell—could cause persons to behave in ways that are contrary to their economic self-interests. Religious moods and motivations are, to quote Geertz, "powerful, pervasive, and long-lasting." They are capable of influencing behavior in ways that are insensitive to economic consequences. Conflict theory does not normally take into account such forces.

Conflict theory stresses conflict and dissension, and the role of self-interests in shaping behavior. It deemphasizes the harmony, consensus, and interrelatedness which functionalists point to. There is no shortage of data on conflict within religious groups, but given all of the conflict which does exist, most groups cohere surprisingly well.

Summary

Irrespective of the ultimate truth or fiction of a religious ideology, religion has certain kinds of social effects or consequences. These consequences are what most interest sociologists. Functional theorists tend to focus on the beneficial role religion plays. For example, at an *individual* level religion may offer a sense of meaning in life, sacralize and give certainty to a system of moral values, and establish a sense of belonging. Religion thereby affects an individual's sense of identity. Furthermore, religion can also serve *societal* functions. By providing a sense of values and beliefs around which a social consensus is formed, religion may contribute to social coherence and harmony. This is especially true for societies in which there is only one religious tradition.

On the other hand, religion is sometimes characterized by conflict—experiencing *internal* discord and/or contributing to conflict in the *larger* society. Dissension itself may be either beneficial or disruptive, healthy or unhealthy. Conflict theorists tend to focus on dissension, disruption, and change. Conflict theorists also tend to emphasize the role of self-interests in human behavior, including supposedly religious behavior.

Conflict and functional theories need not be mutually exclusive. They each offer important insights and each have blind spots in their views of society. We will be incorporating insights and analysis from both perspectives in this book. No analysis which relies on only one perspective can offer a rounded understanding of the relationship between religion and society.

The central fact to keep in mind is that the balances of harmony versus dissonance and of value consensus versus interest-group coercion will vary from one society to another. Furthermore, the amount of integration or conflict within religious groups varies significantly (Baptists have experienced more schisms and have generated far more sectarian groups than Episcopalians). Moreover, it is not just the people in the group who may be in harmony or discord. Within any religious group, the various elements of religion themselves may or may not be well integrated. In the next chapter we will explore the integrity and dissonance among such elements as belief, ritual, symbol, and world view.

4

Religious Experience, Symbol Systems, and World Views
Integrity and Dissonance in Religion

Having investigated the ways in which religion functions in society and in individuals' lives, it is appropriate next to investigate the interrelationships of religion's elements. Nonrational religious experience, myths, rituals, symbol systems, world views, and ethos are all part of this complex phenomenon we call religion. Scholars are interested in how each of these facets relates to the others and which one may be primary. Social scientists are also interested in what happens when secular modes of thinking and views of the world begin to replace religious ones. In some cases, secular understandings have come to replace traditional myths within the religious community— a process that is called modernism. What happens to a religion when this takes place? As we shall see, scholars are far from agreement on the question. One of the results may be a conflict between laity and some of the highly trained clergy in the interpretation of myths, rituals, and symbols. The lack of agreement as to the meaning of central symbols or myths may disrupt the group.

We shall begin by exploring the roles of religious experience, myths, rituals, and symbol systems and by investigating the relationships among them. We shall also discuss the way in which these specific manifestations of religion are related to the more intangible elements of world view and ethos. Then we will turn to an investigation of secularization and to the conflict between folk and official versions of a religion.

Experience of the Holy

Many social scientists define religion in terms of the sacred/profane distinction. For these scholars, the essence of religion has to do with a unique and extra-ordinary experience—an experience that has a sacred dimension and is unlike everyday life. According to some scholars, all religious phenomena evolves out of this seminal experience—the experience of the holy (James 1958; Otto 1923; O'Dea 1966). Such an experience is often called *nonrational*, for it is neither rational nor irrational. These nonrational experiences are described by those who have them as being outside the usual categories of logical, systematic reasoning. They are not illogical; they are simply nonlogical. These experiences seem to defy the normal categories of language. Whether a nonrational experience is the essence of all religious behavior may be debatable; that such mystical experience is one important aspect of the complex phenomenon we call religion is not. It is appropriate, then, to focus initially on the experience of the holy.

Emile Durkheim in 1915 was one of the early scholars to discuss characteristics of the sacred. Using a broad description of religious experience which he believed would be applicable in all cultures, Durkheim (1965) defined the sacred realm as one which both attracts and repells individuals. The sacred is not only attractive, it is also repugnant; it is not only capable of being helpful, it is also dangerous. This *ambiguity* rests in part in the attribution of great *power* to the sacred; because of the overwhelming power that it possesses, it holds the potentiality of being either beneficial or harmful. Nevertheless, the attraction of the sacred is not based primarily on utilitarian considerations. The sacred is conceived as a *nonempirical* force that is considered *intrinsically valuable.* As such, it places a moral obligation on the worshiper and imposes certain ethical imperatives.

Durkheim was fascinated by the importance his primitive informants attached to sacred taboos—rules which prohibit immoral or impure behavior. People do sometimes violate these rules, however, and in doing so they become unclean and unfit for the sacred realm. Durkheim also noted that mere participation in the secular world could cause one to become tainted. Ritual purification before reentering the presence of the sacred was necessary, and this often involved a rather elaborate process. For Durkheim, this emphasized the fact that the sacred was radically different than the profane world. Certain places and times were set aside as special and as belonging to another dimension of reality.

Rudolf Otto explored the nature of the religious experience in his classic book, *The Idea of the Holy* (1923). In that work, Otto insists that there is a tendency of people in Western culture to reduce the holy to rational concepts about God. By analogy to human life, the holy has been attributed with certain qualities that can be understood, debated, and defended in intellectual terms. It is Otto's contention that this intellectual or rational focus is a confusion of the original idea of holiness. He believes that holiness originally had a much larger dimension, a dimension that cannot be entirely reduced to intellectual *concepts.* Hence, Otto attempts to describe the *experience* of the holy, rather than describing the holy itself. He insists that the experience of the holy is so unique that one can never fully understand his description unless one has experienced it. While the experience of the holy is beyond rational or ethical conception, the experience seems universally to bring forth a "creative consciousness." A person is profoundly humbled as he or she senses an utter dependency and unworthiness before the holy. (See Exhibit 4–1.) Rational and moral conceptions about religion come only much later, as an outgrowth of the experience itself.

Otto elaborates on the quality of this experience, which he calls the *mysterium tremendum et fascinosum.* He identifies five qualities of the *mysterium tremendum.* First, the individual is filled with a sense of awe and fear. The word *tremendum* itself expresses the tremor or terror that Otto feels is part of the experience. The story of Moses awed and frightened by the burning bush provides an example of feelings a religious experience generates. Second, one feels overwhelmed by the absolute unapproachability of the *numinous* (Otto's word for the holy). Durkheim's concept of the sacred as a dangerous force is obviously shared by Otto. The ancient Hebrew prohibition against even mentioning the name of Yahweh because of His absolute

Exhibit 4–1 _____

Personal Accounts of Religious Experiences*

I remember the night, and almost the very spot on the hilltop, where my soul opened out, as it were, into the Infinite, and there was a rushing together of the two worlds, the inner and the outer. It was deep calling unto deep—the deep that my own struggle had opened up within being answered by the unfathomable deep without, reaching beyond the stars. I stood alone with Him who had made me, and all the beauty of the world, and love, and sorrow, and even temptation. I did not seek Him, but felt the perfect unison of my spirit with His. The ordinary sense of things around me faded. For the moment nothing but an inefiable joy and exaltation remained. It is impossible fully to describe the experience. It was like the effect of some great orchestra when all the separate notes have melted into one swelling harmony that leaves the listener conscious of nothing save that his soul is being wafted upwards, and almost bursting with its own emotion. The perfect stillness of the night was thrilled by a more solemn silence. The darkness held a presence that was all the more felt because it was not seen. I could not any more have doubted that *He* was there than that I was. Indeed, I felt myself to be, if possible, the less real of the two. (1958:66).

I have on a number of occasions felt that I had enjoyed a period of intimate communion with the divine. These meetings came unasked and unexpected, and seemed to consist merely in the temporary obliteration of the conventionalities which usually surround and cover my life. . . . Once it was when from the summit of a high mountain I looked over a gashed and corrugated landscape extending to a long convex of ocean that ascended to the horizon, and again from the same point when I could see nothing beneath me but a boundless expanse of white cloud, on the blown surface of which a few high peaks, including the one I was on, seemed plunging about as if they were dragging their anchors. What I felt on these occasions was a temporary loss of my own identity, accompanied by an illumination which revealed to me a deeper significance than I had been wont to attach to life. It is in this that I find my justification for saying that I have enjoyed communication with God. Of course the absence of such a being as this would be chaos. I cannot conceive of life without its presence (1958:70).

In that time the consciousness of God's nearness came to me sometimes. I say God, to describe what is indescribable. A presence, I might say, yet that is too suggestive of personality, and the moments of which I speak did not hold the consciousness of a personality, but something in myself made me feel myself a part of something bigger than I, that was controlling. I felt myself one with the grass, the trees, birds, insects, everything in Nature. I exulted in the mere fact of existence, of being a part of it all—the drizzling rain, the shadows of the clouds, the tree-trunks, and so on. In the years following, such moments continued to come, but I wanted them constantly. I knew so well the satisfaction of losing self in a perception of supreme power and love, that I was unhappy because that perception was not constant (1958:303).

_____

* From William James, *Varieties of Religious Experience* (New York: New American Library, 1958), originally published in 1902.

power and unapproachability provides an example. One can also see elements of unapproachability in many high churches that allow only the clergy to enter the chancel area. Some cathedrals even have a screen that hides the altar from the congregation. To go behind the chancel without proper ritual purification would be to risk death. This leads us to the third characteristic: power, energy, or urgency. Otto claims that in describing the experience of the numinous, people use such symbolic language as "vitality, passion, emotional temper, will, force, movement, excitement, activity, impetus." Clearly, the holy has tremendous power, which reinforces its unapproachability and awefulness. Fourth, the experience of *mysterium tremendum* causes an awareness of the "wholly otherness" of the holy. The mystery of the experience lies in its unfamiliar and nonempirical nature. The holy is utterly unlike the profane. Fifth, one feels a sense of fascination with and attraction to the numinous. Although it is potentially terrifying, the holy also elicits a sense of wonder and a feeling of ultimate goodness. Hence, it commands a sense of ethical imperative. According to Otto, this experience of *mysterium tremendum* is the universal foundation and source of all religious behavior. Thomas O'Dea has followed Otto's lead by suggesting that all other forms of religiosity are generated from this nonrational religious experience. We shall return to O'Dea's treatment when we discuss secularization.

Otto's description of the essential religious experience is corroborated in most respects by other scholars who have studied mystical experience. However, there are many people who consider themselves devout believers who have never had one. The emphasis of many mainline denominational congregations is much more intellectual than Otto would suggest. As a theologian, Otto maintains that the experience of the numinous ought to be at the heart of religion. Herein lies the problem. Otto has claimed to *describe* a universal pattern, but he has normative expectations that endorse a particular experience as more religious than others. Hence, he makes a value judgment about some persons being less religious because they have not experienced the numinous as he describes it.

Some theologians emphasize the immanence (proximity, involvement in human life) of God rather than the transcendence (wholly otherness) of God. Are they less religious? They certainly don't think so. Or to use another example, one does not observe mystical experience as being central (or even common) among Unification Church members (Moonies). Is the Unification Church, therefore, not a religion?[1] By making a value judgment about what one ought to do to be religious, Otto has departed from purely empirical observation. Religiosity is multidimensional. The kind of experi-

---

[1] The assumption here is that loyalty to a charismatic leader is a somewhat different experience than a firsthand mystical experience as described by Otto.

ence Otto describes is vital to religious life for many people, but it is not the only source of religious conviction.

Religious conviction is more than ideas. In order fundamentally to influence lives, religion must have an emotional component, something that makes the ideas or belief systems "seem uniquely realistic."[2] A nonrational experience often provides such an impetus to belief.

Andrew Greeley offers clarity to this discussion of the role of sacred experiences. In his analysis of "sacredness" and the extra-ordinary quality of religious experience, he grants that the sacred is usually removed from everyday existence. Yet, he writes, "not everything that is extraordinary is sacred." The important point is that the sacred is something that is treated with profound reverence and respect. Greeley capsulizes his argument with an important twist:

> [People have] a tendency to sacralize [their] ultimate systems of value. Even if one excludes the possibility of a transcendent or a supernatural, one nonetheless is very likely to treat one's system of ultimate explanation with a great deal of jealous reverence and respect and to be highly incensed when someone else calls the system of explanation to question or behaves contrary to it. It is precisely this tendency to sacralize one's ultimate concern that might well explain the many quasi-religious phenomena to be observed in organizations which officially proclaim their non- or even anti-religiousness. The communist, for example, may vehemently deny the existence of a "totally other" and yet treat communism and its prophets, its dogmas, its code, and its ritual with as much respect as does the devout Christian approach [Christianity] (1972:9).

Rather than citing an experience of the sacred as the source of all religious behavior, Greeley suggests that whatever we value very highly (ultimately), we tend to sacralize (to make sacred). Sacredness, then, may be the *result* of a valuing process rather than the primal *cause* of all other religious activity. Greeley does not suggest that experiences of the holy are always secondary, he merely points out that the relationship between values, beliefs, and the sacred may be more complex than Otto, Eliade, and O'Dea would have us think.

Since not all forms of extraordinariness are religious, Greeley offers a clarification. There are two kinds of extraordinariness that traditionally have been called religious. One has to do with the need to make sense out of life, the need for a meaningful interpretation of events. The second has to do with the need for belonging, the need to feel a relatedness to other persons, to humanity, and to the universe. "Sacredness, then, relates to [humanity's] experience of the need for meaning and the need for belonging, as well as the fulfillment of these needs" (Greeley 1972:16). The sacred experience, then (to speak strictly from the human side of it), has

---

[2] The reader may recall this phrase from Geertz's definition of religion.

appeal insofar as it can help persons make sense of the world and feel a sense of belonging. Greeley's approach reintroduces the rational element that Otto was so eager to deemphasize.

Greeley's interpretation is also more consistent with a number of empirical studies than is Otto's. Otto had implied that it was difficult, if not impossible, to be truly religious unless one has had a profound experience of the *mysterium tremendum*. Yet Gordon Allport has reported that in a study of college students who rated religious sentiment as significant in their lives, only 17 percent cited mystical experience as a major influence in their religiosity. After studying many variables affecting one's propensity to hold strong religious convictions, Allport concludes: "The lesson we learn . . . is that the psychological roots of religious sentiment . . . are very numerous" (1950:44). He further insists that there is "no single and unique religious emotion, but rather a widely divergent set of experiences that may be focused upon a religious object" (1950:5).

Several conclusions can be drawn regarding nonrational religious experiences. First, they vary greatly in *intensity* from one person to another. Second, they vary in *content*. The Eskimo shaman makes a spiritual journey to the bottom of the sea to visit Sedna and to appease her for violations of taboos (Barnouw 1982). The Sioux holy man experiences a visit by 48 horses which approach in groups of 12 from the 4 cardinal directions (Neihardt 1961). The Christian mystic[3] may see the Holy Virgin, experience the love of Jesus, or hear the voice of God. The Buddhist mystic may experience "nonbeing" or "utter unity with the universe." The content, or at least the interpretation of the experience, is defined in culturally familiar terms.

Third, nonrational experiences vary in *frequency*. For some, mystic experience becomes a goal in itself and may even take on the form of a full-time occupation. This attitude is particularly common among certain Eastern religions, especially in Buddhist monastaries in Asia and in Hare Krishna temples in the United States. But some Roman Catholic religious orders have established monastaries in which the pursuit of religious experience becomes the principal goal.

Fourth, the *people who value and expect* a religious experience are those who report having had one. Abraham Maslow (1964) insists that probably everyone has had at least one nonrational "peak experience," but that some people do not value such experiences and therefore dismiss them as insignificant or bizarre or even forget them altogether. Other researchers (Glock and Stark 1965; Hood 1970; Davidson 1975; Wimberly et al. 1975; Straus 1979) insist that people who desire such experiences may cultivate behaviors

---

[3] Some writers reserve the word *mystic* solely for Eastern religions with their search for spiritual unity with the universe. Others, following Troeltsch, use the term to refer to any nonrational religious orientation which denies the importance or reality of the social order. However, most writers use mysticism in a broader sense to refer to any nonrational experience which the actors define as sacred.

and attitudes which make it likely that they will have them. This view suggests that social expectation helps to cause such experiences. For example, Wimberly et al. found that many born again commitments were not life-changing events, but affirmations of existing values. In any case, a positive attitude toward peak experiences (including conversions) is highly correlated with reports of having experienced them.

Some form of nonrational religious experience seems to be at the root of religious behavior for many people. Such an experience gives impetus and emotion to belief systems. However, the assumption (by Otto, Durkheim, O'Dea, and Maslow) that a mystical or nonrational experience is the only source of religious conviction may be overdrawn. As Greeley points out, people have a tendency to sacralize the things they value most highly and which give meaning and purpose to their lives. Note, for example, the sense of sacredness which accompanies ceremonial handling of the American flag. The directions which accompany the newly purchased flag emphasize a sense of reverence and awe that should be maintained when caring for the flag. (See Exhibit 4–2.) Such sacredness is not caused by a mystical experience, but is created in the presence of a valued symbol. The sacralization of objects or beliefs places them above question; it insures their absoluteness. Hence, that which we value highly tends to be perceived in reverent or sacred terms.

Anyone who doubts the fact that a firsthand religious experience can be very important need only observe the major surge of born again and pentecostal movements in Christianity in the 1970s. The emphasis of each of these movements is the assurance and sense of certainty provided by a personal experience of the holy. Furthermore many of the Eastern religions which grew rapidly in the 1970s placed heavy emphasis on nonrational religious experience. While an experience of the *mysterium tremendum* may not be the sole source of religious behavior, a sense of sacredness is clearly one important aspect of the complex phenomenon called religion.

Myth and Ritual

When Americans speak of religion, they usually think of a belief system. Indeed, many social scientists have even attempted to measure religiosity by questioning subjects on their agreement or disagreement with certain orthodox religious beliefs. Even the practice of referring to faithful members of a religious group as believers is indicative of this focus. But as we shall see, belief and ritual are quite interdependent, and in the case of some religious groups, ritual is the more important.

Myth

Religious beliefs are usually expressed in the form of myths. By myth, the social scientist does not mean untrue or foolish beliefs. Nor does the

Exhibit 4–2

The American Flag as a Sacred Symbol

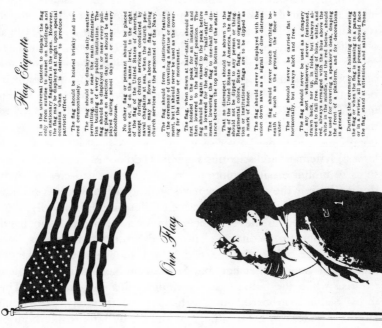

Our Flag

Flag Etiquette

It is the universal custom to display the flag only from sunrise to sunset on buildings and on stationary flagstaffs in the open. However, the flag may be displayed at night upon special occasions when it is desired to produce a patriotic effect.

The flag should be hoisted briskly and lowered ceremoniously.

The flag should be displayed daily, weather permitting, on or near the main administration building of every public institution. The flag should be displayed in or near every polling place on election day and should be displayed during school days in or near every schoolhouse.

No other flag or pennant should be placed above or on the same level, to the right of the flag of the United States of America, except during church services conducted by naval chaplains at sea, when the church pennant may be flown above the flag during church services for the personnel of the Navy.

The flag should form a distinctive feature of the ceremony of unveiling a statue or monument, but it should never be used as the covering for the statue or monument.

The flag, when flown at half-staff, should be first hoisted to the peak for an instant and then lowered to the half-staff position. The flag should be again raised to the peak before it is lowered for the day. By "half-staff" is meant lowering the flag to one-half the distance between the top and bottom of the staff.

That no disrespect should be shown to the flag of the United States of America, the flag should not be dipped to any person or thing. Regimental colors, State flags, and organization or institutional flags are to be dipped as a mark of honor.

The flag should never be displayed with the union down save as a signal of dire distress.

The flag should never touch anything beneath it, such as the ground, the floor or water.

The flag should never be carried flat or horizontally, but always aloft and free.

The flag should never be used as a drapery of any sort whatsoever, never festooned, drawn back, nor up, in folds, but always allowed to fall free. Bunting of blue, white, and red, always arranged with the blue above, the white in the middle and the red below, should be used for covering a speaker's desk, draping the front of a platform, and for decorations in general.

During the ceremony of hoisting or lowering the flag or when the flag is passing in a parade or in a review, all persons present should face the flag, stand at attention, and salute. Those present in uniform should render the military salute. When not in uniform, men should remove the head-dress with the right hand holding it at left shoulder, the hand being over the heart. Men without hats should salute in the same manner. Aliens should stand at attention. Women should salute by placing the right hand over the heart. The salute to the flag in the moving column should be rendered at the moment the flag passes.

When the National Anthem is played and the flag is not displayed, all present should stand and face toward the music. Those in uniform should salute at the first note of the anthem, retaining this position until the last note. All others should stand at attention, men removing their head-dress. When the flag is displayed, all present should face the flag and salute.

★ ★ ★

The National Flag represents the living country and is considered to be a living thing emblematic of the respect and pride we have for our nation. Our flag is a precious possession. Display it proudly.

There are certain fundamental rules of Heraldry which, if understood generally, indicate the proper method of displaying the flag. The right arm, which is the sword arm and the point of danger, is the place of honor. Hence, the union of the flag is the place of honor or the honor point.

The National Emblem is a symbol of our great country, our heritage and our place in the world. We owe reverence and respect to our flag.

It represents the highest ideals of individual liberty, justice and equal opportunity for all.

social scientist identify myth with legends, fairy tales, or folk tales (Kluckhohn 1972:94). Myths, as opposed to the latter phenomena, usually carry with them an element of sacredness. As we have seen from the earlier discussion, that which is sacred is normally that which helps one make sense out of life. Hence, myths are stories or belief systems which help people understand the nature of the cosmos, the purpose and meaning of life, or the role and origin of evil and suffering. Myths explain and justify specific cultural values and social rules. They are more than stories that lack empirical validation; they serve as symbolic statements about the meaning and purpose of life in this world. One sociologist of religion has gone so far as to suggest that all religious symbols (including religious myths) are in a fundamental sense *true* (Bellah 1970a:93). He does not argue their literal veracity, but he insists that symbolic systems of meaning are true in so far as they speak to the fundamental human condition. Hence, they need to be taken seriously. Myths have a powerful impact on the subjective (mental) orientation of persons because they communicate and reinforce a particular world view or a particular outlook on life.

After undertaking an in-depth study of the Hare Krishna, Stillson Judah insists that " 'myth' is actually the highest subjective reality to the devotee. It is the vehicle [which carries one] to inner integration. [Humans] can only live without 'myth' at [their] peril" (1974:196). Judah goes on to suggest that what liberal religion needs for revivification is not a new theology, but a new mythology. "A new theology would only result in a new rationalization. . . . The real need is for a powerful mythic statement about the world" (1974:196). We will discuss the rationalization of myths in the form of systematic theology later, but what is important here is a recognition of the emotional power of which myth is capable. For many persons, logical, systematic and scientific statements do not capture one's imagination so as to mobilize one's emotional resources. The capacity of myths to do this is precisely the reason they have such power in the lives of individuals.

A Central Eskimo myth may serve to illustrate. Historically, the Central Eskimo believed in the existence of a woman, Sedna, who lived at the bottom of the sea. Sedna was once an Eskimo girl. However, against the wishes of her father, she married a bird and went to an island to live. Her father came to get her, but Sedna's husband caused a violent storm to arise while the father was returning Sedna to her home. The father threw Sedna overboard, but she hung on desperately. He chopped her fingers to pieces with his knife, and she finally sank to the bottom of the sea. The pieces of fingers turned into the various sea mammals—whales, seals, and walruses.

Eskimo women in particular were constrained by many taboos or moral prohibitions. For example, when seals were killed and brought home, certain behaviors were prohibited until the seal had been cut up: the skins from the sleeping platform could not be shaken out, women could not comb their hair, and young girls could not take off their boots. After the cutting

Exhibit 4–3 _____

Myths Can Create Powerful Moods and Motivations in People

The God that holds you over the pit of hell, much as one holds a spider, or some loathsome insect over the fire, abhors you, and is dreadfully provoked: his wrath towards you burns like fire; he looks upon you as worthy of nothing else, but to be cast into the fire; he is of purer eyes than to bear to have you in his sight; you are ten thousand times more abominable in his eyes, than the most hateful venomous serpent is in ours. You have offended him infinitely more than ever a stubborn rebel did his prince; and yet it is nothing but his hand that holds you from falling into the fire every moment. It is to be ascribed to nothing else, that you did not go to hell the last night; that you was suffered to awake again in this world, after you closed your eyes to sleep. And there is no other reason to be given, why you have not dropped into hell since you arose in the morning, but that God's hand has held you up. There is no other reason to be given why you have not gone to hell, since you have sat here in the house of God, provoking his pure eyes by your sinful wicked manner of attending his solemn worship. Yea, there is nothing else that is to be given as a reason why you do not this very moment drop down into hell.

O sinner! Consider the fearful danger you are in: it is a great furnace of wrath, a wide and bottomless pit, full of the fire of wrath, that you are held over in the hand of that God, whose wrath is provoked and incensed as much against you, as against many of the damned in hell. You hang by a slender thread, with the flames of divine wrath flashing about it, and ready every moment to singe it, and burn it asunder; and you have . . . nothing to lay hold of to save yourself, nothing to keep off the flames of wrath, nothing of your own, nothing that you ever have done, nothing that you can do, to induce God to spare you one moment.*

The mythology of heaven and hell, and the belief that one who is not saved by God will go to hell, is vividly expanded by Jonathan Edwards in this passage. By emphasizing this myth and elaborating on it, he sought to create powerful, pervasive, and long-lasting *moods* (awe of God's power, humility, fear of God) and *motivations* (repentence, change of attitudes, and behavior). Readers might find it instructive to attend several different religious services in their communities and listen to the symbolism of the language. What myths are being played upon? What moods do the clergy intend to create with these myths? What motivations are sought? What is the symbolic role of emotionally laden language in these services? Another exercise would be to read sermons from clergy of various theological persuasions to identify the symbolic power of language in creating moods and motivations.

* From Jonathan Edward's sermon, "Sinners in the Hands of an Angry God" (preached in 1741), in *Jonathan Edwards: Basic Writings*, ed. Ola Elizabeth Winslow (New York: New American Library, 1966), pp. 159–160.

was complete, products from land and sea had to be cooked in different pots. Many other taboos were related to food preparation, to giving birth, and to menstruation. If any of these taboos were broken, a vapor was believed to emanate from the body of the violator. That vapor sank through the ice, snow, and water, and settled in Sedna's hair as dirt and maggots.

Since she had no fingers, Sedna could not comb out this debris. In revenge, she would call the walruses and seals (which were once her fingers) to the bottom of the sea, and the people would face starvation. Salvation came only if a shaman (Eskimo holy man) entered into a trance, traveled spiritually to the bottom of the sea, combed Sedna's hair, appeased her, and discovered who the offenders were. When he returned, all offenders were required to confess their sins, or taboo violations, openly. The seals then returned (Barnouw 1982:231–234).

Sedna was not a benevolent deity. She was vengeful and had to be obeyed. She was the cause of much anxiety, fear, and even hostility. The Sedna myth served to create these moods of fear and anxiety in people, which then motivated them toward certain types of behavior (obeying of taboos and prohibitions). This myth reinforced an overall world view that the world is a hostile environment, that the future is frought with danger and may be jeopardized by human acts, that survival depends on conforming behavior and obedience to rules by everyone, and that negative behavior will always be reflected back to the actor in some devastating form. The Sedna myth served to solidify and sacralize the general Central Eskimo outlook on life.

Ritual

Although Americans tend to think of belief as the central component of religion, ritual appears to be equally important. In fact, Louis Schneider (1970:23) points out that ortho*praxy,* not ortho*doxy,* is central to Islam. That is, precise conformity in ritual behavior (e.g., prayers five times a day facing Mecca) is what is mandated for the faithful, not total conformity in theological interpretations.[4]

A careful observation of human behavior is enough to make one aware of the great attraction of humans to ritual experiences. Consider, for example, the elaborate pageantry and ritual of a Shriner's convention, or a Masonic lodge, or a De Molay installation. Football games always begin with the playing of the national anthem, and colorfully uniformed marching bands perform. Many meetings of secular civic groups begin with a ritual pattern: the pledge to the flag and a prayer. And for many people, marriage is not legitimate unless the couple has been through a ceremony, however brief. Although common-law marriage (marriage without benefit of ceremony or marriage license) is perfectly legal in 13 states, many people still feel the ceremony is what makes marriage legitimate.

The examples above do not involve a sense of sacredness or ultimacy, and I do not suggest that they are particularly religious phenomena. My point is merely that there is something about human beings to which ritual

---

[4] Schneider is actually citing earlier observations by Wilfred C. Smith and Gustave von Grunebaum.

and pageantry appeal. At a time when many denominations are making their worship liturgies *less* formal, many secular organizations seem to be generating *more* elaborate pageantry! Perhaps this is because the myth systems associated with church rituals are no longer capturing the imagination of many people; hence, the formal ecclesiastical rituals seem hollow rather than awe inspiring. We will return to this issue, but the elaboration of nonsacred ritual at such events as the Olympic Games is quite interesting (or are these rituals and events *really* nonsacred?).

Religious ritual usually involves affirmation of the myths and gives emotional impulse to the belief system. Stillson Judah provides an example when he discusses the role of chanting by Hare Krishna members: "The power of this chanting should not be underestimated. The enthusiasm of the devotees leaping in ecstasy with upraised arms before the shrine can be contagious for many" (1974:95). Not only is the mood contagious; Hare Krishna members insist that complete acceptance and understanding of the belief system is attained through chanting. Judah cites a number of devotees who made comments like: "Although we may not understand something when it is given to us, it comes to us through faith. It's revealed to us through our continuing efforts in chanting" (1974:169).

Ritual may involve the enactment of a story or myth, or it may symbolically remind one of the mythology of the faith by moving participants through a series of moods. Perhaps a brief analysis of a ritual familiar to many readers will help to illustrate the point.

Biblical theology was based on the idea that God had a covenant (or contract) with the chosen people. If they obeyed the commandments and worked to establish a kingdom of justice and righteousness, then God would protect them and provide for them. The scriptures maintain that the Hebrew people got into trouble whenever they broke the covenant, forgot the demands of justice, and ignored the sovereignty of God. In these circumstances, the prophets called the people back to the covenant. The prophets assured them that if they would repent and renew their covenant, Yahweh would forgive them. The New Testament renews this theme, with Jesus calling the wayward to repent and promising God's forgiveness. The most important sacrament in the Christian church is Communion (alternatively referred to as the Lord's Supper, the Eucharist, or the Mass). In instituting this practice, Jesus claimed to be inaugurating a new covenant. Covenantal theology, then, is a basic Christian mythology or belief system.

Many Protestant Christians are not consciously aware that the liturgy (or ritual) in which they participate is based on this theology. In fact, many lay people believe that the order of a worship service is rather arbitrary, that the minister randomly intermixes hymns, prayers, a confession, scripture, anthems, and other liturgical devices. Let us look however at a consistent pattern that prevails in many American Protestant liturgies. The samples provided in Exhibits 4–4 and 4–5 will serve as illustrations. These two

Exhibit 4–4

Order of Worship: Model A

First United Presbyterian Church

October 12, 1980, 10:45 A.M.

The beginning of the organ prelude is a call to silent personal preparation for the worship of God.

Service of Praise

Prelude: Sonata I in F Major, Felix Mendelssohn
    Andante. recit.
    Allegro assi vivace

* Introit

Call to Worship

† Hymn of Praise: no. 96, "Praise Him! Praise Him"

Service of Confession

† Prayer of Confession (in unison)

Who are we, Lord, that we should confess you? We can hardly speak for ourselves; how could we speak in your name? We believe in your Word, but our minds are often full of doubt. We trust your promises, but our hearts are often fearful. We remember that we have been baptized, but we often forget to respond to your grace. Captivate our hearts, that we may know the love which you have given us in your Son. Amen.

† Personal Silent Confession

† Assurance of Pardon

* Ushers will seat those waiting.

† Congregation will please stand.

Service of Proclamation

† Apostles' Creed

† The Gloria Patri

Children's Sermon

Anthem: "The Lord's Prayer," John Zaumeyer (children will leave for Junior Church following the anthem)

Scripture Reading
    Habakkuk 1:2–3; 2:1–4 (pew Bible, p. 1017)
    2 Timothy 1:3–13, p. 287
    Luke 17:5–10, p. 107

Hymn of Proclamation, no. 140, "In the Cross of Christ I Glory"

The Message: "Celebrating the Faith"

The Morning Prayer

Service of Commitment

Moment of Fellowship and Sharing; please sign and pass "registration sheets"

Prayer of Intercession and Lord's Prayer

Offertory: Sonata IV, Felix Mendelssohn
    Andante religioso

† Doxology

† Hymn of Dedication: no. 405, "Come, Come, Ye Saints"

† Charge to the Congregation

† Benediction

† Benediction Response: The Choir

† Postlude: "Choral Song," S. S. Wesley

We are delighted to welcome guests and newcomers to our worship today! We invite you to sign the registration sheet and to share in the Fellowship Hour following the service this morning in Fellowship Hall.

Exhibit 4–5

Order of Worship: Model B

Trinity United Methodist Church

Fourth Sunday in Lent, March 20, 1977

The Preparation

The Chimes and the Lighting of the Altar Candles

The Greetings

The Organ Prelude

Our worship of God begins with the music of the prelude. Let us listen to the music. Let us read the words of the hymns we will sing today. Let us center our thoughts before God. Let us be silent, opening our lives to God.

The Call to Praise

Pastor: Let us gather together because of our need for renewal as persons."
People: "We offer our worship to God who renews us for his service."
Pastor: "So, the Lord be with you."
People: "And with you also."
Pastor: "Lift up your voices."
People: "We lift them up unto the Lord."

* Hymn of Praise: "Love Divine," no. 283

Acts of Self-Examination

Jesus's Summary of the Law of God

The Confession (*prayed by all in unison*)

"Merciful God, we confess before you our failures which everybody knows, our failures that are a burden to us and our failures that do not bother us because we have gotten used to them.

"Father, forgive us.
"Send the Holy Spirit to us.
"And by your mercy,
"Help us to know that we are called to live knowing we are wanted and accepted by you."

Kyrie Eleison, p. 838

The Assurance of God's Love

* Congregation will stand for these acts of worship.

The Proclamation

* Affirmation of Faith (see insert)

* Gloria Patri, no. 792

The Scripture Session: II Corinthians 5:17–21

Anthem: "Alone Thou Goest Forth," Powell; Senior Choir

The Scripture Lesson: Luke 15:11–32

* Hymn: no. 131, "Come, Holy Ghost, Our Hearts Inspire" (Children in grades 1–3 may go to Junior Church during the singing of the last verse of the hymn)

Sermon: "The Man Christ Jesus, 4. His Wholeness"

The Response

The Prayers

    For Ourselves and Our Needs
    For All Humanity
    Of Thanksgiving

The Lord's Prayer and Chorale Response

Offering Our Gifts and Dedication of Ourselves to God

Offertory: "Diapason Movement," Boyce

Attendance Registration

(While the offering is being received, will the person at the end of the pew sign his or her name to the attendance pad and pass it on to the next person. Return it to the person who started it.)

* The Presentation: "The Doxology," no. 809

* The Prayer

* Hymn: "Where Cross the Crowded Ways of Life," no. 204 verses 1, 2, 5, 6

* The Blessing and Choral Response

* The Chimes and Extinguishing of the Altar Candles

* Moments of Christian Greeting, Welcome, and Fellowship: "I should like you to shake hands all around as a sign of Christian love." (I Corinthians 16:30, Phillips trans.)

Organ Postlude: "Andante Maestoso," Corelli

are used because they explicitly articulate the development of the service through subheadings.[5] However, most liturgies are based upon a logical pattern that moves worshipers through successive movements or moods. While there is some variation in the order of Protestant worship services, the majority of mainline American churches tend to follow, in rough outline, the themes developed in these liturgies. Let us examine the relationship between these liturgies and the mythology of the divine covenant.[6]

At the outset of the service, the liturgy is designed to create a mood of awe and praise. The architecture of the church may also enhance this sense. Many church bulletins request that worshipers sit in silence and focus their attention on a rose window, on some other symbol, or on "the presence of God."[7] The prelude is frequently a piece of music that will lift one's spirits. The call to worship draws one's attention to the reason for gathering: to worship and praise God. The congregation then joins together in a hymn of praise which is frequently a joyful, uplifting song of adoration.

Shortly after the congregation is made aware that it is in the presence of God, the mood shifts. Although most of the worshipers were in the same church dedicating their lives to God just a week before, the liturgy attempts to make them aware of the fact that they have not always lived in a way consistent with Christian values. They are reminded that in the push and pull of daily living, they have said the unkind word or failed to do a loving deed (sins of commission and sins of omission). The values they professed on Sunday they may have betrayed by Wednesday (if not on Sunday afternoon). Hence, the second mood or theme of this worship liturgy is a "service of confession." No one can be loving or just or self-sacrificing or righteous all of the time, and the liturgy leads participants to acknowledge their lack of consistent faithfulness. For this reason confession is sometimes called an "act of honesty" (between oneself and God). But this liturgical movement does not end on a note of guilt. Confession is followed by "words of assurance," "assurance of pardon," or "word of new possibility." At this point the congregation is assured by the minister (often through quotation of a biblical passage) that persons "who sincerely confess their sins and who renew their commitment to God, are forgiven."

---

[5] Most Protestant services do not have the subheadings printed in the order of worship to show the change of mood. Some that do have subheadings may emphasize three movements—while others have four. For example, model A differs sequentially from model B in that the latter subsumes the "service of praise" and "service of confession" under a single heading: Service of Preparation. These samples are illustrative of patterns which prevail in approximately two hundred church bulletins from various denominations which I have collected over the past 10 years.

[6] I first became aware of this basic and recurring pattern through Paul Johnson's book, *The Psychology of Religion* (1959). Johnson discusses the psychology of worship by analyzing several different liturgies from different denominations or faiths. The application of this Protestant liturgy draws on Johnson's analysis, though it is a bit more specific than his earlier work.

[7] Those interested in a symbolic interactionist analysis of behavior in a liturgical setting might want to see Hesser and Weigert (1980).

The covenantal theme of repentance prior to renewal of the covenant is enacted.

The liturgy then moves to a third phase, an "affirmation of faith," or "service of proclamation." This phase is frequently the major part of Protestant services. The congregation may repeat a creed or covenant, listen to an anthem or other special music, sing a hymn of proclamation, listen to scripture, and hear a message (sermon) delivered by the minister. In this phase of the ritual, the emphasis is on celebrating God's love, remembering and rehearing the Word of God, and remembering the demands of the covenant. Infant baptisms are usually a part of this movement, although churches that practice only adult baptism and view it as an act of commitment may include it as part of the final movement.

The final movement of most Protestant liturgies is a service of dedication. This part of worship calls for a response to God's word by the congregation. The movement is characterized by a monetary offering (a symbolic act of giving of one's self), concerns of the church or announcements from the pulpit, a hymn of dedication, a charge to the congregation, and a benediction. In some churches the third and fourth phases of the liturgy (proclamation and dedication) may be merged into one. In this case, some acts of dedication and commitment (such as the offering) may actually precede the sermon. However, the hymn of dedication always follows the sermon. In the more evangelical churches, this hymn may be followed by an "altar call"—a request for members to make a public commitment by coming forward and standing before the altar.

It should not be inferred that all Protestant worship through history has followed this mood sequence. The pattern described here has come down from John Calvin, who articulated a rationale for the order of worship which corresponds roughly with the pattern and the theology identified here. However, Zwingli, another reformer of Calvin's day, felt that the climax of the service should be confession. The rest of the service was to build a sense of guilt in the worshipers. This influence can be seen in Puritan liturgies of colonial America. Some denominations continue to be influenced by the Zwingli tradition in their liturgical formats. Furthermore, some pentecostal churches and Christian sects do not have a consistent pattern of worship. The rationale for the order of worship is insignificant, for emotion is judged far more important than thought patterns.

It is also interesting that much of contemporary Protestant worship emphasizes proclamation and commitment. The Catholic Mass seems to place more stress on the service of praise. This reflects a fundamental difference in Protestant and Catholic views of worship (Pratt 1964). The Roman Catholic Church has historically taken an objective approach to the Mass. The emphasis was on glorification of God, and the liturgy was designed with that in mind. It was best to have a congregation present at the celebration of Mass, but if no one came, the Mass would go on. On the other hand, a Protestant minister would scarcely think of conducting a full service of worship if no congregation gathered. The more subjective emphasis of the Protestant denominations—especially the ones that have a more informal, low church tone—is on how the worship affects the worshipers themselves. Hence, the beliefs about worship itself significantly affect the order of a liturgy and the themes it includes. Obviously, liturgies for funerals, marriages, and other special occasions will not necessarily conform to the pattern described above.

From the example provided, it may be seen that ritual and belief are often closely intertwined and tend to be mutually reinforcing. That is, they tend to provide an interrelated *system*. It is noteworthy that sample surveys have consistently found a high correlation between regular attendence at rituals and a high level of acceptance of the belief system of the denomination. However, it is also true that many people are unaware of the logical progression of the worship liturgy and of the theological basis for its order. Hence, the liturgy is viewed as just so many hymns, prayers, and scripture readings in random order. Given this fact, and given the fact that some people attend church for purely status reasons (as a demonstration that they are good citizens) it is not surprising that the correlation between ritual attendance and doctrinal orthodoxy is far from perfect.[8]

Relationship between Myth and Ritual

As has been suggested, ritual in many cases may precede myth. Judah, for example, insists that "chanting is the primary prerequisite" in conversion to the Hare Krishna movement (1974:170). Some scholars have gone even further by suggesting that in terms of chronological development, ritual emerges first and myth develops later to justify the existence of the ritual. Franz Boaz particularly emphasized the primacy of ritual, and the secondary explanatory role of myth (Kluckhohn 1972:95).

However, the process may develop the other way as well. (Kluckhohn 1972:95–96). The Mass is clearly an example of a ritual based on a sacred story. Another example is the Ghost Dance, a religious ritual based on a dream or vision by Wovoka, the Paiute holy man whose trance in 1889 regenerated a powerful religious movement among Native Americans. In this case, the interpreted dream provided both a mythology and a command to perform a ritual (LaBarre 1972:229ff). Clyde Kluckhohn emphasizes the complex relationship between these elements of religion:

> [T]he whole question of the primacy of ceremonial or mythology is as meaningless as all questions of "the hen or the egg" form. What really is

---

[8] It is important to keep in mind that the operationalization of doctrinal orthodoxy has tended to rate people higher on orthodoxy if they view scripture literalistically. Hence, the measures themselves need careful interpretation.

important is the intricate interdependence of myth with ritual and many other forms of behavior (1972:96).

In some cases both myth and ritual may be viewed as factors dependent upon a third component: mystical or nonrational experience. This, of course, was the position of Otto (1923) and, more recently, of Thomas O'Dea (1966). Van der Leeuw (1963:49) has also written that awe, once established, "develops into observance." The experience of awe may be so fascinating and attractive that a ritual is established to try to elicit or recreate that experience. Furthermore a mythology is generated to try to explain or make sense of the experience (O'Dea 1966:24, 40–41). At this point it seems fair to conclude that no generalization can be made about which of these three factors is primary, for there is wide variation between cultures and even within cultures. For that matter, there may even be variation within the same religion, as each denomination or sect of that faith emerges in accord with its own internal dynamic.

The image presented here of highly integrated ritual and myth needs a word of caution. The discussion of the Protestant liturgy suggested a high degree of integration and interdependence between ritual and belief system. However, that integration is largely a matter of interpretation; that is, this integration is to a considerable extent in the eye of the beholder. The participant *interprets* the ritual and myth as mutually supportive, hence it *is* mutually supportive for that person. However, many cases have been found in which diverse tribal peoples practice the same ritual, but interpret that ritual as expressing very different myths. Likewise, people holding the same belief system may celebrate those beliefs with very different ritual patterns. In summary, we can say that beliefs, ritual, and religious experience are important components of what we call religion, that they are usually interrelated and mutually supportive, and that the integration of the three is itself largely a matter of interpretation by the believer.

As readers attend religious services in their own communities they may be interested in asking themselves: What is the rationale for the order of this liturgy? How are myth and ritual intertwined and mutually supportive, or is there no apparent relationship? What does the ritual mean to the *members* of this group?

The Importance of Symbols

The reason why myths and rituals normally have a close relationship is that they are both manifestations of a larger phenomenon—a system of symbols. Elizabeth Nottingham emphasizes the unifying function of symbols:

> [I]t is not hard to understand that the sharing of common symbols is a particularly effective way of cementing the unity of a group of worshipers.

It is precisely because the referents of symbols elude overprecise intellectual definitions that their unifying force is the more potent; for intellectual definitions make for hairsplitting and divisiveness. Symbols may be shared on the basis of not-too-closely-defined feeling (1971:19).

Certainly this is one reason that symbols are important. Geertz (1958:422) emphasizes a slightly different reason that symbols are critically important when he writes: *"Meanings can only be stored in symbols:* a cross, a crescent, or a feather. Such religious symbols, dramatized in rituals or related in myths, are felt somehow to sum up what is known about the way the world is" (my emphasis). Edmund Leach's research on the symbolic power of rituals supports this view. Leach has studied rituals as "storage systems" which encapsulate knowledge. He maintains that ritual provides an important form of economical thinking among many tribal peoples. Meaningful information and important knowledge are encapsulated in ritual in a way analogous to the loading of computer chips with information in our culture. Rituals are viewed by Leach as vessels which carry powerful symbols and which authoritatively transmit a world view and an ethos (Leach 1972:333–337).

A consideration of certain elements in the Catholic Mass will illustrate the power of symbols. As the celebrants come before the altar, they genuflect and cross themselves. Although the act may sometimes be perfunctorily executed, making the sign of the cross acts to remind believers of a particular event. The cross has meaning because it reminds the participant of a sacred story, a particular life, and a divine event. The theological interpretation of the event may vary somewhat from one celebrant to another, but with the regularized pattern of crossing oneself, the centrality of Christ on the cross will not be forgotten. The stained-glass windows may have symbols meaningful to the early church or perhaps depictions of Jesus in a well-known scene. These symbolic representations also bring to mind a whole series of events and stories that are part of the sacred myth. When the priest says, "Take, eat, this is my body," another central event is recalled. At certain points in the Mass, the congregation kneels. This act is a gesture of humility, and is to remind one of an utter dependency and humility before God. In each case, the entire story does not have to be repeated in detail. If the myth is well known, and if the symbolic meaning of the ritual action is understood by the celebrant, then all that is necessary to elicit certain moods and motivations is to introduce the symbol itself. The symbol stores meaning and can call forth certain attitudes or dispositions.

In the Jewish tradition one can see the same power of symbols in a religious festival such as the Seder meal. Even a Gentile cannot help but be moved by the symbolic reenactment of the escape from Egypt. The eating of bitter herbs, which actually bring tears to one's eyes, reminds one of the suffering of the ancestors. The unleavened bread, the parsley, and the haroseth each has symbolic value in recalling a sacred story. This symbolic reenactment confirms in the minds of the Jews where they have been, who they are, and what task lies before them. A sense of identity and a sense of holy mission is powerfully communicated through the ritual.

Geertz's definition of religion articulates very well the important role of symbols: "Religion is a system of symbols which acts to establish powerful, pervasive, and long-lasting moods and motivations in [people] by formulating conceptions of a general order of existence." The symbol systems are important in that they act in people's lives. Ritual and myth, then, are important as symbol systems. In this text, the concept of religion has stressed world view (conceptions of a general order of existence) and ethos (powerful, pervasive, and long-lasting moods and motivations) as central elements. Hence, the next issue before us is the relationships among world view, ethos, and symbols.

World View, Ethos, and Symbols

World view refers to the intellectual framework within which one explains the meaning of life (including one's cosmology). Myths are specific stories or beliefs, the net effect of which is to reinforce a world view (Wuthnow 1981). A single story may not be sufficient to convince someone that God is in charge of the universe and all is well. However, a series of many such myths may serve to reinforce such an outlook on life. World view is a more abstract concept than myth; it refers to one's mode of *perceiving* the world and to one's general overview of life. In this sense, a world view is more taken for granted and less questioned. Many individuals may not be fully conscious of the alternative types of world views and many never question the fact that their perception is influenced by intellectual constructs. Whether one is optimistic or pessimistic in outlook is strongly influenced by one's world view. (See the passages from Jonathan Edwards in Exhibit 4–3.)

One's world view is also closely related to one's ethos. "A people's *ethos* is the tone, character, and quality of their life, its moral and aesthetic style and mood; it is the uderlying attitude toward themselves and their world" (Geertz 1958:421). Ethos refers to *attitudes* about life (moods, motivations) while world view refers to an *intellectual* process (concepts of a general order of existence).[9] Both attitudes and concepts are essential to the establishment of a sense of meaning in life. The world view is confirmed and made to seem objective by the ethos. The set of concepts is placed beyond question and is made absolute by the sacred mood in which it is transmitted. Further-

---

[9] It may be helpful for readers to review the material on Geertz's definition of religion in Chapter 2. The distinction between moods (which he describes as "scalar" or as having to do with depth of feeling) and motivations (which he describes as "vectorial" or directional) is elaborated. Both moods and motivations are part of the ethos.

more, this basic attitude (ethos) is justified and made reasonable by the world view. So in a well-integrated religious system, the ethos and world view are mutually reinforcing.

Symbols, according to Geertz, play the central role of relating the world view to the ethos. Symbols have power because they hold images of how things *are* and how they *ought to be*. On both the intellectual and emotional levels, they transform fact into value. The function of sacred symbols is to encapsulate or summarize the system of meaning, and to deliver that meaning system with power and authority at appropriate times. Geertz discusses the symbolic significance of the circle among the Oglala Sioux as an example:

> For most Oglala the circle is but an unexamined luminous symbol whose meaning is intuitively sensed, not consciously interpreted. But the power of the symbol, analyzed or not, clearly rests on its comprehensiveness, on its fruitfulness in ordering experience. Again and again the idea of a sacred circle, a natural form with a moral import, yields, when applied to the world within which the Oglala lives, new meanings; continually it connects together elements within their experience which would otherwise seem wholly disparate and, wholly disparate, incomprehensible (1958:423).

So symbols have power: they are instruments that help people interpret the events of life. In so doing, they also affect one's outlook on life (optimistic, pessimistic, and so on).

Many other scholars have commented on the world view or "world construction" aspects of religion. The lack of a consistent cosmology to explain events and to justify one's values and lifestyle can be disrupting and disorienting. Peter Berger asserts that society is the guardian of order and meaning, not only at the level of social structure, but at the level of individual consciousness. Sacred images help to preserve order in the structures of society and in the structuring of the individual mind. "It is for this reason that radical separation from the social world, or anomie, constitutes such a powerful threat to the individual. The individual loses his orientation in experience. In extreme cases, he loses his sense of reality and identity. He becomes anomic in the sense of becoming worldless" (Berger 1967:21).

Durkheim suggested long ago that the experience of anomie[10] can be so unsettling that it can result in suicidal behavior. The feeling of a firmly rooted world view, with certain and definite moral rules and regulations, is a compelling need for many humans. Geertz (1966:16) insisted that his tribal-society respondents were quite willing to abandon their cosmology for a more plausible one. What they were *not* willing to do was abandon it for no other hypothesis at all, leaving events to themselves.

In line with this emphasis, Mary Douglas has offered an insightful interpretation of biblical taboos. Not all taboos are health related as was once

---

[10] Anomie may be defined as a lack of purpose, identity, or ethical values; social rootlessness.

maintained. Some taboos have to do with protecting the distinction between sacred and profane. Still others have to do with those things that are anomalies (unexplainable phenomenon) to the accepted world view.

In the process of socialization, a child learns to think in terms of categories of language and in terms of theories or explanations extant in a culture. When new information is received, it is interpreted in terms of those accepted categories of thought. New experiences and new information are assimilated into the present world view. When an experience does not seem to fit into this mold, the person experiences *dissonance* (internal cognitive conflict). According to cognitive psychologist Jean Piaget, one is likely to revise and reorder one's world view when too much dissonance occurs. However, a good deal of dissonant information can be tolerated by certain techniques. This is precisely where Mary Douglas claims that taboos enter the picture. Many taboos have to do with avoidance of those things that violate one's world view (Douglas 1966; 1968).

The food taboos of the Old Testament provide an excellent example. In order to understand the abominations of Leviticus, we must go back to the creation story in Genesis. Here a threefold classification is presented, with the earth, the waters, and the firmament as distinct realms. Leviticus develops this scheme by allotting to each element its proper kind of animal life. Douglas (1966:55) summarizes:

> In the firmament two-legged fowls fly with wings. In the water scaly fish swim with fins. On the earth four-legged animals hop, jump, or walk. Any class of creatures which is not equipped for the right kind of locomotion in its element is contrary to holiness. Contact with it disqualifies a person from approaching the Temple. Thus anything in the water which has not fins and scales is unclean (Lev. 11: 10–12).

Contact with anything that is "contrary to nature" causes a person to be unclean and unfit to enter the temple—for example, anything in the water which does not have fins and scales. Hence catfish are unclean because they have whiskers and no scales; they violate the principles of creation as spelled out in this world view. Creatures which have two legs and two hands, but which walk on all fours, are unclean. Thus, animals which have hand-like front paws (the weasel, the mouse, and the mole) are explicitly taboo because they violate the law of creation. An animal with hands, but which perversely uses its hands for walking, does not fit into the proper scheme of things. Anything that creeps, crawls, or swarms upon the earth is also defined in Leviticus as an "abomination." "Eels and worms inhabit water, though not as fish; reptiles go on dry land, though not as quadrupeds; some insects fly, though not as birds. *There is no order in them*" (Douglas 1966:56, my emphasis).

Among these pastoral people, cloven-hoofed and cud-chewing animals are the proper sort of food. Wild game is edible only if it seems to conform to these characteristics. But animals which do not conform in *both* respects are unfit as food. The pig and the camel are both cloven hoofed, but they do not chew a cud. Douglas points out that the failure to conform to these two necessary criteria for defining animals as acceptable food is the only reason given in the Old Testament for not eating pork; no mention is made of pigs' scavaging habits.

Douglas offers a fascinating and well-documented thesis: many taboos function to protect the culture's world view and to provide a category for those things that don't make sense (anomolies). They are simply abominations which are dirty and to be avoided.[11] Other aspects of order may also be protected or reinforced by taboos. Beliefs about women being unclean during their menstruation and in need of purification functioned to remind them of their inferior social position. The insistence in the New Testament that women cover their head in church served a similar function. Men and women were viewed as fundamentally different. This was symbolically emphasized by men keeping their hair short and women keeping theirs long. Anything that threatened this essential distinction (essential to that world view) was an abomination (it threatened concepts of order). Douglas demonstrates vividly that protection and preservation of the world view is very important in understanding much religious behavior.[12]

Much of Peter Berger's writing has to do with the need for one's world view to seem authoritative, certain, and compelling. In the midst of alternative paradigms and cosmologies, one's world view may become fragile and vulnerable. Hence the vulnerability of a world view is concealed in an aura of sacredness (Berger 1967:33). Without a basis in a convincing world view, social values would not seem compelling and social stability itself may be threatened. Clifford Geertz came to the same conclusion through cross-cultural analysis of religion:

> . . . mere conventionalism satisfies few people in any culture. [R]eligion, by fusing ethos and world-view, gives to a set of social values what they perhaps most need to be coercive: an appearance of objectivity. In sacred rituals and myths values are portrayed not as subjective human preferences but as the imposed conditions for life (1958:426–427).

In conclusion, we might simply point to the complexity of the relationships among the various components of religion. In terms of the integration of these elements into a coherent religious system, we might summarize with the following four points: (1) Ritual and myth tend to be mutually reinforcing as symbol systems. (2) Symbols (including rituals, myths, and artifacts),

---

[11] Another explanation of the abominations of Leviticus, popular among some Jewish scholars, is that they were antiassimilation laws. They forbade activities which were popular among other peoples in the geographic region and thereby limited interaction with and assimilation to these other groups.

[12] For a more detailed discussion of the use of taboos to maintain sex roles, color bars, and class lines, refer to the section on The Functions of Religion in Chapter 3.

encapsulate the world view and ethos of a people. Hence they can elicit powerful emotional responses and (by repetition) help to reinforce a general world view. (3) The ethos and the world view are themselves mutually reinforcing. (4) Together they provide a compelling basis for social values (see Exhibit 4–6).

A problem may arise when a religious system is not so well integrated and mutually reinforcing. Geertz has himself described the social and cultural disintegration that can happen when ritual, myth, social values, and social structure do not harmonize (Geertz 1957:531–543). Some measure of conflict between these elements can be tolerated and is normal. This is the advantage of symbols: they can unify individuals who each adhere to the symbol, but who attach alternative meanings to it. However, some scholars believe that the lack of a common, shared world view can eventually become a problem for a pluralistic society. Their argument is that lack of agreement

Exhibit 4–6

The Interrelationship between the Elements of Religion

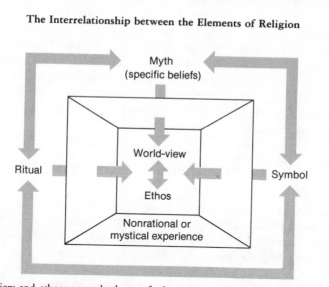

World view and ethos are at the heart of what we mean by religion. Yet these concepts are abstractions from experience; an individual's world view and religious ethos (moods and motivations) are so pervasive and so taken for granted that the subject may not be fully conscious of all their dimensions. These abstractions are made concrete and are reinforced by more concrete expressions of religiosity: ritual, myth, and symbols. Each of these is interrelated and acts to confirm the ethos and world view. Frequently the entire religious realm seems uniquely compelling because of a nonrational religious experience. Some groups may emphasize some of these elements more than others (e.g., religious experience may be more important than unquestioned belief in the myth). Variations in interpretation of any of these may also lead to considerable conflict within the group. In actual practice, religion always has a good deal more internal inconsistency than this diagram would suggest. Hence, it is important to bear in mind that this model is idealized. It does represent a strain toward integrity that is a very real part of all religion. It is also true that when glaring incoherence in this system and conflict in interpretation of the elements becomes severe, some form of religious change is likely to take place.

on the big picture, the unifying ideology or outlook, leaves the culture without a unifying core. Barbara Hargrove goes so far as to suggest that public school teachers may be left with no common framework for interpreting data. If this occurs, teachers will only be able to impart "disjointed facts" (Hargrove 1979:186).

It is a maxim of the social sciences that "facts do not speak for themselves; they must be interpreted." The difficulty in a heterogeneous culture is that there is no agreement on which big theory really makes sense and explains the meaning of life. The overriding, integrating world view which religion provides for many cultures is not a uniting and integrating factor in a pluralistic one. For most science teachers in the past several decades, evolutionary theory has provided the big picture, the overriding theory which explains the relationships among the data. With the creationist movement, this big picture is being challenged in the courts. Some functionalists view the lack of an integrated culture—with a core of common assumptions about the way things are—as devastating to social life.

This cultural diversity, combined with the multiple interpretations of religious symbols, leads us to explore two interesting developments. The first has to do with the impact of the scientific world view on modern society and on religion. This is referred to as secularization, or modernism. The second issue emanates in part from this secularization process. It has to do with the development of folk and elite versions of the faith. The theological elite sometimes interpret scripture, myths, and rituals quite differently from the way the common laity view them.

Secularization: Modification of a World View

Secularization has been discussed by many social scientists and by scores of theologians. There seems to be some consensus that it is a matter of considerable import, but its definition varies greatly. We have no agreement on exactly what secularization is, what causes it, and what effects it might have. It has been viewed as a decline of religion, as a lessening of the sphere of the sacred, or as a tendency of religion to become worldly. The point of agreement seems to be that traditional religious symbols are no longer a unifying force for industrialized society. The modern empirical scientific world view has replaced the miraculous religious world view. Truth and knowledge are gained through double-blind, crossover studies rather than through visions or religious intuition. People look to science and technology to solve problems. As a means of compensating, religionists have developed systematic theologies which are logical, coherent, and rational. Mythology has given way to empiricism, both in the secular world and within religion itself.

That a process of change has taken place in the world view of the Western world is unquestioned. How to understand and evaluate it is more problematic. A number of writers feel that this spells the decline of religion. (Some report this with delight; others are aghast.) Several social scientists are alarmed that it could mean a collapse of the entire society (see especially Peter Berger). Still others maintain that it is a healthy process that will strengthen the influence of religion. They acknowledge religious change, but do not see this change as decline (Parsons, Yinger, Bellah). Others (like O'Dea) view secularization as increased emphasis on logic and reason and a decline in the emphasis on myth and nonrational experience. In any case, a change in the foundations of the world view of Western culture is at stake. It is appropriate to explore the process of secularization as discussed by several key theorists.[13]

Berger: Secularization as the Loss of Sacredness and the Decline of Social Consensus

Peter Berger (1967, 1979) is very much alarmed by the process of secularization. He sees this process as having many adverse effects on individuals and on the society as a whole.

Berger defines secularization as "the process by which sectors of society and culture are removed from the domination of religious institutions and symbols" (1967:107). The function of religion in providing unifying symbols and a unifying world view is extremely important in Berger's view. He insists that a society's *constructed world* (his term for world view) is very fragile. It must be protected by being clothed in an aura of sacredness. The critically thinking empiricist allows that nothing is sacred; that is, nothing is beyond study and question. The world construction of the scientist is based on causality and logic. Since individual thinking is valued, the scientifically oriented society allows and even encourages a plurality of world views. In fact, Berger asserts that "the phenomenon called pluralism is a social-structural correlate of the secularization of consciousness" (1967:127). But he implies that pluralism is not necessarily a good thing. A multiplicity of world views may make all world views seem relative. None of them can be taken as absolute and above doubt (1979:15–20). This has fostered an "acute crises" for individuals by creating a sense of anomie. This lack of meaningfulness in life, referred to by some psychologists as *existential vacuum* or *existential anxiety*,[14] can be extremely disorienting to individuals. Berger (1967:125) insists that the introduction of critical thinking about one's world view "was bought at the price of severe anomie and existential anxiety."

The dysfunctions of allowing pluralism of world views and of reducing

---

[13] We will return to the issue of whether traditional forms of religion are declining in Chapter 10. There are empirical data on trends in church membership and church attendance in that chapter. These are often interpreted as indicators of secularization in our society.

[14] Viktor Frankl's terms (1967).

the realm of the sacred is not limited to individuals. Pluralism also poses threats to the stability and workability of the entire society. Berger is a functional or consensus theorist in the fullest sense of the word. He believes that commonly held beliefs, values, and symbols are the glue that hold a society together. He maintains that a society cannot long exist without a discoverable core of common purposes. Religion has always played this role, and Berger is alarmed that the absolute and uncompromising imperative of religion has been relativized. "Religion no longer legitimates the world. Rather, different religious groups seek, by different means, to maintain their particular subworlds in the face of a plurality of competing subworlds" (1967:152). Because of this, individuals become aware of the fact that there are a plurality of possible religious views—each potentially legitimate—from which they must choose. The fact that one consciously selects a religious orientation (rather than being compelled by the conviction that there is only one possible view) automatically makes the choice relative and less than certain. Berger does not view this situation as one in which the individual is free to choose—an option now available to individuals. Rather, each person *must* choose. The net effect is a diminishing of the power of religion in the lives of people. To use Geertz's phrase, it is the difference between holding a belief and being held by one. Berger laments that "religious traditions have lost their character as overarching symbols for the society at large, which must find its integrating symbolism elsewhere" (1967:153).

Berger concludes that religion must either accommodate, "play the game of religious free enterprise," and "modify its product in accordance with consumer demand," or it must entrench itself and maintain its world view behind whatever socioreligious structures it can construct (1967:153). A religious group that takes the first course tends to become secularized from within and to lose its sense of transcendence or sacredness. It focuses on "marketing" the faith to a clientele that is no longer constrained to "buy." In the process, the faith may be severely compromised and changed. If it fails to accommodate, the religion may be charged with being an "irrelevant" minority faith that does not respond to the needs of the society.

Berger is himself no passive observer. He is appalled by the secularization of religion, and he emphatically supports religious entrenchment. Theologically speaking, Berger is a conservative, and he is alarmed. His own theological position has shaped his perception of religion and its relationship to society. This is not necessarily a criticism of Berger, for the same can be true of any social scientist who studies religion. Facts are interpreted through some paradigm—some overriding explanation of how things are. Hence, one's own religious posture tends to shade one's view of the potential threat or benefit of secularization (Johnson, 1979).

The causes of secularization are many. Berger points out that some of the causes lie within the Judeo-Christian outlook itself. Old Testament theology acted to despiritualize the world. Only God was sacred, and the world was not viewed as being inhabited by spirits. The world was given to humanity to *use*. This outlook allowed an attitude to develop that God's people have the responsibility to manipulate and control resources. Humanity was instructed to have dominion over the earth, and this attitude allowed for the later development of science and technology (Berger 1967:113ff). Another possible factor in this secularization process may have been the institutional specialization of religion. The concentration of religious activities and symbols in one institutional sphere automatically defines the rest of society as "the world"; it becomes the profane realm removed for the most part from the jurisdiction of the sacred (1967:123). By enabling the growth of science and technology, and by limiting the scope of religion to a particular institution, Judeo-Christian religion may itself have promoted secularization.

Berger believes the causes of secularization are complex; he also believes the effects are potentially destructive. The unifying power of religious symbols and the integrating function of a common religious world view are very important for social stability. The lack of a single world view, couched in sacred symbols and an aura of absoluteness, is Berger's fundamental concern. Hence, he believes that secularization—the removal of many sectors of society and culture from the domination of religious institutions and symbols—is a critical process in the relationship between religion and modern society.

Parsons and Bellah: Secularization as Religious Evolution and Development

Talcott Parsons (1963) and Robert Bellah (1970c) have treated secularization as part of the increasing complexity and diversity of modern industrial society. Religion, both as institution and as individual belief system, has become increasingly differentiated from the rest of society. According to Parsons and Bellah, it has simultaneously become more of a private affair. However, they do not see this as a negative change. The possibility of consciously *choosing* one's religious outlook, rather than being *given* a theology, may make religion *more* important to the individual. Parsons insists that Christianity may still have a great effect on Western society; after all, the institutions of the Western world were developed by people who were under the influence of the Christian ethos and the Christian world view. Moreover, private religiosity will continue profoundly to affect public behavior; ultimate values cannot help but affect an individual's "system of action." In fact, much of the influence of religion will be unconscious: "Modern man, working in a large corporate structure that is infused somewhat by Christian ideas, with himself directed somewhat by the Christian ethic, may be behaving religiously a good deal of the time, though the fact that he is influenced by religion may not be immediately clear to him because the influence is both indirect and implicit" (Greeley 1972:134).

Bellah would agree with Berger that religious institutions exert less direct influence on secular institutions than in the past. But he explains this change as a process of religious evolution rather than decline. A more detailed discussion of this concept of religious evolution might help readers to grasp Bellah's view of the contemporary religious scene.

It is necessary first to understand Bellah's definition of religion and his treatment of evolution. Bellah defines religion as "a set of symbolic forms and acts which relate [persons] to the ultimate conditions of [their] existence" (Bellah 1970:21). The reader can see from this that Bellah uses a very inclusive definition of religion, and that the focus of his investigation is on the evolution of symbols. The increase in the complexity of symbols is correlated with an increase in the complexity of social organization. Through this process of evolution, religion is able to do more than reaffirm the present social structure; it can challenge the current norms and values of the secular society and offer an alternative culture. Hence, the latter stages of evolution represent an increased autonomy of religion relative to its social environment. Bellah does not suggest that the evolutionary process is inevitable, irreversible, or unidirectional. He simply suggests a general trend of increasing differentiation of religion from the rest of the society.

Bellah has posited five stages in the evolution of religion: primitive religion, archaic religion, historic religion, early modern religion, and modern religion. The most simple form of religion is exemplified by the Australian aborigines. The symbol system of this type of group focuses on a mythical world, and that mythical world provides a model for understanding the real world. The mythical world is peopled by spirits, but the spirits are not greater than humans. Through ritual, people identify with these mythic or spiritual beings. There are no separate or distinctive religious roles, social structure, or organization. Religion is an undifferentiated part of the culture; hence it serves to unify the culture and enhance the stability of the social structure. Religion does not serve as a lever for social change.

In archaic religion, the spiritual beings have more power and influence than in primitive religion. They are more than models, as they are attributed with power and authority in their own right; they are capable of actively influencing everyday life. Hence, prayer, sacrifice, and other means of communication are established to make contact with these superhuman beings. The development of differentiated religious roles and organizations occurs, but those roles and organizations are still under the control of the political hierarchy. Religion still functions primarily to sanctify the status quo. In fact, the close relationship between religious and political systems is sometimes manifested in a form of divine kingship. Families with high political status usually control the higher-status religious roles as well. The world view is essentially monistic, with the energies of the gods focused on the realm of existence in which humans live. In other words, the religion is essentially this-worldly. The religious symbol system is still not autonomous from the secular symbol system; hence, the religious world view does not offer an alternative to that of the predominant culture.

The distinguishing characteristic of historic religion is that the religious realm is entirely different from that of the secular realm. Historic religion truly emphasizes the distinction between sacred and profane worlds. This dualism usually leads to a rejection of the empirical world and its values in favor of the divine realm. Historical religion is otherworldly in the fullest sense of the word. Its emergence is a significant development because at this stage religion becomes more than tribal loyalty. Historic religions affirm the existence of a single God who is God of all peoples and all tribes. Furthermore, the concept of a separate and independent realm of existence involves the articulation of an alternative model of what the world really is and what is expected of humans. A tension between the religious culture and the secular culture is now possible as each demands the loyalties of the individual. A differentiated religious organization also emerges as a separate institutional structure. As a somewhat autonomous entity, both institutionally and in terms of symbol systems, religion becomes a source of social and cultural change. Political actions may be judged by standards the political authorities do not control.

Early modern religion carries forth a similar pattern in the dualism of the world view and in the autonomy of religious institutions. However, the negative view of the empirical world is modified. While salvation is still viewed as a reward in another realm, one's salvation is worked out through one's personal relationship with God and one's personal demonstration of faithfulness in this world. Bellah traces the beginning of early modern religion to the Protestant Reformation. The Protestant reformers deemphasized the mediating role of the religious organization, and stressed the "priesthood of all believers." Hence, salvation became a matter of individual responsibility and of ethical action in this world. Loyalty and devotion to God was viewed in terms of the conduct of everyday life rather than frequency of attendance at religious ritual.[15] This emphasis meant that secular institutions (law, education, politics) became appropriate arenas for expressing values and attitudes that one derived from a religious view of the world. Religion may provide an alternative view of the world and establish the motive for change, but other institutions may be used as power bases to initiate the change. The society is characterized by increased tension and conflict as various groups seek to establish their concept of the good society or of the Kingdom of God on Earth. Religion has become a more private

---

[15] This raises some interesting questions about the measures of religiosity which view religious action strictly in terms of church attendance and view application of religion to everyday life as a variable.

affair in the sense of not being controlled or determined by public officials, yet the arena for expressing one's religious values has become the arena of public policy and social ethics.

Modern religion is a phenomenon which Bellah believes is currently emerging, although he is quick to point out that the nature of this stage and even its existence are somewhat speculative. Bellah suggests that we are currently undergoing a transformation of religion that involves further privatization and less organizational control. He maintains that new forms of religiosity are emerging. The new form of religious expression is characterized by a breakdown in the dualistic view of the world (with its two realms of existence). This is being replaced by a grounding of religion in ethical life in this world. The world view is less otherworldly, but still involves a symbol system that "relates persons to the ultimate condition of their existence." In this sense, he views the world view as profoundly religious. Bellah writes: "The analysis of modern [humanity] as secular, materialistic, dehumanized, and in the deepest sense areligious seems to me fundamentally misguided, for such a judgement is based on standards that cannot adequately gauge the modern temper" (1970:40). The attempts by several key social scientists to discover "invisible religions" is in keeping with this emphasis on new forms of privatized religion (Luckmann 1967; Yinger 1969, 1977; Wuthnow 1973, 1976b).

Religious evolution is seen by Bellah as an increase in the complexity of symbol systems and in the complexity of the organization of society.[16] The later stages of the evolutionary process allow individuals to make choices as to which world view they will accept. Furthermore, individuals have more autonomy in being able to think for themselves and create their own system of meaning. This allows for greater freedom, and in this sense may be viewed as an advancement for humankind.

Parsons and Bellah each treat secularization as the process by which religion has become a private matter, and they believe that such secularization is taking place. However, if secularization is referred to as a process by which religion decreases in importance and by which it has less influence on one's world view and on social behavior, then Bellah and Parsons would deny that secularization is occurring. Differentiation of world views and pluralization of the culture is evaluated in positive terms. It represents progression of society rather than regression and dissolution.

---

[16] Bellah's theory of religious evolution must be understood within the confines of his operational definition of evolution. Bellah stresses increased differentiation and complexity as the essence of evolution. The natural sciences stress variation and selective retention as the key elements in evolution—factors on which Bellah does not elaborate in his essay. For this reason, some social scientists question whether Bellah's theory is truly evolutionary. Readers should be cautioned that evolution is used in a very specialized way by many scientists and social scientists, while others use the term rather freely to describe the emergence of increasingly complex forms from simpler ones. For a comparison and contrast of biological and sociocultural concepts of evolution, see Lenski and Lenski (1978).

It has been the group that Berger accuses most of having secularized religion—the theological liberals—who have been most actively involved in "social concerns" struggles (civil rights, antiwar movements, and so on). While these movements are themselves not always explicitly religious, many participants are motivated by theological convictions. Many theological liberals have deemphasized the concept of the sacred, but have emphasized that all of life is to be understood in theological terms. Hence, they have *broadened* the scope of religion,[17] even while accepting a rational, empirical understanding of the world. Such theologians as Harvey Cox have celebrated the secularization of religion as a healthy sign (1965). Bellah and Parsons have personally identified with this more liberal strain of theology, and they are not inclined to think of it as less religious or as a sign of the decline of religion. Bellah, like Yinger, is interested in discovering new forms of religion rather than focusing exclusively on traditional expressions.

One difficulty with the theory of secularization presented by Parsons and Bellah is that it is developed on such a high level of abstraction that it is virtually impossible to prove or disprove. Their theory represents a complex analysis of the evolution of symbol systems and of the relationships between symbol systems and "action orientations." The theory is significant and deserves attention; but there is no way to measure or test it empirically. Hence, one cannot validate or invalidate the theory with the accuracy many social scientists prefer.

O'Dea: Secularization as Rationalization and Religious Decline

Thomas O'Dea's approach to secularization takes a somewhat different tact. O'Dea follows Otto's thesis that the essence of religion is the experience of the *mysterium tremendum.* All belief systems or myths are outgrowths of this experience; they are attempts to explain that primary encounter. Moreover, ritual and myth act together to *recreate* the experience at specific times. For O'Dea, religion is not primarily a rational or intellectual phenomenon. However, secularization involves the systematizing of beliefs in logical, rational terms. O'Dea's nonrational concept of religion leads him to the conclusion that secularization represents a decline in religion.

O'Dea (1966:81) suggests that secularization consists of two related transformations in human thinking: "the *desacralization* of the attitude toward persons and things . . . [and] the *rationalization of thought.*" The realm of the sacred is greatly reduced in scope and may even be abandoned altogether. This concept is consistent with Berger's treatment of secularization. However, O'Dea places especially heavy emphasis on the rationalization

---

[17] Berger strongly opposes this sort of broadened scope of religion. He insists that religionists have no business bringing theology into the arena of politics (Berger 1981). Yet he defines the narrowing of the influence and scope of religion as secularization and decline.

process. Here he refers to confidence in reason, logic, and scientific investigation as the primary means of understanding the world. "The evolution of an idea of the world no longer sacred, and one understandable by human reason, means the emergence of a world where *mysteries are replaced by problems*" (O'Dea 1966:86). Not only has Western culture become secularized in this way, but religion has been too. Philosophical theologies—theologies which are based upon systematic logic and which incorporate the findings of science—have been developed and taught at many universities and seminaries. For example, the systematic theologies of Paul Tillich and Henry Nelson Weiman focus on human experience and human knowledge rather than on Bible stories. They view God as the source of creation, human experience, and knowledge. For this reason, *all* human experience is appropriate for theological reflection, not just certain religious stories. Scientific evidence is considered as a legitimate starting point for theologizing. Furthermore, a norm of logical consistency and coherence is foremost in most philosophical theologies, and becomes a measuring stick for truth. Such theologies are rational meaning systems; they generally deemphasize mythology. O'Dea devotes considerable attention to this shift "from *mythos* to *logos*"—from myth to logic. This involves the *demythologizing*[18] of biblical material. It also includes recasting biblical perspectives so that they are consistent with the modern scientific world view.

O'Dea cites Max Weber's thesis that ascetic Protestantism had contributed to the rationalization of economics and other spheres of social life. According to Weber, this rationalization process allowed bureaucratic structures to develop in the Western world. O'Dea cites the Weberian thesis and concludes that the rational, ascetic, this-worldly character of Protestant Christianity had much to do with the secularization of Western culture.[19] He also insists that theology becomes highly rationalized and systematic only with the development of a professional clergy. It is the religious elite that are intent on internal theological coherence and consistency. O'Dea points out that the Mormon church, which has no full-time professional clergy, has not significantly rationalized its belief system.

O'Dea believes that the emphasis on rationality, causal logic, and empiricism tends to lead to disbelief in a transcendent God. Since the world can be explained by science, the need for a transcendent reference fades, and large numbers of people cease to be interested in religion. The secularization of culture begins a process that results in atheism—the decline of religion. Furthermore, the religious belief systems that emerge from systematic theology emphasize rationality and emanate from intellectual activity. Since O'Dea views religion as primarily an outgrowth of a religious *experi-*

---

[18] Theologian Rudolf Bultmann's term (1958).
[19] The Weber thesis will be explored in more detail in Chapter 8.

ence, this secularization process within religion is viewed as a process of decline.

Conclusions Regarding the Process of Secularization

Many questions remain regarding secularization. First, is it an inevitable process? Second, are some religions more secular than others? Third, does continuing secularization mean a decline of religion, and perhaps its eventual dissolution? Fourth, are this-worldly religions always more secular than otherworldly ones? However, before these and other questions can be answered, some consensus needs to emerge as to what secularization really is.

Many treatments of secularization focus on a decline of religion. But how one defines religion makes a great deal of difference—as one can see from the discussions of Berger, Parsons, Bellah, and O'Dea. Robert Bellah and Milton Yinger insist that religion in America is not declining, it is simply changing. They can assert this, in part, because of the definition of religion they use. Powerful, meaning-providing symbol systems are not fading out of existence. Berger's definition of secularization as "a reduction in the sphere of influence of religion" is based on a different definition of religion. What is needed is a nonevaluative definition of secularization which includes the concerns of the various authors.

Benton Johnson suggests that we define secularization as a "process of change that involves a decline of the supernatural element in systems of meaning" (1979:25). Whether this represents a decline of religion depends on whether a belief in the supernatural is part of one's definition of religion. Johnson's definition of secularization allows us to speak of degrees of secularization; it avoids the supposition that secularization is an irreversible process; and it allows the study of naturalistic and philosophical theologies without assuming that they are less religious. Johnson's definition neither presupposes a definition of religion nor makes a value judgment about secularization. It is a definite step toward clarity and consensus—at least with regard to the meaning of the word *secularization.*

It is likely that the increased rationalization of belief systems and the accommodation of those systems to scientific insights have resulted in a decrease in emphasis on the supernatural. Hence, rationality in culture and in religion *would* seem to be a central correlate with secularization. This does not automatically imply a decline in religion; this judgment depends on one's definition.

The question of whether secularization is a pervasive and continuing process has been debated heatedly. One problem is how one measures the phenomenon. Some studies have involved surveys in which the orthodoxy of the public is measured. But is lack of orthodoxy—assent to certain traditional religious beliefs—an adequate measure of secularization? A person may disagree with orthodox statements and still have a supernatural outlook. Other studies have focused on church attendance or church affiliation. The purpose was to measure a decline in religious involvement. But we have just suggested that "decline of religion" is not a helpful definition of secularization. A person may have a profoundly supernatural world view, but not be affiliated with a denomination. Abraham Lincoln and Ralph Waldo Emerson are both examples of nonorthodox and unaffiliated people who had a profound belief in the supernatural. A third method of demonstrating the secularization trend has been to point to the decline in church attendance and in supernatural beliefs among youth and young adults. But as Greeley (1972:142–150) and Newport (1979:547–549) suggest, disbelief and disaffiliation are phenomena that seem characteristic of young people in many eras of history. The evidence suggests that nonbelieving young adults are likely to be solid church people with strong religious beliefs by the time they are in their mid-30s. Student-age disaffection is not new, and it does not provide convincing evidence of a new and permanent swing away from religion. Although Greeley uses the concept of the sacred in his definition of religion, he does not think there is hard evidence of a decline of religion in America. Wuthnow (1976b, 1976c) concurs that age *is* a critical factor in reduced church involvement and agrees that many unchurched young people will become traditionalists of the future. However, he also insists that his data show a net decline in theistic meaning systems—a trend which he believes is likely to continue with that age cohort into their later years.

The significance of secularization lies in the fact that the world view of Americans has become increasingly empirical and scientific. That is, scientific validation has become more authoritative than biblical literalism for many people, and technological control of the world has largely replaced magical or miraculous control. Generalizations in this area must be tentative, and significant counter trends must not be ignored. However, it does appear that empiricism and the scientific outlook has lessened the tendency to use supernatural explanations or supernatural cures for ailments. Wuthnow (1976b) insists that his San Francisco Bay area sample demonstrated a substantial increase in "social scientific" meaning systems.[20] I do not interpret this as a decline in religion, for meaning systems and their related value systems continue to be necessary for human existence. On the other hand, the rationalization process—the movement from mythos to logos—has created some problems for a pluralistic society. One has to do with the glue

---

[20] Social scientific meaning systems, according to Wuthnow, interpret the cause of events in terms of social, cultural, and social-psychological factors. Of course, the cause and the meaning of events are not necessarily the same. Wuthnow's research is convincing in establishing the decline of confidence in supernatural causes. It does not necessarily indicate that social scientific meaning systems establish meaning in the sense of a "why"—a sense of *purpose*.

that holds the society together. If there is no consensus on the big picture, there is increased likelihood of anomie and of societal conflict. This is an important issue in a pluralistic society and may be the source of much conflict. I do not believe the problem is deserving of the alarm evidenced by Berger, however. Second, we see within denominations and within local congregations, a divergence in world views. Some faithful members may celebrate certain rituals, symbols, and myths as representative and expressive of a particular world view. Others in the same congregation may interpret those same stories, rites, and symbols in accordance with a very different world view. The ethical imperatives drawn from those world views may also be widely divergent. Hence, the stage for conflict within the religious group is set. Rather than gathering on the Sabbath to reinforce one's world view and ethos, the religious gathering may be a source of dissonance and stress. Secularization from within has tended to undermine the previously established integrity among symbol systems, world view, and ethos in American Christianity. The lack of integrity at this level may be disconcerting to believers and may cause social conflict and schisms. Whether this creates a great opportunity for needed change or is a process to be alarmed about depends on one's perspective. Readers may be interested in exploring their own assumptions as to whether American religion is undergoing a period of decline or one of constructive change and modernization.

Official and Nonofficial Religion

This leads us to another consideration. The conflict between Christian modernism and more conservative Christianity has frequently been a conflict between theology professors, professional clergy, and church bureaucrats on the one hand, and common folks on the other. Jeffrey Hadden focused particularly on this issue in his book, *The Gathering Storm in the Churches* (1970). The problem underlying his study was an allegiance to a common symbol system by two groups of people, but the attribution of entirely different meanings to that symbol system. The two groups were the ecclesiastical officials and the laity of the various Christian denominations.

Gustav Mensching (1964) has described several distinctions between the folk religion of tribal peoples and the world religions which attempt to be universalistic. While folk religions preserve the local culture and customs, world religions tend to evolve a complicated rational theology, a system of ethics based on that theology, a formal cultic ritual, and a professional clergy that protects, preserves, and elaborates the theology, ethics, and liturgy. However, world religions also tend to develop folk versions of the faith. The masses are seldom moved by complicated rationalized theologies, and a localized version of the religion evolves. Hence, most world religions have within them an official and a folk version of the faith which blends

Exhibit 4–7 _____

The Attack by Conservative Christians on "Secular Humanism": A Conflict Theory Perspective

Most of the discussion of secularization in this chapter has followed a line of argument which has dominated thinking in sociological and theological circles. However, an alternative sort of perspective is provided by conflict theory. The following will provide a conflict theory analysis of the antisecular and antipluralistic movement in America.

Some religious groups have been very vocal in denouncing the trend in American society toward pluralism and away from public expressions of religiosity. The outcry by some groups about the banning of prayer in the schools is one example. In these cases, pluralistic policies are attacked as *secular humanism*—a term which carries loaded meanings of atheism and antigodliness. Conflict theorists point out that the objections are coming primarily from conservative Protestants—not Jews, or Catholics, or Muslims, or members of other groups. It was generally not the faith of these latter groups which was being expressed in public gatherings. Meanwhile, some Protestants feel there is a decline of religion because their own religion is no longer being voiced in "nonreligious" settings. In fact, a conflict theory analysis would point to this outcry against pluralistic policy as a thinly veiled conflict over power and prestige in the society. For the conflict theorist, groups act in their self-interests; many times these groups will define anything that threatens the power and prestige for their own group as degenerate or immoral. The conflict theorist may view the popular discussions of pluralism and secularization as part of a larger power play by Protestants as they seek to sustain their position of privilege in American culture and society.

with local customs, beliefs, and myths. Sometimes ethnic groups within the nation have their own unique interpretation of a faith. This is another form of folk religion, which may also diverge from the official form of that faith.

There are two central dimensions to the conflict between official and folk religion which will concern us here. The first has to do with the relative importance of rationality: official religion tends to develop a systematic theology. Theology professors, publications' editors, directors of boards of social concerns, and other clergy in the bureaucratic structure may struggle with the relationship between science and mythos. They may develop rather secularized theologies or they may develop orthodox theologies which may require mental gymnastics to understand. In either case, the theology is founded on a principle of logical consistency and coherence. (The theology is to be consistent within itself even if it does not relate to everyday experiences and perplexities of lay people). Sometimes the theological elite engages in the demythologizing or remythologizing of biblical stories.[21] All the while the common lay person may not be troubled at all by the lack of logical congruence in the theology. Many people seem to be quite comfortable with a highly incoherent assortment of beliefs and practices. Furthermore, they may be quite satisfied with traditional myths—and find the demythologized or revised versions rather sterile. In fact, the laity of some churches are hostile to the idea of exegesis and biblical criticism. The rise in this century of snake-handling cults and other mystical beliefs among the laity may suggest that secularization is more a phenomenon of the clergy—the elite of trained religious professionals—than of common folk. In fact, the growth of charismatic groups, the rise of biblical fundamentalism, and the decline in membership in liberal churches may suggest that emphasis on myth and emotion in religion are the felt needs of many Americans. Rationalized theology may be less capable of providing a powerful, pervasive and long-lasting system of meaning for the average person. Systematic theology can offer a logical world view, but it does not normally generate the ethos necessary for a vibrant and alive religion. Andrew Greeley argues that conflict over the world view of science and that of religion is not a concern of most Americans.

> To some extent American believers have been able to avoid the conflict between science and religion by simply denying that it exists. Whether this is intellectually honest or not may be questioned, but the point remains that it has been successful; religion and science can go on their merry ways, not conflicting with each other very much, despite the arguments of some elite religionists and elite scientists that they should (1972:106).

The struggle for logical coherence and consistency in theology is only one aspect of the divergence between folk religion and official religion. A second and equally important factor is the desire on the part of the elite to make the faith relevant to all cultures and all peoples. Hence, the theology and ethical principles of the faith are articulated in such a way that the faith does not appear culture bound. The desire is to emphasize those principles of the faith which would have universal appeal. The values and attitudes which are specific to one particular culture are downplayed. The folk religion, on the other hand, involves a synthesis of the historic faith with local customs, values, beliefs, and traditions. The myths and symbols of the religion may be interpreted in such a way that they confirm and justify the local concepts of morality. The ethnocentric biases of the community may be so strong that this localized version of the religion

---

[21] Remythologizing is a process of recasting or reinterpreting myths in a way that is compatible with secular, scientific thinking. Peter Berger insists that the demythologizing strategy of dealing with secularization is theologically bankrupt and will ultimately lead to a denial of the existence of any supernatural realm (Berger 1979:93–113).

may seem to be the only true understanding of the faith. Due to the modification of a religion so that it is compatible with a particular culture, some
writers distinguish folk religion from "true religion" (Southwold, 1982).
However, the terms *true Buddhism* or *true Christianity* involve unwarranted
value judgments. Frequently, official religion is also a modified version of
the world view originally set forth by the founder of the faith. Each usually
represents consistency with the original tenets in certain respects and deviation in other ways. Neither official nor folk religion is entirely static.

Folk religion is certainly not limited to the laity nor is official religion
restricted to the clergy. However, the religious professionals who have
extensive training are more likely to recognize that the historic faith has
undergone modifications in different eras and in various cultures. The professionals are likely to seek out the universalistic elements of the faith, and
to be cautious about identifying local customs as its only legitimate expression. Meanwhile, the abstract formulations of systematic theologians and
ethicists may seem sterile and unsatisfying to the untrained layperson. What
they seek is an assurance that their own concept of morality is absolute.
Therefore, acceptance of elite versions as opposed to folk versions of the
faith tends to be correlated with the extent of professional and theological
training.

The Moral Majority is an excellent case in point. This group, founded
by the Reverend Jerry Falwell of Virginia, is an organization established
to restore moral values to American society. It has supported many traditional Christian values. However, Christian theologians from Europe and
from other parts of the world have been appalled by what they consider
a warping of Christianity. The Moral Majority has taken many traditional
American values and attitudes and presented them as basic to Christianity.
Many of these have never been part of Christian theology or ethics, and
in fact some of them are antithetical to the historic position of Christian
churches.

The Moral Majority has taken the position, for example, that the only
moral and Christian stance is one that favors a balanced federal budget.
While many Americans favor such a position and while there may be good
economic reasons for a balanced budget, there seems to be no biblical or
theological grounding for such a viewpoint. The Moral Majority has taken
positions opposing the Equal Rights Amendment and the Strategic Arms
Limitations Treaty; it has supported the development of the MX missile
system and increases in defense spending. Congressional representatives
and senators who disagree have been labeled immoral and unChristian (Berger 1981; *Newsweek,* September 1980:32, 35). These moral imperatives
do not seem to be based on any biblical or theological foundation, but
they are part of the culture, values, and beliefs of many Americans. Some
Christian theologians find it inconceivable to claim that Christian morality
supports spending money on war-related goods at the expense of feeding

hungry people in the world. They claim that this is directly contrary to the historic position of the Christian church.

What we see in the Moral Majority is a powerful folk religion which has blended Christianity and Americanism. It has endorsed the American way of life, the free enterprise system of economics, and middle-class American values and life styles as central to Christianity. In fact, those who are true believers and make donations to the Thomas Road Baptist Church in Lynchburg Virginia (Falwell's church) are sent an American flag lapel pin—an interesting symbol to represent faith in Jesus. Falwell's potential for wide appeal is due to his synthesis of two primary loyalties of many Americans: Christianity and patriotism.[22] (Civil religion, that is, theologizing about the significance of the nation and of the national culture will be discussed in more detail in Chapter 10.)

As Wade Roof has pointed out, folk religion involves a loose constellation of values, norms, and beliefs—some of which are religiously based and some of which are culturally based. The posture of most official religions is that ethical positions are expected to emanate almost entirely from theological beliefs (1978:54–55). To some extent, any religion must bend and adapt if it is to have wide appeal in a given culture. The values of the faith must be, at least in some basic respects, compatible with the values of the culture in which it hopes to have adherents. In this sense, all American Christianity is influenced by American values and culture. The official group of trained professionals who seek to articulate a universalistic Christianity are not exempt from this influence. But, while no religion is totally independent from localized mores and outlooks, some do have a more universal appeal than others.

Several scholars have treated the conflict between church officials and the laity as a struggle over power (Berger 1981; McGuire 1981). The trained professionals who work in the national headquarters of the denomination may exercise their authority and come to see the church as the national organization. The laity in the local churches may see the church as the local congregation. The parish minister serves as a buffer between these two views of the church (Hargrove 1979:266). The conflict is over the ultimate source of authority: Who has the right to speak for the church? Who has the right to act in behalf of the entire denomination?[23]

---

[22] The propulsion of the Moral Majority into public awareness was due to substanial media exposure, including cover story attention by national news magazines. The media credited this and other similar groups with the conservative swing in the 1980 elections. Actually, two empirical studies conducted in the early 1980s revealed that the Moral Majority does not have a wide base of support and had very little real influence on the elections (Yinger and Cutler 1982; Shupe and Stacey 1982).

[23] Peter Berger (1981) insists that the conflict is a type of class conflict between those who manipulate economic production (the business class) and those who earn their living by manipulating symbols in our society (a new class of academics, clergy, and helping professionals).

Meredith McGuire goes a step further in pointing to the controls the professionals in the hierarchy establish to ensure the continuance of their power and privilege. (Refusal to ordain women is one such method of control.) She demonstrates that women have been systematically excluded from significant roles in the official religion and have frequently been required to wear head coverings and/or veils as a means of setting women apart and reminding them of their inferior status. On the other hand, women have often had important roles in the emergence of nonofficial religion. Hence, nonofficial religion has served an important function in allowing for religious leadership by very able women (McGuire 1981:88). This raises an important point: not all nonofficial religion is necessarily folk religion as we have defined it here. Hence, we may define *nonofficial religion* as any "set of religious and quasi-religious beliefs and practices that is not accepted, recognized, or controlled by official religious groups" (McGuire 1981:83).

McGuire's insight is important; she insists that there is more than one process that can lead to the emergence of nonofficial religious groups. For our purposes here we may distinguish two. First, common laypeople may reject the emphasis on rationality and on abstract universalistic concepts. In place of this systematic, logical theology, they may affirm a localized version of the faith which incorporates many of the local attitudes, values, and customs. On the other hand, nonofficial religion may arise through disenfranchized groups seeking to exert their own leadership skills and express their own religiosity. In this case, emergence of nonofficial religion is largely a result of exclusivity on the part of the official elite. McGuire also points out that official religion has traditionally affirmed masculine values and concepts, and the substantial involvement of women in nonofficial religion represents a search for alternative expressions of religiosity (1981:103).

This line of investigation suggests that more work is needed to understand fully the relationship between official religion and its various nonofficial forms. While folk religion may be one type of modification of official religion, other nonofficial variations of Christianity include faith healing, spiritualism (attempts to communicate with the dead), astrology, and stichomancy (the method of receiving a divine message by randomly opening the Bible and pointing blindly to a passage.) Hence, nonofficial religion often coexists with official religion. Many people who participate in nonofficial religion or who hold folk religious beliefs are also lay leaders in mainline denominations. In any case, the world view of nonofficial religion is often quite different from the official religion of the trained specialists.

Melford Spiro (1970) has pointed out that in the past, study of the religions of other parts of the world tended to focus on what the religious gurus and the clergy believed and practiced. He felt that the study of the folk religion of Buddhism was much more interesting and important than the official religion of Buddhism.[24] It is the latter which is more frequently explored in philosophy of religion texts. Likewise, most sociological studies in this country have tended to focus much more on official religion than on nonofficial religion. In fact, the measures of religiosity have often gauged it in terms of conformity to official positions. Increasingly, social scientists have sought to understand both the religious orientation of the elite and the religion of the common folk. Both forms are important parts of the religiosity of a society. An understanding of this difference between the theology of the highly trained theologians and that of the common folk can help in understanding intradenominational conflict. The religious needs of these two groups are somewhat different. The felt need among the highly educated (whether clergy or not) is for logical coherence and consistency and for an understanding of the faith that is not culture bound. This is not a felt need for many other faithful members. In fact, many members are looking for a metaphysical grounding for the cultural beliefs and values that they learned as children. The difference in needs within a religious group and the attribution of alternative meanings to the same symbol system are two sources of the variations in styles of religious expression. We shall explore this matter somewhat further when we discuss the evolution of religious groups and schisms within them (Chapter 7).

Summary

Nonrational religious experiences, myths, rituals, and symbol systems are all related to the ethos and world view of a religion. Frequently, there is a perceived integrity between these elements, and they are mutually reinforcing. It is nearly impossible to identify one as primary—at least when one is referring to religion as a general phenomenon. However, specific groups may emphasize one or more of these and deemphasize others. When a religious group begins to undergo change, the relationships between these elements of religion may be less direct. This can be terribly disorienting to members of the group, and they may be quite emotional in denouncing "heretics" who offer a different interpretation of the symbols, the myth, or the ethos. When integration of the elements is threatened, the religious group strains to regain the old unity, strives for a new synthesis, or splits into several groups.

We will turn next to the social psychology of conversion and commitment to a religious ideology or religious group, and how these are related to mental health or mental illness.

---

[24] For a recent discussion of official and folk Buddhism (including a critique of Spiro) see Southwold (1982).

The Social Psychology of Conversion and Commitment

In the previous chapter we viewed elements within a religion as being relatively integrated and stable. Dissonance and change were viewed as aberrations and as unusual phenomena. Yet, most religions give considerable attention to the process of personal change or transformation. In this chapter we will investigate the change of world views which is expected and even anticipated by religious practitioners.

Certainly any radical change in the sense of identity and the values of individuals is worthy of study, and the processes of conversion and of becoming committed to a religious group have been of interest to social scientists for some time. William James and other psychologists explored conversion at the turn of the century. But conversion and commitment is significant for yet another reason. Sociologists are interested in the reasons why some religious groups prosper and others collapse. Out of thousands of religious cults[1] that get started, only a few survive more than a decade or two. There are a number of factors that determine which groups will or will not persist. Among these are (1) the group's recruitment strategies and the ability to convert new recruits (Lofland 1977), (2) the depth of the commitment which is engendered in members (Kanter 1972), (3) the institutionalization of the group (Weber 1947), and (4) the ability of the group to mobilize and focus its resources effectively (Bromley and Shupe 1979). With the recent expansion of religious cults in the United States there has been an intensified interest in the first two. In this chapter we will look at some of the recent research on the social psychology of religious conversion and commitment. Relevant also to this concern for cult growth, we will discuss possible criteria for assessing whether religious conversion and commitment enhances or retards mental health. In the following chapter we will address the issues of institutionalization and mobilization of resources.

Much of the recent research on conversion and commitment has focused on nonconventional groups—the "new" religions. Perhaps this is to be expected. Conversion to a group which affirms the basic values of the dominant society does not seem as mysterious and puzzling to most people as conversion to a cult. Persons who convert from Methodism to Catholicism have not engaged in terribly unconventional or "abnormal" behavior. The individual who departs from his or her Episcopal heritage in order to join a congregation of Reform Jews is somewhat more of a curiosity because the change involves adherence to a different religion and an acceptance of minority group status. However, the person who gives up all of his or her possessions to join a religious commune is even more of an enigma to the average American. Anyone who would shave his head, wear a pink

---

[1] The terms *sect* and *cult* will be treated in more detail in Chapter 7. For our purposes in this chapter we will define a sect as a new expression (or a renewed form) of a *traditional* religion. We will define a cult as the nascent organization of a *new* religion. It involves a break from the traditional religions in a society and the creation of a nonconventional form of religion (Stark and Bainbridge 1979).

gown, and chant "Rama Krishna" all day is terribly puzzling and somewhat frightening to many middle-class Americans. The charge of brainwashing seems a ready explanation for this otherwise inexplicable behavior. The general curiosity about the reasons for conversion and commitment to non-conventional groups has led to significant research in this area.

The term *conversion* refers to a process of "turning around" or changing direction in life. Specifically, it refers to a change of world view. It often is viewed as a sudden crisis event, but the process can also be a gradual one. In any case, conversion represents a transformation in a person's self-image.[2] The change is often symbolized by a change of name (e.g., Saul became Paul in the Christian tradition, and more recently Cassius Clay became Mohammed Ali in the Muslim tradition). Since conversion to a nonconventional group often involves a more radical and complete change for persons than conversion to a mainline denomination, it is possible that the conversion process differs for different groups.

Unlike the study of cults, most treatments of conversion within conventional denominations has been rather phenomenological (accepting the explanations of subjects on their own merits). Little research has been conducted on the application of role theory or reference-group theory to mainline church conversions. It may be, however, that the process of conversion to conventional groups has certain parallels with the process of conversion to cults. We will begin by assessing conversion to cults and will then consider the trends in mainline denominations.

The method of *sustaining* commitment to a nonconventional group would also seem to differ from that used by conventional religious groups. What we will find is that the commitment mechanisms do differ, but probably more in intensity than in kind. Religious sects and cults normally demand a very high degree of commitment.[3] Much can be learned about commitment by analyzing the social psychology of these new religious movements. By modifying the theories to allow for the differences between cults and mainline churches, we may gain significant insights into conventional religious commitment. We shall conclude the chapter by presenting an alternative model for analyzing conversion, commitment, and mental health: cognitive structuralism. This theoretical perspective is based on a different set of

---

[2] Sometimes the term *conversion* is used to refer to a significant intensification of a set of values which have been dormant or secondary in a person's life. In this case, the person has "turned around" in that priorities have been reestablished and the person's sense of identity is revised. If the sense of personal identity and values are not somehow transformed, the individual may be said to have experienced a revival of faith, but not a conversion.

[3] Bainbridge and Stark (1980a) discuss several different types of cults: cult movements, client cults (which serve therapeutic or magical functions), and audience cults (which dispense their world view through newspapers or books but which have no organized group). In their typology, cult movements are religious groups which normally demand intense commitments. Client and audience cults do not. I concur with Bainbridge and Stark that the latter two are not really religious. I do not believe they are really cults, for the same authors have insisted that cults are new religions (Stark and Bainbridge 1979).

assumptions and presents the issues in a somewhat different light. Offered this alternative perspective, students may see how different paradigms can lead social scientists to entirely different sets of research questions and different sets of conclusions.

The Social Psychology of Sect or Cult Membership

Are Cults Engaged in Brainwashing?

One of the most often heard comments by Americans is that religious cults engage in brainwashing. Many concerned parents have had their children kidnapped and deprogrammed. At the time of the mass suicide of nearly a thousand cult members at Jonestown, the mass media seemed particularly eager to engage in discussions of brainwashing in the cults. The types of beliefs which are held by cult members often seem outrageous to nonbelievers; they cannot imagine anyone accepting such doctrines unless they were brainwashed. Furthermore, the zealotry of a son or daughter, a person who once seemed rational and even-tempered, can be so shocking that only reference to some form of mind control could seem to explain it. If one desires legitimacy for the mind-control theory, one needs only to point to two authors who have been researching the cults and who have been on numerous television talk shows. These writers have interviewed dozens of former cult members, the parents of cult members, and deprogrammers. They have developed an elaborate theory of mind control which suggests that the potential recruit is put through an experience that makes his or her brain overload, short-circuit, or "snap" (Conway and Siegelman 1978).

Despite the strong public opinion and the intricate theory of Conway and Siegelman, there is little or no evidence of brainwashing in the best-known and most frequently attacked religious movements (Unification Church or Moonies, Hare Krishna, and Divine Light Mission).[4] The problem with the snapping thesis is that the research is based strictly on reports from those already opposed to these religious movements. Conway and Siegelman made no attempt to engage in firsthand observation of the groups. Reports by trained social scientists who have observed the conversion and commitment processes (both as overt observers and as covert potential re-

---

[4] There is some evidence of a near total control environment, with inducement of utter exhaustion and threats to the lives of individuals and their families in Jonestown (Moberg 1980). Hence, there may be a few isolated cases in which converts experience something similar to Korean brainwashing procedures. This seems to be the exception, however. In fact, Robbins and Anthony (1978) claim that the brainwashing metaphor is a weapon to suppress nonconformist religious groups. Shupe and Bromley (1978) go a step further in claiming that the anticult accusations are akin to the witch hunts of an earlier era.

cruits) indicate that the data used by Conway and Siegelman is extremely biased (Davis and Richardson 1976; Lofland 1977; Bromley and Shupe 1979, 1981; Judah 1974; Downton 1979; Richardson and Stewart 1977; and Balch 1980). To understand the shortcomings of Conway and Siegelman's method, readers might consider an analogous situation. If I were to try to understand the social processes in the local Presbyterian church or in the Lion's Club, and I interviewed *only* people who were highly dissatisfied and left that organization, I would not have an accurate or holistic understanding of that group. It may be fruitful for students to list reasons why this would be an inadequate procedure. While the snapping explanation provides an intricate and complex theory of cult conversion, it bears little resemblance to what actually takes place.

While the public is often attracted to the brainwashing thesis, most people have little idea what brainwashing actually is. The term has a specific meaning in the language of the social psychologist. It is usually used to refer to a process by which persons are *involuntarily* caused to adopt a belief system, a set of behaviors, or a world view. In order to force a person to make such a change, one must have total physical control over the individual. The captors must control all the necessities of life and be able to control life and death itself. The captor must be in a circumstance in which no alternatives and no other choices seem available. Even in such a total control situation, only small numbers of American soldiers yielded to the brainwashing techniques of the North Koreans in the 1950s. And most of the acquiescences to the North Korean and Chinese torture procedures were merely verbal. The Americans were eager to return to their previous culture as soon as the total control situation was alleviated. Only about a dozen men were permanently converted by North Korean thought reform out of thousands that experienced the severe treatment (Farber, et al. 1951:271–272). Clearly, religious cults (in which there is much movement in and out of membership) do not hold the same sort of physical control over members' lives that was experienced by prisoners of war held by the North Koreans or the Chinese.

When most Americans use the term *brainwashing,* they have in mind some form of hypnotic trance or mysterious mind control. The implication is that the cults manipulate the minds of potential recruits so that the latter are unwitting and somewhat passive victims of the process. The actual studies of conversion and commitment suggest otherwise. For example, Roger Straus insists that the recruit to a cult is actively involved in choosing to be converted. "The act of conversion, we find, is not a terminal act. Rather, guided by the principle that the way to be changed is to act changed, the new convert works to make conversion behaviorally and experientially real to self and others. . . . It is not so much the initial action that enables the convert to experience a transformed life but the day to day actions of living it" (Straus 1979:163). Rather than a passive paradigm, Straus insists that the recruit is "an actively strategizing seeker" who wants the conversion experience and goes to considerable effort to cause it to happen.[5]

J. Stillson Judah came to the same conclusion when he discovered that conversion is a very gradual process among the Hare Krishna. Emotional commitment to the group ("experiential conversion") often occurs before the recruit even knows what the religious group believes. An "intellectual conversion," or an acceptance of the belief system, comes much later and is consciously *chosen* by the devotee (Judah 1974:168). "Conversion and the consequent transformation in the devotee's life are probably only *apparently* immediate. More generally it is a multi-faceted process that continues over a long period" (1974:178). Another scholar points out, "Brainwashing, thought reform, and coercive persuasion are all terms that focus attention on psychological change as if minds must be altered to change behavior" (Balch 1980:142). But changes in behavior frequently precede changes in thought patterns. More important, changes in behavior can occur without change in beliefs, and many cult members play a devotee role without *ever* fully adopting the ideological framework of the group (Balch 1980).

The cults are not, by and large, involved in putting people in a hypnotic brainwashed trance. On the other hand, many cults do engage in deliberate manipulation, and it is this that alarms many people. Many cults do have a totalistic (all-or-nothing, for-us-or-against-us) world view. They also play heavily on guilt feelings and manipulate facts to gain conversions. This distortion is sometimes referred to by the Moonies as "divine deception." The end (conversion) is believed to justify almost any means, including deception and manipulation. To suggest that the cults are not engaged in brainwashing, then, is not to imply that cult conversion is conducive to mental health. Whether or not the cults are involved in mind control depends largely upon how one defines that term.[6] Regardless, the labeling of a process does not explain it. Let us turn then to an explanation of the actual process at work in the conversion and commitment of persons to these religious cults.

Chronologically, of course, conversion precedes commitment. However, in terms of understanding the social psychology of the two related phenomena, it is logical in this context to treat commitment first. The ultimate outcome of conversion is to elicit a cadre of loyal and committed members.

---

[5] A team of researchers came to a similar conclusion regarding conversions during Billy Graham crusades (Wimberly et al. 1975).

[6] The term *mind control* does not have the same sort of specific meaning for social psychologists as does the term *brainwashing*. Mind control is presumably any manipulation of a person so that he or she does something contrary to self-interests. But if an advertising campaign induces me to buy a car that I cannot afford, have the advertisers engaged in mind control? If persons risk arrest or lose property in order to stand up for something they believe, has their mind been controlled by someone? The problem with the word *mind control* is that it is vague. It has basically been used as a label to stigmatize certain groups.

Hence, we will first explore the way in which a group creates and maintains a high level of commitment. Only after we have an understanding of commitment theory will we turn to a discussion of conversion—the process by which one moves from the status of nonbeliever or marginal member to that of highly committed devotee.

Kanter's Theory of Commitment

Rosabeth Kanter became interested in the elements of commitment while studying utopian communities and communes. She wanted to investigate factors which caused some communities to survive while others dissolved. Some communities were destroyed by hostile neighbors, many others failed because of internal schisms and jealousies, but Kanter became interested in internal factors that were present in *successful* communes. Clearly, living an austere lifestyle with all things shared in common demanded a high level of commitment. She defined success in terms of ability to survive for 25 years, and then proceeded to study 9 successful communities and 21 unsuccessful ones. The result of her research was to identify a number of mechanisms which are a part of the rules, regulations, and social organization of successful communities. These seem to apply to a variety of different types of organizations, but the theory is particularly applicable to religious movements.

It is appropriate to begin with a sociological definition of commitment. Kanter writes:

> A person is committed to a group or to a relationship when he himself is fully invested in it, so that the maintenance of his own internal being requires behavior that supports the social order. A committed person has . . . a feeling that the group is an extension of himself and he is an extension of the group (1972:66).

She goes on to suggest that this sort of commitment involves three major aspects of a social system: retention of members, group cohesiveness, and social control. Hence, commitment occurs on three different levels: commitment to the organization itself, commitment to other persons in the group, and commitment to the rules, regulations and mores of the group. Any group or institution may elicit one or more of these types of commitment. While they are interrelated, they are also distinct aspects of social organization that can be analyzed separately. Each of the three levels of commitment involves two mechanisms which enhance commitment.

Instrumental Commitment. At the instrumental level, the individual must be convinced that continued association with the group or organization is worth the time and effort it demands. Hence, the individual engages in a sort of cost/benefit analysis. At the cognitive or thinking level, the commit-

ted individual must conclude that the profits associated with continued participation are significant and well worth the time and energy expended. Furthermore, if individuals feel that there would be substantial cost associated
with leaving the group, the institution stands to gain in its retention of
members. Two organizational mechanisms tend to enhance instrumental
commitment by influencing this cost/benefit ratio. They are *sacrifice* and
investment.

> Sacrifice means that membership becomes more costly and is therefore not
> lightly regarded nor likely to be given up easily. Investment is a process
> whereby the individual gains a stake in the group, commits current and future
> profits to it, so that he must continue to participate if he is going to realize
> those profits. Investment generally involves the giving up of control over
> some of the person's resources to the community (Kanter 1972:72).

Members of sects and cults are frequently asked to make substantial sacrifices. Many times a comfortable life has been sacrificed for the rigor of
an austere lifestyle, in which numerous popular recreational and social activities are denied. Devotees may be forbidden alcohol, drugs, or coffee, and
they may find that card playing, social dancing, and movies are disallowed.
For example, Judah writes of the attitude of the Hare Krishna:

> The devotee must be ready to relinquish anything material for the satisfaction
> of Krishna. He must be ready to give up something that he strongly desires,
> while accepting something he does not like. He should concern himself with
> the material only when absolutely necessary (1974:91).

Such attitudes of asceticism or self-denial are frequently found among sectarian and cultic groups. Kanter shows that this sacrifice is quite functional
for commitment. "Once members have agreed to make the 'sacrifices', their
motivation to remain participants increases. Membership becomes more
valuable and meaningful. Regardless of how the group induces the original
concessions or manages to recruit people willing to make them, the fact
is that those groups exacting sacrifices survive longer. . . . The more it
'costs' a person to do something, the more 'valuable' he will consider it,
in order to justify the psychic 'expense' " (Kanter 1972:76). Sacrifice causes
a person not to want to leave because leaving would be to admit that the
sacrifices were not worthwhile. Whether consciously or unconsciously, people do not like to admit that they have made foolish sacrifices. Hence,
once a part of the group, demands for self-denying behavior act to increase
and sustain members' commitment.

The other mechanism which enhances instrumental commitment is investment. While people sacrifice by not using their time, energy, and resources
in activities they might otherwise find enjoyable, they are expected to invest
that time, energy, and money in the group. Many cults require at least a
tithe (usually 10 percent of earnings), and many require that the devotee

turn over *all* of his or her earnings to the organization (the Divine Light Mission, the Hare Krishna, and the Unification Church provide a few examples). To the extent that investments are irreversible, the investment becomes even more important. The donation of all one's worldly goods is often not reversible if the person later decides to leave the group.

The devotee may also be required to invest substantial amounts of time in the group. The expectation of the Church of Jesus Christ of Latter-Day Saints (the Mormons) that young male members devote two years proselytizing or missionizing is a good example. Likewise, the hours of public chanting among the Hare Krishna are manifestly designed to enhance commitment. "Public demonstration of one's belief is not only a means of gaining converts, but also a way of strengthening one's own faith" (Judah 1974:177).

Research by social psychologists has indicated that the act of making a public statement on any issue is one of the most important factors in solidifying one's commitment. If you were asked to serve on a panel to discuss the benefits your university offers to the community, the likelihood increases that you would be willing to make a financial donation to that university. You would have invested time and energy in defending the school's importance. Furthermore, after you have taken a stand in favor of something, you may tend to perceive any attack on that organization as an attack on you. You don't want to lose face, so you would likely become defensive in behalf of the institution. Likewise, the public chanting of the Hare Krishna, the door-to-door proselytizing of the Mormons, and the airport fund-raising efforts of the Moonies all serve to reinforce commitment.

The important factor in understanding retention of members is that a group which requires little investment and little or no sacrifice is likely to elicit little instrumental commitment. Persons may be committed at other levels, but commitment to the organization itself will be low. Because world-transforming cults usually exact a high cost (alienation from family, rejection of opportunities of an affluent life, and so on), they must emphasize the benefits and deemphasize the costs. Moreover, their major source of recruitment will be among those who do not yet have much invested in the status quo. It is for this reason that youth are the major target of most cults. In conventional religious denominations, the recruitment process need not be so intense and need not be limited to a particular clientele; the *costs* of joining a conventional group are much less severe. Regardless, some measure of instrumental commitment is important for any organization.

Affective Commitment. Affective commitment refers to an emotional dependence upon the group. Its members become one's primary set of relations, an important reference group. In the case of cults, the group may develop a strategy by which it becomes the *only* reference group of the members. But affective ties are important in conventional religious groups as well. In a Detroit study of the relationship between religion and other aspects of social behavior, Lenski (1963) found that communal involvement (close interpersonal relationships with persons of the same faith) was a more important variable than associational involvement (participation in the organization or institution itself). Affective commitment is of central importance in religious behavior. Andrew Greeley has suggested that while meaning functions may be *primary*, the belonging functions are often chronologically *prior*. We see this clearly as we explore the commitment and conversion processes in modern cults. For example, "warmth and friendship among the devotees" was one of the reasons most frequently cited by members for original attraction to the Hare Krishna movement. (Judah 1974:153–154). It is also noteworthy that the Moonies consciously look for signs of isolation or symbols of transience—like backpacks—to identify prospective converts (Bromley and Shupe 1979:172). Such persons are less likely to have other affective commitments and are more likely to be in need of a group that can offer emotional support.

The affective commitment process involves two mechanisms: detachment or *renunciation* of former ties, and *communion* with the new group. The cults often demand that new recruits not contact their families for the first few weeks or months. And this emphasis may continue. Among the Hare Krishna, for example, "Progress depends on willingness to give up the company of anyone who is not a devotee" (Judah 1974:91). Renunciation of one's former friends, family, and social groups may involve defining outsiders as evil or as insignificant. For example, a Hare Krishna devotee responded in the following way when asked whether he corresponded with his parents:

> No, not really. Sometimes they write me a telegram. They want to know where I am so I tell them, but I am a "sannyasi." We're not supposed to do all these things anymore. Your parents are so temporary. When I speak to my mother on the phone, it's like a stranger. . . . My father is Prabhupad. He raised me. My father didn't raise me. What is a father? A father is one who . . . gave me this material body. But what is that relation? It's a relation of bone and stool and blood. That's all it is. But he didn't raise me. I raised myself in the street as much as I could. I raised myself, but he didn't tell me anything to do. Prabhupad, he raised me. He told me what to do—how to live like a human being, how to elevate myself. My father never told me anything. He didn't know himself. He is not a bad boy, but he didn't know. He had sex life and he had me, somehow or other. So my relation with my parents I just see in terms of blood and stool and meat eating and taking alcohol. My father is Prabhupad and my mother is the scripture (Judah 1974:179).[7]

Among the Amish, the Bruderhof, the early Christian church, the early Mormon church, and other nonconventional religious groups, we find high

---

[7] Judah emphasizes that this is, "the extreme position of the Sannyāsis."

boundaries and a tendency to define nonmembers as degenerate, evil, or confused. Hence, contacts with outsiders are limited and are controlled by norms that make those interactions rather formal, ritualized affairs. This formal and somewhat defensive relationship with nonmembers may cause the latter to think that devotees are behaving strangely and that they must be in some sort of trance. Actually, what has happened is that devotees have changed their affective ties: those who were once significant others have now been supplanted by another reference group. The experience of being treated as a stranger—and as a rather suspect stranger—may be confusing and disconcerting to the family member. Certainly confusion, hurt, and anger are understandable responses. No one likes to be treated as a degenerate or as an inconsequential person, least of all by a family member. Nonetheless, it is important for the public to recognize that the process of conversion and commitment to cults has to do with a change of reference groups, not an hypnotic trance.

The second affective mechanism is communion. While new recruits are removed from former reference groups, they are warmly embraced and provided with a high degree of emotional support in the new reference group. The Moonies are very intentional about this process, which they refer to as "love bombing." Particularly for isolated persons, transient people, or loners, this intensity of concern and emotional warmth may be the most significant experience of family that the individual has known. Many communes and religious groups refer to themselves as family, for the group actually becomes a surrogate family for the members. It is also not surprising that many of the early recruits to the Hare Krishna were individuals who were part of the hippie counterculture and were already alienated from their families.

It is not necessary to focus only on cults to see the importance of this process. Most of the more conservative churches with high retention rates have extensive meetings and social events. If a person attends church on Sunday morning, has another worship experience on Sunday evening (perhaps preceded by a potluck dinner), attends the men's prayer breakfast or the women's prayer group on Tuesday morning, goes to Bible study on Wednesday evening, and serves on a committee of the church, he or she has little time or energy for other social commitments. The other persons attending those functions become one's primary social relations. Some of the mainline churches which do not seem to elicit the same kind of intense commitment are lacking in programs that develop close and supportive interpersonal relationships among members. In fact, Hare Krishna members frequently cited a lack of meaningful friendships in their original religious group as a reason for leaving that faith (Judah 1974:151). In contrast to this, the communal living arrangements among the Hare Krishna, the Moonies, and many other such religious groups create intense feelings of unity, of brotherhood and sisterhood, of oneness.

Kanter points out that communal sharing, communal work (a common task on which devotees feel they are working together), regularized group contact, persecution by outsiders (the common enemy), and group rituals can all function to enhance group solidarity and affective commitment. The group rituals are noteworthy in light of our discussion in Chapter 4 about the role of ritual. Kanter maintains that nearly all successful communes engage in a good deal of group singing. The chanting of the Hare Krishna and the singing among the Moonies may significantly contribute to group solidarity. Kanter maintains that the rhythm and melody provide a feeling of group unity or communion—regardless of the content of the songs (Kanter 1972:100). Hence, when the Moonies sing such songs as "This Land Is Your Land," the very act of singing is what is important. The words may have only secondary significance.

Once recruits become a part of the group and begin to identify its members as their best friends, they may come to realize that the group has an internal stratification system. Some people are more highly respected than others. Since one wants to be liked and respected by one's new friends and colleagues, obedience to the rules becomes important. As one receives responsibilities and is recognized for contributions to the group, one has begun to climb the stratification ladder. Having taken a step or two up the ladder, the individual has made an initial *investment* in the group. Hence, a desire to be liked and to win the approval of one's new significant others (affective commitment) leads naturally to instrumental commitment. Commitment to the group members and commitment to the organization are intertwined.

Retention of members, especially among cults with world-transforming views, depends upon an ongoing set of primary relationships with believers. Bromley and Shupe report that when Moonie devotees are not harboured in supportive environments, defections are very high (1979:184). The insistence on endogamy (marriage only to individuals within the group) is one way to ensure interlocking relationships, and the Reverend Moon has been quick to recognize this. If one's spouse and eventually one's children are within the faith, then defection from the church will also involve separation from one's family of procreation. By ensuring endogamous marriages, a set of interlocking and mutually reinforcing relationships are created. The Unification Church (the Moonies) stresses this affective dimension of commitment. One of the dilemmas that has faced the Unification Church is that although communal relationships are critical to commitment, the organization confronts the inevitable process of evolving a bureaucratic organization (as it increases in size). The dilemma is how to develop a complex organization (which is inherently impersonal) without destroying the personal touch that is necessary to survival. The development of committed family units is a critical strategy to counteract the potentially damaging effects of bureaucratization.

Moral Commitment.   The third level of commitment refers to commitment to the norms and values of the group, including the ideology itself. If the group is to develop in a coherent way, members must accept the mandates of the ideology as it is formulated by the leaders. To put it another way, the leadership must be able to control the group in order to direct its development. Since religious groups do not have military powers or total economic control over the entire populous, they are limited in the extent to which they can coerce members to obey the norms of the group. They must depend on voluntary compliance. The control issue is more problematic for groups which deviate from the dominant society, for compliance with the religious group means deviation from the dominant culture. Hence, the cause of the group must seem compellingly true, eternal, and just. There are two mechanisms which can enhance the moral commitment of devotees: *mortification* and *transcendence.*

The mortification process places heavy emphasis on the willfulness, egotism, selfishness, and conceit of people, and this generates a sense of profound humility. This is done by emphasizing that without this group or the faith perspective of this charismatic leader, the members would be worthless degenerates. For example, Oneida was a religious commune in upstate New York which survived for 33 years in the mid-1800s. It is a fascinating community, but is especially remarkable because it is the only free-love commune[8] to survive for such a long period of time. One reason Oneida proved so viable is because of a practice called mutual criticism. This involved a public confession of all one's faults, weaknesses, temptations, and areas of needed growth. Furthermore, the assembled members would add to the confession if the confessor failed to include everything. The founder of Oneida, John Humphrey Noyes, was especially forthright and aggressive in probing a person's inner feelings and motives.

The journals and diaries of members offer a fascinating account of how members perceived this process. They uniformly reported that after such a session, they felt utterly humble and worthless. But the more important emotion (and perhaps the more surprising one) was a feeling of utter exhilaration and joy. Kanter writes that "the use of mortification is a sign that the group cares about the individual, about his thoughts and feelings, about the content of his inner world. The group cares enough to pay great attention to the person's behavior, and to promise him warmth, intimacy, and love . . . if he indicates he can accept these gifts without abuse" (1972:105).

---

[8] Oneida's system of complex marriage meant that any adult man and any adult woman might engage in sexual relations on a given night. However, there were many norms that guided these practices. In this sense, the *free love* term which is commonly applied to Oneida is somewhat of a misnomer. Oneida defined itself as a biblically based and profoundly religious community. The members did not view their sexual practices as promiscuous (Carden 1969; Parker 1935).

Much like the self-revealing mechanisms used in the encounter group movement, the act of being emotionally naked before others whom one trusts seems to engender ecstatic feelings of intimacy and union with one's associates. But recognizing the feeling of worthlessness and humility is also important in understanding why people follow the leadership of the group with such unquestioning loyalty. Any personal initiative, critical thinking, or alternative explanation of things will be defined as egoistic, self-centered, and self-aggrandizing behavior. Any challenge to the doctrine of the group is a sign of "the Devil at work" in the individual or an indication of a lack of humility. In either case, the person may be demoted in the stratification hierarchy of the group. This demotion may induce humility if the other techniques did not.

Many other groups could be cited for similar mechanisms to induce feelings of humility or individual worthlessness. For example, Synanon (a drug rehabilitation center which turned into a cult) required a 72-hour session of confession and mutual criticism. All members were to undergo this process, known as "heat," once a month. Regardless of specific variations in the way different cults engender the attitude, a sense of personal worthlessness, sinfulness, and self-centeredness is very functional for the group. When people are convinced that they are truly insignificant as individuals, they are more humble and more willing to obey their superiors.[9]

This leads to the second process: transcendence. Although the person may feel worthless as an individual, his or her life has ultimate and eternal meaning as a member of the group. The group offers a hope of final victory which obliterates the meaninglessness of mundane existence. The group offers the Truth, and claims an exclusive hold on that Truth. Nowhere else, members believe, can one gain these insights and participate in this victory! This generates a sense of mystery and a feeling of awe for the leaders. Eventually, of course, that awe must also be routinized so that the members have a feeling of awe for the organization or the movement itself. For example, part of the reason that Oneida members felt such exhilaration following a mutual criticism experience was that they believed they were part of a group that would eventually make *all* the difference in the state of the world. Although the person felt worthless as an individual, his or her life would be significant in the long run. By participating in a group that was believed to be of ultimate importance, the individual could feel a sense of transcendence and ultimate worth. These processes of deemphasizing the individual, glorifying the group, and creating a sense of awe

---

[9] This mortification process is the process most akin to Chinese thought-reform techniques as described by Lifton (1969). In the cult situation, however, people *voluntarily* undergo mortification.

Exhibit 5–1

Kanter's Commitment Theory

Type of Commitment	Processes which Enhance This Commitment
Instrumental Commitment (Commitment to the *organization*)	1. Sacrifice 2. Investment
Affective commitment (Commitment to the *members*)	1. Renunciation 2. Communion
Moral commitment (Commitment to the *ideas* as spelled out by the leaders)	1. Mortification 2. Transcendence

about the group's ideology are the foundation stones of moral commitment.[10]

What happens to moral commitment, however, when the ideology changes? The ideology of the Moonies has changed significantly over the past 20 years. Bromley and Shupe found that such changes do not negatively affect commitment. This is largely because commitment is based more directly on social ties (affective commitment) than on commitment to the ideology (1974:107). However, it is also important to remember that the moral commitment may focus on awe for the leadership. This allows for a process of "continuing revelation" so that an ideology can evolve and change without severely challenging the basic commitment to the rules, regulations, and values of the group. Of course, there may be some who reject the innovations and remain orthodox, especially if the original charismatic leader is no longer alive. We can see this among some Mormons who continue to affirm the legitimacy of polygamy even though the official church hierarchy has reversed that earlier doctrine.

Some of the mechanisms which contribute to commitment in sects and cults are antithetical to many denominations. The doctrine of the priesthood of all believers in some mainline groups[11] tends to contradict the strict spiritual hierarchy system of many sectarian and cultic groups. Second, the emphasis on open-mindedness and tolerance of others in most mainline denominations counters the sectarian emphasis that one's group has the

---

[10] One of the fascinating characteristics of many devotees of the Divine Light and Hare Krishna Movements is that they report an active preconversion search for a guru or an authority who could show them "the way." A predisposition to follow an authority seems to have been present in many cases. Judah reports that in the Hare Krishna movement obedience to and love for one's spiritual master is exactly the same as obedience to and love for Krishna (God). Hence, the surrender of one's will is total (1974:94–95). This suggests that persons who already have a totalistic (all-or-nothing) world view are much more likely to become members.

[11] This doctrine is historically Protestant, but is not equally applied in all Protestant denominations nor in all congregations of any denomination. Furthermore, many local Catholic groups incorporate this concept, and downplay rigid concepts of spiritual status.

whole truth, the only truth, and the exclusively held truth. The high boundaries of "us" and "them" have been falling away as the more moderate and liberal denominations have stressed cooperation and ecumenism. Third, and perhaps most important, the more liberal clergy in mainline denominations have tended to emphasize an "I'm O.K., You're O.K." theme that counters the sectarian denigration of one's self. In fact, many clergy explicitly work to enhance a positive self-image on the part of members of their congregations. They see a positive self-image as essential to mental health and well-being. As we will see later, this positive self-image is conducive to mental health, but it does not particularly enhance commitment to a group's ideology. People who respect themselves and their own ideas are more likely to engage in independent and critical thinking. Liberal clergy argue that critical thinking may not be conducive to institutional conformity, but it is important for mentally healthy adults. They maintain that religions which encourage dependency are not allowing individuals to nurture their God-given creativity. Hence, liberal churches may have lower levels of commitment (as defined by Kanter) because of their emphasis on individuality and personal self-esteem. We will return to a discussion of religion and mental health later in this chapter.

Many different types of groups and organizations use one or more of the commitment mechanisms discussed by Kanter. The unique quality of religious groups with a nonconventional world view is that they must elicit and sustain a very high level of commitment. The cults and sectarian groups that survive are those which utilize all or most of the commitment processes discussed here. Deviant religious groups are unique primarily in the high intensity and large number of commitment mechanisms used.

Commitment, then, can be commitment (1) to the organization, (2) to the group members with whom one has strong emotional ties, or (3) to the ideology and the moral rules of the group as they are interpreted by the group's leaders. Often, commitment at one level will lead to commitment at another. While it is possible for people to be committed at only one level, nonconventional religious groups normally demand commitment at all three levels. This is especially true of groups that expect to transform this world.

This takes us to an investigation of the conversion process. How does one move from apathy to total commitment? How is it that people come to the point of committing their lives and resources to these groups?

Lofland's Theory of Conversion

In his study of conversion among the Moonies, John Lofland points to a sequence of factors which operate to move a person from nonmember status to committed devotee.[12] Lofland's theory is based on the "value-added" model of Neil Smelser (1963), which maintains that a social movement or process may best be understood by identifying "successively accumulating factors." According to this perspective, it is the cumulative effect of many different factors that gives rise to specific types of behavior. The presence of any one or two factors, without the occurence of necessary prior elements, will not result in the same outcome. Hence, events must come about in the prescribed sequence.

Lofland emphasizes that earlier conditions serve to *activate* later ones; the emphasis is not strictly on temporal order. In other words, condition number 6 in the sequence of events may have existed for many years without resulting in the inclination to join a religious cult. Only after the occurence of conditions 1 through 5 does condition 6 become significant in moving a person toward affiliation with the group in question.

Only persons who experience all of the conditions are likely prospects for conversion to a religious cult. Hence, the experiencing of these conditions helps to determine who will convert and who will remain uninvolved. "The sequential arrangement of the conditions may be conceived as a funnel"; that is, they "systematically reduce the number of persons who can be considered available for recruitment" (Lofland 1977:31). A large portion of the population may experience stress or tension, the first condition. A somewhat smaller portion of the population may adopt a religious problem-solving perspective, the second condition. The third factor may apply only to a segment of *that* population, and only a few who experience the first three conditions may confront the fourth. Hence, the number of converts, and who those converts are, is largely a function of the proper sequencing of events in the lives of individuals.

This conversion theory was developed through the study of nonconventional religious groups. Whether it is applicable in its entirety to the more mainline religious groups may be debated. However, some of Lofland's insights do seem to be generic,[13] and they may help us to understand the process of becoming committed to *any* religious group.

Lofland maintains that there are three *predisposing conditions* in the individual which must be present for the individual to be susceptible to cult influence. If these predisposing conditions are operative, the *situational contingencies* become relevant. The predisposing conditions are attributes of individuals (dispositions, attitudes, outlooks) which exist *prior* to contact with the cult.

---

[12] Several other sequential theories of conversion have been set forth by social scientists, but most follow a schema quite similar to Lofland's. Those interested in another example of this sequential model (based on research with the Divine Light Mission) might want to see Downton (1980).

[13] Generic means applicable to other situations.

1. **Tension.** Lofland writes, "It would seem that no model of human conduct escapes some concept of tension, strain, frustration, deprivation, or the like, as a factor in accounting for action" (1977:35). Indeed, it is a commonly accepted maxim of the social sciences that personal change is generally the result of some felt need for change. This implies a dissatisfaction with the status quo. "This tension is best characterized as a felt discrepancy between some imaginary, ideal state of affairs, and the circumstances in which [potential recruits] actually saw themselves" (Lofland 1977:35). Some sort of tension or dissatisfaction with life is a necessary condition to incline a person toward affiliation with a cultic religious group. But this condition is certainly not sufficient by itself. It may be worked out in a psychiatrists's office, in a political campaign designed to change social conditions, or in any one of a dozen different ways.

In societies such as our own that undergo a great deal of change, persons often experience anomie or normlessness. They feel that they are without roots. Clearly this anomie creates a great deal of stress in persons. The tension caused by anomie may be resolved in any one of several ways: suicide or affiliation with absolutistic religious groups are two of the possible responses. But anomie is not the only source of stress that can cause dissatisfaction with one's status quo. There are other sources as well, and the Unification Church consciously seeks to take advantage of them. Since the Moonies are well aware of the importance of tension, they make a point to visit college campuses during final exams week. The stress felt by students provides a necessary predisposing condition for recruitment. Regardless of its source, some form of tension, frustration, deprivation, or dissatisfaction provides the first necessary condition for a person to be favorably inclined to religious proselytizers.

2. **Religious Problem-Solving Perspective.** The second personal characteristic is an inclination to solve problems by turning to religious leaders or religious methods rather than to political or psychiatric ones. Only when a person begins to attach religious or spiritual meaning to events does the individual become amenable to the message of religious groups.[14] Downton maintains that youth members who came out of the counterculture developed a religious orientation as a result of the use of drugs. The hallucinatory experiences resulted in a strong belief in a spiritual dimension to life which had not previously been a component of the world view of these youths. Young people were not favorably inclined toward the Divine Light Mission and the Guru Maharaji until they first sensed that religion was a viable problem-solving route (Downton 1979). Hence, Lofland posits that a spiritual outlook is necessary before a potential recruit will take seriously the message of a proselytizing group.

---

[14] Note that Lofland assumes a supernatural dimension to be intrinsic to religion.

3. Religious Seekership. Lofland insists that among the Moonie converts there was a dissatisfaction with the conventional religious groups and a feeling of being a religious seeker. Virtually all of the converts had church-hopped or had drifted from one religious group to another. They had already concluded that the world view of the religion in which they were raised was inadequate. The new converts had identified themselves as seekers of truth. However, not all seekers were converted. For a seeker to be genuinely attracted to the Unification Church and to be a likely convert, he or she must have had a world view that was generally compatable with Unification theology. Lofland insists that the importance of cultural conduciveness is sometimes overemphasized and exaggerated. However, he does point out that before a person would show interest in the Moonies, he or she apparently must already have held two general belief patterns: (1) a conviction that there is an active supernatural realm from which spirits intervene in the material world, and (2) a belief that every object has a purpose, every event a meaning, and every person a divine task to perform. He found that biblical fundamentalism, millenarian expectations, and many other beliefs that would seem to be important were far from universal.

In the 19th century the Ghost Dance religion spread rapidly among Native American nations. However, it failed to attract the Navaho. The Ghost Dance religion predicted the rise of the dead, but the Navaho were afraid of ghosts. Hence, rather than celebrating such a future event, they refused to have anything to do with this movement. Similarly, it appears that at least a gross congruence of world views between the potential recruit and a religious cult is necessary. The Shakers might provide another example. They were able to get both married couples and singles to join their group, though they required absolute celibacy of their members. Success in gaining converts stemmed from the fact that they recruited from a society that already defined sexual relations as debased. Presumably, they would have a hard time finding recruits among a people who practice a fertility orgy. Uniform congruence does not seem to be necessary, but a general compatibility of outlook seems to be so for a potential recruit actually to become a convert. Hence, self-defined religious seekership, with a compatible world view, is the third dispositional factor Lofland identified.

Each of the above factors seemed to be necessary components in the outlook or disposition of potential recruits. These factors were present *before* the individuals encountered the religious group which they eventually joined. The situational contingencies to be discussed next become significant only if these first three components are already present.

4. Turning Point in Life. The converts to the Unification Church had reached important turning points in their own lives. "Each had come to a moment when old lines of action were complete, had failed, or had been or were about to be disrupted, and when they were faced with the opportunity or necessity for doing something different with their lives" (Lofland 1977:50). Potential converts had recently migrated, had lost or quit a job, or had graduated from, dropped out of, or flunked out of college. We need more information on what kinds of crises incline a person to turn toward a religious group. Lofland found that marital dissolution and illness seldom served this turning-point function. Apparently, some types of turning points stimulate the meaning and belonging needs more profoundly than others. Nonetheless, persons who are not at turning points in their lives are not likely to be responsive to the proselytization attempts of unconventional religious devotees (Moonies, Hare Krishna, and so on). Turning points are times of new beginnings when investment in the status quo is minimal.

5. Close Cult Affective Bonds.   In Lofland's study of the Moonies, almost all recruits were gained through preexisting friendship networks. The Moonies learned that cognitive appeals to ideology (with a focus on the moral commitment level) did not win converts. As the Moonies became aware of this, they gradually began to modify their recruitment strategy. Lofland emphasizes that they "learned to start conversion at the emotional rather than the cognitive level" (1977:308). In other words they learned that affective levels of commitment precede moral levels of commitment.

6. Weakening of Extracult Affective Bonds.   Because of migration away from one's family or because of disaffection from it, an individual may experience isolation, alienation, or loneliness. Such a person is more in need of emotional support as he or she faces a turning point than is one who has a close network of friends and family. As has been pointed out, Moonies consciously look for signs of transiency (backpacks, individuals who are alone). The person who has no other immediate reference group is less likely to have someone oppose or intervene in the conversion process. Without another individual or group to offer an alternative interpretation of the group, the individual is more likely to be drawn into that group. Furthermore, without another significant reference group, the process of renunciation of the outside is much less complicated.

7. Intensive Interaction.   Lofland maintains that some Moonies are only verbally committed, that is, they have not fully experienced the final condition of total commitment. This condition solidifies commitment to the group through intensive interaction, including communal living. In this way "moral-level commitment" is enhanced by providing "communion" with the group. Once the intensive interaction provides a sense of unity and oneness, the devotees actively *want* to believe the ideology. By consciously working on strengthening their faith, they come really to believe the ideology, to feel a sense of awe about the leader, and actually to uphold the

Exhibit 5–2 _____

Lofland's Conversion Model

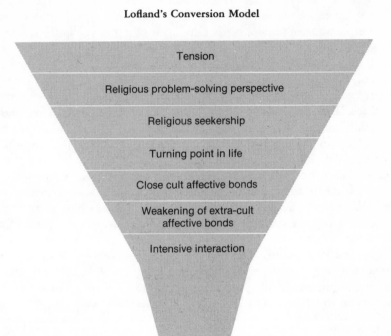

| Tension |
| Religious problem-solving perspective |
| Religious seekership |
| Turning point in life |
| Close cult affective bonds |
| Weakening of extra-cult affective bonds |
| Intensive interaction |

One might view Lofland's model as a "filtering" of people. Each step involves a filtering out of some people and a filtering or even funneling in of others. Those who have experienced the first six filters become "verbal converts." They must go through the seventh step as well to become "total converts." Total converts really believe the theology or ideology of the group. Verbal converts feel committed to the members of the group, and they verbally assent to belief, but they are not yet really committed at a "moral level."

group's values. The conversion becomes total, and commitment becomes intense at all three levels.

Critique of Lofland's Model

For a decade and a half, Lofland's model of conversion has been used widely by sociologists studying cults and sects. However, several have voiced reservations about it in recent years. The most direct challenge has come from David Snow and Cynthia Phillips (1980), who studied the conversion process in an American Buddhist movement. They suggest that several of Lofland's stages may not be common to all cults. First, Snow and Phillips question whether personal tension is necessarily higher for persons who enter cults than for the general population. They cite self-report survey data which suggests that tension is high among the entire population. Moreover, they question whether the intensity and duration of stress is really higher for those who join cults. Much of the report of tension may be a retrospective interpretation—reading into an earlier situation something that was not felt to be present or important at that time. The ideology causes a reinterpretation of previous experience. This can be seen in the comments of converts reported by Snow and Phillips in Exhibit 5–3.

It is also possible that religious conversion actually *creates* the increased tension. We discussed in Chapter 3 the view of A. R. Radcliffe-Brown that religion sometimes creates tension and anxiety in order to provide social solidarity. Snow and Phillips follow this line of analysis. They suggest that while tension may well exist in the convert, it may sometimes be a *result* of joining the group and of having a new interpretation of the meaning of events. For example, belief that the world will soon end or that all nonmembers are evil—including one's family members who refuse to join—may cause great stress. Furthermore, it may cause one to redefine one's premembership status as depraved and stressful. Meanwhile, the group-induced tension may contribute to in-group boundaries and may thereby facilitate group solidarity.

Snow and Phillips also insist that a religious problem-solving perspective was not a prerequisite to persons becoming members of the cult they studied. They point out that ideological congruence was *facilitative,* but *not necessary* for persons to become active members. Furthermore, they found that new

Exhibit 5–3 _____

Tensions and Personal Problems as Factors Leading to Conversion

Male, Caucasian, single, under 30: When I joined I didn't think I was burdened by any problems. But as I discovered, I just wasn't aware of them until I joined and they were solved.

Female, Caucasian, single, under 30: After I attended these meetings and began chanting, I really began to see that my personal life was a mess.

Male, Caucasian, single, under 30: Now as I look back I feel that I was a total loser. At that time, however, I thought I was pretty cool. But after chanting for a while, I found out that my life was just a dead thing. The more I chanted, the more clearly I came to see myself and the more I realized just how many problems I had had.

Male, Caucasian, married, over 30: After you chant for a while you'll look back and say, "Gee, I was sure a rotten, unhappy person." I know I thought I was a saint before I chanted, but shortly after I discovered what a rotten person I was and how many problems I had.

The reports of cult members cited here would seem to support the thesis that tension and unhappiness are factors which contribute to cult conversion. However, these reports may represent substantial revisions or reinterpretations of precult experiences. This involves assignment of motives and use of an interpretive schema which was learned from the cult. Hence, the perception of prior strains and problems may be a *result* of conversion rather than a cause of it. The passages quoted here are generally typical of those made by devotees to cult researchers. However, these statements are chosen because their wording illustrates the retrospective nature of the analysis: "as I discovered, . . . I wasn't aware of them until . . ."; "after I attended these meetings . . . I really began to see"; and "as I looked back. . . ."

Source: Quoted in David A. Snow and Cynthia L. Phillips, "The Lofland-Stark Conversion Model: A Critical Reassessment, *Social Problems,* April 1980, p. 430–437. Used by permission.

members did not always define themselves as religious seekers. Many who joined the Buddhist group they studied had not been active in other religious groups. Some claimed that they had probably always been seeking religious truth, but had not been aware of what they really wanted until they found the *Nichiren Shoshu* movement. Again, this revised interpretation of one's previous experience *may* be a function of reading things into prior experience so that present behavior makes sense. Such self-reports must be analysed with sensitivity to the possibility of bias in the data.

Likewise, the question as to whether one was at a turning point in one's life at the time one encountered a religious group is a matter of interpretation. "Whether a particular situation or point in one's life constitutes a turning point is not a given, but is largely a matter of definition and attitude. There are few, if any, consistently reliable benchmarks for ascertaining when or whether one is at a turning point in one's life. As a consequence, just about any moment could be defined as a turning point. . . . We again face the problem of retrospective reporting" (Snow and Phillips 1980:439).

Finally, Snow and Phillips insist that it is not necessary that members have weak extra-cult affective bonds. They suggest that the necessity of this element may depend on several factors. The extent to which the group's values represent a break from values and perspectives of one's family is very important. If group membership does not involve a transformation of the values one shares with one's family, then alienation from family is unnecessary. Moreover, the tendency toward isolation may be related to the extent to which the group is particularistic (the extent to which it insists that it has the exclusive path to truth or salvation). Finally, isolation of members from extra cult relationships may be a phenomenon of groups with a revolutionary, idiosyncratic, or peculiar world view. Weakening of extramovement ties by cults may be a strategy to neutralize the stigma which nonmembers attach to the group. If outsiders are neutralized as a reference group, then their opinions are not a threat to the group. If the cultic group is not stigmatized, then the strategy of alienating members from nonmembers is less important.

Interestingly, Snow and Phillips did find that both recruitment through affective bonds and sustaining members through intensive interaction were critical. In fact, they describe conversion in the Buddhist group they studied as conforming to the same pattern of verbal commitment followed only much later by total commitment.

Actually, Lofland has himself offered a modification of his original theory, insisting that it may not be as universally applicable as he thought. He now suggests that there appear to be several conversion processes and that different types of groups tend to employ different processes. Lofland and Skonovd (1981) discuss six different conversion motifs with each involving a slightly different series of factors. Some conversions are induced by nonrational experiences, others involve a more intellectual process of study, and still others stress affective ties and belonging functions. Lofland and Skonovd also suggest that different modes of conversion may be more common in different epochs of history. Hence, the heavy emphasis on nonrational experience by William James and Herbert Otto earlier in this century may have been due to the fact that mystical modes of conversion were more common then, while affective modes have been more widely employed by groups in the 1960s, 70s, and 80s. It is interesting to note, however, that of the six conversion motifs outlined by Lofland and Skonovd, four emphasize belonging and group participation *prior to* belief. Intense involvement normally precedes total conversion. In the case of contemporary sects and cults, this sequence seems to be universal.

Summary and Conclusions

In the early years, the conversion strategy of the Unification Church focused on cognitive conversion or "moral level" commitment. Eventually, the Moonie strategy for conversion changed. It involved getting potential recruits to attend a weekend retreat where the devotees could "love bomb" the recruits and attempt to establish close personal bonds. The strategy is not primarily one of brainwashing, but focuses on transference of reference groups. If the new cult is able to establish itself as the primary—and perhaps the *only*—reference group, the new recruit is well on his or her way to full commitment. Cognitive or moral level commitment comes later. One person who experienced the love bombing but who did not join the Moonies reported on the powerful influence of this technique:

> I wanted to break through my feeling of isolation badly enough that right then it almost didn't matter what they believed—if only I could really share myself with them. I think that moment may be exactly the point at which many people decide to join the [cult] (Lofland 1977:311).

It is worth noting that many devotees castigate themselves or feel guilty if the belief system doesn't seem to make sense. They already feel a commitment to the religious group, and their lack of cognitive conformity (moral commitment) is interpreted as a personal fault or lack of faith. Lofland quotes any number of deeply committed devotees who confessed that full intellectual acknowledgement was slow in coming. It is also evident that these converts wanted desperately to believe. They chose to believe; they were not forced against their will. Many others who have studied cults point to the same phenomenon (Bromley and Shupe 1979; Downton 1979; Balch 1980; Judah 1974).

Again this must not lead us to a simplistic conclusion that affective commitment is *always* chronologically prior to moral or ideological commitment. The order *may* be reversed. There are many historical examples of persons who have had mystical experiences that changed their lives. For example, in the case of Saint Paul, it certainly appears that ideological conversion preceded any close affective bonds with members of the Christian community. Any one of the types of commitment (affective, instrumental, or moral) may come first. Nonetheless, some researchers have found that belonging functions tend to be prior in mainline churches (Roof 1978:205) and in charismatic congregations (McGaw 1980), and the current evidence strongly suggests that in the majority of conversions to cults, affective commitment comes first.[15]

Once an individual develops close affective bonds, he or she is likely to want respect from his or her new friends. In order to gain approval, the new convert will behave in ways that will provide continuing affirmation and support. In other words, the recruit begins to invest time, energy, and other resources in the movement and in its goals. The person may begin to raise money, proselytize, chant, or engage in other public activities that enhance instrumental commitment. Any public witness is very important in deepening a recruit's sense of personal investment. Once the new devotee begins to move up the internal stratification system of the group, his or her sacrifice and investment continues to deepen. Not only does the commitment change in degree (it intensifies), it also changes in nature (becoming more instrumental). It is for this reason that religious movements must provide appropriate roles for newcomers, and must provide career possibilities within the movement. If the instrumental commitment is to continue beyond one's youthful years, the religious organization must provide investment opportunities for people in various stages of the life span. Again, this intensified affective and instrumental commitment is particularly important for groups with a nonconventional world view. If devotees begin to develop extracult bonds, the religious commitment begins to weaken.[16]

I hope the foregoing analysis has served several purposes. First, the claims of induced hypnotic trances by groups such as the Moonies or the Divine Light Mission can be put to rest. Second, our discussion hopefully provided students with tools of analysis they may apply to specific religious groups they choose to study. Third, leaders of voluntary civic organizations may be helped to understand some of the components of commitment. In the town in which I live, one church recently arranged its parking lot spaces so that persons who attend church are parked four deep. Cars parked in the middle of the lot cannot move until those ahead of them have moved. The assumption is that no one will be interested in remaining after the

---

[15] This does not negate the affirmation that the meaning function is primary. The meaning function is primary in that it is closer to the manifest purpose of religion. Chronologically, however, the belonging function seems to come first.

[16] This treatment of commitment and conversion has been both rational and sociological. Many psychologists of religion point to the importance of mystical or sacred experiences in the conversion process. I have not intentionally downplayed the role of nonrational experiences. The fact is simply that such experiences do not seem to be central to most of the new religious movements. Furthermore, my intent is to reveal the social dimensions of conversion, for the purpose of this text is to provide a sociological analysis of religion. The foregoing discussion of conversion and commitment is not intended to be comprehensive or all-inclusive.

worship service to chat with friends and acquaintances. If one does not leave immediately, he or she may be blocking three other people from leaving. The very structure of the parking lot has mitigated against affective-level commitment. Persons who are responsible for any voluntary organization (Jaycees, PTAs, international clubs, churches, or whatever) could benefit from being aware of the elements of commitment. Many successful organizations utilize some of the commitment mechanisms outlined by Kanter; Alcoholics Anonymous and Amway Corporation are two examples from the social service and business sectors of society. Such groups do not apply all the mechanisms (such as renunciation) nor do they apply them with the intensity of the cults, but the commitment process itself is similar.

Finally, the theory of commitment and conversion described in this chapter is particularly relevant to religion in Western culture. Presumably, the theory should apply to non-Western religions as well, but this is hypothesis rather than fact. For example, Zen Buddhism is highly individualistic. Whether reference groups or affective bonds to other Buddhists is as important in that movement as it is in most current American cults is yet to be established. Furthermore, empirical research on "multiple conversion motifs" (varieties of conversion processes) may prove fruitful in understanding similarities and differences in conversions in disparate cultures (Lofland and Skonovd 1981).

"Switching" among Mainline Denominations

Changes of denominational affiliation by Christians have become common in modern American society. Such "switching" of denominations does not necessarily involve a conversion, but it does involve a change of commitment. Moreover, the patterns have been pervasive enough that church administrators and social scientists have begun to explore why some denominations are growing and others are declining. This primarily involves interpretation of general statistical indicators of growth or decline of entire denominations rather than participant observations and interviews. The attempt has been to discern from these statistical data the reasons for change of commitment among religious groups.

Dean Kelley's book, *Why Conservative Churches Are Growing* (1972) initiated a renewed focus on this phenomenon of church membership growth and denominational switching. Kelley's thesis is that people are attracted to churches that have strict standards of membership and which expect members to invest much of their time and resources in the group. He claims that conservative churches (fundamentalist, charismatic, and evangelical) are growing rapidly while liberal churches are declining. Exhibit 5–4 provides the type of data which Kelley used. Readers can see the decline in United Methodist, United Presbyterian, United Church of Christ, and Episcopal denominations. He believes people are switching to more conservative denominations (Churches of God, Nazarenes, Seventh Day Adventists, Jehovah's Witnesses, Southern Baptists, Mormons). The reasons he cites for conservative church growth are basically congruent with Kanter's theory of commitment.

However, Kelley's interpretation of data has been challenged from several sources. It appears that most of the converts to the conservative churches are rejoining after a period of absence, or they are coming from other conservative congregations. The conservative churches actually seem to be growing because of two factors: (1) recruits from other evangelical or fundamentalist groups, and (2) a high fertility rate in conservative churches. In one study, less than 10 percent of the new members to conservative churches were converts from outside the evangelical community (Bibby and Brinkerhoff 1973). On the other hand, liberal churches seem to be drawing a much larger percentage of their new members from the more conservative churches. The movement of denominational switching is not primarily from liberal churches to conservative ones, but vice versa.[17] Yet, the fact remains that membership figures for conservative churches are growing while for liberal churches they are declining.

The pattern, then, is that most church members who switch move from the more conservative to the more liberal churches (Bibby 1978:132). Nonetheless, the liberal churches do not *retain* members as well as conservative churches. When people leave liberal churches, they are likely to cease affiliation with any church (Newport 1979:549). Hence, the growth of conservative churches and the decline of liberal churches makes sense, despite the trend of switchers to move from conservative to liberal churches. The conservative churches employ more commitment mechanisms, and they retain members better. This fact, combined with recruitment of former members, a higher fertility rate, and more religious training in the home for children seems to account for better overall membership trends among evangelicals, fundamentalists, and religious sects (Newport 1979; Bibby and Brinkhoff 1973).[18]

It is important to recognize the predominate reasons for denominational switching. The shift to liberal churches does not seem to be primarily an attraction to modernistic theology. What happens is that people tend to worship with others of a similar socioeconomic class. As people are upwardly

---

[17] Switching seems to be primarily to the high-status and the very low-status churches, and away from middle-status congregations. Hence, the movement is not entirely in one direction (Newport 1979:538).

[18] Hoge and Roozen (1979:322) report that, over time, birth rates have been the most consistent correlate with growth and decline of church membership. They insist that "contextual factors" (aspects of the larger society which the churches cannot control) have usually had a greater affect on church membership levels than have "institutional factors" (policies or actions within the church itself).

Exhibit 5–4

Church Membership Statistics, 1940–1980, For Selected U.S. Denominations

Denomination	1940	1950	1960	1970	1980
American Lutheran Church	(1,129,349)[a]	(1,587,152)[a]	2,242,259	2,543,293	2,353,229
Assemblies of God[b]	198,834	318,478	508,602	625,027	1,064,490
Baptist General Conference	N.A.	48,647[c]	72,056	103,955	133,385
Christian and Missionary Alliance	22,832	58,347	59,657	112,519	189,710
Christian Church (Disciples of Christ)	1,658,966	1,767,964	1,801,821	1,424,479	1,177,984
Church of God (Anderson, Ind.)	74,497	107,094	142,796	150,198	176,429
Church of God (Cleveland, Tenn.)	63,216	121,706[e]	170,261	272,278	435,012
Church of Jesus Christ of Latter-Day Saints	724,401[d]	1,111,314	1,486,887	2,073,146	2,811,006
Church of the Brethren	176,908	186,201	199,947	182,614	170,839
Church of the Nazarene	165,532	226,684	307,629	383,284	484,276
Episcopal Church	1,996,434	2,417,464	3,269,325	3,285,826	2,786,004
Free Methodist Church of North America	45,890	48,574	55,338	64,901	68,477
Jehovah's Witnesses	N.A.	N.A.	250,000	388,920	565,309
Lutheran Church in America	(1,988,277)[a]	(2,395,356)[a]	(3,053,243)[a]	3,106,844	2,923,260
Lutheran Church-Missouri Synod	1,277,097	1,674,901	2,391,195	2,788,536	2,625,650
Mennonite Church	51,304	56,480	73,125	88,522	99,511
Presbyterian Church in the U.S.	532,135	678,206	902,849	958,195	838,485
Reformed Church in America	255,107	284,504	354,621	367,606	345,532
Reorganized Church of Jesus Christ of Latter-Day Saints	106,554	124,925	155,291	152,670	190,087
Roman Catholic Church	21,284,455	28,634,878	42,104,900	48,214,729	50,449,842
Salvation Army	238,357	209,341	254,141	326,934	417,357
Seventh-day Adventists	176,218	237,168	317,852	420,419	571,141
Southern Baptist Convention	4,949,174	7,079,889	9,731,591	11,628,032	13,600,126

United Church of Christ	(1,708,146)[a]	(1,977,418)[a]	(2,241,134)[a]	1,736,244
United Methodist Church	(8,043,454)[a]	(9,653,178)[a]	(10,641,310)[a]	9,584,711
United Presbyterian Church in U.S.A.	(2,158,834)[a]	(2,532,429)[a]	3,259,011	2,423,601
Wisconsin Evangelical Lutheran Synod	256,007[d]	307,216	348,184[f]	407,043

The data provided in this table will give an indication of the growth and/or decline of various denominations. While the numbers are quite interesting, caution must be maintained in interpreting these statistics. First, these are figures reported by the denominations themselves. While reliability and completeness in statistical reporting were among the criteria used in selecting the bodies, there are differences in reporting procedures by various denominations. For example, the Roman Catholic Church reported all individuals from the time of baptism. Since Catholics practice infant baptism, their figures include infants and small children. Many Protestant denominations report only church members. Hence, their figures include only those above the age of 12 or 13 and who have gone through confirmation. Finally, some denominations remove members from their "active" rolls who do not make financial contributions, attend church, or otherwise participate in the life of the church. (They do this to lower the "per head" tax to the denomination and to keep accurate records of active members.) Inactives are held on an "inactive list," but they are not reported in these statistics. Finally, those interested in total numbers of denominational families (e.g., all Methodists or all Baptists) would not get complete figures from this table. Many small sectarian offshoots of each denomination are not reported here.

The pattern to which Kelley points may be seen if readers compare recent membership patterns of the United Presbyterians, United Methodists, United Church of Christ, and Episcopalians with those of the Churches of God, the Nazarenes, the Assembly of God, the Church of Jesus Christ of Latter-Day Saints (Mormons), the Jehovah's Witnesses, the Southern Baptist Convention, and other conservative groups.

It is important to remember that these are crude figures of growth and decline. Studies which indicate direction of switching have been based on surveys that asked switchers about their present and former denominations. Obviously, such figures provide more specific data for analysis.

[a] Statistics listed in parentheses are composite totals for each of the denominations which eventually merged to form the group listed here.
[b] Assemblies of God statistics for 1971 and later are full membership statistics.
[c] Data for 1952.
[d] Data for 1939.
[e] Data for 1951.
[f] Data for 1961.
N.A. = not available.
Source: Constant H. Jacquet, Jr., ed., *Yearbook of American and Canadian Churches, 1982*, (Nashville: Abingdon Press, 1982). Copyright National Council of the Churches of Christ in the United States of America, 1982. Used by permission.

mobile, they often change their denominational affiliation. It is not clear whether the move to a denomination of higher status is usually a planned "image-enhancing" strategy or merely a function of joining a church where one has a friendship network (co-workers and colleagues). In any case, the move to higher-status churches is commonly a move to a more modern or liberal theology, for the high-status churches tend to be more modern in theology. For someone who is in a professional occupation or who has moved up the social ladder, the more modern, secular theology may be appealing. A world view which accepts the advances of science may provide more personal coherence and meaning to a highly educated scientist than does a world view which rejects Darwin. Regardless of reasons, changes in socioeconomic status do seem to be the major source of denominational switching (Newport 1979; Hoge and Carroll 1978).

A second important factor is denominational intermarriage. When a person marries someone of the same religion but of a different denomination, one of the two is likely to switch. According to Newport (1979) this comprises a significant proportion of religious switchers. Hence, the "friendship network" factor is extremely important in this case as well (one's spouse being the "friend").[19]

Newport concludes that "the present evidence argues against the notion that Americans pick and choose their religious affiliation on the basis of some well thought-out and *theologically* based criteria" (1979:550). He goes on to say that this does not imply a total absence of theological considerations, but that such concerns appear, from current evidence, to be secondary.

It is clear that denominational switching is not the same as an internal conversion experience. Much of the change from one denomination to another is a matter of merely changing organizational membership. The feeling of belonging—because of friendship networks or because of socioeconomic homogeneity—seems to be the primary influence in this decision. Belief patterns are significant, but moral and instrumental commitment seems to follow affective attachment in the majority of cases. Most frequently, such mainline denominational switching never does result in a change of world view.

We really do not have much empirical research on conversion in mainline denominations. Although the pattern of affective-level commitment followed by instrumental and moral commitment seems to hold for cult conversions and for denominational switchers, we cannot simply conclude that *conversion* within mainline religious groups follows the same pattern.[20] This is a hypothesis that needs testing. It is reasonable to assume that conversion happens

---

[19] Hoge and Roozen (1979) report that marriages in which partners continue to belong to different denominations are highly correlated with religious inactivity.

[20] Roof (1978) maintains that even among mainline denominations, the reasons for affiliation and involvement in churches and the process for becoming committed is different for liberals and conservatives (cosmopolitans and locals).

in a variety of ways, depending on personality characteristics, the cultural climate, and the emphasis of the particular religious group in question.

Part of the problem in understanding conversion in mainline groups is that the rhetoric of religious groups can be misleading. What is sometimes called a conversion is often a ritualized reaffirmation of a world view already held. Many adolescent "converts" at revivals and crusades do not really change their world views. They merely go through an experience by which they publicly affirm the faith in which they have been socialized since infancy. This is a significant experience, but it is not necessarily conversion as that has been defined here. In fact, Billy Graham (who leads many of these crusades) defines conversion as a "change in the direction of one's life to a totally new direction" (quoted by Wimberly et al. 1975:162). According to the research by Wimberly et al., most of those who respond to the crusades are not really converts by Graham's definition.

Sometimes individual decisions at revival meetings or worship services do represent a change. In such cases the public act of commitment usually serves simply as the final step in the consolidation of a new identity which may have been taking form over several months. Hence, the American public uses the word *conversion* to refer to (1) a radical and somewhat sudden change in world views, (2) a consolidation and confirmation of a gradual modification in one's world view, or (3) a reaffirmation and renewed commitment to a world view which has been held for a long time. Only the former two processes are properly called conversions, yet the latter is what occurs most commonly at revivals, crusades, and religious youth rallies (Wimberly et al. 1975).

My purpose in this section has been simply to demonstrate that affective commitment is important in both cults and churches. Reference group influences have often been ignored in the past by psychologists studying conversion, but these reference group factors deserve our attention.[21] We dare not ignore Kelley's basic thesis that the growing churches are those that emphasize uncompromising theological principles and strict conformity. For one thing, it is the strictness that induces the high levels of commitment and retention. Beyond that, however, it *may* be that downwardly mobile people are more concerned with theology (answers to questions about the *meaning* of life), and upwardly mobile people are more concerned with social functions—composition of church membership (Newport 1978:538).[22] It is true, after all, that most switching is toward the high-

---

[21] In a study of Methodists who had dropped out of active participation in their churches, Hartman (1976:40–42) found that a lack of affective ties was the central factor. United Methodist churches were losing members because the affective commitment was weak. This also supports the thesis that belonging is an extremely important factor in church participation patterns.

[22] Such conclusions must be acknowledged at this stage of research as tentative. At least one researcher believes that the opposite is true: Wade Roof believes that meaning functions are more important among liberal cosmopolitans and belonging functions are more critical for conservatives who are oriented to local issues. (Roof 1978:207.)

status churches and the very low-status sects, and away from middle-status congregations. Kelley and his critics may both be right.

Religious Commitment and Mental Health

I have maintained that the conversion and commitment process in most cults is not brainwashing. Nevertheless, one may ask whether these religious groups contribute to emotional immaturity and dependence. After all, this is the primary concern of those opposing cults. However, the same question may also be asked of the more conventional religious groups. In order to answer this question we would first need to define maturity and mental health. For many people, any person or group which does not follow "normal" social behavior and values is considered immature or unhealthy. Maturity and mental health are considered to be synonymous with social conformity.

Most of the religious heroes, saints, and holy persons of the major world religions, however, have deviated significantly from the norms and values of their native culture. Certainly Jesus was not a well-adjusted and conforming member of Hebrew society. He dared to be different. He challenged the status quo and offered alternative interpretations of religious doctrine. He championed the cause of the poor, broke up families (insisting that disciples follow him), and claimed to have power over death itself. And his disciples were certainly no better adjusted to their society. Most of them were beaten and persecuted, and several were eventually put to death for their nonconformist behavior.[23] Later Christian saints have been reported to talk to flowers and commune with nature—clearly strange and inexplicable behavior. Calvin, Luther, Wesley, Fox, and many other reformers could be cited for their refusal to conform to the expectations and norms of their day. Many present-day theologians insist that to be a Christian is to refuse to be fully adjusted to the values and expectations of one's society. Although my examples are drawn from the Christian tradition, one could point to the same lack of societal adjustment on the part of religious leaders in most of the major world religions. It would seem that we would either need to admit that religion is counterproductive in producing well-adjusted, mentally healthy adults, or we must define mental health and emotional maturity in a more generic way.

Even if we move beyond a social conformity definition of mental health, it is clear that religion has often contributed to narrow-mindedness, to guilt complexes, and to emotional dependency. Howard Clinebell has written:

---

[23] No one knows for sure how most of the disciples died. The tradition is that most died martyrs' deaths. It is known that Stephen was stoned to death in Jerusalem, and church historians believe that Paul was beheaded and Peter was crucified in Rome (Walker 1970).

> American Protestantism has frequently made critical and tragic errors in
> its presentation of the Christian religion—errors which have contributed to
> emotional and spiritual conflict and immaturity in our people. Most of those
> errors find a focus in a stern, legalistic, absolute, and Pharisaical moralism
> which is the characteristically American form of Protestantism (1965:27).

Many persons with severe guilt complexes have been debilitated by the
stern moralistic religious training of their youth. This has led some psychologists of religion to explore the religion of the "healthy minded" and that
of "sick souls" (James 1958).

In his *Religious Factors in Mental Illness,* Wayne Oates (1955) emphasizes
that it is important not to exaggerate the role of religion in mental illness.
"Sick religion" is both cause and effect, and even where it is a cause of
mental illness, it is not the sole cause. Oates went even further by suggesting
that lack of a sense of meaning or purpose in life seemed to be more of
a mental health problem than did "unhealthy religion." In a mental hospital
where he conducted research, over half of the patients indicated no evidence
of current religious interest or of past religious influence. This proportion
of the population was, of course, much higher than the general population.
Rodney Stark (1971) and C. Kirk Hadaway (1978) have also found a
positive correlation between religious involvement and a sense of well-being.
Provision of some sense of ultimate meaning in life may be one of the
necessary components of mental health (Frankl 1962). Religion tends to
address itself to this need for meaning and purpose. Clearly, religion is
capable of affecting one's mental state, but the relationship between religion
and mental health or religion and mental illness is not a simple one.

Much of the research has offered contradictory findings (Sanua 1969).
Part of the problem has been that religiosity has sometimes been simplisti-
cally defined (using only a single dimension, such as frequency of church
attendance). Furthermore, mental health has also often been defined in
terms of a single factor (life satisfaction, reports of anxiety, authoritarianism,
and so on). A more holistic concept of mental health is needed. Some
attempts have been made to formulate a generic and holistic (multidimensional) concept of mental health. We cannot explore the multiple components of mental health in depth here. However, Howard Clinebell
(1965:30–54) has specified 12 criteria for assessing how conducive any
religious group or religious ideology is to mental health. His assumptions
about a mentally healthy person will be clear from the criteria. They should
not be accepted as the final word on the matter, but may provide a helpful
starting point in further explorations of the relationship between religion
and mental health. Clinebell's criteria or tests for mentally healthy religion
are:

1. *"Does a particular form of religious thought and practice build bridges or barriers
   between people?"* Healthy religion may be identified as one that contributes to
   understanding, cooperation, and emotional bonds between people.

2. *"Does a particular form of religious thought and practice strengthen a basic sense of trust and relatedness to the universe?"* Eric Erikson's developmental psychology emphasizes the critical importance of basic trust in a healthy and productive personality. Some groups seem to emphasize a conspiracy world view, inhabited by evil or ill-willed people or spirits. Clinebell maintains that such a religious world view is not conducive to mental health.

3. *"Does a particular form of religious thought and practice stimulate the growth of inner freedom and personal responsibility?"* Autocratic leadership and authoritarian dogmatism may result in unhealthy dependency, fear, submission, and guilt. Religion is also capable, however, of facilitating a sense of self-worth, self-confidence, interdependence, and individual responsibility.

4. *"Does a particular form of religious thought and practice provide effective means of alleviating guilt? Does it provide well-defined, significant, ethical guidelines, or does it emphasize ethical trivia?"* Some religions emphasize the minutae of everyday behavior, such that the person is preoccupied with legalisms. (The Shakers specified which foot one was to step out of bed with.) Mentally healthy religion helps one make moral decisions, but it also provides for forgiveness and a new start if one makes immoral or unethical choices. Clinebell maintains that liberal Protestant churches have often not taken the feelings of guilt seriously and have often failed to provide adequate means for reduction of guilt (forgiveness).

5. *"Does a particular form of religious thought and practice increase or lessen the enjoyment of life? Does it encourage a person to appreciate the affective or feeling dimension of life?"* Of course many religious groups would insist that enjoyment of this life is insignificant or trivial. At this point we can see how difficult it is to develop a concept of mental health which does not rest ultimately on value judgment about what is important in life. Nonetheless, Clinebell insists that from an empirical point of view, enjoyment of life is an important component of mental health. Certainly sensitivity to feelings is also part of being a whole and healthy personality.

6. *"Does a particular form of religious thought and practice handle the vital energies of sex and aggressiveness in constructive ways or in repressive ways?"* Clinebell insists that "there is no more revealing test of the mental health impact of a religious approach than its handling of sex and aggressiveness. . . . When persons label these drives as 'bad' in themselves, they must either deny their existence (repression) or stagger under a deadening load of guilt feelings." In either case, the results for mental health and emotional maturity may be devastating. Puritanical attitudes toward sex are not intrinsic to Christianity, although they have frequently emerged in American Christianity.

7. *"Does a particular form of religious thought and practice encourage the acceptance or denial of reality? Does it foster magical or mature religious beliefs? Does it encourage intellectual honesty with respect to doubts? Does it oversimplify the human situation or face its tangled complexity?"* Many religious groups would want to argue with Clinebell over what is "reality" and what is "mature religious belief," but he seems to suggest three principles. First, he insists that life is filled with uncertainties and ambiguities. Many religious groups have a simplistic all-or-nothing, good versus evil view of the world (totalistic). Clinebell maintains that a refusal to admit to ambiguity in life is immature and unhealthy. Second,

he insists that religion "mitigates against full mental health when it encourages people to ignore their honest doubts." Here he accepts the position of Tillich and H. R. Niebuhr in maintaining that faith is more than just an absence of doubt. Third, Clinebell seems to endorse here the liberal theological position that religious beliefs should not be contrary to logic or to empirical evidence. "Mature religious beliefs" are juxtaposed against "magical" beliefs, suggesting that beliefs which are contrary to empirical investigation are immature. Clinebell's own world view is evident in this criterion.

8. *"Does a particular form of religious thought and practice emphasize love and personal growth or does it emphasize fear?"* All the research on childhood development indicates that an environment of love, acceptance, and mutual trust is conducive to personal growth and emotional maturity. The hellfire and brimstone preaching of Puritan New England was certainly not a model of religion if mental health is a concern.

9. *"Does a particular form of religious thought and practice give its adherents a philosophy of life that is adequate in providing a sense of ultimate meaning, purpose and value?"* Clinebell cites Viktor Frankl's thesis that meaning or purpose in life is an intrinsic human need. In fact, Frankl's logotherapy system of treatment is based on the theory that an existential vacuum (lack of meaning or purpose in life) is a major cause of personality problems. Mentally healthy religion helps releave this vacuum by providing an adequate "frame of orientation" or "object of devotion."

10. *"Does a particular form of religious thought and practice encourage the individual to relate to his unconscious through living symbols?"* Clinebell writes: "If a religious approach is to enhance personality health, it must take the deep, unconscious aspects of the mind seriously, encouraging its participants to keep open the lines of communication with this hidden world which profoundly influences everything we do." Symbolism is the language both of the unconscious and of religion. Religious groups which make symbols concrete and interpret them literally may retard the vitality of the symbols. Healthy religion recognizes the importance and power of symbolic language, but avoids literal and absolutistic interpretation of the symbols.

11. *"Does a particular form of religious belief and practice accommodate itself to the neurotic patterns of the society or endeavor to change them?"* Contrary to the equivalence of mental health with social conformity, Clinebell insists that a healthy religion will object to social injustice, prejudices, and the like. He writes, "One mark of a maturity-motivating religious approach is that it is concerned with the redemption of society as well as of individuals. . . . Rather than preaching peace of mind or adjustment to society, it challenges persons to creative discontent and nonconformity to the sick side of our culture."

12. *"Does a particular form of religious thought and practice strengthen or weaken self-esteem?"* The research regarding the importance of self-esteem for a healthy and productive personality is overwhelming. Religion which is destructive of that self-esteem may therefore be identified as unconducive to mental health.

Having viewed Clinebell's criteria, three comments seem to be in order. First, it is not the *conscious purpose* of religion to facilitate mental health. Hence, it is understandable that many religious groups would object to such criteria. Clinebell is interested in the subjective consequences of religion—which is of little interest to many devout believers. Second, employment of Clinebell's criteria in the evaluation of the mental health consequences of religious groups would quickly reveal that present-day cults are not the only religious groups that may retard mental health and emotional maturity. In fact, virtually every religious group would get a mixed rating. In some ways, the cults do seem to be especially guilty of creating emotional immaturity by emphasizing utter dependency on a cultic leader or group. They also create a simplistic world view (totalistic) and play heavily on guilt feelings. But some observers who have studied cults have pointed to significant personal growth and expansion of self-knowledge among cult members. For example, Downton argues that for many members of the Divine Light Mission dependency is a stepping-stone to independence and autonomy (1979:156, 177, 210).

On the other hand, religious groups that are considered legitimate may be destructive of mental health in some respects. Robert Jay Lifton, who studied brainwashing in China, suggests that many conventional religious groups are totalistic, which is not conducive to mental health (1969:419–472). Clinebell's criteria may be helpful in that it causes us to identify the *specific ways* in which a religious group *retards* or *enhances* mental health. This surely would be an improvement over the broadside generalizations which have often been leveled only at the nonconforming religions.

Finally, a word must be said about Clinebell's criteria themselves. Any attempt to identify maturity or mental health must ultimately involve some value judgments. Clinebell's assumptions and his world view reflect the empiricism of the social sciences. Although he is himself a Christian theologian, he utilizes a rational, secular perspective. While many religious people would find his philosophical assumptions acceptable, others who reject religious modernization would challenge the basis of his concept of mental health. For our purposes, as social scientists studying religion, empiricism is the only defensible position. Nonetheless, the social scientist must recognize that any definition of mental health is bound to be fraught with value judgments.

The social scientist may also question whether there is a Western bias underlying these criteria. Are they (or any criteria) applicable in all cultures? Is it possible to define mental health in a way that has cross-cultural validity? Rational, secular empiricism is a product of Western philosophy. Can this empiricism define health or maturity in a way that is not biased in favor of Western religious thought? Empiricism, after all, involves a specific world view.[24]

Clinebell's tests provide a helpful starting point for thinking about the

---

[24] Wuthnow (1976b) treats social science itself as being a meaning system or world view which is replacing theistic outlooks for some people.

relationship between religion and mental health. However, none of the 12 points should be considered above criticism. The purpose of presenting these criteria is to stimulate thought on the part of the reader regarding the meaning of mature or mentally healthy religion. Rather than defining mental health in terms of one or two factors further research needs to be based on a holistic understanding of the many dimensions of mental health. Each of these 12 items (or some other such list) would have to be operationalized into specific statements that can be tested empirically.

The religion and mental health issue is an important one. The kidnapping and deprogramming of cult devotees is usually justified on the basis of the mental incapacity which the group's conversion process supposedly creates. Are these cults engaged in behavior that is categorically different from other religious groups, or are deprogrammers violating the civil liberties and the First Amendment rights of individuals? The answer may rest in part on whether religious cults are determined to be *uniquely* guilty of undermining mental health. On the other hand, even if religious cults are not conducive to a healthy personality structure, many will challenge the constitutional rights of parents to kidnap and deprogram their children. The question of the effects of the cults on mental health will not *necessarily* resolve the legal question.

There is another way to approach the issue of religion and mental health. One could focus on developmental psychology and emphasize that both human needs and human perception will vary, depending upon one's position in the life cycle. Furthermore, one may be more susceptible to totalistic world views in some stages of personal development than in others. Also, one may be more susceptible to the affective processes of cults when one is in certain phases of development (e.g., E. Erikson's [1963] identity or intimacy stages of personality development). There are many developmental theories that could be explored in relationship to religion, but we will conclude this chapter by exploring one perspective that may offer insights into several of the issues discussed here.

An Alternative Theoretical Approach to Conversion and Commitment: Structuralism

In most of this chapter, we have viewed religion from a traditional sociological perspective. We have discussed such central sociological concepts as roles, reference groups, and group functions. However, there is another significant theoretical perspective on religion, values, and mental processes which deserves our attention. This approach, called *cognitive structuralism*,[25]

---

[25] Cognitive structuralism is so named because it posits an innate structure in the minds of all persons, regardless of cultural background.

is more psychological than sociological in character, for it has to do with perception and with the development of cognitive processes. However, the sociologist would be seriously remiss to ignore research on the subject, for it raises some important issues which could alter our understanding of (1) conversion, (2) the development of a person's world view, and (3) the nature of commitment.

The structuralist approach emerged from the research on cognitive development conducted by Jean Piaget and his followers.[26] Piaget has identified a sequence of steps that occur in intellectual development, steps through which every individual in every culture must progress. He maintains that each stage represents a way of understanding or making sense of experience. Furthermore, he insists that movement through each of these stages is an innate characteristic of the developing human mind. This insight may have important implications for understanding world views. For example, Ronald Goldman, who applied Piaget's approach to religious education, maintains that a child in the concrete operational stage (7–12 years old) is legalistic and literalistic. Hence, the child at this stage will understand biblical stories literally regardless of how they are taught (Goldman 1964:165). Only when the child enters the formal operational stage of thinking can he or she understand biblical stories as mythical symbols. Each stage, therefore, represents a kind of world view—or at least profoundly affects one's world view.

According to Piaget, a person does not move to a new stage until he or she experiences cognitive dissonance, an internal, intellectual conflict that forces one to face the fact that one's present interpretation of experience is inadequate. Change comes about in one's world view as one matures intellectually. Each change of stage, in one sense, represents a sort of conversion. It should be clear that this theory is primarily concerned with changes in the intellectual sphere. Insofar as religious conversion represents a change in world view, structuralist research may offer significant insights.

Basing his research upon this structuralist position, Lawrence Kohlberg has developed a theory of moral development. (Kohlberg 1971, 1980; Duska and Whelan 1975; Wilcox 1979.) The implications of the research go well beyond strictly moral decision making; the theory has to do with one's world view. Kohlberg maintains that all persons, regardless of religious background or culture, move through the same sequence of stages. His cross-cultural research suggests that one's formal religious affiliation and one's culture may affect the rate at which one advances through the stages, but not the sequence. Furthermore, Kohlberg and his followers maintain that no one ever skips a stage.

---

[26] There is another school of structuralism which has emerged from anthropological research. We will be limiting our discussion to the work of Piaget and Kohlberg. Students interested in structuralism may also want to explore the anthropological work of Claude Levi-Strauss, Levi-Bruhl, and their followers.

Kohlberg's research is conducted by giving children moral dilemmas in which two values are in conflict (e.g., the right to property versus the value of human life). The child is asked what would be the right thing to do in each situation (see Exhibit 5-5). The specific answer (e.g., whether or not Heinz should steal the drug) is of much less interest to the structuralists than is the *rationale* that is given. The researcher asks, "*Why* is that the

Exhibit 5-5 _____

Examples of Moral Dilemmas Used by Kohlberg

A. Judy was a 12-year-old girl. She had saved up from babysitting and lunch money for a long time so she would have enough money to buy a ticket to a rock concert that was coming to her town. Her mother had promised her that she could go to the rock concert if she saved the money herself. She had managed to save up the $5 the ticket cost plus another $3. Later her mother changed her mind and told Judy that she had to spend the money on new clothes for school. Judy was disappointed and decided to go to the rock concert anyway. She bought a ticket and told her mother that she had been able to save only $3. That Saturday she went to the performance, telling her mother that she was spending the day with a friend. A week passed without her mother finding out. Judy then told her older sister, Louise, that she had gone to the performance and had lied to her mother about it.

1. Should Louise, the older sister, tell their mother that Judy had lied about the money or should she keep quiet? Why?
2. What would be the best reason for Louise to keep quiet? Why?
3. Louise thinks about how it would influence Judy in the future if Louise tells. What influence on Judy's future should Louise consider? Why?

B. In Europe, a woman was near death from a special kind of cancer. There was one drug that the doctors thought might save her. It was a form of radium that a druggist in the same town had recently discovered. The drug was expensive to make, but the druggist was charging 10 times what the drug cost him to make. He paid $200 for the radium and charged $2,000 for a small dose of the drug. The sick woman's husband, Heinz, went to everyone he knew to borrow the money, but he could only get together about $1,000, which is half of what it cost. He told the druggist that his wife was dying, and asked him to sell it cheaper or let him pay later. But the druggist said, "No, I discovered the drug and I'm going to make money from it." So Heinz got desperate and broke into the man's store to steal the drug for his wife.

1. Should Heinz steal the drug? Why?
2. Which is worse, letting someone die or stealing? Why?
3. What does the value of life mean to you, anyway?

C. In a country in Europe, a poor man named Valjean could find no work, nor could his sister and brother. Without money, he stole food and medicine that they needed. He was captured and sentenced to prison for six years. After a couple of years, he escaped from the prison and went to live in another part of the country under a new name. He saved money and slowly built up a factory. He gave his workers the highest wages and used most of his profits to build a hospital for people who couldn't afford good medical care. Twenty years had passed when a tailor recognized the factory owner as Valjean, the escaped convict whom the police had been looking for back in his hometown.

1. Should the tailor report Valjean to the police? Why?
2. Suppose Valjean were reported and brought before the judge. Should the judge have him finish his sentence or let him go free?
3. From society's point of view, what would be the best reason for the judge to have Valjean finish his sentence?

right thing to do?" It is the answer to this question that is critical in understanding one's moral stage, for each stage represents a mode of reasoning
and an outlook on life. Only by understanding the individual's rationale
can one determine his or her outlook. For example, two people may agree
on what is right in the case of Heinz, but one person may be responding
to selfish interests while the other is concerned with philosophical reflections
about what would be just for everyone. Kohlberg has done longitudinal
studies on the same individuals for a span of almost 25 years. Based on
these extensive longitudinal studies, he has identified three levels of thinking
with two stages at each level, six stages in all.[27]

Preconventional Level

A tiny infant has no sense of right or wrong. The infant simply experiences
the world. But gradually that child comes to realize that some behaviors
result in punishment. Playing with electrical plugs may result in a shout
of "No!" from the parents and a slap on the hand. Even before developing
the ability to talk, the child begins to sense that some behavior is wrong.
The child has begun to enter level 1. At this preconventional level, the
person is entirely *egocentric* in outlook. Right or wrong is gauged strictly
in terms of the consequences for that individual. The person's outlook is
quite literally "looking out for number one." The person is not able to
project into a role other than the one he or she is currently experiencing.
Small children are egocentric in their perception; and Kohlberg maintains
that some adults have remained at this level.

There are two stages at the preconventional level. The first of these is
the punishment-obedience orientation. At this stage the child is concerned
first and foremost about obeying superiors in order to avoid punishment.
"Wrong" is whatever one gets punished for and "right" is whatever powerful people want. In a very real sense, the person believes that might makes
right. The stage is egocentric because the individual is concerned only with
avoiding punishment for himself.

The stage 2 person is still egocentric, but he or she is more calculating
in determining right from wrong. The person is willing to risk the possibility
of being caught and punished if the potential reward is great enough. A
person at this stage engages in a cost/benefit analysis with his or her own
needs and desires as the criteria for evaluation of cost and benefit. At this

---

[27] One criticism of Kohlberg's work is that he used only males in his original studies.
One feminist researcher insists that the stages which Kohlberg identifies are somewhat different
for girls and women than for boys and men (Gilligan 1982). Other feminist researchers
maintain that the six stages are present for both sexes, but the specific moral issues may
differ somewhat for the two sexes (content differs but the structure of the stages is the same).
Research on a possible sex bias in Kohlberg's theory continues. It may be a decade or more
before we have adequate longitudinal data on the moral development of girls so that comparative data is available on both sexes. Perhaps only then can the issue be adequately resolved.

stage the person recognizes the need for friends and social relationships. The concept of justice or fairness in such relationships is reciprocity. A stage 2 person would help a friend if the friend would reciprocate, but if the individual doesn't think the friend would help in a similar situation, then aid may be withheld. Justice means that "I'll scratch your back if and only if you will scratch mine." The bottom line in any relationship at stage 2 is "what's in it for me."

Conventional Level

The second level is the conventional level. In this level, the individual begins to realize the importance of the social group. Conformity to the social group takes on extreme importance and the individual is willing to sacrifice his or her own needs and desires for the sake of the group. One common definition of the socialization process is "convincing individuals to *want* to do what they *must* do (for the society to survive)." At the conventional level, the person is thoroughly socialized such that social norms and social needs are internalized in the individual. The conventional level of thinking focuses on reducing egocentrism. On the other hand, the conventional level usually heightens ethnocentrism.[28] This level includes stages 3 and 4.

Stage 3, interpersonal sharing, is oriented toward pleasing significant others or conforming to a reference group in order to be liked. First and foremost, the individual wants to conform to the norms of the group or the expectations of specific other people. Kohlberg sometimes calls this the "nice boy/nice girl" stage. When I was a child I remember visiting frequently with an older woman. Sometimes her expectations for my behavior were more limiting than the norms in my own home. If she would scold me for misbehaving when I felt I had done nothing wrong, I would question why that behavior was inappropriate. The answer was always the same: "What will the neighbors think?" I have no idea what stage I might have been operating on at that time, but the woman was clearly thinking at stage 3. Her criterion for right or wrong behavior was always what someone else would think. (This reference point was not limited to her conversations with children.) The stage 3 person wants to conform to the expectations of those with whom she or he has a face-to-face relationship.

Eventually, the person is likely to discover that if everyone conformed only to the expectations of his own family and friends, the entire society might collapse. Survival of a society requires laws, and it requires that the citizens obey the laws. Maintenance of the social order at all costs becomes

---

[28] Ethnocentrism is the tendency to assume that one's own society's norms, values, and cultural patterns are the only moral standards. It is manifested in a closed-minded and narrow loyalty to one's own culture, and a prejudice against other ways of life.

the criterion for "right." The person at this stage (stage 4) is likely to be a great advocate of law and order. Obeying authority is extremely important to such a person, not because of fear of punishment, but because the social system must be preserved. Again, persons at this stage are very ethnocentric, but the circle of loyalties has expanded beyond one's immediate acquaintances; one's loyalties now include one's nation. The battle cry that one often hears during wartime is indicative of this stage: "Our country, right or wrong." Such a statement suggests that loyalty to country is so strong that moral questions are irrelevant; not even God dare criticize her! What is right is what is good for my country. Furthermore, wrong is defined in terms of the law. A person at this stage is not even particularly concerned with whether the law is just for everyone.

Principled Level

The third level, with stages 5 and 6, is the principled level. Kohlberg maintains that 80 percent of the American population has not reached this level. He also suggests that this level is usually not attained until the person is at least in his or her early 20s. Some simple tribal societies may not have anyone above a stage 4, although all industrialized societies have people at this level of thinking.[29] Kohlberg's principled level involves a decision-making procedure that is based on well-defined social and ethical principles. The thinking is more abstract and one considers many more factors in order to determine a just solution to a problem. At this level the individual defines morality in terms of fairness for everyone, not just for self or for one's own group. Rather than being egocentric or ethnocentric, the person at this level attempts to develop moral principles that are *universalistic.*

The fifth stage is referred to as social contract thinking. Unlike the person at stage 4, the individual at stage 5 asks whether a law is just before deciding whether it should be obeyed. The person emerging from stage 4 thinking usually goes through a process of relativism: do your own thing. However, relativism is hardly the material for building a just and stable society. Soon the individual learns that his or her rights are limited by the rights of the neighbor. As the adage goes, one's right to swing an arm is limited by the proximity of a neighbor's nose. Hence, the person begins to think in terms of how to construct a legal system (a social contract) in which the rights of each individual can be protected. Laws are to be obeyed if they are agreed upon by the members of the society and if they are indeed fair to all members of that society. Furthermore, the stage 5 thinker is interested in procedural justice and insists that due process must be protected. Maintenance of due process is at least as important as the conviction

---

[29] Insofar as Kohlberg is pointing to principled thinking as being more complex and differentiated, he seems to be confirming Robert Bellah's scenario of religious evolution (discussed in Chapter 6).

Exhibit 5–6 _____

Kohlberg's Stages of Moral Development

6. Universal ethical principles	Decision making based on ethical principles which are logically comprehensive, consistent, and universal.	Principled (universalistic) level
5. Social contract orientation	Protect individual rights and liberties; concern with due process. Justness of laws important.	
4½. Relativism phase		
4. Societal maintenance orientation	Maintain social order for its own sake; "Law and order" is highest priority.	Conventional (ethnocentric) level
3. Interpersonal sharing orientation	Desire to be liked; loyalty to in-group.	
2. Instrumental relativist orientation	Cost-benefit analysis; "You scratch my back, and I'll scratch yours."	Preconventional (egocentric) level
1. Punishment obedience orientation	Avoidance of punishment; deference to powerful people.	
0. No concept of moral imperative	Tiny infant who does not yet have language.	

of any given lawbreaker for due process protects the civil liberties of the innocent. The framers of the United States Constitution were excellent examples of stage 5 thinkers.

Stage 6, the universal ethical principle orientation, emphasizes respect for human personality as a supreme value. Moral decisions are based on well-thought-out ethical principles. These are logically comprehensive, universal, and consistent. They are not concrete rules (like the Ten Commandments) but abstract ethical guidelines for decision making. Mahatma Gandhi and Martin Luther King, Jr., are examples of such thinkers, but one could also point to the ethical systems of a number of philosophers and theologians.

Typically, a person is in a given stage for two or three years. It is possible, however, for a person to "freeze" at a particular stage. Some adults, for example, have never progressed beyond the very egoistic preconventional level. Progress in moral thinking, when it does occur, is stimulated by two factors: (1) hearing a moral rationale that is one stage higher than the person's current stage (2) at a time when one is experiencing cognitive dissonance. (A moral argument that is more than one stage above the individual's present thinking is simply unintelligible to that individual. Hence, many college ethics courses may be confusing to students if the text is written at stage 6 thinking and the students are operating at stage 3 or 4.)

Kohlberg has also insisted that a person always moves *up* the sequence of stages. Although the person may freeze at a particular stage, he or she will not regress. This is the one proposition which seems to be most widely questioned. Other researchers maintain that the sequential development is not irreversible. Kohlberg grants that a person at a higher stage may succumb to social pressures and may go along with a group that is operating at a lower stage of thinking. Nevertheless, the person does not really believe the moral rationale of the group. Moral *behavior,* then, is affected by both affective and intellectual processes. *Knowing* what is right (by thinking through the moral implications) is *necessary* but *not sufficient* in determining behavior. This latter part of Kohlberg's argument is well taken, but his evidence is still not entirely convincing that a stage 3 person, surrounded by a reference group of stage 2 people, could not regress in both thinking and behavior.

Finally, Kohlberg points out that although he has identified a developmental process that humans go through, this does not automatically mean that persons *ought* to go through these stages or that the stage 6 person is more moral. That is a value judgment rather than a description by a social scientist.

Structuralist theory presents a slightly different lens for viewing the issues discussed in this chapter. It can have significant implications for our understanding by suggesting a different set of considerations. Let me suggest four ways in which structuralist theory might alter the way one views conversion and commitment.

First, the structuralist position raises some interesting questions about one's definition of conversion. Kohlberg and other structuralists[30] are quick to emphasize that the structure of one's thinking is different from the content. One can have stage 3 liberal Christians, stage 3 fundamentalist Christians, stage 3 Moslems, or stage 3 Buddhists. A change from one of these groups to another—with the change of beliefs and practices that are appropriate to members of the new religious group—is what is normally called conversion. Romney Moseley (1978) has suggested, however, that such a change might be called lateral conversion. A change of content of religious beliefs occurs, but the individual still operates within the same stage of perception. Moseley reserves the word *conversion* for changes involving change of con-

---

[30] James Fowler (1981) has recently published his work on a theory of faith development that bears many similarities to Kohlberg's schema. Space does not allow exploration of both theories, but readers interested in exploring further the structuralist perspective will want to consult Fowler's work. Some of the insights elaborated here are gleaned from Fowler's chapter on conversion.

tent *and* change of stage (e.g., from a stage 2 Christian to a stage 3 Buddhist). A number of structuralists insist that change of stage is as important in transforming one's world view as a change of one's specific beliefs.

The importance of stage changes as transformations of one's world view can be illustrated by looking at the differences in interpretations of a religion by persons in different stages. A person in stage 2 is likely to interpret the teachings of Christianity in terms of reciprocity. Such a person serves God with the expectation that God will reciprocate, and that individual does unto others so that others will return the favor. A person in stage 4 tends to interpret the essence of Christianity as maintenance of the religious system (in unchanged form) and rigid adherence to rules (such as the Ten Commandments). Stage 2 and stage 4 thinkers have very different views of the basics of Christian thought. Furthermore, level 2 interpretations (stages 3 and 4) differ markedly from those of level 3 (stages 5 and 6). Since level 2 thinking involves extreme loyalty to in-group norms, persons at this level are likely to be particularistic (believe that only their own group offers truth and salvation). A change to level 3 (stage 5) requires a radical reinterpretation of world-view to a universalistic and inclusive outlook.

All of this raises the question as to whether a change of stage, without a change of religious group, can be considered a conversion experience. Some writers insist that conversion involves a significant alteration in one's values and beliefs; a change in the content of one's beliefs is assumed. However, the intensification of a belief system so that one's priorities are reordered has also been referred to as conversion by many scholars. Many converts at revivals and crusades are persons who have undergone a radical *alteration* in the *interpretation* of their faith but they have not changed religions. Not all scholars consider a significant reinterpretation of an existing faith to be a conversion experience, but if one does grant that this falls under conversion, then it is also possible to describe a change of stages as a sort of conversion too. I know one minister whose theology has changed drastically over the past 20 years. He has not joined a new religion, nor has he changed denominations. Neither has he had a nonrational experience which might be called a born again encounter. Yet, he describes his gradual change as a type of conversion, and he utilizes moral development theory to explain it.

Kohlberg and other developmentalists insist that each change of stage represents a change of outlook—a modification of world view. For this reason structural theory raises some interesting questions about our concepts of conversion. Structuralists are not in agreement about whether a stage change is a form of conversion, but it is at least possible, using structuralist concepts, to distinguish several types of conversion: stage conversion (same religion, new stage), lateral conversion (same stage, new religion), and diagonal conversion (new stage, new religion). Sociologists would likely

Exhibit 5-7 _____

A Structural Model of Types of Conversions

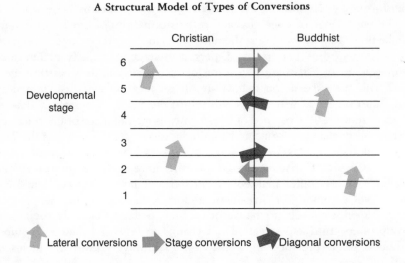

differ widely on whether stage conversions are really a form of conversion, but most would probably reserve the term conversion for those changes that include modification of *social behavior* (either involvement in a new group or intensified participation in a group one formerly belonged to).

A second possible contribution of structuralist theory is that it introduces a new factor as the primary inducement to certain types of conversion. Piaget, Kohlberg, and other structuralists stress that stage changes are induced by cognitive dissonance. This suggests that in conversions involving a change of stage (stage conversions or diagonal conversions), intellectual conflict is central. Whether such conflict is also operative in lateral conversion is unclear.[31] It may be that lateral conversions are more likely to follow an affective motif (belonging and participation preceding belief) while diagonal conversions may normally follow an intellectual motif (change of belief comes first). At this point these are speculations. The role of *intellectual* conflict in conversions may become clearer as structuralist research on religion continues.

A third insight of the structuralist perspective is that a person's stage of moral thinking may serve as an important conducive factor in conversion itself. In reading Lofland's study of the *Doomsday Cult,* one cannot help but notice the predominance of stage 2 and stage 3 thinking among members (1977:210–211). This raises two interesting questions. Are persons at certain stages more likely to join particular groups? Is an individual's moral

_____
[31] Insofar as some people convert to a different religion because the world view of their former religion does not explain the anomalies of life, cognitive dissonance would seem to be operative in lateral conversions as well. Such dissonance would seem to be a factor in the religious seekership element described by Lofland.

development stage a predisposing or deterring condition for recruitment to any one group? If so, perhaps it should be added to Lofland's list of factors. Second, is the conversion and commitment process any different for stage 5 people than for stage 2 or 3 people?[32] For example, are stage 5 thinkers less inclined to affective conversions and more predisposed to intellectual or mystical conversion motifs? Kohlberg, Fowler, and other structuralists stress that those at later stages are more willing to be nonconformists. Hence, it would be logical that they be less likely to be influenced by affective conversion motifs which stress reference group factors. Alternatively, are persons at stage 2 or stage 4 attracted by one conversion strategy more than by others? At this point we have only interesting speculations which need empirical investigation. Much research is needed to validate and expand structuralist theory and to explore the implications of the theory for understanding religion.

A fourth potential contribution of structuralist theory has to do with one's criteria of mental health. I have already mentioned Kohlberg's warning that his developmental sequence is a *description* of stages, not a *prescription*. In other words, a description of stages does not presuppose that one ought to progress through these stages. Having warned against this naturalistic fallacy of logic, however, he proceeds to develop a philosophical argument that each higher stage *is* a more adequate (healthier?) means of making moral decisions. Wearing the hat of a philosopher, Kohlberg argues that persons not only *do* go through successive stages but that they *ought* to be encouraged to grow and develop toward the principled stages of thinking.

If one accepts Kohlberg's philosophical argument,[33] one may have a guideline for evaluating whether a given religion contributes to mental health. Religious groups which encourage higher-level thinking or which facilitate growth beyond the lower stages might be considered "healthier" religions. If the natural evolution is considered in a positive light, then any group or belief system which retards that growth and causes a freeze at an earlier stage can be defined as "unhealthy." (Kohlberg and his followers are still not entirely certain as to all the factors which cause a person to stagnate at a given level.) In this way, the moral development theory can be used to assess the relationship between religion and mental health. There are some dangers in this approach, and one must never assume that the value judgment problem has been avoided just because one employs a theory based on empirical research. A statement of ought is always a value statement. In fact, many sociologists resist the use of this sort of sequential stage theory because such theories often contribute to labeling and to judg-

---

[32] My hunch is that it is. I suspect that a person who thinks at stage 5 would be much less likely to abdicate personal decision making, accept mortification, and passively obey the authorities of the religious group. Stage 5 thinkers value independent thinking too highly to abdicate personal responsibility for their own thoughts and actions.

[33] This is a big "if"; many social scientists resist acceptance of the stages as *prescriptions* of how one *ought* to develop as a person.

mental evaluations that undermine the posture of objective, disinterested scholarship. It is viewed as a threat to the norm of cultural relativism (remaining nonjudgmental toward other cultures).

This is a brief treatment of cognitive structuralism. I hope it will provide the reader with an alternative view of factors which affect a person's world view and which therefore may affect conversion and commitment. Clearly, structuralism offers a different starting point for understanding human behavior, and it causes the researcher to look for different variables. At the present time, there is no comprehensive structuralist theory of conversion—but some researchers are working on it. (Moseley 1978, and Fowler 1981.)

As a project to deepen understanding of theories discussed in this chapter, students may want to list ways in which Kohlberg's theory is similar to that of Kanter and Lofland. Likewise, specify ways in which structuralism is in conflict with the approaches of Kanter and Lofland. How might these theories complement and correct one another? By addressing issues such as these, students can develop their own skills in comparison, contrast, and synthesis.

Summary

There is much we still do not know about the social psychology of religion, for religious behavior is complex to say the least. The foregoing discussion should provide students with an understanding of some of the major theoretical currents and issues that are now being explored.

What we do know is that commitment may involve an intellectual commitment to an ideology or to a world view, an emotional commitment to the other members of the group, or an instrumental commitment to the organization itself. While conversion to cults is often viewed by the popular press as an intellectual transformation, research suggests that affective commitment to other members comes first, followed by instrumental and intellectual (moral) commitment. Hence, our suggestion that belonging functions are prior in religious cults, even if meaning functions are primary. Many researchers are finding belonging functions to be the initial element in many people's decision to affiliate with mainline denominations or to switch denominational commitment. On the other hand, nonrational religious experiences or theological arguments may be the first and foremost elements of commitment for many people; hence, one must be wary of overgeneralizations. There are probably multiple conversion processes some of which are more affective and some of which are more intellectual in nature. We are only beginning to understand these processes and the factors which make one process more or less amenable to certain persons and to particular periods of history.

Conversion and commitment may contribute to or detract from mental health, depending upon the content of the ideology and the structure of the group. We have suggested a multidimensional approach to assessing the relationship between religion and mental health and have found that probably all groups would get a mixed rating. Clearly, the cults are not the only religious groups capable of undercutting mental health. Finally, we have viewed an alternative paradigm for analysis of moral and religious thinking. Structuralism offers a very different approach for understanding transformation of world views and the factors which affect those transformations.

Certainly the survival of any new religious movement depends on the group's ability to recruit and convert new members and then to sustain their commitment. However, if the group is to survive it must also address certain institutional matters. It is to these remaining issues of group viability which we now turn.

6

Emergence and Viability of Religious Movements
Routinization of Charisma, Mobilization of Resources, and Maintenance of Plausibility

Maintaining a high level of commitment from members is necessary for a group to survive. Such commitment, however, is not sufficient to ensure the group's ongoing viability. In this chapter, we will be looking at the development of any religious group from its beginning as a fledgling cult to its status as an established and stable religion. Ever since Max Weber first developed the proposition that new religious movements generally start out as cults headed by a charismatic leader, much of the sociological work in religion has evolved around the concept of charisma. Therefore, we shall begin by exploring that. But Weber insists that charisma is inherently unstable; if the group does not institutionalize, it will die shortly after the founder dies. Many cults never make the transition and therefore never develop into viable religious groups. Even if a group does institutionalize, the process of institutionalization is itself fraught with dilemmas, usually causing changes in the religious movement. A second process which affects survival involves mobilizing resources on behalf of the group and minimizing its potential opposition. For religious groups that pose a challenge to the structure of the existing society, this mobilization of resources is a major issue in their survival and success. Finally, a religious group will not survive for long unless the world view seems plausible (believable) to the members. Religious groups construct "plausibility structures" to make their view of the world seem uniquely realistic. Furthermore, certain types of religious beliefs tend to be self-validating to members, reinforcing plausibility. We shall explore these processes in the emergence of a religious group, indicating that the way in which resolution of these issues occurs determines whether a group will survive and in what form. In the following chapter we will examine various types of religious groups and will discuss the factors that sociologists look for in trying to understand any particular one.

Charisma and the Charismatic Leader

Max Weber was the first sociologist to write extensively on the importance of charismatic leadership. He maintained that new religions generally get their impetus from the attraction of a charismatic leader, a dynamic person who is perceived as extra-ordinary and set apart from the rest of humanity. Weber writes:

> The term "charisma" will be applied to a certain quality of an individual personality, by virtue of which (s)he is set apart from ordinary [people] and treated as endowed with supernatural, superhuman, or at least specifically exceptional powers or qualities. These are such as are not accessible to the ordinary person, but are regarded as of divine origin or as exemplary, and on the basis of them the individual concerned is treated as a leader (Weber 1947:358–359).

The charismatic leader is able to use this power to mobilize followers and to create within them a sense of mission.

Weber insists that charismatic leadership is not to be judged as intrinsically good or evil, for it could be either. The point is that some individuals come to be regarded as exceptional and perhaps even divine by followers or disciples. Although the followers do not necessarily experience the *mysterium tremendum* in quite the way it is described by Otto (see Chapter 4), they do become convinced that their charismatic leader is a direct agent of God, or perhaps God incarnate. Believers may feel a sense of mystery and awe in the presence of such a leader. The feelings of members of the Unification Church for the Reverend Moon provide one example. He is believed to be the new Christ, God incarnate. Whatever he says is believed to be true simply because he said it.[1]

Later writers, building upon Weber's concept, have elaborated the difference between charismatic and ideological leaders. Margrit Eichler (1972) suggests that the charismatic leader is the source of truth simply because he or she utters it. The ideological leader, on the other hand, is one whose leadership comes from an ability to articulate clearly or to interpret a particular belief system. Final authority rests outside the person, but the leader is the primary interpreter. This distinction is consistent with much of Weber's writing about charisma, although, at other times he uses the term *charisma* in a broader context and seems to accept many types of leadership as charismatic. Hereafter, we shall reserve the concept of charismatic leader for those whose authority resides in their very personhood or in their utterly unique relationship with the deity. What they say does not need to be legitimated or confirmed by some other source. What they say is viewed as truth itself.

One element of charismatic leadership that Weber thought to be especially important was its antiestablishment and revolutionary tendencies.[2] He be-

---

[1] This is a different sort of religious experience than Otto describes. Nonetheless, some elements of this phenomenon are quite similar to those described by Otto and by Durkheim (see Chapter 4). Although the absoluteness of power and unapproachability are not as pronounced as with the *mysterium tremendum* experience, the charismatic leader's authority is nonempirical, total, and unquestionable. The charismatic person offers the only source to truth or salvation, and in this sense has a good deal of power. Hence, the leader has a considerable amount of "personal space"; that is, he or she may be approached, but not too closely. A second important characteristic of the charismatic authority is that it is "specifically outside the realm of everyday routine." Like Durkheim's concept of the sacred, charisma is foreign to the profane world. The experience is based on something beyond the ordinary empirical world. Hence, we might identify this awe in the presence of a charismatic leader as an alternative form of nonrational religious experience.

[2] Peter Berger has shown that Weber's assumption was based in large part on the most recent biblical scholarship of his day. Current Old Testament scholarship, based on new evidence and different assumptions, points to the prophet or charismatic leader as a member of the establishment and not as an isolated individual. Although the prophet often was part of the establishment, he did challenge the status quo and in this sense was quite revolutionary. (Berger 1963.)

lieved that charismatic authority is intrinsically unstable and is antithetical to social order.

> Charismatic authority is specifically outside the realm of everyday routine and the profane sphere. In this respect, it is sharply opposed both to rational, and particularly bureaucratic, authority and to traditional authority. . . . Both rational and traditional authority are specifically forms of everyday routine control of action; while the charismatic type is the direct antithesis of this. Bureaucratic authority is specifically rational in the sense of being bound to intellectually analyzable rules, while charismatic authority is specifically irrational in the sense of being foreign to all rules. Traditional authority is bound to the precedents handed down from the past and to this extent is also oriented to rules. Within the sphere of its claims, charismatic authority repudiates the past and is in this sense a specifically revolutionary force (Weber 1947:361–362).

Weber was emphatic in asserting that the Old Testament prophets were not spokesmen for some economic group. Their interests were explicitly religious, although there were social and economic implications to their messages. Weber was interested in the power of ideas in bringing social change. More recent research has focused on why people attribute superhuman powers to others. This line of research has stressed the fact that adherence to a charismatic leader and the development of a charismatic cult is likely when certain social conditions prevail.

Social Processes in the Evolution of a Charismatic Group

Sociologists do not usually accept the theory that charismatic leaders are "Great Persons" who are able to bring change solely by the dynamism of their personalities. In its simplist form, the great person theory suggests that some individuals are so dynamic and magnetic that they could transform any culture. The current evidence suggests otherwise; certain conditions in the society may be conducive or nonconducive to the rise of a charismatic leader. Anthony Wallace has explored this issue and has identified a series of somewhat overlapping stages in the revitalization of a culture. His scenerio describes the process by which a charismatic leader comes to influence a culture—whether it be the entire culture or a particular subculture.

Wallace (1972) approaches the process of transformation as a crisis of meaning. He uses the term *mazeway* to refer to an individual's concept of nature, society, culture, personality, and body image and of the relationship between each of these. He is interested in the process by which a whole culture may change its mazeway, or what we have called its world view. Wallace points out that when one is under severe stress, one's world view provides explanations and specifies actions for the reduction of that stress. However, if one is under stress, particularly chronic stress, and the current cognitive orientation does not provide effective channels for its reduction, the person must choose between tolerating stress and changing his or her outlook on life. Wallace writes, "Changing the mazeway involves changing the total gestalt[3] of his image of self, society, and culture, of nature and body, and of ways of action" (1972:505). Wallace even goes so far as to insist that all organized religions are survivals from the mazeway reformulation that occurred at an earlier time of cultural crisis and individual stress.

The first phase in the development of a revitalization movement is a "steady state" period. At this point, the established cultural processes are able to meet most of the needs of the majority of the population. Varying levels of stress may be experienced by members of the society, but most stress is tolerable. In cases where it is not, deviant coping mechanisms (including psychosis) may be employed. Some cultural modification may occur, but at rates which are sufficiently gradual that social stability is not threatened.

During the second phase, larger numbers of individuals may begin to experience increased stress. Many types of factors may interfere with the effectiveness of the cultural system: political subordination, pressures to acculturate to a larger cultural matrix, military defeat, economic displacement, epidemics, and so on. While the individual may be able to tolerate some increased stress, eventually a level may be reached that demands a search for alternatives. The system of meaning which justifies social relationships is no longer adequate; cultural norms begin to weaken and explanations which are to help people cope with bafflement, suffering, and injustice no longer suffice.

When individuals begin to ignore cultural norms and to explore new behaviors and new ways to reduce stress, the culture may enter a period of distortion, the third phase. The culture begins to "wobble" as it experiences internal distortion: the elements of the culture are no longer related in a harmonious way.[4] This rise of anomie, or normlessness, is itself a source of further stress. As people become aware of the incongruities of the culture and the inadequacy of the current world view, they may experience disillusionment, apathy, and meaninglessness.

Other scholars have pointed out that revitalization movements may be induced by either anomie or by alienation. *Anomie* is the feeling of frustration that results when the rules of the game are unclear. It is frustration due to a lack of consistent cultural expectations. *Alienation* is the feeling of

---

[3] A gestalt is one's total view of things, including the interrelationships of specific aspects of life.

[4] Wallace's research was conducted in relatively simple homogeneous societies in which a single religion served to enhance cultural unity and provided the meaning system.

frustration that results when the rules are clear, but when one feels left out of the social matrix. The norms seem foreign and the institutions seem beyond one's control or one's meaningful participation. While anomie is normally a result of rapid cultural' change, alienation frequently occurs in rather stable societies. In short, persons may experience great stress and subcultural groups may endure substantial wobble due to either anomie or alienation. Disillusionment, apathy, and meaninglessness are results of both processes (Hargrove 1979: 283–290).

The fourth phase is the period of revitalization which contains six steps or substages: mazeway reformulation, communication, organization, adaptation, cultural transformation, and routinization. (See Exhibit 6–1.) First, one individual experiences some sort of abrupt and dramatic moment of insight which seems to offer an explanation of the "real" nature of the culture's problems. Wallace refers to this as *mazeway reformulation*. A sense of unity or wholeness is perceived by this individual, and is defined as a revelation or inspiration. Although other scholars seriously question his broad generalization, Wallace insists that the perceived unity is almost always based on the hallucinatory vision of a single individual. This person usually comes to be seen as a prophet who explains the cause of the cultural malaise (some form of immorality or violation of norms) and the solution (a set of prescriptions for moral and/or ritual behavior). This solution provides a new mazeway by which one's experiences in that society seem meaningful.

After the prophet has formulated a new mazeway, he or she *communicates* that world view by preaching and exhorting members of the society to repent and reform. As new converts are made, the beginnings of *organization* take shape. A small clique of special disciples provides the inner circle and the nucleus of the campaign for conversion. Hence, there comes to be a hierarchy of members: the prophet, the disciples, and the followers.

Exhibit 6–1 _____

The Emergence of a Revitalization Movement with a Charismatic Leader:
Wallace's Scenerio

1. Steady state
2. Period of increased stress
3. Period of cultural distortion (cultural wobble) as traditional meaning systems break down.
4. Period of revitalization
   a. Reformulation of the world view by an individual—inspired by a nonrational experience or "hallucinatory vision."
   b. Communication of the world view to others.
   c. An organization emerges.
   d. Adaption or modification of the world view for greater "fit" with existing cultural values.
   e. Cultural transformation—as large numbers of people accept this new meaning system.
   f. Routinization (or institutionalization) of the meaning system.
5. New steady state.

The leader is held to be charismatic in the sense that Weber used the term.

Many revitalization movements have a revolutionary—or at least antiestablishment—message. Insofar as a group does bear a message which is hostile to the status quo, it will experience resistance from significant portions of the society. To be widely accepted, the group must gain some measure of legitimacy. In order for this to happen, the original doctrine may be modified or *adapted* by the prophet. In response to criticisms and affirmations, various beliefs may be played down and eliminated or emphasized and elaborated. Hence, the original vision may be modified so that it has a better "fit" to the personality patterns and cultural assumptions of the population. If cultural conduciveness is not present at the outset, it may be achieved through continuing revelations of the leader. Those who have studied the Unification Church have commented on the modification of the Reverend Moon's original proclamation of Korea as the chosen land. Once in the United States, Moon recognized a central role for the United States. After all, not many Americans were likely to convert to a religion that glorified another country and assigned only secondary significance to their own country and ethnicity. Continual expansion of any religious movement may be dependent upon such adaptation of the world view.

As increasing numbers of people come to accept the new mazeway, or world view, a *transformation of attitudes and behavior* may take place in the entire culture or in a significant subculture. The movement may then come to be *routinized* or institutionalized, and a new steady state established.[5]

A number of other scholars have discussed the influence of charismatic leaders and how they come to be viewed as extra-ordinary. Many social psychologists have pointed out that people who are experiencing some sort of stress or anomie are likely to attribute extra-ordinary powers to someone who offers hope. Attribution is somewhat like projection as a psychological process: other people are perceived to have particular qualities because the viewer wants to see those qualities in the person. Hence, social circumstances are very important in the development of a charismatic movement. If the charismatic leader were in a social climate that did not have intense cultural strains, he or she would likely be viewed as an ordinary citizen or possibly as mentally deranged.

Nonetheless, once the charismatic leader has emerged and developed a following, it is necessary for the group to undergo a transformation. Charismatic leadership is not only revolutionary, it is inherently unstable. Hence, the movement undergoes a process which Weber referred to as the "routinization of charisma."

---

[5] Wallace was describing this process as a cultural transformation of an entire nonindustrialized society. However, revitalization movements are certainly not limited to homogeneous and relatively simple societies. Hargrove (1979:284ff) treats fundamentalism as a nativistic or revitalization movement in modern America.

The Routinization of Charisma

If the religious movement is to survive for any significant period of time, a stable set of roles and statuses must be established and a consistent pattern of norms generated and adhered to. Hence, the nature of the charismatic authority is transformed.

> In its pure form charismatic authority has a character specifically foreign to everyday routine structures. If this [religious movement] is not to remain a purely transitory phenomenon, but to take on the character of a permanent relationship . . . it is necessary for the character of charismatic authority to become radically changed. Indeed, in its pure form charismatic authority may be said to exist only in the process of originating. (Weber 1947:363–364).

The community gathered around a dynamic leader must evolve into one with a stable matrix of norms, roles, and statuses. This process of routinization (developing stable routines) is commonly referred to by sociologists as institutionalization. Any group which fails to institutionalize its collective life simply will not survive.

Institutionalization serves both ideal and material interests of followers and leaders. The *ideals* of the group can be furthered only if it survives and only if it mobilizes its resources. Hence, institutionalization serves the ideological interests of adherents. But the followers and the leaders also have a *material* stake in the survival of the group. Insofar as they have invested time, energy, and financial resources in the group, they are likely to feel that they have a vested material interest in its survival and success. Therefore, the inherent forces working for routinization are strong.

Perhaps the most critical test of a group's routinization is the way it handles the issue of succession. When the charismatic leader dies, the group may quickly disperse. However, many people have a vested interest in the survival of the group and will seek to ensure its viability. But who will provide the group with leadership? And how will that decision be made?

The transfer of power to the next designated leader has important implications for the subsequent evolution of the group. First, the charisma which was once identified with a personality must be associated with the religious ideology and with the religious organization. The group, the body of beliefs, and perhaps a written record (a scripture) become sources of veneration. This more stable source of authority in itself changes the character of the group. Second, a decision-making process must be sacralized as the divinely appointed method of choosing the successor. This method may involve the designation of a successor by the original leader, some form of divinely sanctioned and controlled election, the drawing of lots, a hereditary succession, or any one of a number of other procedures. In any event, the followers must recognize the new leader or leaders as the legitimate heir(s) to leadership. Otherwise, the group may be torn by schisms as various splinter groups identify different persons as the rightful leader.

The new leader or group of leaders is not likely to possess the same sort of unquestioned authority that was vested in the personhood of the original leader. Some of the awe and respect will have been transferred to the teachings and to the continuing organization itself. The rules and values of the group must be attributed with transcendent importance in and of themselves. Commitment is now to the organization and to the ideology of the movement, and the authority of the new leader(s) may be restrained by these stabilizing forces. No longer are the sayings of the leader taken as true simply because that person said them. They must be evaluated in light of what the original leader said and did.

Another issue of routinization has to do with provision of a stable economic base. If some members are to devote full time to the service of the leader and the movement, then a continuing and consistent source of income must be provided. This may come from some obligatory payment to the organization by members who are employed in secular positions (a tithe), from members begging or soliciting (as done by Hare Krishna and Moonies), or from the establishment of some industry sponsored by the organization (as in the Bruderhof production of Community Playthings or, in the mid-19th century, Oneida's production of steel traps). However accomplished, this provision of a stable source of income is a critical part of the routinization process. Without this financial base, there can be no full-time clergy, administrative staff, or other regular employees. If there are no career opportunities within the organizational structure, instrumental commitment may begin to wane. Furthermore, some type of full-time administrative staff may be necessary if the group is growing and expects to continue expanding.

Sometimes routinization is a slow process which occurs largely after the death of the leader. After the death of Jesus, his disciples were a band of frightened and discouraged individuals. Through a series of experiences they became convinced that Jesus had risen from the dead and their faith was renewed. However, it was the new convert, Paul (previously known as Saul of Tarsus), who was responsible for the expansion of the group, for he universalized the faith and recruited Gentiles on an equal basis with Jews. Paul also established organizational links between the various congregations. He collected money from his Gentile converts which was given to the parent organization in Jerusalem, and he traveled from one congregation to another forging a bond between them and creating a loyalty to himself. In fact, the parent group often sought to undermine his authority, and Paul constantly had to work at maintaining his position of leadership. (By most accounts, Peter and James, leaders of the Jerusalem church, were not adept at organizational matters. However, in the early period they felt that Paul was wrong to allow Jew and Gentile converts to eat together and to be treated as equals.)

Paul established norms and expectations which were spelled out in his teachings and in his epistles. He often "corrected" local congregations because they had begun to follow norms that had emerged spontaneously out of the group. He assumed authority and was sought out as the person to resolve conflicts and to define customs and mores (e.g., whether women could worship without a head covering, and what format the love feasts should follow). He also authorized teachers at various churches. In fact, in his later epistles he even referred to bishops and deacons. These officials appear to have been local ones at the time, but eventually the roles expanded to be more centralized with broad supervisory functions. The routinization process was by no means complete by the time of Paul's death, but it was well underway. It is clear that Paul was the organizational genius who initiated the institutionalization process; it was his organizational initiative that eventually resulted in that bastion of European religious life, the Roman Catholic Church.

So in some cases, a later organizer initiates institutionalization of the faith after the death of the charismatic founder. In other cases, the charismatic leader also happens to be an excellent organizer (the Reverend Moon seems to be both charismatic leader and primary organizer of the Unification Church). In any event, the routinizing function must be performed.

Perhaps the most important test of the routinization of charisma is that of determining leadership succession. However, normalization of roles and statuses, establishment of relatively stable norms, and provision of a stable economic base usually have to be addressed long before succession becomes an issue. If routinization does not occur, the viability of the group for any substantive period after the death of the original leader is unlikely.

Weber did not believe that charismatic leadership was limited to religious groups. For example, many political movements are initiated and guided by charismatic figures. However, Weber did imply that virtually all religious cults are formed around charismatic leaders. Weston LaBarre (1972) has insisted even more strongly that *all* religions begin as charismatic cults. Scholars are not in agreement on this.[6]

---

[6] This will be discussed further in Chapter 7. For an analysis by two scholars who do not think a charismatic leader is necessary, see Bainbridge and Stark (1979). They believe that a cult can gradually emerge as a process of subcultural evolution. Individuals may gradually create a "deviant" subculture through group interaction processes and may "mutually convert" each other to the group's world view through a series of many small steps. They also insist that a sect which is faced with hostility may gradually emerge into a cult. The problem with the Stark and Bainbridge proposal for our uses is that many of the "cults" they studied were not religious, including most of those which were created by subcultural evolution. Since we have defined the cult as a fledgling organizational stage of a new religion, most of the spontaneously created groups which they describe would not be considered cults by our defini-

It does seem safe to say at this point that most religious groups that seek to establish a new religion (as opposed to a new denomination of an existing religion) are founded by charismatic leaders. (Such groups are called *cults*). In *sectarian* movements (religious groups which seek to reform or renew the traditional religion) a charismatic leader is not a prerequisite. Sectarian movements may take place without members becoming utterly dependent on the authority and inspiration of one person. For example, scriptural literalism may be the basis of a religious reform movement. One person may be the primary interpreter of scripture, but what the individual says is not considered true simply because he or she said it. This is an example of an ideological leader as opposed to a charismatic one (Eichler 1972).[7] Regardless, if a new group is to prosper and survive, it must undergo a process of institutionalization. Its extent and form will vary from group to group, but some routinization must take place. But institutionalization itself creates new problems or dilemmas.

Dilemmas of Institutionalization

As Thomas O'Dea puts it, "religion both needs most and suffers most from institutionalization" (1961:32). While institutionalization is necessary, it tends to change the character of the movement and to create certain dilemmas that all routinized religions face.

The Dilemma of Mixed Motivation

When the enthusiastic band of disciples is gathered around the charismatic leader, there is a single-minded and unqualified devotion to the leader and to his or her teachings. The followers are willing to make great sacrifices to further the cause, and they willingly subordinate their own needs and desires for the sake of group goals. However, with the development of a stable institutional structure, the desire to occupy the more creative, responsible, and prestigious positions can stimulate jealousies and personality conflicts. Concerns about personal security within the organization may cause members to lose sight of the group's primary goals. Mixed motivation occurs when a secondary concern or motivation comes to overshadow the original goals and teachings of the leader. Conventions of clergy sometimes debate

---

tion. If subcultural evolution—without a charismatic leader—is possible for a cult, it is a rare phenomenon. Certainly the sect-to-cult movement can be documented, but the only sects which undergo this transformation seem to be those which have charismatic leaders.

[7] For an example of a sectarian group with an ideological leader (rather than a charismatic one) see discussions by Arnold and Arnold (1974) and Zablocki (1971) on the Bruderhof. The Bruderhof is a Christian communal society with settlements in New York, Pennsylvania, Connecticut, and several places in Europe.

pension plans and insurance programs more heatedly than statements of mission (O'Dea 1961:33).

It is important to recognize the dilemma in this process. Religious institutions do need to provide for the economic security and well-being of their full-time professionals if they expect them to maintain high morale and commitment. Likewise, if those professionals are to be satisfied and fulfilled by their work, they need to feel that they can really utilize their creative talents and abilities. These secondary concerns are important to the individuals in question. The problem for the organization is that these secondary matters can take on primary importance for some members and subvert the original sense of mission.

Such secondary concerns may come to the surface while the charismatic leader is still alive. For example, at the time of the Last Supper, Jesus's disciples got into an argument over who was the most important and who would have the most exalted position in the Kingdom of God (Matthew 18:1; Mark 10:37). However, such self-oriented motivations can be rather easily overcome by a simple command of the charismatic personality. Mixed motivation is more likely to develop when the group's sense of security is institutionally based rather than charismatically based. Later generations are much more likely to belong to the group for reasons unrelated to the teachings of the charismatic leader.

In the 1960s one American inner-city congregation voted to spend tens of thousands of dollars to air-condition the sanctuary and sandblast the building's facade. The church was located on the edge of a black ghetto where poverty, unemployment, and inadequate health care were rampant. The congregation chose to use its resources to make the sanctuary more comfortable when it was very hot (on four or five Sundays per year) and to beautify the building so that it could be "a symbol of prestige and grandeur in the community." Prestige and personal comfort would seem to be a wide mark from the unselfish sacrifice and service called for by the founder of Christianity: "the least of you shall be the greatest." In this congregation, where social status became a primary goal in church decisions, mixed motivation would seem to have taken its most extreme form.

The Symbolic Dilemma: Objectification versus Alienation

In Chapter 4 we explored the importance of symbols in religion. In order for a community to worship together, a common set of symbols must be generated which meaningfully express the world view and the ethos of the group. However, this process of projecting subjective feelings on to objective artifacts or behaviors can proceed to the point that the symbols no longer have power for the members. As O'Dea puts it, "Symbolic and ritual elements may become cut off from the subjective experience of the participants. A system of religious liturgy may come to lose its resonance with the interior dispositions of the members. . . . In such a case the forms of worship become alienated from personal religiosity" (O'Dea 1961:34).

We have already explored the fact that variant interpretations of a symbol in a religious community can have devisive effects (Chapter 4). But according to O'Dea, symbols may also become utterly meaningless to members of the religious community. Many Christian churches have stained glass windows which depict a fish. This was a powerful symbol to the early Christians. In Greek, the first letters of each word in the phrase, "Jesus Christ, Son of God, Savior" spelled the word *fish*. The fish came to be used as a coded symbol of insiders: a drawing of a fish identified one as a Christian to other believers without giving one's Christian identity away to Roman soldiers. Hence, a representation of a fish became an important symbol of solidarity and conviction for Christians, a highly persecuted group. Most modern-day worshipers do not know the origins of the fish as a symbol of faithfulness, and the symbol does not enhance the worship experience. In this case, the symbol is treated with indifference rather than with hostility. In any event, the fish is no longer a powerful symbol which acts to solidify the group, create powerful moods and motivations, and reinforce the world view.

At the Last Supper, Jesus gave his disciples a cup and told them that it represented the "new covenant." He asked each to drink from the cup. A short time before this he had told the disciples that they could not drink the "cup" from which he must drink, and a few hours after the supper he prayed, "Take this cup from me." In each case, the concept of drinking from a cup had a symbolic reference to accepting an obligation or responsibility.

At that Last Supper, the act of drinking from a common cup may have been as powerful a symbol to the disciples as its contents. The ritual was substantially an act of commitment. Since sharing a common cup is not a symbol of a contract or covenant in our society, much of the original symbolism is missing for the average Christian. The communion service is still a powerful ritual enactment for most Christians, but at least part of its symbolic meaning may have changed over the centuries. Many churches focus exclusively on what is in the cup, and few congregations share a single chalice.

In other cases, the symbols may come to be seen by some as a barrier to communication with the transcendent. The antisymbolism of the Puritans, who rejected stained glass windows and identified Roman Catholic stations of the cross as "idols," provides an example. In the minds of these people the visual symbols had come to symbolize an overbearing bureaucratic organization rather than a transcendent experience. Such alienation from established forms, symbols, and rituals can lead to either apathy toward religion or radical revolt and reformation of the faith.

The process of developing objective, observable symbols which express a deeper subjective experience is part of the process of institutionalization. Symbols are necessary to bind a group together and to remind them of a common faith, but that very objectification of experience into symbols may eventually create problems. If the symbols lose their power and meaning for members, the group must either create new symbols or it will face internal problems of meaning and belonging.

The Dilemma of Administrative Order: Elaboration of Policy versus Flexibility

As a religious group grows and enters the process of institutionalization, it may develop national offices and a bureaucratic structure. In so doing, a set of rational policies and regulations may be established to clarify the relationships between various statuses and offices in the organization. Like the federal government or any other bureaucratic structure, these rules and regulations and the plethora of interrelated departments and divisions may create an unwieldy and overcomplicated structure. Ecclesiastical hierarchies are no less susceptible to red tape than any other bureaucratic structure. And as O'Dea points out, attempts to modify or reform the structure may run into severe resistance by those whose status and security in the hierarchy may be threatened. Resolution of the dilemma of administrative order may be impeded by the existence of mixed motivation. Many persons within the hierarchy may view reorganization as a threat to their own security or positions of power and prestige.

Again, the dilemma must be recognized as such. Students sometimes see unwieldy organizational complexity and excessive rules and regulations as silly and unnecessary. However, people in complex organizations frequently feel a profound need for guidelines for decision making. The search for concrete policy in the face of some new problem is common in any large, formal organization. If no policy has been clearly established, people look to the resolution of similar cases in the past. The precedent often then becomes an unwritten rule. The development of elaborate and sometimes overly complex policy is a natural outgrowth of the desire of people to know how to solve problems and deal with unusual cases. People at lower levels in the organization do not feel comfortable making decisions without the sanction of those with more authority, or without consensus in the group. Yet, this felt need for clearly articulated policy can mean that an organization is run entirely by rigid rules and regulations. Not only is this uncomfortable and frustrating, but it greatly reduces flexibility.

A group of clergy appointed to a committee to screen candidates for ordination and ministry do not feel authorized to establish their own standards for ordination. They want to know what guidelines have been set by the denomination as a whole. If none are available they would likely seek to have some guidelines formally approved to help them make decisions. (In the absence of formally approved policy, their own decisions may take on the authority of official policy.) The guidelines which are adopted may specify a college degree and a seminary education from an accredited university and theological school respectively. However, years later an ordination screening committee may encounter a case in which an individual brings impressive experiential credentials and enthusiastic letters of reference, but holds degrees from nonaccredited institutions. Does the committee have the authority to wave the national guidelines in this case? Whatever the members decide, their decision may be seen as a binding precedent for future cases. Policy continues to be elaborated, but it may also restrict a group in its ability to be flexible with new circumstances.

John Fry (1975) believes that the United Presbyterian Church, USA has recently been caught in this dilemma of administrative order. In the late 1960s, the United Presbyterians, USA modified the organizational structure of the denomination. One goal was to create greater participation in building the budget of the church and in setting priorities; a parallel concern was to establish increased accountability for the use of church funds. The budget process which was set up put the national office for planning, budgeting, and evaluation in a facilitative role and removed its power to set policy directions. The procedure for building a budget, which was spelled out in the church governance document, called for an elaborate process of collaboration and negotiation between national, regional, and district offices (general assembly, synods, and presbyteries). Once the budget was set in place, national offices were given diminished room for flexibility, for they no longer were granted as much authority to determine priorities and respond to emergencies as once was the case. This procedure reduced the likelihood that a board in the church hierarchy would allocate funds to radical groups or individuals who seek social change (as the Council on Church and Race did for the legal defense of Angela Davis, a black militant involved in a highly publicized trial in the early 1970s.[8]) But the policy also hampered the ability of the church leaders to offer aggressive leadership and to tackle important (and controversial) issues. Fry believes the church has been "trivialized," that the elaborated policy has tied the hands of the church and left it with only bland, marginally important issues to address as its social outreach. He is convinced that the church's sense of mission

[8] A member of the Communist Party in the United States, Angela Davis had been controversial as a professor at UCLA. In 1970, an effort to free two black prisoners and a black defendant resulted in a shoot-out in the Marin County, California Courthouse, and the weapons used were found to be registered in Angela Davis' name. She was charged with kidnapping, conspiracy, and murder. She insisted that she was innocent, and her defenders believed that she could not get a fair trial in the political atmosphere of Marin County. Her black militance and her Communist Party affiliation had become as important in the pretrial publicity as her guilt or innocence. Eventually, she was acquitted of all charges.

has been retarded due to an unwieldy bureaucratic process for building budgets and an excessive concern for concensus and harmony within the church. In this case, Fry thinks that the balance between accountability and flexibility has shifted so far in one direction (accountability) that a dilemma has turned into an outright dysfunction.

The Dilemma of Delimitation: Concrete Definition versus Substitution of the Letter for the Spirit

In the process of routinization, the religious message is translated into specific guidelines of behavior for everyday life. The general teachings about the unity of the universe or about the love of God must be translated into concrete rules of ethical behavior. If this is not done, the religious belief system may remain at such an abstract level that the ordinary person does not grasp its meaning or its import for everyday living. The meaning of many of Jesus's teachings were not understood even by his disciples until he gave specific illustrations or elaborated through parables. In the ancient Hebrew tradition, the covenant which Abraham had made with God was comforting, but in order to understand the human obligations in it, specific ethical codes were spelled out. The Torah, the first five books of the Hebrew Bible (the Christian Old Testament) is a record of this religious law.

However, in the process of translating the outlook of the faith into specific rules, something may be lost. Eventually, the members may focus so intently upon the rules that they lose sight of the original spirit or outlook of the faith. The religion may then degenerate into legalistic formulae for salvation and/or may become moralistic and judgmental in a way inconsistent with the original intent of the founder (O'Dea 1961:36). The legalism and ritualism of the late classical period of pharisaic Judaism provides one example. The fundamentalistic and rule-bound interpretations of Islam by the leading ayatollas of Iran provide another example; their posture is clearly inconsistent with the central thrust of Islam. The woodcut print by Robert Hodgell (Exhibit 6–2) illustrates his view of some segments of Protestantism in the United States. It expresses more eloquently than words the problem created when the letter of the religious ethical code becomes more important than the spirit of that code.

Hence, the dilemma is created: the abstract moods, motivations, and concepts must be made concrete so that common lay people can comprehend their meaning and implication for everyday life. However, by translating the spirit of the faith into specific moral rules and ritual requirements, the possibility is established that later generations may become literalistic and legalistic about those rules and may miss the central message.

Exhibit 6–2 _____

Substitution of the Letter for the Spirit
The Fundamentalist: Linocut Original by Robert O. Hodgell

Used by permission of R. O. Hodgell.

The Dilemma of Power: Conversion versus Coercion

If a religious group is to stay together and sustain its common faith, conformity to the values and norms of the group must be ensured. While occasional deviation from established norms may not threaten the group, most of the beliefs, values, and norms of the faith must be adhered to most of the time. In its early stages, the religious group is comprised of members who have personally converted to the group. They feel a personal loyalty to the charismatic leader, or they have had a nonrational conversion experience, or they have been motivated to internalize the faith through some other process. But later generations, who have grown up within the religious organization, may never have personally experienced anything that compelled them to accept the absolute authority of the faith in their own lives—or the authority of the religious hierarchy to interpret the faith. They may be inclined to challenge official interpretations. While such challenges can also come in the first generation, internalization of the authority structure is usually more complete in the first generation of believers than in later ones (O'Dea 1961:37).

In order to maintain the integrity of the organization and ensure consensus in their basic world view, religious organizations may resort to coercive methods of social control. Excommunication is one procedure. When Sonia Johnson, a Mormon, took a public stand in 1979 in favor of the Equal Rights Amendment, the Mormon hierarchy informed her that her stance was heretical. When she refused voluntarily to accept the position of the church and the authority of its leaders, she was excommunicated. Likewise, other religious bodies have excommunicated members who fail to conform to basic doctrinal or ritual standards. Of course, in some periods of history the unorthodox were subject to torture and death. Regardless of the specific methods used, the maintenance of conformity through coercion rather than conversion is significant. Conformity due to internalization of norms is much more powerful and lasting than the use of coercion, but *voluntary* internalization of the norms by *all* members is difficult to sustain. Therefore, an institutionalized religious organization may come to rely on coercive methods as a last resort to maintain conformity and consensus.

The Dilemma of Expansion: Rationalized Structure versus Communalism

In the early phases of development, much of the members' sense of commitment comes from the sense of belonging and the feeling of community. As we found in our chapter on conversion and commitment, a sense of belonging is a critical element in the commitment of members of new religious cults. But membership growth is also important; if the group fails to grow and expand its influence, the members' morale may waiver and the sense of mission and destiny may fade. As the group does grow, it will soon reach the point when the members do not all know each other, and it becomes necessary to develop rational structures and procedures for decision making. Hence, the process of institutionalization may undermine the sense of communalism (belonging). Affective commitment must then be reinforced by instrumental and moral commitment. (Discussed in

Chapter 5.) In fact, instrumental commitment may become primary, although it is based—consciously or unconsciously—on a cost/benefit analysis. Instrumental commitment heightens a person's sense of loyalty based on advantages accrued to the individual. This would seem to play into the dilemma of mixed motivation in a very direct way. When the individual's commitment hinges in large part on the question, "What's in it for me?" the problem of mixed motivation has become a reality.

Most religious groups establish local congregations which are relatively stable and which fulfill much of the need for affective commitment. However, Bromley and Shupe (1979:253) found this rational structure versus communalism dilemma to be one of the most significant facing the Unification Church in the mid-1970s. The original sense of communalism was being lost in the process of bureaucratization. The development of a rational structure was mandatory for the coordination of this large and growing organization. But as this happened, the close interpersonal caring and sharing that had attracted many persons into membership was beginning to wane. By creating permanent vocational opportunities within the organizational structure, Moon was able to reinforce the possibilities of instrumental commitment. People could develop their careers as expressions of commitment to the group. Moon also performed mass weddings, sometimes with hundreds of people married at one ceremony and to partners designated by Moon himself. This ensured endogamous marriages. It also meant that leaving the group would involve separation from one's spouse and (eventually) from one's children. In this way, Moon made the marriage bond a form of affective commitment to the group. (Bromley and Shupe 1979:191). As this illustrates, it is possible to find alternative ways of generating the affective type of commitment. But the fact remains that when an organization expands to the point that a bureaucratic structure is needed, the affective commitment mechanisms will have to be transformed to account for the loss of communalism.

The fact that a group's growth means that members can no longer know all other members in itself means a change in the group's character. Growth also means that eventually the group must develop task specialization. As this happens, the common member does not know what is happening in all areas of the organization. Some individuals or special groups gain almost autonomous control over their own area or department, and they may use that platform to influence policies, budget allocations, and goals of the entire organization. As Ronald Johnstone (1975:110) puts it, "a bureaucracy, once formed, tends to take on a life of its own, initiates and implements policy partly of its own making, and may begin to direct the larger organization of which it is a specialized part in new directions." Frequently, most lay members do not know who the leaders of their denominational church divisions are and are not even fully aware of policy decisions their church hierarchy makes. Nonetheless, those policies are implemented with the aid of donations by local churches. While common members provide the financial support, an elite group of people, unknown to most of the laity, decide how to spend it. This can be the basis of internal organizational conflict, especially if the elite supports causes that the laity oppose (civil rights, women's liberation, or liberationist movements in the Third World).

Institutionalization as a Mixed Blessing

The process of institutionalization is a mixed blessing (or perhaps a necessary curse) for religion. If a new cult does not institutionalize, it is not likely to last long. The absence of routinization will mean that the group will expire with the death of the charismatic leader. The particular pattern of routinization will vary from group to group, and some organizations become more bureaucratic and centralized than others. For example, some religious bodies have successfully routinized without establishing a professional clergy, while others have highly trained professionals as ministers and a hierarchy of area ministers, bishops, and archbishops. The student of religious organizations will find considerable variation in the extent and style of institutionalization, but some form of routinization is essential.

Of course, there are other reasons why religious bodies develop increasingly complex institutional structures which are decreasingly responsive to local congregations. One reason is that such institutional expansion and organizational alliances are necessary if a group is to reach some of its goals. A single congregation may not be able to afford to sponsor a mission hospital in an impoverished country, so it joins with other churches in the denomination. But in creating such collaboration, the local congregation relinquishes its right to determine how the money will be spent. Such policies are made at another level: the denomination's board of discipleship or board of missions. Or a group of local congregations from several denominations may unite to establish a low-income housing unit for the poor or the elderly, or may cosponsor an alcohol treatment center or a family counseling center for the community. Again, a board of directors is established to determine policy, and the local congregation loses some of its autonomy and control over its resources.

Other forces for ecumenical cooperation may strike even closer to home. For example, several denominations may develop a joint board for producing Sunday School materials. Such a cooperative venture reduces the cost for each of the denominations and allows them to hire highly trained specialists in religious education to design the curricula. In so doing, each denomination may get much higher quality materials than it would if each congregation or each denomination tried to create its own. However, it does mean that the local congregation reliquishes some control over the content (Johnstone 1975, 109). The board which directs policy is now interdenominational. These examples may help to illustrate the fact that bureaucratization often helps groups achieve positive goals. Hence, religious groups are not just pushed into institutionalization for survival's sake. They are also "pulled" (attracted) into it in order to accomplish greater things.

Despite the necessity of institutionalization, certain changes in the character of the group occur in the process. Changes in motivation for membership, alienation from the symbol systems, development of unwieldly bureaucratic structure in the organization, substitution of moralistic legal codes for the spirit of the original teachings, employment of coercion to ensure conformity and consensus within the group, and loss of a sense of communalism are some of the problems institutionalization generates. Avoiding these problems by avoiding institutionalization is simply not at option; rather, renewal movements, revivals, and other processes of regeneration are the means by which religious groups seek to overcome these dysfunctions. As we shall see in the next chapter, the rebellion against routinization is one reason for the development of new sects. Much of the internal conflict and many of the schisms in denominations are due to the need for regeneration and a need to restate the faith in terms that are compelling to a new generation facing different problems of social meaning.

Even if a group goes through the process of institutionalization, it may face opposition from other groups and institutions in the society. Routinization is necessary, but not sufficient, to ensure survival. We turn next to an analysis of resource mobilization.

Mobilization of Resources and the Viability of Religious Movements

The "resource mobilization perspective" is emerging in the sociology of religion.[9] Proponents of this perspective insist that viability is much more complex than a simple matter of institutionalization. They suggest that the type of world view the group holds combines with organizational and environmental factors in determining its success or failure. Unlike Kanter, Lofland, Downton, and others who maintain that viability depends primarily on the ability of the group to elicit commitment, resource mobilization theorists emphasize appropriate types of organization and adaptation for specific types of religious movements (Bromley and Shupe 1979:19–24).

The resource mobilization perspective maintains that the ability of any group to achieve its goals is limited by the self-interests of other groups and by other change-resistant forces. Hence, success can be realized only if the group is able to mobilize or activate resources in its own behalf.

---

[9] Resource mobilization theory was actually developed by Mayer Zald and his associates. For a discussion of the resource mobilization perspective, see Zald and Ash (1966); McCarthy and Zald (1977); and Zald and Berger (1978). Bromley and Shupe will be discussed here because they have applied this perspective to religious organizations.

Such resources include financial support, political clout, favorable public attitudes (legitimacy), and the time and energy of members. The resource mobilization perspective, then, stresses the interactive process between the religious group and the larger society. Decisions regarding internal organization, methods of recruitment, and formulation of doctrine are often profoundly affected by societal response. The form and character of any religious group is a product of this interaction and is not solely a result of a sect's internal dynamics.

The problems of resource mobilization vary significantly for different types of groups, and one way of identifying these is to focus on the extent and level of change they seek to implement (Aberle 1966:315–333). Extent of change refers simply to the totality or partiality of change; level of change has to do with change being personal or societal in nature. The *transformative* group seeks total change of the entire social structure. Moderate reforms are considered insufficient; a complete overhaul of all aspects of society and culture is mandated. Bromley and Shupe emphasize the totalistic nature of the expected change by referring to such groups as world-transforming movements. The Unification movement is an excellent example.

The second type of group is the *reformative* group. This seeks partial change in the social structure. Change in individuals is considered insufficient; the society itself must be reformed. On the other hand, the extant society and culture are not viewed as utterly depraved. They simply need modification and fine tuning. The third type of group has a *redemptive* focus; it seeks total change in the individual. Changes in the organization of society are seen as secondary to personal conversion. In some cases, societal changes may even be considered utterly insignificant. The emphasis is on change of heart and mind: the remolding of personality. Groups which stress *alternative* change are interested only in partial change in the individual. Some religious movements stress faith healing or place the emphasis on personal devotion and piety. The convert is to change his or her world view and behavior relative to one particular aspect of life, but change in political or economic views or in one's interpersonal relationships is considered unnecessary.

Most groups do not focus exclusively on individual or structural change. Frequently, a change at one level is seen as the precursor to change at another. Nevertheless, a primary emphasis on change at one level or the other is usually discernible.

The problems of resource mobilization for each of these types of groups are somewhat different. Those which have only minor impact on the loyalties and resources of individuals and which do not call for radical changes in the social order are much less likely to threaten the interests of others in society. Because of this, they are also less likely to meet with hostility and the stigmatizing labels of outsiders. As we found in Chapter 5, groups which have not been stigmatized normally do not require isolation of members from nonmembers[10] (Snow and Phillips 1980). Isolation of members from family ties can be a major cause of hostility toward new religious groups, and avoidance of this strategy can mean circumvention of a vicious cycle of stigmatization and defensive responses.

Furthermore, if no stigma is attached to the group and no hostility directed toward it, the group may be able to work cooperatively with conventional units of society, gain access to resources through many different persons in the society, and therefore not need to demand the total resources of its members. Since mobilization of resources by such groups is met with much less organized resistance, survival rates are somewhat higher. (In fact, the major problem of resource mobilization may be simply one of stimulating enough commitment so that members do not become apathetic and withdraw their support. Conflict from outsiders does function effectively to strengthen in-group loyalty.)

The Church of Christ, Scientist, which was begun in the 1860s, provides an example of a nonrevolutionary group which coexisted rather harmoniously with other social institutions. Mary Baker Eddy, the founder of the church, interpreted the central teachings of Christianity as guidelines for mental, physical, and spiritual health. She believed that disease, sin, and death are caused by mental error and can be overcome by right thinking. The world view was highly otherworldly and very individualistic. Her teachings did not threaten the social order. Rather they called for changes in individuals. Furthermore, these changes did not require a radical break from one's family or from other nonmembers. The Christian Scientists received minimal stigmatization or hostility from outsiders (compared to world-transforming groups like the Moonies of our own day). In fact, their membership was and is comprised largely of rather affluent and well-established people. Mobilization of financial resources has never been as severe a problem for the Christian Scientists as it has been for groups like the Hare Krishna (which demands total commitment) or the flying saucer cult (which has an idiosyncratic message).

Transformative or world-transforming groups are likely to experience great resistance from other institutions and from persons who have a vested interest in the status quo. Such groups demand not only total commitment of individuals, but threaten the entire social structure with radical change. This may earn the group the label of "subversive." Reformative groups (which seek partial change of the social structure) will also encounter opposition from institutions and persons with vested interests, but the opposition is not likely to be as intense or as widespread. Redemptive groups (which seek total change of individuals) will receive most of their opposition from

---

[10] However, groups which are highly *particularistic* (feel that salvation and truth can be attained only through membership in their own group) may weaken ties to nonmembers, regardless of whether their belief system is revolutionary or not.

individuals (especially family members) who have affective ties to the devo-tees. Since individuals have less power to apply against a group than does an institution, resource mobilization will be somewhat less problematic for redemptive groups than for transformative and reformative ones. Of course, if family members are sympathetic to the group or are themselves recruited, there may be little opposition to redemptive groups even from family mem-bers. Groups which stress alternative change (partial change of individuals) normally face the least amount of opposition from institutions or from indi-viduals with affective ties to members.

The internal development of a religious group is therefore influenced by the type of change the charismatic leader espouses and by the response of the larger society to the movement. Since the world-transforming or transformative group is likely to experience the most severe conflicts with the larger society and to have the most problems with gaining legitimacy, it is appropriate to focus our attention on the resource mobilization problems in this type of group.[11] Bromley and Shupe have developed their theory specifically on the basis of their research on the Unification Church. The Moonies believe that the world as we know it is soon to end, and that the new era will be structured under a world government apparently headed by the messiah, the Reverend Moon. This new government will be a form of theocracy (government by God or by the agents of God—the clergy). Clearly, the world is to undergo a radical political reformation.

Bromley and Shupe (1979:25) point out that any group must choose a strategy for change from three possibilities: coersion, bargaining, or persua-sion. The use of coercion by a world-transforming group is appropriate only if the group has access to substantial political or military resources. Otherwise, the group will be quickly crushed by defenders of the status quo. The bargaining strategy involves use of existing resources to exchange with outsiders so that outsiders are manipulated into the desired changes. Such a strategy is possible for reformative movements which may use their buying power or political influence to further their cause. However, this strategy involves compromise and reciprocity. The world view and goals of the world-transforming group will usually not allow such compromise and cooperation with the existing structures. For a relatively small and powerless group which hopes to transform the world, persuasion is the only viable strategy available. Hence, all of its resources must be mobilized to persuade people that the changes the group advocates are in the best interests of everyone.

The resources that the group has available are quite diverse. The first is a compelling ideology. The ideology of the world-transforming movement

---

[11] Resource mobilization theory has also been applied to world-transforming groups more than it has to others. Hence, there is more information available using this theory to understand transformative groups than there is on other types of groups.

is characterized by its forecast of total, imminent, and cataclysmic change in the structure of society. Those who are prepared and help in this transformation will be exalted in the new era, and those who do not heed the message will be doomed to some horrible fate. The new era is envisioned as manifesting values and priorities which are very much in contrast with the depraved values of the current social order. The role of devotees in the new era is usually clearly defined by the ideology; understandably, the devotees are expected to have positions of power and prestige. Such an ideology can motivate members through its promise of awesome rewards and/or punishments. Furthermore, the day of transformation is viewed as so imminent that little time is left for preparation. This outlook can be a powerful spur to the mobilization of the personal resources (time, energy, money) of believers.[12]

Bromley and Shupe maintain that the leadership of world-transforming movements is characteristically charismatic. Since the source of authority is vested in the person of the leader, the entire structure of the organization tends to be pyramidal, from the leader and disciples down. This allows tremendous centralization of the decision-making process and enhances the implementation of those decisions. Moreover, the unique authority of the leader even justifies control over the daily lives and personal concerns of members.

In terms of organization, the world-transforming movement usually has strong communal tendencies. This sense of familial bond and close affective ties enhances commitment. However, as the organization grows, a bureaucratic structure is established for more effective administration. To use resources wisely and efficiently, the organization must delineate lines of authority and areas of responsibility. This, in turn, tends to undermine the sense of community and the affective basis of relationships which are central to group commitment. This creates the dilemma of expansion which was discussed earlier.

World-transforming movements must also engage in intensive socialization practices. Since the group hopes to instill values that are antithetical to those of the larger society, they must take the socialization of members seriously. Particularly, since a small number of people from the larger population are likely to be candidates for recruitment, the group must hold on to those members it does manage to interest in the movement. This intensive socialization is important in mobilizing and maintaining the personal resources of recruits.

These factors are critical in mobilizing and maintaining resources within the movement. But outside forces are also critical to the movement's viabil-

---

[12] Of course, the monumental goal of transforming the entire society may also cause disillusionment among members if they perceive little accomplishment of—or even significant movement toward—their goal. Methods of dealing with this problem will be discussed in the next section.

ity. The first external factor is the environmental context. In social environments that have large numbers of alienated or discontented people, the ground is fertile for the growth of world-transforming movements. In social contexts that have few discontented members, such movements will not find many people receptive to their message of alienation and transformation. For the most part, world-transforming movements are not able to do much about creating favorable conditions, but they try to capitalize on them when they do exist. They may also make adaptations in their message and their appeal if they move to new social environments with different sources of tension and dissatisfaction. Hence, world-transforming movements may make internal adjustments in order to fully exploit the resource of discontentment.

If transformation movements are to succeed through a strategy of persuasion, they must gain wide publicity. Social visibility is paramount to the achievement of their aims. However, if they are to gain converts, their visibility must be in a context of legitimacy. They must be viewed as unique and as worthy of attention, but they must also be considered noncontroversial and nonsubversive. In some cases this is quite difficult to achieve. After all, their goal *is* subversive! They wish to undermine the present social order and replace it with one of their own.

This creates a serious dilemma for the group. Mobilization of resources means gaining general public approval and support, but the ideology demands an uncompromising opposition to the status quo. This means that the group must either conceal its real goals and purposes for a while (the Moonies call this divine deception) or they must modify their ideology. For example, by suggesting that the present government has some ordained role in the transformation process, temporary cooperation with the current social order may be justified. Eventually, this may lead to more permanent accommodation to the values and standards of the larger society. The desire for legitimacy and the need to lessen public resistance are powerful drives for the movement. How a group resolves this dilemma will make a significant impact on subsequent developments in the organization and ideology.

Finally, the larger society may become aware of the revolutionary nature of the world-transformation movement and may impose measures to monitor or control the development of the group. The antiestablishment posture of the group may lead it to endorse unconventional and even illegal behavior. Formal legislation may be passed to limit the activities of the group, and ad hoc vigilante-style groups (e.g., deprogrammers) may be formed to undermine its work.[13] Clearly, such developments restrict the ability of the group to mobilize forces on its behalf.

---

[13] Bromley and Shupe refer to the anticult deprogrammers as engaged in a modern-day form of witch-hunting. See Anson Shupe and David Bromley's book, *The New Vigilantes: Deprogrammers, Anti-Cultists, and the New Religions* (1980).

The resource mobilization perspective makes an important contribution to the sociology of religion. It demonstrates that the viability of a group depends on more than the implementation of commitment mechanisms or a few simple steps of routinization. Resource mobilization theory requires a force-field analysis, an investigation of all the social forces which may be operating to advance or retard the success of the group. Depending on the extent and level of change advocated, there may be differing forces operating to resist the group's ambitions. The world-transforming movement is likely to experience the most severe resistance and face the most problematic dilemmas. However, the *response* of any new religious group to social resistance will largely determine its future. Not only will its viability be affected, but the group's composition, organization, and goals will be shaped by the decisions and compromises that are made. The resource mobilization perspective emphasizes that even internal affairs, such as the world view or belief system, are shaped in large part by interaction with the surrounding culture. Bromley and Shupe (1979) have demonstrated such changes within Moonie theology, and Thomas O'Dea's study of the Mormons (1957) shows similar theological accommodations in that group.[14]

Although routinization and mobilization of resources are both important, a group may also be unviable if its beliefs or world view are implausible, or if the culture changes so that the basis for establishing truth is modified. It is to this issue of plausibility that we turn next.

Plausibility of the World View

Another important factor in the survival of a religious group is the plausibility or believability of the world view. If everyday events or if scientific explanations seem to disprove the religious world view, the survival of the group may be threatened. If the belief system is viewed as implausible or unrealistic, it is unlikely to offer much sense of meaning and purpose in life. One widely respected sociologist of religion, Peter Berger, has devoted much of his writing to the exploration of *plausibility structures.* These are social interactions and processes within a group which serve to protect and sacralize the shared meanings and outlooks of the group.[15] Much of Chapter 4 was

---

[14] We might note here that only an historical analysis is capable of revealing these patterns. The ahistorical procedure of classical functionalism could never reveal these modifications of world view. Hence, much of the sociology of religion research from the 1930s until the 1960s is lacking in this sort of analysis.

[15] It is worth noting that plausibility is an important issue for maintenance of any ideology, be it political, economic, or whatever. All social systems establish plausibility structures to reinforce belief in the status quo. In fact, Stuart Hills (1980) maintains that one of the problems in understanding deviance is that it is necessary to break through the "mystification" of conformity and deviance. He insists that all societies tend to mystify and label appropriately those behaviors which either support or threaten the status quo, thereby increasing the stability of

concerned with this issue, and the emphasis in Chapter 5 on the importance of affective commitment in maintaining moral commitment points to the same phenomenon. Belief systems, if they are to survive, must be rooted in a social base and reinforced through symbols, stories, and rituals which create a sense of sacredness or absoluteness about the beliefs. An understanding of the religious group as a reference group is particularly critical to any analysis of plausibility. Individuals are capable of accepting all sorts of strange beliefs if enough other people seem convinced. It is a basic maxim of social psychology that individuals look to others for a definition of the situation if they are uncertain themselves.

Even if a plausibility structure exists, however, the belief system may be subject to disproof or may be counter to common sense. If a religious leader stakes his or her reputation on a specific time, date, and year when the end of the world will come, the movement may be in serious trouble the day after the predicted apocalypse.

But one should not assume that problems of plausibility are limited to doomsday groups. Wade Clark Roof maintains that liberal Protestantism is currently experiencing strains in theological plausibility. This is partially because the plausibility structures in liberal Protestant groups tend to be weaker, but the problem does not end there. Liberal Protestants are inclined to accept scientific method and scientific knowledge as authoritative, and these are based on naturalistic explanations. Scientific causal analysis does not accept supernatural intervention as a factor. Laws of nature or natural factors are used to explain everything from the origin of the universe to an individual's mystical experience. For some liberal Protestants and Catholics, this naturalistic explanation is not a problem. They simply accept a remythologized meaning system (modernism) which suggests that God works through natural processes, including psychological ones. For others, scientific explanations seem to dismiss the need for belief in God. In fact, studies have shown that a small but significant percentage of American church members do not believe in God (Roof 1978:88–89), or at least are unsure of his existence. (Glock and Stark 1966:5). For some people, scientific explanations threaten to make the religious view of reality implausible.

Even a book like this, with its psychosocial explanations of religious behavior, is threatening to many people. The type of analysis it presents may cause some readers to question the plausibility of their own faith. The tendency to view religious behavior through a naturalistic lens may trouble

the existing system by making conforming behavior seem uniquely moral and "right." However, it is easy for people—including social scientists—to misunderstand much of deviant behavior because the plausibility structures that define deviance are so deeply rooted that they are taken for granted. In effect, Hills has taken Berger's concepts of the social construction of reality and the mystification of social structure and applied them to the field of criminology. This entire field of examining the social forces which cause people to accept the validity of social beliefs is known as the sociology of knowledge.

some readers, for we are approaching commitment and conversion through reference-group theory rather than attributing these processes entirely to the Holy Spirit. Sociology provides a lens for viewing reality; it has its own assumptions and world view. While we attempt to avoid either a theistic or an atheistic bias, some readers might consider the naturalistic mode of interpretation an attempt to debunk theism.

We cannot resolve these issues of plausibility here, but it is important to recognize that in a pluralistic society, people are constantly exposed to meaning systems which seem to contradict their own. The most severe problems of plausibility occur for members of the world-transforming groups, who expect the transformation of the world imminently. What happens to the belief system when time drags on and the end does not arrive? We have already seen the mobilizing power that is inherent in millenialism, but how can such a view be sustained? Plausibility structures are important, but if one's religious group teaches that the millenium was to come on April 23, and this is May 1, something more than a reference group is needed to make the world view believable. If they are going to survive, world-transforming movements must develop belief systems that are self-validating.[16]

One of the important characteristics of the ideology of many sects and cults is *dualism,* the belief that reality is ultimately a battle between the forces of good and evil. Frequently, evil is personalized in the form of Satan or the Devil. Dualism is very functional in sustaining plausibility of an otherwise implausible world view. Since plausibility is essential for the survival of a group, dualism is often a significant factor in those groups which hold deviant world views. In other words, groups which have a world view that contradicts the scientific and "commonsense" explanations are more likely to survive if they have a world view that is dualistic.

Lofland's description of the role of dualism in the Unification Movement provides an interesting example. He articulates one of the central postulates of their world view as follows:

> Anything that hinders or hurts a [member] or the group or an outsider who is assisting is an attack by Satan's spirits. Anything that helps a [member] or the group or an outsider who is assisting is an act of helping or leading by God's spirits (Lofland 1977:197).

Hence, "whether expectations are fulfilled or not, the believer cannot lose. He derives confirmation from any outcome" (1977:197). This dualism is not merely an interesting characteristic of many new religious movements in America; it is central to their appeal. Meredith McGuire emphasizes this point when she writes, "The tidiness and order of the dualistic interpreta-

---

[16] For a fascinating study of a doomsday group which dissolved after its prediction failed, see Festinger, Riecken, and Schachter, *When Prophecy Fails* (1956).

tion of the world are part of the basic appeal of such movements. Dualistic figures of Good and Evil simplify the world for people who are overwhelmed by the ambiguity and complexity of modern life" (1981:35). The sense of normlessness is crushed by the absoluteness of the answers which dualism provides.

Furthermore, once the dualistic perspective is adopted, it appears to be self-validating. Lofland explains that the Moonies fed upon the conventional mass media to confirm their world view. When national and international events reflected unrest, deterioration, and disorganization, the devotees were jubilant. Surely this was evidence to everyone that the end was near! Surely this victory by Satan would convince people to repent and join the Unification cause. If a month went by when no tragedies occurred, this was because God was restraining Satan for some special reason:

> April had no new major crises because it was the month of Parent's Day, the [Moonie] equivalent of Christmas. God restrained both Satan and himself for the occasion, but they redoubled their efforts in May, and the stock market plummeted the week of May 21 (Lofland, 1977:200).

These interpretations were not limited to major world crises. Such news items as the collision of two ships or the suicide of a lonely 40-year-old secretary were confirmations of their world view. Not only does dualism offer a nice neat explanation of the meaning of events, but the world view can be constantly confirmed by viewing news events in its own light.

Moonies often attend religious rallies of other groups in hope of finding seekers whom they might recruit. Being constantly exposed to other preaching would seem to be a potential threat to the plausibility structures of the Unification movement. However, Lofland reports that the opposite was the case. "If a church was ill-attended, people were falling away from the churches in these last days; if well attended, people were seeking for truth, but not finding it there. If it was housed in a new building, the church was resorting to external appearance to compensate for its inner death; if in an old building, people were falling away" (1977:203). Furthermore, if a minister preached a message that in any way resembled a dualistic world view, that minister was viewed as a covert ally and was thought to be a convert secretly teaching the "Divine Principles" to Christians.

Of course, many other religious groups are also dualistic. The Jesus People, many pentecostal and most fundamentalistic groups, and the Appalachian Snake-Handling Cult (a folk version of Christianity) are a few examples of dualistic religious groups. In each of these cases, dualism provides for a simple plausibility process. On the other hand, the expectation of a catastrophic end to the world in the near future has caused some doomsday prophets to set a specific date upon which the Final Judgment will commence. Recently, a California-based group awaited the end in August 1981. Followers of the fundamentalist preacher quit their jobs and sold all of their property as a sign to God of their faith. Other preachers and lay people influenced by the writings of Hal Lindsey are expecting the end of the world in the late 1980s. What happens to such groups when the date passes?

In many cases, passage of the doomsday date results in the movement's collapse. However, the Unification Church has passed several critical dates established by the Reverend Moon. In these cases, the ideology was modified by simply proclaiming that the end of the world will come in several phases. The cataclysm which was expected was simply declared to have occurred— but in the unseen realm. Some Christian groups which predicted the end of the world have similarly modified their stance. In some cases, they simply set a new date. However, only so many dates can come and go without group morale waning and religious plausibility declining. A more effective strategy is to proclaim that the new era is now in progress, but that only the "saved" or the "elect" are able to see or experience the transformation. This has been the strategy of the Jehovah's Witnesses for whom the millennium began in 1914. In any case, basic dualism can continue to provide a simplistic and self-validating system of meaning.

Other plausibility mechanisms can also be used effectively to create apparently self-validating belief systems. When a body of scripture—whether it's the Koran, the Bible, or the Book of Mormon—is believed to be literally and absolutely true, passages within those scriptures which testify to the veracity of the contents reinforce the believer's conviction. All other forms of evidence (scientific or otherwise) can be readily dismissed if they contradict those scriptures. The sacred scrolls become the final authority on all things, and the sense of sacredness which surrounds that scripture makes anything in it seem plausible. In this case, the utter respect for the scripture serves as a self-validating plausibility structure.

Close-knit reference groups and awe-inspiring rituals and symbols serve as important plausibility structures. However, the content of a belief system is also important. For those groups which reject the outlook of the dominant culture, dualism provides a world view that not only offers to explain the meaning of events, but also provides a neat tautology (circular reasoning) that allows for self-validation of the world view. It is not surprising, then, that many of the new religious movements, especially the world-transforming ones which have managed to survive, are dualistic.

An Exercise in Application: The Development of the Shakers

The processes described in this chapter may become more meaningful to readers if applied to a single group. There are many studies of specific religious groups which students could use to exercise their skills in applying (and critiquing) these theories and concepts. In the following pages, I will briefly outline the development of one religious group in America so that readers can begin to identify these processes in a group.[17]

The United Society of Believers in Christ's Second Appearing—commonly known as the Shakers—was founded in England by Ann Lee. "Mother Ann," the illiterate daughter of a blacksmith, was born in 1736. When she was 23, she—along with her family—joined an enthusiastic religious group derogatorily known in the community as the "Shaking Quakers." William Pitt was assuming political power at the time, and England was entering an era characterized by change and popular unrest. As so often happens, social change and upheaval spawned a number of religious movements (e.g., George Whitefield and the Wesleys were simultaneously producing a revival that resulted in Methodism).

The Shaking Quakers acquired their name because during worship services the members would fall into trances in which they would quiver and shake or manifest other frenzied behavior. Most people believed them to be "demented hooligans." They were sometimes attacked by mobs (which only solidified their commitment to each other and strengthened boundaries against outsiders). On a number of occasions they were imprisoned for Sabbath-breaking (their style of worship was considered indecent and even blasphemous).

While incarcerated in a Manchester jail in 1770 for just such a charge, Ann Lee experienced a vision in which she witnessed "the original sin." She believed that the sexual act was the cause of all evil and suffering in the world. (She had always felt guilty about engaging in sex with her husband, and when her four children each died in childbirth she was convinced that their deaths were divine judgments on her for her concupiscence). She emerged from the jail with such conviction and sense of mission that she quickly emerged as the central leader of the Shaking Quakers. In fact, she was referred to as Mother Ann, and the woman who had previously led the group became known as "the female equivalent of John the Baptist." Mother Ann was believed to be Christ incarnate. Since God had come the first time in male form, it seemed only reasonable to the group that in the Second Coming Christ would be female.

Mother Ann was prone to visions. One such revelation compelled her to believe that the group was being called to America, and she and the Shakers emigrated in 1774. However, this strange group—which refused to bear arms and which had a British leader—was suspected of being a band of spies when the Revolutionary War broke out the following year. Furthermore, the insistence on celibacy among members was highly reminiscent of the requirements of the Catholic clergy. Many of the New England

---

[17] The most thorough scholar on Shaker life is Edward Deming Andrews. Although his publications on the group are numerous, students interested in reading more about the United Society will want to start with Andrews' book, *The People Called Shakers* (1963). For somewhat briefer accounts see Holloway (1966); Kephart (1976); Nordhoff (1966); or Noyes (1966).

colonists therefore accused the Shakers of papalism—an especially derogatory label among bigoted Protestants. The Shakers were run out of many New England towns—in some cases they were dragged to the edge of town by their hair. At one point, 10 Shakers were jailed for their teachings. Their doctrine that married life was immoral clearly and directly challenged conventional society. Married persons who joined the group were required to separate. Such a policy earned the Shakers a label as family breakers.

The Shakers again responded to the hostility by drawing more closely together, by developing a particularistic outlook (with high boundaries between "we" and "they"), and eventually by establishing communal societies so they could withdraw from contact with the larger society. Their imprisonment for their teachings also served another function: an otherwise little-known movement gained tremendous notoriety.

Shaker theology stressed a negative attitude toward humanity. People were viewed as inherently depraved, but salvation was possible if people would only confess their sins and reform their lives. The outlook—especially in the early years—was also highly dualistic, and anything that opposed the group or its beliefs was identified as satanic. Perhaps the most novel aspect of Shaker theology was the insistence on God's bisexuality. God was believed to be both male and female, and was manifest in the bisexuality of all creation. (Hence, the explanation that in the Second Coming, Christ would be in female form.) The Shakers rejected both the Christian doctrine of the Trinity and the belief in physical resurrection. The resurrection is not a future event, Lee insisted, but occurs to each individual at the time of confession and personal acceptance of "the new life." Salvation and resurrection were *individual* experiences.

Lee also stressed a return to primitive or pentacostal Christianity with its five central principles: common property, celibacy, pacifism, separation of church from government, and belief in the power of spirit over physical disease. The last principle was the only one they felt they had not completely mastered. The insistence that the sexual act was the source of all evil and depravity in the world was a central Shaker doctrine, but it was not an uncommon sentiment in the 18th century. The fact that others in the culture shared this view allowed for group expansion. When social attitudes toward sexuality changed, the Shakers found recruitment of new members extremely difficult.

Upon entering the United Society of Believers, a person was required to make a total confession of his or her previous life. It was recognized that sometimes these confessions take several years to complete because a person may come only gradually to realize the full depravity of his or her former existence. When persons became a part of the group, they were also expected to engage in testimony and in seeking new converts.

Ann Lee died in 1784 after an intense two-year missionary tour of the eastern states. The Shakers had faced bitter opposition and many attempts to discredit them during this tour, but they had also gained many converts. The group was not yet living a communal life, but Ann Lee had predicted its necessity. Indeed, she had justified this requirement because of the precedent of the early church, but if the group had not become communal, it may well have dissolved. The persecuted members needed a haven; they needed the emotional and financial support that a communal society could offer; and they needed the plausibility structure that intense social interaction would provide. Furthermore, given the resistence the group experienced, its members needed to mobilize personal resources. When the group did finally become communal, all possessions were given to the group or were sold and the money from the sale donated to the Shaker society. All members worked together, giving their skills, time, and energy in the service of the United Society of Believers.

But Ann Lee died before this communal society became a reality. Many converts fell away when the charismatic leader died, and even the faithful were nearly overcome with doubts and fears. But Ann had established James Whittaker (Father James) as her successor and the passing of leadership occurred without major internal conflict. Whittaker had come from England with Ann Lee; his knowledge of her teachings and his outstanding ability as a speaker made him the generally acknowledged leader. But his own death came less than three years after Mother Ann's. He had dedicated the group's first meetinghouse in New Lebanon, New York, but the communal society was not yet in operation. Nor had a procedure been established for choosing the next successor.

When the devotees gathered in the first assembly after Father James's death, the choice of leader loomed large. They waited prayerfully for divine inspiration, and eventually several members arose, each declaring that the spirit of God had spoken: Joseph Meecham would be the new "chosen one." And it was Meecham who became the organizational genius in the United Society. He galvanized the followers into a unified band, established norms of behavior, and set up a central committee to make administrative decisions. Without the influence of Meecham, the Society would almost surely have collapsed (Andrews 1963:54).

One particular challenge which Meecham had to address was providing a stable economic base. However, once the communal society was established, it soon became highly productive. The Shakers were an extraordinarily resourceful people, having made, by some accounts, upwards of three thousand inventions during the course of their existence. Among their most notable were the flat-head broom (such as you might use to sweep your porch), the common clothespin, a threshing machine, a turbine water wheel, the circular saw, the vacuum pan for evaporating liquids (eventually leading to evaporated milk), the first metal writing pens, and the first one-horse wagon used in this country (Andrews 1963:113). The Shakers refused to take out patents, and their ideas were often stolen and patented by others.

But the group was able to support itself adequately because the inventions allowed for a high degree of efficiency in work.

Shaker worship services were emotional and spontaneous. They included speaking in tongues, singing, dancing, and frenzied seizures. In the early years the services seemed chaotic to outsiders with each individual expressing religiosity in his or her own way (see Exhibit 6–3). Later, the services became ritualized; complex group dances evolved which had a systematic pattern that many of today's marching bands might envy. (Men marched or danced as one unit; women performed in an opposite unit. See Exhibit 6–4.) Positions of hands and feet were highly symbolic in those early days. Hands with palms up represented openness to the spirit of God, and children[18] were trained to sit or dance during worship with palms heavenward. Eventually, the Shakers became rather rigid about their insistence on adherence to certain behavior patterns, many of which had originally been moral precepts or had served as symbolic gestures (see Exhibit 6–5). However, the singing, dancing, and other emotional outlets during their ritual produced a tremendous feeling of group solidarity. The idea of continuing revelation seemed a real possibility to members when they saw it occur at their frequent worship gatherings. The highly emotional services and the intense group interaction created an extraordinarily strong plausibility structure.

However, the belief in continuing and spontaneous revelation eventually became a problem. Since anyone could have a revelation, the leaders had little control over the development of doctrine. The emphasis on spontaneity left the group open to all sorts of non-Shaker proclamations. Eventually, each person who had a revelation was required to report it first to the executive committee of the Society, which would rule on whether the vision or insight was true or not. Only then would the whole society hear the message. This was certainly a cumbersome procedure, but it illustrates well the transformation which occurs after the charismatic leader has died and charisma is routinized. While Ann Lee lived, she had the authority to interpret other people's dreams or inspirations. The means of sustaining conformity and control is more complicated when such a leader passes from the scene.

At their peak in the 1830s, the Shakers had 6,000 members living in 18 communities in the United States. Most of the settlements were in New England or in upstate New York, although there were also several Shaker villages in Ohio and Kentucky. As social attitudes toward sexuality changed in America, the Shakers did not compromise their stance that sexual expression is the root of all evil. It became increasingly difficult to recruit members

---

[18] Some members had been married and had children prior to joining the group. This was one source of the children. In later years the Shakers were also known for raising orphans (at a time before most communities had county homes for orphaned children).

Exhibit 6-3

Observers' Descriptions of Shaker Worship

In the best part of their worship every one acts for himself, and almost every one different from the other: one will stand with his arms extended, acting over odd postures, which they call signs; another will be dancing, and some times hopping on one leg about the floor; another will fall to turning round, so swift, that if it be a woman, her clothes will be so filled with the wind, as though they were kept out by a hoop; another will be prostrate on the floor; another will be talking with somebody; and some sitting by, smoking their pipes; some groaning most dismally; some trembling extremely; others acting as though all their nerves were convulsed; others swinging their arms, with all vigor, as though they were turning a wheel, etc. Then all break off, and have a spell of smoking, and some times great fits of laughter. . . . They have several such exercises in a day, especially on the Sabbath. . . .

*****

When they meet together for their worship, they fall a groaning and trembling, and every one acts alone for himself: one will fall prostrate on the floor, another on his knees and his head in his hands; another will be muttering over articulate sounds, which neither they or any body else understand. Some will be singing, each one his own tune; some without words, in an Indian tune, some sing jig tunes, some tunes of their own making, in an unknown mutter, which they call new tongues; some will be dancing, and others stand laughing, heartily and loudly; others will be druming on the floor with their feet, as though a pair of drum-sticks were beating a ruff on a drum-head; others will be agonizing, as though they were in great pain; others jumping up and down; others fluttering over some-body, and talking to them; others will be shooing and hissing evil spirits out of the house, till the different tunes, groaning, jumping, dancing, druming, laughing, talking and fluttering, shooing and hissing, makes a perfect bedlam; this they call the worship of God.

The Reverend Valentine Rathbun, Sr.

About thirty of them assembled in a large room in a private house,—the women in one end and the men in the other,—for dancing. Some were past sixty years old. Some had their eyes steadily fixed upward, continually reaching out and drawing in their arms and lifting up first one foot, then the other, about four inches from the floor. Near the centre of the room stood two young women, one of them very handsome, who whirled round and round for the space of fifteen minutes, nearly as fast as the rim of a spinning-wheel in quick motion. . . . As soon as she left whirling she entered the dance, and danced gracefully. Sometimes one would pronounce with a loud voice, 'Ho, ho' or 'Love, love,'—and then the whole assembly vehemently clapped hands for a minute or two. At other times some were shaking and trembling, others singing words out of the Psalms in whining, canting tones (but not in rhyme), while others were speaking in what they called 'the unknown tongue,'—to me an unintelligible jargon, mere gibberish and perfect nonsense. At other times the whole assembly would shout as with one voice, with one accord. This exercise continued about an hour. . . .

Exhibit 6–3 *(Concluded)*

This done, several of the young people, both men and women, began to shake and tremble in a most terrible manner. The first I perceived was their heads moving slowly from one shoulder to the other,—the longer they moved the quicker and more violently they shook. The motion proceeded from the head to the hands, and the whole body, with such power as if limb would rend from limb. The house trembled as if there were an earthquake. After this several young women embraced and saluted each other; two men embraced and saluted each other; a third clasped his arms around both, a fourth around them, and so on, until a dozen men were in that position, embracing and saluting. I did not observe any man salute or embrace a woman, or any woman a man. . . .

Senator William Plumer

Quoted in Edward Deming Andrews, *The People Called Shakers,* new enlarged edition (New York: Dover Publications, 1963) pp. 28–30. Used by permission.

Exhibit 6–4

Square Order Shuffle

Shaker worship was originally emotional and spontaneous. Eventually, highly ritualized dances in group formations evolved as part of the liturgy—with the men as one unit and women as another. Even the position of hands was viewed as symbolic of an inward spiritual attitude.

Photograph from Edward Deming Andrews, *The People Called Shakers* (New York: Dover Press, 1963), p. 189. By permission.

Exhibit 6–5 _____

Excerpts from Shaker "Orders and Gifts"
(posted in the sister's retiring room)

Every person must rise from their beds at the sound of the "first trumpet," kneel in silence on the place where you first placed your foot when getting out of bed. No speaking in the room unless you wish to ask a question of the sister having the care of the room, in that case whisper. Dress your right arm first. Step your right foot first. At the sound of the "second trumpet," march in order, giving your right side to your superior. Walk on your toes. Fold your left hand across your stomach. Let your right hand fall at your side. March to your workshop in order. No asking unnecessary questions.

Quoted in Mark Holloway, *Heavens on Earth,* 2nd ed. (New York: Dover Publications, 1966), p. 73. Used by permission.

to this celibate society, for this central belief no longer seemed plausible to many Americans. Furthermore, the fiery passion for evangelism had faded over the generations. The group was no longer able to mobilize the energy and resources of a substantial number of people. The motivations for membership had gradually been transformed. Most of the new members by the turn of the century were orphans who had been raised within the Shaker society. They had been socialized as Shakers rather than joining as committed converts. Today only a handful of elderly Shaker women live in the one remaining New Hampshire Shaker Village.[19]

Summary

Many religious movements appear to get started through the dynamism of a charismatic leader (Jesus, Mohammed, Sun Myung Moon, Ann Lee). The individual is viewed as an agent of God or perhaps as God incarnate (in the flesh). What that person says is held as true simply because he or she said it. However, Weber held that charisma is inherently unstable, and if a group is to survive it must routinize. That is, it must develop norms, roles, and statuses; it must transfer the sense of awe from the individual personality to the teachings and the organization; and it must make provisions for succession of the leader when he or she dies. As these policies are spelled out and various statuses gain specialized job descriptions, the movement is taking its first steps toward institutionalization. Many decades later the group may be highly bureaucratized.

_____

[19] There are several historic Shaker villages which have been kept up by historical societies, but only one is still owned and occupied by Shakers.

Some new religious groups are started by ideological leaders rather than charismatic ones. They are the interpreters of some scripture or other ideological source that is inherently authoritative. But even in cases where an ideological leader initiates a new religious group, routinization is essential if the group is to survive.

There may be other forces leading to institutionalization as well. Accomplishment of major goals calls for a high degree of organization and efficiency. In order for some goals to be achieved, alliances with other organizations may be required. This means the development of commissions, boards, and divisions to direct these projects.

Regardless of the cause of institutionalization, it brings many changes in the religious movement itself. Bureaucracies take on a life of their own, somewhat independent of the lay members, and tend to influence the workings of the whole organization. As we pointed out in Chapter 4, this sometimes results in official and folk versions of the faith. Over time, the institutionalized religion will also have to face the dilemmas which routinization creates. Institutionalization is a necessity, but it has mixed consequences for the group.

If the group is to survive, it must gain access to basic resources, and gain members' commitments of time, energy, and finances. But it also must acquire a niche in the society. Since its claim on resources may conflict with those of other groups and institutions, the group must keep from being crushed or crowded out by other groups. If the religious ideology calls for a radical political transformation, it may be defined as subversive and may be opposed through political and legal channels. Understanding of the continued existence or the collapse of the group may call for a force-field analysis. In other words, one must understand the social forces which oppose the group and the forces mobilized by the group to protect its interests. The viability of the group may depend on its ability to mobilize resources on its behalf.

Finally, continued existence of the group depends on its ability to make its world view seem plausible. Geertz's definition of religion, discussed in detail in Chapter 2, stresses the importance of plausibility structures even in the definition:

> A religion is a system of symbols which acts to establish powerful, pervasive and long-lasting moods and motivations in [people] by . . . formulating conceptions of a general order of existence and . . . *clothing these conceptions in such an aura of factuality that . . . the moods and motivations seem uniquely realistic* (my emphasis).

Symbol systems, rituals, close-knit reference groups, and other mechanisms which make the belief system seem "uniquely realistic" are called plausibility structures. Besides the development of plausibility structures, some groups develop a world view that seems to be self-validating. Dualism (the belief in a good spiritual force which opposes an evil force) is such a belief system. Everyday experiences, when interpreted through dualistic assumptions, can appear to validate those very assumptions. Although circular reasoning is used, many people view their system as "proven" by everyday events. Other methods may be used to maintain plausibility, but if the religion is to survive, the world view it sets forth must seem uniquely believable and even compelling.

Survival of a religious group, then, depends on a basic level of routinization, an ability to mobilize resources in its behalf and defuse forces which oppose it, and an ability to maintain the plausibility of the world view. Groups cope with each of these issues in a variety of ways; hence, there are many types of religious organizations. In the next chapter we will explore types of religious groups and what sociologists look for in trying to understand any particular religious movement.

Analysis of Religious Groups and Organizations
Religious Typologies and Choice Point Analysis

In the previous chapter we explored the social factors which contribute to the survival of a religious group. We saw that religious groups vary a great deal and undergo significant changes in the process of development. In order to conduct research on religion and make generalizations about religious behavior, social scientists have categorized groups with significant similarities into types, comparing and contrasting characteristics of churches, sects, denominations, and cults. As Milton Yinger has pointed out, this procedure of referring to particular types of groups has shortcomings. "Classifications are in one sense arbitrary. They oversimplify the data by disregarding what are held to be minor differences in order to emphasize what are thought to be major similarities. They are constructs of the mind, not descriptions of reality" (Yinger 1970:251).

Generalizations about any social behavior can be made only by comparing and contrasting phenomena that are in some respects similar. However, it is essential that the conception of various types be as clear, precise, and accurate as possible. Otherwise, the concepts themselves may cause confusion, misunderstanding, and faulty generalizations. Some sociologists think that the concepts of church, sect, and denomination have produced just such confusion; they have been used in a variety of ways by various researchers, and there is no consensus as to the meaning of the terms. Nonetheless, many scholars continue to try to clarify these terms because they feel that they continue to be valuable as analytical tools. As we explore the way in which such terms as *church, sect, denomination* and *cult* have been used, it is important to keep in mind that they provide only one of many possible ways to organize the data and to think about religious groups. But they also represent the predominant mode of comparing religious groups in recent decades.

The goal of this chapter is to help students know what to look for when analyzing any specific religious group. What is it that the sociologist looks for in analyzing religious groups? We will begin by investigating the development of the church-sect typology and will conclude by exploring a more open-ended method of comparing and contrasting religious groups and movements. The first method is most useful in making *generalizations* about various types of religious groups (nomothetic approach); the latter procedure is particularly helpful in trying to describe the *unique* dynamics of any particular group (ideographic approach).

Church, Sect, Denomination, and Cult

The Church-Sect Typology

Weber and Troeltsch.   Most discussions of the church-sect typology begin with the work of Ernst Troeltsch, a German theologian and social philosopher. Actually, the concepts of church and sect can be traced back to Troeltsch's teacher, the eminent German sociologist, Max Weber.[1] Weber emphasized that the sect is an exclusive group. To be a member, one must meet certain conditions, such as adherence to a particular doctrine or conformity to particular practices (like adult baptism or abstinence from alcohol). Membership in the sect is voluntary, limited to adults, and involves a commitment by the members. The church, on the other hand, is viewed as an inclusive group that encourages all members of the society to join and which requires less specific commitment and conformity (Weber 1963:65).

Troeltsch included Weber's defining criteria, but he expanded the concept to include many other factors. In the process, the emphasis was shifted. Troeltsch was a theologian concerned primarily with Christian ethics and social concepts. For Troeltsch, the central characteristic of the church is its acceptance of the secular order. The sect, on the other hand, tends to reject the social order and to maintain a prophetic ministry. Hence, the church is characterized by "compromise" of Christian values and accommodation to the secular society. Clearly, *compromise* is a value-laden term. What is compromise to one person is not to another. (Eister 1967). While Weber's criteria of sect and cult avoided this value judgment, Troeltsch's formulation has been more widely used—probably because social scientists have been intrigued with the multidimensionality of his scheme.

The generalizations drawn by Troeltsch in 1911 were significantly influenced by the particular location and era in which he studied. This is true, of course, of all sociological research, and it is important for the researcher to be aware of both cultural and historical bias. Troeltsch was well aware that his generalizations were limited to Christian European culture. He was interested in describing the correlation of factors that characterized religious groups there and at that time. He suggested that many of the correlations he was identifying might not apply to American Christianity. What Troeltsch did hope to accomplish was to demonstrate a correlation between certain patterns of organization, particular theological orientations, and specific ideas about society. He was preeminently a social philosopher and Christian ethicist.

The *sect,* as identified by Troeltsch (1931), is a group which stresses the volitional aspect of membership. Therefore, it emphasizes adult commitment. (Infant baptism is forbidden.) Membership is exclusive, with certain criteria established for acceptance into the fold. A conversion experience, as evidence of one's transformation from a degenerate state, is usually neces-

---

[1] It is unfortunate that sociologists have tended to use Troeltsch's definition of church and sect, for Weber's use of the terms actually seems to have greater utility for today. His distinction is simpler and is based on sociological rather than theological criteria. Nonetheless, we will discuss Troeltsch because his formulations have so profoundly influenced later developments in church-sect typology.

sary. The community also maintains a judgmental attitude toward nonmembers, for they view themselves as the "faithful remnant" of God's people. Violation of the moral principles of the group or rejection of doctrine is frequently punishable by expulsion from the group. Salvation is achieved by personal perfection or by one's moral worthiness. Since this involves overcoming of worldliness, austerity or asceticism (self-denial) is frequently the norm.

Sects also tend to emphasize the priesthood of all believers, at least as an ideal. They are characterized by a high level of lay participation and a deemphasis on the role of the clergy. In fact, in many cases the clergy have no formal training, and in others the clergy may be dispensed with altogether. Church polity is normally democratic. The sect is also hostile or indifferent to secular society and to the state, drawing its members primarily from the poorer classes and from other socially disenfranchized groups. Social status in secular society is not a source of power and prestige within the sect—personal charisma and spirituality are the foundations of sectarian respectability.

Finally, the sect tends to be fundamentalistic in its theology. The emphasis is on regeneration of the original (biblical) expression of the faith as the only legitimate one. Frequently the Sermon on the Mount is identified by such groups as a sort of Christian manifesto. Later writers have added to Troeltsch's observations the view that sectarian worship is typically informal and allows for spontaneity of expression by the congregation. In summary, the sect is a religious protest against established religion and against secular society.

The *church* is a more open and accepting expression of the faith. Membership in the church is determined largely on the basis of birth. Rather than stressing adult baptism and conversion experiences, emphasis is on the religious education of children. Growing into the faith is viewed as a natural process that requires no abrupt change or reversal in one's life. In fact, membership is inclusive and may coincide with geographic or national boundaries. Acceptance into the organization is largely a formalized procedure not closely guarded or protected. Furthermore, deviation from accepted doctrine does not normally result in expulsion. Churches do not want competing religious groups, and if they are to encompass everyone, they must allow for compromises and be tolerant of variations.

Churches stress that salvation is granted through the grace of God, not through individual effort. God's grace is believed to be transmitted through church sacraments as administered by the church hierarchy. Hence, leadership in the church is provided by a highly trained professional clergy which is duly authorized (ordained) to administer the sacraments and to oversee all other church operations.

In its relations with the larger (secular) society, the church tends to adjust to, compromise with, and support the existing values and structure. Social stratification within the church usually mirrors that in the secular world. Finally, the theology of the church may be either orthodox or modernistic, but the original revelation is not the only source of truth. The historic positions of the church in various eras have legitimacy in their own right. Later scholars have added that worship in the church is orderly and formal, with much less opportunity for emotional and spontaneous expression.

Troeltsch also described another type of religious group which has received less attention by scholars. He described as *mystics* that cadre of loosely associated individuals who emphasize nonrational personal experience as the cornerstone of religion. More recent scholars have called this mystic movement a cult (Becker 1932; Nottingham 1971; McGuire 1981). We will return to a discussion of the concept of cult later. At this point it is interesting merely to note that Troeltsch was aware that some religious expressions did not seem to fit on his continuum from sect to church. In fact, mysticism almost defied classification because there appeared to be so little organization, so little discipline or control of members, and so little sense of being a member of anything.

One shortcoming of Troeltsch's study is that he does not give us many clues as to what social conditions are likely to generate which kinds of groups. A second problem, in terms of contemporary utility of the typology, is that he has suggested a correlation of *many* variables, some sociological, some theological. While these particular constellations of factors may have been present in European Christian groups up until the beginning of the 20th century, we see many religious groups today that combine these factors in different ways (Knudsen et al. 1978). Troeltsch never intended his typology of church and sect to be applicable cross-culturally or in all eras of history, but for several decades after his work was published, social scientists attempted to employ it in just such a generalized way.

Recent attempts to revise the typology have hinged largely on which one or two sociological factors should be the determining ones in the identification of a sect or a church. Theological differences, on the other hand, are sometimes used to distinguish different *subtypes* of sects or denominations (Wilson 1970). The lasting contribution of Troeltsch is his suggestion that a religious group may move from sect to church. His scheme stimulated significant refinements by Niebuhr and others.

Niebuhr.   The next major attempt to develop the church-sect typology was undertaken by H. Richard Niebuhr in his work *The Social Sources of Denominationalism* (1957). Here he tried to identify the *social conditions* which cause the formation of each type of group. Niebuhr was an American theologian whose primary interest was religion and society. He approached the topic from a normative perspective (that is, he was interested in moral implications and what *ought* to be the social ethic of a Christian group).

Although the social scientist attempts to avoid such value judgments,

Exhibit 7-1 _____

Characteristics of Sects and Churches as Delineated by Troeltsch and Niebuhr

The Sect	The Church
1. Volitional membership (emphasis on adult conversion and commitment).	1. Membership largely on the basis of birth (emphasis on religious education of children).
2. Exclusive membership policy—closely guarded.	2. Inclusive membership—may coincide with national citizenship or geographic boundaries.
3. Particularism—judgmental attitude toward those who do not accept the one true path; self image that of the "faithful remnant" or the "elect."	3. Universalism—acceptance of diversity and emphasis on the brotherhood and sisterhood of all humanity.
4. Small faithful group.	4. Large, bureaucratic organization.
5. Salvation achieved through moral purity, including ethical austerity or asceticism.	5. Salvation granted by the grace of God—as administered by church sacrament and church hierarchy.
6. Priesthood of all believers; clergy deemphasized or nonexistent; lay participation high.	6. Leadership and control by highly trained professional clergy.
7. Hostile or indifferent to secular society and to the state.	7. Tendency to adjust to, compromise with, and support existing social values and social structures.
8. Fundamentalistic theology—only the original revelation is an authentic expression of the faith.	8. Either orthodox or modernist theology—formulations and interpretation of the faith in later periods of history are legitimate in their own rights.
9. Predominently a group of lower-class persons or those otherwise socially disenfranchized. (Worldly prestige is eschewed and spiritual or charismatic qualities become the basis for internal stratification).	9. Membership comprised of upper and middle-class people, but with professional classes controlling most leadership positions. (Stratification of the society is reflected within the church.)
*10. Informal, spontaneous worship.	*10. Formal, orderly worship.
*11. Radical social ethic—emphasizing the equality of all persons and the necessity of economic equality.	*11. Conservative social ethic—justifying the current socioeconomic relationships.

* Stressed by Niebuhr but not by Troeltsch.

Niebuhr's work is important, for he described the sect and the church as stages or points in the development of a religious group. He clearly placed these concepts in a framework of religious group evolution and added a new type, the denomination. He also moved beyond Troeltsch by pointing out ways the *internal* structure of a group causes a group to be transformed from one type to another.

Like Troeltsch, Niebuhr viewed the difference between sect and church as hinging on compromise. At the outset of his book he wrote, "Denominationalism in the Christian church is . . . an unacknowledged hypocrisy. It is a compromise made far too lightly, between Christianity and the world.
. . . It represents the accommodation of Christianity to the caste-system

of the world" (1957:6). He viewed the division of the Christian churches into different and exclusive denominations as antithetical to the fundamental values and teachings of Christianity. Certainly, this tendency to schisms and separateness has not declined since Niebuhr's observations in 1929. Protestants, in particular, have a continuing penchant for generating new reform groups. Not only are there many pentecostal and fundamentalist groups with unique and sometimes lengthy names,[2] but the mainline groups have many subdenominations. There are, by one recent count, 23 brands of Baptists, 17 varieties of Methodists, 14 versions of Lutheranism, and 9 forms of Presbyterianism (Jacquet 1982:108–110).

Niebuhr also felt that social inequality in the society at large is contrary to the basic principles the founder of Christianity set forth. As he put it, "The inequality of privilege in the economic order appears to contain a fundamental denial of the Christian principle of brotherhood and to be symptomatic of an unhealthful state of society because it is contrary to the divine law." Hence, accommodation to a society with social prejudices and social inequities is an implicit rejection of Christian values (Niebuhr 1957:8–9). Niebuhr did not hesitate to make a value judgment based on Christian ethics: denominationalism is evidence of evil within Christendom. For Niebuhr, the emergence of the church is caused by a deterioration of Christian social ethics. The reemergence of a sect is an attempt to recapture and reassert the Christian concern for social justice and equality. In the desire to be successful (as defined in worldly terms), the church discards this prophetic ministry and thereby ignores the basic thrust of the faith, the establishment of the just society—the Kingdom of God.

Niebuhr pointed out that the existence of different denominations is not due to mere ideological differences, as is often believed. Rather, the plurality of different Christian groups represents differences in race, nationality, social class, and region of the country. The fact that racism, nationalism, regionalism, and class are the *real* basis of denominationalism appalled Niebuhr. As a theologian, he was aghast at the way religious ideology was used to justify the economic self-interests of the powerful. He pointed out that groups from different social classes tend to develop different theological outlooks. Hence, the *source* of the schism is *social*. The stratification system of the society causes a division between people who are supposedly of the same faith. But the groups erroneously identify their differences as purely ideological or theological. The stratification of society invades both the social organization of Christianity and its theology.[3]

Over a period of time, the tendency of Christian groups is to compromise

---

[2] The group that apparently has the distinction of having the longest name is The House of God, which is the Holy Church of the Living God, the Pillar and Ground of the Truth, Inc. (Jacquet 1982:62).

[3] We will take a closer look at the relationship between religion and social class and religion and racism in Chapters 8 and 9, respectively.

the values of the faith and adopt the secular world's values and inequities. This is a tendency toward the church type of religious group. On the other hand, the disfranchized often recognize the compromises of the faith, and call the faithful back to radical commitment. This sectarian reaction is a means of renewal and revitalization of the faith. Niebuhr also pointed out that sectarian zeal seldom lasts more than a generation. The first generation of sect members stress adult conversion and commitment, but they also establish religious education programs for their children. Eventually, the children are accepted into full membership on the basis of their knowledge of the faith. Personal conversion and dramatic life changes are deemphasized in later generations as *knowledge* of the faith (memorized Bible passages and so on) becomes the membership criterion. Often the later generations also experience upward social mobility and are no longer disfranchized. The sect gradually institutionalizes, comes to desire a trained professional clergy, deemphasizes a personal conversion experience as the basis of church membership, and begins to accommodate to the stratification system of the society.

Although Troeltsch had suggested a process of movement from sect to church, it was Niebuhr who elaborated the point and described the forces causing the change. He developed the sociological use of the term *denomination,* another type of religious group which represents a midpoint in the continuum between sect and church.

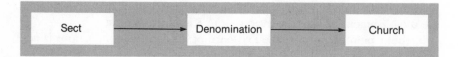

The key to understanding the movement from sect to denomination is the development of religious education programs. First, the focus on education reflected a departure from the emphasis on an abrupt change of life through conversion. Religion could be taught; it was not solely the result of a spontaneous and emotional conversion experience. Second, in most sectarian groups the development of religious education programs represented the first stages of institutionalization. Impersonality and orderliness (lack of spontaneity) were marks of the trend to denominationalism, and both of these were normally results of institutionalization. Hence, Niebuhr viewed the emergence of Sunday Schools as an important benchmark in the movement toward becoming a denomination. A second indicator was the relative emotionalism or sobriety of the religious rituals. The emotionalism of sectarian worship helped to sustain the high levels of commitment to this countercultural group. With the decline of emphasis on firsthand conversion experience, a more literate, rational, and orderly worship style began to predominate (1957:63).

Like Troeltsch, Niebuhr's formulation emphasized compromise (a value-laden criterion) as the primary basis for distinguishing sect from church. He also indicated a high level of correlation between many diverse factors. Although his description may have been accurate for many religious groups of his day, we can point to many that have some features of the sect and some of the denomination. For example, many of the more emotional, conversion-oriented Christian groups of today (born again Christians) deemphasize the importance of a trained professional clergy as necessary to transmit the grace of God; they downplay the necessity of orderliness and solemnity in worship; and they stress the centrality of a personal conversion experience. Yet, many of these same groups are not radicals that object to the stratification system and speak forcefully on behalf of the poor. Many of them support the current economic system (the status quo) and defend the national values of the United States. They are well acculturated. Niebuhr would probably assert that they are not manifestations of early Christianity, but further forms of compromise. After all, he might say, they do not restore the original *social ethic* of Christianity. However, this does not solve the problem that a large number of groups do not seem to fit the typology. The definition of types is still problematic.

Furthermore, some religious groups do not seem to fit Niebuhr's sequential model—with new groups returning to the purity of the original faith. Stephen Steinberg (1965) has analyzed the emergence of Reform Judaism from Orthodox Judaism as a reform group resembling the church model. Reform Judaism did not represent a protest against the "perversion of true religion" and did not call for a return to the "old ways." Rather, it represented a fuller acculturation or modernization of the faith. This new group was rejecting what members considered an excessive tie to the past on the part of the parent body. It is important, therefore, to keep in mind that Niebuhr describes the predominant trend, but the sequential pattern of sect → denomination → church is not universal.

Nonetheless, Niebuhr's formulation is important for several reasons. First, many later developments were built upon his conceptualization. Therefore, an understanding of later formulations is facilitated if we understand Niebuhr. This is particularly true relevant to his sequencing of types and the trend to move from sect to denomination to church.

Second, Niebuhr identified some of the social conditions which may give rise to different types of groups, both internal and external factors. A conflict between the group's ideology and the values of the larger society is one factor. The Christian social ethic calls for a feeling of brotherhood and sisterhood of all peoples and for the establishment of a society that is just and equalitarian. The conflict between such an imperative and the social realities of inequality, prejudice, and warfare may create group schisms. Some believers may want to modify the faith so as to be "realistic," while others may insist on adherence to the original social ethic. Hence, conflict between ideology and social reality may generate schisms and new groups.

Another factor that contributes to the emergence of new groups is frustration with the impersonality of highly bureaucratized religion. Some individuals desperately seek a religion which enhances interpersonal ties and a sense of belonging. Likewise, some persons may rebel against the lack of spontaneity and affectivity in the worship of church-type groups. The quiet, orderly worship of an Episcopal church may not satisfy some people. The scholarly and rational sermon of a Presbyterian minister may not enhance the sense of worship for a migrant farm worker with little formal education. Hence, different emotional and cognitive styles of worship may generate different formulations of the faith and different types of groups.

A final factor that generates differences is purely external to the nature of the religion itself. Denominations or other religious groups may form around ethnic, racial, or class lines. Religious scholars, including both theologians and social scientists, continue to emphasize the central role of ethnicity in the formation of denominations (Marty 1972; Greeley 1972:108–126).

Although there are many difficulties with Niebuhr's typology, he did point beyond the typology itself and suggested some of the social sources (within groups and external to them) that cause the formation of different sorts of religious groups.

Continuing Formulations.   Various sociologists have continued to clarify the concepts of sect and church and to identify factors which contribute to the formation of one type of group as opposed to another. Werner Stark (1967) and Benton Johnson (1963) have suggested that a value conflict with the dominant society should be the central criterion that distinguishes the sect. Stark even goes so far as to suggest that all sects are countercultures. The insistence on reducing the church-sect typology to one defining characteristic is an attempt to clarify the use of the term and to avoid a confusing typology which does not always correspond with social realities. Many of the elements used in the past vary independently of each other. There is a definite need for increased precision in the use of these terms. In short, there has been a recent movement toward simpler conceptualizations, as originally suggested by Weber.

Johnson suggests: "A church is a religious group that accepts the social environment in which it exists. A sect is a religious group that rejects the social environment in which it exists" (1963:542). Using this single criterion, the classification of a group will not depend on its intrinsic qualities (extent of institutionalization; emphasis on conversion and voluntary adult commitment, and so on). Rather, classification of a group would depend on the nature of its relationship to the larger culture in which it resides. Johnson points out that the use of this criterion involves a shift in the classification of some groups. For example, the Roman Catholic Church has always been considered the best example of a church. In the United States, the Catholic Church has represented a minority group that has sometimes been at odds with the predominant values and policies of the country.

Johnson would suggest that in the United States, Catholics are more toward the sectarian end of the continuum.

One problem with this criterion has to do with which value conflicts are so significant as to warrant classification as a sect. The "dominant value system of the United States" includes many different values, attitudes, and beliefs. These various values may themselves be found independent of one another. For example, no one who studies the Church of Jesus Christ of Latter-Day Saints (Mormons) can fail to notice the emphasis on hard work, family values, individualism, and national loyalty. Yet, there are significant ways in which the Mormons have deviated from cultural values of this country. Although most of the above-mentioned values were part of the value orientation of this group in the 19th century, the Mormons also endorsed the practice of polygyny (one man with two or more wives). Non-Mormon neighbors and the federal government were firmly opposed to this policy. The conflict between the Mormons and Gentiles at one point became violent. In 1857, President James Buchanan commissioned federal troops to move into Utah, and the resultant skirmishes are referred to as the Utah Mormon War. (O'Dea 1957:101–111).

Is conflict over one value perspective (such as polygyny) enough to classify a group as sectarian, or must there be conflict in several major areas? Or is it merely the intensity of the conflict—degree of tension between the group and the surrounding culture—that is the defining factor? Of course, intense conflicts may also arise over issues other than value orientations or religious beliefs. In fact, much of the prejudice against the Mormons was due to conflict over scarce resources and valued lands. The problem was not strictly a conflict of value orientations, but one over who would possess what *both* groups valued. Johnson would recognize the early Mormons as a sect, for they were in intense conflict with their larger social environment. But students should recognize that conflict and harmony are not always mutually exclusive. A group may be in consensus with the dominant culture on some issues and in intense discord on others.

Perhaps the most significant difficulty with this value-conflict criterion is highlighted by Johnson himself. Many groups commonly recognized as sects actually socialize in dominant-society values. Although they seem to be in conflict with the dominant society, many holiness sects are alternative modes of enculturating people in that society's values. (Johnson 1961). He writes, "It may well be that one of the most important functions of the conversionist bodies in the United States, both now and historically, has been to socialize potentially dissident elements—particularly the lower classes—in the dominant values which are our basic point of reference. The differences sociologists have seen between the Protestant 'churches' and the Protestant 'sects' may be matters of taste, rhetoric, and expressive symbolism . . . far more than they are matters of basic value orientation" (1963:547). Yet, some sectarian groups, like the Old Order Amish, do provide an alternative value orientation that does not lead to eventual acculturation. The use of value conflicts with the dominant culture is one way to distinguish sects from churches, but this defining criterion is not without its shortcomings.

Several sociologists have emphasized social conflict as either a *cause* of the rise of sects or as a *variable* within them, rather than as their defining characteristic. Some scholars suggest that a sect's development is the result of continuing interaction between the religious group and the host society. Three critical factors have been identified that determine the evolution of the sect: (1) the centrality or sacredness of the values and norms that the sect rejects or protests against; (2) the tolerance of protest in the host culture; and (3) the strategy of the sect in expressing its protest (e.g., aggressive militancy versus withdrawal) (Redekop 1974). This view recognizes that many sects are in intense conflict with the dominant society, but it also affirms the thesis that some sects acculturate members into the values of the dominant society. With sects playing either role, conflict with the society hardly seems an appropriate definition of sectarianism. It is this sort of variability that caused one scholar to suggest that perhaps extent of institutionalization should be the central defining characteristic of sects and churches (Greeley 1972:24–25). In any event, the trend is toward a simplified definition of church and sect (e.g., see Knudsen et al. 1978).

Like many contemporary scholars, Milton Yinger holds that Troeltsch's concept of church and sect includes too many variables, many of which are not highly correlated in actual groups. Unlike Johnson, he prefers to use several factors in defining sects, denominations, and churches. Yinger reduces Troeltsch's list of characteristics, which includes both sociological and theological factors, to strictly sociological variables. He suggests three that seem to him to be central, and he establishes a helpful model that lends insight into types of groups and their evolution. The three criteria suggested by Yinger are these:

1. The degree to which the membership policy of the group is exclusive and selective or open and inclusive.
2. The extent to which the group accepts or rejects the secular values and structures of society.
3. The extent to which, as an organization, the group integrates a number of local units into one national structure, develops professional staffs, and creates a bureaucracy (Yinger 1970:257).

Yinger points out that in actual cases, the first two variables are very closely correlated. Those groups which reject secular values are likely to be exclusive and selective in their membership policies, and those groups that accept secular values are likely to be inclusive and open in their membership.

By using the first two factors as one component and the extent of institutionalization as the other, Yinger develops a model that suggests several different types of groups (see Exhibit 7–2). This two-dimensional model is capable of showing a progression from sect to church, but it also demonstrates that increased institutionalization may occur somewhat independently from membership policy and from the acceptance of secular values. There are pressures (discussed in Chapter 6) which cause groups to evolve generally from the types in the lower left side of the grid toward those in the upper right side. Nonetheless, the rate, the direction, and the extent of this evolution is not inevitable. Whether a group stabilizes as an established sect or continues to acculturate to the stage of institutional denomination or ecclessia has to do with the group's belief system. A group which focuses on individual anxiety, sin, and salvation will acculturate rather easily. Sects whose primary concern is social evils and injustices are more likely to become established sects and may never move to the ecclesiastical or denominational stages (Yinger 1970:266–268; Wilson 1970:233–242).

There are two types of religious organizations that will not fit this schema. The first is the shamanistic religion of many nonindustrialized societies. The religion is universally held by all members of that society. It does not pose values which are antithetical to the secular values, for it serves as a sort of glue that helps unify the culture. On the other hand, religion in such a culture is not highly institutionalized. Yinger calls such a religion a Universal Diffused Church, for it is diffused through the culture rather than being specialized and maintaining its own autonomous organization. The second case that does not fit is the Universal Institutionalized Church, which most perfectly fits Troeltsch's description of the church. This is best exemplified by the highly institutionalized Roman Catholic Church of the Middle Ages. It was universal in that no other religion had a significant influence in Europe; national boundaries and religious loyalties were therefore coextensive, with Roman Catholic Christianity playing a major factor in the culture of medieval Europe.

These two exceptions highlight an important fact: the existence of sects and denominations is a phenomenon of pluralistic societies. In fact, scholars have maintained that the pure form of church Troeltsch described is impossible in a democratic and pluralistic society. Likewise, the Universal Diffused Church is a phenomenon of only very simple and homogeneous societies; it is not found in complex and heterogeneous ones.

I have found Yinger's conceptualization to be particularly helpful, for he reduces the number of variables to be considered, and at the same time shows how several different types of groups can emerge. The primary value of his schema is in identifying *several* possible patterns in the *evolution* of groups.

In short, some sociologists insist that the concepts of sect and church can be useful tools of analysis only if the criteria for defining them are greatly simplified. Others feel that church-sect theories have become such a hopeless hodgepodge of definitions and variables that the terms themselves have no real meaning or utility. (Goode 1967; Muvar 1975; Greeley

Exhibit 7–2

Yinger's Schema, Types of Religious Organizations (modified)

I. Inclusiveness of membership
II. Extent of acceptance of societal values

	Low			High
		Universal institutionalized church		
III. Extent of organization, complexity, and distinctiveness of the religious structures — High 4.	Null	Rare (Seventh Day Adventists)	Institutional denomination (The Church of God)	Institutional ecclesia (Episcopal Church)
3.	Null	Established or institutionalized sect (Old Order Amish)	Diffused denomination (Beachy Amish Mennonite)	Diffused ecclesia (Christian Scientist)*
2.	Sect movement (the Bruderhof)	Established lay sect (Amana Church Society)	Rare	Rare
1. Low	Charismatic sect (The Way)	Null	Null	Null
		Universal diffused church		

Measurement of III. above.

	Are local religious units integrated into a national organization?	Are there religious professionals?	Is there a bureaucratic structure?
4. Most complex	yes	yes	yes
3.	yes	yes	no
2.	yes	no	no
1. Least complex	no	no	no

* The Church of Jesus Christ, Scientist has a bureaucratic structure, but no professional clergy. This church does not seem to fit the nomenclature of diffused ecclesia, but it does fit two of the three criteria of institutionalization

Source: J. Milton Yinger, *The Scientific Study of Religion* (New York: Macmillan, 1970), p. 261–262, examples added. Used by permission.

Exhibit 7–3

Sects Have Been Identified by a Variety of Defining Characteristics

	Max Weber	Ernst Troeltsch	H. R. Neibuhr	Benton Johnson	Andrew Greeley	J. Milton Yinger
1. Volitional membership (emphasis on adult membership, personal conversion experience, high level of commitment).	X	X	X			
2. Exclusive membership policy (membership closely guarded and expulsion practiced for violation of norms).	X	X	X		X	X
3. Particularism (belief that only members of the in-group are saved).		X	X			
4. Lack of complex organization (local group with no national organization or bureaucratic structure).		X	X		X	X
5. Belief that salvation is achieved through moral purity (including ethical austerity or asceticism).		X	X			
6. Clergy role deemphasized or nonexistent (lay participation high; priesthood of all believers stressed).		X	X			Subsumed under 4
7. Conflict with host society (rejection of secular values; hostile or indifferent to the state).		X	X	X		X
8. Fundamentalistic theology (only the original revelation is the authentic expression of the faith).		X	X			
9. Lower-class or disfranchized group (group membership comprised primarily of socially disadvantaged persons).		X	X			
10. Informal, spontaneous worship (expectation of spontaneous, emotional expression of faith in corporate worship).			X			
11. Radical social ethic (emphasizing the equality of all persons and the necessity of economic equity).			X			

1972:77–79) Still others persist in using multidimensional definitions of sects and churches, but describe any particular group only with the adjectives "sect-like" or "church-like." Using this procedure, a scholar acknowledges that of five or six items used to operationalize sectarianism, a group may qualify as a sect on most but not all. Likewise, a group may be called church-like if it conforms to *most* of the specified characteristics of a church (Winter 1977; Demerath 1965). Rather than describing pure types, these scholars simply attempt to describe groups as being closer to the sectarian or the ecclesiastical end of a continuum. This procedure is useful for those interested in demonstrating correlations of a style of religious organization (sect-like or church-like) with certain social attitudes or social circumstances (e.g., the amount of gender prejudice or the socioeconomic status of group members). This procedure is not helpful for those interested in tracing the patterns of religious group evolution. When this is the theoretical issue one wishes to pursue, a simplified definition of sectarianism and ecclesiasticism is needed. In any case, students of religion should be sure they understand how sect and church or sect-like and church-like are defined and measured in any specific study they read.

In Chapter 8 we will look more closely at studies which have traced the relationship between social attitudes and church-like or sect-like groups. In the following pages we will continue to focus on the issue of religious group evolution.

Social Conditions which Generate Each Type of Group

We might summarize this discussion of churches, denominations, institutionalized sects, and sects by reviewing the factors which seem to cause the emergence of new groups. Niebuhr pointed to three. First, when Christian denominations begin to ignore the original concern of the faith for poverty and inequality, sectarian groups are likely to arise. As members of those sects (who are disproportionately from the lower classes) begin to achieve some affluence, the sect begins to accommodate secular values and becomes comfortable with the status quo. The group begins to denominationalize. Those persons who are still economically disfranchised are likely to break again from the group and reject social inequality as contrary to the original ethic of the faith. One cause of sectarianism, then, is the existence of social inequality.

Second, Niebuhr pointed out that some groups are expressions of ethnic values and national loyalties. In such cases, the belonging function operates to separate German Methodists from other Methodists and Italian Catholics from Irish Catholics. The sense of ethnic belonging, then, had become a source of division within Christendom.

Third, Niebuhr pointed out that churches and denominations become bogged down in bureaucratic structures. Some sect movements are expressions of a desire for religious groups that are smaller, more informal, and less under the control of a professional clergy. Sectarianism, then, is sometimes an expression of rebellion against complex organizational structure.

Fourth, he believed that sectarian movements are sometimes spawned by a desire for more spontaneity and more emotional expression in worship. Worship in the denominations tends to become formal, orderly, and highly intellectual. Niebuhr pointed to both internal and external factors in the emergence of new religious groups. However, his emphasis on the sect-to-denomination transformation was on internal factors (i.e., institutionalization).

Whether and how a sect develops into a denomination also depends largely on how the larger society responds to this new group. If the values of the dominant culture the sect challenges are central ones, if the host culture does not have a tradition of religious freedom and tolerance, and if the strategy of the sect is aggressive militance (rather than avoidance and withdrawal), the group will either be crushed or will reinforce its antiestablishment posture. If the group does survive, its acculturation is likely to be very slow. In fact, such a group may remain forever an established sect. On the other hand, if the dominant cultural values the sect rejects are tangential, if there is a tradition of religious tolerance in the host culture, and if the strategy by which the sect mobilizes its resources is inoffensive, the group may accommodate and become acculturated rather quickly. The movement from sect to denomination is determined in large degree by outsiders' response to the group (Redekop 1974).

As we discovered in the previous chapter, the internal belief system of the group is also important in the evolution of a group. If a sect's definition of evil and corruption is individualistic (matters of personal decision making and individual determination) then acculturation and accommodation is likely. If evil is considered to be social in nature, if the structures of the society are defined as incompatible with religious values, then the group is less likely to denominationalize. The Quakers (Society of Friends) have a very strong *social* ethic. Although they are not really persecuted in contemporary American society, the Quakers remain an institutionalized sect. In this case, the resistance to denominationalizing is internal (based in their social ethic) rather than external (Yinger 1970:267).

Brian Wilson (1959) has identified several different types of sects depending on their theological orientation. Using his classifications, he points out that some types of sects are more likely to denominationalize than are others. He maintains that groups which have a theological orientation encouraging a simple ascetic lifestyle are more likely to generate an affluent membership. Affluence often leads to accommodation. Those sects that do not stress asceticism are slower to accommodate.

But an even more important point is made by Wilson when he demonstrates that the movement toward denominationalism is largely a function of an expanding economy. As members become more affluent, they tend to acculturate to the values of the dominant society and lose their fervor for revolution or reform. Since opportunities for upward mobility are most likely in a climate in which the economy is growing, the state of the economy may affect the likelihood of a group becoming a denomination or stabilizing as an institutionalized sect. Stagnant economics are more likely to generate rather permanent sects. Wilson believes that both internal belief systems and external factors in the society affect the group's subsequent development, but he puts more emphasis on external forces (i.e., an expanding economy).

The formation and evolution of any group is the result of many interacting processes: the social standing of members, ethnic factors, survival forces which impel a group to institutionalize, responses of outsiders to the group and its message, the belief system of the group, and the state of the economy in the host society. Both internal and external forces determine its evolution.

Thus far, however, we have discussed only the development of sects, institutionalized sects, denominations, and churches. How does the term cult fit into all of this?

The Concept of Cult

The term *cult* has been used by sociologists in three distinct ways. For one group of theorists, a cult is a small religious group which has a highly committed membership, lacks a bureaucratic structure, is led by a charismatic leader, and holds some esoteric or occult ideas. By defining cult in this way, some social scientists have identified the cult as the earliest phase of a cult-sect-denomination-church continuum. These theorists use the term *cult* where Yinger uses the term *charismatic sect.* This sort of definition seems to be the one most often used by the popular press when describing the growth of cults in America. However, it is not currently used by very many sociologists of religion.

A second procedure (an attempt to elaborate Troeltsch's mysticism category), emphasizes the lack of internal discipline and the loose-knit structure in the cult. Following Howard Becker's formulation (1932), the cult is seen as an urban, nonexclusive, loosely associated group of people who hold some esoteric beliefs. They are kindred spirits who have some common views relative to one particular aspect of reality, but such persons may also belong to other, more conventional, church groups. The presence of a charismatic leader is common, but certainly not necessary. The Spiritual Frontiers Fellowship provides an example. It is a group of people who believe firmly in life after death and in various forms of parapsychology. They emphasize spiritual healing, the power of mind over matter, and the possibility of communication with the dead. They hold occasional workshops and lecture/seminar programs to expand their understandings and to inspire one another to deeper belief in the power of the spirit. Much of the membership consists of professional people who are well educated, belong to main-line denominations, and do not think of themselves as esoteric "kooks." The group has no charismatic leader; in fact, authority is at a minimum. Commitment to such groups is nondemanding, and membership is likely to be transient. The cult, in this case, is viewed not so much as a precursor to the sect, but as a separate and distinct type of religious phenomenon. The chief defining characteristics of the cult are the loose structure and the lack of application of the world view to all aspects of life. A number of sociologists utilize this approach in defining cult (Becker 1932; Notting-ham 1971; Hargrove 1979; McGuire 1981).

A third approach is to define the cult as the beginning phase of an entirely new religion. The group may be loosely structured or it may demand tremen-dous commitment, but it must provide a radical break from existing religious traditions. This approach to identifying the cult is also used by a number of sociologists (Glock and Stark 1965; Stark and Bainbridge 1979; Yinger 1970; Nelson 1968; and Johnstone 1975). While both of these latter defini-tions have their advocates, the third approach seems to be emerging as the more common one and seems to me to provide a more helpful analytical tool. Perhaps the term *occult* (or some similar term which avoids negative connotations) could be used to refer to such religious groupings as the Spiritual Frontiers Fellowship, Silva Mind Control, Transcendental Medita-tion, astrology groups, and flying saucer groups (who believe UFOs are messengers from outer-space gods). Such loose-knit groups may eventually emerge into cults. In this text, however, we will be using the third approach.

Charles Glock and Rodney Stark define cults as "religious movements which draw their inspiration from other than the primary religion of the culture, and which are not schismatic movements in the same sense as sects whose concern is with preserving a purer form of the traditional faith" (Glock and Stark 1965:245). This emphasis distinguishes a cult from a sect in that the latter attempts to renew or purify the prevailing religion of the society while the cult introduces a new and different religion. Some-times it is difficult to determine whether a religious movement is attempting to renew or replace the traditional religion, for a new religion often tries to gain legitimacy and acceptability by exaggerating its continuity with exist-ing faiths. Nonetheless, the issue of whether a group is trying to purify or to replace the traditional religion of a society is central to this concept of cult. Milton Yinger, after his careful development of the sect-denomina-tion-ecclesia grid, turned to a treatment of the cult:

> [Some religious groups] do not appeal to the classical, the primitive, the "true" interpretation of the dominant religion, as the sect does, but claim to build *de novo*. The term *cult* is often used to refer to such new and syncretist movements in their early stages. It often carries the connotations of small size, search for a mystical experience, lack of structure, and presence of a charismatic leader. They are similar to sects, but represent a sharper break, in religious terms, from the prevailing tradition of a society (1970:279).

The Unification Church provides an interesting example. The members of this group believe that Sun Myung Moon is the messiah. They accept his doctrine that Jesus was supposed to have been the Son of God, but that he failed in his mission and got himself killed. Jesus provided a partial salvation (purely spiritual), but he failed to redeem the social, economic, and political structures of this world. Since Jesus failed in the total task which was assigned to him, God has now blessed and empowered the Reverend Moon to fulfill this divine role. Obviously, such a doctrine is a sharp break from traditional Christianity. While the organizational structure and the conflict with the predominant societal values cause the Moonies to appear to be a sect, the development of a new and unique religious doctrine distinguishes them from the sects. In order to gain legitimacy and acceptance, however, the Unification Church has downplayed these radical doctrines and has stressed its endorsement of traditional American values (anti-Communism, importance of family life, and so on).

The Church of Jesus Christ of Latter-Day Saints provides another example (despite their claim to being a Christian denomination). Although they believe that Jesus was the messiah and they believe in the Bible, they also have a second book which they hold as sacred scripture. The new scripture (The Book of Mormon) came from Joseph Smith's "translation" of some golden plates which he found in upstate New York. Smith taught that prophets in the early Americas had made a written record of messages from God and of the visit which Jesus made to this continent. The last of these prophets buried the written record on golden plates, and Smith was told in several visions where to find them and how to translate them. The Mormons emphasize that they are a branch of Christianity, but many of their theological innovations are not accepted as Christian doctrine by other Christian groups (such as the belief that unmarried individuals can never attain celestial heaven, the highest of their levels of heaven). The early Mormons were an example of a cult rather than of sectarian reform.

Although the issue of whether a group is initiating a new religion is the central one in defining a cult, there are several other characteristics that are common in cults. While sects often place a strong emphasis on the authority (perhaps even literal authority) of scripture, cults frequently stress mystical, psychic, or ecstatic experiences. There is not a categorical difference between the two groups on this, but cults seldom use previously existing scriptures as a sole source of truth. In fact, it is not uncommon in the United States for cults to generate their own scriptures. The Mormons are one example, and the Unification Church has also been generating a written record which seems to be taking on the aura of sacred scripture. This penchant for scriptural basis is probably caused by the scriptural (written record) orientation of American culture. Cults in other cultures do not ordinarily generate new scriptures. Hence, if the traditional religion emphasizes the role of scripture, the cult is likely to develop its own alternative form of "written word."

Another pattern which prevails in many cults is the centrality of a charismatic leader. A charismatic leader is a person who is believed to have extraordinary insights and powers (discussed in Chapter 6). Such a person is attributed with certain divine qualities, and is believed to have direct and unique contact with the supernatural. It is the unique insights of these individuals that are the basis for the alternative faith. While most cults are clearly founded by such charismatic leaders, some sociologists believe that cults can also develop in a more spontaneous way—through "spontaneous subcultural evolution" (Bainbridge and Stark 1979). Such cults, like the groups that focus their faith on the saving power of unidentified flying objects (UFOs), are usually more loosely structured and more democratic. They have no identifiable charismatic figure, but stigmatization and hostility by outsiders may force adherents to draw more closely together and raise boundaries against outsiders. Such groups usually start out as nonreligious subcultures, but may eventually emerge into esoteric cultic groups with a world view and ethos that contradicts those of the dominant society. (Nelson 1968:357–358; and Bainbridge and Stark 1979:291–293). Hence, Bainbridge and Stark believe that there are really three different ways cults may emerge: through the process of spontaneous subcultural evolution; through the dynamic leadership of a charismatic leader who genuinely believes in the veracity of his or her teachings;[4] or through the leadership of a charismatic "entrepreneur" who sees religion as a money-making scheme. (Some "charismatic leaders" do indeed seem to be con men who are manipulating religion as a means of gaining power and wealth.) Social scientists are therefore not in agreement on the *necessity* of a charismatic leader in the formation of a cult.

Externally, the sect and the cult look much alike. Both rebel against the predominant cultural values, both lack trained professional leaders and a bureaucratic structure, and both insist on a stringent membership policy which requires significant commitment (although the cult may not require this in its very earliest stage of development). The cult, like the sect, is also capable of institutionalization. In fact, some institutionalization is necessary if the group is to outlive its founder. The evolution of sects and cults is comparable as indicated in Exhibit 7–4.

This diagram, while oversimplifying the process, does suggest the parallel manner in which these two types of groups may evolve. If we allowed for the two-dimensional analysis Yinger proposes, we would have a more

---

[4] Bainbridge and Stark make a value judgment about these leaders by referring to them as "psychopathic characters." We discussed the issue of religion and mental health in Chapter 5. I prefer to avoid labeling all of these leaders with a pejorative term. Some of them do seem to be "psychopathic," but others are merely protesting the "sick side" of American culture and may be more mentally healthy in many respects than those who perpetuate the status quo. By allowing only two categories of charismatic leaders (conscious manipulators and "sincere" psychopaths), Bainbridge and Stark introduce an unwarranted value judgment.

Exhibit 7–4 _____

Evolution of Sects and Cults

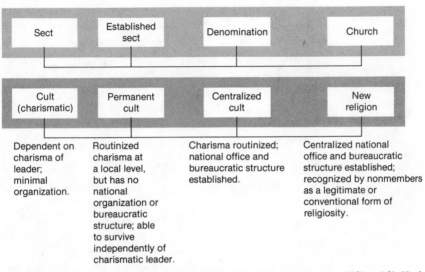

Sect	Established sect	Denomination	Church

Cult (charismatic)	Permanent cult	Centralized cult	New religion

Dependent on charisma of leader; minimal organization.

Routinized charisma at a local level, but has no national organization or bureaucratic structure; able to survive independently of charismatic leader.

Charisma routinized; national office and bureaucratic structure established.

Centralized national office and bureaucratic structure established; recognized by nonmembers as a legitimate or conventional form of religiosity.

From Geoffrey K. Nelson, "The Concept of Cult," *Sociological Review*, November 1968, p. 360. Used by permission of Routledge and Kegan Paul LTD.

accurate picture: institutionalization and accommodation to secular values do not necessarily occur at the same rate.

To understand fully the evolution of a sect or cult, we must give attention (1) to the hostility toward the group within the dominant society, and (2) to the strength of the desire for legitimacy within the deviant group. In other words, we must take into account the pressures at work on a group as it attempts to mobilize its resources and to counter opposition to its existence. Bainbridge and Stark (1979:293) insist that hostile forces may cause a sectarian group to become a cult; as its beliefs are modified to define its separateness, it develops a unique world view. They refer to the People's Temple of Jonestown as an example of this sect-to-cult movement. With this added variable which affects the development and self image of a group, our view of sect and cult emergence becomes more complex. (see Exhibit 7–5).

Clearly, no one graph is capable of demonstrating the many factors that affect the evolution and development of a particular religious group. This one looks at sects and cults from a slightly different lens than does the one developed by Yinger. The important point here is that both sects and cults lack organizational complexity and are similar in rejecting the values of the secular society. However, the sect views its role as one of purifying the traditional faith by calling members back to what are believed to be core principles. Cults represent the nascent stages of the development of

Exhibit 7–5

Social Forces and Sect-Cult Transformation

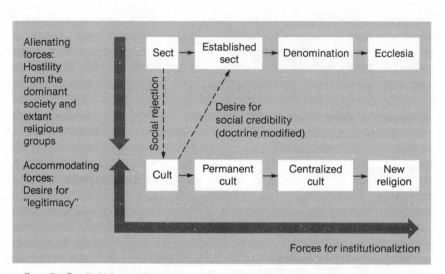

Alienating forces: Hostility from the dominant society and extant religious groups

Social rejection

Sect → Established sect → Denomination → Ecclesia

Desire for social credibility (doctrine modified)

Accommodating forces: Desire for "legitimacy"

Cult → Permanent cult → Centralized cult → New religion

Forces for institutionaliztion

From Goeffrey K. Nelson, "The Concept of Cult," *Sociological Review,* November 1968, p. 360. Used by permission of Routledge and Kegan Paul LTD.

a new or a syncretistic religion. Other factors may affect the evolution of a sect or a cult, but the institutionalizing and accommodating tendencies frequently cause sects to become denominational in form. The cult usually either dies out or institutionalizes into a new religion.

If all of this seems terribly complex, it is because the evolution of religious groups *is* complex. Various scholars have focused on different aspects of religious group evolution and therefore have defined such terms as *sect, cult,* and *denomination* in alternative ways. This is an important point for the new student of religion to bear in mind when reading a study that discusses sects and cults. Readers should always be sure they understand how an author defines his or her terms and how those terms were operationalized or measured.

Theories about sect-to-church transformations are generalizations about how this change *normally* occurs. It may or may not be precisely descriptive of the process as it occurs in a specific group a reader chooses to study. Furthermore, such terms as *sect, cult, established sect,* and *denomination* are normally not ones that can be *permanently* assigned to a group. They simply describe organizational characteristics of a group at a *particular moment* in its history. With this in mind, church-sect theory can enable us to describe the normal process of organizational change in religious collectivities. References to church-like or sect-like groups also allow us to identify similarities of religious style among certain religious groups and differences in character with others at any given time. One recent development in church-sect theory is the use of such adjectives as sect-like and church-like to describe the religiosity of individuals—regardless of the groups those individuals belong to (Demerath 1965). This has yielded fruitful insights, but students encountering such a study should be sure they understand how church-like and sect-like were operationalized.

In short, if one seeks to generalize about how most groups evolve and the stages they go through, the concepts of church, sect, and denomination can be helpful. However, if one wants analytical tools for understanding one specific group in depth, the choice point analysis is more profitable than a broad label of sect, cult or denomination.

Elements in the Analysis of a Religious Group: Choice Points

Studies seeking *generalizations* about social behavior are called nomothetic analyses. Most sociological studies tend to be nomothetic in character, for the discipline of sociology tends toward generalizing about social behavior. We compare similar types of phenomena in order to formulate theories about the causes or the consequences of a certain *type* of activity, behavior, or structure.

Some scholars, however, are more interested in simply *describing* the *unique* development and character of one *specific group*. The accurate description of a social group, without any attempt to prove or disprove a larger theory, is referred to as idiographic analysis. Idiographic analysis has been most typical of history as a discipline, although some anthropologists—influenced by Franz Boas[5]—have also insisted on purely idiographic studies. Church/sect concepts were originally developed to describe differences between groups, but over the years those distinctions have been used as a basis for generalizations about religious groups and as the foundation for building theories. Hence, church/sect theory today is essentially nomothetic.[6] Readers interested in simply describing a particular religious group as it currently exists (idiographic analysis) may find the choice point concept to be considerably more useful than church/sect distinctions.

---

[5] Boas insisted that if one was studying a group with the goal of comparing or contrasting groups or of proving a specific theory, a bias would enter the study. The observer would notice only that which he or she set out to notice and would screen out data that did not fit. He believed that nomothetic orientations had resulted in distorted descriptions of other cultures. For this reason he insisted that a moratorium be called on nomothetic studies; anthropologists should simply seek to describe as accurately as possible. Only after massive amounts of accurate and "uncontaminated" data had been collected should anthropologists begin to interpret them.

[6] Some social scientists believe that church/sect theory has been of limited value for generating valid generalizations. The problem may be that church/sect concepts were formulated for descriptive purposes (see discussion of Troeltsch), not for purposes of budding a general theory.

Andrew Greeley (1972) suggests that persons who wish to understand a religious group are *not* well served if they simply have a list of eight or ten different *types* of groups, each with its own typical characteristics. Rather, a researcher should have a list of "things to look for" when trying to understand a group (Greeley 1972:21–28). He provides a list of eight dimensions, with each arranged on a continuum.[7] For example, he suggests that the theology of a group may range on the continuum from extreme orthodoxy to extreme modernism. Other scholars have also used this procedure, referring to it as a "choice point" analysis (O'Dea 1978:134; Winter 1977:105–137). By choice point these sociologists simply suggest that religious collectivities choose a direction or an emphasis on certain critical issues in their group life. The social scientist identifies the choices made by a group on those specific points. The nature of each of those choices will profoundly affect a group's style and character. The purpose is not to classify a specific group as representative of a particular *type* of group, but to recognize its unique character. Choice point analysis is favored by those who undertake idiographic studies.

No one list satisfies everyone, for different scholars notice different patterns as significant. Nonetheless, the following discussion will indicate some of the most commonly identified elements that sociologists notice or look for when investigating any new religious group. Each of these variables may affect the character of a religious group and its members' behavior. Certain factors tend to be highly correlated in most groups (making them more sect-like or church-like), but here we will emphasize the fact that the following variables can be found in all sorts of combinations in any one group. Hence, we will discuss them independently.

1. Theology: Reversionism/Orthodoxy/Modernism

There is frequently a strain in the theology of any religious group which has been in existence for a significant period of time. What we look for here is the mode of interpretation or the source of doctrinal *authority*. One thrust is for the group to adhere to the original formulation of the faith as articulated by the charismatic leader and the early cadre of faithful followers. This emphasis stresses the purity of the original revelation, and attempts to preserve the tradition. In American Christianity, this also may involve a literal interpretation of scripture (fundamentalism). We shall call this emphasis reversionism, for it involves a concerted effort to avoid contemporary modification of the world view and to *revert* to the original formulation of the faith.

---

[7] Greeley's list includes the theology (modern/orthodox), ritual (high church/low church), liturgy (Apollonian/Dionysian), organization (church/sect), attitudes toward clergy (person of *God*/person of God), piety (incarnational/eschatological), ethics (systematic/situational), and world view (pessimistic/optimistic). (Greeley 1972:21–28).

In other cases, later historical revelations and interpretations are also viewed as authoritative (as in the case of the authority of papal proclamations in the Roman Catholic tradition and the authority of interpretations of scripture by earlier rabbis in Orthodox Judaism.[8]) The truth of any contemporary doctrine is still assessed in terms of its conformity to earlier doctrines, but not limited to the original formulations. This approach is generally referred to as orthodoxy.

The third approach is to explain the faith in a way consistent with the predominant attitudes, beliefs, values, and assumptions of contemporary culture and experience. In this instance, new knowledge from science is accepted and incorporated into the theology of the group.[9] Revelations from an earlier era are treated as important, but the emphasis is on what God is saying to contemporary culture. Since earlier revelations were received in an age when many of the laws of science were not yet discovered, the world view of that earlier group is thought to contain less than the whole truth. This theological approach is referred to as liberalism or modernism. Rather than being thought of as given from some external source (the absolute and immutable imperatives of divine revelation), meaning is considered something that is created and continually discovered as humans interact with their environment. The process is sometimes referred to as "inductive" since the starting point for theological reflection is human experience. The starting point for theological reflection for reversionism and orthodoxy is the religious tradition.

Most religious groups seek acceptance and legitimacy in the culture. Hence, they tend to modify the original concepts in subtle and unconscious ways. Frequently, they are not aware of modifications which occur over time, and they defend current belief as if it were an intrinsic doctrine of the faith. For example, many present-day Christians are convinced that the principles of capitalism, as an economic system, are entirely consistent with Christianity. In fact, they may go to great lengths to identify Christianity with capitalism and against communism. Yet, Tawney has shown in his investigation of the writings of Luther, Calvin, and the Roman Catholic Church that the central principles of capitalism were thought at that time to be antithetical to Christian faith (see Chapter 8). Another example is

---

[8] Although there is an insistence among Orthodox Jews that the Torah is the inerrant word of God, the Talmud and other commentaries by rabbinical authorities are normally used to interpret or elaborate Jewish theology. In some cases, however, Orthodox Jews have treated the Torah as being a complete statement which is above interpretation or commentary. It is to be followed literally. This tendency represents a reversionist movement within Orthodox Judaism. Each specific congregation of Orthodox Jews must be analyzed carefully before one determines whether it is orthodox in the sense that I have used that term or whether it has this reversionist tendency.

[9] Berger distinguishes between two forms of modernism or liberalism. Those interested in more subtle or refined distinctions in modernism should see his book, *The Heretical Imperative* (1979).

the evangelical Christian groups that support increases in defense spending by the U.S. government. Interestingly, during the first several centuries of the Christian church, it was taken for granted that all Christians must also be pacifists. In each of these cases, the faith was modified to be consistent with general values and beliefs of the larger culture. The point is, fundamentalist and orthodox groups are somewhat *selective* in what they view as authoritative and binding from the past. Nearly all groups, including those generally considered more conservative or orthodox, tend to modify the earlier doctrines in light of current circumstances and cultural norms.

On the other hand, nearly all religious groups seek roots in some tradition. The sense of being identified with a worthy tradition and the acceptance of the truths of an earlier revelation have profound appeal. Even the most liberal groups constantly struggle to understand how their current formulations of the faith can be consistent with an earlier tradition and revelation. Groups which do not have this sense of an authoritative historical tradition often lack vitality. After all, if science and contemporary culture have all the answers, why call oneself Christian (or Jewish or Buddhist) at all? Interestingly, many liberals and/or their children do eventually opt for this sort of secularism. This continuum suggests the very issue that Troeltsch discussed in his sect/church dichotomy: To what extent is a group clinging to earlier formulations of the faith, and to what extent modernizing and compromising its sense of historical roots?

As we have seen in the discussion of cults, some groups are not interested in revitalizing the existing religion; they offer a new alternative. Hence, when one observes a cult, one does not find reversionism, orthodoxy, or liberalism, but the beginnings of what may become a new religion. As this group evolves into a new religion (if it does survive) one can find the same tension between original doctrine and accommodation to the culture. With the cultural changes of each succeeding decade, the tension increases until the new religion may have its own schism between orthodoxy and modernism. (For example, there are some fundamentalist sects of Mormonism which still cling only to the original teachings of Joseph Smith and do not accept later revelations).

2. Ritual: Simple Church/High Church, Dionysian/Apollonian

The ritual of any particular group may be viewed in terms of two different continua (Greeley 1972). The first has to do with the formality or informality of the worship atmosphere. The simple church is characterized by a simple liturgy, a casual, unpretentious atmosphere, and a lack of elaborate artwork, architecture, or musical productions. The low-church ritual represents the belief that elaborate ceremonies create a barrier to real worship; God is believed to be best encountered in the simple things in life. The high-church style of worship emphasizes the transcendence and majesty of the deity. In this instance, majestic liturgy is combined with overwhelmingly beautiful architecture, art, and music. Worship of the deity calls for the maximum in human effort, and the beauty of the service is itself expected to create a sense of awe and wonder within the worshiper.

The second continuum has to do with the ritual's primary appeal. Some religious rituals appeal to emotions, while the worship services of other groups appeal primarily to logic and reason. The Apollonian[10] orientation stresses logical understanding. The deity is believed to communicate with persons through their minds; humans are conceived largely as rational beings. In fact, some Christian denominations stress that this is the primary way in which persons are "in the image of God." Apollonian worship, therefore, tends to be cerebral, reserved, and sober. Dionysian liturgy, on the other hand, is based on the premise that the deity speaks to humanity primarily through emotions. In this case, humanity is viewed as more than rational; nonrational, ecstatic experience is viewed as the essence of religion. The liturgy may also allow for more spontaneous expression of the faith, sometimes incorporating shouting, dancing, seizures, glossolalia (speaking in tongues) and other emotional expressiveness.

As Exhibit 7–6 suggests, the ritual of any group may tend toward one end of the continuum or the other on each of these, so that four different patterns may be identified: simple-church Dionysian, simple-church Apollonian, high-church Dionysian, and high-church Apollonian.

To a person raised in one style of ritual, other forms of liturgy may have a disconcerting effect. The individual may feel alienated and even offended by a liturgy style that is unfamiliar. In teaching the sociology of religion, I often require students to visit worship services which differ significantly from their own tradition. One young man from a simple-church Dionysian background was asked to attend a very high-church Episcopal service. The congregation used the Book of Common Prayer, stood whenever passages from the Gospel were read, knelt during prayer, and engaged in other traditional acts unfamiliar to the student. He later responded that he felt like a piston inside an enormous engine: up, down, up, down. Although he is a devout Christian, he was alienated and frustrated by that particular style of service. Likewise, one middle-aged woman in my class attended a pentecostal service. She was a member of a high church Lutheran congregation. She found the spontaneity and the "lack of decorum and dignity" to be most unsettling. A negative response is not always forthcoming from such visitations. Many students have found a different mode of expression to be most refreshing. This is particularly likely if a person has become somewhat alienated from his or her own tradition.

Most religious groups are likely to have both Dionysian and Apollonian

---

[10] Nietzsche (1924) used the terms *Apollonian* and *Dionysian* to classify Greek tragedies. Ruth Benedict (1934) was the first social scientist to employ them in the analysis of a total culture. Greeley (1972) first used them for the comparison of liturgies.

Exhibit 7–6 _____

Characteristics of Religious Rituals

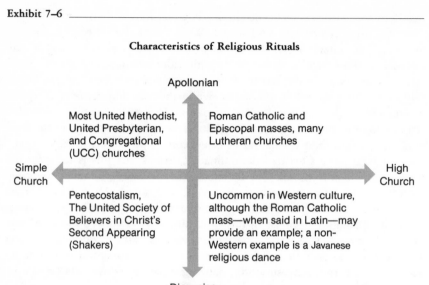

Apollonian

Most United Methodist, United Presbyterian, and Congregational (UCC) churches

Roman Catholic and Episcopal masses, many Lutheran churches

Simple Church

High Church

Pentecostalism, The United Society of Believers in Christ's Second Appearing (Shakers)

Uncommon in Western culture, although the Roman Catholic mass—when said in Latin—may provide an example; a non-Western example is a Javanese religious dance

Dionysian

elements in their liturgy. After all, if religion has both world view and ethos, it must include both cognitive and affective dimensions. If we recall the close relationship between world view and ethos components of religion, then we surely would be mistaken to assume that one religion is entirely emotional in orientation and another is strictly cerebral. Religious groups differ only in the *emphasis* they place on intellect as opposed to emotion. Many logical and rationally developed sermons are sterile in terms of affect, but other aspects of the service may appeal to the emotions. On the other hand, I have heard many sermons that have worked a congregation into high emotional pitch, but which seemed to me to be devoid of logical consistency or substantive content. Nonetheless, they do seem to reinforce the world view of the members of *that* congregation. Readers may find it instructive to discover their own preferences in religious ritual.

3. Organization: Ecclesiastical/Sectarian

As we have seen, an important element in the character of any religious group is the extent of the group's institutionalization. There are many issues one could explore in trying to understand a group's pattern of routinization and internal organization. Complexity of the organizational structure, the existence of an ordained clergy and the nature of their credentials, and the restrictiveness or openness of the group's membership policy are among the most important organizational factors in the development of the group.

A. Complexity of Structure: Highly Institutionalized/Small Group.

In the desire to keep religion authentic, there is often a tendency to want to abolish bureaucratic structures and maintain a simplified communal atmosphere. Yet, if the group is to survive and if it begins to expand, the development of some institutional structure becomes necessary. This may involve the affiliation of local units into a larger regional or national organization. When this occurs, a bureaucratic structure is likely to emerge to coordinate and guide the national organization. With the emergence of such a pattern, one has the development of an increasingly complex organizational structure. This issue of structural complexity has been elaborated earlier in this chapter and in the previous one.

B. Clergy: Formally Trained/No Clergy. In attempting fully to understand the organizational structure of a group, one also must understand the role of clergy in it. In the more complex structures, one usually finds full-time religious professionals. Often the person is ordained or otherwise authorized for leadership in the organization on the basis of extensive training and educational credentials. In the smaller groups, however, one often finds more emphasis on a priesthood of all believers and a rejection of formal academic training as a qualification of leadership. The leader may be chosen on the basis of personal qualities or some other criterion which ignores formal educational credentials.

Some groups which deemphasize both formal training and personal charisma elect their clergy by lot. The Amish, for example, nominate several candidates for office by a congregational vote. Then they have each candidate choose a Bible from several provided. The one who chooses the Bible which has a slip of paper with a prayer on it is the new *Diener* (servant). (Schreiber 1962:131–134; Hostetler 1968:89) This method is used because the Bible says the disciples decided on a new apostle (after the death of Judas) by drawing lots (Acts 1:26). Formal training of clergy is neither valued nor expected by the Amish; the final determination is believed to be made by God, since only God can determine the outcome of such a chance process as drawing lots. In the case of some other religious groups, the decision may be made to eschew the whole idea of an elite group of ordained leaders. The group simply does not have a formal clergy.

In most cases in Western culture, the emergence of a formally approved clergy accompanies the increase in organizational complexity. However, the Christian Scientists are a denomination which has an international bureaucratic structure, but they have no clergy. They do have religious professionals who run the bureaucracy, but not a separate class of members who are more sacred or who are set aside for exemplary living, performance of sacraments, or any other uniquely exalted role. Hence, religious groups may be assessed in terms of the credentials required of those who are designated leaders, attitudes of the members toward those leaders (the extent to which there is deference to and a sense of awe for the ordained clergy), and the difference between leaders and other members in their relative powers and responsibilities. Some groups that do have professional clergy do not expect those clergy to have more power or to be more "holy."

C. Membership Policy: Restrictive/Open.   Membership may be highly selective and may require a good deal of commitment, or it may be open to virtually all members of the larger society. At the outset, a group may emphasize its position as the faithful remnant and may wish to limit membership to the truly dedicated. The requirement of only adult membership is often imposed to ensure that individuals do not become members simply because they were born into the group. An act or statement of personal commitment is frequently expected at the time of initiation. As a group grows, however, more emphasis may be placed on expanding membership. In many, one is initiated into the group at birth and is assumed to be a part of it unless one explicitly rejects the faith. Frequently, a more open membership attitude accompanies an increase in organizational complexity. However, it is sometimes possible to find a small religious group that has a simple organizational structure and an open membership policy. Likewise, one may encounter a group with a complex organizational structure and a membership policy that allows only those adult members who make a significant pledge of commitment and conformity to the group.

4. Relations with Secular Society: Withdrawal/ Transformation/Acceptance

In one sense, the membership policy of a religious group may indicate attitudes toward the prevailing culture and relations with the secular society. But relations with the outside world need to be understood in more depth than one can gain simply by perusing the group's membership policy. In fact, the relations with the secular society can be very complex, and they should be analyzed with a good deal of care. Each religious group may rebel against certain values and patterns of the dominant society, and may strongly affirm other prevailing cultural themes.

As we have already seen in this chapter, the more highly institutionalized religious bodies are more likely to affirm the basic value structure of the prevailing culture, and the less complex groups have frequently rejected that culture and structure. However, it is also true that many holiness sects and other apparently countercultural groups have actually provided alternative modes of accommodation and adjustment to secular society (Johnson 1961). Many sectarian groups, like the snake-handling Christians of Appalachia and many pentecostal temples found in small-town America, are intensely patriotic. They affirm basic American values and support the free enterprise economic system in this country.

On the other hand, some mainline denominations have bureaus and boards which have supported socialistic programs, have charged American patriotism with being a form of idolatry (worship of the nation rather than worship of God), and have sent aid to liberation groups in the Third World. Seemingly "un-American" stances have also been taken by a number of local congregations affiliated with such mainline denominations as the United Church of Christ, the United Presbyterian Church, USA, the United Methodist Church, and the Unitarian Universalist Association. Many of the more sectarian groups have been appalled by these stances and have come to the defense of the prevailing cultural norms. Ironically, it has sometimes been the establishment groups that have advocated change and the sectarian groups that have resisted it.

These stances have not been a matter of the establishment churches advocating modernization and secularization. Many of their controversial stances have been based on a biblical concept of social justice. Support for racial goals and affirmative action policies by denominational bureaus has often been based on scriptural concepts of corporate justice rather than on the more individualistic concepts of justice prevalent in secular American culture.

While acceptance of the dominant culture is one mode of relationship, rejection of the culture through withdrawal is another. Withdrawal may reflect a rejection of this-worldliness or an attempt to create a faithful society within this world. Some religious groups define all of this world as evil and under the control of Satan. Life in the flesh (in this world) and life in the spirit are juxtaposed as opposites. They have no expectation of ever transforming this world into the Kingdom of God. They simply await the Apocalypse, the day when God intervenes in human history, destroys the world as we know it, and begins a new age.

Other religious groups reject the secular culture, but not because they believe that life in this world is inherently depraved and evil. They simply believe that the *specific* culture which surrounds them is antithetical to their espoused faith. Hence, they may retreat to their own community and attempt to maintain a remnant of true believers. They attempt to create a good and faithful society in the midst of a larger, depraved culture. The Amish serve as one example of this; other illustrations include the Koinonia Community in Georgia (Lee 1971), the Oneida utopian community in upstate New York (Carden 1969; Parker 1935), and Arthur Gish's energy-efficient Christian commune in southern Ohio (Gish 1973).

Some groups seem to reject many of the values and structures of the dominant society, but they are not content to withdraw into their own commune. Rather, they choose to participate in the secular society and seek to transform it. In some cases, the group maintains that the Kingdom of God is this-worldly, and they choose to transform secular society by working within its structures. Rather than viewing this world as inherently evil or depraved, they seek to transform it into a just or a "Godly" society. They may hope to change the secular culture so that it will be consistent with sacred values. Some transformationists do not really expect ever to succeed fully in their task, but they believe God requires that the faithful express their devotion by working for a more humane and just social order. The mainline denominational churches which have objected to prevailing cultural norms are usually transformationists in their conception of church and society. Likewise, militant sects can be very aggressive in their attempts to bring change. Transformationists run a very wide gamut, from those who see the need for only modest corrections in the society to those who insist that the entire value system and social structure needs radical alteration (world-transforming movements).

As we have already seen in this chapter and in the preceding one, the relationship of a religious group to the host society may be affected by many factors, both internal and external to the group. The historical causes of a current relationship may be significant in fully understanding the dynamics of any given group. In any case, rejection of the dominant culture through withdrawal is usually viewed as a sect-like response, while acceptance of the secular culture is generally viewed as a church-like response. Attempts to transform the dominant culture may be undertaken by militant sects or by conventional denominations, the difference usually resting in the extent of change that is proposed.

5. Realm: This-Worldly/Otherworldly

Although some sociologists have defined religion as otherworldly in orientation, Max Weber pointed out that the realm in which God's action is identified (or in which the ultimate victory over evil is expected) may be either this-worldly or otherworldly. The religion of the Old Testament is filled with interpretations of God's action in *this* world and with the expectation of the Kingdom of God *on earth*. On the other hand, there are strong strains within the Judeo-Christian heritage that point to salvation in an afterlife. Heaven, or the Kingdom of God, in this case is believed to be an experience of another realm. Similarly, those who await the end of the world at any moment expect that the ultimate victory over evil, suffering, and injustice will transpire in an utterly transformed realm. Rather than assume that all religion is otherworldly, the careful student of religion sets out to discover the orientation of a group. Most religious groups do believe in some sort of God or gods. Since the deity is not usually experienced directly through the five senses, most religions affirm a realm of existence which transcends this world. But the ultimate arena of divine action and the locus of the Heavenly Kingdom may be anticipated in this world and in human history.

For those who define religion as ultimate concern or as a set of symbols that act to create a world view and an ethos, religion can clearly be this-worldly. Hence, if one uses a broader definition of religion (see Chapter

2) one may insist that there are many this-worldly religions in American society. The question of realm, then, is concerned with the location of the final victory over suffering, death, and injustice.

6. Piety: Doing (active)/Being (passive)

Piety has to do with one's devotion to religious principles and practices, and it can take several different forms. In one sense, devotion is the *means* by which one seeks to achieve holiness or an ultimate victory over death, suffering, and injustice. Regardless of whether one's orientation is this-worldly or otherworldly, religious people develop practices which are designed to enhance and glorify that which is viewed as sacred.

"Doing," or "active," piety implies that individuals are to participate in creating their own salvation and/or establishing the Kingdom of God. The doing form of piety is one in which the individual views himself as an "instrument of God." The doer may also practice asceticism—suppression of personal desires and needs in order to advance to a divine goal.[11] The lifestyle and behavior of the individual is believed to have an impact on the ultimate scheme of things. Some otherworldly doers believe they are earning their own salvation in an afterlife. They believe that the morality of their lives in this world will determine their eternal destiny. Others view their activity as a *response* to the experience of divine grace: they seek to respond to God by serving God's purposes. This-worldly doers are often instrumentalists: they emphasize that their actions are ultimately affecting the transformation of life on this earth. The goal in this case may be to help create the Kingdom of God. Hence, asceticism stresses the efficacy of human action: the behavior and lifestyle of persons does make a difference.

The "being" form of piety (sometimes called mystic or passive piety) pays much less attention to human effort and much more to human experience and to an individual's *character* (quality of spirit). The holy is something that is simply experienced. Salvation is viewed as a gift that cannot be earned and humans are viewed as being utterly incapable of contributing to God's kingdom. Insofar as the individual's behavior is important, the stress is usually on righteous character or on virtue. The emphasis is not on what one does, but on what one wants to be. Attitudes and intentions are stressed more than actions.

Otherworldly mystics may emphasize nonrational experience of the holy as the only step toward salvation. Sometimes self-denial (asceticism) is used as a *technique* to purify their spirits and to enhance mystical experiences. This-worldly mystics may believe that prayer, meditation, proper performance of certain rituals, or the quality of an individual's character may affect the actions of the supernatural in this world. Some religious groups

---

[11] The term *asceticism* means self-denial.

assert that changes in this world will come about through the power of positive thinking or through individuals having proper attitudes. Norman Vincent Peale, the well-known Protestant minister, is one advocate of this view, but the same approach can be seen in such cults as est. Some passive pietists believe that such problems as world hunger can be solved by will power. In fact, some groups assert that medical surgery can be performed through mind power—without benefit of scapel or other surgical tools and equipment. The key is purity and intensity of concentration.

One difference between doing and being piety is that the former has some *empirical* likelihood of success, while the latter is based on a nonempirical strategy. For this reason, activist piety is sometimes referred to as part of the "rationalization" of religion. Whether the goal is this- or otherworldly, the means may be based on nonrational, mystic procedures or on sacrifice and deliberate effort by humans to achieve the goal.

In most cases, doing and being forms of piety are found together. In fact, in some groups the two responses may be so blended that it is nearly impossible to determine which is primary. However, in most instances there is a discernible emphasis on either doing or being as the proper form of expressing one's piety.

7. Scope of the World View: Narrow-Range/ Wide-Range Vectors

Anthropologist Clifford Geertz (1968) has suggested that religion may be studied in terms of the "scope" of its impact on adherents. For some persons, religion is one of many concerns in life, blocked off into a separate sphere, having little to do with economic behavior, political opinions, or corporate affairs. For such persons, religion is a private affair which may be of profound importance in the life of the individual. However, the individual insists that it is one's responsibility as a citizen to "render to Caesar that which is Caesar's." Clergy are not expected to meddle in political affairs, and religion is believed to have little or nothing to do with business transactions. W. T. Jones (1972) suggests that such a person views reality through "multiple, narrow-range vectors." Life is seen as many separate and distinct realms.

Empirical research by Lenski and others has shown that such a view of the world is hardly uncommon among Americans. In fact, Lenski (1963) has found a correlation which suggests that those who are more orthodox in theology are more likely to have a multiple, narrow-range vector world view. Such an outlook does not mean that religious beliefs are less meaningful or are less firmly held. On the contrary, Geertz (1968:111–117) holds that the "force" of one's belief (or the intensity of one's conviction) may be quite unrelated to its scope. Indeed, this tendency to a narrow-range vector may be precisely the reason that the 54 percent of Americans who said that religion was very important to them also reported that their religious beliefs have no effect on their ideas of business or politics (Yinger 1970:48).

On the other hand, many religious people consider religion the lens through which all other institutions are to be understood.[12] In this case, religious norms, attitudes and motivations are expected to affect all of life. The demands of religious ethics may be enforced with absolute and uncompromising vigor. Many religious communes and utopias are developed as a means to create a lifestyle which conforms fully to religious principles of morality. Jones (1972) describes such a world view as a "unitary wide-range vector." Actually, any ideology can serve as such a lens for interpreting reality. In China after the ascension to power by Mao Tse-Tung, communism provided the lens for understanding and viewing all behavior. As one reads the accounts of brainwashing or thought-reform techniques used in China, one cannot help but be struck by the way in which every aspect of life was reinterpreted. Some social psychologists refer to such an outlook as totalism (Lifton 1969).

The concept of narrow- or wide-range vectors remains at an impressionistic stage of analysis. Much more work is needed to clarify how to measure or test the differences in people's world views. In some religious groups it is difficult to determine whether the group has a multiple narrow-range world view or a unitary wide-range one. For one thing, in many religious collectivities we find a variety of outlooks, shaped in part by the teachings of that religion but also in part by personality characteristics developed in one's childhood and by many other factors as well. Moreover, there is often a difference in the scope of the official and folk versions of a faith, and one must distinguish which is being described in any particular group.

Nonetheless, the concept of scope may still provide insights. The development of a world view with multiple narrow-range vectors can allow religious persons to accommodate radical and/or ascetic demands of their faith to a comfortable, luxurious lifestyle. This can be done without any sense of

---

[12] The tendency of social scientists who use a broad definition of religion (Yinger, Geertz, and this author) is to assume that religion almost always has considerable force and scope. Note for example, the definition of faith in Chapter 2. Faith is identified as the organizing principle of life, as that which gives meaning and purpose to all of life. Likewise, Geertz defines religion as a system of symbols which act to create powerful, pervasive, and long-lasting moods and motivations in people by formulating a general order of existence. . . ." The implication is that religion affects all of life, or that *whatever* is the central value that does affect all of life is one's religion. Geertz points out that all people seem to be "more or less religious," but that those of us who study religion tend to put too much emphasis on the "more" and not enough on the "less." For those of us who find a broad definition of religion most useful, it is imperative that we be cognizant of this potential bias in our study of religion. Some people may not have one central organizing principle or value which gives meaning to life. Whether or not the world-view advanced by a particular *conventional* religious group is broad or narrow is a matter that needs to be explored in each specific case.

Exhibit 7–7 _____

Religious Scope: Wide or Narrow Range of Influence

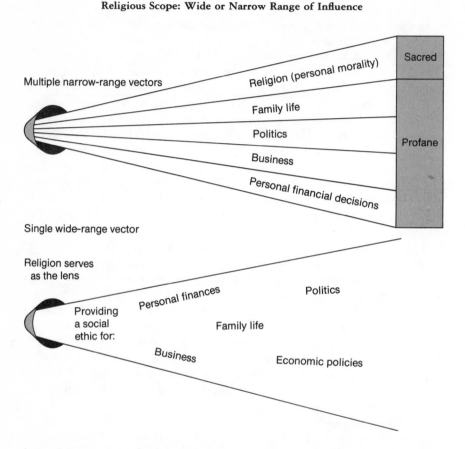

inconsistency. A multiple-vector outlook allows the person to view each aspect of life as distinct and separate. Likewise, the uncompromising (and often self-righteous) behavior of many Christian groups can be understood as part of a totalistic (unitary, wide-ranged) world view.[13]

Choice Point Comparisons of Three Religious Groups

The use of choice points may be clarified if we illustrate with three specific congregations. In this section I will offer a brief comparison of an Old

_____

[13] Descriptively, we find that people in mainline denominations are more likely to have multiple, narrow-range outlooks and people in sects have unitary wide-range world views. Hence, several sociologists have identified multiple narrow-range world views as church-like and unitary perspectives as sect-like. However, this seems a highly questionable practice since the official posture of most denominations is that religion should affect all of life.

Order Amish congregation (25 families), a United Presbyterian church in a small town in the Midwest (500 members), and the Mother Church of the Church of Jesus Christ, Scientist, in Boston (large urban congregation).

In theology, the Amish are reversionists. However, they differ from many fundamentalistic groups. Most Protestants believe that if a behavior is not explicitly forbidden in the Bible, it is acceptable. The Amish teach that if a behavior is not explicitly endorsed in the New Testament or practiced by Jesus and his disciples, it is forbidden. Since the Bible never mentions electricity, telephones, or automobiles, they are forbidden. In many Amish communions, however, this opposition has been softened; gasoline engines are allowed on the farm for processing grain, but automobiles are forbidden. This has led to schisms (there are now 17 different Amish communions or subgroupings). The ruling bishop in each area rules on specific behaviors and inventions Amish members wish to introduce. He must determine whether an innovation is consistent with or a violation of New Testament principles.

The small-town Presbyterian church is quite modern in its theology. The minister seeks to interpret theological maxims in terms of the findings of contemporary science. The technological age is embraced: the marvels of the computer age are discussed from the pulpit, a group meets to study what science and technology might offer for the future, and educational seminars explore how to theologize or find some ultimate meaning in these trends. The Bible is studied, but one emphasis here is to discover how the ancestors reflected theologically. Many biblical maxims are viewed as anachronistic in our own day.

The Christian Science church has a more orthodox theology. The Bible, particularly as interpreted by Mary Baker Eddy, is considered authoritative. No sermon is preached at Sunday services; rather, lessons prepared by the national office are read by lay readers. This means that every congregation of Christian Scientists hears the same message, and no local clergy can modify or modernize it. Christian Science theology would not be considered orthodox by many other Christian denominations. Mary Baker Eddy taught that sickness is an illusion of the mind which can be overcome by right thinking. Even death was viewed as unreal, for the mind, or spirit, continues. The rather exclusive emphasis on health represents a divergence from most Christian theology. However, the outlook of the Mother Church is orthodox as we have used that term in this chapter; it remains faithful to its own traditional or historic affirmations, and it affirms that the original revelations (in the Bible) are properly understood only through later historical interpretations.

Amish ritual is simple and Apollonian. The church meets in a family home or in a barn, rotating to different homesteads every two weeks (services are every other Sunday). No order of worship is printed, no stained glass windows grace the service, and no trained choir performs. Although the service is simple, it is not a highly emotional one. In stark contrast to services of the Shakers (see Exhibit 6–3 in the previous chapter) the Amish services are orderly and reserved. The service normally lasts three or four hours; in fact, each of the sermons (there are frequently two or three) may run nearly an hour. Their purpose is usually to reinforce ideas or beliefs rather than stimulate emotions.

The Presbyterian congregation is also simple and Apollonian in ritual. Although there is a printed order of worship, the service is rather relaxed and informal. While a choir sings an anthem each Sunday and the organist makes maximum use of the beautiful new handcrafted organ, the congregation occasionally reacts with applause for especially well-performed pieces of music. The minister will joke with the congregation, and sometimes members will respond with witty banter. During the service, members will stand to make announcements. The overall thrust of the service is on concepts and ideas. While the minister appeals to emotions in sermons, the thrust is clearly cognitive.

Boston's Mother Church has a high-church ritual,[14] again with an Apollonian thrust. When one enters the cavernous sanctuary, one has the feeling of standing in a great cathedral. The size and beauty of the architecture is enough to inspire a sense of awe. The organ is one of the largest and most versatile in the world. The service is orderly and dignified. Musical performances are met with an awed silence. The appeal of the service is to the intellect rather than to emotions. While the net effect of the service is to create powerful moods and motivations, these emotions are not expressed through frenzied behavior.

In terms of organization, the Amish are quite sectarian. While there are more than 80,000 Amish in the United States, they are divided into 17 groupings, many of which are "not in communion" with each other. There is no national office or bureaucratic structure. The clergy (ministers and bishops) have no formal theological training, having been chosen by lot. In fact, they continue with their full-time occupations in farming or farm-related services. Membership in an Amish communion is highly restrictive. It is nearly impossible to become Amish (they grow in numbers due to large family size). On the other hand, young people who do not accept the tenets of the faith and do not conform to group norms will risk the *Meidung* ("shunning" or excommunication).

The Presbyterian congregation is part of a highly institutionalized network. The session of the church must send in their books and records annually for overview by higher authorities. The national network produces

---

[14] The high-church style may be, in part, a function of congregational size. A more informal atmosphere often prevails in smaller group settings. (Some large Presbyterian churches have a high-church liturgy.) However, most small-town Christian Scientist services are considerably more formal than pentecostal churches of the same size. The liturgy is, by its nature, rather formal in the Christian Scientist Church.

study materials and sets national priorities which the local congregation is asked to implement. The clergy are approved by a board which screens candidates carefully and ensures that they have proper credentials (a theological degree from an accredited seminary). Local membership in the congregation is open, with members being asked only to assent to certain theological affirmations before the entire congregation. Expulsion is unheard of (although clergy can be "defrocked").

Christian Scientists also have an elaborate national headquarters, with their own division of publications. In fact, the impressive complex of buildings which houses the national offices stands beside the Mother Church in Boston. However, unlike most church-like groups, the Christian Scientists have no ordained clergy. Worship services are led by readers who read a prepared script, the same in every Christian Science church in the world on that Sunday. Church membership is open, with few "tests" of conformity or risks of expulsion.

In its relationship with the larger society, the Amish demonstrate a posture of withdrawal. Normally they do not vote and, as pacifists, they refuse to serve in the armed forces. In most communities their children attend separate schools (one-room schoolhouses in some cases), and do not go beyond the eighth grade. The Amish do pay taxes, however. They have rather high boundaries between themselves and outsiders, referring to all non-Amish persons as "English."

The Presbyterian congregation accepts the larger society, although a few of the members have become involved in social movements which seek to change particular aspects of it. The church has a Peace Study group and the Session (ruling body of the local church) has endorsed a nuclear weapons freeze campaign. The church supports other organizations which address various social problems (a shelter for battered women, an antihunger program, and mission projects which seek to alleviate racism in society). However, most of the programs which the church has supported have been ones which lessen existing suffering rather than ones which seek to transform the basic structure of society. (However, sometimes the proclamations from the national church are considerably more sweeping in nature. One publication in 1982 involved a scathing attack on the basic economic policies of the Reagan administration and advocacy of a more equalitarian society.)

Basically, acceptance also characterizes the Christian Science church. The theological postures that illness, death, and disease are illusory, and that suffering is a state of mind, tend to weaken any inclination to bring change through social action. The theology has a profoundly individualistic thrust. Of course, the rejection of medicine has led Christian Scientists to withdraw from that aspect of society and to generate their own alternative to doctors for childbirth; they have their own cadre of midwives. Although they demonstrate withdrawal in this one area, the general relationship to society for the Church of Jesus Christ, Scientist, is one of acceptance.

Amish and Christian Scientist congregations focus on an otherworldly realm as the ultimate solution to human suffering. The goal of the Amish is otherworldly salvation. As Hostetler (1968:50) writes, "The Amish show little interest in improving the world or their environment. They profess to be 'strangers and pilgrims' in the present world." The physical world is viewed merely as a testing ground—a transitory phase in which the destiny of one's soul may be determined. Christian Science stresses the idea that one can begin to live on a spiritual plane in this world—if one gets past the physical and realizes the true nature of human existence. Indeed, one can overcome illness and disease. Hence, there are this-worldly consequences of faith, but the ultimate solution lies in another realm of existence. This other realm will be most fully realized in an afterlife.

The minister of the Presbyterian church is much more this-worldly. He believes there is a life after death, but also is convinced that the otherworldly realm is of secondary concern for Christians. The primary task of Christians is to build a world of peace and justice. References to the Kingdom of God are essentially this-worldly, with a premillenial expectation that God is at work subtly transforming the structures of society. Christians, therefore, are called to participate in the ongoing work of God in the world. The afterlife will take care of itself. In a sense, the minister is less interested in individual salvation from hell than he is with *social* redemption from greed, bigotry, warfare, and social injustice. While the minister and some of the laity are this-worldly, many members are very otherworldly. For these people the ultimate answers to suffering, pain, and injustice are located in an afterlife. One senses a fundamental conflict beneath the surface of this church, for the symbols of the faith have very different meanings to members. The church continues, however, with few visible signs of this underlying dilemma. For the most part, the members continue to ignore fundamental differences in ideology and cultivate strong belonging ties.

In style of piety, the Amish are doers. They are convinced that their actions and behavior are important, but not because of the effect on this world. They believe that the way they live their lives will ultimately affect their eternal salvation. They seek to avoid contact with the "depraved" ways of the world and believe that only the righteous remnant will be saved. They are otherworldly in outlook, but they do seek to *work out* their own salvation, to "win" their salvation by righteous behavior and godly lifestyle.

As one peruses the sermons of the minister at the First Presbyterian Church (sermons are printed each week and made available to the congregation), one can identify the occasional influence of Martin Luther's theology: God's love is irrespective of one's deeds. God's grace is a gift freely given. However, a more common theme is the emphasis on persons creating their own future, on doing. Humans are free to choose and are responsible for their own destiny. A frequently expressed sentiment in church devotionals and in educational gatherings is that God's work is accomplished through human hands and feet. The laity are as likely as the minister to express this faith in the ultimate efficacy of human action, both in influencing this-worldly affairs and in shaping the individual's spiritual destiny.

The Christian Scientist idea that sin, suffering, and disease are mental errors and have no existence in reality leads to a somewhat more passive form of piety. The individual must change his or her frame of reference and correct errors in thought. If the individual lives on the purely spiritual plain, then most problems will evaporate; they were really illusions anyway. Human action is not viewed as being particularly effective, but a change of human consciousness or awareness is believed to be of utmost importance. Mary Baker Eddy was emphatic in stressing mind over matter and in asserting that the power of the mind far surpasses the physical laws of science and medicine. She believed that health and wholeness are realized through a mystical process (Eddy 1886). An activist lifestyle or other behavioral expressions of the faith were not central to her theology. The emphasis is on the state of one's "being."

In terms of world view the Amish have a unitary wide-range outlook in which every aspect of life is seen in religious terms. The bishop rules on new farming innovations, and all facets of life are scrutinized for consistency with religious principles—or at least they are supposed to be. Religion provides the lens for understanding all of life and for determining a wide range of everyday behaviors. As Hostetler (1968:49–50) says, religion for the Amish is "pervasive and associated with a total way of life, not a specialized activity."

The minister of the small-town Presbyterian church also preaches that all of life should be understood through a theological lens. Adult educational discussions are often sprinkled with comments by lay people about the application of their faith to everyday life and to understanding political and economic trends. A question often raised is: How do we understand where God is at work in current history and contemporary social processes? However, one can also hear comments, especially by less-involved members, that question what the minister's sermon or the adult church school lesson had to do with religion. Some people have left the church because the minister was always talking about politics, or economic policy, or international relations rather than focusing on "religion." If the pattern in this Presbyterian church is at all similar to that found in other mainline denominations, a very large number of the members probably have a multiple-vector world view.

Christian Scientist theology has had a much more narrow scope from its inception. Mary Baker Eddy attacked modern science and medicine, but her theology was individualistic. Basically, it ignored the structures of society, focusing instead on individual suffering. (For this reason the movement appealed primarily to the middle class rather than the lower class.

This is unlike most sectarian movements, and the rather rapid transformation of the movement from a sect-like to a church-like style is due to its middle-class clientel.) The net result is that Christian Scientist worship today still tends to present a narrow emphasis on health and wholeness of the mind. Political or economic policies are not topics which are scrutinized. The world view is much narrower in its scope than the official position of the United Presbyterian Church or of the Amish.

Each of the religious groups discussed here has its own distinctive style. Choice point analysis allows one to sense the uniqueness of each group and avoids the pigeonholing effect of simply labeling a group as a sect or a church. None of the groups fits all of the criteria in multidimensional definitions of sect-like and church-like. Of course, the Amish fit most of the characteristics of a sect, but their Apollonian style of worship is more church-like. The Christian Scientists probably vary farthest from typical patterns. They have a highly centralized bureaucracy (a church-like characteristic), but they ordain no clergy (a sect-like pattern). Although they reject the precepts of modern science and medicine (bastions of the society) and offer a mystic route to health, they also practice a worship style that is church-like (high-church Apollonian). By emphasizing the uniqueness of the combination of characteristics in any given group, the choice point procedure is useful for those wishing simply to describe the style of a particular group (an idiographic description).

Summary

In attempting to classify different styles of religious groups, Weber and Troeltsch described different *types* of religious groups. Troeltsch's description of the sect and the church was more multidimensional than Weber's. Niebuhr elaborated the typology even further by adding the denomination and discussing several added variables that he believed were correlated with the types. He also generalized about the typical mode of religious group evolution—from sect to denomination to church and back to sect. This began several decades of theorizing and generalizing about each type of religious group. The conceptions of church and sect had been transformed from purely descriptive tools to theory-building ones.

The lack of precise correlation of the many variables in multidimensional formulations led to changes in church/sect theory. One recent move has been to simplify the number of factors which are used to distinguish a sect from a denomination or church. Some scholars suggest using a single variable (Johnson; Greeley); others (such as Yinger) use two or three variables and identify several subtypes of religious groups (charismatic sect, established sect, diffused denomination, institutionalized denomination, and so on). This procedure has contributed to the identification of alternative paths of religious group evolution, depending on the independent rates at which a group may institutionalize and accept the values of the dominant society. Such approaches describe a multilinear process of group evolution rather than the unilinear evolution depicted by Niebuhr. Some social scientists continue to utilize the multidimensional conception of sects and churches, recognizing that few groups will fit all the criteria. In this case, a group which fits most of the typical characteristics for a sect or a church is described as sect-like or church-like.

The concept of cult has also been added to the types of religious groups. While the concept of cult has been used in various ways by different scholars, I have (with Nelson, Yinger, Bainbridge and Stark, and others) distinguished the cult as a new (or imported) religious movement in a society. This is differentiated from the sect which represents the regeneration of a traditional religion in that society. The cult, like the sect, goes through processes of institutionalization and modification. But if it survives and eventually gains legitimacy in the society, the cult is viewed as a new religion rather than as a denomination of existing religions. As in the case of the sect, many social forces affect the development of the cult and shape its style and character.

Church/sect theory has been helpful in generalizing about the "typical" pattern of religious group evolution. It has also been useful in identifying correlations between styles of religiosity (sect-like or church-like) and such variables as socioeconomic status (as will be discussed in chapter 8). In short, church/sect theory has been widely used to make generalizations about religious groups which are in some ways similar (nomothetic studies). However, for those who seek simply to describe the unique character of a specific group, choice point analysis may have greater value. Choice point analysis involves an investigation of the choices a specific group makes on critical points. The combination of these choices (which may vary independently) determine the unique style and character of a group. Scholars who are attempting to describe a group accurately and are not interested in the development of theory are likely to use some form of choice point analysis.

While choice point analysis has great utility for idiographic studies, some sociologists interested in nomothetic issues have also turned to it. For example, when Glock and Stark (1966) undertook a study of anti-Semitism among Christians, they operationalized such variables as theological orthodoxy (actually fundamentalism or reversionism) and particularism (the belief that only members of one's own group have a true religion) and correlated those directly with measures of prejudice toward Jews. They were not interested in how churches or sects as types contributed to prejudice. Rather, they sought to study independently the relationship of each choice point to prejudice.

The concepts of church, denomination, sect, and cult still have utility for sociological study of religion, but the trend seems to be away from dependence on these distinctions and toward various forms of choice point studies. Increasingly, the interest is in how each choice independently affects behavior or attitudes rather than in the net effect of several variables on behavior. Independently tracking the effects of many different variables has become possible only in recent times as social scientists have gained the invaluable assistance of the computer.

Both choice point and church-sect studies have been utilized in gathering data for the following two chapters. There we will see illustrations of the way in which religion affects and responds to its social environment. We will also see that a religion can affect the host culture in various ways—sometimes even in contradictory ways (for example, simultaneously contributing to both tolerance and prejudice). In the next chapter, we will examine the relationship between religion and social stratification. In Chapter 9 we will scrutinize the role of religion in relationship to racism and sexism in American society.

8

Religion and Social Stratification: Interactive Process

In this chapter and the next we will examine the interactive relationship between religion and the social structures and processes of the larger society. These chapters are designed to illustrate the sociological method of analysis; they are certainly not exhaustive treatments of the influence of religion on other social structures.

One of the important elements of social structure is the stratification system. In this chapter we will explore the relationship between one's position in the stratification system and one's religious orientation. We will see ways in which socioeconomic circumstances affect religion and ways in which religion, in turn, impacts economic behavior. We shall begin by investigating the role of religion as a causal variable that affects one's economic behavior.

269

Religion and Economic Behavior: Religion as a Causal Variable

Weber's Protestant Ethic Thesis

Among the important factors determining the social status of individuals in any society are the economic behavior of those individuals and the nature of the economic system itself. The question which has interested many scholars has been, "To what extent does religion affect economic behavior?" The landmark study on this issue has been Max Weber's seminal work, *The Protestant Ethic and the Spirit of Capitalism,* for it has generated an incredible amount of research and discussion.

Weber's study was undertaken in response to two issues. First, he was interested in the relationship between religion and economic activity. This study was one of a series of comparative studies of religion and its affects on economic development[1] (Weber 1951; 1952; 1958b; 1963). In the first sentence of chapter 1 of *The Protestant Ethic,* Weber points out that Protestants tend to be more affluent than Catholics and to occupy the higher-status positions in virtually all industrialized societies. He was interested in the relationship between religious affiliation and social stratification, including the differential effects of various faiths.

Second, Weber wished to address a larger theoretical issue. He hoped to provide a corrective to the simple economic determinism of Karl Marx. Marx had maintained that one's economic status was the principal determining factor in all behavior. He felt that it was fruitless to try to understand human behavior as an expression of values, ideals, or beliefs. Marx believed that beliefs and values are a *result* of economic forces, that one's ideas and ideals act to justify one's economic fortunes—or to compensate one for a lack of economic fortune. Religion served to justify and sacralize the current social arrangements. Because of this, it helped to reinforce the status quo and served to retard change. For Marx, values, beliefs, and ideals do not serve as primary causal forces; they are secondary factors that result from economic forces.

Marx recognized that beliefs—including religion—could serve as *proximate* causes, even as he insisted that they are not *ultimate* causes. He acknowledged that humans are active agents and that beliefs organize and propel one's action. It was for this reason that he stressed the importance of the working class changing from "false consciousness" to "class consciousness." He also emphasized that religion often served as an opiate of the masses—again revealing his awareness of the role of beliefs and ideas on action. Without

---

[1] These comparative studies included investigations of Confucianism and Taoism, Hinduism and Buddhism, and ancient Judaism. Weber's interest was in the way religious beliefs encourage or discourage the development of rational business enterprise.

ignoring this awareness, it is also accurate to say that Marx believed ideas are powerfully conditioned by material (or economic) circumstances. Economic forces were viewed as the principal factors in shaping human behavior; ideas, values, and beliefs were only proximate influences, and were themselves largely shaped by economic forces. Religion, which deals in values, ideals, and beliefs as its primary currency, was viewed as a relatively unimportant force, at least for those interested in the principal factors that cause social change or ultimately shape human behavior.

Some writers have claimed that Weber's study was intended as a direct refutation of Marx, but this clearly was not the case. Weber agreed with Marx's contention that economic self-interests have a powerful effect on the beliefs and values of people. Yet, Weber viewed this position as only a partial truth. He insisted that while economics can affect religion, religion can also affect economics. In fact, he held that Protestantism (especially Calvinism) was a significant force in the formation of capitalism as an economic system. Rather than being a *refutation* of Marx, Weber viewed his study as a modification or corrective to the overly simplistic analysis by Marx. While he accepted Marx's view that people behave in ways that enhance their own self-interests, Weber felt that perceptions of self-interest were not limited to the economic realm. A religious self-interest (e.g., concern over salvation) could also motivate people.

In *The Protestant Ethic and the Spirit of Capitalism,* Weber attempted to identify how religious beliefs and self-interests had affected economic behavior. In focusing on the Protestant "ethic" he was really referring to the overall perspective and sense of values of Protestantism. He felt that the breakthrough from the feudalistic to the capitalistic economic system was substantially enhanced by this particular world view. In sum, he felt that ideas could be important factors that facilitate social change, including changes in the economic system.

In order for capitalism to thrive, several conditions had to be met. There had to be a pool of individuals with the characteristics necessary to serve as entrepreneurs. They had to be individualistic, and had to believe in the virtues of hard work and of simplicity of lifestyle. Protestantism tended to create a supply of such people. Although economic self-interests create such people today, Weber maintained that the original pool was formed largely by people motivated by religious beliefs and self-interests.

One of the primary concerns of people in the 15th and 16th centuries was their eternal salvation. One way to be assured of salvation was to serve God directly. If one was called by God to the priesthood or to holy orders in a monastery, one seemed to have a better chance of eternal salvation. But Martin Luther developed a different concept of divine service. He stressed the priesthood of all believers and insisted that one could be called by God to a variety of occupations that served humanity. This new concept of a calling is referred to as the doctrine of vocation, for the word *vocation* means calling. According to Luther's teachings, one may be called to many types of secular positions, as well as to the priesthood. Since secular positions were also viewed as service to God, any form of work could be a means of expressing one's faith. Hard work became a way of serving and glorifying God. Idleness or laziness, by logical extension, came to be viewed as a sin. While Luther initiated this concept of vocation and held to it in principle, it was the Calvinists who fully implemented it. In fact, Calvin even suggested that when a person was hard at work, he or she was most in the image of God.

Industriousness was an essential quality for the emergence of a class of entrepreneurs, and this quality was a central virtue among Calvinists. But it was not enough for people simply to develop an ethic of hard work. The rational investment of earnings was also critical. The Protestant emphasis on asceticism and on delayed gratification served to enhance this aspect of capitalistic enterprise. Asceticism was a major theme in the preaching of a number of reformers, for the pleasures of the world (gambling, drinking, secular forms of entertainment, and luxuries) were all viewed as sinful and evil. God required a simple, even austere, lifestyle. Calvin even described self-discipline as the "nerves of religion"; hence, self-denial became a central virtue. This denial of present desires was accomplished because of the principle of *delayed gratification.* Believers were willing to forgo pleasures now for the promise of much greater rewards in the future. In the case of the reformers, the future rewards were anticipated in the afterlife. Nonetheless, the principle of delayed gratification is an important one for the development of economic capital. In fact, Weber defines capitalism as the systematic investment of time and resources with the hope of significant returns in the future (profits). The idea of denying one's immediate desires in the hope of a greater return in the future was basic to both Calvinism and to capitalism.

Among many of the early Protestants—and especially among the Calvinists—hard work was a moral and religious duty; but since income from one's industriousness was not to be spent on luxuries or sensual pleasures, the only thing to do was invest it. Among Methodists and certain other Protestant sects, excess income was to be given to the poor.[2] But according to R. H. Tawney (1954), the Calvinists felt that people who were impoverished were poor simply because they were lazy.[3] Not wishing to contribute to this wickedness, the Calvinists were not inclined to donate much of

---

[2] John Wesley's economic ethic was "*earn* all you can, *save* all you can, and *give* all you can." He was extraordinarily hardworking and ascetic in his own lifestyle, but he gave nearly three fourths of whatever he earned to the poor or for the establishment of churches and schools. Hence, he did not accumulate great wealth.

[3] This generalization applies to the Calvinists—the followers and successors of Calvin— much more than to Calvin himself. Calvin's own teaching stressed generosity (Calvin 1952:34–44).

their income to the needy. Most of their profits were available for investment. This created a situation in which increased amounts of capital were available in the society and economic growth was enhanced.

Other characteristics of Calvinism were also significant. One of the important doctrines in Calvin's theology was that of predestination. According to this doctrine, God has already decided who is saved and who is damned. One's fate is predetermined and there is really nothing a person can do about it. This doctrine might easily have resulted in a sense of fatalism, despair, and despondency. But in this case, people coped with their anxiety about whether they were saved by acting as if they were. Of course, this would not improve their chances, but any impious or un-Christian behavior would only ensure to themselves and others that they were damned. Righteous behavior would not earn a person a position in heaven, but one's behavior was believed to be an outward sign of one's eternal status. Being righteous, thrifty, hardworking, and ascetic was a way of hedging one's bets. When so much was at stake, it seemed foolish to take chances.

Furthermore, this predestined state placed one in a position of radical individualism. One was not saved because of anything others did or because of the groups one belonged to. One was strictly on one's own in this matter of salvation. Weber (1958a:104–107) writes: "In what was for the man of the age of the Reformation the most important thing in his life, he was forced to follow his path alone to meet a destiny which had been decreed for him from eternity. No one could help him. . . . In spite of the necessity of membership in the true church for salvation, the Calvinist's intercourse with his God was carried on in deep spiritual isolation."

Since an attitude of rugged individualism was important for the entrepreneur, the sense of religious individualism provided a compatible outlook. In fact, Weber suggests that the religious individualism may have partially predated and thereby contributed to the attitude of economic individualism. Economic individualism, in turn, means that individuals make rational economic decisions based on their own self-interests. Once capitalism is formed, according to Weber, it is capable of sustaining its own individualistic motivations. But he suggests that religious self-interests and beliefs may have contributed to the original formation of capitalism.

Finally, Calvin taught that regardless of one's eternal salvation, everyone is to glorify God and to work for the creation of a Divine Kingdom on earth. In fact, Calvin emphasized that the proper aim of humanity is not personal salvation, but the glorification of God through the sanctification of this world. This focus created a strong this-worldly component to the theology, for one's labors in transforming this realm—the here-and-now—were the best indicators of one's devotion to God. Later Calvinists (Puritans) reinforced the inner-worldly (or this-worldly) element even further by suggesting that one's socioeconomic status was an indicator of one's spiritual grace and eternal destination. Delayed gratification and asceticism became increasingly this-worldly and rational (i.e., based on concrete self-interest).

Due to certain beliefs, then, 15th-century Europe was supplied with (1) an increasing supply of capital for investment, and (2) a pool of individuals who had the values and attitudes appropriate to becoming entrepreneurs. While these characteristics were not *sufficient* to bring on the development of capitalism, they were *necessary*, and Weber believed that religion had contributed to the formation of the capitalistic system of economics by supplying these characteristics. He maintained that a religious outlook had influenced the economic behavior and financial fortunes of individuals (Protestants becoming more affluent than non-Protestants), and also had contributed to the development of a new economic system. Contrary to Marx, Weber felt that religion was capable of being a cause of economic conditions—not just a result.

Weber's thesis has been highly controversial and has generated a large number of essays and research projects. Some scholars have argued that Calvinism had little to do with the development of capitalism. Some insist that the beginning of colonialism (with its influx of new capital resources) and changes in postmedieval technology sparked the advent of capitalism. Others emphasize the fact that capital was available for entrepreneurs through Jews and through Catholic bankers in urban areas. In these cases, the concurrent rise of capitalism and Protestantism is seen as a simple coincidence (Samuelsson 1961). The outlook described as the Protestant ethic is viewed as insignificant—or at least its uniqueness to Protestants is denied.[4]

Other writers have basically agreed with Weber, but have suggested modifications in his thesis. For example, R. H. Tawney (1954) suggests that most contributions of Protestantism to the development of an individualistic and laissez-faire economic system were entirely latent. He points out that in the Middle Ages, the Catholic Church held usury (lending money for interest) to be on a par with adultry and fornication.[5] Not only was lending money at interest considered immoral, but prosperity itself was viewed as a source of spiritual corruption. Both of these attitudes were carried over to various extents in the teachings of the reformers.

Luther, who represented a rural peasant orientation, was particularly opposed to self-interested individualism and to laissez-faire policies. Furthermore, he felt that it was immoral to make money through investments, lending, or any form of speculation. He held to a labor theory of value—the idea that one should be rewarded financially only in proportion to the labor one actually performs.

Calvin, on the other hand, was much more urban and secular in back-

---

[4] Those interested in detailed critiques of Weber's Protestant ethic thesis will want to see Tawney (1954), Hudson (1949), Fanfani (1936), Robertson (1959), Green (1959), and Samuelsson (1961).

[5] It was for this reason that Jews were looked to as sources of capital; they were willing to lend money at interest because usury was not defined as immoral within the Jewish tradition.

ground and orientation. Although he was no defender of laissez-faire capitalism, he did believe that capital investment was essential to a healthy economy. Hence, he insisted that there was nothing inherently evil about investing or lending money at moderate interest. However, he did insist that no interest should be charged the poor, and he put strict ethical guidelines on economic activity. He also remained deeply suspicious of the spiritual effects of economic prosperity. At one point he commented, "Wherever prosperity flows uninterruptedly, its delight corrupts even the best of us," and at another time he suggested that "prosperity is like rust or mildew." In fact, Calvin's distrust of the influences of money, is revealed in his considerable ambivalence about usury. One English clergyman who studied Calvin's theology commented that "Calvin deals with usury as the apothocarie doth with poyson" (cited by Tawney 1954:94). It seems clear that at the manifest level, both Protestants and Catholics believed that "the spirit of capitalism is foreign to every kind of religion" (Samuelsson 1961:19).[6]

Tawney grants that Protestantism may have unconsciously contributed to the early development of capitalism, but even as it did so, the reformers were preaching against certain practices that were later taken for granted as an integral part of the free enterprise system. In fact, he insists that the massive accumulations of wealth that were acquired by later industrialists were not the result of the Protestant ethic or of thriftiness. Such capital was acquired by unscrupulous exploitation of people and resources, and by manipulating speculations that were euphemistically called "opportunities." Tawney agrees with Weber that Calvinistic theology and ethics (such as recognizing the legitimacy of capital investment) contributed to the *advent* of the free enterprise system, but he feels that early Protestant ethics were quite incompatible with the free-for-all capitalism of the 18th, 19th, and even 20th centuries. Moreover, he felt that capitalism would probably have made its entrance even without the contribution of Protestantism. Calvin's endorsement of investment was viewed by Tawney as largely an *accommodation* to existing forces.

This brings us to another critique, the view that rather than causing asceticism, individualism, and a work ethic, Calvinism was simply an agreeable theology to those who already held these values and attributes. According to this position, people became Calvinists because Calvinism justified and even sacralized beliefs, behaviors, and outlooks which those people already practiced. The lonely individual risk of salvation paralleled the financial risks of venturesome entrepreneurs. We will return later to this issue of *elective affinity* (the attraction of persons to a religious world view because it justifies one's self-interests and one's current outlook).

---

[6] Samuelsson, citing Fanfani, suggests that not only were the religious ethics of Christianity alien to capitalism; he also asserts with this statement his belief that the spirit of capitalism arose quite independently of any religious influence.

Empirical Research

There have been some efforts to prove or disprove Weber's thesis through empirical research in the modern world. Perhaps the most well-known study was undertaken by Gerhard Lenski (1963) in suburban Detroit. He conducted in-depth interviews with 656 people—Protestants, Catholics, and Jews. He attempted to test the Weberian thesis in several ways. First, he asked people to rank the following in order of importance in a man's job:

1. Receiving a high income.
2. Having no danger of being fired (job security).
3. Being able to work short hours and having lots of free time.
4. Having chances for advancement.
5. Feeling that one's work is important and provides a sense of accomplishment (Lenski 1963:89).

Although items 1 and 4 reflect the popular usage of the term *Protestant ethic,* Lenski points out that only item 5 is consistent with the original concept of vocation and Weber's treatment of the Protestant ethic.

Lenski found that Catholics were somewhat more likely to respond with 2 or 3 as first choices, while Protestants more often responded with 5. Part of the difference may have been due to the fact that Protestants were more highly represented in the professional classes, while Catholics were largely in the working class. But even when he held social class constant, he found a difference between Protestant and Catholic answers. The differences between the groups were not large (54 percent of Protestants versus 44 percent of Catholics responded with statement 5), but Lenski held that they were still significant. Jews ranked second in the number of 5 responses (48 percent) and ranked the highest on the number of positive answers to 2 and 4. Lenski insisted that the differentials between groups, especially between Protestants and Catholics, were shrinking as more ethnic groups (largely Catholic) were being acculturated into the American value system.[7]

As a second means of measuring the Protestant ethic, Lenski sought to ascertain the attitudes of people toward installment buying. Installment buying (have now, pay later) seemed to Lenski to be the utmost rejection of the principle of delayed gratification. A critical attitude toward installment buying would be a position consistent with the Protestant ethic. Again, Lenski found white Protestants more critical of installment buying and more in tune with the Protestant ethic than Catholics—but only by about 5 percent. Interestingly, Jews were the most in tune with the Protestant ethic, being most highly critical of installment buying (56 percent versus 44 percent for white Protestants).

---

[7] He also believed that black Protestants—who ranked lowest on the Protestant ethic scale—were affected in their attitudes largely by racial discrimination and the legacy of slavery. Hence, he felt that secular social forces were more responsible for their socioeconomic status and their economic outlooks than was their Protestant heritage.

As a third means of assessing the impact of religion on economic attitudes and behavior, Lenski compared active church members with nominal members (members in name only). He found that the sons and daughters of devout Protestants were more likely to be upwardly mobile than were the sons and daughters of nominal Protestants. Conversely, he found that the sons and daughters of active Catholics were more likely to be downwardly mobile than were the children of marginal Catholics. This, he suggests, provides evidence of the contrary influences of Protestantism and Catholicism on socioeconomic behavior. (There were not enough Jews in the sample to permit a reliable analysis on this item). While Lenski used other means to operationalize and measure economic attitudes and behavior, he essentially felt that the evidence strongly supported the Weberian thesis:

> With considerable regularity the Jews and white Protestants have identified themselves with the individualistic, competitive patterns of thought and action linked with the middle class, and historically associated with the Protestant Ethic or its secular counterpart, the spirit of capitalism. By contrast, Catholics and Negro Protestants have more often been associated with the collectivistic, security-oriented, working-class patterns of thought and action historically opposed to the Protestant Ethic and the spirit of capitalism (1963:113).

Subsequent researchers, especially the Catholic priest Andrew Greeley, have come up with findings quite contrary to Lenski's. Greeley's research suggests no significant difference between Protestants and Catholics in concepts of vocation or in upward mobility. In fact, some of the evidence indicates more upward mobility for Catholics than for Protestants. The conflict between these two sociologists and their partisans has been intense on this issue. Although Lenski and Greeley have been the primary spokespersons for the contrasting positions, numerous others have conducted research too.

First of all, sociologists have not been able to agree on the question of whether Protestants do, in fact, tend to have higher social status than Catholics. Three studies indicated that Protestants generally do (Lenski 1963; Crowley and Ballweg 1971; Porter 1965); three indicated no differences (Gockel 1969; Goldstein 1969; and Mueller 1971a); one found Catholics to have higher status (Mueller and Lane 1972); and one found that liberal Protestants had higher status than Catholics but that fundamentalist Protestants did not (Morgan et al. 1962).

Many more studies have been done on status *mobility* of persons from various religious groups, and the results are equally mixed. Seven studies found Protestants to be more upwardly mobile than Catholics (Lenski 1963; Mayer and Sharp 1962; Crowley and Ballweg 1971; Jackson et al. 1970; Organic 1963; Weller 1963; and Goldstein 1969); one found that Catholics had higher mobility (Alston 1969). Ten found no differences in mobility when such important variables as educational level and ethnicity were held constant (Featherman 1971; Mueller 1971a; Schuman 1971; Warren 1970; Greeley 1963, 1969a; Kohn 1969; Glenn and Hyland 1967; Lipset and Bendix 1959; and Mack et al. 1956).

One difficulty is variations in the way various scholars have operationalized social mobility; two researchers reported higher social mobility for Protestants if one defined mobility solely in terms of occupation, but if one utilized other factors (such as education, income, and achievement orientation), the results showed little difference.[8] A second problem is that none of the studies distinguish clearly between current and previous religious affiliation of respondents. Hence, there is no control which would clearly identify religious affiliation as cause or as consequence of social mobility. Third, most studies do not distinguish between Protestant denominations—they are all lumped together. Weber's thesis never suggested that all forms of Protestantism equally enhance upward social mobility of believers, but only those with a particular world view or set of values (a strong work ethic, emphasis on asceticism, and an individualistic thrust). Nor did he insist that it was only Protestants who might hold those views. A more direct measure of the Protestant ethic is needed so that variations within groups can be identified rather than just variations between groups.

The matters of whether modern-day Protestants manifest the characteristic outlooks of the Protestant ethic more than do Catholics and whether it makes any difference is still not satisfactorily answered for many sociologists. For many others it seems to be a moot point. If evidence presented by Lenski and others proved to be accurate, it would offer some plausability to Weber's thesis, but it would clearly not prove it. On the other hand, if present-day Catholics are more upwardly mobile than Protestants, we would not have disproved the possible effects of a Protestant ethic at the time capitalism was coming into predominance. Moreover, the rational pursuit of wealth (spirit of capitalism) is so thoroughly secularized in the Western world that it has become independent of any one religious tradition. Weber himself had pointed out that the spirit of capitalism had quickly secularized and gained a standing independent of any theological impetus.

Finally, Weber's study was not intended as a narrow contrast of Protestants and Catholics, with an implication that only Protestants were capable of developing the outlook of the entrepreneur. Weber was suggesting that *any* sacred milieu which stressed certain values and outlooks—individualism, asceticism, and an ethic of hard work—was conducive to the development of capitalism and to the affluence of those holding those views. He only asserts that historically, Protestant reformers developed those values somewhat earlier than did the Catholic Church. In short, an empirical study in *contemporary* society does not prove or disprove a theory about the role of religion in a previous era.

---

[8] For reviews and interpretations of the various studies cited here, see Bouma (1973), Gaede (1977), and Riccio (1979).

Regardless of whether Protestantism contributed to the rise of capitalism, the idea that one's beliefs may affect one's economic standing is still popular. Many commentators besides Weber have suggested that when a broad concept of vocation combines with asceticism, the result is an increased likelihood of affluence for members of that group. John Wesley, the founder of Methodism, pointed this out with some alarm, for he felt that economic affluence was one of the most corrupting forces to spiritual growth:

> How then is it possible that Methodism . . . though it flourishes now as a green bay tree, should continue in this state? For the Methodists in every place grow diligent and frugal; consequently they increase in goods. Hence they proportionately increase in pride, in anger, in the desire of the flesh, the desire of the eyes and the pride of life. So, although the form of religion remains, the spirit is swiftly vanishing away.
>
> Is there no way to prevent this—this continual decay of pure religion? We ought not to prevent people from being diligent and frugal; we must exhort all Christians to gain all they can, and to save all they can; that is in effect to grow rich. What way then can we take, that our money not sink us into the nethermost hell? (Wesley 1943:208).

Likewise, Liston Pope (1942) found that asceticism and a theological concept of hard work in holiness sects were factors in the economic development of southern mill towns. One can see a similar phenomenon at work among Black Muslims. Ghetto blacks who were once impoverished began to have somewhat improved economic circumstances when they lived under the severe Muslim asceticism and the Islamic insistence that all work should be for the greater glory of Allah. These cases suggest that certain outlooks can be *conducive* to economic prosperity. However, there are many factors in the economic development of any group, and one would be foolish to maintain that any one set of beliefs is capable of single-handedly changing one's economic fortunes.

The Amish are a case in point. In Amish culture, asceticism and hard work are among the most important virtues. Clearly they have a strong Protestant ethic. The Amish are generally pretty comfortable financially, and they usually have some savings. However, they are certainly not what one might call wealthy by normal American standards. The refusal to use modern technology and to harness efficient forms of energy (gasoline engines, electricity, and so on) means that there are substantial limits to their productive capacity. At the outset of the Protestant Reformation, the reformers had to establish standards for assessing the morality of social behavior. They upheld the Bible, and not the church hierarchy, as the standard against which all behavior was measured. As mentioned previously, for most Protestants, anything that was not specifically forbidden in the Bible (especially in the New Testament) was acceptable. For the followers of Jacob Amman, anything that was not expressly endorsed in the Bible was forbidden. Since the Bible does not say it is acceptable to depend on electricity, motor cars, tractors, telephones, or other such innovations, they are *forboden.* The Amish have refused to use most modern technological innovations.

So even if a group has a Protestant ethic, its members will not necessarily become highly affluent. Their access to natural resources, their access and willingness to use technology and other efficient sources of energy, and the economic opportunities available to that group within the larger social structure all affect economic development of the group and its members. No amount of asceticism and work ethic among black Americans will fully counteract the structural discrimination they experience. A profound work ethic combined with an emphasis on asceticism *may contribute* to affluence, but they are certainly *not sufficient* to bring prosperity.

Although many sociologists question the effectiveness of the Lenski study—or of any contemporary empirical research—in proving or disproving the Weber thesis, the study can still be very instructive to the sociology student. First, it demonstrates how sociologists go about measuring and testing a theory in a survey method of research. Students can get some notion of how sociologists attempt to infer sets of values without asking direct questions about such abstract concepts as delayed gratification. Furthermore, Lenski's study is important in that it uncovered some other interesting correlations between religion and economic behavior.

First, Lenski found that people who were "devotional" in their religious orientation were more likely to be influenced by their faith in economic and political matters than were those who were "orthodox." Devotionalism was assessed by inquiring of respondents whether they prayed at least once a day to ask God for personal guidance and direction. Those who answered positively were considered "devotionalists." Denominational orthodoxy was assessed by asking the following six questions:

1. Do you believe there is a God, or not?
2. Do you think God is like a Heavenly Father who watches over you, or do you have some other belief?
3. Do you believe that God answers people's prayers, or not?
4. Do you believe in a life after death, or not; if so, do you also believe that in the next life some people will be punished and others rewarded by God, or not?
5. Do you believe that, when they are able, God expects people to worship Him in their churches and synagogues, *every* week, or not?
6. Do you believe that Jesus was God's only Son sent into the world by God to save sinful men, or do you believe that he was simply a very good man and teacher, or do you have some other belief? (Lenski 1963:56).

Affirmative answers to all of these questions were necessary for a person to be considered orthodox. Orthodoxy reflects an intellectual commitment, while devotionalism is more behaviorally oriented (i.e., prayer). One might expect that most persons who are high on the orthodoxy measure might also be high on devotionalism, but this was not the case. Lenski found that the two varied rather independently. While the two orientations are certainly not logically contrary, neither are they highly correlated empirically (Lenski 1963:26).

Lenski found that those who were high on orthodoxy tended to compartmentalize life into discrete categories: family life, religion, economics, and so on. In other words, those who were denominationally orthodox had a world view best characterized as multiple narrow vectors (see choice point analysis in Chapter 7). On the other hand, devotionalists tended to have a single, wide-vector world view and were more likely to apply their faith to everyday life. Religion had much more effect on the economic and political attitudes of devotionalists than it did on the orthodox. This is most interesting in that a person's overall world view appears more important than his or her *specific beliefs*.[9] Clearly, a religious world view can affect behavior in ways that cannot be assessed by simply asking if one agrees with certain doctrines. World view is a much deeper concept than belief, and we are only just beginning to learn how to identify and assess a person's world view.

Second, Lenski attempted to measure whether religion affected people through institutional affiliation and by participation at services, or through reference group factors (having most of one's friends and one's spouse from the same religious orientation). One might expect associational and communal involvement to be rather highly correlated, but the correlation was far from perfect. In fact, Lenski suggests that there was "almost no relationship" between them (1963:24). Lenski was especially interested in those cases in which the correlation was very low: (1) persons who attended worship services regularly and participated in the institutional life of the church, but who had a majority of friends from other denominations or were married exogamously, and (2) persons who were *not* active in the institutional church, but who married endogamously and retained friendships that were religiously homogeneous.

He concluded that religion may influence a person either through a formal structure or through an informal network of friends, but overall communal involvement appears to be the more important variable.[10] However, he also found instances in which the two had differential effects—one contributing, for example, to racial tolerance and the other to racial bigotry. It is important for the student of religion to remember that religion can affect behavior and attitudes through many different channels. Lenski's observation is significant because of its attempt empirically to measure some of these different influences.

---

[9] This is one reason I stressed the broader concept of world view in my definition of religion (see Chapter 2).

[10] This ought not be surprising, given the many studies (cited in Chapter 5) which indicate the extreme importance of affective commitment (commitment to members and sense of belonging to the group). Instrumental commitment (to the organization or institution) comes much later, and appears to be less tied to moral commitment (commitment to the group's ideology).

Religious Ethics and Economic Action

Thus far, we have pointed to unconscious or indirect ways in which religiosity affects people's economic action. But religion can also affect the economic behavior of individuals directly—through "moral boycotts." In such cases, definitions of morality and immorality by religious groups are significant in that these groups use their economic clout to influence non-members and to coerce them into moral behavior.

In the late 1960s and early 1970s, the Catholic Church in America sponsored an organization called Project Equality. Many Protestant churches also joined this effort. Member churches were asked to contact all employers and ask them to develop affirmative action policies in hiring. An affirmative action policy simply requires that when there is a job opening, the employer take affirmative or positive steps to ensure that discrimination doesn't occur unintentionally. If an employer goes to a local employment agency when job openings occur, that employer may not be purposefully discriminating. But if there is discrimination in housing, and if the employment bureau is in an all-white suburb, then only white middle-class people may find out about the opening. A more qualified candidate may fail to obtain the job due to lack of information about it. Hence, *unintended* discrimination would have occurred, and Project Equality wanted to eliminate that possibility.

In the case just given, an employer would contact not only the employment agency in that suburb, but would also notify offices in the minority sections of town. If one were seeking a new college graduate, the employer would contact not only the well-known universities that are predominately white, but would also make a special effort to notify the placement offices at predominately black colleges. This would ensure that qualified minorities would know about the job, and would have an equal chance to apply. The most qualified candidate would then be hired. (Affirmative action is sometimes confused with job quotas or with favoritism to minority candidates. Quotas are viewed by some people as reverse discrimination).

If a business, service company, or supplier refused to adopt an affirmative action program, churches would cease doing business with the company and would encourage church members to patronize other firms. Project Equality then printed a booklet listing companies which did have affirmative action/equal opportunity hiring policies and encouraged church people to reward these companies with their business. It is difficult to establish how much economic impact this policy actually had, but use of financial resources to influence social policies is a continuing issue for churches.

Some congregations which have endowment funds have invested in certain companies so they could attend stockholder meetings and insist that the corporation no longer make certain types of weapons (nerve gas, napalm, neutron bombs, and so on) or that companies cease their cooperation with and implicit support of oppressive governments in the Third World. For example, making investments in the Republic of South Africa and paying taxes to that government help stabilize the Afrikaner economy and may thereby perpetuate its racist system of apartheid. Some churches have insisted that American corporations withdraw from investment in those countries which violate human rights (Seidman 1979). In this way, churches have used their economic clout to influence social policies and to create what they believe to be a more just society.

Of course, there is often disagreement about what the moral issues are. The examples above are the types of issues that more liberal congregations are likely to address, for social and economic justice is frequently defined as the central issue in Christian social ethics for many liberals. Other groups, like the Moral Majority, have defined sexual innuendo on television to be of central import, and they have proposed boycotts against companies that sponsor shows they have defined as immoral. Other groups have focused on other issues, but the procedure is similar. Still others have suggested that the use of economic power as coercion and as a means of establishing policies which one considers moral is inappropriate in a pluralistic society. The procedure has itself been challenged as morally questionable. Students may want to discuss whether the use of institutional resources to bring change is justifiable. Regardless of one's position, the fact remains that religious definitions of morality and the strategies of religious groups to attain a moral or "good society" have affected the economic behavior of many individuals.

In conclusion, religious orientation can affect economic behavior. There is evidence, however, that religion is more likely to affect one's behavior if it takes the form of a single, overall world view than if it represents only one of several ways of looking at things. Because their religious views permeate virtually all aspects of their lives, devotionalists are more influenced by their religious views than are those who are orthodox. Furthermore, the evidence suggests that religion influences the economic and political views of individuals more through participation in informal communal networks than through participation in the formal structure. Regardless, the sacralization of specific values or outlooks may affect one's economic behavior. While one's socialized values may not be sufficient to change one's socioeconomic position, they may contribute to such a change.

Social Class and Religious Involvement

Whether or not one accepts Weber's explanation of causality, the fact remains that denominational affiliation is correlated to social class. The pattern of religious affiliation by social class is demonstrated in the table in Exhibit 8–1. Taken as a whole, no denomination is class exclusive. However, at a

Exhibit 8–1

Socioeconomic Profiles of American Religious Groups

Denominational ranking by social class, 1952*
(figure in parenthesis represents percentage of
that group that is "upper class").

Atheistic/Agnostic	(33.3)
Christian Scientist	(24.9)
Episcopal	(24.1)
Congregational	(23.9)
Presbyterian	(21.9)
Jewish	(21.8)
Reformed (Christian)	(19.1)
Methodist	(12.7)
Protestant (undesignated)	(12.4)
Lutheran	(10.9)
Christian (Disciples)	(10.0)
Protestant (small bodies)	(10.0)
Roman Catholic	(8.7)
Baptist	(8.0)
Mormon	(5.1)

Denominational differentials for educational level and income,
1972–1976†

	Education (mean number of years)	Income (mean)
Jewish	13.7	$14,350
Episcopal	13.6	14,100
Presbyterian	13.1	13,200
Congregational	13.1	12,045
Methodist	12.0	10,085
Catholic	11.7‡	10,820§
Lutheran	11.6	10,400
Other Protestant	11.6	9,385
Baptist	11.0	9,245
Sectarian	10.9	8,080

(No specific data are provided for Christian Scientists, Reformed,
Disciples, or Mormons in Roof's recent study)

Note: One must be cautious about comparing the 1952 data with the more recent information, for the methods of measuring social class are not identical. However, they do both suggest a rather stable correlation of certain denominations with the upper, middle, and lower classes respectively. The biggest change has been in the relative position of Catholics. Data provided by Roof (1979) and Greeley (1981) suggest that this change is due to the continuing assimilation of Catholic ethnics into the economic mainstream and to location of Catholics in cities (where income opportunities are greater).

* Source: Herbert Schneider, *Religion in 20th Century America*, (Cambridge: Harvard University Press, 1952) p. 228. Used by permission.

† Source: Wade Clark Roof, "Socioeconomic Differentials among White Socioreligious Groups in the United States," *Social Forces*, 58 (September 1979). Copyright © The University of North Carolina Press. Used by permission.

‡ Educational levels for Roman Catholics vary substantially depending on ethnicity, with those who have been in this country longer generally ranking higher than more recent Catholic immigrants. For example, Irish Catholics had a mean educational score of 12.7 years, while Spanish-speaking Catholics had a mean educational level of 10.3 years.

§ Income levels for Roman Catholics vary substantially depending on ethnicity, with those who have been in this country longer generally ranking higher than more recent Catholic immigrants. For example, the mean income for English and Welsh Catholics was $12,900, for Irish Catholics it was $11,940, for Italian Catholics it was $11,275, and for Spanish-speaking Catholics it was $7,860.

local level, congregations tend to be more class segregated than this exhibit would indicate. In other words, a large downtown Baptist church in a southern community may have a large percentage of upper- and middle-class people from that town. On the edge of town, a smaller Baptist church may be attended almost entirely by working- and lower-class persons. Likewise, the Congregational churches (United Church of Christ) in big cities in the northeast tend to draw the more highly educated population. But in a small town in upstate New Hampshire, where only two or three churches serve the community, the Congregationalists may draw heavily from the lower- and middle-class population. Probably no local congregation is totally class exclusive, and some congregations are relatively well integrated in terms of class. Nevertheless, the tendency is for local congregations to be somewhat more segregated by social class than the above table indicates.

There are many reasons for the correlation between social class and denominational affiliation. We discussed one explanation in the previous section: the belief system of some denominations may enhance the members' likelihood of worldly success. A second explanation deals with the relationship of the theology to the secular order. Some theological orientations endorse the present social order as ordained by God (a modern-day version of the divine right of the king); others insist that religion has little or nothing to do with the social order and that religious ethics is concerned only with personal motives and intentions. In either case, members of the privileged classes would not find their self-interests threatened. On the other hand, some religious groups (such as the Bruderhof) define affluence as the root of evil and glorify the life of poverty and self-denial. Still others attack the social order and advocate a restructuring of the socioeconomic system (much like the radical reformation of the Anabaptists).[11] In these groups members of the privileged classes might find themselves very uncomfortable, while the lower classes would find either solace or hope for the future. In this case, class differences between denominations would be due to elective affinity; people choose a religious group which fits their own socioeconomic circumstances. We will explore this view more thoroughly in the next section.

A third reason for class differentials may be a simple matter of like-seeking-like. Those of similar educational level may be drawn by common interests, common speech patterns and other homogeneous characteristics. A highly educated person may not return to a church in which the minister demonstrates little scholarship and uses bad grammar. The visitor simply feels uncomfortable. Likewise, a person with little education may feel alienated and lost in a church where the minister delivers a scholarly sermon based on tightly argued logic. Such a sermon may seem utterly irrelevant and

---

[11] For a more detailed treatment of the social ethics of specific groups or of specific eras, see Troeltsch (1931), H. R. Niebuhr (1951), and Forell (1966).

uninspiring to the visitor. Moreover, when people move to a new community, they sometimes join churches which are attended by their colleagues at work. This pattern of affiliation is based on the tendency to associate with people who are in some respects similar. Common socioeconomic background is one factor in this feeling that others are somehow similar.

A fourth explanation is based on this like-seeking-like concept. This view suggests that as people move from one social status to another, they tend to change their religious affiliation. Hence, advocates of this explanation take a position precisely opposite of the Weberian thesis. Rather than suggesting that religious beliefs may cause social mobility, these theorists insist that changes in religious affiliation frequently *follow* changes in social status. This is so because people are more comfortable with persons of the same socioeconomic standing or because they are using religious affiliation as a way of reinforcing their upward social mobility. (See the discussion of religious switchers in Chapter 5).

This explanation is a controversial one. Nelsen and Snizek (1976) studied this theory of "musical pews," using data from a national election sample. They concluded that there is no evidence to support the idea that denominational switching follows social mobility. Newport (1979), using data from previous studies combined with new survey information from the National Opinion Research Corporation, insists that his evidence does support the theory. More empirical evidence is needed and perhaps a more sophisticated treatment of variables is necessary. It may well be that this explanation holds for some types of groups or for some types of people, but not for others. At this point our tools of analysis are still too crude to make firm generalizations.

Finally, class differences in denominational affiliation may sometimes be explained by matters of history and ethnicity. In this country, the Episcopalians, Congregationalists, and Presbyterians are the denominations which have been well established for the longest period of time. Christian Science— also a high status denomination— was founded more recently, but it was founded in this country and is not a product of recent immigration. Lutherans, who occupy higher status in certain European countries, represent somewhat more recent arrivals in this country. The highest-status positions were already occupied, and the German and Scandinavian immigrants have had to work their way up the social ladder from the bottom. Persons from these ethnic backgrounds are also located in more rural areas of the United States. Hence, they tend to rank lower on such status indicators as educational level, cash income, and occupational prestige. Likewise, the Roman Catholic population includes many Irish, Italian, and Hispanic Americans whose immigrating ancestors date back only one or two generations. These original immigrants had to accept unskilled labor positions. Their descendants have only gradually been integrated into higher-status positions. They have not had the same period of time to accumulate family fortunes.

Perhaps even more important than denominational affiliation by social class, however, is the research which has focused on ways in which one's social class seems to affect one's style of religiosity. In Chapter 2, we discussed some of the ways in which religiosity has been operationalized. Some of the early studies on religion and social class used attendance as the prime indicator of religious commitment. Since upper-class people tend to be more regular in church attendance, it appeared that the upper and middle classes were considerably more "religious" than the lower classes. When researchers began to use multidimensional measures of religiosity, a rather different pattern emerged. Fukuyama (1961) found that among Congregationalists, people who ranked high in socioeconomic status also scored highest for church attendance[12] and for religious knowledge (biblical teachings and the theological orientation of the denomination). On the other hand, lower-class members scored higher on devotionalism (personal religious experience, daily prayer, and so on) than did higher status Congregationalists. This led to more in-depth studies by N. J. Demerath (1965) and by Rodney Stark (1972).

Demerath did an in-depth case study of one denomination (Lutheran) and followed it with survey data from four other denominations for comparison (Congregationalists, Presbyterians, Disciples of Christ, and Baptists). He began by distinguishing two types of religiosity: church-like and sect-like. Church-like religiosity was operationalized in terms of attendance at Sunday worship services, participation in parish activities, and involvement in secular civic organizations. (The rationale for the last one was that sectarians usually withdraw from worldly organizations and reject the current social order, while church-like people viewed civic involvement as an expression of one's faith). Sect-like commitment was operationalized in terms of the number of close friends in the congregation (communal involvement), extent to which the religion provided aid and direction for everyday living, and disapproval of the minister's participation in community affairs.[13]

Demerath found that within any given denomination, an individual's style of religiosity is highly correlated to his or her socioeconomic status. More important, Demerath suggests that members of different social classes who belong to the same church may be active in different ways and may have quite different needs met by the same organization. The higher a Lutheran's

---

[12] Virtually all of the studies in the 1950s, 1960s, and early 1970s found that church *attendance* was higher among those with high socioeconomic status. However, three empirical studies in the late 1970s have challenged this assumption—claiming that socioeconomic status has very little effect on attendance at religious services (Mueller and Johnson 1975; Davidson 1977; Alston and McIntosh, 1979).

[13] The validity of this last item as an indicator of sect-like religion may be questioned. Clergy from sect-like groups are often involved in community affairs, but affairs of a different sort than their mainline counterparts. Not many sectarian ministers would join conventional civic clubs such as the Rotarians, but they may be involved in antimilitary movements (many "sectarian" groups are pacifist) or in local efforts to close an X-rated movie theater.

social status, the more likely he or she is to participate in church-like ways. The lower the social status, the more likelihood there was of sect-like participation. The same pattern held for the other four denominations as well. Exhibit 8–2 shows the percentages of people for each social class and in each denomination who rated high on church-like commitment.

Exhibit 8–2 _____

Percentage of Those High in Church-Like Involvement

Denomination	Individual Status			
	Upper	*Middle*	*Working*	*Lower*
Congregationalists	65	62	46	34
Presbyterians	67	55	45	36
Disciples of				
Christ	73	63	55	42
Baptists	67	54	37	32
Lutherans	51	45	32	24

Source: N. J. Demerath III, *Social Classes in American Protestantism* (Chicago: Rand McNally, 1965), pp. 87, 118. Used by Permission.

Rodney Stark used a somewhat different procedure. He did not begin by defining which patterns were characteristic of church-like or sect-like commitment, but simply looked for correlations and patterns. He found that participation at religious rituals, a high degree of religious knowledge, and high involvement in voluntary church organizations and activities were strongly correlated to high socioeconomic status. He then suggested that these three dimensions of religiosity are generally indicative of church-like commitment. On the other hand, he found that orthodoxy (actually biblical literalism), reports of having had a religious experience, personal devotionalism (such as daily prayer), communal involvement (reports that most close friends are members of the same church), ethicalism (application of religious principles to everyday life), and particularism (belief that only members of one's own denomination will be saved) are inversely related to socioeconomic status (Stark 1972:494). Stark notes that high-status church members participate to a greater degree in those activities which reinforce their respectability and confirm their worldly success. Lower-class persons are religiously active in ways that will offer comfort and solace and will provide compensations for one's lack of worldly success. Stark (1972:495) and Demerath (1965:xxi) independently conclude that differences in religiosity between the social classes are not ones of *degree* so much as ones of *kind* or *style* of involvement.

Several other empirical studies using various measures of churchness and sectness, have also found both church-like participation and sect-like participation within each denomination—and have found socioeconomic status to be the critical variable affecting a member's orientation (Dynes 1955; Winter 1977). However, one recent study has introduced a new variable which also needs to be taken into account. Davidson (1977) studied four congregations representing two different denominations. He found that one's specific congregational membership (for example, a predominantly middle-class Methodist church versus a predominantly lower-class Methodist church) was a more important variable in affecting a person's style of religiosity than his or her *individual* socioeconomic status. Each local congregation affirms certain behaviors or beliefs as central and applies informal group norms to enforce that style of religiosity. Davidson also found that an individual's socioeconomic status had less impact on conservative community-like groups (where belonging functions and informal norms were important) than in liberal audience-like congregations (where the sense of community was less strong).

Of course, denominational affiliation is also significant in shaping one's religious style. Various denominations stress different styles of religiosity and while there is substantial variation within each denomination, there is also very significant variation *between* denominations. In short, one's socioeconomic status, one's denominational affiliation, and one's *local* congregational membership are all significant interacting variables which affect one's style of religiosity (Stark 1972; Davidson 1977).

The bulk of the empirical research on social status and religiosity suggests that persons with high status are more likely than lower-class persons to be committed at an instrumental level—through investment of time and money in the formal structure (Estus and Overington 1970). Lower-status persons are more likely than higher-status persons to be committed at the affective level—through close friendship networks.[14]

Expressions of religious commitment tend to be significantly affected by socioeconomic status in other ways as well. Not only do people of different social classes tend to affiliate with different denominations, but members of the same denomination who are of different socioeconomic status tend to participate in the life of the church in different ways and for different reasons. Furthermore, the overall socioeconomic level of a *local* congregation affects the style of religiosity of that group[15] and members may be affected in their religiosity as they conform to the norms of their local congregation. Socioeconomic status is certainly not the only important factor affecting one's style of religiosity, but it is an important one.

---

[14] At this point, there is little evidence on differences in moral commitment—commitment to the belief system itself—because the belief systems are articulated differently. For a discussion of types or levels of commitment, see the section on Kanter's commitment theory in Chapter 5.

[15] Predominant socioeconomic status is of course not the only important factor in shaping a congregation's style of religiosity. The educational background and the personality characteristics of the minister are also extremely important, and regional, denominational, and ethnic factors may have important impacts on congregational style.

Theology as Social Ideology

In earlier chapters we discussed the fact that one of the functions of religion is to address issues of meaning. When people experience suffering or encounter injustices, they want to know why—or why me? Why is it that the good often seem to encounter suffering and hardship while the evil seem to flourish like the green bay tree? On the other hand, when a family member or a good friend meets tragedy or death, people sometimes question, "Why couldn't it have been me?" The arbitrariness of suffering causes people to want an explanation; the world should make sense—it should have some ultimate meaning. If these events do not make sense, then life somehow seems a cruel joke. Any belief system which attempts to explain the reasons for evil, suffering, and injustice by placing them in a divine master-scheme is referred to as a *theodicy*.

In trying to make sense out of the world and out of human experience, religious ideologies frequently provide explanations for the inequalities which exist in the social system. Sometimes religious beliefs endorse the current social system as established under divine will. For example, the present social arrangements may be viewed as God's divine plan, or the structures of this world may be viewed as a testing ground established by God to determine the truly faithful. On the other hand, the structures of this world may be viewed as the province of an evil force (e.g., Satan). This latter view is more likely to be found among lower-class sects. Since lower-class persons are more likely to experience frustrations with the existing social system and to feel it is unjust, they are likely to have a rather different theodicy. Max Weber maintains that the lower their social class, the more likely people are to adhere to an otherworldly religion (Weber 1963:91).

The theodicies of the lower classes are essentially "theodicies of despair" or "theodicies of escape" while theodicies of the upper classes tend to be those "of good fortune." People who are socially oppressed and who are experiencing a great deal of suffering need some explanation of a deeper justice or a deeper meaning which will ultimately prevail. In many lower-class sects, financial affluence is defined as the root of avarice and as a sign of evil. Human experience is divided into worldly and spiritual realms; and attachment to the second of these requires a rejection of worldly success. This rejection makes economic deprivation much easier to bear, for poverty is espoused as a noble choice; it is made a virtue. In fact, a frequent text for preachers in lower-class Christian sects is the saying by Jesus, "It is easier for a camel to go through the eye of a needle than for a rich man to enter the Kingdom of Heaven." The saying is likely to be understood literally and as applicable to the present day. (In affluent churches, this saying is often treated as a comment directed specifically at the rich young ruler Jesus was addressing or strictly at the rich people of that day and age. Its application to today's world is minimized.)

Other devices can also be used to make deprivation and suffering meaningful. When the ancient Hebrews were exiled from their homeland and were made slaves of the Babylonians, their plight seemed hopeless and many of them felt their God had forsaken them. These people awaited a messiah figure who would rescue them and take them back to their homeland. (The expectation of a messiah was a distinctly Jewish theodicy.) The messiah, they believed, would be a military general who would show forth the power of God with his mighty leadership. But the messiah did not come. Eventually a prophetic genius came along who rearticulated the theodicy. He insisted that the ultimate victory would come not through military might, but by the ability to endure suffering. The suffering of the Jews was part of God's master plan to provide salvation to all of humanity. The messiah figure was recast as a "suffering servant." Suffering was not meaningless; indeed it was a high calling. Release from the suffering would come in Yahweh's time—only after the divine purposes had been fulfilled. The idea of being a chosen people was preserved by being redefined. Rather than being chosen for privilege, the Jews were chosen for service. They were hand-picked to be God's tools to transform the world. Jews have been persecuted and oppressed for 2,500 years, yet their theodicy of suffering has sustained them and held them together. Second Isaiah (Isaiah 40–55) was the first to articulate a theodicy for their oppression.[16]

This provides only one of many possible examples of religious groups which recast their theology and world view to fit their social circumstances. Groups which are comprised of members of the privileged class also develop theodicies to justify their good fortune. As Weber puts it (1958:271), "the fortunate is seldom satisfied with the fact of being fortunate. Beyond this one needs to know that one has the *right* to good fortune, . . . that one 'deserves' it." Elizabeth Nottingham elaborates:

> Almost equally important for a society [as a theodicy of disprivilege] is a morally acceptable explanation of its successes. Since a successful society often enjoys its worldly accomplishments at the expense of less fortunate peoples, its members are frequently driven to find a moral formula that will not only provide positive meaning for their own good fortune but also will help diminish any guilt they feel about the less happy situation of other groups (1971:126).

One reason for differential denominational affiliation by social class may be that the theodicy of one denomination may have a better fit with the needs and concerns of those in certain circumstances. Weber (1958b:62–

---

[16] Theodicies of disprivilege will be discussed in more detail later—in the section on religion and minority status.

63) referred to the tendency for members of certain social and economic groups to be drawn to certain religious beliefs as elective affinity. Hence, Weber himself recognized that many people during the reformation whose fortunes were rising may have been drawn to Calvinism. Calvin's emphasis on individualism and his refusal to condemn usury as intrinsically evil may have attracted upwardly mobile people. This could be seen as a modification by Weber of his earlier suggestion that Calvinist beliefs caused upward mobility. No doubt Weber would assert that both processes are at work; upward social mobility and Calvinistic beliefs were mutually reinforcing.

Not only is the view of the present social system rather different in the theologies of different socioeconomic groups, but the basic virtues and vices tend to be different. Liston Pope and H. Richard Niebuhr have both elaborated on differences between affluent and lower-class churches. Pope did a study of lower-class Protestant churches attended by mill workers and compared them to the high prestige "uptown churches" in a North Carolina community. He found that in the mill worker world view, the world is a battlefield where God and Satan struggle for each individual soul. The sacrificed "blood of Jesus" and Bible reading by the faithful are the critical elements which allow God to be victorious in any given situation. As one mill minister summarized it, "You have to carry a bucket of blood into the pulpit to satisfy these people." (Pope 1942:88) H. Richard Niebuhr (1957) has further pointed out that the lower-class concept of the deity is one of a comforter, protector, and savior. The role of God is to "take care of His people."

The chief decisions that control the lives of unskilled laborers occur at a level that they cannot control directly. Likewise, Pope found that the mill workers viewed their role in the supernatural realm as one of observer, cheerleader, and marginal supporter. The battle is viewed as one between superpowers (the Lord and the Devil), and it is largely the action of a third party (the sacrifice of Jesus) which will determine the outcome. This passive observer posture is typical of lower-class religiosity, especially for those groups stressing a theodicy of escape. A content analysis of hymns used in lower-class congregations illustrates the emphasis on dependency, alienation from this world, and blood sacrifice. Notable also is the negative concept of human character and of one's self evaluation ("such a worm as I"). (See Exhibit 8–3 for examples.)[17]

Alienation from upper-class values is also expressed in lower-class concepts of immorality, for upper-class forms of amusement are typically viewed as vices. Pope summarizes the mill workers' view of sinful behavior: "The principal sins, in the eyes of mill villagers, are such uptown 'worldly amuse-

---

[17] Of course, the hymnals of the various denominations carry many of the same hymns. In analysis of differences in hymns, two factors can be viewed as significant: (1) the character of hymns which are *not* common to upper- and lower-class hymnals, and (2) differences between denominations in the *popularity* of those hymns which *are* common to all of the hymnals.

ments' as playing cards, dancing, gambling, drinking, and swimming with members of the opposite sex" (Pope 1942:88). Niebuhr has also stressed the social ethic inherent in lower-class expressions of Christianity. It is not only the individual who needs saving it is the whole social system. The current social arrangements are often viewed as unjust and inequitable; hence, they are in need of redemption and transformation. In fact, sin is not just thought of as wrong actions, but as a "state of being" which is all-pervasive. Sin is a depraved condition which infects both the individual soul and the fabric of society.

Another characteristic of lower-class churches, pointed out by H. Richard Niebuhr, is a high degree of emotionalism in the worship services. One explanation of this is that religious liturgies may provide an emotional outlet for frustrations and humiliations experienced in the society. Weston LaBarre discusses the extreme emotionalism in snake-handling churches of the Appalachian hills. The members are impoverished, many having only a few years of formal education. Some are illiterate. While their religious life involves shouting, dancing, seizures, and trances, these people are not more emotional in everyday life than any other Americans. LaBarre (1962:174) comments that for these poor folks of rural Tennessee and Kentucky, "their church is the only place were they can freely and spontaneously *feel* and act out their feelings."

In the upper classes, economic prosperity is defined as a blessing of God or even as a sign of divine favor. Moreover, members of the upper classes are accustomed to controlling their own destinies. Their outlook stresses individual accomplishment, a positive assessment of their ability to change things in this world, and a high valuation of individual initiative. In fact, Niebuhr suggests that the American middle and upper classes[18] characterize the deity as "energetic activity" and as a being who expects the same sort of productive activity from humanity. "The conception of God which prevails in bourgeois faith is that of dynamic will." (Niebuhr 1957:84) This set of values is vividly illustrated by the hymns which are sung in upper- and upper-middle class churches (see samples in Exhibit 8–4).

Equally important is the way in which conventional secular norms and values are embraced in upper-class churches. Pope points out that in the mill town he studied, the concepts of sin in the affluent uptown churches emphasize premarital sexual relations, failure to pay one's debts, participating in "shady business activities," failure to live up to one's contracts or agreements, and lack of involvement in social and civic obligations. Pope also found that upper-class church members were more likely to view religion

---

[18] H. Richard Niebuhr focused on the characteristics of what he called the "middle-class" churches—but since he was juxtaposing them against the lower-class churches, it is clear that he was describing the religious tendencies of all nonpoor—including both middle and upper classes.

Exhibit 8–3

Hymns in Churches of the Less Affluent

"Nothing but the Blood"

What can wash away my sin? Nothing but the blood of Jesus;
What can make me whole again? Nothing but the blood of Jesus.
Oh! precious is the flow That makes me white as snow;
No other fount I know, Nothing but the blood of Jesus.

Nothing can for sin atone, Nothing but the blood of Jesus;
Naught of good that I have done, Nothing but the blood of Jesus.
Oh! precious is the flow That makes me white as snow;
No other fount I know, Nothing but the blood of Jesus.

This is all my hope and peace, Nothing but the blood of Jesus;
This is all my righteousness, Nothing but the blood of Jesus.
Oh! precious is the flow That makes me white as snow;
No other fount I know, Nothing but the blood of Jesus.

(Baptist hymn)

"A Gathering in the Sky"

There'll be a great gathering in the sky
When all of God's children get home
We'll join the happy millions as they sing
There around the great white throne
I'm speaking of a big tent meetin'
Where we never shall say good-bye
I'm longin' for the day
When I hear my savior say
There's a gathering in the sky.

One by one we passed through the valley dim,
Our load seems hard to bear;
But I'm going to a great reunion,
Where people's not afraid of prayer.
There'll be alot of old time singing,
Somewhere up there on high.
It seems I can hear them saying
There's a gathering in the sky.

(Rural Appalachian hymn)

"Remember Me"

Alas! and did my Savior bleed? And did my Sov'reign die?
Help me, dear Savior, Thee to own, And ever faithful be;
Would He devote that sacred head For such a worm as I?
And when Thou sittest on Thy throne, Dear Lord, remember me.

Was it for crimes that I have done He hung upon the tree?
Help me, dear Savior, Thee to own, And ever faithful be;
Amazing pity! grace unknown! And love beyond degree!
And when Thou sittest on Thy throne, Dear Lord, remember me.

(Nazarene hymn)

"No One Understands Like Jesus"

No one understands like Jesus, He's a friend beyond compare;
Meet Him at the throne of mercy, He is waiting for you there.
No one understands like Jesus, When the days are dark and grim:
No one is so dear as Jesus—Cast your ev'ry care on Him.

Exhibit 8–3 *(Concluded)*

No one understands like Jesus, Ev-ry woe He sees and feels;
Tenderly He whispers comfort, And the broken heart He heals.
No one understands like Jesus, When the days are dark and grim;
No one is so dear as Jesus—Cast your ev'ry care on Him.

(Country and Western hymn
used in Independent Baptist and
Methodist Sects)

★ ★ ★ ★ ★

In lower- and working-class churches, the hymns frequently depict the world as a place of suffering and hardship, and the inherent worth of the individual is viewed rather dimly ("Naught of good that I have done"; "a worm such as I"). Sin is viewed as a state of being rather than as a specific action. A major focus is comfort in this world combined with hope for the next. Finally, the decisive action which determines one's changes is not accomplished by the individual, but by some external force or action (the sacrificial blood of Jesus).

as a specialized sphere of life. Religion is generally viewed as a good and levitating force in society, but upper-class citizens believed that religious organizations ought not meddle in political or economic matters.[19]

Niebuhr also pointed to the narrowing of the scope of religiosity among the affluent, indicating a transformation in the concept of Christian ethics. He insisted that as the lower-class sect emerges into a denomination and develops a middle-class clientele, it tends to lose its social ethic and its emphasis on social evils and injustices. The concept of Christian morality is individualized, focusing on personal actions and motives. Niebuhr suggests that the problem of *individual* salvation becomes far more urgent for middle-class church members than the problem of *social* redemption. From the perspective of the affluent, nothing is substantially wrong with the social system which would require its "redemption."[20]

Niebuhr points out that in the process, the conception of sin is changed

---

[19] As we noted earlier, Lenski found the same pattern in his study of religion in Detroit: upper-class people were more likely to be theologically orthodox and to categorize religion as a realm separate from economics and politics. Lower-class persons were more likely to be devotionalists and were more likely to apply their religion to everyday life. In other words, members of upper-class churches were more characterized by a multiple, narrow-vector world view than were members of the lower classes. The sociology student should be cognizant, however, that this generalization refers to a statistically significant difference which exists between the groups; there is clearly not a categorical difference between the classes in these matters.

[20] Davidson (1977) finds no difference between individuals or between congregations of different socioeconomic background on horizontal beliefs (beliefs about helping other people and loving one's neighbor). Niebuhr's point is that the *way* in which help is offered may differ; helping individuals cope with their problems is quite different from changing the structure of society itself. During the 1960s and 1970s liberal denominations began to address the issue of structural change. The difference between classes in how Christians think help should be offered may still exist, but the difference is probably much less significant now than it has been for most of American history.

Exhibit 8–4 _____

Popular Hymns in Affluent Denominations

_____

"O Brother Man, Fold to Thy Heart"

O brother man, fold to thy heart thy brother;
Where pity dwells, the peace of God is there;
To worship rightly is to love each other,
Each smile a hymn, each kindly deed a prayer.

Follow with reverent steps the great example
Of him whose holy work was doing good:
So shall the wide earth seem our Father's temple,
Each loving life a psalm of gratitude

(Congregational hymn)

"I Sing a Song of the Saints of God"

I sing a song of the saints of God Patient and brave and true,
Who foiled and fought and lived and died For the Lord they loved and knew
And one was a doctor, and one was a queen, And
one was a shepherdess on the green: They were all of them
saints of God, and I mean, God helping, to be one too.

They loved their Lord so dear, so dear, And his love made them strong;
And they followed the right, for Jesus' sake, the whole of their good lives long.
And one was a soldier, and one was a priest, And
one was slain by a fierce wild beast: And there's not any
reason, no, not the least, Why I shouldn't be one too.

They lived not only in ages past, There are hundreds of thousands still:
The world is bright with the joyous saints Who love to do Jesus' will.
You can meet them in school or in lanes, or at sea, In
church, or in trains, or in shops, or at tea; For the saints of
God are just folk like me, And I mean to be one too.

(Episcopal hymn)

"Rise Up, O Men of God"

Rise up, O men of God! Have done with lesser things;
Give heart and soul and mind and strength To serve the King of kings.

Rise up, O men of God! His Kingdom terries long;
Bring in the day of brotherhood And end the night of wrong.

Rise up, O men of God! The Church for you doth wait,
Her strength unequal to her task: Rise up, and make her great!

Lift high the cross of Christ! Tread where His feet have trod.
As brothers of the Son of Man, Rise up, O men of God. Amen

(Presbyterian hymn)

* * * * *

In upper- and middle-class churches, the hymns frequently express a positive value of this-worldly activity, an affirmation of individual self-worth, a high valuation of individual initiative and accomplishment and a sense that persons are in charge of their own destinies. In one of these hymns, Jesus is depicted as an *example* to humankind rather than as a bloodied sacrificial Lamb. Furthermore, the saints of God are depicted in one hymn as common folks rather than as a highly committed elect.

in a very fundamental sense—a sense much more important than simply a matter of upper-class churches defining different behaviors as sinful. Whereas the lower-class churches focus on sin as a state of being, the middle-class churches limit their concept to sins—specific actions or personal characteristics. In the middle classes, "sin is not so much a state of soul as a deed or a characteristic; it is not so much the evil with which the whole social life and structure is infected as it is the personal failure of the individual" (Niebuhr 1957:85).

In middle- and upper-class churches, individuals are encouraged to cultivate a sense of self-worth and self-esteem; members do not often sing on Sunday morning about an Amazing Grace that "saved a *wretch* like me" or about how the blood of Jesus was shed "for a *worm* such as I." Such negative self-images are characteristic of lower-class hymnology where the conception of sin is more pervasive. It is the upper-class churches which are likely to respond positively to such theologians as Harvey Cox (1964:xi) when he writes of sin: "I believe a careful examination of Biblical sources will indicate that humanity's most debilitating proclivity is *not* pride. It is *not* the attempt to be more than human. Rather it is sloth, the unwillingness to be everything humanity was intended to be."

As one reviews the hymns in Exhibits 8–3 and 8–4, one can see this difference in emphasis. These distinctions are not a categorical or exclusive difference between upper- and lower-class churches. Clearly, there is wide variation of religious expression and theology within denominations and between persons of the same social class. Niebuhr and Pope describe trends, and attempt to make us aware of the fact that socioeconomic status does affect religiosity in important ways.

Similar class variations are found among other world religions as well. For example, Hinduism in the upper classes of India conforms much more to the official religion of that faith; it is monotheistic and stresses concepts of transmigration of souls (reincarnation). The lower classes have a sort of Hindu folk religion which is polytheistic. Lower-class Hindus tend to identify Hindu statues as gods in themselves (rather than as symbols), and they believe in heaven and hell rather than in reincarnation. In fact, in some areas the folk Hinduism of the lower classes can hardly be recognized as Hinduism at all (Noss 1949:243).

In each society where members of several social classes share a common religion, the faith tends to be modified and reinterpreted to fit the needs and the values of each socioeconomic group. It is difficult to say which socioeconomic group is most faithful to the religious teachings. In the United States, various studies have shown that upper-class church members tend to have much more accurate knowledge of the official teachings. However, lower-class members tend to be more willing to apply their faith to everyday life—including all realms. Perhaps this is why Troeltsch insisted that the "sects" of the lower classes and the "churches" of the upper classes each accurately depicted certain biblical teachings and core themes while they each distorted other central concepts. The important point for our purposes is to recognize that one's social status and one's economic self-interests do tend to affect one's theodicy, and hence one's world-view and one's style of being religious.

Exhibit 8–5 _____

Theodicies, Social Conditions, and the Spread of a Religion to Other Cultures

The ability of a religion to spread to other cultures may be affected by the nature of its theodicy. Most religions in the world are limited to a particular tribe or nation of people. The theodicy is articulated in terms of what is good and bad solely for that one group. The chosen people imagery of the ancient Hebrews (prior to Second Isaiah) tended to view good and evil strictly in terms of the fortunes of their own group. This highly ethnocentric view was repeated in the American doctrine of Manifest Destiny in the 19th century. Many Americans held the view that it was the divine will that America dominate "underdeveloped peoples" (such as Native Americans) in order to "civilize" them. This doctrine justified incredible exploitation of Native Americans in this country and tragic colonialism abroad. The ideology obviously was only intended for one group, Anglo-Americans. The earlier English doctrine of "white man's burden" (the responsibility of whites to "take care of" nonwhite peoples who supposedly could not take care of themselves) is another example of a secularized theodicy.

Religions which focus on tribal ancestors or which define good and evil solely in terms of the self-interests of one nation are not likely to spread and become world religions (ones that are found around the world and in a variety of cultures). Only when the theodicy addresses conditions common to all of humanity will the religion be acceptable in other cultures. The sense of universalism—the idea that the victory over pain, suffering, injustice, and death is appropriate and available for all people—is a first step in a religion diffusing to other cultures. For Christianity, this was implemented by Saint Paul. But even after the religion is articulated in universalistic terms, its spread will be affected by the compatibility of the religious outlook with the values and outlooks in the host culture. One factor in this compatibility is the economic circumstances of the group in question. If the people are impoverished, oppressed, disfranchized, or otherwise in despair, a theodicy of escape is much more likely to take hold. If the people in question are affluent or are otherwise comfortable with their position and their circumstances, a theodicy of despair will not likely have great appeal. The spread of any religion to other cultures is limited in part by the fit between its theodicy and the social conditions of the people hearing the message.

Of course, this discussion would be incomplete if we pointed merely to economic self-interest as a determinant of religious ideologies. An important and interesting phenomenon in today's world is the fact that many denominations whose members are affluent have directly and rather aggressively challenged the structures of inequality and privilege. For example, Congregationalists, Presbyterians, Methodists, Episcopalians, and Catholics all have commissions or task forces on racism, poverty, and social inequities. These task forces do not just attack the problem at an individual level; they challenge the very structure of society and point to *systemic* causes of poverty and racism. They issue statements calling for change—sometimes for radical change—in the basic social and economic structures of society.

Many of the liberal positions taken by the National Council of Churches and by various denominational boards, of course, have not been supported by a majority of the lay constituencies of the churches (Hadden 1970; Jenkins 1977). These controversial policies have been formulated and approved by highly trained professionals who are insulated from direct contact with conservative laity. Jenkins (1977) suggests that because these religious professionals are not paid in proportion to their level of training, their major sense of occupational satisfaction comes from their sense of mission—the sense that they are involved in a moral issue of great importance and that they are making a significant contribution to its resolution. The fact that they work for causes which are *not* in their own self-interest is part of their professional identity and serves to enhance their self-esteem. Because these officials are somewhat removed from the local congregations and have a good deal of autonomy, they are able to develop programs that may not be supported by their affluent and often conservative constituency.

However, bureaucratic control by liberal clergy is only part of the reason that denominational boards of middle-class churches have championed causes of the poor, for there are also many relatively affluent church members who are highly supportive of programs—denominationally sponsored or otherwise—which challenge the status quo. This concern for the disprivileged among affluent congregations appears to be stimulated by religious teachings. The prophets of the Bible consistently called for social justice as the primary indicator of true religious expression, and this theme is frequently developed in the adult education materials of the Catholic Church and most mainline Protestant denominations.

This ethical or prophetic theme is also central to the Reformed branch of Judaism. Although Jews are generally among the more affluent members of American society, they have often championed the cause of blacks and other minorities. For example, it was largely Jews that founded the National Association for the Advancement of Colored People (NAACP) and the National Urban League, two organizations which have been instrumental in fighting for equal rights for blacks.

Likewise, migrant farm workers (predominantly poor Mexican-Americans) have received support from affluent Christian and Jewish congregations which send financial aid to the United Farm Workers and encourage church members to participate in boycotts of grapes, lettuce, and other products. The boycotts end only after wages are increased, conditions improved, and a union contract is signed. However, this usually means increases in the cost of the produce. In other words, affluent church members knowingly boycott goods with the ultimate result that they must pay higher prices. Such behavior is not in the narrow self-interests of these affluent individuals, yet they persist in this behavior because they are convinced that it is the moral thing to do.

The point I wish to make is that while the theology of a group has a tendency to be shaped by the group's economic circumstances and self-interests, the causal relationship can run the other way. Theological teachings can cause people to behave in ways that one might not expect from looking only at their socioeconomic circumstances. Religious teachings can become a tool for justifying one's self-interests, or they may cause one to advocate positions which run counter to one's own economic interests. The reasons for this lie in theodicies which people adopt. In the following section we shall see that a theodicy may mobilize people to action, or it may encourage accommodation and passivity.

Religion and Minority Status

Is Religion an Opiate for the Oppressed?

A good deal of recent sociological research has focused on the religion of the disprivileged. This has been stimulated by a debate over the role of religion for the poor: Does it act as an opiate of the masses or does it inspire the dispossessed to militancy? Karl Marx maintained the former, that religion gave the poor a feeling of solace and a hope of compensation so that they would not rebel. They were, in essence, drugged. Those that hold to this position insist that religion serves as a tool of control for the dominant economic class and ethnic group. Critics have maintained that when European missionaries went to regions which were later colonized, they had the Bible while the natives had the land. When the missionaries left, the natives had the Bible and the Europeans had the land (Marx 1967:95). While examples of this view that religion is a tool of exploitation abound, they neither provide proof nor establish causality.

Other researchers point to contrary data, such as the fact that most civil rights leaders have been members of the clergy and the fact that as many as 60 percent of the members of the Congress of Racial Equality (which became a militant black civil rights group) are weekly church attenders. Many historical analyses have also found that black religion was frequently a motivating force in slave revolts, for religion asserted the intrinsic human worth of slaves (Wilmore 1972). Scholars from several disciplines have utilized a variety of research methods to clarify the relationship between religion and concern for alleviating social injustices. Our treatment in this section will focus on the function of religion in minority groups—specifically ethnic minorities.[21]

One landmark empirical study of the effects of religion on blacks in the United States was conducted by Gary Marx (1967). Using a sample

---

[21] The sociologist uses the term *minority* to refer to groups which have less power to control their destiny than do others. It does not mean the group is necessarily smaller in numbers. (Blacks comprise three fourths of the population of the Republic of South Africa, but they are still referred to as a minority group). In the United States women, homosexuals, the handicapped, and the elderly are often referred to by sociologists as minority groups. In suggesting that we will be focusing on *ethnic* minorities, I wish to make clear that we will not be treating these other groups in this section.

survey method of research, Marx discovered that blacks who were members of higher-status (and predominantly white) denominations were more likely to be militant in their civil rights positions than were those from lower-class churches or sects (including exclusively black churches and sects). A militant black was defined as one who *actively* and *consistently* opposed discrimination and segregation.[22] Percentages of blacks who were militant for each denomination were as follows: Episcopalian, 43 percent; United Church of Christ, 42 percent; Presbyterian, 36 percent; Catholic, 36 percent; Methodist, 28 percent; Baptist, 25 percent; and sects and cults, 15 percent (Marx 1967:99). For most scholars, the fact that blacks in lower-class churches were more passive was not really unexpected; but the evidence that blacks in *entirely black congregations* were more passive than blacks in predominantly white congregations was something of a surprise to many sociologists.

Marx also correlated several measures of religiosity to civil rights militance. He found that infrequent church attendance and indifference to religion were positively correlated with militancy. Eighteen percent of those who attended church more than once a week were militant while 32 percent who attended less than once a year were activists (Marx 1967:101). When asked how important religion is to the person, 22 percent of those who said "extremely important" were militant, while 62 percent of those who answered "not at all important" were militant (Marx 1967:100). Marx also found that orthodoxy was inversely related to militancy.[23] When he combined these factors into an overall index of religiosity, he found a negative relationship between religiosity and militance. Furthermore, the finding held even when he kept certain key variables constant: age, sex, denomination, and region of the country in which the respondent was raised (see Exhibit 8–6). Marx concluded that there apparently is an "incompatibility between piety and protest."

Seymour Lipset, by doing a cross-cultural political analysis, has come to a similar conclusion, but offers an added dimension to Marx's investigation. He maintains that rigid fundamentalism and dogmatism are based on the same underlying personality characteristics, attitudes, and dispositions as political radicalism. In fact, he insists that the most radical political movements often have developed from seedbeds of religious fanaticism. However, he also points out that religious fanaticism and political fanaticism tend to serve as functional alternatives; one usually finds only one or the

---

[22] Marx asked seven questions to determine attitudes toward civil rights policy. Only those who answered with activist responses to at least six of the questions were considered militant. Those who gave activist responses on three, four, or five questions were classified as "moderates." Those who took activist responses on two or fewer were called "conservatives."

[23] The way in which Marx operationalized orthodoxy may be open to some question. He used three items to measure orthodoxy: having no doubt about the existence of God, about the existence of the Devil, and about the existence of the afterlife. The second of these is not accepted by all Christian denominations as a central tenet of faith or as "orthodox."

Exhibit 8–6

Militancy Related to Religiosity by Age, Sex, Place of Upbringing, and Denomination
(percent militant; number of respondents shown in parentheses)

| | Index of Religiosity | | | | | | |
	Very Religious		Quite Religious		Not Very Religious		Not at All Religious	
Age:								
18–29	20	(25)	28	(110)	35	(55)	43	(37)
30–44	22	(54)	31	(161)	37	(59)	53	(58)
45–59	21	(63)	21	(117)	24	(33)	52	(21)
60 +	13	(67)	11	(96)	26	(19)	*	
Sex:								
Women	18	(133)	21	(286)	32	(76)	42	(38)
Men	20	(76)	28	(199)	33	(90)	52	(86)
Where raised:								
Deep South	16	(122)	19	(255)	25	(61)	38	(29)
Border states	29	(49)	28	(104)	31	(42)	54	(35)
Non-South	16	(38)	32	(126)	41	(63)	60	(52)
Denomination:								
Episcopalian, Presbyterian, or Congregationalist	17	(12)	39	(23)	46	(13)	58	(12)
Catholic	10	(10)	31	(49)	40	(20)	54	(28)
Methodist	35	(23)	20	(76)	36	(28)	50	(12)
Baptist	17	(161)	23	(325)	30	(101)	46	(68)

* Three out of six respondents scored as militant.

Source: Gary Marx, *Protest and Prejudice: A Study of Belief in the Black Community* (New York: Harper & Row, 1967), Copyright © 1967 by Anti-Defamation League of B'nai B'rith. Reprinted by permission of Harper & Row, Publishers, Inc. Table 66, p. 103.

other at any given time (Lipset 1960:107–108). In this respect, his finding supports that of Gary Marx. Lipset's study adds a new insight, however, because of its diachronic (historical) methodology. He found that in certain circumstances, religious groups may be the spawning ground for political militancy, but in the process of development these militant groups frequently become less religious (at least in the traditional sense of the word). The sample survey method used by Gary Marx would not indicate this type of pattern, for it focused on attitudes at one given time period.

Other sociologists have challenged Marx's findings more directly by questioning the accuracy of his data on black religion. Follow-up studies have indicated a much more varied effect of black religiosity. Nelson, Madron, and Yokley (1975) have provided empirical data which demonstrates that black religion sometimes does stimulate social change. In another study, Hunt and Hunt (1977) found that, regardless of denominational affiliation, blacks who are church-like in their religiosity are more likely to be inspired to militancy than are blacks who are sect-like. When this variable is held constant, the inverse relationship between militancy and church attendance disappears. A more in-depth understanding of the world view or the theodicy of a subjugated group is necessary before one can predict passivity or militance.

Theodicies and Levels of Activism

The world view of many sectarian groups is otherworldly. The reality or at least the importance of this world is denied except for its function as a testing ground. Only the faithful will be saved and will reach heaven in the afterlife; only the true believers will have "pie in the sky in the sweet by and by" (as it is sometimes referred to affectionately by believers and derisively by skeptics). This afterlife experience is expected to commence for each individual immediately after death. This sort of otherworldly religion is frequently associated with passivity in this-worldly affairs. Members of the dominant social groups are usually more than happy to have their subordinates believe that vindication will come only after death. Slave owners in this country often had that sort of doctrine preached to their slaves, and coupled it with warnings that the saved would be those who lived out their status in this world without causing any trouble.

Another sort of world view is eschatological. In the eschatological world view the ultimate victory over suffering and death will commence at some future time in history. Eschatology may take either of two forms: progressivism or millenarism. Furthermore, millenarism sometimes has a subtype known as apocalypticism.

In the progressive view, the day of perfection will be reached when God and humanity have worked together to attain it. This involves a gradualistic concept of social evolution. The view is based on the idea that God is the creator and rules over the earth. God's master plan is for the evolution of the world into an ever more humane, just, and Godly kingdom (the Kingdom of God on Earth). But it is believed that God will not establish this without human effort and participation. In this evolutionary eschatology, trust in God is often equated with trust in the goodness of God's creation. Believers are to look for signs of God at work in this world and are to become actively involved in the material world. Progressive eschatology was characteristic of much of the Social Gospel movement in America at the turn of the century. In a somewhat modified form, this sort of outlook—with its positive view of this world—continues to be a force in many mainline denominations and is the predominant view of Reformed Jews.[24]

---

[24] Actually, this worldly eschatology is the predominant theodicy in most of the Hebrew and Christian Bibles. In the entire Jewish Bible (the Christian Old Testament) the idea of life after death is mentioned only four times. Salvation was expected to be this-worldly and was anticipated within history. God was thought to be in charge of creation and of history, both of which were viewed as good. The idea of the soul as something separate from the body which would live on after the material body died was an idea introduced by the Greeks and is found in later rabbinical writings and in the Christian New Testament.

Another form of eschatology, millenarism, assumes that the transformation of the world will be sudden rather than gradualistic and will be inaugurated primarily by supernatural powers. Norman Cohn, a historian who has done extensive comparative studies of millenarism, points to five defining characteristics of these movements. The millenarian vision is:

a. Collective, in the sense that it is to be enjoyed by the faithful as a group.
b. Terrestrial, in the sense that it is to be realized on this earth and not in some otherworldly heaven.
c. Imminent, in the sense that it is to come both soon and suddenly.
d. Total, in the sense that it is utterly to transform life on earth, so that the new dispensation will be no mere improvement on the present but perfection itself.
e. Accomplished by agencies which are consciously regarded as supernatural (1964:168).

The word *millennium* means a thousand years and refers to the new age to come. Although the term originates from the New Testament prediction (in the Book of Revelation) that Jesus will return and rule for a thousand years, the word is also used to refer to non-Christian groups with this sort of world view. Hence, millenarians are those people who await a future event by which the Kingdom of God or the New Age will begin. Many millenarian Christians have their own life-after-death scenerio. This involves a bodily resurrection of the dead at the time the new age begins. This is a rather different concept than the belief that eternal life for an individual begins immediately after death and that the spiritual world is coexistent with the material. Nonetheless, many people hold some combination of both beliefs and are not much troubled by the need for coherence and consistency in their theodicy.

The concept of salvation for millenarians, then, is time oriented, terrestrial (although life on earth in the new age will be quite different from present life on earth), and collective (rather than individualistic). Although the transformation will ultimately be accomplished by supernatural forces, humans do have an active and important role in preparing the way. Life in this world is viewed as a time of suffering and of being tested, but the new age will mean the advent of a new social order where justice prevails.[25]

For disadvantaged groups, the millenarian view offers great hope for the future. Frequently, groups that hold this view are highly emotional in their religious expression and become fanatical in their efforts to inaugurate

---

[25] Each of these theodicies (salvation in an afterlife, progressive eschatology, and millenial eschatology) are within the mainline tradition of Christian theology and are given different emphasis by various denominations. For example, one study revealed that 94 percent of the Southern Baptists felt that Jesus would definitely return to earth some day. By contrast, only 13 percent of the Congregationalists fully believed in that prediction (Stark and Glock 1968:34). This is one reason that the procedure of operationalizing orthodoxy only in terms of one of these views and then assuming that those who are more orthodox are also more religious is suspect.

the new age. Hence, it is not uncommon for millenarian groups to precipitate active revolt against the established authorities. Yonia Talmon writes

> Comparative analysis seems to indicate that, generally speaking, the more extremely millenarian a movement is the more activist it is. . . . There seems to be a correlation between the time conception of each movement and its position in the *passivity-activity continuum*. Movements which view the millennium as imminent and have a total and vivid conception of redemption are, on the whole, much more activist than movements which expect it to happen at some remote date. . . . It would seem that truly great expectations and a sense of immediacy enhance the orientation to active rebellion while postponement of the critical date and lesser expectation breed passivity and quietism (1965:527).

Talmon points out that millenarism has enjoyed popularity at all levels of society at one time or another. The theodicy of the Unification Church is millenarian, yet the members have been recruited substantially from relatively affluent middle- and upper-middle-class families. This provides a contemporary example of millenarism that is not rooted in economic dispossession. Nonetheless, it has normally been a religion of *deprived groups*— oppressed peasants, the poorest of the poor in cities and towns, and populations of colonial countries. The millennial outlook usually develops as a reaction to especially severe hardships and suffering. Talmon writes: "Many of the outbursts of millenarism took place against a background of disaster— plagues, devastating fires, recurrent long droughts that were the dire lot of the peasants, slumps that caused widespread unemployment and poverty and calamitous wars" (1965:530). In most cases, millenarism is a phenomenon of ethnic groups which have endured sustained subjugation. The predisposing factor is the gap between the socioeconomic expectations of a group and their actual ability to satisfy their needs.

For example, when simple tribal societies encounter complex ones, there are generated enormously inflated expectations without an adequate development of institutional means for their satisfaction. This was the case in the Cargo cult of Melanasia where exposure to an American military base caused poor indigenous peoples to feel frustrated with their own lack of possessions. Their response was to develop a mystical cult around a flag pole. They believed that if they cracked the mystical marching code of the soldiers, an airplane loaded with cargo for the natives would arrive. The discrepancy between desire and reality is often bridged by millenarian hope. The millennial hope, in turn, sometimes leads to action.

One can also see the correlation of millenarism with "relative deprivation" in the American lower-middle class. For example, Ohio lost many jobs and some of its population in the late 1970s as industries moved to states where energy costs would be less (the Sun Belt). When this combined with the impact of the economic recession of the early 1980s, many people lost jobs. Furthermore, the predictions for the future were gloomy, and many working- and middle-class people began to doubt the American dream of prosperity and plenty in the future. It is noteworthy that at the same time there has been a substantial growth of millenarism in Ohio.

Exhibit 8–7 _____

Milleniarian Anticipation Expressed in Hymns

"Jesus Comes"

Watch ye saints with eyelids waking, Lo, the pow'rs of heav'n are shaking;
Keep your Lamps all trimmed and burning, Ready for your Lord's returning.
Lo! He comes, lo! Jesus comes; Lo! He comes, He comes all glorious!
Jesus comes to reign victorious, Lo! He comes, yes, Jesus comes.

Kingdoms at their base are crumbling, Hark, His chariot wheels are rumbling;
Tell, O, tell of grace abounding, Whilst the seventh trump is sounding.
Lo! He comes, lo! Jesus comes; Lo! He comes, He comes all glorious!
Jesus comes to reign victorious, Lo! He comes, yes, Jesus comes.

Nations wane, tho' proud and stately, Christ His Kingdom hasteneth greatly;
Earth her latest pangs is summing, Shout, ye saints, your Lord is coming.
Lo! He comes, lo! Jesus comes; Lo! He comes, He comes all glorious!
Jesus comes to reign victorious, Lo! He comes, yes, Jesus comes.

"Our Lord's Return to Earth Again"

I am watching for the coming of the glad millennial day
When our blessed Lord shall come and catch His waiting Bride away
Oh! my heart is filled with rapture as I labor, watch and pray
For our Lord is coming back to earth again.
Oh! our Lord is coming back to earth again, Yes, our Lord is
   coming back to earth again, Satan will be bound a
   thousand years, we'll have no tempter then,
After Jesus shall come back to earth again.

Then the sin and sorrow, pain and death of this dark world shall cease
In a glorious reign with Jesus of a thousand years of peace;
All the earth is groaning, crying for that day of sweet release,
For our Jesus to come back to earth again.
Oh! our Lord is coming back to earth again, Yes, our Lord is
   coming back to earth again, Satan will be bound a
thousand years, we'll have no tempter then,
After Jesus shall come back to earth again.

* * * * *

These two hymns express vividly the revolutionary and earthly expectations of the millennial vision. The first stresses the collapse of the present social order and the destruction of kingdoms. The second expresses a mood of waiting until the supernatural does its work. Compare the messages to those in the hymns in Exhibits 8–3 and 8–4.

One must be wary of simplistic generalizations about the kind of social behavior millenarism generates. Some modern millenarian movements are ineffective in their change strategies because they employ mystical methods to bring change; for others the millennium is too distant to motivate members to militancy. Nonetheless, the overall tendency is for millenarians to be activists. Sometimes the activism is directed at the social system and has an empirical likelihood of bringing change. This is what Wallace called a "rational strategy" (see Chapter 6). If people believe that they are responsible to God for helping to overthrow the present social order, their concept of religious duty may, in fact, stimulate social reform.

Unlike the progressivists who see the present order as good and getting better, millennial movements usually seek total transformation of this world—which they view as unjust or even inherently evil. Many groups that begin with a rational approach become progressively more strategic and more rational (more secular?) if they begin to meet with success. This is illustrated by the tendency which Lipset described for religious movements to spawn radical political movements and the political movements, in turn, to lose much of their religiosity (Lipset 1960). Of course, for sociologists who insist that a world view may be religious without being supernaturalistic, these secular political movements are no less religious than their predecessors. They simply have this-worldly and rationalistic systems of faith.

There is one particular type of millenarism which is common among the most destitute—those who feel utterly vulnerable in relationship to another group of people. This form emphasizes much more strongly the idea that the world is evil and controlled by Satan. Contrary to the evolutionary eschatology, this view describes human history as being on a hopelessly *downward* spiral. Ironically, this depressing circumstance is viewed as a sign of hope because it indicates that the end is near. God will intervene in history and bring forth the new age. Nothing humans can do will significantly alter the course of history. The believer can only be ready for the day of judgment, preparing his or her own soul and perhaps engaging in mystical ritual action, such as dancing around a fire (the Ghost Dance) or marching around a flag pole (the Cargo cult) or spreading the word until everyone is informed of the noble story (Seventh Day Adventists and Jehovah's Witnesses). This extreme form of millenarism is called apocalypticism.

Within Christianity, apocalypticism is normally based on a literal interpretation of the Book of Revelation. Its utter rejection of the present age and present world disallows any attempt to bring change. For this reason, it usually leads to passivity in terms of the social structure. Groups or individuals are more likely to adopt this posture and this world view if they are powerless and utterly despairing.[26] If some hope exists of social change through human action, the group or individual is more likely to develop a rational strategy.

Christianity, then, has within it several theodicies, which in numerous ways are quite different. Some congregations and some denominations stress one of them exclusively. Most congregations have some people who do not believe in a Second Coming or in an imminent end to the world;

---

[26] This does not mean that *only* the destitute will develop such a world view, but they are more likely to be inclined in this direction than are those in other socioeconomic circumstances.

Exhibit 8–8

The Apocalyptic World View

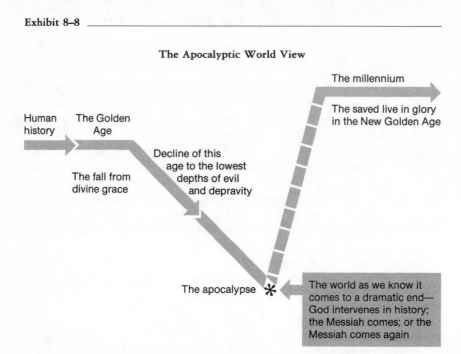

This represents, in broad outline, the apocalyptic view of history. Various groups develop their own scenerio of how the end will occur. For example, some Christian groups believe the millennium is only the precursor to the Golden Age to come. Satan is expected to have a period of rule between the time of the millennium and the true Eternal Age.

Exhibit 8–9

The Progressive View of History

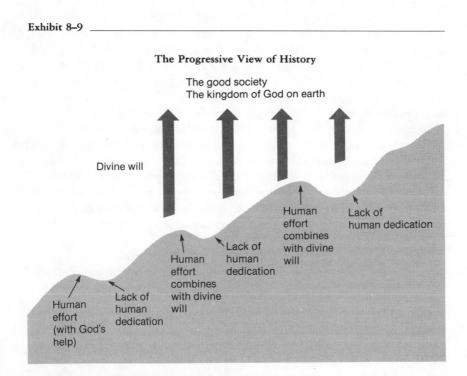

Exhibit 8–10

Apocalypticism in Christian Scripture

Only two books in the Christian Bible are apocalyptic: Daniel and Revelation (sometimes called the Book of the Apocalypse). Several other books (such as the Gospel of Peter, the Gospel of Mary, the Gospel of Thomas, and the Gospel of Infancy) were omitted from the Canon (the Bible) because they were apocalyptic and dualistic (the material world viewed as evil, and the spirit world viewed as good). In fact, as late as the Synod of Laodicea in A.D. 360 church fathers voted explicitly to exclude the Book of Revelation (along with these other books) from the list of books that made up the scripture. Several decades later, at the Provincial Council (A.D. 383 and 392), church leaders decided to include the Book of Revelation. They mistakenly came to believe that it was written by John the Evangelist. (Biblical scholars believe that the Book of Revelation could not have been written by John the Evangelist because it is written in very poor Greek. There are many awkward sentences and some grammatical errors. The Evangelist who wrote the Gospel of John—and possibly John I—wrote in extraordinarily fluent Greek. Furthermore, the Book of Revelation uses speech patterns and refers to historical events which occurred after John the Evangelist's death.)

Despite the inclusion of Revelation in the Canon, the Gnostic Gospels (Infancy, Peter, Mary, and Thomas) were (and are) specifically omitted; their dualistic apocalypticism was considered heretical (Weaver 1975). Hence, only Daniel and Revelation present a consistent apocalyptic world view in the Bible. Daniel was written when the Hebrew people were under the most severe oppression and felt powerless and vulnerable. Likewise, the Book of Revelation was written at a time in the Roman Empire when one could be put to death for being a Christian. But despite the fact that apocalypticism is atypical in the Bible, many Christian sects sustain a world view based primarily on the outlook of these two apocalyptic books. In most cases, this view is adopted by those whose social circumstance makes them feel powerless and vulnerable.

rather they believe in a spiritual world which is coexistent with this world and which is attained by individuals if they have a right relationship with God. Others do not believe in life after death, at least not immediately after death. Rather, they expect the millennium to occur sometime in the future. Many Christians believe a little bit in each of these outlooks, but have no coherent explanation of how the views fit together.[27] The important point is that, depending on which world view is stressed among an oppressed minority group, one may expect very different levels of activism or militance. Those whose hope lies in a coexistent spiritual world which is attained by individual means are frequently passive. Those who hold an apocalyptic view are also usually passive. However, millenarians are frequently activist and militant. For them, religion is not an opiate; it is the inspiration that gives them hope, provides them with vision, and shores up their courage.

---

[27] Lack of logical coherence or consistency is not uncommon; many peoples hold more than one world view, even though those world views may be contradictory in many respects. Spiro (1978) points out that some Chinese say devotions at both Taoist and Buddhist temples; some Japanese worship the gods of both Shinto and Buddhism; certain Singhalese pay homage to both the Hindu *deva* and the Buddhist Gautama; and many Burmese Buddhists believe firmly in the Thirty-Seven Nats (the folk religion of Burma). In many cases, the outlook on life of two theodicies is utterly different, yet local people claim allegiance to both world views.

The progressive view, with its suggestion that the present social system is already a good one and is constantly improving, has little appeal to the oppressed. This view is frequently held by social activists in more affluent religious groups.

Judaism also has within it several theodicies. Reform Jews await a "messianic age" which they believe will be established by combined human and divine effort. Orthodox Jews hold to a belief in a coming messiah who will bring the Kingdom of God into being, will reunite the Jews, and will rebuild the temple. This millenarian view has been especially emphasized in times of Jewish history when oppression of Jews was most severe. A belief in resurrection from the dead was introduced to the Hebrews through the Persians nearly two thousand years ago and is now part of the messianic expectation as well. Another theodicy—the belief in life after death in heaven or purgatory[28] —was also introduced by the Greeks. Orthodox Jews affirm this doctrine as well—even though it represents quite a different theodicy from the more this-worldly messianic expectation. Conservative Jews vary a great deal from one congregation to another in which of these theodicies they emphasize.

Reform Judaism (at least in its official form) does not accept the beliefs in resurrection or in heaven and purgatory. Its members are messianic, but they anticipate a messianic age—a *time* of peace and justice—which will be inaugurated due to the work of God and of many people. They do not expect a single individual to arrive who will solve the world's problems. The confidence of Reform Jews that human action can be effective in bringing significant change is itself a product of a people who are not destitute and powerless. The social circumstances of Reform Jews has allowed for and encouraged this modification of the traditional theodicy. Likewise, the theodicy has justified and encouraged social activism. The Reform branch of Judaism is often noted for being the most prophetic and the most militant in its attempts to bring change.

The Jews have been subjugated and persecuted throughout much of their history, and the theodicies which they have developed have usually been ones of disprivilege. Sometimes the theodicies have motivated Jews to militancy and activism (such as the times of the escape from Egypt and the Maccabean revolt), and sometimes they have called for passivity—waiting for the messiah. There can be little doubt, however, that these theodicies have served to bond the Jews together and have helped to sustain them through incredible hardships.

---

[28] Jews believe that no soul is so evil that it deserves a permanent condemnation. Hence, they have no concept of hell. The worst that can happen to an utterly evil person is that his or her soul will cease to exist, and the person will not be remembered among the living. A person who has lived a life that is less than holy may spend up to 11 months in purgatory, but is eventually united with God. Jewish theology spends much less time on speculations about the nature of the afterlife than does Christian theology.

What we have found is that oppressed peoples frequently adhere to a world view that is either otherworldly or is millenarian; the answer to life's frustrations is sought in a transformed future or in a different realm of existence. Given the subjugation of women throughout the history of the Western world, the role of women in millenaristic movements is especially interesting. Cohn (1964) points out that millennial movements are common when there is a substantial group of wealthy, leisure-class women who are without social function or prestige. He points out that a number of millennial reformers during the Reformation were able to survive because they were sheltered and supported by women of the nobility. These women were experiencing extreme status inconsistency—they had high social status financially and in terms of family political prestige, yet as individuals they had no respected function and could demand little personal prestige or respect. Due to their subordination and their boredom, medieval women of the leisure classes were likely to support millenarians whose primary constituencies were the economically and politically dispossessed.

Max Weber (1963:104–105) also noted that women showed a great receptivity to all religious prophecy except that which is exclusively military in orientation. He emphasized that prophets challenge the status quo and are usually rather equalitarian in their relationships with women. Jesus and Buddha are both cited as examples of charismatic figures who ignored many traditional sex-role norms. Weber also pointed out that equalitarianism of the sexes rarely survives beyond the earliest stages of the sect's existence. Routinization almost always has meant a return to traditional roles. The point here is that at least two outstanding scholars have suggested that women are disproportionately attracted to the type of religious experience that normally appeals to the very poor.

Most recent empirical studies have not shown significant differentiation in religious outlooks between males and females, but this may be due to a failure of researchers to investigate the issue. We certainly know much more about differences in religiosity between members of different social and economic groups than we do about differences in religiosity between males and females. Weber's and Cohn's comments are suggestive of an area of research that deserves our attention: Are women, because of their subjugated position in society, more likely than men to be otherworldly or millenarian? Do men and women differ in other matters of religiosity?

One conclusion can safely be drawn from our foregoing discussion: the experience of social and political disprivilege can have a significant impact on one's world view and on one's style of religious expression. Likewise, the world view and sacred ethos of a group may have a significant effect on how its members respond to the experience of social and political subordination. To understand better the workings of religion in the experience of a specific subjugated group we will turn to an overview of the black church in America.

The Black Church in America

The vast majority of black Americans who are religiously affiliated are members of a Methodist or a Baptist denomination. In fact, Eric Lincoln (1974a:10) has found that 90 percent of the black church members in this country are members of one of the five independent denominations of Baptists and Methodists. Nonetheless, one must be cautious about making generalizations about black religion or the black church in America, for there is tremendous diversity of religious expression among blacks. There is a strong local autonomy emphasis in the independent black denominations, and this means that local churches within the same denomination may vary considerably in theology and in style of ritual. Of course, there is also wide variation in the white denominations, but these denominations tend to be somewhat more centralized. The localistic bias of black churches tends to facilitate local variations and to exaggerate intradenominational diversity.

Gayraud Wilmore (1972:222) points out that in Cincinnati in the 1930s, only 10.6 percent of the population was black, but black churches accounted for 32 percent of all churches in that city. Similar figures reveal the same pattern in Detroit and Philadelphia. Wilmore cites these crude figures as illustrations of the high degree of divisiveness and separation which exists in the black religious community. Perhaps the most important variation in black religiosity is that due to socioeconomic standing. The lower-class churches are characterized by emotionalism and fundamentalism, and the minister is unlikely to have had any formal theological training. On the other hand, the religious expression of the black professional class is quite similar to the religiosity of the white middle class. It is characterized by orderly and rational worship conducted by a well-educated and theologically trained minister. Beyond the variations of Christianity in the black community, there also exist a large number of black religious cults. Yet, regardless of variations within the black community, we can still safely say that black religiosity tends to be more emotional in character than white religiosity.

We are able to discuss the existence of black religion as a distinct phenomenon in large part because the vast majority of blacks do belong to all-black churches. This is not due to theological differences, but to the caste-like nature of American society relative to blacks. During the time of slavery, black Christians were required to occupy the balcony while whites were seated on the main floor. This allowed slave owners to keep track of their slaves and ensure that religious meetings were not used to incite rebellion. Gradually some "trusted" black preachers were allowed to meet separately with slaves to have religious services. This was virtually the only official leadership role allowed black slaves, and it is not surprising that the black pastor enjoyed tremendous prestige and occupied the primary leadership position in the black community for more than a century.

However, it was free blacks who actually founded the independent all-black denominations. In Philadelphia two black clergymen, Richard Allen and Absolam Jones, started the African Methodist Episcopal Church in 1794, and a group of free blacks in New York started the African Methodist Episcopal Zion Church in 1820 (Wilmore 1972:110–119). The segregation in the white churches was unbearable for free blacks. To Allen and Jones, it seemed to be a direct contradiction of the Christian faith. Furthermore, predominately white denominations were very little concerned about the needs of blacks. The ability of all-black churches to minister effectively to the social and religious needs of their people resulted in a tremendous increase in the membership of these denominations, and eventually in the spawning of others. The result is that most black Christians have continued to this day to worship in segregation from white Christians. As one theologian has put it, Sunday morning at 11 o'clock is the most segregated hour of the week in America. It is precisely this separateness which makes it possible to speak about black religion and the black church as a distinct entity.

There are two different schools of thought regarding the origins and central character of black religion in America. One group of scholars believes that the conversion of blacks was a final step in obliterating any remnant of African culture among the slaves. The experience of being torn from their homelands and their families and being involuntarily relocated on a new continent was a stunning experience for the first generation of black Americans. Furthermore, slaveholders frequently had policies that blacks from the same African culture or who spoke the same African language were not to be placed on the same plantation. Hence, no common language, religion, or culture could enhance communication and solidarity among slaves. In fact, members of enemy societies were sometimes thrown together in the most unhappy of circumstances.

At first, the white masters refused to allow their slaves to be preached to, for most Christian denominations maintained that a Christian could not own another Christian. Hence, if a slave converted, the master would either have to give up his or her own church membership or would have to free the converted slave. For this reason, slaveowners prohibited proselytization. Since many Christian missionaries wanted to preach to the Africans, they gradually compromised their position: conversion did not automatically require manumission. Eventually, the slave owners found that religion could be a powerful tool for controlling slaves, for they could use the aura of sacredness to reinforce desirable behavior patterns: submissiveness, industriousness, and obedience. By providing the Negro with a world view that is profoundly otherworldly, slaveowners hoped to replace the last vestiges of African hopes for freedom with a sacred system which the whites could control.

E. Franklin Frazier (1957, 1963) and Arthur Fauset (1944) first developed

the thesis that the Christianization of blacks was the final step in the decultura-
tion of Africans. However, they also pointed out that these African converts
used the imagery of Christianity to forge a religious expression appropriate
to their own needs. In this view, Christianity became functional for the
slaves in that it established a common base for unity and solidarity among
otherwise disparate peoples. This view of black religiosity stresses the fact
that slave religion was a synthesis of white religion and black experience,
and it developed its own unique character and history. The emotionalism
which is characteristic of black churches is attributed to the fact that it
was mostly Baptists and Methodists who evangelized the slaves. Since the
revival-meeting style of those denominations is highly enthusiastic and emotional, it is not surprising that black Christianity was also revivalistic. Furthermore, poorly educated and economically impoverished groups are frequently more emotional in religious expression than more educated and
affluent coreligionists. This would also add to the highly emotional tenor
of black religion.

Other scholars, such as Melville Herskovits (1958), Gayraud Wilmore
(1972), and Joseph Washington (1972), have insisted that slave religion
was influenced by certain patterns of religiosity that are common to many
African religious ceremonies. According to Herskovits, the tendency to
turn to religion rather than to political action to alleviate frustrations is
typical of African cultures. Moreover, the rhythm and motion which characterize the singing, preaching, and congregational responses in black churches
is also common in Africa. Hence, the style of religiosity of the black church
is viewed as a survival of previous cultural patterns much the same way
that the sentence structure of the black dialect is viewed by linguists as a
survival of African languages. The *specific* religious belief systems are granted

---

Exhibit 8–11 _____

Excerpts from a Catechism for American Slaves

Question: What did God make you for?

Answer: To make a crop.

Question: What is the meaning of "Thou shalt not commit adultery?"

Answer: To serve our heavenly Father, and our earthly Master, obey our overseer, and
not steal anything.

These questions from a catechism designed for slaves illustrate the way Christianity was
twisted to serve the interests of the powerful group. Indeed, if black slaves had any accurate
understanding of Christianity it would be surprising. Several denominations established special
catechisms for slaves which were, at best, truncated interpretations of the faith.

Source: Gayraud S. Wilmore, *Black Religion and Black Radicalism* (Garden City, N.Y.: Doubleday, 1972),
p. 34.

to be a product of the new world and of contact with white missionaries, but the *mode of expression* is viewed as uniquely African.

The debate continues between those holding each of these views with some efforts having been made at synthesis (Glenn, 1964). We cannot expect to resolve the issue here, but I do want to highlight the significance of the alternative views. For those who deny that African culture had any real influence on slave religiosity, the characteristic features of the black church are thought to originate in socioeconomic subordination. If this view is correct, the emotionalism of black religiosity may fade, even in all-black churches, as members of those congregations improve their socioeconomic standing.[29]

On the other hand, black religiosity will continue to have a different flavor from white religiosity if the difference is rooted in ethnic differences which are preserved in segregated religious organizations. There is empirical evidence to support both views, but I do not believe that one can fully understand the religiosity of the first slaves without some understanding of their previous experiences of religion. Through the transmission of religion from one generation to the next, the remnants of African religiosity have been passed down to the contemporary black church. Only history will be able to answer the question as to whether assimilation to white American culture and changes in socioeconomic status will result in a more subdued and rationalized religious style among blacks. My own expectation is that the unique, expressive style of the black church will continue.[30]

Regardless of the causes of black religious patterns, there is a consensus that black religion in America does have a unique character (Wilmore 1972; Winter 1977; Johnstone 1975; Cone 1972; Washington 1964, 1972). In fact, Joseph Washington refers to black Christianity in America as a form of folk religion. First of all, the Christianity which was preached to blacks was a truncated and manipulated version of Christian theology; it was designed to help pacify them and compensate them for their inferior position in life (see Exhibit 8–11). Furthermore, religion became the means by which slaves could express their frustrations and their hopes—both of which emanated from their subordinate standing in society.

---

[29] The assumption here is that religious emotionalism is an expression of socioeconomic deprivation (a thesis discussed earlier in this chapter and in Chapter 7). According to this argument, emotionalism will give way to middle-class forms of religiosity—which are more cerebral and more subdued—as blacks achieve economic affluence. A second line of argument is that although the origins of black religious emotionalism were due to socioeconomic subordination, the pattern is now institutionalized and will continue independently of economic changes among blacks.

[30] It is interesting to note that middle-class black theologians, such as James Cone and Gayraud Wilmore, continue to support the emotionalism of the black church. Although they are not personally impoverished, they do not conform to the subdued style of worship of white churches. Most black preachers—despite their economic standing—take pride in the distinctiveness of black preaching and the emotional expressiveness in black worship services.

One of the characteristic expressions of this black religiosity was the Negro spiritual. Surprisingly, few Negro spirituals were Christological; in fact, many do not even mention God (Wilmore 1972:10). The message of most spirituals was an expression of hardship and a hope of freedom. Those spirituals that do focus on Jesus stress his suffering, his experience of being scorned, and his role as liberator. Some spirituals were based on biblical stories (such as "Joshua Fit the Battle of Jericho"), but many were commentaries on contemporary events. "Oh, Lord, What a Morning, when the Stars Begin to Fall" emerged right after Nat Turner's insurrection (1831) when slaves were under the tightest scrutiny. The slaves hoped for that day when the apocalypse would come, the revolution would be successful, and the sky would fall on whites. Washington insists that slaves used the vocabulary of white ministers and the Bible, and that whites believed the Negroes were being socialized in the values which owners wanted. But content analysis of these hymns, combined with reports from former slaves on the role of the spirituals, has suggested a different interpretation. Washington (1964:218) writes:

> The popular view that Negro spirituals are of Christian origin is based upon the preponderance of otherworldly themes, Biblical words, and the instruction and messages of the missionaries. These were the tools the Negroes had at hand. But this view assumes the credulity of the slave. It overlooks the awareness of Negroes that religion was methodically used to hold them in check, and their capacity to use it for other purposes than worship. Thus, the distinction between spirituals being forged from materials presented by Christians and forged from the Christian faith itself is essential . . .

Scholars have found that many spirituals were, in fact, "code songs" which communicated one thing to blacks, while white masters sat by—content that their slaves were getting a heavy dose of otherworldly religion. For example, the spiritual "Let Us Praise God Together, on Our Knees," which is included in the hymnbooks of many mainline white denominations and many sects, was actually a call to a secret meeting of slaves at *dawn*. The chorus of that spiritual is as follows: "When I fall on my knees *with my face to the rising sun,* Oh, Lord, have mercy on me." Likewise, when a slave working in the fields began singing "Steal away, steal away home; I ain't got long to stay here," he or she was indicating this-worldly intentions to other slaves. Participation of the other slaves in the chorus was a way to wish the person well and a promise to try to cover for the slave's absence as much as possible. Some of the spirituals were rather thinly veiled codes, such as the one that went:

I am bound for the promised land;
I am bound for the promised land;
Oh who will come and go with me?
I am bound for the promised land!

"Canaan, Sweet Canaan" did not point only to an otherworldly realm, but it referred to Ohio, Indiana, Illinois, and even Canada. Similarly, references to the Jordan River usually meant the Ohio River. "Swing Low, Sweet Chariot" provides an example. When the underground railroad was ready to take another group of escapees north, blacks could let others at a worship gathering know about it without giving themselves away to white attendants who came to ensure that nothing subversive happened at these religious gatherings. Someone would begin to sing, with great emotion,

> I looked over Jordan [the Ohio River]
>   and what did I see;
> Coming for to carry me home;
> A band of angels [Harriet Tubman or another conductor
>   of the underground railroad]
> Coming after me; Coming for to carry me home [freedom]
> Swing low [deep into the South] Sweet Chariot [the
>   underground railroad]
> Coming for to carry me home.

The slaves at that worship service understood the symbolism and double meanings very well (Cone 1972:88–90).

In some cases it is hard to know whether a particular spiritual was otherworldly in its meaning or a code song. Some spirituals, like "When the Saints Go Marching In" had a definite otherworldly character. Other songs had a here-and-now double meaning, but they were not necessarily calls to action. A biblical theme was being rehearsed, but contemporary characters were clearly identified with historical figures in the story. The spiritual "Go Down Moses" emerged at the time when Bishop Francis Asbury of the Methodist Church was instrumental in formulating antislavery planks in the Methodist code of discipline. Asbury had himself referred to South Carolina as "Egypt" when he had been there to preach (Washington, 1964:210) and that theme was expressed in the chorus of this popular hymn:

> When Israel was in Egypt's land, let my people go;
> Oppressed so hard they could not stand, Let my people go.
> Go down, Moses, way down in Egypt land;
> Tell old Pharoah, Let my people go.
>
> Oh let us all from bondage flee, let my people go;
> And let us all in Christ be free, let my people go.
> Go down, Moses, way down in Egypt land;
> Tell old Pharoah, let my people go.

It doesn't take much imagination to figure out who represented "Moses," "the Israelites," and the "Egyptians" in the eyes of those slaves.

The use of religious language for coded communication is certainly not a new phenomenon, for there are other reports of oppressed peoples communicating in a similar manner. Most biblical scholars believe that the Apocalypse (the Book of Revelation) was a coded message from John the Elder (a prisoner on the Island of Patmos) to his people in the churches of Asia Minor. At that time, one was required to worship the emperor of Rome. Since Christians refused to do so, they were persecuted. The Book of Revelation is an encoded book that is very difficult to translate because many of the symbolic meanings of that day have been lost. An understanding of the double meanings requires fluency in Aramaic and Greek. The book was not destroyed by the Romans, for they viewed it as a harmless fantasy about another world. They never recognized the political references which abound in the book and which served as a resounding criticism of Rome.

Likewise, an acquaintance of mine was a minister in Cuba during and after the revolution in that country. He told me that he occasionally preached against certain of Fidel Castro's policies, but he always did so in code, using the language of the Book of Revelation and other seemingly otherworldly references from Pauline epistles. As he put it, "I had to be careful, for I never knew when a visiting soldier might be in the congregation who might report me for subversive political comments. However, my people knew what I was talking about."

All of this simply serves as a warning against facile generalizations regarding the otherworldliness of the religion of the oppressed. Of course, some blacks did understand Christianity in otherworldly terms, and it served to compensate them and to discourage any rebellion in this world. They believed they would get their just deserts in the next world. The important point here is that slave religion was not a simple adoption of white Christianity; it was a reworked Christianity which had its own character, style, and outlook. Much of the black church today has been influenced by this heritage. Even where the message is otherworldly, political issues have never been entirely foreign to black churches. In fact, Johnstone (1975:276–277) found that most black preachers today feel that it is utterly appropriate to use the church for political purposes. Furthermore, 30 percent of the black ministers interviewed felt it is proper for a minister to tell parishioners how to vote. Wilmore (1972) also points out that while the black church in America has recently gone through a period of quietism, it has historically been more involved in political affairs than its white counterpart.[31]

One reason the black church has been involved in political matters has been the fact that the black preacher was the main spokesperson for the Negro community. During the period of slavery, the role of plantation preacher was often the only leadership role afforded southern blacks. Hence, it became a position of considerable prestige within the black community. Following emancipation, this position continued to be the most important

---

[31] This recent period of quietism may be what is reflected in Gary Marx's research which was cited earlier.

leadership role; the black preacher became the spokesperson for the community and the liason between the dominant white class and the subordinate black one. Since whites often owned the buildings where blacks worshiped and held other clubs over the black community, the black preacher had to be sensitive to the interests of both whites and blacks. This liaison role was certainly not just religious in character. It was often explicitly political.

The preacher's role as the central spokesperson for the community has largely survived to this day. The black church has served since emancipation as the heart of that ethnic community. It has sponsored social and cultural affairs, established insurance programs for members who did not qualify for insurance under white-controlled corporations, started schools and colleges to educate young people, sponsored political debates held in the church sanctuary, initiated economic recovery and growth programs for blacks, and generally served as a community center. In fact, Gunnar Myrdal (1944:938) calls the black church a "community center par excellence." The preacher was the person who gave impetus to most of these programs and thus came to be highly esteemed in the community.

Since the preacher held a position which afforded leadership opportunities and offered status in the community, his was a highly coveted position. Hence, there have often been young would-be preachers waiting in the wings to have their chance to preach and start their own congregations. Perhaps this is another reason for the large number of small black churches, each with its own semiautonomous preacher. The ministry was attractive to energetic blacks because other professions were essentially closed to them. However, there has been a significant decline over the past 40 years in the ratio of blacks in the ministry per 10,000 people in the population as increasing numbers of black Americans enter law, medicine, politics, and other professions (Glenn 1964:638). The black minister no longer holds a monopoly on leadership and status as was once the case. Nonetheless, the preacher still holds a more substantial position within the black community than does his or her white counterpart. It is noteworthy how many black political figures have begun their careers as ministers. Adam Clayton Powell, Andrew Young, and Jesse Jackson are a few of the better-known politician/preachers on a long list of such leaders.

Partially because of the acceptance by the black community of clergy being involved in political affairs, ministers were able to gain ready acceptance as civil rights leaders. Martin Luther King, Jr. provides a particularly good example. King's civil rights speeches were constructed and delivered in the style of black preaching. His nonviolent resistance strategy of the 1950s and 1960s required resistance to injustice, but forbade participants from using violence. He insisted that blacks would change social structures by appealing to the conscience of the nation and by economic boycotts. If a white police officer struck a black protestor, blacks were to resist the temptation to strike back. They were instructed to turn the other cheek and to love their enemies. They were told to hate injustice, but not the person who perpetuated it. They were taught that love would be the weapon by which opponents would be transformed. The mixture of religious teaching and political action did not seem at all inconsistent to King's followers, for they were used to black preachers also being political figures.

It is hard to imagine how the many rallies which King led could have remained nonviolent without the influence of religious teachings. Moreover, when people's homes and churches were being bombed and rallies were dispersed by police officers swinging billy clubs, religion served to shore up the courage and conviction of the people, for they were assured that God was on the side of justice, and ultimate victory was certain. Some black critics of nonviolence, like Rap Brown and Stokely Carmichael, felt that King's religion was another form of opiate and that blacks should fight back. Nonetheless, there is little doubt that the civil rights movement of the 1950s and 1960s gained much of its impetus from a black Baptist preacher—Dr. Martin Luther King, Jr. Even the emphasis on black power and black pride started with King's movement—although these concepts were modified by more militant groups. Clearly the role of the minister has been a central one within the black community in America.

Of course, black religion in America has also included many black sects and cults. There are a great variety of them, each emerging out of the common black experience of subjugation, but each offering its own unique characteristics (Washington 1964, 1972; Wilmore 1973; Lincoln 1973; and Fauset 1944). Perhaps the two best known black cults are Father Divine's Peace Mission and the Lost/Found Nation of Islam (Black Muslims). The Father Divine movement started in 1932 when a man by the name of George Baker opened a mission in Harlem. He took the name of Major J. Devine and quickly gained notoriety by distributing alms among poor blacks. He taught that God is everywhere, everything, and everyone, and eventually his followers came to believe that Devine was God incarnate. Baker then came to be known as Father Divine. Under his direction, the mission developed into a communal living settlement, and maintained extremely high standards of cleanliness and of morality. Although the group was highly ascetic in character, the emphasis was not otherworldly. It was directed toward changing the socioeconomic system. However, the strategy of change involved largely benevolences rather than radical political changes. Because of its moderate stand, it did not incur the opposition of powerful white organizations. The movement spread across the country and was one of the larger black cults in America.

The Lost/Found Nation of Islam is more radical in its outlook, and has considerable influence in many of America's prisons—where much of the proselytization has taken place. The movement started in the summer of 1930 when an Arab peddler came to the ghetto of Detroit. He sold silks and other materials, and preached that black people in Africa and the Middle

East were Islamic, not Christian. Christianity was depicted as the religion of the white people with a white God and a white savior. Being a Christian was equated with worshiping white people and was described as the white society's way of duping blacks into subordinate roles.

This newcomer insisted that whites are incapable of telling the truth, and he sought to tell the real story of black civilization in Asia and Africa. He told fantastic stories about black culture on other continents. All blacks were viewed as Muslims in their origins, and American blacks were called the "Lost Tribe of Shebazz." Many blacks were delighted with his stories of sophisticated and advanced black culture and his insistence on black superiority. It provided a basis for a sense of dignity and pride which was often denied to poor ghetto blacks. Furthermore, the preacher's Arab background lent credibility to his claims of first-hand knowledge of Africa and Arabia.

This preacher, known only as W. D. Fard, developed a substantial following (estimated at 8,000 adherents). One of his devotees was a dynamic black whom Fard renamed Elijah Muhammad. (Muslims refuse to accept the names they received from slavery and accept a new name when they join the Islamic temple.) When Fard mysteriously disappeared in 1934, Elijah Muhammad was named Minister of Islam. One of Muhammad's main disciples, in time, was Malcolm X.[32] There have been many schisms in the short history of the Black Muslims, but the movement has grown and is a significant force in the black ghetto.

The black Muslims originally insisted that only black people could join, although that requirement was modified in the 1970s. As a political/religious group, the Muslims experienced their heyday in the 1960s when black militancy and black pride were gaining momentum. Malcolm X became the primary spokesperson for the Black Muslims and gained national attention as a militant leader until his assassination in 1965. Attention was also focused on the Muslims when such notable sports personalities as Muhammad Ali and Kareem Abdul-Jabbar converted to the Nation of Islam.

The Muslims have been a religious group which is as thoroughly political as it is religious. For them, the distinction between politics and religion is meaningless. They explicitly reject any otherworldly views, so the socio/economic/political structures of this world are of central importance to their view of "salvation." In fact, the ultimate goal of Muslim faith was an autonomous and separate black nation in America. (Whites, they believed, belong in Europe). The Muslims advocated a program of social, economic, and political segregation of blacks from whites. Since the "original man" was declared by Allah to be black, whiteness meant a lack of purity and

---

[32] Malcolm X broke with Muhammad in 1964 after a trip to Mecca. On that trip he learned that the teachings of the Black Muslims were quite different from orthodox Islam. He established the Muslim Mosque, Inc. that same year, but was assassinated in 1965.

truth. In short, whiteness was a sign of evil. (These doctrines were undergoing change in the 1970s in certain Muslim sects).

The Islamic world does not recognize the legitimacy of Muslim theology.
In terms of official Islamic orthodoxy, the teachings of the Lost Nation of
Islam are heretical. In short, the Lost Nation of Islam is a folk religion
(see Chapter 4) which has grown out of the experience of black America
(Washington 1963). But to call such a movement a folk religion is not to
denigrate its importance as a religious movement. Indeed, the Black Muslims
may well be one of the most important religious developments in 20th-
century American religion. Because of the ascetic teachings, the emphasis
on industry and hard work, and the extreme sacrifice and devotion to the
cause, the Lost/Found Nation mobilized a significant amount of financial
and personal resources on its behalf. And since internal discipline is high,
Muslim ministers have also been able to deliver a significant block of votes
to politicians. By acting as a unified front, they are able to make their
presence felt in the larger society (Lincoln 1973).

In Chapter 6 we discussed the fact that sectarian movements are more
common among socially and economically disfranchized groups. Since blacks
in this country are disproportionately represented in this category, it is
not surprising that black religion is characterized by a large number of
sectarian movements. Nonetheless, movements like the Black Muslims and
the Father Divine Mission comprise a relatively small percentage of the
church-affiliated blacks in this country. One interesting phenomena, however, is the trend toward more this-worldliness in mainline black churches.

James Cone is one of the outstanding black theologians of our day, and
his major thrust stresses the eschatological theme in Christianity and deemphasizes the otherworldly one. Cone is one of a number of theologians
who have been articulating a "liberation theology," an emphasis on social
and economic liberation at some future time in history. Otherworldliness
is viewed by Cone and a number of other black theologians as an opiate
to black people. The true world view of Christianity, according to these
theologians, is eschatological. In fact, a Christianity which is not supportive
of black power is viewed as no Christianity at all. They insist that since
Jesus was an advocate of the poor and the oppressed, so also must all true
Christians be. This sort of Christianity would certainly incline believers
toward militancy rather than passivity. It is noteworthy that Cone finds a
rejection of otherworldliness and an endorsement of eschatology (millenarism) to be a first step in making the black church an effective tool of social
and political change.

Black religion in America includes a wide diversity of styles and emphases.
However, religion in the black community is more highly emotional than
most white religiosity, it places a heavy emphasis on freedom and equality
(either in the next world or at a future time in history), and it is characterized
by a distinctive rhythm in singing, preaching, and congregational responses.

Some of the distinctiveness of black religion is probably due to survivals from African religion. Much of it is also due to the distinctive place that blacks have held in the stratification system of American society. Even a brief look at the black church is enough to illustrate the fact that the religion of any group is effected by the socioeconomic status of its members. Furthermore, the outlook the religion fosters may motivate people to seek change, or it may enhance acquiescence. If black theologians who teach at major seminaries—scholars like Cone and Wilmore—are any indication of what the future will be, black ministers are likely to continue to be more politically involved than their white counterparts. Moreover, if these theologians do set a course for the black church (and that is a big "if") then the black church is likely to be increasingly an inspiration to social and economic militancy rather than an opiate. Only time will tell.

Summary

Religion and stratification systems are interrelated and interactive. One's religious outlook—one's values and one's world view—may contribute to one's rise or decline in the socioeconomic system. If one is taught a sacred ethic which requires hard work and simple living, this may enhance eventual accumulation of wealth, although other social conditions must also be present for such social mobility to take place. On the other hand, one's socioeconomic standing may also incline one to a world view which is compatible with one's current circumstances (elective affinity). Religious orientation may be cause or effect of social mobility. Furthermore, the theodicy and style of religiosity of the disprivileged tend to be quite different from that of the privileged, even within the same congregation.

The religiosity of the disprivileged is itself far from monolithic. In some cases, the religion of the disinherited serves as a kind of opiate. This seems especially likely if the world view is otherworldly or apocalyptic. In other cases, the religion of the disinherited provides an inspiration to work for social change.

Religion both influences and is influenced by the socioeconomic system. At this point, the strong consensus among social scientists is that economics is the more powerful variable. In other words, a person's religiosity is significantly affected by his or her position in the stratification system. The effects of religion on the socioeconomic behavior of most people is considerably less pronounced. The Marxian perspective is that economic self-interests affect religion more than religion affects economic behavior. Much to the chagrin of many religious people, the empirical evidence tends to support this view.

9

Religion and Prejudice: Racism and Sexism

In the previous chapter we explored the effects of minority status on the religious outlook of people. In this chapter we shall turn the tables and explore the relationship between religion and the attitudes of members of the majority group. This will allow us to gain a more holistic view of the relationship between religion and social power. There is a second reason for exploring religion and prejudice. The investigation will also allow us to see the complex ways in which religion can affect people by exerting influence as reference group, as belief system, or as institution. Sometimes these aspects of religion can be working at cross-purposes, as we shall see in this chapter. Furthermore, secular forces and conflicts are often the prime cause of prejudice and discrimination, and religion, as the system of meaning, is used to justify existing inequities. Religious forces may be either cause or effect.

This analysis will be limited to a discussion of the influence of Christianity. The decision to focus only on one religious tradition is based on three considerations. First, it is possible to go into more depth if we limit the scope of our application. This chapter, like the entire book, is designed to show students how sociologists of religion attack a particular problem; the goal is to illustrate how sociologists study religion rather than to provide comprehensive data on all religions. By focusing on the tools the sociologist uses for analysis and on the interrelationship of variables, the reader should have an idea about how the sociologist would approach the relationship between religion and prejudice in any religious group. Second, my own background and research in Christian theology and ethics allows me to offer a more comprehensive analysis in this tradition than in others. Third, most of the recent empirical studies on religion and prejudice have concentrated on prejudice among Christians. The discussion will be directed to an understanding of racial and sexual bias. Religion can contribute to other types of prejudice (such as anti-Semitism) and these forms of prejudice will be commented upon but not explored in detail.

Christianity and Racism

Empirical Findings

In the 1950s, empirical studies showed that church members were more racially prejudiced than nonmembers. Despite the fact that Christianity claimed to enhance fellowship and love among people, the research indicated a correlation between Christianity and bigotry. A number of explanations were formulated to interpret this phenomenon. Some scholars attempted to identify factors in the belief system of Christianity which might contribute to prejudice. Others felt that the correlation was spurious, that both prejudice and church membership resulted from some third factor. For example, Gordon Allport (1966) insisted that church membership and prejudice both serve to reinforce feelings of identity and belonging. In people with certain personality characteristics, religion and prejudice fulfill the same psychological functions. Hence, Allport insisted, religion does not cause prejudice; rather, both are caused by personality factors in certain people. Other explanations of the correlation were offered, but the whole debate changed significantly as more sophisticated and refined data were gathered.

In the 1960s, several survey studies revealed that while church members are more prejudiced than nonmembers, the most active members were the least prejudiced of all. The earlier studies had lumped together all members without regard to level of commitment or amount of participation in the life of the church. Since there are larger numbers of marginal members in most churches than there are active members, the statistics were weighted heavily in the direction of marginal member attitudes. The evidence now shows that infrequent church attenders are more prejudiced than nonattenders, but that frequent attenders are the lowest of all on scales of prejudice (Allport 1966:454; Gorsuch and Aleshire 1974:287).

This finding led to several theories and hypotheses. One of the first asserted that some church members are *intrinsically* religious and others are *extrinsically* religious (Allport 1966). Intrinsically religious people join churches because their faith is meaningful to them in and of itself. Such people are committed at what Kanter would call the moral level (see Chapter 5). The meaning functions of religion are central for them. Individuals who are extrinsically religious tend to join churches because of secular advantages. Those who join because of status factors, for example, would be considered extrinsically religious. To use Kanter's formulation of types of commitment, we might say that people who are committed primarily at the instrumental and/or affective levels would be extrinsically religious. The belonging, identity, and status functions are especially important to them. Allport insisted that persons who were intrinsically religious score low on measures of racial prejudice, while persons who are extrinsically religious score high.

As research continues on this issue, it becomes obvious that the variables affecting the relationship between religion and prejudice are complex. For example, Hadden (1970:130–132) found that the specific theological orientation of church members was very important. Fundamentalists are likely to oppose civil rights for blacks, much more so than those of other theological persuasions. Theological liberals are most sympathetic to granting equal rights to minorities, followed by the neoorthodox and then by the conservatives. This finding suggests that it is not enough to know whether a person is intrinsically religious; one must also understand something about the nature of the meaning system itself before correlations can be predicted.

Two other approaches to the correlation have indicated that other factors may be responsible for it. For example, it is possible that prejudice and dogmatism (especially in the form of fundamentalism) are both results of personality factors. We will explore this possibility later when we discuss simple dualism in the world view and how that relates to both prejudice and dogmatism.

Another interesting explanation suggests that prejudice and religious orthodoxy may both be products of social overconformity. Gorsuch and Aleshire (1974) maintain that nonchurch membership and very active membership are both deviations from the American social norm. Hence, they offer the explanation that racial tolerance and level of church involvement both result from an individual's willingness to be a cultural deviant. The key to the relationship, they believe, may be in identifying what factors cause a person to take a stand different from the crowd. They write, "In the American society of the past twenty-five years, a person would have needed a strong internalized value system and a willingness to deviate to be *either* a nuclear church member or to have no contact with the church. It is only such people with unique value systems who could be expected to have rejected the widely accepted norm of racism" (Gorsuch and Aleshire 1974:188).

Another bit of evidence would seem to support this correlation. Allport found that the *most* prejudiced people were those who were "indiscriminately pro-religious." That is, they agreed with all statements which were in any way supportive of religion, including those which contradicted one another. The desire to be generally proreligious, but without giving much thought to the specifics, might be construed as a tendency to conformism. (Being generally proreligion is not necessarily correlated with active church participation.) It is interesting that Allport found indiscriminately proreligious people to be more racially prejudiced than either intrinsically or extrinsically religious people (1966:456).

One difficulty with comparing the various empirical studies is that prejudice has been measured in a number of ways. In most cases, rather broad statements have been used to determine whether a person is prejudiced. However, when statements are articulated in terms of specific behavior, people are much more likely to give prejudicial responses. This was illustrated in a study by Frank Westie, who attempted to discover how thoroughly Americans apply their general values to specific situations. The paired statements in Exhibit 9–1 indicate the discrepancy that can occur when generalized value assertions are translated into specific applications. These represent only a few of the statements Westie used.

In his study of religion and social attitudes, Jeffrey Hadden used specific questions to identify various social attitudes. He concluded that for the laity, religious beliefs and social beliefs operate relatively independently (1970:79–181). (For clergy, theological values were more closely related to social values.) Some scholars have concluded from this that religion has little influence on the everyday life of people. Others have continued to search for differences among religious people, such as intrinsic and extrinsic religiosity to explain the differential effect of religion on people's everyday attitudes. In this chapter, we will explore the possibility that religion may simultaneously contribute to tolerance and to bigotry. In the previous chapter, we discussed the fact that Protestantism may have contributed to the development of capitalism even while the formal positions of Protestant reformers opposed many of its basic principles. Likewise, religion provides countervailing forces which may unconsciously encourage prejudice even while it offers beliefs that would combat it. In the following pages we

Exhibit 9–1 _____

Percentage of Americans Agreeing with General and Specific Value Statements

	General Value Statement	Percentage Agreeing	Specific Value Statement	Percentage Agreeing
A.	Everyone in America should have an equal opportunity to get ahead.	98	a. I would be willing to have a Negro as my supervisor in my place of work.	60
B.	People should help each other.	99	b. If a Negro's home burned down, I would be willing to take his family into my home for the night.	64
C.	Each person should be judged according to his own individual worth.	97	c. I would not mind if my children were taught by a Negro schoolteacher.	67
D.	I believe in the principle of brotherhood among people.	94	d. I would be willing to invite Negroes to a dinner party in my home.	29
E.	Under our democratic system people should be allowed to live where they please if they can afford it.	60	e. I would be willing to have a Negro family live next door to me.	35

Source: Frank Westie, "The American Dilemma: An Empirical Test," *American Sociological Review* (August 1965), p. 531.

will explore various theories and hypotheses which suggest the countervailing influences of religion on racial prejudice.

Racism as a World View

The belief that some categories of human beings are biologically or genetically less human than others is actually a modern phenomenon (Kelsey 1965; Jordan 1968; Mosse 1978). Of course, peoples throughout history have believed that those who had different values, beliefs, or styles of life were stupid or inferior. Ethnocentrism (prejudice based on differences in cultures) is a universal phenomenon. One can also find occasions in history when "outsiders" have been excluded because they were not of the same lineage. But the articulation of a systematic philosophical and "scientific" statement that divides humans into higher and lower orders of being has been given credence only since the 18th century[1] (Jordan 1968; Mosse

_____

[1] The origins of racism are difficult to pinpoint with precision, for the emergence of the concept was gradual. The first systematic effort to classify all of humanity into distinct groups based on physical characteristics was conducted by Francois Bernier in 1684. The first to place humans into a pseudoscientific-ranked order (the "chain of being") was Carolus Linnaeus in the 1730s. Many other efforts to develop a "scientific" system of racial classification ensued. Contributions to the idea that humans could be classified and valued according to physical

1978). George Kelsey (1965) has done an incisive analysis of the modern racist world view and its fundamental difference from the basic world view of Christianity.

The important characteristic of racism is that a person's inherent worth is judged on the basis of his or her genes. The philosophical foundations of racism are naturalistic: "Persons are understood in terms of that which is below themselves—the elements of the world, their animality, specifically their genes. To find out who people are and the quality of their life, we must inquire into their ancestry . . . The question of who a person is, is answered in his or her genetic structure"[2] (Kelsey 1965:56). Persons who are racist feel superior to or of greater worth than someone who has a different genetic structure (different skin color, hair color, facial features, and so on). In other words, their sense of worth is centered on their genes.

At this point, it is instructive for the reader to recall the definition of faith provided by H. Richard Niebuhr (quoted in Chapter 2). Niebuhr says that whatever provides one with a sense of worth and meaning is properly termed one's "god." Elsewhere, Niebuhr talks of faith as "trust in that which gives value to the self" (1960b:16). In fact, the term *worship* refers to a celebration of the center of worth or the center of all other values. Literally, the word *worship* means a state or condition of worth. Kelsey cites Niebuhr's definition of faith, and goes on to explain how racism serves as a faith or world view. He writes, "The racist relies on race as the source of his [or her] personal value. . . . . [L]ife has meaning and worth because it is part of the racial context. It fits into and merges with a valuable whole, the race. As the value-center, the race is the source of value, and it is at the same time the object of value" (Kelsey 1965:27). In fact, the logical means to improve humanity is, from this perspective, selective genetic breeding and maintenance of the purity of the superior race.

Kelsey goes on to discuss the world view of Christian theology. The

---

characteristics were offered by such writers as David Hume in 1748, Johann Friedrich Blumenbach in 1775, Johann Kaspar Lavater in 1781, Christian Meiners in 1785, Peter Camper in 1792, Joseph Gall in 1796, and Charles White in 1799. Meiners was the first to suggest that civilization would decline because of interracial marriages and the degeneration of the white race. The full systematic articulation of modern racial thinking did not occur until the 1850s. In that decade three major tracts were published which formulated the chief tenets of contemporary racism: Robert Knox, *Races of Men* (1850); Carl Gustav Carus, *Symbolism of the Human Form* (1853); and Comte Arthur deGobineau, *Essay on the Inequality of Human Races* (1853–55). Gobineau is commonly cited as the "father of modern racism." Regardless of whether one identifies the beginnings of racism with the Linnean chain of being (1730s) or with the more careful articulations of the late 1700s or with the systematic pseudoscientific statement by Gobineau (1850s), racism is a relatively modern construct in the Western world. For an analysis of the history of modern racism, see Winthrop D Jordan's *White Over Black* (1968) and George L. Mosse's *Toward The Final Solution* (1978).

[2] Some nouns, verbs, and pronouns have been modified by me in order to make the language sexually inclusive.

source of personal worth for the Christian is not found in his or her biological nature, but in one's relationship with God. In this sense, Christian theology has allowed for only one distinction between persons, that between the regenerate and the unregenerate. The means of saving or improving human life is not through biological controls, but through divine grace. Humans have worth because of their relationship with that which transcends them, not because of something they inherit through their genes. By contrast, racism assumes some segments of humanity to be defective in their essential being, and thereby incapable of full regeneration (Kelsey 1965:25). The assumed defect is not one of character or spirit, but a defect of creation: biologically "they" are less human.

Of course, many persons in American society are racist and still consider themselves Christian. Kelsey suggests that such persons are, in fact, polytheists; they worship more than one god. The question is which center of worth is predominate in any given situation. Such persons do not have a *single* world view that gives unity, coherence, and meaning to life. Most of them are unaware of and unconcerned with the logical contradictions in their outlook, or the fact that they are actually polytheists.

The official position of all of the major denominations in the United States is that Christianity and racism are mutually exclusive. Racism is viewed as a form of idolatry (worship of a false god) that is utterly incompatible with Christian theology. The line of argument generally follows the same pattern Kelsey outlined. Yet, despite the fact that racism and Christianity involve assumptions that are logically contradictory, the two ideologies have historically existed together and even been intertwined. (Some of the early formulations of racism were even developed by Christian clergy.) Let us investigate some of the ways that Christendom may have unconsciously contributed to racist thinking.

Sources of Racial Prejudice in Christianity

Christianity may have unwittingly contributed to racism through its world view, its reference-group influences, or its institutional strategies. In the following pages we will explore meaning, belonging, and institutional factors within Christianity which may be conducive to the formation and/or the persistence of racism.

Meaning Factors.   Before discussing aspects of the Christian world view which may have affected the development of racism, it is necessary to make a distinction between types of racism. In his psychohistory of white racism, Joel Kovel (1970) identifies two types of racist thinking. *Dominative racism* is the desire by some people to dominate or control members of another group. It is usually expressed in attempts to subjugate members of the out-group. This is the sort of racism which historically has been predominant in the southern states of the United States. White slaveowners, for example, would live and work in close proximity to blacks, even assigning black women to nurse and care for their young. White men also visited slave row for sexual purposes. Whites did not mind associating with blacks on a daily basis and having contact with them—as long as blacks knew their place! They were not to get uppity or self-assertive.

This sort of racism is quite different from the racism of the North. Here the racism was of the *aversive* variety. Aversive racism is expressed in the desire to avoid contact with blacks rather than the desire to subjugate them. In fact, northerners have often been quite moralistic about the dominative racism of the South, while they were at the same time systematically restricting blacks to isolated neighborhoods and ghettos. Part of the reason that school desegregation has been more problematic in the North than in the South is that aversive racism has resulted in more isolated housing patterns. Therefore, busing has become a more significant cost. Meanwhile, with the weakening of dominative racism in the South in recent years, some evidence suggests an increase in aversive racism there.[3]

Most measures of racism in America have not controlled for these two types of racism. For example, review again the questions in Exhibit 9–1. Does the discrepancy between answers to the general questions and to the specific questions reflect the view that blacks should not have equal rights? Or does it reflect a feeling by respondents that they *personally* don't want to associate with blacks?[4] If the latter is true, respondents would feel that blacks should have an equal right to a supervisory job, but not with the respondent's company. It is also noteworthy that the two specific statements with which subjects most disagreed were those which represented close contact and an ongoing relationship (questions *d* and *e*). Because of the design of most empirical studies, we really do not know how much difference there is between dominative and aversive racism in American attitudes. I do know that many students in my classes have felt that domination of another person was wrong, but by the end of the course had admitted aversive feelings they had not previously recognized.

The distinction between dominative and aversive racism is significant because Christian thought may sometimes contribute to aversive racism even while it fights against dominative racism. Several scholars have pointed to the role of Protestant pietism in the formation of racism. Gayraud S. Wilmore has suggested that certain strains of Protestant theology placed heavy emphasis on the moral purity and perfection of the "saved." The desire for moral

---

[3] In some cases a person may hold to both dominative and aversive racism, and the two types of racism may be mutually reinforcing. For analytical purposes here, I shall focus on the distinctions between the two.

[4] This is a subtle difference, but an important one for understanding prejudice. There should be no implication that aversive racism is less of a problem; indeed, it may be more of a problem because of its subtlety.

purity was especially strong among New England Puritans, and later among the Perfectionists. An important aspect of this puritanism was the desire to *avoid contact* with anything that was evil or could be polluting.

Wilmore relates this to the cultural symbolism of European and American society. Perhaps this is most vividly seen in the color symbolism of the European languages, which is especially noticeable in English. For example, prior to the 16th century, the definition of *black* in the Oxford English Dictionary included the following:

> Deeply stained with dirt; soiled, dirty; foul. . . . Having dark or deadly purposes, malignant; pertaining to or involving death, deadly; baneful, disastrous, sinister. . . . Foul, iniquitous, atrocious, horrible, wicked. . . . Indicating disgrace, censure, liability to punishment, etc.

In discussing this phenomenon, historian Winthrop Jordan goes on to say, "Black was an emotionally partisan color, the handmaid and symbol of baseness and evil, a sign of danger and repulsion. Embedded in the concept of blackness was its opposite—whiteness. . . . White and black connoted purity and filthiness, virginity and sin, virtue and baseness, beauty and ugliness, beneficence and evil, God and the devil." (1968:7). Even much of the art work of this period showed the Devil as dark skinned and the saintly figures as white. This color symbolism cannot be traced particularly to Christian teachings, but Christian responses to persons with dark skin may have been influenced by this symbolic association.

Wilmore insists that areas of the United States which were especially influenced by Puritanism and Perfectionism are more likely than other areas to have strong aversive racism. Pietism—in many forms   emphasized moral purity. Ownership of slaves was often condemned by these groups because it might compromise the moral righteousness of the owner. However, many of these same pietists did not want to have to associate with these dark-skinned people. Although the source of the feelings was probably only partially conscious to the individuals, they often felt that blacks were unclean—in body and in soul. They simply wished to avoid contact. Dominative racism was condemned, aversive racism was not.

Van Der Post (1975:71–77) has a slightly different interpretation of the role of perfectionistic or puritanist theology. He suggests that the desire for inner purity—and the refusal to admit anything negative in oneself—caused pietists to "project" evil onto blacks. His interpretation focuses on projection, but it also suggests that obsession with moral purity and innocence contributed to racism.

Jordan (1968:271–276) documents that among some of the religious groups which opposed slavery, the opposition was based largely on concern for how slaveholding might corrupt the soul of the owner. In this case, the ultimate goal is the purity and righteousness of the dominant group member more than concern for minority group members who were suffering. For example, one of the primary reasons for the abolitionism of Quaker John Woolman in the mid-1700s was that slaveholding created a feeling of superiority and pride in the owners. At that time, pride was considered the most heinous of sins. Since slaveowning caused pride, it was a source of evil. It was domination of another group that was the central problem. By 1776, the Friends were excommunicating any Quaker who owned slaves (Jordan 1968:271).

The Quakers were more effective than most groups at setting up programs to educate blacks and to provide them with resources for economic independence. Their stance against dominative racism was unparalleled among religious groups. Yet, very few blacks ever became members of the Society of Friends. No doubt this was partially because the quiet, contemplative style of worship practiced by the Friends was so unlike the emotional and enthusiastic style of African religious ritual. The emotional expressions of the Baptists and Methodists was more similar to the type of religious expression familiar to blacks. Beyond this, blacks may have felt unwelcome in many Quaker congregations; Quaker pietism may have created an unconscious aversive form of racism among some members of this group. This may be part of the reason for an almost total lack of black converts. Quakers may have been intense about ending domination, but less so about establishing associational ties by including blacks within their own group (Jordan 1968). Wilmore's thesis is that Christian groups may have combatted dominative racism even while they unwittingly contributed to aversive racism.

The Protestant emphasis on moral purity or perfection is perhaps the most important unwitting contributor to the formation of racist attitudes among American Christians. But this doctrinal emphasis contributed primarily to one type of racism and only in the context of certain other cultural attitudes and structural circumstances. Pietism in modern America may not have the same effect. There are other aspects of Christian thought, however, which may contribute to the persistence of racism in American society.

Stark and Glock, among others, have pointed to the importance of the Christian emphasis on free will. The doctrines of sin and salvation are based on the assumption that humans are free and responsible beings. After all, if a person was entirely predetermined in his or her behavior, one could not hold them responsible or guilty for an act. Guilt implies freedom of choice, with the wrong choice having been made. The concept of individual freedom is also the foundation of such socioeconomic concepts as rugged individualism. In this latter case, each individual is viewed as getting his or her just deserts in society because one's circumstances are considered a result of personal choices, lifestyle, and willingness to work hard. As Stark and Glock (1969:81) put it, "Christian thought and thus Western civilization are permeated with the idea that [people] are individually in control of, and responsible for, their own destinies. If I am really the 'captain of my soul' and 'the master of my fate,' then I have no one but myself to thank or blame for what happens to me."

This doctrine is significant in race relations because many conservative Christians put the blame for disadvantage on those who are disadvantaged. Although there is no evidence that the doctrine of free-will individualism contributes *directly* to prejudicial attitudes, it may disincline those who are affluent from helping those who have been subjugated to poverty and discrimination (Stark and Glock 1969). The doctrine reinforces the attitude that those who are down and out are probably getting their just deserts. And—the reasoning goes—if those who are impoverished are not receiving their due, they will better themselves without the help of anyone. Persons who hold such a view are not likely to want to change the institutional structures of society that systematically discriminate. In fact, they are not likely to recognize the existence of institutional discrimination at all. Institutional discrimination refers to policies that discriminate against members of a particular group. Frequently, this is not intentionally directed against members of a particular group, but because members of that group are disproportionally represented in a certain status, they are disproportionally affected.

One example of intentional institutional discrimination is the California Anti-Alien Land Act of 1913, which specified that foreign-born individuals could not own farm land unless they were American citizens or were eligible to become citizens. This in itself does not seem to discriminate unduly against any particular group. However, Congress had previously passed a law which specified that people of Japanese origin were not eligible for citizenship. Likewise, the literacy tests which required that a person be able to read and write before they were allowed to vote in certain southern states in the 1950s were disproportionately disfranchizing to blacks. Blacks were not the only ones who could not vote. Nor were *all* blacks prohibited. But there is no question that illiteracy was higher in the black community, and that blacks were disproportionately affected.

Sometimes discrimination in one institution affects discrimination in another. This is called systemic discrimination. For example, discrimination in education has often led to discrimination in the job market. Since Indians and Hispanics have poorer educational backgrounds, they do not meet the job qualifications for the better-paying jobs in our society.[5] The employer is not purposefully discriminating against members of these ethnic groups, but the net effect is that Indians and Hispanics are underrepresented in

---

[5] In 1969, American Indians under federal supervision had an average of only five years of schooling; 27 percent of adult Indians were illiterate. In 1976, 24 percent of Mexican-Americans had less than five years of formal education; only 33 percent had graduated from high school (Luhman and Gilman, 1980:220–121).

the professional positions in our society. Institutional or systemic discrimination is discriminatory in effect, even if not in intent.[6]

The important point here is that those who hold to a strong doctrine of rugged individualism usually deny the existence or importance of institutional discrimination. Stark and Glock found that those who hold to traditional Christian doctrines of total free-will individual responsibility, and moral retribution (punishment for lack of adherence to moral standards), are more likely to believe in rugged individualism and are less likely to work for the reduction of institutional discrimination. These religious traditionalists often maintain that the only thing necessary to reduce inequality between groups is to teach minority persons to be more responsible for their own lives.

Hence, a particular religious belief (free-will individualism) is correlated to other beliefs (such as rugged individualism) and the entire set of beliefs contributes to apathy about racial discrimination. Clearly, we have no proof that the religious beliefs come first and cause belief in rugged individualism or cause complacency. In fact, it is likely that these beliefs simply justify complacency rather than cause it. They allow people to ignore structural inequality and to benefit from inequality without feeling guilty about it. The religious beliefs do not contribute to the formation of racism, but they do contribute to its persistence.

Religious people may also allow racism to persist because of adherence to a "miracle motif" (Stark and Glock 1969:85). This is the expectation that God will bring change only when the divinely appointed time arrives. Furthermore, change will occur without the benefit—and despite the opposition—of human resources. Hence, human effort is viewed as futile. Since the matter is viewed as being in God's hands, the miracle motif does not inspire members to work for change. Insofar as religious people adhere to this outlook, they are likely to encourage the persistence of racial discrimination by their own lack of action. Fortunately—from the standpoint of combatting racism—the miracle motif is far from universal in the Christian community.

Another set of religious beliefs is also correlated with certain kinds of prejudice. This set revolves around the assumption that one's own religion is uniquely true and legitimate and that all others are false. Only members of one's own group are expected to be saved. Glock and Stark (1966:19–40) refer to this orientation as particularism.[7] Not all religious people are particularistic. However, some groups teach that persons who are members

---

[6] Students who want to explore more fully the subtle workings of institutional discrimination may want to see *Discrimination American Style,* by Joe R. Feagin and Clairece Booher Feagin (1978).

[7] Particularism is a form of ethnocentrism—a concept which may be more familiar to sociology students.

of any other denomination or any other faith are damned. Glock and Stark (1966) found that among Christians, particularism is highly correlated with anti-Semitism. It is also highly correlated with antipathy toward atheists and agnostics. However, they did not find a correlation between particularism and racial prejudice (Stark and Glock 1969:79). This is no doubt due to the fact that both blacks and whites in the United States are predominately Christian.

Particularism would be expected to contribute to racial prejudice in social settings where boundaries between racial and religious groups are coextensive. In other words, in societies where members of one racially identifiable group is Christian and members of another physically identifiable group are Moslems, particularism may contribute to antipathy between them. Hence, particularism is a potential contributor to racial prejudice in certain circumstances, and it was definitely operative in the formation of racism in this country—before blacks were converted to Christianity (Jordan 1968). However, particularism does not currently seem to be a factor in antiblack sentiment in the United States.

Because particularism does contribute to certain kinds of prejudice, a good deal of attention has been given to assessing its relation to hatred of Jews. There are several Christian doctrines which, if narrowly defined, may lead to a particularistic view. Gordon Allport, for example, points to the doctrine of election as a belief system which may contribute to bigotry (Allport 1966:449–450). The doctrine of election is the belief by some people that they are God's chosen people. The issue is whether this doctrine is interpreted as election for service and responsibility or election for salvation. Some charismatics, fundamentalists, and born again Christians emphasize that only those who have experienced the Holy in exactly the way they have are eligible for salvation. Others of these groups may view their religious experience as a unique call to serve humanity; they do not interpret the concept of election in particularistic terms. When the doctrine of election is interpreted in terms of exclusive salvation, it is highly correlated to particularism. Whether it is a cause, as Allport suggests, remains to be established by empirical research.

Another conviction that may contribute to particularism is a belief in a unique divine revelation (Allport 1966:449). This would apply to groups which insist that God has given the sole truth to their group. Hence, certain Christian doctrines may be interpreted in such a way that in-group boundaries are stressed and particularism strengthened. Allport quotes Saint Augustine as saying, "Where truth is known, men have not the right to err" (1966:449). In other words, religious tolerance is intolerable. Certainly this view would seem capable of spurring a variety of out-group prejudices. However, hard empirical evidence on the role of the doctrines of election and unique revelation is needed. The theory that these beliefs have lent themselves to prejudice are highly plausible, but as yet not empirically established.[8]

Despite the fact that official Christianity manifestly opposes racism and encourages a sense of the brotherhood and sisterhood of humankind, certain beliefs may have the effect of increasing certain kinds of prejudice.[9] This brings us to the second process by which religion may contribute to prejudice: reference group loyalties and we/they categories of thought.

Belonging Factors.   Religion may contribute to prejudice through its sense of community and the feeling of belonging. As the religious community becomes a major reference group, people want to conform to the norms of the community in order to feel accepted. Furthermore, as they begin to identify closely with the group, they develop a sense of us and them. In fact, we discovered in Chapter 5 that the creation of strong group boundaries was one technique used to enhance commitment to a religious group (see the discussion of Kanter's theory of commitment, especially affective commitment).

The informal community of believers which provides individuals with a sense of belonging is a very important part of religion. However, the community develops unwritten norms and expectations—some of which may conflict with official religious policy. In an attempt to conform, members may adhere to the informal norms of the community rather than to the official policy of the formal religious organization. It is noteworthy that Lenski (1963:328) found that communal members (who are influenced through the belonging function) were much more likely to be racially prejudiced than were associational members (who were either morally or instrumentally committed). Informal norms and values of the community may be contrary to the official ones but they may be vigorously enforced through informal sanctions (Lenski 1963:334). A group of Lutheran laity at a Sunday afternoon picnic may tell ethnic jokes or may subtly reinforce negative images of blacks, regardless of the minister's sermon that morning to the contrary. The reference group norms are often more powerful in influencing behavior than the idealized norms in the ideology.

Another major theory of racial and ethnic prejudice is based on the tendency of people to accept those who are similar to them and to be suspicious of anyone who is defined as "different." This view of the cause of prejudice

---

[8] Glock and Stark (1966:38–39) have found that biblical literalism is highly correlated with particularism and with prejudice. Biblical literalists stress the uniqueness of biblical revelation and often emphasize the concept of being the elect. However, this evidence does not demonstrate a clear path analysis of the doctrine of election causing particularism and particularism then causing prejudice. The evidence is not hard by empirical standards.

[9] There is one other belief system or outlook that may contribute directly to prejudice: dualism. However, I wish to delay our discussion of dualistic world views and prejudice until certain other theoretical foundations are set forth.

is sometimes called the we/they theory, perhaps best illustrated by an empirical study conducted by Eugene Hartley (1946). Hartley used a variation
of the Bogardus Social Distance Survey, an instrument designed to measure
prejudice toward various ethnic groups. A list of ethnic groups is provided
and respondents are asked to rate the closest relationship that they would
be willing to have with a member of that group. Seven categories are provided, ranging from "would marry a person who is a member of this group"
and "would be willing to have a member of this group as a best friend"
to "would allow only as visitors to my country" and "would exclude from
my country entirely."

Hartley adapted the Bogardus instrument by adding three fictitious
groups: the Danireans, the Pireneans, and the Wallonians. Using a random
sample of college students at eight northeastern universities, he attempted
to measure the correlation between prejudice toward blacks and prejudice
toward these fictitious groups. Hartley found a high level of prejudice toward
these three nonexistent groups: more than half of the respondents expressed
a desire to avoid contact with these people and some respondents wanted
them expelled from the country. Moreover, nearly three-fourths of those
who were prejudiced against blacks and Jews were also prejudiced against
Pireneans, Wallonians, and Danireans. He used this data as evidence that
prejudice is *not* caused by stereotypes (stereotypes are rigid and largely
erroneous images of a particular group or category of people). After all,
no one has a negative stereotype of a group that does not exist. The negative
feelings of respondents toward Danireans, Pireneans, and Wallonians were
based on the fact that these groups sounded unlike the respondents. That
is, their negative reaction was based on a simple issue of whether the people
sounded "similar to" or "different from" the respondents; Pireneans
sounded more like one of them than one of us (Sherif 1976:275). Many
other empirical studies by social psychologists have supported this we/they
theory of the causes of prejudice.

One of the most important functions of religion, as we have seen at
several points in this book, is to provide a sense of belonging, a sense of
group identity, a sense of we. To add to this, a number of Christian groups
place a strong emphasis on particularism (discussed in the previous section).
Such a belief would tend to add to the in-group sense of superiority and
to the distinction between us and them. The belonging function of religion,
then, is capable of contributing to antipathy.

The development of religiously based we/they prejudice is especially
likely in situations where racial boundaries and religious boundaries are
coextensive. The importance of its influences is illustrated by several empirical studies which show higher levels of prejudice against those with differing
belief (e.g., atheists or Jews) than against those of another race (blacks).
(Rokeach et al. 1960; Rokeach 1968; Smith et al. 1967; Byrne and Wong
1962; Byrne and McGraw 1964). But if they practice a different religion

and also look different, the exclusionary tendencies are reinforced even further.

The white Christians who encountered blacks from the 15th to the 18th centuries were meeting people who were different on several counts. In fact, in the 18th century, the words *white, Christian,* and *civilized* were used by many European writers as synonyms for we while the terms *black, heathen,* and *savage* were used interchangeably for they (Jordan 1968). At that point, much of the denigration of blacks was because they were not Christians. We/they religious distinctions, then, may have contributed to the formation of racial prejudice, even if they are not a primary cause of racial prejudice today. Nonetheless, one can see the application of religioracial we/they categories in contemporary Ku Klux Klan literature and in various types of anti-Semitic materials.

At this point, it is helpful to return to a theoretical perspective discussed earlier in this text: cognitive structuralism. This offers an interesting alternative interpretation. In Chapter 5 we explored Kohlberg's theory of the stages of moral and intellectual development. This theory, based on the earlier work of Piaget, maintains that the human mind grows through sequential stages. Kohlberg's research indicates that all humans go through the same steps, but that a person can freeze at any one stage. He discusses three levels of thinking (which translated, might be called egocentric, ethnocentric, and universalistic thinking), and he specifies two stages at each level. (See Chapter 5 for more detail.) Another cognitive structuralist, William Perry, Jr. (1970), has been conducting in-depth research on the overall world view or mode of perceiving the world of college students as they move through stage 3 (Interpersonal Sharing; loyalty to one's own group), stage 4 (Social Maintenance, loyalty to the authority structures of one's community and one's nation), and stage 5 (Social Contract; protection of the rights of all people, regardless of whether they are members of one's own in-group)[10] Perry identifies nine "positions" or modes of perception and elaborates them in much more detail than Kohlberg spelled out in his scheme. We do not have the space here to explore each of Perry's positions in detail, but he does offer some interesting insights into we/they thinking.

Perry has found that people who are in stage 3 according to Kohlberg's classification[11] are extremely dualistic in their thinking. They see "right"

---

[10] Perry does not discuss his research in relation to Kohlberg's stages. His research is on students and how their thinking patterns change during their four years of college. He engaged in an inductive exploration of the patterns of perception of these students and only then tried to interpret the data and develop a theory. Nonetheless, one cannot help but see the correlations of his "positions" with Kohlberg's stages. Hence, I have taken the liberty to discuss Perry's findings in relation to Kohlberg's stages rather than present an entirely new paradigm at this point.

[11] Stage 3 thinkers see right as what is popular with one's closest associates. The primary motive is to be popular and to be accepted by one's in-group.

and "wrong" as absolute categories and have little sense that moral decision making can be highly ambiguous, with many shades of gray. People with this outlook tend to view authority figures, absolute truth, and rightness as closely aligned with one another. Furthermore, all three are synonymous with we. On the other hand, wrongness and they are viewed as identical. Group loyalty at this stage is so strong that it is unthinkable that we could be anything but right. Furthermore, the absoluteness of right and wrong categories contributes to highly dogmatic thinking. Perry calls this outlook "simple dualism."

Through the challenge of the educational process and through cognitive dissonance created in the classroom, Perry's subjects began to recognize the ambiguities of human history and the shades of meaning that can be applied to human behavior. They moved into a position of complex dualism (similar to Kohlberg's stage 4, Social Maintenance) and eventually to relativism and to universalistic commitment. The important point here is that some students perceived the world in terms of simple dualism, and those who were dualistic saw every issue in terms of we and they. This would suggest that *any* belief system or ideology is likely to be perceived and interpreted by some people in categorical terms. It may not be the belief system *or* the reference group per se which causes the prejudicial outlook, but rather the cognitive mode of organizing and interpreting experience. Insofar as some people view all things as categorically right or wrong, and insofar as those persons view right as synonymous with we and wrong as synonymous with they, a fertile ground is tilled for prejudice and antipathy. This suggests that a dualistic world view—regardless of specific religious content—is likely to be related to prejudice. It also suggests that religious particularism may be effect rather than cause. Finally, it offers an explanation for the apparent high correlation between dualism, dogmatism, and prejudice.[12] (The interpretation of causality between reference group and structural theories is compared in Exhibit 9–2.)

Of course, some religious traditions reinforce this tendency by emphasizing the absoluteness and unquestionable stature of their doctrine and their

---

[12] At this point we will lack the hard empirical evidence that might demonstrate a correlation between religious dualism and prejudice, largely because dualism has not been operationalized and studied in relationship to various measures of prejudice. However, we do know that Christian fundamentalists are somewhat more racist than other Christians, and they are much more likely to be prejudiced toward Jews and atheists. Since fundamentalists tend to be dualistic (that is, to view all of history as a struggle between the "children of light" and the "children of darkness"), the correlation between dualism and prejudice would seem to have some empirical support. However, this is very marginal evidence; the correlation between fundamentalism and dualism is far from perfect. We need to have studies which control for this variable more directly. And, even if a correlation is found between religious dualism and prejudice, this does not establish a causal relationship. We would not know whether a dualistic religious outlook enhances prejudice or whether people in an intellectual stage of simple dualism are more likely than others both to be prejudiced and to join groups with a dualistic religious outlook. Perry's research does suggest a new variable which needs to be understood more fully.

Exhibit 9–2 _____

Reference group theory scenerio

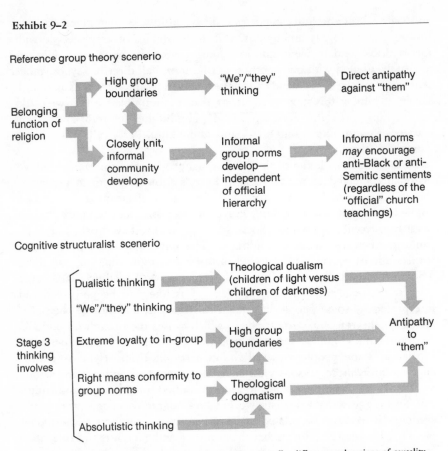

Reference group theory and cognitive structuralism theories offer different explanations of causality.

authority figures (either clergy or charismatic leaders). In fact, questioning the tradition or the correctness of an authority has sometimes been equated with a lack of faith and a decline in status within the group. If one takes the structuralist paradigm seriously, this would mean that many religious groups try to eliminate the sort of cognitive dissonance which leads to intellectual growth and to a reduction in we/they thinking.

Hence, the belonging functions of a particular religion may enhance antipathy toward others in several ways. First, the informal community may develop norms that encourage discrimination, despite the official position of the church. Second, the development of high boundaries between groups can reinforce we/they categories of thought. On the other hand, cognitive structuralists suggest that we/they thinking may be a *result* of persons being in Stage 3 ethical thinking—with its simple dualism, its intense group loyalty, and its dogmatic and particularistic outlook. This view suggests an alternative interpretation of the initial cause. I present this structuralist view so that students can see how a new theoretical perspective can totally change the kinds of questions one raises and the assumptions one makes about causality. Regardless of one's theoretical perspective, religion is known to be related to prejudice insofar as it creates and/or sanctifies we/they thinking.

Institutional Factors

Religion as an institutional structure can affect social behavior somewhat independently from the belief system or the reference group factors. This is perhaps best illustrated by a study of the clergy of Little Rock, Arkansas, in the midst of a major racial crisis.

Ernest Campbell and Thomas Pettigrew (1959) studied the role of Protestant ministers in the school desegregation controversy in 1957. Consistent with other findings, they found that ministers of small working-class sects were supportive of segregation and that most of the clergy of mainline denominations were sympathetic to integration. However, very few of the ministers of mainline denominations spoke out or got actively involved in the conflict. The official positions of their denominations, their professional reference system (other mainline clergy), and their own personal convictions were prointegrationist. Yet, they did not take the prophetic stance which one might expect.

When they did speak out, it was often in generalities, or with references to "deeper issues," or with other techniques which would prevent anyone from taking offense (or from taking their statements too seriously). Social psychologists use the term *aligning actions* to refer to statements which modify the meaning of other statements or actions. When the clergy in Little Rock did discuss the racial crisis with their congregations, they would usually preface their remarks with a comment that softened the impact of the stance. An ethical view can be moderated and made more palatable when a minister begins by saying something such as this: "Everyone has to make up his or her own mind on moral questions. My opinion is simply the opinion of one person and there is certainly room for other views." Such statements allowed ministers in Little Rock to speak briefly to the issue of segregation without raising too much opposition or offending people too deeply. Members of the congregation were, in effect, invited to ignore the comment or to view it as one opinion among many.

Other clergy used the "exaggerated southerner technique," stressing their own deep roots as southerners and their ancestors' positions as plantation owners. Having said this, a few brief comments would be offered on the values of desegregation or at least of peaceful action. Again, the effort was to avoid being cast as an outsider or as a subversive. This technique, like the first, allowed ministers to feel that the issue had been addressed and that a prophetic stance had been maintained. Hence, they could avoid feeling guilty for having ignored the issue. They had not compromised their principles.

Those clergy who spoke out in favor of desegregation used aligning actions such as these. By doing so, ministers avoided becoming isolated and alienated from their congregations, but they also made it easier for congregations to take their ministers less seriously. Moreover, few clergy spoke out against segregation—even with the use of aligning actions.

Of course one reason that the clergy avoided the issue was because their congregations overwhelmingly supported segregation. Since their congregations were important reference groups to the pastors, they were caught between reference groups (the professional reference and the congregational). Furthermore, many held to the position that "you can't teach those you can't reach." They insisted that if members of the congregation were offended by the minister's position, then later opportunities for education and change would be lost. Such factors were no doubt part of the reticence of clergy to take a strong stand, but the most important factors were institutional in character.

Although the official statements of most denominations condemn segregation, the working propositions of the church bureaucracies are such that rewards come to those who do not "rock the boat." Concepts of success in the ministry are related to growth in membership and in church finances. The addition of a new educational wing on the church or the need to build a new and much larger church building are often viewed as signs that the pastor must be doing something right. Moreover, ministers often view harmonious, satisfied congregations as evidence of success. The minister whose church is racked with conflict and is declining in membership is certainly not a prime candidate for promotion to a larger church. Whether the minister is part of an episcopal system (where a bishop appoints clergy to a congregation) or of a congregational system (where a pulpit committee from the local church seeks out a pastor to hire) a reputation for controversy and uncompromising conscience is not an asset. The minister who wants to advance in his or her career keeps the congregation united, the funds flowing, and the membership stable and/or increasing.

This process provides an excellent illustration of O'Dea's "dilemma of mixed motivation." Clergy were torn between two motivations: being faithful to the prophetic teachings of the church on the one hand and enhancing their careers by doing that which is necessary to be "successful" on the other. Many felt that they would work on one of the goals first (building their careers) and would later take on the hard task of speaking their consciences forthrightly. Yet, some observers were skeptical of such a strategy. One Little Rock minister who did speak out had this to report:

> I talk to the young ministers and I ask them why they aren't saying anything. They say no one will listen to them, they aren't known and their churches are small. But wait, they say, until we get big churches and are widely known. We won't be silent then. Then I turn to the ministers in the big churches and I listen to them trying to explain why they have done so little. Their answer is a simple one; they say they have too much to lose. Only recently,

one such man said to a group I was in, "I've spent seventeen years of my life building up that church, and I'm not going to see it torn down in a day" (Campbell and Pettigrew 1959:120–21).

A complex set of factors plays upon a minister and affects decision making. Some of them may create pressure which calls for contradictory behavior. Just understanding the belief system of a religion is by no means sufficient to understanding the behavior of religious persons. In the case of racial bigotry in Little Rock, the official position of most denominations called for prophetic forthrightness by the clergy, but at the same time they provided concrete rewards (promotions to bigger churches) for taking the road of least resistance. In effect, the institutional procedures operated to reward those who were restrained in their comments or even complacent about the entire matter. The silence by the clergy, in turn, created an environment in which it seemed that everyone shared the same view. Conformity to norms of prejudice was easy, for few people were saying anything to create cognitive dissonance or to challenge the reference group norm. In such a case, religion is *not* a factor in *causing* prejudice, but in failing to oppose prejudice forthrightly, the churches *contributed* to the *continued existence* of racism.

Of course, religious institutions are also very capable of using their influence to combat racism. For example, the Roman Catholic Church was instrumental in starting a program known as Project Equality (discussed in Chapter 8). This involved churches using their buying power to reduce racial discrimination by requiring all of their suppliers to adopt affirmative action policies. Some businesspeople became angry with their church for such coercion and cut off their pledges, and some local churches discontinued the activity because of this response. Nonetheless, many national church offices remained members of Project Equality (as did some local congregations). This suggests only one of many ways in which churches have used their corporate influence to bring change, particularly at the level of the national denominational office. In fact, several studies have indicated that the more insulated the official church hierarchy is from the local congregation, the more likely they are to emphasize equalitarian stances (Wood 1970; Beck 1978). Several studies show that southern Catholics have been less likely to discriminate than members of congregationally based Protestant churches in the South. This has been largely because bishops, who are not directly responsible to the local congregation, have been willing to advocate strongly the official church posture. (Fenton 1969).

My point is that institutional factors may work to enhance racial prejudice and discrimination or to combat it. But just knowing the official position of the denomination does not give the whole picture. Just as the religious belief system may have countervailing influences within it, so also may the religious institution provide motivations and influences that run counter to the official doctrine. It is simplistic to say that religion contributes to bigotry or it contributes to tolerance. First, it is necessary to know what interpretation of Christianity one is talking about: pietist, fundamentalistic, orthodox, liberal, and so on. Second, any given religious group may be contributing to tolerance in some respects while simultaneously contributing to exclusivity and prejudice in other ways. Our discussion of the countervailing influences of religion has been only illustrative of the process. A comprehensive analysis would take another book in itself.

Our focus on ways that religion sometimes *contributes* to bigotry is only part of the picture. Religious prejudice is frequently an expression of other conflicts within the society at large. That is, religious prejudice is frequently effect rather than cause.

Social Conflict and Religious Expression: The Conflict Perspective

It often happens that religious prejudice is actually a reflection of larger social conflicts rather than their cause. In this case, religion may be acting purely as a justification for discriminatory behavior; the out-group is defined as spiritually inferior so that members of the in-group do not feel guilty about their blatantly unjust behavior. This perspective is an important contribution of the Marxian theory of social conflict. Marxian analyists look to nonreligious causes of prejudice, although they recognize the role of religion in maintaining social inequities.

Perhaps the most important theory of racial and ethnic discrimination is that which insists that prejudice and discrimination are caused by conflict over scarce resources. Some items in any society are scarce and nondivisible or nonsharable (or at least are viewed as such). The best jobs, the best housing, the best educational opportunities (admittance into a professional school), and social status are examples of items that are viewed as scarce and over which there may be conflict.

Vander Zanden (1972) develops this theory of ethnic group conflict by pointing to three variables which are central in discrimination and prejudice. First, when two groups are in conflict over some scarce resource, the likelihood of prejudice is very high. It is interesting to note the increase in anti-Arab sentiments in this country after the energy crisis began in the 1970s (with Arabs controlling oil resources). Second, when the two groups in conflict are aware of their differences because of physical differences (skin color, facial features) or cultural differences (dress, language, beliefs), prejudice and discrimination are even more likely to occur. Group distinctions allow for strong feelings of we and they. Third, where one of the groups has more power to control access to scarce and valued resources, discrimination and prejudice are nearly universal. The more powerful group uses its power to control the resources. It then develops stereotypes of the out-group in order to *justify* discriminatory behavior and to make that behavior seem morally right. Religion is frequently a part of this moral justification.

An important point here is that prejudice and discrimination are enhanced if the groups in question differ not only in their economic interests, but also in their physical appearance, their language, their culture, and their religion. In cases where two groups differ in all of these ways, it is common for the conflict to be justified and highlighted in religious terms. Native Americans were freely exploited and their lands taken from them because they were "heathens" who needed to be "civilized" (which usually meant "Christianized"). Likewise, many southern states had laws which forbade conversion of slaves during the early period of the slave trade. The slaveowners were afraid that if blacks held the same religious beliefs as whites, owners would be forced to free their chattel. Once this idea passed, justification for discrimination came to be based more intensely on color than on religious affiliation.

The central point is this: when lines of differentiation between people in racial characteristics, cultural backgrounds, language, religious orientations, and economic self-interests are coextensive and mutually exclusive, antipathy is likely to occur. Although religion is one cause, it is not necessarily the primary cause. However, religion may be used as the primary justification for hostility. After all, if they are immoral heathens and infidels who are damned by God, treating them with something less than respect seems quite reasonable and moral. It must therefore be recognized that what seems on the surface to be religious prejudice may, in fact, be caused by conflicts between groups that seek control over the same scarce resources. The source of the conflict is primarily economic.

The conflict in Northern Ireland represents a situation in which economic, religious, and ethnic boundaries are coextensive. The Protestants are the landowners and are of Scottish descent. The Catholics tend to be poor laborers who are fiercely loyal to the concept of an independent and united Ireland. The conflict is referred to as one between Protestants and Catholics, but religion is not the sole or even the primary cause of the conflict. The medieval crusades of Christians against the Moors were also justified on religious grounds, but the conflict was rooted in economic and ethnic interests as well.

In social circumstances, where members of an ethnic group are not necessarily of the same social class or the same religious group, the likelihood of religiously based prejudice is reduced. Likewise, where members of a particular religious group do not share the same ethnic background or economic interests, the likelihood of prejudice is somewhat diminished and religious justifications for discriminatory behavior are also reduced. Hence, religion often acts to reflect larger social conflicts. The student of religion must be wary of overgeneralizing about religion as a cause of social conflict. In any given situation, religion may well be a cause of conflict, but each case must be evaluated in terms of the specific social setting and the specific world view of the religious group.

Christianity and Sexism

Empirical Findings

The contributions of Christianity to racial prejudice have been somewhat indirect and subtle. Sexism[13] in Christianity has been more explicit and widespread, although there are significant variations among religious groups. Actually, we have much less empirical research available on religiosity and sexism than we have on religion and racial attitudes. Most of the studies available contrast church members with nonmembers or they compare sex-role attitudes between denominations. As we have already seen, multidimensional studies yield considerably more insight than the simpler measures. Those studies which have used multidimensional analyses have been limited to studies of college students. Hence, they reveal attitudes only among the better-educated (and perhaps more achievement-oriented) segment of the population.

Although the present state of our knowledge is somewhat limited, researchers have turned up some interesting findings. We can say that generally those who are nonaffiliated tend to score lower on measures of sexism than those who are church members (Bayer 1975; Dempewolff 1974:674; Henley and Pincus 1978:86–87; Lipman-Blumen 1972; Martin et al. 1980; Mason and Bumpass 1975:1216; McMurry 1978; Meier 1972; Tedlin 1978). But unlike the studies of religion and racial prejudice (in which the most active church members were least prejudiced), the most active church members have been found to be most likely to hold sexist attitudes (McMurry 1978:90). The correlations are not extremely high, but they are significant.

One study compared the effects of 13 different variables on sex-role traditionalism and found religious affiliation to be the most important single factor (Martin et al. 1980). Individuals who are fundamentalistic in their religious orientation are more likely than other religious persons to insist that women "stay in their place" (Hesselbart 1976; Thornton and Freeman

---

[13] Sexism refers to any behavior which discriminates against a person because of sex and any ideology which maintains that one sex is intrinsically and immutably superior to the other. We will be dealing in this chapter primarily with ideologies or belief systems which define women as inherently inferior. Sex bias may be manifest in either of two related concepts: rigid sex-role expectations or concepts of gender. Sex roles are tasks which are assigned to males or females. Concepts of gender are ideas about the innate personality characteristics and capacities of the "normal" female (femininity) or of the "normal" male (masculinity). Sex roles are usually justified on the basis of gender concepts.

1979), while members of liberal denominations are more likely to favor equality of the sexes. Nonetheless, increased levels of religious involvement in any denomination have generally correlated with higher levels of sex prejudice.

Another study used the distinction between intrinsic and extrinsic religious orientations, which Allport had used in studying racial prejudice, and applied it to a study of sex bias. However, in the case of sexism it was intrinsic religiosity (valuing religious experience for its own sake and not because of secondary rewards) which correlated with prejudice (Kahoe 1974). Furthermore, one's *present* religiosity and affiliation have been found to be more important predictors of sex-role attitudes than one's childhood religious orientation (Lipman-Blumen 1972; Welch 1975). All of this would suggest that there might be something intrinsic about Christian theology that contributes to sexist attitudes. Such a finding would indicate that the relationship between religion and prejudice is quite different in the cases of racism and sexism.

Of course, these findings are open to continuing investigation. One recent study of university students found no significant correlations between religious orientation and sex role attitudes (Barrish and Welch 1980). This new study may offer different results because of different methods of measuring sex bias and religiosity. Or, alternatively, the study may reflect a change in attitudes that has occurred in those religious communities located near college campuses. At this point our conclusions must be tentative, but the current evidence indicates that the relationship between religion and prejudice is different in the cases of racism and sexism respectively. Let us explore the factors that seem to contribute to sex bias among Christians.

Sources of Sexism in Christianity

As with racial prejudice, we will investigate three ways that religion may be related to sex bias: meaning factors, belonging factors, and institutional factors.

Meaning Factors. One might expect that Kelsey's thesis on Christianity and race might apply to women as well. After all, Christian theology has stressed that one's worth is not founded in one's chromosomes, but in one's relationship to God. Basing one's sense of self-worth on gender rather than on skin color would seem to be no less a form of idolatry. Indeed, logic would seem to require such a position. However, the history of sex bias is much longer than that of racial bias. Sexism is not a modern phenomenon; it is deeply rooted in the religious and philosophical traditions of the Western world. Sexual differences have been viewed as creations of God and sexual inequality has frequently been viewed as God-ordained. Hence the meaning system has often reinforced sex roles (tasks designated as "women's work" or "men's work") and concepts of gender (concepts of "masculinity" or "femininity"). Because sexism is so much a part of the history of the Western world, it is appropriate that we briefly explore sex-role attitudes in Western philosophical and religious thought. Obviously we can only scratch the surface in the space we have here, but it is instructive to note some of the views held at various points in history by influential religious and philosophical thinkers and by religious bodies.

Because of the increase of women theologians and biblical scholars, more attention has been given in recent years to sex-role and gender assumptions in the Old and New Testaments. Familiarity with the original Hebrew, Greek, and Aramaic has allowed women scholars to find patterns that were previously overlooked. For example, the Hebrew language has two different words which have commonly been translated as *man*. One of these, *'adham*, is a generic term which refers to all of humanity. The other word, *'ish* refers specifically to males. Since both terms have been translated into English as *man*, some of the subtle implications are lost in the translation. The passage in Genesis which says that God created man is written with the term *'adham*. Hence, it would read "God created humanity in his own image, male and female he created them." Here the scriptures are less sexist than some people assume when they are limited to English versions (Bird 1974; Trible 1979).

Elsewhere it is clear that the scripture was written for males, as in the books of law (Bird 1974). The legal code is divided into apoditic law (moral commandments) and casuistic law (case law). The apoditic law is written primarily to men in that the literary voice and the examples are relevant to males. The Tenth Commandment provides a good example: "You shall not covet your neighbor's house; you shall not covet your neighbor's wife, or his manservant, or his maidservant, or his ox, or his ass, or anything that is your neighbor's." Not only does the passage specify wife rather than the more general term spouse, but the wife is included in a list of property that was owned exclusively by men. Furthermore, the Hebraic second person pronoun, which we translate as *you*, had masculine and feminine forms (similar to the way our third person pronoun has masculine and feminine forms: he and she). In the Ten Commandments, as in most of the apoditic law, the masculine form of the second person pronoun was used. Clearly the community was being addressed only through its male members. Note as another example the audience which is being addressed in Exodus 22:22–24: "You shall not afflict any widow or orphan. If you do . . . then your wives shall become widows and your children fatherless."

Similar assumptions are part of the casuistic law, in which punishments for committing proscribed acts are spelled out. Most casuistic law begins with the formula "If a man does X, then. . . ." But the term *man* here does not translate as the generic term *person*, for it is the masculine term *'ish* that is used. In those instances in which laws were articulated for women, they often served to remind them of their inferior position. Women were defined as unclean during their menstrual period and were unfit to enter the temple for seven days after the birth of a son. By comparison, women were unclean for 14 days after the birth of a daughter! Such contamination was not normally associated with the natural bodily processes of men.

Of course, the attitudes toward women are not consistent in the Old Testament, for it was written over a period of many centuries and contains many types of literature. The book of Proverbs, for example, depicts women primarily as sources of great wisdom. But the overall effect is clearly that women have a subordinate position. Even much of the symbolic action is limited to males; the primary symbolic act which represents the covenant with God is circumcision. Hence, only men could be ritually inducted into the covenanted community of God's people. Clearly, there were elements of intrinsic sexism in the early biblical period. Such attitudes are taken particularly seriously today by those Christians who accept the totality of the Bible as literally true.

Of course, Christian thought has been more than just a continuation of Judaism; historically it represented a synthesis of Hebrew and Greek world views. Many of the early theologians drew heavily from Greek philosophers. The Greek tradition was actually more explicitly sexist than was Hebrew culture. Aristotle's biological and political sciences, for example, depicted free Greek males as the embodiment of rationality. Such rationality was to be the ruling force in the good society and the "spirit people" (males) were obligated to subjugate the "body people" who were represented by slaves, barbarians, and women (Ruether 1975:14). Furthermore, Aristotle taught that every male seed should normally produce its own image in another male. Females were the result of an accident or aberration in the womb in which the lower material substance of the female womb subverted and warped the higher characteristics of the male. Women, clearly, were viewed as defective human beings (Ruether 1975:15).

Even before Aristotle, the assumption was common that reason and affectivity were mutually exclusive and were associated with good and evil respectively. Plato had taught that the sexual act lowered people to the frenzied passions characteristic of beasts. The world of nature and of natural impulses was viewed as depraved and corrupted while reason was viewed as the path to true goodness and spirituality. Moreover, reason was identified with males; passion and natural creation (in the form of childbirth) were associated with females.

This sort of dualistic world view is characteristic of nearly all philosophical systems in classical Greece. Religious historian Rosemary Ruether maintains that such hierarchical dualism[14] is universally associated with sexist thinking. Women are invariably associated with the "lower" processes and with

---

[14] Hierarchical dualism refers to any belief system which divides all of life into two distinct realms, one of which is higher than the other (This world/other world; darkness/light; carnality/spirituality; reason/emotion; and so on).

worldiness. Women are viewed as the cause of passion and are believed to be preoccupied with it; furthermore, they are identified with worldly creation because of their biological function in childbirth. Ruether insists that dualistic thinking—in which the empirical world is defined as evil and the spiritual world is viewed as good—may have an inherent sexist bias. Ruether maintains that much of the sexist bias in Christian history comes from the Greek, not the Hebrew, legacy. She writes that, unlike Christianity and Greek philosophy, "Hebrew religion, especially in its preexilic period, is not a religion of alienation that views nature as inferior or evil" (Ruether 1975:187). (We will return to the relationship between dualism and sexism in the next section.)

The New Testament Gospels depict a much more positive view of women (Ruether 1975; Parvey 1974). Jesus himself violated many of the sex-role taboos of his day. He allowed women to join his traveling group (Luke 8:1–3) and encouraged them to sit at his feet and learn (traveling and studying with a rabbi were viewed as very improper for women in that day). Jewish law also defined any woman with a flow of blood as unclean and polluting and it forbade Jewish males from speaking alone to any woman who was not their wife. Jesus deliberately disregarded both taboos (Mark 5:25–34; Matthew 9:20–22; Luke 8:43–48; John 4:27). He frequently contrasted the faithlessness of the religious leaders with the profound faith of poor widows and outcast women. In that day, unattached women were considered suspect and were to be avoided. His comments would certainly have been insulting and sacrilegious to many people (Luke 4:25–29).

Even his own ministry was modeled after the role of women, for Jesus taught that the role of the faithful was not one of glory and fame, but of service. He capped his ministry by washing the feet of his disciples, a task normally assigned to women or servants, and at the time of his greatest disappointment outside the gates of Jerusalem, he described himself as feeling like a "mother hen"—an interesting analogy because of its feminine connotation. Finally, after Jesus had been killed, it was only the women followers who remained faithful. Other examples could be used, but few scholars question that the Gospels are among the least sexist books in the Bible.

If the Gospels were remarkable for their lack of sexism; the New Testament epistles are another matter. Many people have a view of Saint Paul as one of the world's worst misogynists. He ordered women to obey their husbands, he told them not to speak in church, and he held to the old Hebrew belief that women serve men, and only men could serve God. Much has been written on these passages; they are frequently used today in conservative congregations to reinforce traditional roles. However, there are numerous references to women preachers who were sent by Paul or who accompanied him. In actual practice, he did not prohibit women from leadership roles.

Paul was a complex personality who often lacked consistency among his radical theology, his social teachings, and his behavior. It was Paul who asserted that in Christ, "there is neither male nor female." The society in which he lived was much more extreme in its sexism, and by comparison he appears liberal (Parvey 1974). For example, some Christians of that day were much influenced by Gnostic philosophy and attempted to synthesize it with Christian doctrine. These Gnostic Christians taught that women were not worthy of becoming Christians, at least not unless they first became males. The Gnostic Gospel of Thomas (which was never accepted as part of the biblical canon) stated boldly, "For every woman who makes herself male shall enter the kingdom of heaven" (cited in Bullough 1973:113). It was this sort of influence from Greek philosophy that Paul combatted in stating that in Christ there is no distinction between men and women. But despite his efforts, the Gnostic view of women as defective humans found its way into the scriptures. Vern Bullough points to this when he concludes, "the most misogynistic statements in the scriptures appear not in the epistles of Paul but in the Apocalypse (the Book of Revelation)" (1973:103). John the Elder describes the procession of the redeemed as a company of virgin *men* "who have not been defiled with women." Obviously, women were viewed as lesser beings who were not capable of being saved.[15] The influence of Gnosticism can be clearly seen in this final book of the New Testament.

Although he rejected Gnostic misogynism, Paul was the one who emphasized so heavily the sin of Adam and Eve, and he clearly believed that the responsibility for original sin lay with Eve. The implication is that women are an easier mark for the forces of evil. Interestingly, the role of Eve in original sin is nowhere mentioned in the Old Testament except in the first few chapters of Genesis. Yet, this was to be a major theme in Christian doctrine for many centuries to come. Tertullian, one of the early church fathers, picked up on this theme and continually reminded women that each one of them was an Eve, "a devil's gateway." He held women responsible for being "the first deserter of the divine law" and wrote to them, "You are she who persuaded him who the devil was not valiant enough to attack. You destroyed so easily God's image, man. On account of your desert—that is, death—even the Son of God had to die" (cited by Bullough 1973:114). Hence, women were held responsible for the crucifixion! At a much later time, Martin Luther also emphasized that a woman was responsible for the Fall. While he generally opposed ridicule of women in public, he did on one occasion follow his comments on the story of humanity's

---

[15] It is noteworthy that early Christianity was not dualistic (O'Dea, 1966:52). In fact, the Book of Revelation was held to be heresy by many church leaders for the first few centuries of Christendom. It was excluded from the Canon until a vote by church leaders at the Provincial Council in A.D. 392 made it an official part of the Christian scriptures (Weaver 1975:68). (See the discussion in Chapter 8 on millenarism and apocalypticism.)

Fall with the directed observation, "We have you women to thank for that!" (cited in Bullough 1973:198). So it was that the Adam and Eve story became a much more important justification of misogynism in Christian history than it ever was in the ancient Hebrew tradition.

Although the story of the Fall and the guilt of Eve became a justification for sexist attitudes, such scholars as Ruether have pointed to dualistic theology as a more basic cause. When the world view separates the world into two distinct realms, with the worldly realm governed by the passions and being inherently evil and with the heavenly realm governed by rationality and being inherently good, women and men are commonly identified as beings of one or the other of these realms. Such dualistic theology also frequently associates the sexual drive as worldly, ruled by passion and evil. As a cause of sexual arousal in men, women have often been identified with the evil, worldly, and passionate side of the polarity. This occurs because men usually have the *power* to apply the labels of good and evil and to make their labels stick.

Saint Augustine, a highly influential theologian for centuries, held to the Platonic view that passion was evil and that the sexual act lowered humans to the frenzied and unthinking level of beasts. Hence, he taught that when the sexual act was performed, it should be done without emotion or feeling. The man was to plant his seed in the woman with the same dispassion as a farmer sowing seeds in the furrow of a field. So appalled by passion was Saint Augustine that he held the male erection to be the essence of sin. He waxed at some length and in horrified disgust about the "hideous" and uncontrollable (irrational) nature of the male erection. But if the erection was the essence of sin, it was clear who was responsible for causing it: women! (Ruether 1974c: 164–165). In fact, this sort of projection of sexual lust on women and a general view of women as temptresses was so common among Christian theologians that Bullough (1973:98) concludes: "Sometimes it almost seems as if the church fathers felt that woman's only purpose was to tempt man from following the true path to righteousness. . . . Many of the church fathers seemed to find it difficult to follow their ascetic ideals and obviously felt the task would have been somewhat simpler if women did not exist."

Because sexual activity was viewed as corrupting (if not outright evil), a life vow of chastity was considered a more holy mode of life. But Ruether has studied the rationale for virgin lifestyles in the early church and has found a consistent pattern: virginity caused women to *rise above* their (innately evil) natures, but it caused men to *fulfill* their (innately good) natures (Ruether 1974c:160). Further, celibacy was *one* Christian lifestyle for men. For women it was the *only* path to holiness. In fact, Augustine and Jerome suggested that for women the choice between childbearing and celibacy was a choice between shame and glory (Bullough 1973:119). Eventually the feeling that sexual activity was depraved and evil led to a new doctrine about the birth of Jesus. Since Jesus was to have been born of an uncontaminated womb, Mary herself came to be viewed as a source of purity. In the medieval period, the doctrine of immaculate conception was articulated. According to this doctrine, Mary was herself born of a virgin; hence, her womb was a sinless environment. Clearly, the obsession with sex as evil was reaching extreme proportions.

One can also see the increase in misogynism at the time of the Protestant Reformation as it is manifested in Christian art. For many centuries, the Prince of this world (Satan) was sculpted as a handsome, attractive man as viewed from the front. As one walked around the statue, one would see that the back was a hollow shell, eaten by worms, frogs, and snakes. The imagery was powerful in its condemnation of this-worldly values. In the 14th century, however, the image of this-worldliness became "Frau Welt," a beautiful and alluring young woman from the front. But again, the back side of the figure was decayed and infested with snakes, frogs, rats, and other vermin. The image of evilness and worldliness had become female (McLaughlin 1974:253–254). Furthermore, the physical attraction of a beautiful woman was identified with baseness and corruption. This trend in Christian art was expressed in both Protestant and Catholic circles.

A negative view of sexual experience has frequently been correlated with negative attitudes toward women. However, Bullough (1973:140) uses Islam as a means of comparison and finds that in that tradition, although sexual activity is defined as good and as part of God's creation, women are still severely exploited. In fact, the Koran compares women to fields in need of cultivation and it advises men to cultivate them frequently. In this context, women are viewed instrumentally, as objects to be used. So while a negative view of sexuality is almost always correlated with subjugation of women (Bullough 1973), a positive view of sex is no assurance that women's fortunes will rise. Furthermore, this example makes clear that the tendency to justify women's subordinate status and the treatment of women as sexual objects is certainly not limited to Christianity. In fact, one pair of researchers concluded, "In no religious system do women's dominant metaphors derive from characteristics other than their sexual and reproductive status, while for men sexual status has little to do with religious representation and participation" (Hoch-Smith and Spring 1978:2).

Sexism continued in the Protestant Reformation. The Protestant reformers abolished the requirement of celibacy among the clergy and reemphasized the childbearing role as a holy vocation, and one might expect that this would result in a lessening of sexism. Nonetheless, sexism can be seen in the writings of Luther, Calvin, John Knox, and other prominent reformers. In fact, "The First Blast of the Trumpet against the Monstrous Regiment of Women" was published by John Knox in 1558 and stands to this day as one of the most misogynistic statements in Christendom. Moreover, the removal of Mary as a primary religious figure of adulation left Protestantism without a major saint or model who was female (Ruether 1975; Douglass 1974).

Protestantism also contributed to sexism in other ways. In the previous chapter we explored Max Weber's thesis regarding the Protestant ethic and economic development. Weber also maintained that the Judeo-Christian world view in general and Calvinism in particular contributed to the objectification of this world; that is, the material world was increasingly viewed in instrumental terms. The world was despiritualized (in the sense that inanimate objects were viewed as being without spirits). Humanity was to have dominion over the material world, and all material things were valued only in terms of their satisfaction of human need and desires. Hence, the Judeo-Christian outlook—and Protestantism in particular—contributed to a rational outlook in which the natural world was to be wisely (and responsibly) *exploited*. A number of scholars insist that this is one reason that science and technology developed more quickly in the Western world.

Rosemary Ruether (1975:186, 191) claims that because women have always been viewed as closer to nature (as creators of new life), they have frequently been objectified (or evaluated in purely utilitarian terms) along with other natural phenomena. The suggestion is that Protestantism thereby helped to create a more instrumental outlook on life and on human relationships in Western culture. In so doing, it contributed to an attitude that women are objects to be exploited and used.

Wilmore has also suggested that the Protestant ethic, in creating a more instrumental or utilitarian outlook on the material world, has contributed to an instrumental attitude toward blacks. Slaves were "thingafied"—seen as objects to be used rather than as persons with intrinsic worth. The utilitarian outlook of Calvin allowed for great technological strides, but it may also have had negative consequences for human relationships. Its ultimate consequence may have been to despiritualize not only nature but certain categories of people as well.

Although women were viewed for centuries as spiritually more vulnerable than men and as a source of evil influence, an interesting shift occurred in America in the 19th century. As opposed to the sternness and harshness of 18th-century American Christianity, the sentimentality of the 19th century was clearly more "feminine" in tone. Barbara Welter (1976:94), who refers to this as the "femininization of American religion," writes: "When . . . a more intuitive, heartfelt approach was urged, it was tantamount to asking for a more feminine style." Welter points out that the most popular hymns written at that time stressed passive and accepting roles. Such hymns as "Just As I Am, without One Plea," "To Suffer for Jesus Is My Greatest Joy," and "I Need Thee Every Hour" illustrate a pattern in hymnody of exalting dependency, submissiveness, and a willingness to suffer without complaint as Christian virtues. These were also viewed as feminine characteristics and as feminine virtues in 19th-century American culture. In contrast, the ideal characteristics of the male were embodied in the aggressive, independent, self-sufficient industrialist. This transformation of American religion was perhaps most noticeably seen in the imagery of Jesus. In the 18th century, he had been viewed as the stern taskmaster and as the exalted ruler of God's kingdom. In the 19th century, the major characteristics attributed to Jesus were loving self-sacrifice, tenderheartedness, and willingness to forgive those who injured him.

Given the mixed signals that men were receiving about masculine and Christian virtues, it is not surprising that male church attendance dropped off and religion came to be viewed as a woman's concern. As depicted in almost any popular novel or sermon of that day, women were more spiritual, more noble, and more generous than men. As Welter put it, "Womanhood was believed to be, in principle, a higher, nobler state than manhood, since it was less directly related to the body and was more involved with the spirit; women had less to transcend in their progress" (1976:95). Religion also came to be viewed as less rational (Ruether 1975). Rationality was associated with science, technology, and industry, all of which were male-dominated spheres. Women were now viewed as more religious than men and as the transmitters of morality, but still not as highly rational. The clergy, who were still almost entirely male, were sometimes viewed as naive, unknowing, and incapable of understanding business practices. As religion was feminized, the leaders of the church were also attributed with feminine virtues and vices (Ruether 1975:76–77).

Although women came to be seen as more spiritual, this happened at a time when religion was having decreased influence on the affairs of the world. Commerce and politics were increasingly secular and governed by principles of secular rationality. At the very time when women were being identified with religiosity, religion was being demoted to a less influential position in society. In fact, the feminization of religion may have occurred precisely because religion was being dislodged from direct access to political power; it was becoming identified as a concern of the home and of the individual. This loss of social power was equated to taking on a more feminine role in society. To state it in its most negative form, to be religious was to be unknowing, lacking in power, and guided by naive sentimentality rather than by realism and reason. The stereotypes of women as irrational and emotional had remained constant, but the role of religion in society—and hence its image—had changed significantly.

We have explored several ways in which religious ideology has been related to sex roles and concepts of gender. What is needed at this point is more empirical evidence to validate the hypotheses set forth here, especially on Ruether's theory of a relationship between dualism and sexism. There is some empirical evidence that lends support to Ruether's thesis. Fundamentalist Christians are frequently dualistic in their theology; they also score much higher than other Christians on measures of sex bias. A correlation appears to exist. On the other hand, fundamentalist groups and Christian sects have proportionally more clergywomen than do the mainline denominations, despite the fact that they tend to be more dualistic. Dualism and sexism *may* be closely related, but there appear to be other variables at work which we have not yet clarified. One such variable appears to be the extent of institutionalization of a group; the more complex the religious organization becomes, the less likelihood there has been of women being ordained. (This will be explored later in this chapter.)

Continued research is also needed on the reasons why nonfundamentalist church members rate higher on sexism scales than nonmembers, and why active members seem to be more sexist than inactive members. One theory is that the long history of sexism in theology has carried over into the present day and that, unlike racial bias, sex bias has been *intrinsic* in Christian theology. Another thesis suggests that religious sexism operates more implicitly. This theory maintains that contemporary theological language may have a subtle psychological effect which contributes to sex bias. Some congregations are attempting to do away with the use of male nouns and pronouns in reference to God, the exclusive use of male terms in church hymns, and male pronouns in liturgies and prayers. Empirical evidence on the effects of these patterns is as yet inconclusive, primarily because the research on these topics is in its infancy. For any young sociologist who is looking for a research project, this field is wide open. At this point we can only conclude that Christianity has a long history of sex bias which has continued into many present-day congregations. In many cases this sexist bias appears to have been transmitted through the ideology or the meaning system. However, there may be other patterns of religious behavior that are equally important or even more important than beliefs in maintaining gender prejudice.

Belonging Factors.   When members of conflicting ethnic or racial groups also belong to different religious groups, the likelihood of religiously based prejudice increases. However, in most religions in the industrialized world, men and women are not utterly segregated. Men and women are members of the same families and are members of the same religious organizations. Hence, it might seem that we/they distinctions would not occur. Nonetheless, the distinction of we and they between male and female is often given sanction in religious groups. Among Orthodox and Hasidic Jews, men and women sit separately during worship. The same pattern has prevailed among certain Protestant groups in America, such as the Shakers and the Old Order Amish. Such religiously sanctioned segregation of the sexes would seem to reinforce we/they distinctions which are part of the larger culture: males and females are viewed as different species.[16]

---

[16] Actually, Shaker women had a more equalitarian position than did their sisters in the secular culture. In this case, the segregation of the sexes was to help maintain the policy of celibacy.

Another case of sexual segregation has been the Roman Catholic practice of maintaining monasteries and convents for male and female devotees. Originally, this practice was designed to maintain celibacy, for the celibate life was viewed as more holy. However, it was only celibate males who articulated theological doctrine. It was those same celibate males who sometimes felt sexual desires and who blamed women for creating these "unholy" feelings. Clearly a form of aversive prejudice developed toward women and exacerbated the dominative patterns that already existed. Hence, the segregation of males and females may have contributed to we/they distinctions. Since it was men who developed the formal theological positions of the church, the we/they social pattern may have been an important factor in the development of explicitly sexist theology.

Of course, the sexual segregation was not an entirely negative factor for many of the women in the convents. They were able to work in jobs that otherwise would have been denied to women. Since they were free of childbearing and childrearing responsibilities, they could devote their lives entirely to careers (teaching, nursing, and so on). Moreover, many nuns advanced to positions of organizational leadership and responsibility within the convent that would have been denied them in the larger secular society. Hence, the effects of such segregation were mixed: some women gained freedoms and opportunities otherwise unavailable, but the system may also have heightened sexism among the men by highlighting we/they distinctions.

Earlier in this chapter we discussed William Perry's (1970) thesis regarding simple dualism in the world view of some people and how that might relate to racist categories of thought. Such dualism also seems to have been a factor in the development of sexism. As we found earlier, the person who has a simple dualistic outlook is likely to think in terms of we and they. This is quite interesting in light of the comments by a number of Western philosophers and theologians. For example, Saint Augustine discussed the relations between a husband and his wife and compared it with the mandate by Jesus to "love your *enemies.*" Clearly, he viewed males and females as categorically different.

There were other ancient philosophers whose tendency toward basic dualism was equally pronounced. Pythagorus viewed the universe as divisible into two opposing principles: light versus darkness, odd versus even, right versus left, good versus evil, and male versus female. Light, odd, right, good, and male were in one category; dark, even, left, evil, and female were in the other (Bullough 1973:107). Likewise Saturnius, a Gnostic leader, believed that God had created two kinds of people, the wicked and the good. He believed that men represented the good and women the inherently evil. Satan, the god of evil, was believed by Saturnius to be the foremost advocate of marriage and reproduction since that was how evil was continued in this world (Bullough 1973:112). Philo, the early Christian theologian, insisted that the world was made up of two realms:

the created world dominated by sense perception and feelings, and the heavenly realm characterized by rationality. Women were defined as inferior since they were people of this world (oriented to feelings and the senses). Men, on the other hand, were people of the heavenly realm since they represented the rationality of the soul. Progress, according to this view, meant giving up the female gender! (Bullough 1973:109).

Hence, it may be that dualistic ideology is not the cause of sexism (as Ruether suggests), but merely a correlate. In other words, it may be that persons in a particular stage of intellectual development (simple dualism) are likely to hold a certain type of theology (dualistic), are likely to engage frequently in simplistic we/they thinking, and are likely to be highly sexist. Cognitive structuralism may offer an alternative view as to which is cause and which is merely correlate. On the other hand, it may be that dualistic theology and simple dualism—as a cognitive mode of understanding the world—are mutually reinforcing and *together* tend to create high boundaries between people.

Informal norms within the religious community may cause people to adhere to prejudicial attitudes in order to feel accepted—regardless of the position of the church hierarchy or of denominational official theology. In order to feel included—a sense that one belongs—one may feel compelled to laugh at jokes about women and to accept the prevalent attitudes and norms regarding the proper place of women. The social sanctions for not conforming to informal norms and expectations can be much stronger than those associated with violation of the official norms of the denomination. The penalty for ignoring the informal, unwritten standards is social exclusion; the reward is a sense of belonging. The official position of the denomination frequently lacks such immediate and concrete reinforcements. Hence, the informal culture of the group and the desire to belong may be more important in shaping attitudes than the group's formal or official posture.

The belonging function of religion, then, may enhance sex bias in several ways. Insofar as the religious outlook stresses the fact that males and females are utterly different, the sense of we versus they may be heightened. This may lead to suspicion and prejudice, especially in person's who are in a simple dualism stage of intellectual development. Second, the informal community which provides the sense of belonging may have informal norms that foster sexism. This leads to the next major way in which religion may enhance sex bias—the formal organizational structure itself.

Institutional Factors.   Perhaps the most vexing problems of religious prejudice toward women lie in institutional patterns. After a study of Christianity and Islam, Vern Bullough concludes, ". . . regardless of what a religion teaches about the status of women, or what its attitudes toward sex might be, if women are excluded from the institutions and positions which influence society, a general misogynism seems to result" (1973:134). We have already seen that denigration of women became part of the theological system (meaning system). This would not likely have occurred if women were also in positions to formulate and shape the official theology of the church. For this reason, denial of ordination becomes a significant issue. Furthermore, as long as a significant distinction is made between clergy and laity, and as long as the clergy are looked up to as leaders, as those most in tune with God and as the legitimate messengers of God, the denial of ordination to women affirms their inferior position among the "people of God."

Many women scholars believe that ordination of women is a key issue: "By this exclusion the church is saying that the sexual differentiation is—for one sex—a crippling defect which no personal qualities of intelligence, character, or leadership can overcome" (Daly 1970:134; see also Ruether 1975:75). When the Church of Jesus Christ of Latter-Day Saints (Mormons) refused to ordain blacks, it was widely recognized as a statement about the inferiority of black people.[17] Yet, some of the same denominations which were critical of the Mormons have opposed ordination of women. In this latter case, the argument that denial of ordination was a statement of inferiority was vigorously denied. Most of the theologically trained women seeking ordination have not found the denial convincing. Furthermore, the lack of women in leadership positions can subtly influence attitudes, especially of small children. The absence of women in important positions often communicates to children—much more vividly than any words to the contrary—the social inferiority of females.

The reasons for exclusion of women from ordination are noteworthy. Some scholars trace this exclusion back to Saint Paul who, in keeping with the contemporary attitude toward women, wrote that women were not to speak in church. However, I have already pointed out that he did not vigorously follow that policy himself. At least one historian has traced the original restriction on ordination to Constantine. When Christianity became the official religion of the Roman Empire, it came under some of the cultic attitudes then prevalent. Specifically, religious leaders were to maintain ritual purity. Since women were viewed as unclean at particular times of the month because of natural biological processes, they were unfit for ministry (Ruether 1975:71). And since males dominated the priesthood and formulated the theology, women were continually defined as unfit. In fact, in the 13th century Thomas Aquinas adopted Aristotle's view that women are defective males—biologically, morally, and intellectually. He held that the male seed should normally result in another male. Only if the mother's blood caused a defect in the fetus did the child result in a "misbegotten male" (a female). Hence, he reasoned that only men could fully represent Christ (the perfect human being) in the ministry. Such a rationale would not likely have occurred if women had been part of the hierarchy all along.

---

[17] The Mormon church began to ordain blacks in 1978.

But the fact is that they were not, and given the belief that females were less human (basically and irreversibly defective) it is somewhat surprising that women were allowed even to be baptized. Total exclusion of women from religious participation is not unknown in the world.

The insistence on the ritual purity of the priest in performing the Mass is one reason given in contemporary America for not ordaining women. The belief that only men can represent the perfection of Christ has also been offered. Sometimes the feelings run deep on this issue. Given the feminization of American Christianity which was discussed earlier, it would seem appropriate for women to be in leadership roles. Many lay people feel that women are more religious than men and that the ministry is a somewhat feminine role. (It is viewed as a nurturing role occupied by people who are "naive" about the "real world.") The sex-role conflicts of many male clergy may be reflected in the pronouncement by one Episcopal clergyman that to ordain women would be "spiritual lesbianism" (cited in Ruether 1975:78). This strange (but emotionally laden) term suggests that ordination of women is seen by some clergymen as a threat to their own sexual identity as ministers. For some strange reason, the ordination of women was interpreted as a sexual perversion.

Most major denominations *have* recently accepted women for ordination, and the official church pronouncements reject sexism and endorse equality for women at all levels. One recent study has even indicated a willingness by rather large majorities of church members to have a clergywoman. (Lehman 1981:105–106). Despite all this, few theologically trained women are receiving appointments to large congregations. They continue to be placed in positions as assistant ministers, as directors of religious education, or as the sole minister in small, struggling congregations which have very low salary scales. If the official position of these church hierarchies is that women are equally competent and should be placed in positions of leadership, why is this not happening? The answer seems to lie in the inherent biases and goals of complex organizations.

Edward Lehman, Jr. (1981) approaches the issue of women in the ministry from the resource mobilization perspective. Once an organization is in existence, it tends to take on characteristics and needs of its own, the most important being viability. If the organization is to survive, it must mobilize and control critical resources: the financial support of members, the skills, time and energy of members, members' compliance with role requirements, and so on. However, in such voluntary organizations as churches, people must be convinced rather than coerced into compliance. Members who are not convinced can simply withdraw their support from the organization. (See the discussion on the dilemma of power: conversion versus coercion in Chapter 6.) Part of the problem for voluntary organizations is that members experience few negative consequences for *not* participating. Political and economic organizations control many basic resources, so one can be severely incapacitated by refusing to play by the rules. It is the lack of coercive control that makes commitment mechanisms so important for voluntary organizations. (See the discussion of commitment in Chapter 5.) Regardless, the leaders and committed members of an organization will hold the survival of that organization to be the highest priority. This sort of built-in value system tends to play against women in the ministry.

Although Lehman's research on American Baptist churches indicated that a majority of church members had no objection to having a woman minister, three fourths of them felt that "most church members" were opposed to having a woman pastor. Furthermore, the more active a member was in the life of the church, the more likely he or she was to be negative about the idea of a woman minister. The primary concern was that having a woman as minister would cause controversy and conflict, and such conflict might result in members leaving the church or withholding financial support. Since this sort of action could threaten the continuation of the entire organization, the controversy is studiously avoided. In virtually all churches, the pulpit committee or search committee is elected from representative areas of the church life. In almost all cases, the members of the committee are chosen from among the most active members in the church. Hence, pulpit committees normally have a built-in bias to avoid anything which is controversial or might result in conflict.

Lehman found that churches which were growing were least likely to consider a clergywoman. Where things were going well, members saw little reason to risk everything on a potentially divisive action. So the churches which were "healthiest" from an organizational standpoint were least likely to accept a woman pastor. The churches already in serious trouble, with declining enrollment and dwindling financial resources, had little to lose in accepting a clergywoman. In fact, their members often reasoned that it was better to have a first-rate clergywoman than a second-rate clergyman. And since women have harder times finding positions, they will more often accept lower-paying appointments than will equally qualified males.

Although the official position of the denomination may encourage local churches to accept women in positions as senior pastors, organizational concerns regarding viability often play against that. The local congregation is simply more interested in promoting and maintaining its cohesiveness and stability than in responding to denominational resolutions. When denominational statements are perceived as being in conflict with local congregational needs, there is seldom much question about which will prevail in the end (Lehman 1981:109).

Virtually all denominations have some sort of executive minister who is responsible for a geographical region. These area ministers or district superintendents are supposed to act as "pastors to the pastors," and implement official church policy. Furthermore, these organizational functionaries are usually the ones to whom pulpit committees go when they seek a new minister and to whom ministers appeal when they desire a move. The specific organizational pattern and the official titles vary from one denomination to another—as does the amount of authority of these officials over the congregations in their district. Although the role and job descriptions vary, one expectation remains rather constant: a major function of officials in this position is to maintain harmony in the congregations. Furthermore, an area minister may appear to be doing a poor job if a large number of congregations in that area withdraw from the denomination or radically reduce their pledges to the national organization. To be recognized as successful and to be a candidate for career advancement, the regional official must cultivate intrachurch harmony. The institutional reward system tends to favor caution. Although most of the executives of the American Baptist churches Lehman interviewed felt that clergywomen were just as competent as clergymen, they also shared the perception that laypeople would balk at the placement of a woman pastor. Their tendency was to avoid rocking the boat. So although these executives were charged with responsibility for implementing official church policy, they often did not press potentially controversial issues. Lehman writes: "An important theme in these patterns is the executives' role of maintaining organizational viability, especially in the local churches" (1981:114).

Meanwhile, the seminaries are educating increasing numbers of women. Since the number of male applicants to seminaries has declined in the past decade and since the average level of academic ability of male candidates has also declined, the tremendous increase in women theology students[18] has allowed theological schools to continue without lowering their standards. In effect, this same organizational need—survival—has driven many seminaries to admit women to preministerial programs. Once granted a degree, however, women have difficulty finding a suitable appointment, and the seminaries at this point do not have adequate organizational structures or sufficient influence on local churches to place their graduates.

The major issue of this section is how the ordination of women and their placement may perpetuate assumptions of female inferiority in our culture. The lack of women in positions of church leadership may affect the way people think about males and females. This is especially likely to influence the thinking of children, mentioned earlier. Furthermore, the lack of women in the hierarchy has allowed explicit sexism to be expressed by theologians and to go unchallenged by anyone with similar credentials.

The current trend (at least as it is expressed in the official resolutions of most major denominations) is in the direction of ordaining and appointing clergywomen. Some denominations continue to deny ordination to women, the most notable example being the Roman Catholic Church. Of the mainline

---

[18] Lehman reports a 570 percent increase of women Master of Divinity students in one decade in Baptist seminaries (1981:114).

Protestant denominations, the last to ordain women was the Protestant Episcopal Church in 1976, and controversy still rages over the issue in some areas of that church.[19] But as we have seen, even in those denominations which have been more aggressive in endorsing ordination of women, clergywomen have a hard time gaining positions in larger churches, unless they settle for an assistantship or a directorship of religious education. The problem is not one of outright prejudice as much as one of organizational goals and assumptions taking precedence over other considerations.

One fact is highlighted by this exploration of institutional factors: religion is both a world view (set of beliefs, attitudes, and outlooks) and an institution in society. Understanding of religious behavior can never be limited to one or the other. As an organization in society, religious bodies are often influenced by purely organizational considerations. In many ways, the organizational considerations take precedence. Hence, a strictly philosophical analysis of belief systems can never provide anything more than a partial analysis of religious behavior. It is precisely the interplay between social forces and belief systems which fascinates the sociologist of religion.

The central theme of this unit thus far has been that Christianity has often contributed to sex bias through its meaning system, its belonging and identity functions, and its institutional reward systems. Many denominations are currently trying to reverse these trends, but the countervailing forces of sexism are deeply embedded. But there is more to this web of behaviors than the fact that religion may have caused or contributed to gender prejudice. It is also true that religion may sometimes simply be the arena in which larger social conflicts are expressed and justified. In this case, religion is primarily a reflection of conflict rather than a cause. A number of scholars feel that this perspective is more helpful in understanding the witch-burning craze of Europe.

Social Conflict and Religious Expression: The Conflict Perspective

We discussed earlier the fact that racial prejudice is often caused by deeper economic conflicts between groups and is then justified on religious terms. Obviously, both sexes are represented in each social class, ethnic group, and religious organization in the Western world. Nonetheless, Marxian conflict theory can be useful in understanding religious expressions of sexism. When social tension and conflict are at a peak, it may find expression in the religious realm. For example, in traditional patriarchal societies, beliefs in the innate avarice and pollution of women are related to women gaining

---

[19] The only schism in the Episcopalian church occurred in 1976, largely over the ordination of women. Other divisive issues included adoption of a new prayer book and advocacy of certain social policies by the Protestant Episcopal Church. The splinter group—which does not ordain women—is known as the Anglican Church of North America.

independence from men (Douglas 1966; Gluckman 1965). One anthropologist has also pointed out that belief in evil female witches almost always occurs when women are attaining economic independence from males (Hoch-Smith 1978). In other words, negative religious views of women frequently develop at precisely those times when men are losing the economic advantages of having a subordinate female class to serve their needs. Mary Nelson has explored the foundations of the European witch burnings of the 15th to 18th centuries and has found the Marxian conflict perspective to be particularly helpful in understanding this phenomenon.

Interestingly, belief in the existence and efficacy of witchcraft was for many centuries considered a pagan superstition, an illusion or fantasy which originated in dreams. Until the 13th century, the belief that there was such a thing as a witch was considered by church officials to be superstitious nonsense (Bullough 1973:223; Nelson 1975:336; Ruether 1975:89–101). It is true that sorcery was practiced by some Europeans—a legacy of pre-Christian folk religion. Herbs and potions were used to cure illnesses and to ward off evil spirits. This folk religion affirmed the existence of all sorts of supernatural forces and evil spirits which inhabit the earth, and a sorcerer was often used to ward off misfortune. The Christian missionaries and church hierarchy believed that as local communities were Christianized, such magical fears and beliefs would disappear. In fact, when inquisitors in the 13th century began to run out of heretics to prosecute, they appealed to the Pope to let them extend their jurisdiction to sorcery. But Pope Alexander IV held to the official church position that witchcraft and sorcery were illusions. The appeal was denied; the pope would not have church officials prosecuting something that didn't even exist except in the minds of the superstitious. At an earlier time, Charlemagne had imposed the death penalty for killing a supposed witch (Clark and Richardson 1977). Nonetheless, by 1426, the church would be punishing as a heretic anyone who even used the services of a "witch" (Nelson 1975:336–338).

During the period from 1400 to 1700, between 500,000 and a million people were burned as witches (Ruether 1975:89; Nelson 1975:336). Most of these victims were women. In fact, the loss of lives was so staggering that it has been referred to by some scholars as a holocaust. Hugh Trevor-Roper (1967:16) reports that "in twenty-two villages 368 witches were burnt between 1587 and 1593, and two villages, in 1585, were left with only one female inhabitant apiece." This sort of massive attack on women represents a kind of genocide, but one which focuses on one sex rather than on an ethnic or religious group. Perhaps *gynocide* is a more appropriate term.

A number of scholars have sought to address the question: Why were women identified as witches? This is not the case in all cultures. In fact, in many hunting/gathering and agricultural societies, witches are exclusively males. Witchcraft carries a prestigious and highly protected status in these societies, and women are frequently excluded from the ranks entirely. Nonetheless, in Reformation Europe it was overwhelmingly women who were tried as witches.

It was not until 1484 that Pope Innocent VIII issued a bull making witchcraft a form of heresy and empowering inquisitors to eradicate this cancer from Christendom. Two Dominican priests, armed with this authority, wrote a book that became the handbook for witch-hunters. *The Malleus Maleficarum* (*The Witches' Hammer*) by Jakob Sprenger and Henry Kramer became a classic statement of misogynism as it articulated the reasons why women were witches. These authors claimed that the term *female* came from the word *femina*, which meant lacking in faith. The basic premise of the *Malleus* was that witches are pawns of the Devil, and that the Devil recruits his agents through carnal lust. As they put it in the *Malleus,* "All witchcraft comes from carnal lust, which in women is insatiable." In fact, the inquisitors taught that witches ride broomsticks at night to "black Masses" in which they fornicate with the Devil and feast on roasted children. (Nelson 1975:335–336).

It appears that the distinction made between witches (which henceforth were strictly female) and wizards or warlocks (which were the male counterpart) was a product of this period. It was only the female sorcerers who were duped by carnal lust. Since women were viewed as fickle, feeble in intelligence, spiritually weak, and innately carnal, they were considered to be much more vulnerable to Satan than men. Furthermore, since the Devil was viewed as male, it was clear that his paramours would be female. As Rosemary Ruether put it, "the devil was a strict heterosexual!" (1975:97). Clearly, the most evil sort of sorcerers were (female) witches, for only they engaged in sex with the Devil. Hence, even the application of different terms for male and female sorcerers (wizard or warlock versus witch) had a sexist foundation.

From the *Malleus* it was clear that witches were dangerous for three reasons: they took away men's generative powers (both economic and sexual); they killed infants, frequently while the babes were still in the womb; and they indulged in sexual intercourse with no goal of childbearing, but for the pure gratification of sexual lust. Surprisingly, Mary Nelson suggests that all three of these charges against women had some foundation in reality.

Witch-hunts always seem to arise at times of profound social upheaval, which was certainly the case in Europe during the period in question. "The development of an industrial system of producing goods and urban living patterns made the medieval family structure obsolete and required changes in the make-up of the labor force. Both of these new conditions made it necessary for women to step outside their traditional social roles" (Nelson 1975:343). The property-holding function of the medieval family made it necessary for women primarily to bear male heirs and to maintain the household. But industrialization required people to move to the city, and cash

Exhibit 9–3 _____

Excerpts from the Malleus Maleficarum

. . . Since women are feebler both in mind and body, it is not surprising that they should come under the spell of witchcraft. For as regards intellect, or the understanding of spiritual things, they seem to be of a different nature from men; a fact which is vouched for by the logic of the authorities, backed by various examples from the Scriptures. Terence says: Women are intellectually like children. And Lactantius (Institutiones, 3) No woman understood philosophy except Temeste. And Proverbs 11, as it were describing a woman says: As a jewel of gold in a swine's snout, so is a fair woman which is without discretion.

But the natural reason is that she is more carnal than a man, as is clear from her many carnal abominations. And it should be noted that there was a defect in the formation of the first woman, since she was formed from a bent rib, that is, a rib of the breast, which is bent as it were in a contrary direction to a man. And since through this defect she is an imperfect animal, she always deceives. For Cato says: When a woman weeps she weaves snares. And again: When a woman weeps she labours to deceive a man. And this is shown by Samson's wife, who coaxed him to tell her the riddle he had propounded to the Philistines, and told them the answer, and so deceived him. And it is clear in the case of the first woman that she had little faith. . . . And all this is indicated by the etymology of the word; for Femina comes from Fe and Minus, since she is ever weaker to hold and preserve the faith. And this as regards faith is of her very nature, although both by grace and nature faith never failed in the Blessed Virgin, even at the time of Christ's Passion, when it failed in all men.

Therefore a wicked woman is by her nature quicker to waver in her faith, and consequently quicker to adjure the faith, which is the root of witchcraft.

* * * * *

If we inquire, we find that nearly all the kingdoms of the world have been overthrown by women. . . . Therefore it is no wonder if the world now suffers through the malice of women.

And now let us examine the carnal desires of the body itself, whence has arisen unconscionable harm to human life. Justly may we say with Cato of Utica: If the world could be rid of women, we should not be without God in our intercourse. For truly, without the wickedness of women, to say nothing of witchcraft, the world would still remain proof against innumerable dangers. . . .

Let us consider another property of hers, the voice. For as she is a liar by nature, so in her speech she stings while she delights us. Wherefore her voice is like the song of the Sirens, who with their sweet melody entice the passers-by and kill them. For they kill them by emptying their purses, consuming their strength, and causing them to forsake God.

* * * * *

To conclude. All witchcraft comes from carnal lust, which is in women insatiable. See Proverb 30: There are three things that are never satisfied, yea, a fourth thing which says not, It is enough; that is, the mouth of the womb. Wherefore for the sake of fulfilling their lusts they consort even with devils. More such reasons could be brought forward, but to the understanding it is sufficiently clear that it is no matter for wonder that there are more women than men found infected with the heresy of witchcraft. And in consequence of this, it is better called the heresy of witches than of wizards, since the name is taken from the more powerful party. And blessed by the Highest Who has so far preserved the male sex from so great a crime: for since He was willing to be born and to suffer for us, therefore He has granted to men this privilege.

Source: Jakob Sprenger and Henry Kramer, *Malleus Maleficarum*, ed. and trans. by Montague Sommers (New York: Benjamin Blom, 1970), pp. 44–47. (Originally published in 1486.)

income became increasingly important; in some cases it was necessary for wives to seek work. As women entered the labor force, they entered into direct competition with men for jobs. In so doing, they did "threaten the generative force" of some men. Many women engaged in sorcery or became midwives because, in a society that did not offer women many job opportunities, these activities did provide a source of income. But these midwives and herbalists were taking business which otherwise would have gone to male doctors. So it was not only laboring-class males whose economic generative powers were threatened.

Second, since families could not afford to support members who did not work, women were expected to marry when they came of age. Unmarried daughters either joined convents or had to fend for themselves. Many young men at this time joined trade guilds in order to make a living, but most guilds had regulations forbiding apprentices from marrying until they were well established in the trade. This usually meant they were in their 30s or 40s before they could marry. For this reason, there were many young women who could not find husbands, had difficulty finding a job which would support them, and yet were on their own. Some of these women found employment and displaced men from their work; others turned to prostitution. In the latter case, they "participated in sex with no eye to childbearing and for the sole purpose of satisfying sexual drives" (albeit of the male partner!).

Finally, the economically marginal family in the city found children to be a tremendous financial liability. Various forms of birth control were used, including coitus interruptus and abortion. There is also some evidence that infanticide increased significantly. This meant that "babies were being killed, many of them while still in the womb" (abortion).

The events that so alarmed witch-hunters were to some extent occurring, and women came to be blamed for these things. Nelson insists that women were not merely scapegoats; they were in fact competing with men for jobs. It is noteworthy that witch-hunters accused primarily women who were *independent of men*—widows, divorcees, and never-marrieds—and women who *deviated from the established norms*—midwives, healers, and individuals who were considered very wise. The witchcraft hysteria was a religious expression of larger social conflicts: conflict regarding (1) sex roles, (2) the role of the family in society, (3) the morality of contraception and birth control, and (4) priority rights of one sex to employment. In the midst of these social conflicts, two forces emerged to entice women to return to the traditional role. One was the great increase in the veneration of the Virgin Mary. Mariolatry became a cultic obsession as she was made a model of traditional female virtue. Second, fear of being accused of witchcraft caused women to think twice before they deviated from accepted norms of proper female behavior (Nelson 1975:344).

Remnants of pagan sorcery did exist in Europe during the time of the witch-hunt hysterias, but they existed before and after as well (Murray 1921). Only an understanding of the tensions caused by social upheaval can adequately explain the impetus behind the massacre. On the other hand, recent research on collective behavior makes it clear that social tension is necessary but not sufficient to cause a collective movement (Smelser 1962). Such factors as a conducive "generalized belief system" must be present. Ruether picks up on this insight and insists that the general belief system of post-medieval Europe must be taken into account in understanding the witch-hunts. She maintains, with Murray, that pagan sorcery practices did exist and were commonly used by village folk. There also existed a folk belief in supernatural forces and spiritual beings which could be controlled through magic. Since women tend to be more involved in folk religion and folk magic than men (largely because women have been denied full access to official religion) women were much more vulnerable to charges of witchery (McGuire 1981:89–103). But perhaps the most important shared belief was the view that women were more carnal than men. The theology of the day was one of ascetic dualism: the self-denying children of light were in perpetual conflict with the lascivious children of darkness. And ascetic Christianity identified carnality with femaleness and spirituality with maleness (Ruether 1975:91). This assumption allowed the easy association of evil and witchcraft with women. If an understanding of ideology is not enough to explain the witchcraft hysteria, neither is the existence of social tension in itself. It was the combination of the world view *and* the tensions involved in the changing social structure (in sex roles, economics, and family structures) which allowed for this religiously sanctioned holocaust.

There are three major explanations for the decline of the witch hysteria. Hugh Trevor-Roper (1967) has maintained that witchcraft declined because of a general scientific enlightenment that made belief in witches implausible. This approach assumes that the movement died when belief was undermined. Clark and Richardson (1977:120) suggest that the witchcraft hysteria came to an end because a new male/female equilibrium was established so that men were no longer threatened by new sex-role relationships. "If the persecution of witches was rooted in male anxiety about the sexual power of women, an anxiety that burst forth in persecution as the old patriarchal culture was disintegrating, then the witch craze would end only as women attained a new status and men began to find themselves relatively secure with it."

A third view is that charges of witchcraft had come to be used as a blatant form of secular political exploitation. Enterprising judges were accusing rather wealthy people of sorcery because the judges were allowed to keep all property confiscated from witches (Nelson 1975:342; Ruether 1975:104–105). Witch-hunts came to an end when the self-interests of the powerful were threatened. Political structures were modified so that local judges lost their unchecked capacity to exploit people for their own benefit

(Nelson 1975). This view is illustrated in the way the brief witch hysteria of Salem, Massachusetts (1692) came to an abrupt halt: it ended when powerful and prestigious members of the community were accused as witches and used their influence to stop it (Erikson 1966; Bonfani 1971).[20] Less powerful members of the society had not been able to shed the label of "witch" so easily.

Witch-hunts never became as massive nor were the penalties as severe in England during the period of time when witchhunts prevailed in southern and central Europe. This may have been in large part because women already had a more secure and independent role in England than in the rest of Europe. Some scholars insist that Puritanism—although far from a champion of women's rights by today's standards—gave women a more independent and respected position than did other religious traditions of the day. Although punishment of supposed witches did occur in England and was sometimes initiated by Puritans, the social climate was such that changes in sex roles were not viewed as such a dire threat to the interests of men. (Anderson and Gordon 1978.)

All of this points to the effects of social processes on religious behavior and attitudes. Marxian theorists suggest that religious discrimination is often merely an expression of deeper economic and political conflicts. Social conflict between men and women over jobs and family roles was central in the witch-hunt holocaust which was sanctioned by the Christian church. However, without the presence of a world view that made this discriminatory action toward women seem right and just (that is, consistent with the laws of the universe) it is unlikely that it would have taken place.

Summary

Christianity may contribute in subtle ways to the development and persistence of racism, sexism, and other ethnic prejudice, even if its official posture mitigates against such prejudice. First, antipathy may be fostered, consciously or unconsciously, through the meaning system. Second, prejudice may be

---

[20] The causes of the witch hysteria of Salem are somewhat different from those of the three-century-long hunt in Europe. In Massachusetts, 20 people were hanged or pressed to death (14 of whom were women), and 150 others were being held in prison when the hysteria abated. The hysteria had lasted only one year, and within four years colonialists were holding yearly fasts to repent for their behavior. In 1709, the General Court also ordered a small payment to surviving victims as a redress of damages. The general atmosphere of skepticism combined with a threat to the interests of the powerful to bring this movement to an end. However, misogynistic theology was not the central theme in the American hysteria. In fact, based on a study of sermons and inspirational literature, Laurel Ulrich (1980) suggests that Puritan New England between 1668 and 1735 was much less sexist than Europe at the time of the witch-hunts. The Salem witch-hunts are better explained by theories of collective hysteria.

passed on through the we/they boundaries and through informal norms of the community. The belonging function can stress exclusivity and hostility. Finally, formal institutional structures may contribute to the persistence of prejudice by rewarding behaviors other than prophetic ministry.

One cannot make generalizations about Christianity as a whole on any of these characteristics. Some Protestant Christian groups, for example, have been remarkable for their lack of prejudice. The Shakers believed in a female Christ figure (Mother Ann Lee), and the Christian Scientists were founded by a female charismatic leader (Mary Baker Eddy).[21] Nor can one generalize from one form of prejudice to another. Certainly the religious processes which have fostered racism have been quite different from those that contributed to sexism. But the foregoing discussion should serve to illustrate the complex way in which any given religious body can have countervailing influences. This is precisely why the sociologist who studies religion is not satisfied simply with an investigation of official beliefs of a denomination or world religion or even a study of the beliefs of the common folk. Religion can influence human behavior in a variety of ways.

Not only is Christianity capable of contributing to ethnic and sexual prejudice, but religious prejudice is often a *reflection* of larger conflicts in the society. In this instance, religion is effect rather than cause. In any case, our discussion points to the interactive relationship of religious values and behavior with the social conditions of the society at large.

For the sociologist, any attempt to understand religion must include some understanding of the social dynamics which surround it. Religion—the world view, ethics, and symbol system that provide any social context with a sense of meaningfulness—both affects and is affected by the social structure in which it exists. This is the important contribution of those who wish to understand religion from a sociological perspective.

---

[21] Two other religious movements have been notable for their father and mother Godhead: the Mormons, and the Transcendentalists under Margaret Fuller.

Religion in Contemporary Society: Current Trends

As we have seen throughout this book, social scientists do not always agree on the roles religion plays in society. Hence, it is not surprising to find that observers differ widely in their interpretation of current trends and in their projections of the future of American religion. Some believe that religion has undergone a recent resurgence. Others see a tremendous decline in the face of secularization. Still others maintain that religion is neither growing nor declining, but undergoing transformation. These variant interpretations are due in part to differing definitions of religion. Furthermore, alternative methods for operationalizing religiosity have yielded data that contrast significantly. We shall explore these issues in this chapter as we investigate current trends and anticipate future prospects for religion in the United States.

Reading the Trends in Traditional Religious Commitment

Resurgence of Religion in the United States?

Those who maintain that a major religious revival is underway in the United States point to the rise of new religious movements. For example, the born again movement has gained a great deal of media attention in recent years. A Gallup poll in 1976 (with a sample of 1,553 Americans) indicated that half of Protestants and a third of the total American public have had a born again experience (*Newsweek,* October 25, 1976:68). In a 1979 survey conducted by Princeton Religion Research Center, 33 percent of American teenagers reported a born again experience (1980:70). If these figures are correct, 50 million Americans attest to some sort of personal religious experience or personal commitment.[1] Two recent candidates for the American presidency, both of them successful in their bids, have found it politically expedient to play heavily upon their religious commitments (Jimmy Carter in 1976 and Ronald Reagan in 1980).[2] While skeptics of the resurgence have pointed to a decline in church building programs, supporters of this view point out that extraordinary increases in spending for mass media evangelism show a shift of priorities in spending, not a decline. Indeed, the expansion of religious programming on television (sometimes called the electronic church) has been remarkable. However, an increase in programming does not automatically signal a growth in new believers or a deepened commitment to the faith by present members. (In Chapter 5 we discussed different types of commitment and the fact that financial giving may occur independently of commitment to an ideology.)

Others who suggest a growth of religion in America point to the nontradi-

---

[1] Actually, the term *born again* is a broad one which includes many types of experiences. Depending on the group, being born again may entail a personal religious experience, an adult baptism, glossolalia (speaking in tongues), or a gradual experience of deepened commitment. For example, 33 percent of the teenage respondents in the Princeton sample reported being born again, but 27 percent described being born again as a gradual process of deepened religious commitment and only 6 percent pointed to a specific, sudden experience (Princeton Religion Research Center 1980:70).

[2] Jimmy Carter placed considerable stress on his born again status in 1976, and Ronald Reagan endorsed evangelical groups and affirmed fundamentalist concepts in the 1980 campaign. In both cases, public affirmations of religiosity were considered a boon to the candidates' political aspirations. This is viewed by some commentators as evidence that religion is undergoing a resurgence in public life. In the past several decades, presidents were generally expected to believe in God and to attend church occasionally, but a *profound* religious commitment was not much of an asset. In fact, an overly strong religious commitment might well have been a liability.

tional religious movements—the cults. The increase of cult membership in the 1960s and 1970s indicates to some observers an intense search for meaning among young people. While traditional religious organizations and ideologies may have failed to provide it for many, these new religious movements show that religion is gaining new popularity among young people. No one knows the number of members in most cults (the groups and their detractors both tend to exaggerate substantially the number of followers). Anticultists estimate that as many as 3 million Americans are involved in one of the one thousand cultic movements in the United States, and another 6 million are involved in meditation groups, such as Transcendental Meditation and Yoga (Conway and Siegelman 1978:11–12). A more cautious estimate is that perhaps a million and a half Americans are involved in cultic movements in this country (Johnstone 1975:317).[3] Since we have no accurate figures on the number of people in cults 25 or 50 years ago, it is difficult to estimate how much of a growth these numbers represent. One fact is clear, religious cults are more visible around major college campuses now than they were several decades ago. It appears that some young Americans seem to be opting for a new form of religion rather than opting out of religion altogether.

One other source has caused some observers to believe that traditional religiosity has undergone a revival. According to data reported on denominational membership, the conservative denominations (Southern Baptist, Nazarene, Assembly of God, and so on) are the ones which are growing and the moderate and liberal denominations (Episcopal, United Church of Christ, United Methodist, United Presbyterian, and so forth) are declining (see Exhibit 5–4 in Chapter 5). Dean Kelley, an official of the National Council of Churches, maintains that people have been switching to more conservative denominations because the latter seem more certain of their claims to truth and because they require a strict and uncompromising commitment (sacrifices and investments). Other researchers, using better controls on their data, have challenged this thesis. They report that most switching is from conservative denominations to more liberal ones and from liberal ones to "no religion" (Newport 1979). These researchers grant that conservative denominations have been growing more rapidly than liberal ones, but they insist that the increase in crude numbers has been due to higher birth rates among the more conservative denominations. (For more detail, refer to the discussion of religious switchers in Chapter 5.)

There are some signs of renewed religious intensity in America, much

---

[3] Even this figure may be high. Johnstone uses estimates by Peter Rowley (1971) who estimates the number of people who are even loosely associated with a cultic group. For example, the figure of 600,000 persons associated with Scientology is apparently the number who have ever taken a Scientology course. Those who have studied Scientology in depth put the number of active participants at 30,000 (Whitehead 1974). Even a well known group like the Unification Church has only about two thousand *devoted* members, although there are a much higher number of people loosely associated with the movement (Lofland 1977; Bromley and Shupe 1979).

of which took social scientists by surprise. But most social scientists claim that these are still small minority movements or temporary aberrations in an overriding trend of religious decline.

Decline of Religion in the United States?

Those who maintain that religion is in a declining pattern point to drops over the past several decades in the percentage of the population who are formally members of a congregation and the percentage attending religious services on a weekly basis (see Exhibit 10–1). The trend is clearly downward. Of course, these indexes only show institutional expressions of religion, not religion as a world view. Church membership tends to be a particularly poor measure of personal religiosity (Demerath 1965). Church attendance is a somewhat better indicator, but as we found in Chapter 8, it is correlated highly to some dimensions of religiosity (religious knowledge, doctrinal orthodoxy) and not to others (reports of personal religious experience, devotionalism, ethicalism, and communal involvement). But affiliation and attendance are not the only items which have suggested a decline in the influence of religion. In recent years, fewer people respond positively when asked whether they think religion is increasing its influence on everyday life. Furthermore, the number of people who report that they believe in life after death or that they have "no doubts about the existence of God" has also declined. This has caused a large number of sociologists to conclude that religion is in a declining mode.

Berger, O'Dea, and others have written extensively about the process of secularization, which they believe to be antithetical to religion. Parsons and Bellah concur that certain transformations of religion have taken place, and while they do not view these processes as evidence of a decline in religiosity per se, they do believe that traditional forms of religion are fading (see Chapter 4). In fact, not many sociologists have argued against the basic thesis that traditional religiosity is declining in America.

There are, however, a few sociologists who have recently sought to disrupt this consensus. One of these dissenters, Andrew Greeley (1969b; 1972), insists that no long-term decline has taken place. While there may be some recent drops in affiliation from the extraordinary high of the 1950s, church affiliation and church attendance is far ahead of historical averages for the nation as a whole. There is strong evidence to support his position; historians claim that in 1800 less than 10 percent of the population belonged to churches and only about 20 percent[4] attended religious services (Hudson

[4] Hudson estimates church membership at 1 out of 15 members of the population, with attendance at about 3 times that number. Membership was very low because it was highly restricted. Church membership as a percentage of the population increased particularly because criteria for such membership were relaxed. However, even using present day definitions of religious affiliation, Hudson (1973:130) claims only about 40 percent of the population would have identified themselves as church members. Such a figure is far below contemporary figures in America.

Exhibit 10-1

Percentage of American Adults Attending Church on an Average Week

Source: *Yearbook of American Churches.* New York: National Council Press, 1960–1972, and *Yearbook of American and Canadian Churches.* Nashville: Abingdon, 1973–1982. Used by permission.

Church membership, 1936–1979 (based upon those *saying* they are members)

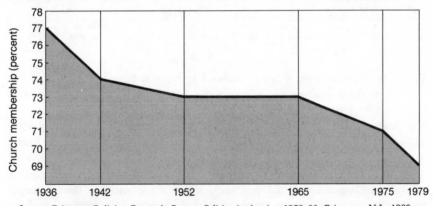

Source: Princeton Religion Research Center, *Religion in America, 1979–80.* Princeton, N.J., 1980, p. 37. Used by permission.

These figures indicate those who claim church membership in a sample survey. However, respondents sometimes report that they are members of a particular denomination even though the local congregation no longer has that person on their active membership roles.

1973:129–130). By 1850, only 16 percent of the population were members of religious organizations (see Exhibit 10–2).

Greeley interprets any recent reversal in church growth patterns as part of a normal cycle. But he even doubts that a really significant downturn in recent religious involvement has taken place at all. He argues that there has been a decline in some dimensions of religiosity and an increase in others. For example, he found that among Protestants there was a decrease

Exhibit 10–2 _____

Church Membership as a Percentage of the American Population, 1850–1970 (based upon denominational reports of membership)

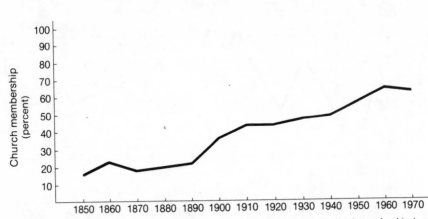

While short-term statistical figures seem to indicate a tremendous decline in church membership (see Exhibit 10–1), the long-term figures make the downturn of the past two decades appear slight. These long-term statistical figures must also be evaluated with caution. Prior to the 1920s, some churches counted only the heads of families as members and others counted only adult members. Some denominations now report all baptized members—including infants. Note also the difference in self-reports and denominational reports of church members for the years 1936–1979 as reported in Exhibits 10–1 and 10–2.

Source: *Yearbook of American Churches.* New York: National Council Press, 1960–1972, and *Yearbook of American and Canadian Churches.* Nashville: Abingdon, 1973–1982. Used by permission.

in the number of people who believed in heaven (down 4 percent), but a small increase in the number that prayed three times a day or more (up 2 percent). Among Catholics, he found a small decrease in the number that prayed three times a day or more (down 3 percent), but a net increase in participation in church activities (up 3 percent). Among Jews, he found a substantial decline in the number that believed in God (down 21 percent) or in life after death (down 18 percent), but a significant increase in active church involvement (up 12 percent). In all three groups, fewer people reported that religion was important in their own life, but in all three there was an increase in the percentage who engaged in weekly Bible reading. Moreover, Greeley suggests that religion is less important to people in that they don't think about it all of the time or when making everyday decisions. But it does provide a sense of ultimate meaning in life, and it establishes an important sense of belonging and fellowship. In this role as a significant reference point, religion may have more influence over the individual's behavior than it did as an abstract set of beliefs and principles. (As we found in Chapter 8, communal processes usually are more important factors in affecting behavior than are associational ones.) Greeley insists that exclusive loyalty to religious ideology—in which all of one's attitudes are scrutinized for their consistency with religious doctrine—is a phenomenon that has been rare in the history of human religions (Greeley 1972:142).

As for faith in the principles of science, declines in otherworldliness, and a waning sense of the sacred, Greeley sees little among the common laity. Secularization, if it exists at all, is a phenomenon of religious elites (the clergy, theologians, and religious officials). Even among graduate students at 12 of the top universities in the United States, where one would expect the most secularization, Greeley reports that only a modest decline in religious affiliation has taken place. He insists that minor downturns in several indexes of religiosity have caused many sociologists to make sweeping generalizations about a long-term and pervasive pattern. He believes this interpretation has grossly exaggerated the facts.

Several other scholars have agreed with Greeley and offered other data which challenge the thesis that religion is caught in a long-term process of decline. Hoge and Roozen (1979) and Wuthnow (1976c) have argued with Greeley that the downturn is short term. They insist that short-term trends cannot be explained by long-term processes (such as secularization). Hoge and Roozen explain growth and decline trends with several interacting variables. They point out that social and cultural changes in the larger society (values, beliefs, socioeconomic conditions, and so on) can affect patterns of religious affiliation and membership. These are referred to as "contextual factors." However, in order to understand growth and decline of any given denomination or local congregation, one must also understand the affects of "institutional factors," which may either mobilize people or alienate them. They point out that the membership factors in churches are affected by national and local contextual factors, by national institutional factors (in a denominational hierarchy) and by local institutional factors (in a local congregation). Church membership and attendance in the nation at any given time is influenced by these factors—and at any given time there are likely to be countertrends that strengthen or weaken church ties in various denominations and in various regions of the country (Hoge and Roozen 1979:319–327). These counterforces explain the irregularity of church membership patterns as the force-field changes from time to time.

Rigney, Machalek, and Goodman (1978) have also found irregular variation in religiosity. Using longitudinal data on seven measures of religiosity, they found a long-term pattern of decline in some areas (e.g., annual contributions to religious organizations and to charities as a percentage of all per capita expenditures, religious books published as a percentage of all books), a pattern of long-term increase in one area (church membership as a percentage of the total population), and irregular variation in others (percentage reporting regular church attendance, church construction as a percentage of all construction). They conclude that there are clearly countervailing forces at work in American religiosity, and that secularization is "not a unitary process." However, one factor pervades all attempts to discern long-term trends in religiosity, an unfortunate lack of reliable and comparable historical data (Rigney et al.:1978).

Conclusion

By way of summary, we can point to three important issues that affect one's interpretation of the data: one's definition of religion, one's interpretation of the privatization factor, and one's understanding of the youth factor. For those who hold to a substantive definition of religion (religion as a belief in the supernatural), religion seems to be in decline. For those who use a functional definition (religion as that which provides a sense of meaning in life), religion is changing but is not necessarily declining. Most of the statistical data which indicates a decline in religiosity and a rise in secularization is based on a substantive definition of religion. A decline in orthodoxy is viewed as a decline in religiosity, and orthodoxy is often measured with questions about belief in the Devil, in the virgin birth of Jesus, and in Jesus' ability to walk on water. Among Catholics, belief in the infallibility of the pope in matters of faith and morals is often a criterion of orthodoxy, and hence of religiosity. The assumption behind these measurement devices is that religion and science are antithetical. Hence, a move from a fundamentalist or conservative theological stance to a liberal one is interpreted as a decline in religiosity—an interpretation most liberals would reject.

Much of the survey data is based on the idea that religion must be otherworldly. Those who do not believe in life after death are said to be less religious. Talcott Parsons (1964) and Max Weber (1958) have insisted that religion is not necessarily otherworldly. Hence, a decline in otherworldliness is not necessarily an indication of a decline in religiosity. Theologian Harvey Cox is an interesting example. He claims that secularization is the fulfillment of a central biblical theme: liberation from superstition and from animism (the belief that all material objects have spirits). A profoundly this-worldly orientation is deeply biblical, he asserts. A number of liberal theologians concur with this view. For these religious scholars, secularization and religiosity are not antithetical; an increase in one is not interpreted as a decline in the other. In this book we have also discussed the Lost/Found Nation of Islam (the Black Muslims) and the Cargo cult as religions, yet both groups are profoundly this-worldly in their world view. The point I wish to make here is that some of the data which have shown declines in religiosity have measured only certain expressions of religiosity.

The tendency to measure religiosity in terms of adherence to specific beliefs is clearly understandable, for we have seen that religious systems tend to "freeze" their world views and encapsulate them in beliefs which are supposedly immutable. But as societies change, these beliefs can come to be implausible or irrelevant. It is interesting to note the emergence of process theology among the religious elite at a time in which social change seems to be the only certainty. One of the fundamental principles of process theology is that change is indisputable, inescapable, and eternal. Not even God is viewed as immutable and absolute, but rather as changing and evolving. Even the deity is "in process." Many observers view this as a further accommodation to society and as evidence that religion is losing ground— even within its own ranks—to the secular world view.

As we have seen in this text, the accommodation of a religious world view is certainly not new, and is not necessarily evidence of a decline. Few people would describe the theology of John Calvin as antithetical to religion, yet his system of belief accommodated Christian thought to the emergence of capitalism (see Chapter 8). Few view Second Isaiah as less religious than his predecessors, even though he accommodated the Hebrew theodicy to account for the secular exigencies of the exile. Sociologists who define the accommodation of contemporary religious beliefs to secular social realities seem to be placing a value judgment on our contemporary transition which they would not think of doing to earlier transitions.

A second issue in interpreting religious trends has to do with how one understands the process of the privatization of religion. Sociologists from a wide range of perspectives (Berger, Luckman, Parsons, Bellah) have maintained that religion has increasingly become a private, individual affair. Each individual is able to choose his or her religious orientation from a wide range of religious "entrepreneurs." Religious beliefs are not givens which seem to be unquestionable and imbedded in the very nature of reality. The modern citizen can *choose* his or her form of religiosity. Berger views this as hazardous for religion;[5] Parsons and Bellah see it as a healthy sign.

Related to this privatization is the fact that religion comes to have an ever narrower scope of direct influence. With the differentiation of institutions and the specialization of functions of these institutions, religion is seen (at least by Berger) as having less impact on the society as a whole. Another way to say this is that increasing numbers of people have a multiple narrow-vector world view rather than a single integrated wide-vector world view. This assertion that religion has a narrowed scope is still at the stage of hypothesis. We have no hard empirical data by which we can compare contemporary world views with historical outlooks. Furthermore, those who use a functional definition of religion may insist that the "real" religion of a people is that which has scope. One's real system of meaning may be something other than traditional doctrines which one affirms only verbally. According to this definition of religion, a person's "real faith" is *always* manifest in his or her daily life—even if he or she does not consciously call that faith religion.

If it can be established that there *is* an increase in multiple narrow-vector world views, another interesting possibility occurs: traditional religion may be undergoing simultaneous revival and decline. Clifford Geertz (1968)

---

[5] In his earlier work (1967) Berger suggests that privatization is disastrous for both traditional forms of religion and for society as a whole. His more recent work (1979) suggests certain offsetting advantages of individualized religion. But despite certain benefits, individualization continues to be viewed by Berger as a threat to *traditional* forms of religiosity.

discusses the difference between force and scope in religion. *Force* refers to the intensity with which people hold their beliefs, *scope* to the influence of one's religious symbols and ideas on other areas of life. It is possible (and again, this is hypothesis) that the increase in born again and charismatic movements represents an increase in force of traditional religiosity for some Americans, but that traditional religiosity is simultaneously declining in scope. Students may want to explore their own assumptions about what it means to be religious. Can religion exist without scope? Or are those belief systems something other than the true meaning system of individuals? Does the current growth of traditional religiosity represent an increase in force but not in scope? How would a sociologist go about proving or disproving this thesis? How would you design a research model?

Finally, any interpretation of religious trends must come to terms with the youth factor. The increases in the 1970s of those reporting "no religion" were largely younger members of the adult population. Some observers have felt that this bodes ill for religion, since young people would not be sustaining the churches in a few years and would not be raising their children in a religious context. Hence, the major form of recruitment—procreation and religious socialization within the home—would not be sustaining the churches in future decades. Other observers have pointed out that religious inactivity in the teens and early 20s is not a new phenomenon. It is a normal developmental process most generations have experienced. Most people, by their early to mid-30s, join churches and see that their children get some religious training. This generation, it is claimed, will be no different.

Still others claim that the religious apostasy of the current generation is due to the unique experiences in young adulthood which these individuals have endured. Americans who are just now reaching their mid-30s grew up in an atmosphere of political assassinations (John Kennedy, Martin Luther King, Jr., Robert Kennedy), radical politics, the Vietnam War, and the Watergate scandals. All these events occurred when this generation was at an impressionable age. Their effects on this particular age group may be lasting. The group may have developed—with more frequency than most generations—a larger number of cynical personalities or larger numbers of individuals who seek political solutions to problems. The group of young people who were born 10 years later may have been less aware of the events of the 1960s and may be more inclined to involvement in traditional religious organizations (Wuthnow 1976c:862; Newport 1979:547, 549). At this point it is too early to know which of these interpretations is correct.

Overall, there appears to be a recent reduction in traditional forms of religion and especially in institutional expressions of Christianity. At this point, it is premature to predict how pervasive and how long-lasting this trend will be. In terms of church affiliation and attendance at worship services, there is a reversal of the growth pattern which lasted for several decades. However, current affiliation and attendance patterns remain ahead of their levels for the early 1800s—in what were supposed to have been the "good old days" of high levels of religious commitment.

Exhibit 10–3 _____

"No Preference" in Religion as a Correlate of Age, 1980*

Age	Percentage
18	11
19	11
20	12
21–24	14
25–29	13
30–34	11
35–39	8
40–44	6
45–49	6
50–59	4
60–69	4
70 and older	3

The proportion of people responding "no preference" when questioned about their religious preference has increased significantly since the 1960s. In 1967, 2 percent of the population responded with this answer. By 1979, 8 percent expressed no preference. In 1980 the number was 7 percent. Most of the increase was related to age, since it is mostly young adults (ages 18–32) whose religious involvement fades. The debate is whether the current group of young adults lived through social upheavals which permanently affected their sense of religiosity or whether—like their elders—they will also join churches as they become parents and decide that they want their children raised in a church context. Part of the increase from 1967 to 1979 in "no preference" may be due to the fact that the very large number of people who were born during the baby boom (1947–1960) were in their late teens, 20s, and early 30s during that period. Many of the baby boom people are still in that age group; by 1990 those born during the "birth dearth" (late 1960s and early 1970s) will be in that critical age range.

* Source: Gallup Poll, 1980. Reported by the Princeton Religious Research Center, 1981. Used by permission.

Alternative Forms of Religion

A number of social scientists maintain that declines in traditional measures of religiosity are not indicators of a decline of religiosity itself, but rather signal a change to new forms. Some of these are nontheistic and some even lack a supernatural dimension. For this reason, many sociologists prefer to call these processes "quasi-religious phenomena" or "functional alternatives to religion." Regardless of what one calls them, these value perspectives provide many people with a sense of purpose in life and with a center of worth (which is the etymological basis for the word *worship*). When any ideology or value system becomes a meaning system—one which defines the meaning of life, death, suffering, and injustice—it usually takes on a sacred cast in the eyes of the adherents.

Sometimes we are so familiar with these sacred meaning systems in our own culture that we are only partially conscious of them; we take them for granted as a part of the way things are. Some sociologists who use a functional definition of religion seek to discover these value perspectives which underlie American culture and which serve as a world view or a faith system. This requires a distinction between what people *say* they value or believe and what their *behavior* reveals about their values or beliefs. When someone thinks he or she ought to believe something is desirable (e.g., daily exercise) but fails to act on that belief, phenomenologists refer to the belief as a velleity rather than a value. A value is something a person feels is so important that he or takes action upon it. The acid test of value, according to this perspective, is action. (We discussed the difference between a value and a velleity in Chapter 2.) In the same way, some social scientists have sought to go beyond the verbal affirmations of people regarding their religion to discover the actual faith systems or meaning systems of Americans. In the following pages we will explore three types of meaning systems which serve as alternative forms of religion or quasi-religious dimensions of American culture.

Civil Religion

Emile Durkheim maintained that all cultures have a religious dimension. In fact, Durkheim believed that religion represents a sanctification of society and that the true object of worship is society itself. The sense of sacred imperative was viewed as essential to social maintenance since it convinces people to do that which they might not want to do. They become willing to make sacrifices on behalf of the larger society and set aside their individual self-interests. Moreover, the sense of sacredness provided a source of social unity and harmony; Durkheim viewed a set of common values as mandatory for a society's survival. While not all of these assumptions are shared by most contemporary sociologists, many do believe that there is a religious dimension to all cultures.

In many societies, the sense of unity and common meaning is provided by a traditional religion. If a single religion is held by an overwhelming proportion of the population, it may serve as a source of national unity and religious officials may explain the fortunes and misfortunes of the nation in terms of the traditional religious symbols and values. However, in a religiously heterogeneous society, no one religious group can serve this function. In fact, religious groups may become sources of civil conflict and hostility rather than harmony and unity. In a pluralistic society, something other than traditional religions must serve as a basis for social consensus and for defining the meaningfulness of national activity (Cole and Hammond 1974). Hence, pluralism requires a new meaning system—which becomes sacralized and serves as a form of religiosity.

Such national religions are referred to by social scientists as *civil religions*. (The term was originally coined by Jean Jacques Rousseau.) John Coleman (1970:70) offers a formal definition: "Civil religion is the set of beliefs, rites, and symbols which relates a person's role as citizen and his society's place in space, time, and history to the conditions of ultimate existence and meaning." This system of meaning can be a supplementary one which complements the traditional religiosity of citizens, or it may become a primary source of devotion and commitment in itself. Socially, civil religion serves to define the national purposes in transcendent terms and acts as an expression of national cohesion. In short, it offers a nondenominational theodicy for the nation.

In the United States, civil religion is expressed through myths, rituals, national holidays (holy days), celebrations of the lives of national "saints," visitations to national "shrines," and sacred treatment of national symbols. The mythology of American civil religion began early in the nation's history. In the speeches of some of the first presidents and in sermons of some of the colonial preachers, America was treated as the "promised land." In fact, in his second inaugural address, Thomas Jefferson explicitly compared the founding of the new nation to the founding of Israel, and Europe was defined as the contemporary Egypt—from which God's people had fled. This began a long process of myth development which has grown through the past two hundred years. The belief in the American Dream, the American Way of Life, and the fundamental goodness of America is expressed with reference to a supernatural blessing: "America, America, God shed his grace on thee, and crown thy good with brotherhood from sea to shining sea." Hymns such as these evoke a profound sense of reverence, for they express a deeply ingrained mythology.

Civil religion is also expressed through the rituals that take place on such high holy days as Memorial Day, the Fourth of July, and presidential inauguration days. The ceremonials on these days express central American values and inspire a feeling of unity and a sense of transcendence. The meaning of the nation is believed to transcend individual lives and is more important than contemporary events. Hence, the nation is viewed as having a transcendent dimension (greater purpose), even if it is not a supernatural one. The effort to stop Hitler and "make the world safe for democracy" provides one example. More recently, the space shuttle program and moon landings provided a sense of national accomplishment and collective identity.

National ceremonies tend to emphasize this theme of the transcendent purpose of the nation. Most such celebrations occur around national shrines which are themselves capable of eliciting a feeling of awe—for they symbolize both the transcendence of the nation and the sacrifices made on its behalf. Examples of national shrines are the Washington and Lincoln memorials in Washington, D.C., the Capitol building, the Tomb of the Unknown Soldier, war cemeteries, and the birthplaces or burial sites of American presidents. In an excellent analysis of the symbolism of a Memorial Day celebration in an American town, Lloyd Warner discusses the unifying quality of these rituals and symbols: "The cemetery and its graves become the objects of sacred rituals which permit opposing organizations, often in conflict, to subordinate their ordinary opposition and to cooperate in expressing jointly the larger unity of the total community through the use of common rites for their collective dead" (Warner 1953:24–25).

Since some sociologists view these ceremonials as the central expression of civil religion, content analyses of speeches and newspaper articles on Memorial Day and the Fourth of July and analyses of central themes in presidential inaugural addresses have become an important means of studying this phenomenon. There are also other national holidays, but they tend to be of somewhat lesser significance as expressions of civil religion: Thanksgiving (which George Washington in 1789 first made a national holiday so that citizens might thank God for the blessings of this land and this nation), President's Day (birthday celebrations for Washington and Lincoln), and Labor Day (a time to celebrate the accomplishments of American labor and the upward social mobility provided for Americans through the labor movement).

The paramount sacred object in this religion is the American flag. The importance of this symbol can be seen not only in the prescribed handling of the flag (see Exhibit 4–2 in Chapter 4), but in the intensity of the outrage when the stars and stripes are "desecrated"—treated inappropriately. Particular national heroes or saints also serve as focal points for veneration and myth development. Washington and Lincoln are the most important and most widely recognized saints, and are paid homage on President's Day. For some people, Presidents Jefferson, Wilson, Franklin Roosevelt, or Kennedy are key figures. Sometimes folk heroes (like Betsy Ross, Daniel Boone, or Charles Lindberg), business tycoons (who symbolize the rags-to-riches mythology), and military heroes (who symbolize courage and a willingness to sacrifice for the nation) are given honored status and held up to children as exemplary of the American Way. In many quarters, Martin Luther King, Jr., has become a saint of the civil religion because of his efforts to apply the motto "freedom and justice for all" to all Americans. These national saints serve as inspirations and as behavioral models much as Saint Francis, Mother Seton, or Saint Teresa of Avila do in the Christian tradition.

Many observers of this American civil religion have been appalled by it, labeling it as idolatry or as "American Shinto."[6] But Robert Bellah,

---

[6] Shintoism is a Japanese religion (the state religion prior to 1945) which involves worship of ancestors and ancient heroes, a glorification of national accomplishments, a deification of the emperor of Japan, and a profound reverence for nature.

the most widely cited scholar investigating civil religion in America, has argued that this phenomenon needs our careful attention no less than any other form of religiosity. Bellah has focused primarily on references to God or to the transcendent realm in the Declaration of Independence, Washington's Farewell Address, the inaugural addresses of various presidents,[7] and other formal speeches made at times of transition or times of crisis (e.g., Lincoln's Gettysburg Address and John Winthrop's landing sermon before the Pilgrims debarked from their ship at Salem). Bellah finds that references to God and to the transcendent mission of America are pervasive in these formal addresses. Even our pledge of allegiance mentions that we are a nation "under God" and our currency is stamped with "In God We Trust." But this religiosity is clearly *not* Christianity. Civil religion is limited to affirmations which members of any denomination or sect can accept—including non-Christians. While this public theology has a distinctly Protestant style to it, and is much influenced by the Protestant ethic, it is not a form of Protestant Christianity.

Bellah claims that the civil religion has gone through three major trials which have called for refinement and revision in its theology. The first major crisis was the Revolutionary War. Out of that testing of will and purpose emerged the imagery of Washington as a Moses who led us out of bondage. The Judeo-Christian imagery of God working in history was and is the clear paradigm for our civil theology. The second major crisis was the Civil War. The imagery of the Gettysburg Address sets the stage for this next phase of civil theology. Lincoln consistently used rebirth imagery in his ode to "these honored dead." He repeatedly used phrases such as "brought forth," "conceived," "created," and "a new birth of freedom." Not long after he delivered that speech, Lincoln himself became "our martyred President," who "gave the last full measure of devotion." Bellah points out that the theme of sacrificial giving of one's life was indelibly written into the civil religion. Lincoln became the martyr who gave his life so that the nation might live—an interesting repetition of the Christian theme of a martyred savior.

Bellah asserts that America is currently in the midst of its third time of trial as it struggles with its sense of mission in a world of poor nations. Furthermore, the Vietnam War and the Watergate scandal left many Americans cynical. The covenant with God seemed to have been broken, for America has seemed to ignore its end of the agreement. (Bellah 1975). Bellah believes that the way we work through this crisis—the way we define the meaning of contemporary events and current American standing in the world—will be of critical importance in the development of the American character in the next century.

---

[7] Every president has made reference to God or to divine will and divine guidance in an inauguration ceremony.

Bellah (1970b:185) insists that "without an awareness that our nation stands under higher judgment, the tradition of the civil religion would be dangerous indeed." It would be dangerous because it would serve only to sanctify the status quo and the current social structures, regardless of whether they are just. He denies that the conservative function is the only role of civil religion in America. American civil religion is also prophetic; that is, it proclaims judgment on America when it fails to live up to its creed. The ideals of the nation provide a foundation for criticism and improvement. For example, Martin Luther King, Jr., delivered a critical speech about his hopes for the nation, and it proved deeply moving to the American people because his dream was "deeply rooted in the American Dream" (see Exhibit 10–4). Sidney Mead (1974) has also insisted that civil religion is not just the American Way of Life or a sanctified ethnocentrism. It is the aspirations of the nation and is therefore essentially prophetic in nature. Failure to live up to the national aspirations and goals—which he sees as very noble in nature—provides the basis for judging the nation. According to Bellah and Mead, civil religion guards against governments doing whatever they want to do and then sanctifying their actions; civil religion provides a *standard of judgment* for national policy. Bellah states the case very clearly when he writes:

> Religion and morality and politics are not the same things, and confusing them can lead to terrible distortions. But cutting all links between them can lead to even worse distortions. The concept of civil religion simply points to the fact that some links between them seem to exist in all societies. At its best civil religion would be realized in a situation where politics operates within a set of moral standards, and both politics and morality are open to transcendent judgment (1974:271).

Martin Marty (1974) has pointed out that civil religion can be either prophetic or priestly. While it may provide a basis for judgment and correction, civil religion has often served simply to endorse the status quo. In this case, the nation is not "under God"; rather the name of God is simply used to sanctify the actions of the nation. In fact, Marty had earlier referred to the priestly type of American civil religion as American Shinto—a label intended to be derogatory, for Marty viewed this form of religiosity to be idolatrous. (Marty is not only an historian, but a theologian and an ordained Lutheran minister).

Bellah recognized the same phenomenon when he contrasted the inaugural address of John Kennedy in 1961 with that of Richard Nixon in 1973. Bellah claims that Nixon's version of civil religion was one in which God gave blessing and sanction to the actions of the United States. Kennedy's speech called the nation to a higher calling which only God would ultimately judge. Hence, just as there are several theological interpretations of Christianity, so also are there several interpretations of American civil religion.

Exhibit 10–4 _____

I HAVE A DREAM

I say to you today, my friends, that in spite of the difficulties and frustrations of the moment, I still have a dream. It is a dream deeply rooted in the American dream.

I have a dream that one day this nation will rise up and live out the true meaning of its creed: "We hold these truths to be self-evident: that all men are created equal."

I have a dream that one day on the red hills of Georgia the sons of former slaves and the sons of former slaveowners will be able to sit down together at the table of brotherhood. . . .

I have a dream that my four little children will one day live in a nation where they will not be judged by the color of their skin but by the content of their character.

I have a dream today. . . .

I have a dream that one day every valley shall be exalted, every hill and mountain shall be made low, the rough places will be made plains, and the crooked places will be made straight, and the glory of the Lord shall be revealed, and all flesh shall see it together.

This is our hope. This is the faith with which I return to the South. . . . With this faith we will be able to work together, to pray together, to struggle together, to go to jail together, to stand up for freedom together, knowing that we will be free one day.

This will be the day when all of God's children will be able to sing with new meaning "My country 'tis of thee, sweet land of liberty, of thee I sing. Land where my fathers died, land of the Pilgrim's pride, from every mountainside, let freedom ring."

And if America is to be a great nation this must become true. So let freedom ring. . . .

From every mountainside, let freedom ring.

When we let freedom ring, when we let it ring from every village and every hamlet, from every state and every city, we will be able to speed up that day when all of God's children, black men and white men, Jews and Gentiles, Protestants and Catholics, will be able to join hands and sing in the words of that old Negro spiritual, "Free at last! Free at last! Thank God almighty, we are free at last!"

—*Martin Luther King, Jr.*

Martin Luther King's "I Have a Dream" speech delivered at the March on Washington in 1963 is a major formulation of American civil religion. Although King was a Baptist preacher, he appealed not to values which are uniquely Christian, but to ones that would be compelling to Americans of any religious stripe. He quotes scripture only once, and that was from the Old Testament—thereby appealing to Jews as well as to Christians. This speech provides an example of the prophetic role of American civil religion.

Source: C. Eric Lincoln, *Is Anybody Listening to Black America?* (New York: Seabury, 1968), pp. 65–66 (abridged).

This creates an interesting irony, for precisely those symbols and beliefs which are supposed to unite the country often become the basis of conflict. Advocates of civil rights for blacks and members of the Ku Klux Klan both appeal to the American Way and to quasi-religious American values in defense of their stance. Likewise, both advocates and opponents of other social movements have based their stance on a version of the American civil religion for this serves as the legitimizing ideology of any movement.

Not only does American civil religion have prophetic and priestly versions, but it also has official and folk versions. Will Herberg (1955) undertook a study of American religiosity in the 1950s and claimed that Protestants, Catholics, and Jews in America were all worshiping the American

Way of Life. Herberg was focusing primarily on the priestly functions of the civil religion, but more important, he was interested in the views of average Americans. He found Americanism to provide the most important set of values and to serve as the most central faith system for most Americans. Herberg maintained that the core beliefs of the traditional religions (such as belief in Jesus Christ as the Son of God) were only peripheral in the lives of most church members. The central sacred system of beliefs was the American Way of Life. Regardless of whether this set of beliefs was accompanied by a deity, it appears to be the operating center of values and hence the central religion of America. Herberg's interest was not primarily in formal pronouncements of presidents at their inaugurations or in civil religion as it is expressed in formal documents (such as the Declaration of Independence). Rather he focused on the everyday values and sense of sacredness of the common American.

While Bellah and Mead have focused on the "official" civil religion, Herberg and others have studied its "folk" version. Some scholars have done content analyses of Fourth of July newspaper editorials (Thomas and Flippen 1972) or such popular events as the "Honor America Day" (July 4, 1970) sponsored by Billy Graham and Bob Hope (Streiker and Strober, 1972). Still others have distributed questionnaires to a random sample of the population to determine their attitudes and beliefs (Wimberly 1976; Wimberly et al. 1976; Wimberly and Christenson 1981). In each of these cases, the studies tapped the civil religiosity of the common folk rather than the official aspirations of the nation.

Clearly, civil religion is complex and multifaceted. At the risk of oversimplifying, we can identify at least four types of civil religion: (1) official-prophetic, (2) official-priestly, (3) folk-prophetic, and (4) folk-priestly. However, the empirical evidence suggests that folk versions of American civil religion are much more frequently priestly in character. It is the official version which is likely to have a prophetic dimension.

Bellah (1974, 1975), Marty (1974), Herberg (1974), and other commentators have agreed that a civil religion which entirely lacks a prophetic dimension can be dangerous, for it tends simply to serve the interests of those in power and to enhance that power by sacralizing it. Those writers who have studied the folk version of civil religion have seen little that was prophetic; hence, they have been highly critical of it.[8] But these critics have often compared the best of traditional religion with the worst of the civil religion. On the other hand, Mead is highly critical of the narrowness and bigotry of traditional religiosity, and points to the universal values of the civil religion. He simply compares the best of civil religion with the worst of the traditional religions. Bellah suggests that like any form of

---

[8] Coleman (1970:75) suggests that recent opposition to civil religion by Protestant religious leaders may have occurred simply because control of civil religion was dropping out of *their* hands!

Exhibit 10–5 _____

Operationalizing Civil Religiosity

Most studies of civil religion have relied on content analyses or participant observation studies. In studies where a survey method is used, the researcher must operationalize civil religiosity. It is not easy to formulate questions which reveal both official and folk versions of civil religion in both their priestly and prophetic forms. The items below have been used to operationalize civil religion—with a 5-point scale ranging from strongly agree to strongly disagree. Some questions, such as 6, are asked in such a way that a positive response would imply a rejection of civil religiosity—for civil religion endorses religious pluralism in the nation. Students may want to try formulating their own series of questions which might measure the civil religion dimension of respondents.

1. America is God's chosen nation today.*
2. To me, the flag of the United States is sacred.*
3. Human rights come from God and not merely from laws.*
4. If our government does not support religion, government cannot uphold morality.*
5. We should respect the President's authority since his authority is from God.†
6. National leaders should not only affirm their belief in God but also their belief in Jesus Christ as Lord and Savior.†
7. God can be known through the experience of the American people.†
8. The founding fathers created a blessed and unique republic when they gave us the Constitution.†

---

* Ronald C. Wimberly and James A. Christenson, "Civil Religion and Other Religious Identities," *Sociological Analysis* (Summer 1981): p. 93.

† Ronald C. Wimberly, Donald A. Clelland, and Thomas C. Hood, "The Civil Religious Dimension: Is It There?" *Social Forces,* June 1976, p. 893.

---

religion, civil religion may be good or bad. His major plea is that we take it seriously as an alternative form of religiosity in America (Bellah 1974; 1975).

Many nations have spawned a civil religion because of its role in uniting a pluralistic country. A fundamental part of building a new nation is the development of a common ethos or set of values and loyalties. Furthermore, the meaning of the new political arrangements must be spelled out. Civil religion is not a phenomenon limited to American life (Coleman 1970; Markoff and Regan 1981; McGuire 1981:166–179). In some cases, civil religion may be established by a national government which tries to abolish traditional religiosity and replace it with national loyalties and a transcendent meaning to the nation. The Soviet Union provides one example of this type of secular civil religion. In other cases, civil religion is not expected to replace the traditional religion, but is designed as an added dimension to existing religions. This style is illustrated in the requirement of the Roman Empire that in addition to their own god or gods, all subjects had to worship the emperor. A variety of systems of civil religion can be found—some sponsored by traditional religion, some in conflict with it—but all pluralistic societies seem to have an element of "national religiosity."

A number of scholars believe that while many Americans attend churches and have memberships in traditional religious groups, the central meaning system of these people is Americanism (their "true" religion). For these people the flag is a more important symbol of their religion than is the Star of David or the cross, and the Fourth of July is a more celebrative and meaningful holiday than Easter or Passover. This sort of analysis is by no means limited to social scientists. Theologian H. Richard Niebuhr was emphatic in his insistence that nationalism was a greater threat to Christianity than atheism. No doubt patriotism has effectively replaced traditional religions as the operative faith of many people (Wimberly et al. 1976).

But for many Americans, two systems of faith seem to operate simultaneously, sometimes complementing, sometimes conflicting with each other. When conflict occurs, one coping strategy is to adopt a world view with multiple, narrow vectors. Most of the time, Americans are probably no more aware that they hold two rather different meaning systems than are the Burmese who hold to both Buddhism and the folk religion of the Thirty-Seven Nats or the Chinese who say devotions at both Taoist and Buddhist temples. There is a strain toward coherence and logical consistency in the world view of most people, but in any given instance the strain may be large or small. Students should never underestimate the capacity of humans to overlook or ignore incoherence and logical inconsistency in their meaning systems. Nor should they overemphasize the cognitive aspects of religion at the expense of affective dimensions. People will often hold to a meaning system because it makes them feel like an accepted member of the group or because it helps them feel significant. Logical consistency is often of secondary importance.

Regardless of one's personal evaluation of civil religion, the student of religion must keep in mind that it serves functions for the individual and for the society as a whole. American civil religion provides a sense of ultimate meaning to one's citizenship. It causes people to feel good about themselves as participants in the nation. It is not likely to disappear soon from the American scene. Not only is it likely to endure, but the particular style and character of American civil religion in the future is important, for civil religion may be influential in shaping the course of the nation. As for the personal religiosity of most Americans, some blend of traditional and civil religiosity is likely to continue.

Invisible Religions

Several other scholars have stressed the individualization of religion—the way in which each individual in modern society constructs his or her own meaning system by drawing from many popular philosophies. Perhaps the most important work developing this thesis is that by Thomas Luckmann (1967). Luckmann uses an extraordinarily broad definition of religion, referring to it as the "symbolic universes of meaning" which infuse all of life with a sense of transcendent purpose. He emphasizes world view as an elementary and universal manifestation of religion (1967:52–53). In this respect, Luckmann's definition of religion is similar to other functional definitions (Yinger, Geertz). But rather than limiting religion to macrosystems of meaning—meaning systems which address death, suffering, and injustice—he seeks to understand world view at all levels of generality and specificity. He insists that "No single interpretive scheme performs the religious function. It is rather the world view as a whole, as a unitary matrix of meaning" that defines one's identity and serves as one's religious orientation (1967:55–56). In essence, he points to personal identity as "a form of religiosity" (1967:70). A person's sense of identity—his or her values, attitudes, dispositions, and sense of self-worth—are part of his or her religiosity, because all of these are related to feelings about what makes life worth living. These are "invisible" forms of religion in that they do not have the social manifestations one normally associates with religion.

This is certainly a broad definition. Many social scientists have objected that it makes everything religious—or makes nothing at all specifically religious. They make an important point. The aspect of this definition which I find intriguing is that Luckmann has defined religiosity in a way very compatible with that of a number of contemporary theologians. H. Richard Niebuhr, Paul Tillich, and a number of other modern theologians have strongly resisted the idea that one's faith or one's religiosity is expressed primarily through cognitive beliefs. Rather, they insist that one's faith is most fully manifested in everyday assumptions, in actions, and even in personality structure. Hence, Niebuhr and Tillich seek to discover one's "real" center of worth by exploring the issue of what one ultimately trusts. Given the fact that some of the most widely acknowledged theologians (whose trade is meaning systems) have defined religiosity similarly to Luckmann, his formulation deserves our attention.

Luckmann believes that as society has become increasingly complex, and as institutions have specialized their sphere of influence, traditional religions have had an influence over a decreasing range of human behavior and thinking. Combined with this is the tendency of traditional religions to freeze their systems of belief so as to make them seem more eternal, absolute, and unchanging. At the same time, technological, political, and economic changes have continued to occur; indeed, in the modern Western world change occurs at ever increasing rates. Luckmann maintains that this has caused traditional forms of religion and orthodox meaning systems to become irrelevant to the everyday experiences of the common person. He denies that this represents a decline of religiosity. The common person is as religious as ever, but the religiosity of the laity has taken on new forms. Luckmann insists that claims of a decline in religiosity are due to the fact that sociologists have usually asked questions which measure only traditional religiosity (church affiliation and attendance, belief in traditional doctrines, and frequency of prayer).

In the modern world, people derive their sense of meaning by drawing on a wide range of popular philosophies. Each of these competes for the loyalties of the citizen, who is basically a consumer at the marketplace. The product which each popular philosopher is selling is a world view—with its own center of worth or system of values, and its own definition of what makes life worth living. Popular religious tracts, *Playboy* magazine, psychological theories expressed in best-selling books and in *Reader's Digest*-type magazines, and underlying themes and values communicated through television programs can all affect a person's sense of the meaning of life and one's individual "philosophy of life." *Playboy* is very explicit about expressing a consistent philosophy and set of personal values. Unrestricted personal expressiveness and the desirability of substantial economic affluence are among those values most worthy of a person's effort.

Other organizations, social movements, or businesses also compete in the philosophy-of-life marketplace. Libertarianism is a political movement which exalts the rights of the individual to seek his or her own self-interests without interference. The prime formulator of libertarianism was the late Ayn Rand, whose newsletter was faithfully read by believers and whose public addresses packed houses with enthusiastic followers.[9] Ayn Rand stressed individual initiative and the survival of the fittest, and believed that altruism was the worst sort of vice. Selfishness, if one followed the logic of her argument, was the most exalted virtue and would ultimately lead to the best type of society. At the opposite end of the political spectrum, Marxism offers a coherent outlook on life and a constellation of values which promises to bring a better life in the future through collective action and collective consciousness. Each of these social movements offers a philosophy of life and a set of values which compete with traditional religions in defining the meaning and purpose of life.

Even business enterprises, like Amway Corporation, seek to motivate by stressing the primacy of financial independence, the value of the American Way[10] of free enterprise economics, and the rewards of close friendship with other distributors. In fact, the regular Amway weekend regional rallies can be analyzed as plausibility structures (see Chapter 6) which operate to reinforce the believability of the values and outlook presented by the corporation. Most individuals develop their own personalized meaning system or philosophy of life by drawing from many such sources in modern life, including the traditional religions. However, traditional religions are

---

[9] In her later years, Ayn Rand spoke only once a year—at the Ford Hall Forum in Boston. Since I was living in Boston in the early 1970s and normally attended these forums, I happened to hear her. I was amazed to find that people had flown in from various cities as far away as New Orleans and London for the sole purpose of hearing her speak. People who were not members of the forum but who wanted to hear her waited in line all day to gain entrance.

[10] The name Amway is expressive of this exaltation of the American Way.

only one source of such meaning systems, and they are normally blended with other outlooks in the faith system of any given individual.

Berger, Parsons, and Bellah, it may be recalled, also stressed the privatization of modern meaning systems (see Chapter 4, the discussion of secularization). Parsons and Bellah view the process as a good and healthy sign. Berger points to the phenomenon as evidence of a decline in religion. While Luckmann does not see the process as indicative of a decline in religion, neither does he view it as a particularly healthy trend. When individuals must construct their own meaning systems, those systems may seem less eternal and less compelling. The individual may, therefore, experience anomie or normlessness. On the other hand, those who do construct a sustainable meaning system often develop one which is so privatized that it offers meaning only to the individual—ignoring the larger social structure. Because many privatized meaning systems in modern society exalt the autonomy of the individual (self-realization, individual social and geographic mobility, and so on) the locus of meaning is in the individual biography (Luckmann 1967:109). With this locus of meaning, individuals are not likely to make sacrifices on behalf of the larger society. If this orientation continued indefinitely, the needs of the society itself would go unmet. For this reason, the privatization of religiosity could be unhealthy in the long run for the larger society.

Hence, Luckmann insists that religiosity is not declining in the modern world; it is undergoing transformation. An alternative form of religiosity has been developing—a form which does not look like religion to many people because it lacks the institutional structures and the conventional dogmas characteristic of traditional religions. Luckmann insists that an alternative form of religiosity is emerging and that it needs to be understood as a modern manifestation.

Luckmann's thesis has drawn a great deal of attention. Several attempts have been made to measure the relative influence of traditional religious views and other "popular" meaning systems in personal philosophies of life. The results are mixed: Machalek and Martin (1976) found evidence to support Luckmann's thesis regarding invisible religions; Nelson et al. (1976) did not. Bainbridge and Stark (1981) studied lay attitudes toward traditional religious doctrines and found that they may not be as impotent and irrelevant to the average citizen as Luckmann implies. On the other hand, Wuthnow (1973) found substantial variations in the personal theologies of seminary students—many departing significantly from traditional Christian theology. In any case, most social scientists would grant that the meaning systems of most Americans seem to be somewhat eclectic, with traditional religiosity, patriotism, and other value systems converging. At the present time, we do not know for sure whether this phenomenon is any more common in the modern world than it was in past eras. Furthermore, our tools of analysis are at present so crude that it is difficult to make significant generalizations about privatized systems of faith in America.

Readers may find it interesting and worthwhile to reflect on their own sense of meaning and their own system of values. Do all your values evolve out of a traditional religion? Most of them? Some of them? What other sources have affected your outlook on life? What about the sense of meaning and the personal values of your friends and acquaintances? Does it make sense to you to refer to personalized systems of meaning as a form of religiosity? Why or why not? Do you agree with Niebuhr when he says whatever provides one with a sense that life is worth living is his or her god and that one's center of values is what one truly worships? Is it essential for a meaning system to address the meaning of death in order for it to be called religion? These are important issues which have divided sociologists in their approaches to studying religion and in their generalizations about religious trends in this country.

Quasi-Religious Movements

Loosely integrated societies—in which the intensity of commitment to cultural tradition is low—are more likely than tightly integrated ones to generate cults and other nontraditional social movements (Stark and Roberts 1982). So it is not surprising that in the United States—a pluralistic and rather loosely integrated society—there are many religious cults and other quasi-religious movements. Some of these movements hold rather esoteric beliefs; others are based on concepts from popular psychology and from the "human potential" movement. Among the quasi-religious movements we will discuss in this section, none attracts a large following, and most do not attempt to articulate a comprehensive world view which explains the meaning of death, suffering, and injustice. Nonetheless, they have collectively affected a significant segment of the American population—especially in urban areas.

Quasi-religious movements are cult-like in character, and many sociologists have treated them as cults.[11] However, in Chapter 7 I defined a cult as a new religious movement which offers a world view, theodicy, or set of beliefs which departs significantly from traditional religious groups.[12] If a group or movement does not provide a world view that addresses the issues of suffering, death, and injustice, it is not a religion and therefore not a cult in the sense that we have used that word. Nonetheless, there

---

[11] As we found in Chapter 7, cults have been defined in a number of ways. Those who have followed the tradition of Howard Becker in defining cults as religious movements with little sense of group coherence or group cohesion are likely to view these movements as cults.

[12] The Divine Light Mission, the Unification Church and the Hare Krishna provide particularly good examples of cults.

are social movements and organizations in the United States which address themselves to issues of world view, transcendence, or ultimate fulfillment in at least partial ways. Like the invisible religions Luckmann discusses, these outlooks and beliefs can affect the world view of adherents and their overall state of religiosity. Furthermore, some of these movements continue to elaborate their perspectives on life and eventually do develop theodicies and evolve into cults. Some are closer to becoming cults than others, but at this point it will suffice to identify them collectively as quasi-religious movements.

One such orientation is astrology, a set of beliefs about impersonal forces in the universe which profoundly influence human life on earth. These forces can be "read" or predicted through an understanding of the stars. The zodiacal sign under which a person is born is thought to influence significantly (or even determine) one's personality structure and one's thinking processes. Astrology is not a new phenomenon, nor is it limited to any particular age group. It is not organized around a particular group of people (there is no church), there is no ordained clergy or other sanctioned leadership hierarchy, and there is no formal doctrine. Yet, certain principles and beliefs which are transmitted through books and word of mouth are common to those who believe in astrology.

A surprisingly high number of Americans believe in astrology. According to a study conducted in San Francisco (Wuthnow 1976a:158) approximately 10 percent of the respondents reported that they are "firm believers." Many others follow the horoscopes printed in newspapers, know their zodiac sign and the characteristics of persons under that sign, and "half-believe" in the efficacy of astrology (that is, they are not full converts, but they remain open to astrology and believe that there is probably something valid about it). In fact, only 4 percent of those interviewed in the San Francisco study were "firm disbelievers." In this respect, astrology is sometimes integrated into the world views of persons who are members of mainline religious groups. Their religiosity is a synthesis or blend of a traditional religion and astrology. For others who are not active in traditional religious groups, astrology may play a more significant role in their overall world view.[13] One study found that astrology seems to serve as an alternative to conventional religion for some people—especially marginal or subjugated members of society: the poorly educated, nonwhites, females, the unemployed, the overweight, the unmarried, the ill, and the lonely (Wuthnow 1976a:167).

Another form of quasi-religious movement has focused more on the development of untapped human capabilities. Transcendental Meditation, Silva Mind Control, Scientology, and est are examples of this type of movement. Transcendental Meditation is a meditation technique which bears some re-

---

[13] Among those who are in mainline religious groups, the fatalism and predestination emphasis of astrology may be countered somewhat by Jewish or Christian perspectives.

semblance to yoga. Its advocates insist that it is not a new religion, and practitioners include both people who are active in traditional religious groups and those who are by traditional measures nonreligious. Some persons use this technique as a means of relaxation, others seek to tap the "cosmic consciousness" which is the ultimate source of energy in the universe.

T.M. was started in the late 1960s by a Hindu teacher, Maharishi Mahesh Yogi. It involves chanting a *mantra*—a word, phrase, or sound which is given to each recruit. A mantra is not to be shared with others, but chanting one and concentrating exclusively on it offers one a channel to inner bliss. T.M. masters maintain that such social problems as war, poverty, crime, and racism would disappear if everyone would engage in transcendental meditation. They maintain that if everyone were in tune with the cosmic consciousness, such problems would not exist. People would be more relaxed and more able to fulfill their cosmic purposes (Needleman 1970:134). T.M. claims it is not a religion, but only a discipline of meditation. While it was founded by a Hindu leader, it is used by some Christians and by persons unaffiliated with any religious group. In fact, a poll conducted in 1972 indicated that approximately 4 percent of the American public practice T.M. (Princeton Religion Research Center 1980:34). While this includes only a small percentage of the population, it does mean that a much larger number of people are involved in T.M. than in any of the religious cults which have received so much attention.

Silva Mind Control, Scientology, and est are movements which are more highly organized and which have an internal stratification system. All three are related to popular psychology and parapsychology (belief in clairvoyance, telepathic communication, and psychic healing), and all three are based on education models. Silva Mind Control offers to train people in "psychic powers," while Scientology and est offer to help people become "clear" and to maximize their human potential. The more courses one takes, the higher one moves in the stratification system of the group. This, of course, enhances instrumental commitment, for one makes a financial investment (the courses are not cheap) and begins to rise in the system of respectability and esteem within the group (Bainbridge and Stark 1980b; Bainbridge 1978; Wallis 1977). Some observers view these movements as essentially business enterprises (the courses are substantial sources of income) which sell a popular psychology/self-help product. They do seem to operate on the fringes of both religion and popular psychology. However, Scientology is very explicit about its claim to be a religious movement,[14] and est has increasingly moved in the direction of claiming access to ultimate

---

[14] The original movement started by Ron Hubbard was called Dianetics and was set forth as a *science*. In 1955, Hubbard recast his theories as a religion by incorporating into the Founding Church of Scientology. This was presumably to distinguish his system from empirical investigation so that it could not be disproven by other scientists (Bainbridge and Stark 1980).

truth. (Werner Erhardt, the founder of est, started out in Scientology and later formed his own group. Many of the teachings of est and much of the jargon are borrowed from Scientology.)

The quasi-religious movements discussed here are only illustrative of a number of such movements which offer inner peace, ultimate fulfillment, spiritual expansion, or insights into the "truth" about human existence. Meher Baba, Spiritual Scientists, Association for Research and Enlightenment, Spiritual Frontiers Fellowship, and I Ching are only a few of the many other religious movements one might explore. Whether some of these are actually new religions may be debatable, but they do seem to represent a form of spirituality which might influence traditional religiosity or serve as an alternative mode of religion. For example, a person may use transcendental meditation to relax, to get into deeper touch with his or her inner self, or to tap a cosmic source of energy. Yet, that person may not consider this activity "prayer," and may not respond positively to other traditional measures of religiosity (doctrinal orthodoxy, church attendance, and so on). Likewise, a person who believes in astrology may not be religious in traditional ways, but he or she may have a world view which offers to explain the meaning (or at least the cause) of events. Any empirical studies of religiosity which attempt to explain current trends and likely patterns for the future must take into account the possibility that religiosity is not declining, but is changing in both form and substance.

The nature of religiosity in America does seem to be changing somewhat. World views of Americans, including those who are active in traditional religious groups, appear to be somewhat more this-worldly (or *secular,* if you prefer that term). There also seems to be less willingness to assent to traditional doctrines. This may very well be a sign of an increase in the privatization of religiosity and an increase in syncretistic world views. At this point we have little comparative data for firm generalizations. The meaning systems of people have, no doubt, always been characterized by a good deal of syncretism, but because of changes in access to the mass public due to television and other mass media, self-help groups and others espousing their own philosophy of life probably have more influence on common citizens than in earlier eras. This may account for more individuality in meaning systems.

Whether this is a trend which will have unfortunate consequences for the *society as a whole* remains to be seen. The trend *may* have negative effects for the *established churches:* if fewer people feel committed to the theology which traditional religions espouse, it could involve a decrease in commitment to those organizations. On the other hand, privatization may bestow other offsetting benefits to the society—and perhaps even to religious organizations. Predictions at this point are highly speculative. The recent downturn in traditional forms of religiosity may be the beginning of a pattern, but at present the attendance levels at conventional American churches are much higher than they were in Puritan days and are higher than other industrialized nations in the modern world.

My own interpretation is that religion is not in a declining phase—but readers should remember that I use a broad definition of religion. Systems of meaning which offer to explain the meaning of human events through a world view, an ethos, and a system of symbols are not likely to disappear. However, certain traditional views and certain established religious institutions may well decline in their influence.[15] Whether the reader views this change of religiosity as a decline in religion will be determined largely by his or her operational definition of religion.

Religion and Society: A Continuing Interaction

The Continuing Functions of Religion

Religion is not likely to disappear because it serves an important function in the lives of people. It provides a system of meaning which protects the individual from the terror of chaos and meaninglessness. Geertz (1966) and Evans-Prichard (1972) reported that their informants in nonindustrial societies were quite willing to abandon their theodicy or their explanation of events if a more plausible one came along; what they adamantly refused to do was to give up their explanation for none at all, to leave events to themselves and attribute them with no meaning. While a few academics and other existentialists in modern society may be comfortable with the idea of living in a world where life, death, and suffering have no ultimate meaning or purpose, most people want to know why?—or why me? Like Geertz's Javanese informants, we are also willing to abandon our system of meaning if a more plausible one comes along, but not many of us will abandon it for no explanation at all. And of course, our current religious organizations work very hard to maintain a structure of plausibility so that we will not readily abandon traditional systems.

But religious organizations are also sustained because they meet a secondary need: that of belonging. In a rapidly changing society, in which large numbers of people are geographically mobile, many people live a substantial distance from their extended families. Friendships can fulfill some of the need for close association, but religious groups are common places in which individuals and families seek close relationships. Religious groups provide a continuing sense of identity and belonging for people in a society where everything else seems to change. To be sure, not all religious groups fulfill this function with equal effectiveness, but the fact that cults draw their memberships primarily through the affective commitment process is evidence of its importance in our society.

---

[15] If decline in traditional religiosity does occur, it will likely happen primarily among those of higher socioeconomic standing (Newport 1979) and among persons who are marginal in American society (that is, who are poorly integrated into the social system).

Of course, religion is also dysfunctional in certain respects—such as the contribution of some religious groups to bigotry and narrow-mindedness. In societies in which all members of the society are members of the same religion, religious particularism is probably somewhat functional for the society; external conflict contributes to intrasocietal harmony. In a pluralistic society, particularism may be much more of a problem, for it causes intrasocietal discord. Religion will likely continue to be dysfunctional in certain respects.

The Continuing Conflicts of Religion

Religion will, no doubt, continue to be manifested in a variety of ways, some of them in conflict with one another. As we have seen in this study, religion is manifested in individual faith which may or may not correspond well with the world view set forth by the group. Furthermore, a particular congregation may be in tune with the official position of the denomination or it may hold to a form of folk religion. Beyond this, the system of belief, symbol, and ritual may or may not be well integrated and coherent. And, of course, religion is manifested not only in a world view and ethos, but also in institutions—with roles, statuses, financial resources, and all the dilemmas and dysfunctions that are associated with complex organizations. There is a strain toward coherence and consistency among these various elements of religion, but the fit has never been perfect, and is not likely to be so in the future.

A certain amount of conflict and dissension is likely to be a perpetual feature of religion. This need not be considered an entirely negative statement. Dissonance is the catalyst to change and growth. Many religious groups recognize the good that can come from dissent and disharmony, and refer to organizational or cognitive restlessness as the "movement of the Holy Spirit." Conflict and consensus are closely related phenomena, and all healthy organizations need a good dose of each. Religion is no exception. It is, therefore, safe to predict that religion will continue to be characterized by conflict and dissonance within a context of consensus. The specific mixture of each in a given religious group will affect its character, and perhaps its ability to survive.[16] The existence of conflict—within religious groups and between religious groups—is likely to persist in the future.

---

[16] Obviously too much conflict can destroy a group, but a total consensus is no assurance of survival. A group can create a plausibility structure which enhances a high degree of group harmony. But the belief system may seem utterly implausible to nonmembers, and the group may not recruit enough new members to sustain its survival. The Shakers (who were celibate and had to recruit new members) sustained a high degree of internal consensus, but have faded almost completely out of existence after surviving for two hundred years. This is an extreme example, but it serves to illustrate the point that internal consensus is not a guarantee of survival if the group has an outlook contrary to that of the larger society. Compromise may be necessary for survival, and those same compromises may, in turn, lead to internal conflicts.

The Continuing Interaction of Religion and Society

Religion, in its many manifestations, will no doubt continue to be interrelated with the larger society in a multifaceted and complex manner. We have found, for example, that social conditions affect the likelihood of a cult coming into existence. We have found that one's faith may have an effect on one's economic behavior and on one's economic fortunes, and that one's economic standing may, in turn, influence the type of theodicy one accepts. Among subjugated groups of people, we found that their theodicy was shaped by their social standing and that their response to it (militancy or passivity) was affected by their theodicy.

We also found that various dimensions of the religious system may have contradictory effects on social behavior. Certain teachings of the Protestant reformers were explicitly hostile to capitalistic enterprise, even while other teachings may have unintentionally contributed to the rise of capitalism. We find that in contemporary mainline Protestant denominations, equal treatment of men and women is the official norm. Ordination of women is endorsed, yet institutional factors within the religious system mitigate against clergywomen being hired. Likewise, informal group norms within the religious group may contribute to racism and sexism, even while the official statements of the church repudiate such prejudice. In fact, religious doctrines may firmly renounce one kind of prejudice (dominative racism) even while they contribute unwittingly to another form of antipathy (aversive racism). We have also found that antipathies and discriminatory actions which appeared to be religiously based are sometimes rooted in deeper social cleavages (such as ethnic conflicts) or in other social processes (such as the sex-role conflicts which were at the root of the postmedieval witch-hunts). Religion is sometimes cause of social processes, sometimes effect, and sometimes merely a correlate. It is this complexity of the relationship which makes generalizations so difficult. It is precisely this complexity which also makes the sociological study of religion so fascinating. This complex interweaving of religion and society—in all the various dimensions of the religious system—will also be characteristic of religion in the future.

These generalizations—that religion will continue to serve certain functions, that it will continue to have internal tensions and cause external conflicts, and that it will continue to be interwoven with society in complex ways—are very broad ones. Specific generalizations must be reserved for specific groups. If there is one insight that we can glean from past predictions, it is that one cannot accurately make specific generalizations about such a broad spectrum of groups and behaviors (i.e., religion in general). With the tools of analysis provided in this text, however, readers should have an idea of the way in which sociologists investigate the social processes of any specific group and predict its probable future.

Summary

There is little agreement among sociologists on whether religion is increasing, declining, or simply holding its own in America. Part of the disagreement depends on whether one looks at trends of the past few decades or longer-term patterns. One's definition of religion is also relevant in interpreting the trends. Those using a substantive definition are somewhat more likely to see a decline in religion; those employing a functional definition tend to point to changes in religion—with emphasis on alternative forms of religiosity. Closely related to this is one's assessment of the privatization factor. Some scholars believe the individualization of religion is evidence of its decline; others herald it as indicative of a change that may ultimately strengthen the impact of religion. Finally, the low levels of religious involvement by young adults is interpreted as a sign of lean times ahead for American denominations. However, some scholars maintain that low levels of participation by young adults have been characteristic of every generation and are nothing new. Within a decade or so we should have a fairly firm answer to this latter issue. The others may not be resolved as definitively.

Alternative forms of religion have taken on several forms. One of the most widely studied of these is civil religion—a meaning system which explores the ultimate significance of the nation. This type of "religion" has both prophetic and priestly forms and can be studied in official or folk versions. Other approaches to alternative religions have focused on "invisible" or privatized religion. This involves a study of the world views or ultimate meaning systems which individuals construct from many sources. A third alternative form of religiosity is that provided by quasi-religious movements. These are loosely integrated movements, some based on esoteric beliefs, and others on concepts from popular psychology. These movements normally do not claim to offer a total world view or holistic meaning system, but they influence one's religious outlook. Moreover, some of these movements eventually do claim to offer access to ultimate truth and meaning. Hence, they become religious cults. Loosely integrated and rapidly changing societies like the United States tend to generate more of these quasi-religious movements than more stable and highly integrated societies. The future developments of these groups and their impacts remain to be seen.

Religion is not likely to disappear in the future because it serves important functions in the lives of many people. Although some of the societal functions of religion have changed, meaning and belonging continue to be important human concerns which religion helps to satisfy. In the past, religion has also been characterized by a variety of internal and external conflicts. It seems safe to predict that this pattern will continue. Religion and society interact in many ways, religion being sometimes the cause and other times the effect of social patterns in the larger culture and social structure. One cannot accurately generalize about the effects of religion without specifying a particular religion or even a particular aspect of religion. Likewise, the future impact of religion will be characterized by diversity. The methods of analysis provided in this text should provide readers with an understanding of how to approach any specific religion from a sociological perspective.

Epilogue
The Sociological Perspective on Religion: A Concluding Comment

Sociology seeks to understand the social processes of religion. Because the discipline is limited to empirical investigation, it does not address the truth or falsity of a religious system. The researcher adopts a posture of at least temporary agnosticism. Nonetheless, explanations of cause and effect are offered with only empirically identifiable causes being noted. Hence, the effect is apparently to explain away any supernatural causes. Sociology offers only one lens or one vantage point for understanding religious processes, and it tends to operate within the confines of that vantage point. Other disciplines and other vantage points can offer other insights.

Furthermore, the interpretations of causality which are presented in this book represent the current understandings of sociologists, and the social sciences remain ever open to new data and new perspectives. Like Geertz's Javanese informants, social scientists are willing to accept a new interpretation if it seems more plausible and if the data support it. The discipline will continue to develop, and new data may prove or disprove theories about religious behavior which now seem plausible. Methods of data collection and data interpretation are constantly being challenged and reassessed. Even the naturalistic bias of empiricism—with its stance of temporary agnosticism—is being challenged in some quarters. This naturalistic bias has caused some scholars to posit an alternative assumption; they have attempted to formulate empirical research procedures and sociological theories which assume the reality and efficacy of the supernatural (Garrett 1974; Poloma 1982a). It remains to be seen whether these efforts will bear fruit or are futile attempts to overcome the innate limitations of an empirical discipline.

Regardless, the meaning of a transcendent dimension of life for individuals can never be fully grasped through objective, scientific study. Margaret Poloma (1982b) insists that scientific empiricism is itself a world view and that the determinism of the social sciences can dull one's sensitivity to the mystical, intuitive, symbolic-imagistic side of life.[1] Milton Yinger (1970:2) states the case eloquently:

> No one would claim that the analysis of paint, painter, and patron exhausts the meaning of art; we are becoming cautious about making equivalent claims for the analysis of religion. The scientist must realize that propositions derived from objective study do not exhaust the meaning of things.

With Yinger and O'Dea, I remain convinced that neither theism nor atheism are inherently unsophistocated. Both are assumptions about the nature of the world which deserve our respect.

The purpose of this text has been neither to destroy the faith of believers nor to make believers out of skeptics. The purpose has been to help readers gain insight into the complexity of religion and the relationship between religion and society. In the process, the views of readers (including their world views) may have been changed or modified. Sometimes the insights of social scientists are unsettling, for they challenge our assumptions about reality. But that is the nature of the search for truth—the seeker must be willing to follow the data wherever it leads. Certainly sociology does not offer the *whole* truth about religion or about any aspect of human life, but sociological investigation can *contribute* to a *holistic* understanding of human experience—including religious experience. As I suggested in Chapter 1, sociological study of religion cannot be proven to be directly beneficial to religious faith, but surely ignorance is more harmful in the long run than is disquieting knowledge. Likewise for nonbelievers, ignorance of this phenomenon—which is so important to many people—leaves a gap that prevents a holistic understanding of human behavior.

Future contributions to the understanding of religion will likely require two characteristics: uncompromising academic rigor and an honest recognition of the limitations of our current knowledge. Certainly, there is much that we do not know about religion and about religious behavior. I only hope that my own fascination with the sociology of religion has been contagious to the readers, and that this brief introduction will serve only as the beginning of a continuing study.

---

[1] Wuthnow (1976b) has also treated social science as a world view or an invisible religion. Those interested in pursuing this issue will want to see Polanyi (1946, 1949) as well.

Bibliography

Aberle, David F.
  1966: *The Peyote Religion among the Navaho.* Chicago: Aldine.

Alba, Richard D.
  1976: "Social Assimilation among American Catholic National-Origin Groups." *American Sociological Review* (December):1030–1046.

Alba, Richard D., and Ronald C. Kessler
  1979: "Patterns of Interethnic Marriage among American Catholics." *Social Forces* (June):1124–1140.

Allport, Gordon W.
  1950: *The Individual and His Religion.* New York: Macmillan.
  1966: "The Religious Context of Prejudice." *Journal for the Scientific Study of Religion* (Fall):447–457.

Alston, Jon P.
  1969: "Occupational Placement and Mobility of Protestants and Catholics, 1953–1964." *Review of Religious Research* (Spring):135–140.

Alston, Jon P., and William Alex McIntosh
  1979: "An Assessment of the Determinants of Religious Participation." *The Sociological Quarterly* (Winter):49–62.

Ammerman, Nancy
  1980: "The Civil Rights Movement and the Clergy in a Southern Community." *Sociological Analysis* (Winter):339–350.

Anderson, Alan, and Raymond Gordon
  1978: "Witchcraft and the Status of Women—The Case of England." *British Journal of Sociology* (June):171–184.

Anderson, Charles
  1970: *White Protestant Americans.* Englewood Cliffs, N.J.: Prentice-Hall.

Andrews, Edward Deming
  1963: *The People Called Shakers.* New enlarged ed. New York: Dover Publications.

Argyle, Michael, and Benjamin Beit-Hallahmi
1975: *The Social Psychology of Religion.* Boston: Routledge & Kegan Paul.

Arnold, Eberhard and Emmy
1974: *Seeking for the Kingdom of God: Origins of the Bruderhof Communities.* Ed. by Heini and Annemarie Arnold Rifton, N.Y.: Plough Publishing House.

Bainbridge, William Sims
1978: *Satan's Power: Ethnography of a Deviant Psychotherapy Cult.* Berkeley: University of California Press.

Bainbridge, William Sims, and Rodney Stark
1979: "Cult Formation: Three Compatible Models." *Sociological Analysis* (Winter):283–295.
1980a: "Client and Audience Cults in America." *Sociological Analysis* (Fall):199–214.
1980b: "Scientology: To Be Perfectly Clear." *Sociological Analysis* (Summer):128–136.
1981: "The Consciousness Reformation Reconsidered." *Journal for the Scientific Study of Religion* (March):1–15.

Balch, Robert W.
1980: "Looking Behind the Scenes in a Religious Cult: Implications for the Study of Conversion." *Sociological Analysis* (Summer):137–143.

Balch, Robert W., and David Taylor
1976: "Salvation in a UFO." *Psychology Today* (October):58–66, 106.
1977: "Seekers and Saucers." *American Behavioral Scientist* (July/August):839–860.

Barnes, Douglas F.
1978: "Charisma and Religious Leadership: An Historical Analysis." *Journal for the Scientific Study of Religion* (March):1–17.

Barnouw, Victor
1982: *An Introduction to Anthropology: Ethnology.* 4th ed. Homewood, Ill.: Dorsey Press.

Barrett, William, ed.
1956: *Zen Buddhism: Selected Writings of D. T. Suzuki.* Garden City, New York: Doubleday.

Barrish, Gerald, and Michael R. Welch
1980: "Student Religiosity and Discriminatory Attitudes Toward Women." *Sociological Analysis* (Spring):66–73.

Batson, C. Daniel
1975: "Rational Processing or Rationalization? The Effect of Disconfirming Information on a Stated Religious Belief." *Journal of Personality and Social Psychology* (July):176–184.
1977: "Experimentation in Psychology of Religion: An Impossible Dream." *Journal for the Scientific Study of Religion* (December):413–418.
1979: "Experimentation in Psychology of Religion: Living with or in a Dream?" *Journal for the Psychology of Religion* (March):90–93.

Batson, C. Daniel, Stephen J. Naifeh, and Suzanne Pate
    1978: "Social Desireability, Religious Orientation, and Racial Prejudice."
    Journal for the Scientific Study of Religion (March):31–41.

Bayer, Alan E.
    1975: "Sexist Students in American Colleges: A Descriptive Note." *Journal
    of Marriage and the Family* (May):391–396.

Beck, Marc
    1978: "Pluralist Theory and Church Policy Positions on Racial and Sexual
    Equality." *Sociological Analysis* (Winter):338–350.

Becker, Howard
    1932: *Systematic Sociology*. New York: John Wiley & Sons.

Bellah, Robert N.
    1970a: "Christianity and Symbolic Realism." *Journal for the Scientific Study of
    Religion* (Summer):89–96.
    1970b: "Civil Religion in America." Pp. 168–215 in *Beyond Belief: Essays on
    Religion in a Post Industrial World*. New York: Harper & Row.
    1970c: "Religious Evolution." Pp. 20–50 in *Beyond Belief: Essays on Religion
    in a Post Industrial World*. New York: Harper & Row.
    1974: "American Civil Religion in the 1970's." Pp. 255–272 in *American Civil
    Religion*. Ed. by Russell E. Richey and Donald G. Jones. New York: Harper
    & Row.
    1975: *The Broken Covenant: American Civil Religion in Time of Trial*. New York:
    The Seabury Press.

Belth, Nathan C.
    1979: *A Promise to Keep*. New York: Times Books.

Benedict, Ruth
    1934: *Patterns of Culture*. Boston: Houghton Mifflin.

Benz, Ernest
    1964: "On Understanding Non-Christian Religions." Pp. 3–9 in *Religion,
    Culture, and Society*. Ed. by Louis Schneider. New York: John Wiley & Sons.

Berger, Peter L.
    1961: *The Noise of Solemn Assemblies*. Garden City, New York: Doubleday.
    1963: "Charisma and Religious Innovation: The Social Location of Israelite
    Prophecy." *American Sociological Review* (December):940–950.
    1967: *The Sacred Canopy*. Garden City, N.Y.: Doubleday. Copyright © 1967
    by Peter L. Berger. Reprinted by permission of Doubleday & Company,
    Inc.
    1969: *A Rumor of Angels*. Garden City, N.Y.: Doubleday.
    1974: "Some Second Thoughts on Substantive Versus Functional Definitions
    of Religion." *Journal for the Scientific Study of Religion* (June):125–133.
    1979: *The Heretical Imperative*. Garden City, N.Y.: Anchor Press.
    1981: "The Class Struggle in American Religion." *The Christian Century*
    (February):194–200.

Berger, Peter L., and Thomas Luckmann
    1966: *The Social Construction of Reality*. Garden City, N.Y.: Doubleday.

Berry, Brewton, and Henry L. Tischler
1978: *Race and Ethnic Relations.* 4th ed. Boston: Houghton Mifflin.

Bestor, Arthur
1957: *Backwoods Utopias.* 2nd enlarged ed. Philadelphia: University of Pennsylvania Press.

Bianchi, Eugene C., and Rosemary Ruether
1976: *From Machismo to Mutuality: Essays on Sexism and Women-Men Liberation.* New York: Paulist Press.

Bibby, Reginald W.
1978: "Why Conservative Churches Really Are Growing: Kelley Revisited." *Journal for the Scientific Study of Religion* (June):129–138.

Bibby, Reginald W., and Merlin B. Brinkerhoff
1973: "The Circulation of the Saints: A Study of People Who Join Conservative Churches." *Journal for the Scientific Study of Religion* (September):273–283.

Bird, Phyllis
1974: "Images of Women in the Old Testament." Pp. 41–88 in *Religion and Sexism.* Ed. by Rosemary Radford Ruether. New York: Simon & Schuster.

Bonfani, Leo
1971: *The Witchcraft Hysteria of 1692.* Wakefield, Mass.: Pride Publishing.

Bouma, Gary D.
1973: "Beyond Lenski: A Critical Review of Recent Protestant Ethic Research." *Journal for the Scientific Study of Religion* (June):141–155.
1980: "Keeping the Faithful: Patterns of Membership Retention in the Christian Reformed Church." *Sociological Analysis* (Fall):259–264.

Bringhurst, Newell G.
1981: *Saints, Slaves, and Blacks: The Changing Place of Black People Within Mormonism.* Westport, Conn.: Greenwood Press.

Bromley, David G., and Anson D. Shupe, Jr.
1979: *Moonies in America: Cult, Church and Crusade.* Beverly Hills, Calif.: Sage.
1980: "The Tnevnoc Cult." *Sociological Analysis* (Winter):361–366.
1981: *Strange Gods: The Great American Cult Scare.* Boston: Beacon Press.

Buber, Martin
1958: *Hasidism and Modern Man.* Ed. and trans. by Maurice Friedman. New York: Harper & Row.

Bullough, Vern L.
1973: *The Subordinate Sex: A History of Attitudes Toward Women.* Urbana, Ill.: University of Illinois Press.

Bultmann, Rudolf
1958: *Jesus Christ and Mythology.* New York: Charles Scribner's Sons.

Byrne, Donn, and Carl McGraw
1964: "Interpersonal Attraction Toward Negroes." *Human Relations* (August):201–213.

Bryne, Donn, and Terry J. Wong
1962: "Racial Prejudice, Interpersonal Attraction, and Assumed Dissimilarity of Attitudes." *Journal of Abnormal and Social Psychology* (October):246–253.

Calvin, John
1952: *Golden Booklet of the True Christian Life.* Trans. by Henry J. Van Andel. Grand Rapids, Mich.: Baker Book House.

Campbell, Ernest Q., and Thomas F. Pettigrew
1959: *Christians in Racial Crisis.* Washington, D.C.: Public Affairs Press.

Cannon, Walter B.
1942: " 'Voodoo' Death." *American Anthropologist* (April):169–181.

Carden, Maren Lockwood
1969: *Oneida.* New York: Harper & Row.

Carr, Leslie G., and William H. Hauser
1976: "Anomie and Religiosity: An Empirical Re-Examination." *Journal for the Scientific Study of Religion* (March):69–74.

Chalfant, H. Paul, Robert E. Beckley, and C. Eddie Palmer
1981: *Religion in Contemporary Society.* Sherman Oaks, Calif.: Alfred Publishing Co.

Chambers, Patricia Price, and Paul H. Chalfant
1978: "A Changing Role or the Same Old Handmaidens: Women's Role in Today's Church." *Review of Religious Research* (Winter):192–197.

Christ, Carol P., and Judith Plaskow, eds.
1979: *Womanspirit Rising: A Feminist Reader in Religion.* New York: Harper & Row.

Clark, Elizabeth, and Herbert Richardson, eds.
1977: *Women and Religion.* New York: Harper & Row.

Cleage, Albert B., Jr.
1968: *The Black Messiah.* New York: Sheed and Ward.

Clinebell, Howard J.
1965: *Mental Health Through Christian Community.* Nashville: Abingdon Press.

Cohn, Norman
1964: "Medieval Millenarism: It's Bearing on the Comparative Study of Millenarian Movements." Pp. 168–181 in *Religion, Culture, and Society.* Ed. by Louis Schneider. New York: John Wiley & Sons.
1975: *Europe's Inner Demons.* New York: Basic Books.

Cole, William A., and Phillip E. Hammond
1974: "Religious Pluralism, Legal Development, and Societal Complexity: Rudimentary Forms of Civil Religion." *Journal for the Scientific Study of Religion* (June):177–189.

Coleman, John A.
1970: "Civil Religion." *Sociological Analysis* (Summer):67–77.

Comte, August
1880: *A General View of Positivism.* 2nd ed. Trans. by J. H. Bridges. London: Reeves and Turner.

Cone, James H.
1969: *Black Theology and Black Power.* New York: Seabury Press.
1970: *Liberation.* Philadelphia: J. B. Lippincott.
1972: *The Spirituals and the Blues.* Westport, Conn.: Greenwood Press.

Conway, Flo, and Jim Siegelman
    1978: *Snapping: America's Epidemic of Sudden Personality Change.* Philadelphia:
    J. B. Lippincott.

Coriden, James A., ed.
    1977: *Sexism and Church Law.* New York: Paulist Press.

Coser, Lewis A.
    1954: *The Functions of Social Conflict.* New York: Free Press.
    1967: *Continuities in the Study of Social Conflict.* New York: Free Press.

Cox, Harvey
    1964: *On Not Leaving It to the Snake.* New York: Macmillan.
    1965: *The Secular City.* New York: Macmillan.

Cross, Whitney R.
    1950: *The Burned Over District: The Social and Intellectual History of Enthusiastic
    Religion in Western New York, 1800–1850.* Ithaca, N.Y.: Cornell University
    Press.

Crowley, James W., and James A. Ballweg
    1971: "Religious Preference and Worldly Success." *Sociological Analysis*
    (Summer):71–80.

Daly, Mary
    1968: *The Church and the Second Sex.* New York: Harper & Row.
    1970: "Women and the Catholic Church." Pp. 124–138 in *Sisterhood is Powerful.*
    Ed. by Robin Morgan. New York: Vintage Books.

Darley, J. M., and C. Daniel Batson
    1973: "From Jeruselem to Jericho: A Study of Situational and Dispositional
    Variables in Helping Behavior." *Journal of Personality and Social Psychology*
    (July):100–108.

Davidson, James D.
    1975: "Glock's Model of Religious Commitment: Assessing Some Different
    Approaches and Results." *Review of Religious Research* (Winter):83–93.
    1977: "Socio-Economic Status and Ten Dimensions of Religious Commitment."
    Sociology and Social Research (July):462–485.

Davidson, James D., and Dean D. Knudsen
    1977: "A New Approach to Religious Commitment." *Sociological Focus*
    (April):151–173.

Davis, Kingsley
    1949: *The Human Society.* New York: Macmillan.

Davis, Rex, and James T. Richardson
    1976: "The Organization and Functioning of the Children of God." *Sociological
    Analysis* (Winter):321–339.

DeJong, Gordon F., Joseph E. Faulkner, and Rex H. Warland
    1976: "Dimensions of Religiosity Reconsidered: Evidence From a Cross-
    Cultural Study." *Social Forces* (June):866–890.

Demerath, N. J. III
    1965: *Social Class in American Protestantism.* Chicago: Rand McNally.

Dempewolff, J. A.
1974: "Some Correlates of Feminism." *Psychological Reports* (April):671–676.

Deutscher, Irwin
1966: "Words and Deeds: Social Science and Social Policy." *Social Problems* (Winter):235–254.
1973: *What We Say, What We Do.* Glenview, Ill.: Scott, Foresman.

De Vaux, Roland
1961: *Ancient Israel.* 2 vols. New York: McGraw-Hill.

Doress, Irvin, and Jack Nusan Porter
1978: "Kids in Cults." *Society* (May/June):69–71.

Douglas, Mary
1966: *Purity and Danger.* London: Routledge and Kegan Paul.
1968: "Pollution." Pp. 336–341 in *International Encyclopedia of the Social Sciences.* Vol. XII. Edited by David Sills. New York: Macmillan and Free Press.

Douglass, Jane Dempsey
1974: "Women and the Continental Reformation." Pp. 292–318 in *Religion and Sexism.* Ed. by Rosemary Radford Ruether. New York: Simon & Schuster.

Downton, James V., Jr.
1979: *Sacred Journeys: The Conversion of Young Americans to Divine Light Mission.* New York: Columbia University Press.
1980: "An Evolutionary Theory of Spiritual Conversion and Commitment: The Case of Divine Light Mission." *Journal for the Scientific Study of Religion* (December):381–396.

Dunlap, Knight
1946: *Religion: Its Function in Human Life.* New York: McGraw-Hill.

Durkheim, Emile
1965: *The Elementary Forms of the Religious Life.* Trans. by Joseph Ward Swain. New York: Free Press. (Originally published in London: George Allen and Unwin, 1915).

Duska, Ronald, and Mariellen Whelan
1975: *Moral Development: A Guide to Piaget and Kohlberg.* New York: Paulist Press.

Dynes, Russell R.
1955: "Church-Sect Typology and Socioeconomic Status." *American Sociological Review* (October):555–560.

Eddy, Mary Baker G.
1886: *Science and Health With Key to the Scriptures.* 19th ed., rev. Boston: Published by the author.

Edwards, Jonathan
1966: *Jonathan Edwards: Basic Writings.* Ed. by Ola Elizabeth Winslow. New York: New American Library.

Eichler, Margrit
1972: *Charismatic and Ideological Leadership in Secular and Religious Millenarian*

    Movements: A Sociological Study. Ph. D. dissertation, Duke University. Ann Arbor, Mich.: University Microfilms.

Eister, Allan W.
    1967: "Toward a Radical Critique of Church-Sect Typologizing." *Journal for the Scientific Study of Religion* (April):85–90.

Eliade, Mircea
    1959: *The Sacred and the Profane: The Nature of Religion.* Trans: by Willard R. Trask. New York: Harcourt Brace and World.

Enslin, Morton S.
    1930: *The Ethics of Paul.* New York: Harper & Row.

Erikson, Erik H.
    1963: *Childhood and Society.* 2nd ed. New York: W. W. Norton.

Erikson, Kai
    1966: *Wayward Puritans.* New York: John Wiley & Sons.

Estus, Charles, and Michael A. Overington
    1970: "The Meaning and End of Religiosity." *American Journal of Sociology* (March):760–778.

Evans-Prichard, E. E.
    1937: *Witchcraft, Oracles, and Magic among the Azande.* Oxford: Clarendon Press.

Fanfani, Amintore
    1936: *Catholicism, Protestantism, and Capitalism.* New York: Sheed and Ward.

Farber, I. E., Harry F. Harlow, and Louis Jolyon West
    1951: "Brainwashing, Conditioning, and D. D. D. (Debility, Dependency, and Dread)." *Sociometry* (December):271–283.

Fauset, Arthur H.
    1944: *Black Gods of the Metropolis.* Philadelphia: University of Pennsylvania Press.

Feagin, Joe R., and Clairece Booher Feagin
    1978: *Discrimination American Style: Institutional Racism and Sexism.* Englewood Cliffs, N.J.: Prentice-Hall.

Featherman, David L.
    1971: "The Socioeconomic Achievement of White Religio-ethnic Sub-groups: Social and Psychological Explanations." *American Sociological Review* (April):207–222.

Fenton, John H.
    1960: *The Catholic Vote.* New Orleans: Hauser.

Festinger, Leon; Henry W. Riecken; and Stanley Schachter
    1956: *When Prophecy Fails.* New York: Harper & Row.

Fichter, Joseph
    1954: *Social Relations in the Urban Parish.* Chicago: University of Chicago Press.

Fisher, Miles Mark
    1953: *Negro Slave Songs in the United States.* New York: Citadel.

Fitzgerald, Frances
  1981: "A Reporter at Large: A Disciplined, Charging Army." *The New Yorker*
  (May 18):53–141.

Forell, George W.
  1966: *Christian Social Teachings.* Minneapolis: Augsburg Publishing House.

Fowler, James W.
  1981: *Stages of Faith.* San Francisco: Harper & Row.

Fox, William S., and Elton F. Jackson
  1973: "Protestant-Catholic Differences in Educational Achievement and
  Persistence in Schools." *Journal for the Scientific Study of Religion* (March):65–
  84.

Frankl, Viktor E.
  1962: *Man's Search for Meaning.* Rev. ed. New York: Simon & Schuster.
  1967: *Psychotherapy and Existentialism.* New York: Simon & Schuster.

Frazier, E. Franklin
  1957: *Negroes in the United States.* Rev. ed. New York: Macmillan.
  1963: *The negro Church in America.* New York: Schocken Books.

Fredman, Ruth Gruber
  1981: *The Passover Seder.* Philadelphia: University of Pennsylvania Press.

Fry, John R.
  1975: *The Trivialization of the Presbyterian Church.* New York: Harper & Row.

Fukuyama, Yoshio
  1961: "The Major Dimensions of Church Membership." *Review of Religious
  Research* (Spring):154–161.

Gaede, Stan
  1977: "Religious Affiliation, Social Mobility, and the Problem of Causality:
  A Methodological Critique of Catholic-Protestant Socioeconomic
  Achievement Studies." *Review of Religious Research* (Fall):54–62.

Galanter, Mark, Richard Rabkin, Judith Rabkin, and Alexander Deutsch
  1979: "The Moonies: A Psychosocial Study of Conversion and Membership
  in a Contemporary Religious Sect." *American Journal of Psychiatry*
  (February):165–170.

Garrett, William R.
  1974: "Troublesome Transcendence: The Supernatural in the Scientific Study
  of Religion." *Sociological Analysis* (Autumn):167–180.

Geertz, Clifford
  1957: "Ritual and Social Change: A Javanese Example." *American Anthropologist*
  (February):32–54.
  1958: "Ethos, World View and the Analysis of Sacred Symbols." © *The Antioch
  Review.* 17:4 (Winter):421–437. Reprinted by permission of the editors.
  1966: "Religion as a Cultural System." Pp. 1–46 in *Anthropological Approaches
  to the Study of Religion.* Ed. by Michael Banton. London: Tavistock Publications.
  1968: *Islam Observed: Religious Development in Morocco and Indonesia.* Chicago:
  University of Chicago Press.

Gilligan, Carol
1982: *In A Different Voice.* Cambridge, Mass.: Harvard University Press.

Gish, Arthur G.
1970: *The New Left and Christian Radicalism.* Grand Rapids, Mich.: William B. Eerdmans Publishing.
1973: *Beyond the Rat Race.* New Canaan, Conn.: Keats Publishing Co.

Glazer, Nathan
1957: *American Judaism.* Chicago: University of Chicago Press.

Glenn, Norval
1964: "Negro Religion and Negro Status in the United States." Pp. 623–639 in *Religion, Culture, and Society.* Ed. by Louis Schneider. New York: John Wiley and Sons.

Glenn, Norval D., and Ruth Hyland
1967: "Religious Preference and Worldly Success: Some Evidence from National Surveys." *American Sociological Review* (February):73–85.

Glock, Charles Y.
1959: "The Religious Revival in America." Pp. 25–42 in *Religion and the Face of America.* Ed. by Jane Zahn. Berkeley: University of California Press.

Glock, Charles Y., ed.
1973: *Religion in Sociological Perspective: Essays in the Empirical Study of Religion.* Belmont, Calif.: Wadsworth.

Glock, Charles Y., and Rodney Stark
1965: *Religion and Society in Tension.* Chicago: Rand McNally.
1966: *Christian Beliefs and Anti-Semitism.* New York: Harper & Row.

Gluckman, Max
1965: *Politics, Law, and Ritual in Tribal Society.* Oxford: Basil Blackwell.

Gmelch, George J.
1971: "Baseball Magic." *Transaction* (June):39–41; 54.

Gockel, Galen L.
1969: "Income and Religious Affiliation: A Regression Analysis." *American Journal of Sociology* (May):632–647.

Goen, C. C.
1970: "Fundamentalism in America." Pp. 85–93 in *American Mosaic.* Ed. by Phillip E. Hammond and Benton Johnson. New York: Random House.

Goldman, Ronald
1964: *Religious Thinking from Childhood to Adolescence.* New York: Seabury Press.
1965: *Readiness For Religion.* New York: Seabury Press.

Goldstein, Sidney
1969: "Socio-economic Differentials among Religious Groups in the United States." *American Journal of Sociology* (May):612–631.

Goode, Erich
1967: "Some Critical Observations on the Church-Sect Typology." *Journal for the Scientific Study of Religion* (April):69–77.

Gorsuch, Richard L., and Daniel Aleshire
1974: "Christian Faith and Ethnic Prejudice: A Review and Interpretation of Research." *Journal for the Scientific Study of Religion* (September):281–307.

Greeley, Andrew M.
1963: *Religion and Career: A Study of College Graduates.* New York: Sheed and Ward.
1969a: "Continuities in Research on the Religious Factor." *American Journal of Sociology* (November):355–359.
1969b: *Religion in the Year 2000.* New York: Sheed and Ward.
1970: "Comment on Educational Expectations." *American Sociological Review* (September):917–918.
1971: *Why Can't They Be Like Us?* New York: E. P. Dutton.
1972: *The Denominational Society.* Glenview, Ill.: Scott, Foresman.
1974: *Ethnicity in the United States.* New York: John Wiley & Sons.
1981: "Catholics and the Upper Middle Class: A Comment on Roof." *Social Forces* (March):824–830.

Green, Robert W., ed.
1959: *Protestantism and Capitalism: The Weber Thesis and Its Critics.* Boston: D.C. Heath.

Hadaway, Christopher Kirk
1978: "Life Satisfaction and Religion: A Reanalysis." *Social Forces* (December):636–643.
1980: "Denominational Switching and Religiosity." *Review of Religious Research* (Supplement):451–461.

Hadaway, C. Kirk, and Wade Clark Roof
1979: "Those Who Stay Religious 'Nones' and Those Who Don't: A Research Note." *Journal for the Scientific Study of Religion* (June):194–200.

Hadden, Jeffrey K.
1970: *The Gathering Storm in the Churches.* Garden City, N.Y.: Doubleday.

Hadden, Jeffrey K., and Raymond C. Rymph
1973: "Social Structure and Civil Rights Involvement: A Case Study of Protestant Ministers." Pp. 149–162 *Religion in Sociological Perspective.* Ed. by Charles Y. Glock. Belmont, Calif.: Wadsworth.

Hammond, Phillip E., and Kirk R. Williams
1976: "The Protestant Ethic Thesis: A Social-Psychological Assessment." *Social Forces* (March):579–589.

Hammond, Phillip E., Luis Salinas, and Douglas Sloane
1978: "Types of Clergy Authority: Their Measurement, Location and Effects." *Journal for the Scientific Study of Religion* (September):241–254.

Hargrove, Barbara
1979: *The Sociology of Religion.* Arlington Heights, Ill.: AHM Publishing Corp.

Hartley, Eugene L.
1946: *Problems in Prejudice.* New York: King's Crown Press.

Hartman, Warren J.
　　1976: *Membership Trends: A Study of Decline and Growth in the United Methodist Church, 1949–1975.* Nashville: Discipleship Resources.

Haugk, Kenneth
　　1976: "Unique Contributions of Churches and Clergy to Community Mental Health." *Community Mental Health Journal* (12):20–28.

Hay, David, and Ann Morisey
　　1978: "Reports of Ecstatic, Paranormal or Religious Experience in the U.S. and Great Britain—A Comparison of Trends." *Journal for the Scientific Study of Religion* (September):255–268.

Henley, Nancy M., and Fred Pincus
　　1978: "Interrelationship of Sexist, Racist and Homosexual Attitudes." *Psychological Reports* (February):83–90.

Herberg, Will
　　1955: *Protestant-Catholic-Jew.* Garden City, N.Y.: Doubleday.
　　1974: "America's Civil Religion: What It Is and Whence It Comes." Pp. 76–88 in *American Civil Religion.* Ed. by Russell E. Ruchey and Donald G. Jones. New York: Harper & Row.

Herskovits, Melville
　　1958: *The Myth of the Negro Past.* Boston: Beacon Press.

Hesselbart, Susan
　　1976: "A Comparison of Attitudes Toward Women and Attitudes Toward Blacks in a Southern City." *Sociological Symposium* (Fall):45–68.

Hesser, Gary, and Andrew J. Weigert
　　1980: "Comparative Dimensions of Liturgy: A Conceptual Framework and Feasibility Application." *Sociological Analysis* (Fall):215–229.

Hills, Stuart L.
　　1980: *Demystifying Social Deviance.* New York: McGraw-Hill.

Hoch-Smith, Judith
　　1978: "Radical Yoruba Female Sexuality: The Witch and the Prostitute." Pp. 245–267 in *Women in Ritual and Symbolic Roles.* Ed. by Judith Hoch-Smith and Anita Spring. New York: Plenum Press.

Hoch-Smith, Judith, and Anita Spring, eds.
　　1978: *Women in Ritual and Symbolic Roles.* New York: Plenum Press.

Hoge, Dean R., and Jackson W. Carroll
　　1973: "Religiosity and Prejudice In Northern and Southern Churches." *Journal for the Scientific Study of Religion* (June):181–197.
　　1975: "Christian Beliefs, Nonreligious Factors, and Anti-Semitism." *Social Forces* (June):581–594.
　　1978: "Determinants of Commitment and Participation in Surburban Protestant Churches." *Journal for the Scientific Study of Religion* (June):107–128.

Hoge, Dean R., and David A. Roozen
　　1979: *Understanding Church Growth and Decline, 1950–1978.* New York: Pilgrim Press.

Holloway, Mark
    1966: *Heavens on Earth.* 2nd ed. New York: Dover Publications.

Homans, George C.
    1941: "Anxiety and Ritual: The Theories of Malinowski and Radcliffe-Brown."
    American Anthropologist (April):164–172.

Hood, Ralph W.
    1970: "Religious Orientation and the Report of Religious Experience." *Journal
    for the Scientific Study of Religion* (Winter):285–291.
    1978: "The Usefulness of the Indiscriminately Pro and Anti Categories of
    Religious Orientation." *Journal for the Scientific Study of Religion*
    (December):419–431.

Hostetler, John
    1968: *Amish Society.* Rev. ed. Baltimore: John Hopkins University Press.

Hudson, Winthrop S.
    1949: "Puritanism and the Spirit of Capitalism." *Church History* (March):3–
    17.
    1973: *Religion in America.* 2nd ed. New York: Charles Scribner's Sons.

Hunt, Larry L., and Janet G. Hunt
    1977: "Black Religion as Both Opiate and Inspiration of Civil Rights Militance:
    Putting Marx's Data To The Test." *Social Forces* (September):1–14.

Hunt, Richard A.
    1972: "Mythological-Symbolic Religious Commitment: The LAM Scales."
    Journal for the Scientific Study of Religion (March):45–52.

Jackson, Elton F., William S. Fox, and Harry J. Crockett, Jr.
    1970: "Religion and Occupational Achievement." *American Sociological Review*
    (February):48–63.

Jacobs, Jerry
    1971: "From Sacred to Secular: The Rationalization of Christian Theology."
    Journal for the Scientific Study of Religion (Spring):1–9.

Jacquet, Constant H., Jr., ed.
    1969: *Yearbook of American and Canadian Churches.* New York: National Council
    Press.
    1982: *Yearbook of American and Canadian Churches.* Nashville: Abingdon Press.
    Copyright © 1982 by National Council of the Churches of Christ in the
    USA. Used by permission of the publisher, Abingdon Press.

James, Janet Wilson, ed.
    1980: *Women in American Religion.* Philadelphia: University of Pennsylvania
    Press.

James, William
    1958: *Varieties of Religious Experience.* New York: New American Library.
    (Originally published in 1902.)

Jenkins, J. Craig
    1977: "Radical Transformation of Organizational Goals." *Administrative Science
    Quarterly* (December):568–586.

Jewett, Paul K.
  1980: *The Ordination of Women.* Grand Rapids, Mich.: William B. Eerdmans Publishing.

Johnson, Benton
  1961: "Do Holiness Sects Socialize in Dominant Values?" *Social Forces* (May):309–316.
  1963: "On Church and Sect." *American Sociological Review* (August):539–549.
  1979: "A Fresh Look at Theories of Secularization." Paper presented to the American Sociological Association. Boston, August 27, 1979.

Johnson, Paul E.
  1959: *Psychology of Religion.* Rev. and enlarged ed. Nashville: Abingdon Press.

Johnstone, Ronald L.
  1975: *Religion and Society in Interaction.* Englewood Cliffs, N.J.: Prentice-Hall.

Jones, W. T.
  1972: "World Views: Their Nature and Their Function." *Current Anthropology* (February):79–109.

Jordan, Winthrop D.
  1968: *White Over Black.* Baltimore: Penguin Books.

Judah, J. Stillson
  1974: *Hare Krishna and the Counterculture.* New York: John Wiley & Sons.

Kahoe, Richard D.
  1974: "The Psychology and Theology of Sexism." *Journal of Psychology and Theology* (Fall):284–290.

Kanter, Rosabeth Moss
  1972: *Commitment and Community.* Cambridge, Mass.: Harvard University Press.

Kelley, Dean M.
  1972: *Why Conservative Churches are Growing.* New York: Harper & Row.
  1978: "Comment: Why Conservative Churches are Still Growing." *Journal for the Scientific Study of Religion* (June):165–172.

Kelsey, George D.
  1965: *Racism and the Christian Understanding of Man.* New York: Charles Scribner's Sons. Copyright © 1965 George D. Kelsey. Reprinted with the permission of Charles Scribner's Sons.

Kephart, William M.
  1976: *Extraordinary Groups: The Sociology of Unconventional Life-Styles.* New York: St. Martin's Press.

Kim, Hei C.
  1977: "The Relationship of Protestant Ethic Beliefs and Values to Achievement." *Journal for the Scientific Study of Religion* (September):255–262.

Kluckhohn, Clyde
  1972: "Myths and Rituals: A General Theory." Pp. 93–105 in *Reader in Comparative Religion: An Anthropological Approach.* 3rd ed. Ed. by William A. Lessa and Evon Z. Vogt. New York: Harper & Row.

Knudsen, Dean D., John R. Earle, and Donald W. Schriver, Jr.
1978: "The Conception of Sectarian Religion: An Effort at Clarification." *Review of Religious Research* (Fall):44–60.

Kohlberg, Lawrence
1971: "From Is To Ought." Pp. 151–284 in *Cognitive Development and Epistemology*. Ed. by T. Mischel. New York: Academic Press.
1980: "Educating for a Just Society: An Updated and Revised Statement." Pp. 455–470 in *Moral Development, Moral Education, and Kohlberg*. Ed. by Brenda Munsey. Birmingham, Ala.: Religious Education Press.

Kohn, Melvin L.
1969: *Class and Conformity: A Study in Values*. Homewood, Ill.: Dorsey Press.

Kovel, Joel
1970: *White Racism: A Psychohistory*. New York: Pantheon Books.

LaBarre, Weston
1962: *They Shall Take Up Serpents: Psychology of the Southern Snake-Handling Cult*. New York: Schocken.
1972: *The Ghost Dance*. New York: Dell.

Landis, Benson Y., ed.
1965: *Yearbook of American Churches*. New York: National Council Press.

Leach, Edmund R.
1972: "Ritualization in Man in Relation to Conceptual and Social Development." Pp. 333–337 in *Reader in Comparative Religion*. 3rd ed. Ed. by William A. Lessa and Evon Z. Vogt. New York: Harper & Row.

Lee, Dallas
1971: *The Cotton Patch Evidence*. New York: Harper & Row.

Lee, Gary R., and Robert W. Clyde
1974: "Religion, Socioeconomic Status, and Anomie." *Journal for the Scientific Study of Religion* (June):35–47.

Lehman, Edward C., Jr.
1980: "Patterns of Lay Resistance to Women in Ministry." *Sociological Analysis* (Winter):317–338.
1981: "Organizational Resistance to Women in Ministry." *Sociological Analysis* (Summer):101–118.

Lenski, Gerhard
1963: *The Religious Factor*. Rev. ed. Garden City, N.Y.: Doubleday. Copyright © 1961 by Gerhard Lenski. Reprinted by permission of Doubleday & Co., Inc.

Lenski, Gerhard, and Jean Lenski
1978: *Human Societies*. 3rd ed. New York: McGraw-Hill.

Lifton, Robert Jay
1969: *Thought Reform and the Psychology of Totalism: A Study of "Brainwashing" in China*. New York: W. W. Norton.

Lincoln, C. Eric
1973: *The Black Muslims in America*. Rev. ed. Boston: Beacon Press.
1974a: "The Power in the Black Church." *Cross Currents* (Spring):3–21.

Lincoln, C. Eric, ed.
1968: *Is Anybody Listening to Black America?* New York: Seabury Press.
1974b: *The Black Experience in Religion.* Garden City, N.J.: Doubleday.

Lipman-Blumen, Jean
1972: "How Ideology Shapes Women's Lives." *Scientific American* (January):33–42.

Lipset, Seymour
1960: *Political Man.* Garden City, N.Y.: Doubleday.

Lipset, Seymour M., and Reinhart Bendix
1959: *Social Mobility in Industrial Society.* Berkeley, Calif.: University of California Press.

Lofland, John
1977: *Doomsday Cult.* Enlarged ed. New York: Irvington Publishers.

Lofland, John and Norman Skonovd
1981: "Conversion Motifs." *Journal for the Scientific Study of Religion* (December):373–385.

Luckmann, Thomas
1967: *The Invisible Religion.* New York: Macmillan.

Luhman, Reid, and Stuart Gilman
1980: *Race and Ethnic Relations.* Belmont, Calif.: Wadsworth.

McCarthy, John D., and Mayer N. Zald
1977: "Resource Mobilization in Social Movements: A Partial Theory." *American Journal of Sociology* (May):1212–1239.

McGaw, Douglas B.
1979: "Commitment and Religious Community: A Comparison of a Charismatic and a Mainline Congregation." *Journal for the Scientific Study of Religion* (June):146–163.
1980: "Meaning and Belonging in a Charismatic Congregation: An Investigation into Sources of Neo-Pentecostal Success." *Review of Religious Research* (Summer):284–301.

McGuire, Meredith B.
1977: "Testimony as a Commitment Mechanism in Catholic Pentecostal Prayer Groups." *Journal for the Scientific Study of Religion* (June):165–168.
1981: Religion: The Social Context. Belmont, Calif.: Wadsworth.

McLaughlin, Eleanor Commo
1974: "Equality of Souls, Inequality of Sexes: Women in Medieval Theology." Pp. 213–266 in *Religion and Sexism.* Ed. by Rosemary Radford Ruether. New York: Simon & Schuster.

McMurry, Mary
1978: "Religion and Women's Sex-Role Traditionalism." *Sociological Focus* (April):81–95.

Machalek, Richard
1977: "Definitional Strategies in the Study of Religion." *Journal for the Scientific Study of Religion* (December):395–401.

Machalek, Richard, and Michael Martin
    1976: "Invisible Religions: Some Preliminary Evidence." *Journal for the Scientific Study of Religion* (December):311–322.

Mack, Raymond W., Raymond J. Murphy, and Seymour Yellin
    1956: "The Protestant Ethic, Level of Aspiration and Social Mobility: An Empirical Test." *American Sociological Review* (June):295–300.

Malinowski, Bronislaw
    1931: "Culture." Pp. 621–645 in *Encyclopaedia of the Social Sciences*, Vol. IV. Ed. by Edwin R. A. Seligman and Alvin Johnson. New York: Macmillan. Reprinted with permission of Macmillan Publishing Co., Inc. Copyright 1931, renewed, 1959 by Macmillan Publishing Co., Inc.
    1936: *The Foundations of Faith and Morals.* London: Oxford University Press.
    1944: *A Scientific Theory of Culture and Other Essays.* Chapel Hill: The University of North Carolina Press.
    1948: *Magic, Science, and Religion and Other Essays.* New York: Free Press, (Reprint ed., Garden City, N.Y.: Doubleday, 1954.)

Marett, R. R.
    1914: *The Threshold of Religion.* London: Methuen & Co.

Markoff, John, and Daniel Regan
    1981: "The Rise and Fall of Civil Religion: Comparative Perspectives." *Sociological Analysis* (Winter):333–352.

Martin, Patricia Yancey, Marie Withers Osmond, Susan Hesselbart, and Meredith Wood
    1980: "The Significance of Gender as a Social and Demographic Correlate of Sex Role Attitudes." *Sociological Focus* (October):383–396.

Martin, William
    1979: "Hearts and Minds." *Texas Monthly* (September):260–266.
    1981: "Time of Repentance, Season of Joy." *Texas Monthly* (December):218–224.

Marty, Martin E.
    1972: "Ethnicity: The Skeleton of Religion in America" *Church History* (March):5–21.
    1974: "Two Kinds of Two Kinds of Civil Religion." Pp. 139–157 in *Civil Religion in America.* Ed. by Russell E. Richey and Donald G. Jones. New York: Harper & Row.

Marx, Gary
    1967: *Protest and Prejudice.* New York: Harper & Row.

Maslow, Abraham
    1964: *Religions, Values, and Peak Experiences.* Columbus, Ohio: Ohio State University Press.

Mason, Karen, and Larry L. Bumpass
    1975: "U.S. Women's Sex Role Ideology, 1970." *American Journal of Sociology* (March):1212–1219.

Mayer, Albert J., and Harry Sharp
    1962: "Religious Preference and Worldly Success." *American Sociological Review* (April):218–227.

Mead, Margaret, ed.
    1955: *Cultural Patterns and Technical Change.* New York: New American Library.
Mead, Sidney E.
    1974: "The Nation With the Soul of a Church." Pp. 45–74 in *American Civil Religion.* Ed. by Russel E. Richey and Donald G. Jones. New York: Harper & Row.
Meier, Harold C.
    1972: "Mother Centeredness and College Youths' Attitudes Towards Social Equality for Women: Some Empirical Findings." *Journal of Marriage and The Family* (February):115–121.
Menschung, Gustav
    1964: "The Masses, Folk Belief, and Universal Religion." Pp. 269–272 in *Religion, Culture, and Society.* Ed. by Louis Schneider. New York: John Wiley & Sons.
Middleton, Russell
    1973: "Do Christian Beliefs Cause Anti-Semitism? A Comment." *American Sociological Review* (February):33–52.
Miller, Robert T., and Ronald B. Flowas
    1977: *Toward Benevolent Neutrality: Church, State and the Supreme Court.* Waco, Tex.: Baylor University Press.
Moberg, David
    1980: "Prison Camp of the Mind." Pp. 318–330 in *Society As It Is.* Ed. by Glen Gaviglio and David E. Raye. New York: Macmillan.
Moody, Edward J.
    1977: "Urban Witches." Pp. 427–437 in *Conformity and Conflict.* 3d ed. Ed. by James P. Spradley and David W. McCurdy. Boston: Little, Brown and Company.
Mooney, James
    1965: *The Ghost-Dance Religion and the Souix Outbreak of 1890.* Abridged by Anthony F. C. Wallace. Chicago: University of Chicago Press.
Morgan, James N., Martin H. David, Wilbur J. Cohen, and Harvey E. Brazer
    1962: *Income and Welfare in the United States.* New York: McGraw-Hill.
Moseley, Romney M.
    1978: *Religious Conversion: A Structural-Developmental Analysis.* Ph. D. dissertation, Harvard University.
Mosse, George L.
    1978: *Toward the Final Solution: A History of European Racism.* New York: Harper & Row.
Muelder, Walter G.
    1961: *Methodism and Society in the Twentieth Century.* Nashville: Abingdon Press.
Mueller, Charles W., and Weldon T. Johnson
    1975: "Socioeconomic Status and Religious Participation." *American Sociological Review* (December):785–800.
Mueller, G. H.
    1980: "The Dimensions of Religiosity." *Sociological Analysis* (Spring):1–24.

Mueller, Samuel A.
1971a: "Dimensions of Interdenominational Mobility in the United States." *Journal for the Scientific Study of Religion* (Summer):76–84.
1971b: "The New Triple Melting Pot: Herberg Revisited." *Review of Religious Research* (Fall):18–33.

Mueller, Samuel A., and Angela V. Lane
1972: "Tabulations from the 1957 Current Population Survey on Religion: A Contribution to the Demography of American Religion." *Journal for the Scientific Study of Religion* (March):76–98.

Munsey, Brenda, ed.
1980: *Moral Development, Moral Education, and Kohlberg.* Birmingham, Ala.: Religious Education Press.

Murray, Margaret
1921: *The Witch-cult in Western Europe.* London: Oxford University Press.
1952: *God of the Witches.* 2nd ed. London: Oxford University Press.

Murvar, Vatro
1975: "Toward a Sociological Theory of Religious Movements." *Journal for the Scientific Study of Religion* (September):229–256.

Myrdal, Gunnar
1944: *An American Dilemma.* New York: Harper & Row.

Neal, Marie Augusta
1975: "Women in Religion: A Sociological Perspective." *Sociological Inquiry* (December):33–45.

Needleman, Jacob
1970: *The New Religions.* Garden City, N.Y.: Doubleday.

Neihardt, John G.
1961: *Black Elk Speaks.* Lincoln, Neb.: University of Nebraska Press.

Nelson, Geoffrey
1968: "The Concept of Cult." *Sociological Review* (November):351–363.

Nelson, Hart M.
1973: "Intellectualism and Religious Attendance of Metropolitan Residents." *Journal for the Scientific Study of Religion* (September):285–296.

Nelson, Hart M., Robert F. Everett, Paul Douglas Mader, and Warren C. Hamby
1976: "A Test of Yinger's Measure of Non-Doctrinal Religion: Implications for Invisible Religion as a Belief System." *Journal for the Scientific Study of Religion* (September):263–268.

Nelson, Hart M., Thomas W. Madron, and Raytha L. Yokley
1975: "Black Religion's Promethean Motif: Orthodoxy and Militancy." *American Journal of Sociology* (July):139–146.

Nelson, Hart M., and William E. Snizek
1976: "Musical Pews: Rural and Urban Models of Occupational and Religious Mobility." *Sociology and Social Research* (April):279–289.

Nelson, Hart M., and Hugh P. Whitt
    1972: "Religion and the Migrant in the City: A Test of Holt's Cultural Shock
    Thesis." *Social Forces* (March):379–384.

Nelson, Mary
    1975: "Why Witches Were Women." Pp. 335–350 in *Women: A Feminist
    Perspective*. Ed. by Jo Freeman. Palo Alto, Calif.: Mayfield.

Newport, Frank
    1979: "The Religious Switcher in the United States." *American Sociological Review*
    (August):528–552.

Niebuhr, H. Richard
    1951: *Christ and Culture*. New York: Harper & Row.
    1957: *The Social Sources of Denominationalism*. New York: Meridian Books.
    (Originally published in 1929 by Henry Holt and Company.)
    1960a: *Radical Monotheism and Western Culture*. New York: Harper & Row.
    Copyright 1942, 1952, © 1955, 1960 by H. Richard Niebuhr. Reprinted
    by permission of Harper & Row, Publishers, Inc.
    1960b: "Faith in God and in Gods." Pp. 114–126 in *Radical Monotheism and
    Western Culture*. New York: Harper & Row.

Nietzsche, Friedrich
    1924: *The Birth of Tragedy*. New York: Macmillan (originally published in
    German in 1872).

Nordhoff, Charles
    1966: *The Communistic Societies of the United States*. New York: Dover
    Publications.

Noss, John B.
    1949: *Man's Religions*. New York: Macmillan.

Nottingham, Elizabeth K.
    1971: *Religion: A Sociological View*. New York: Random House.

Noyes, John Humphrey
    1966: *Strange Cults and Utopias of 19th Century America*. New York: Dover
    Publications.

Oates, Wayne E.
    1955: *Religious Factors in Mental Illness*. New York: Association Press.

O'Dea, Thomas F.
    1957: *The Mormons*. Chicago: University of Chicago Press.
    1961: "Five Dilemmas in the Institutionalization of Religion." *Journal for the
    Scientific Study of Religion* (October):30–39.
    1966: *The Sociology of Religion*. Englewood Cliffs, N.J.: Prentice-Hall. Reprinted
    by permission of Prentice-Hall, Inc.
    1968: "Sects and Cults." Pp. 130–136 in *International Encyclopedia of the Social
    Sciences*. Vol. 14. New York: Macmillan.

Ofshe, Richard
    1980: "The Social Development of the Synanon Cult: The Managerial Strategy
    of Organizational Transformation." *Sociological Analysis* (Summer):109–127.

Ogburn, William F.
  1950: *Social Change.* New York: Viking.

Organic, Harold Nathan
  1963: *Religious Affiliation and Social Mobility in Contemporary American Society: A National Study.* Ph. D. dissertation, University of Michigan.

Otto, Rudolf
  1923: *The Idea of the Holy.* Rev. ed. Trans. by John W. Harvey. London: Oxford University Press.

Pahnke, Walter N.
  1963: *Drugs and Mysticism: An Analysis of the Relationship between Mystical Consciousness and Psychedelic Drugs.* Ph. D. dissertation, Harvard University.

Parker, Robert Allerton
  1935: *A Yankee Saint: John Humphrey Noyes and the Oneida Community.* New York: G. P. Putnam's Sons.

Parsons, Talcott
  1955: *Essays in Sociological Theory.* Rev. ed. Glencoe, Ill.: Free Press.
  1964: "Christianity in Modern Industrial Society." Pp. 233–70 in *Sociological Theory, Values, and Sociocultural Change.* Ed. by Edward Tiryakian. Glencoe, Ill.: Free Press.

Parsons, Talcott and Edward A. Shols, eds.
  1951: *Toward a General Theory of Action.* Cambridge, Mass.: Harvard University Press.

Parvey, Constance F.
  1974: "The Theology and Leadership of Women in the New Testament." Pp. 117–149 in *Religion and Sexism.* Ed. by Rosemary Radford Ruether. New York: Simon & Schuster.

Perry, William G., Jr.
  1970: *Forms of Intellectual and Ethical Development in the College Years.* New York: Holt, Rinehart & Winston.

Piaget, Jean
  1950: *The Psychology of Intelligence.* London: Routledge & Kegan Paul.
  1954: *The Construction of Reality in the Child.* New York: Basic Books.

Poblete, Renato, and Thomas F. O'Dea
  1960: "Anomie and the 'Quest for Community': The Formation of Sects Among the Puerto Ricans of New York." *American Catholic Sociological Review* (Spring):18–36.

Polanyi, Michael
  1946: *Science, Faith, and Society.* Chicago: University of Chicago Press.
  1949: "The Nature of Scientific Convictions." Pp. 49–66 in *Scientific Thought and Reality.* Ed. by Fred Schwartz. New York: International Universities Press.

Poloma, Margaret M.
  1982a: *The Charismatic Movement: Is There a New Pentacost?* Boston: Twayne Publishers.

1982b: "Toward a Christian Sociological Perspective: Religious Values, Theory and Methodology." *Sociological Analysis* (Summer):95–108.

Pope, Liston
1942: *Millhands and Preachers.* New Haven: Yale University Press.

Porter, John
1965: *The Vertical Mosaic.* Toronto: University of Toronto Press.

Pratt, James Bissett
1964: "Objective and Subjective Worship." Pp. 143–156 in *Religion, Culture, and Society.* Ed. by Louis Schneider. New York: John Wiley & Sons.

Princeton Religion Research Center
1980: *Religion in America: 1979–80.* Princeton, N.J.: Princeton Religion Research Center.
1981: *Religion in America, 1981.* Princeton, N.J.: Princeton Religion Research Center.

Radcliffe-Brown, A. R.
1939: *Taboo.* Cambridge, Mass.: Harvard University Press.

Redekop, Calvin
1974: "A New Look at Sect Development." *Journal for the Scientific Study of Religion* (September):345–352.

Riccio, James A.
1979: "Religious Affiliation and Socioeconomic Achievement." Pp. 179–228 in *The Religious Dimension.* Ed. by Robert Wuthnow. New York: Academic Press.

Richardson, James T., and Mary Stewart
1977: "Conversion Process Models and the Jesus Movement." *American Behavioral Scientist* (July):819–838.

Richardson, James T., Mary White Stewart, and Robert B. Simmonds
1978: "Conversion to Fundamentalism." *Society* (May/June):46–52.
1979: *Organized Miracles.* New Brunswick, N.J.: Transaction Books.

Richey, Russell E., and Donald G. Jones, eds.
1974: *American Civil Religion.* New York: Harper & Row.

Rigney, Daniel, Richard Machalek, and Jerry D. Goodman
1978: "Is Secularization a Discontinuous Process?" *Journal for the Scientific Study of Religion* (December):381–387.

Robbins, Thomas
1969: "Eastern Mysticism and the Resocialization of Drug Users." *Journal for the Scientific Study of Religion* (Fall):1308–1317.

Robbins, Thomas, and Dick Anthony
1972: "Getting Straight with Meher Baba." *Journal for the Scientific Study of Religion* (June):122–140.
1978: "New Religions, Families, and Brainwashing." *Society* (May/June):77–83.

Robbins, Thomas, and Dick Anthony, eds.
1981: *In Gods We Trust: New Patterns of Religious Pluralism in America.* New Brunswick, N.J.: Transaction Books.

Robertson, H. M.
 1959: *Aspects of the Rise of Economic Individualism: A Criticism of Max Weber and His School.* New York: Kelley & Millman. (Originally published in 1933.)

Robinson, John
 1963: *Honest to God.* Philadelphia: Westminster Press.

Rokeach, Milton
 1968: "The Nature of Attitudes." in *Beliefs, Attitudes and Values.* Ed. by Milton Rokeach. San Francisco: Jossey-Bass.

Rokeach, Milton, Patricia W. Smith, and Richard I. Evans
 1960: "Two Kinds of Prejudice or One?" Pp. 132–168 in *The Open and Closed Mind.* Ed. by Milton Rokeach. New York: Basic Books.

Roof, Wade Clark
 1974: "Religious Orthodoxy and Minority Prejudice: Causal Relationship or Reflection of Localistic View." *American Journal of Sociology* (November):643–664.
 1976: "Traditional Religion in Contemporary Society: A Theory of Local-Cosmopolitan Plausibility." *American Sociological Review* (April):195–208.
 1978: *Commitment and Community.* New York: Elsevier.
 1979: "Socioeconomic Differentials Among White Socioreligious Groups in the United States." *Social Forces* (September):280–289. Reprinted by permission of The University of North Carolina Press.

Roof, Wade Clark, Christopher Kirk Hadaway, Myrna L. Hewitt, Douglas McGaw, and Richard Morse
 1977: "Yinger's Measure of Non-Doctrinal Religion: A Northeastern Test." *Journal for the Scientific Study of Religion* (December):403–408.

Rowley, Peter
 1971: *New Gods in America.* New York: McKay.

Ruether, Rosemary Radford
 1974a: *Faith and Fratricide: The Theological Roots of Anti-Semitism.* New York: Seabury Press.
 1974b: "The Persecution of Witches." *Christianity and Crises* (December 23):291–295.
 1974c: "Misogynism and Virginal Feminism in the Fathers of the Church." Pp. 150–183 in *Religion and Sexism.* Ed. by Rosemary Radford Ruether. New York: Simon & Schuster.
 1975: *New Woman, New Earth.* New York: Seabury Press.

Ruether, Rosemary Radford, ed.
 1974d: *Religion and Sexism.* New York: Simon and Schuster.

Ruether, Rosemary Radford, and Rosemary Skinner Keller
 1981: *Women and Religion in America. Vol. 1: The Nineteenth Century.* San Francisco: Harper & Row.

Ruether, Rosemary, and Eleanor McLaughlin, eds.
 1979: *Women of Spirit: Female Leadership in the Jewish and Christian Traditions.* New York: Simon & Schuster.

Runda, John, and John Seidler
 1980: "Religion and Prejudice: New Evidence and a New Interpretation."

Paper presented to Society for the Scientific Study of Religion. Cincinnati, November 2.

Samuelsson, Kurt
1961: *Religion and Economic Action.* Trans. by E. Geoffrey French. New York: Basic Books. (Originally published in Sweden in 1957.)

Sanua, Victor D.
1969: "Religion, Mental Health, and Personality: A Review of Empirical Studies." *American Journal of Psychiatry* (March):1203–1213.

Schneider, Herbert
1952: *Religion in 20th Century America.* Cambridge, Mass.: Harvard University Press.

Schneider, Louis
1970: *Sociological Approach to Religion.* New York: John Wiley & Sons.

Schneider, Louis, ed.
1964: *Religion, Culture and Society.* New York: John Wiley & Sons.

Schneider, Louis, and Sanford M. Dornbusch
1958: *Popular Religion.* Chicago: University of Chicago Press.

Schreiber, William I.
1962: *Our Amish Neighbors.* Chicago: University of Chicago Press.

Schuman, Howard
1971: "The Religious Factor in Detroit: Review, Replication, and Reanalysis." *American Sociological Review* (February):30–48.

Seidman, Ann
1979: "Why U.S. Corporations Should Get Out of South Africa." *Issue: A Quarterly Journal of Africanist Opinion* (Spring/Summer):37–41.

Shannon, William
1963: *The American Irish.* New York: Macmillan.

Sherif, Carolyn Wood
1976: *Orientation in Social Psychology.* New York: Harper & Row.

Shupe, Anson D., Jr., and David G. Bromley
1978: "Witches, Moonies and Evil." *Society* (May/June):75–76.
1979: "The Moonies and the Anti-Cultists: Movement and Countermovement in Conflict." *Sociological Analysis* (Winter):325–334.
1980: *The New Vigilantes: Deprogrammers, Anti-Cultists, and the New Religions.* Beverly Hills, Calif.: Sage.

Shupe, Anson, and William A. Stacey
1982: *Born Again Politics and the Moral Majority.* New York: Edwin Mellen Press.

Singer, Margaret Thaler
1979: "Coming Out of the Cults." *Psychology Today* (January):72–83.

Smelser, Neil J.
1962: *Theory of Collective Behavior.* New York: Free Press.

Smith, Carole R., Lev Williams, and Richard H. Willis
   1967: "Race, Sex, and Belief as Determinants of Friendship Acceptance."
   Journal of Personality and Social Psychology (February):127–137.

Smith, Huston
   1958: *The Religions of Man.* New York: Harper & Row.

Snow, David A., and Cynthia L. Phillips
   1980: "The Lofland-Stark Conversion Model: A Critical Reassessment." *Social
   Problems* (April):430–447.

Southwold, Martin
   1982: "True Buddhism and Village Buddhism in Sri Lanka." Pp. 137–152
   in *Religious Organization and Religious Experience.* Ed. by John Davis. London:
   Academic Press.

Spiro, Melford
   1966: "Religion: Problems of Definition and Explanation." Pp. 85–126 in
   Anthropological Approaches to the Study of Religion. Ed. by Michael Banton.
   London: Tavistock.
   1970: *Buddhism and Society.* New York: Harper & Row.
   1978: *Burmese Supernaturalism.* Philadelphia: Institute for the Study of Human
   Issues.

Sprenger, Jakob, and Henry Kramer
   1970: *Malleus Maleficarum.* Ed. and trans. by Montague Summers. New York:
   Benjamin Blom. (Originally published in 1486.)

Spretnak, Charlene, ed.
   1982: *The Politics of Women's Spirituality.* Garden City, N.Y.: Anchor Press.

Stark, Rodney
   1964: "Class, Radicalism, and Religious Involvement." *American Sociological
   Review* (October):698–706.
   1971: "Psychopathology and Religious Commitment." *Review of Religious
   Research* (Spring):165–176.
   1972: "The Economics of Piety: Religious Commitment and Social Class."
   Pp. 483–503 in *Issues in Social Inequality.* Ed. by Gerald W. Thielbar and
   Saul D. Feldman. Boston: Little, Brown.

Stark, Rodney, and William Sims Bainbridge
   1979: "Of Churches, Sects and Cults: Preliminary Concepts for a Theory of
   Religious Movements." *Journal for the Scientific Study of Religion* (June):119–
   121.

Stark, Rodney, Bruce D. Foster, Charles Y. Glock, and Harold E. Quinley
   1973: "Ministers as Moral Guides: The Sounds of Silence." Pp. 163–186 in
   Religion in Sociological Perspective. Ed. by Charles Y. Glock. Belmont, Calif.:
   Wadsworth.

Stark, Rodney, and Charles Y. Glock
   1968: *American Piety: The Nature of Religious Commitment.* Berkeley: University
   of California Press.

1969: "Prejudice and the Churches." Pp. 70–95 in *Prejudice U.S.A.* Ed. by Charles Y. Glock and Ellen Siegelman. New York: Praeger Publishers.

Stark, Rodney, and Lynne Roberts
1982: "The Arithmetic of Social Movements: Theoretical Implications." *Sociological Analysis* (Spring):53–67.

Stark, Werner
1967: *Sectarian Religion.* Vol. 2, *The Sociology of Religion: A Study of Christendom.* New York: Fordham University Press.

Steinberg, Milton
1947: *Basic Judaism.* New York: Harcourt Brace and World.

Steinberg, Stephen
1965: "Reform Judaism: The Origin and Evolution of a 'Church Movement.' " *Journal for the Scientific Study of Religion* (October):117–129.

Stevens, Edward
1974: *The Morals Game.* New York: Paulist Press.

Straus, Roger A.
1979: "Religious Conversion as a Personal and Collective Accomplishment." *Sociological Analysis* (Summer):158–165.

Streiker, Lowell and Gerald Strober
1972: *Religion and the New Majority.* New York: Association Press.

Swatos, William H., Jr.
1976: "Weber or Troeltsch? Methodology, Syndrome, and Development of Church-Sect Theory." *Journal for the Scientific Study of Religion* (June):129–144.

Talmon, Yonina
1965: "The Pursuit of the Millennium: The Relation Between Religion and Social Change." Pp. 522–537 in *Reader in Comparative Religion.* 2nd ed. Ed. by William A. Lessa and Evon Z. Vogt. New York: Harper & Row.

Tavard, George H.
1973: *Woman in Christian Tradition.* South Bend, Ind.: University of Notre Dame Press.

Tawney, R. H.
1954: *Religion and Capitalism.* New York: New American Library. (Originally published in 1924.)

Tedlin, Kent
1978: "Religious Preference and Pro/Anti Activism on the Equal Rights Amendment Issue." *Pacific Sociological Review* (January):55–66.

Thomas, Michael, and C. C. Flippen
1972: "American Civil Religion: An Empirical Study." *Social Forces* (December):218–225.

Thornton, Arland, and Deborah Freedman
1979: "Changes in the Sex Role Attitudes of Women, 1962–1977: Evidence From a Panel Study." *American Sociological Review* (October):831–842.

Tillich, Paul
 1957: *Dynamics of Faith.* New York: Harper & Row.

Titiev, Mischa
 1972: "A Fresh Approach to the Problem of Magic and Religion." Pp. 430–433 in *Reader in Comparative Religion: An Anthropological Approach.* 3rd ed. Ed. by William A. Lessa and Evon Z. Vogt. New York: Harper & Row.

Trevor-Roper, Hugh
 1967: "Witches and Witchcraft." *Encounter* (June):13–34.

Trible, Phyllis
 1979: "Eve and Adam: Genesis 2–3 Reread." Pp. 74–83 in *Womanspirit Rising.* Ed. by Carol P. Christ and Judith Plaskow. New York: Harper & Row.

Troeltsch, Ernst
 1931: *The Social Teachings of the Christian Churches.* 2 vols. Trans. by Olive Wyon, with an introduction by H. Richard Niebuhr. New York: Macmillan. (Reprint ed., New York: Harper & Row, 1961; originally printed in German in 1911.)

Turner, Jonathan H., and Alexandra Maryanski
 1979: *Functionalism.* Menlo Park, Calif.: Benjamin/Cummings.

Tyler, Edward B.
 1958: *Primitive Culture.* Vol. II. New York: Harper & Row. (Originally published in London: John Murray, 1873.)

Ulrich, Laurel Thatcher
 1980: "Vertuous Women Found: New England Ministerial Literature, 1668–1735." Pp. 67–87 in *Women in American Religion.* Ed. by Janet Wilson James. Philadelphia: University of Pennsylvania Press.

Ungerleider, J. Thomas and David K. Wellisch
 1979: "Coercive Persuasion (Brainwashing), Religious Cults, and Deprogramming." *American Journal of Psychiatry* (March):279–282.

Van Der Post, Laurens
 1955: *The Dark Eye in Africa.* New York: William Morrow.

Vander Zanden, James W.
 1972: *American Minority Relations.* 3rd ed. New York: Ronald Press.

Vogt, Evon Z.
 1952: "Water Witching: An Interpretation of a Ritual Pattern in a Rural American Community." *Scientific Monthly* (September):175–186.

Walker, Williston
 1970: *A History of the Christian Church.* 3rd ed. New York: Charles Scribner's Sons.

Wallace, Anthony F. C.
 1966: *Religion: An Anthropological View.* New York: Random House.
 1972: "Revitalization Movements." Pp. 503–512 in *Reader in Comparative Religion: An Anthropological Approach.* 3rd ed. Ed. by William A. Lessa and Evon Z. Vogt. New York: Harper & Row.

Wallace, Ruth
　　1975: "Bringing Women In: Marginality in the Churches." *Sociological Analysis* (Winter):291–303.

Wallis, Roy
　　1977: *The Road to Total Freedom: A Sociological Analysis of Scientology.* New York: Columbia University Press.

Warner, W. Lloyd
　　1953: *American Life: Dream and Reality.* Chicago: University of Chicago Press.
　　1961: *Family of God: A Symbolic Study of Christian Life in America.* New Haven: Yale University Press.

Warren, Bruce L.
　　1970: "Socioeconomic Achievement and Religion: The American Case." Pp. 130–155 in *Social Stratification.* Ed. by Edward O. Lanmann. Indianapolis: Bobbs-Merrill.

Washington, Joseph R., Jr.
　　1964: *Black Religion.* Boston: Beacon Press.
　　1972: *Black Sects and Cults.* Garden City, N.Y.: Doubleday.

Weaver, Horace R.
　　1975: *Getting Straight About the Bible.* Nashville: Abingdon Press.

Weber, Max
　　1946: *From Max Weber: Essays in Sociology.* Ed. and trans. by Hans H. Gerth and C. Wright Mills. New York: Oxford University Press.
　　1947: *The Theory of Social and Economic Organization.* Ed. and trans. by A. M. Henderson and Talcott Parsons. New York: Oxford University Press. Copyright © 1947, renewed 1975 by Talcott Parsons. (Originally published in 1925.)
　　1951: *The Religion of China.* Trans. by Hans H. Gerth. New York: Free Press. (Originally published in 1920–21.)
　　1952: *Ancient Judaism.* Trans. and ed. by Hans H. Gerth and Don Martindale. New York: Free Press. (Originally published in 1920–1921.)
　　1958a: *The Protestant Ethic and the Spirit of Capitalism.* Trans. by Talcott Parsons. New York: Charles Schribner's Sons. (Originally published in 1904–1905.)
　　1958b: *The Religion of India.* Trans. and ed. by Hans H. Gerth and Don Martindale. New York: Free Press. (Originally published in 1920–1921.)
　　1963: *The Sociology of Religion.* Trans. by Ephraim Fischoff. Boston: Beacon Press. (Originally published in 1922.)

Weigert, Andrew J., and Thomas L. Darwin
　　1970: "Secularization: A Cross-National Study of Catholic Male Adolescents." *Social Forces* (September):28–36.

Welch, Susan
　　1975: "Support Among Women for the Issues of the Women's Movement." *Sociological Quarterly* (Spring):216–227.

Weller, Neil J.
　　1963: *Religion and Social Mobility in Industrial Society.* Ph. D. dissertation, University of Michigan.

Welter, Barbara
    1976: "The Feminization of American Religion, 1800–1860." In *Dimity Convictions*. Athens: Ohio University Press.

Wesley, John
    1943: *Selections from the Writings of the Rev. John Wesley, M. A.* Compiled and arranged by Herbert Welch. Nashville: Abingdon Press.

Westie, Frank
    1965: "The American Dilemma: An Empirical Test." *American Sociological Review* (August):527–538.

Whitehead, Harriet
    1974: "Reasonably Fantastic: Some Perspectives on Scientology, Science Fiction, and Occultism." Pp. 547–587 in *Religious Movements in Contemporary America*. Ed. by Irving I. Zaretsky and Mark P. Leone. Princeton, N.J.: Princeton University Press.

Wilcox, Mary M.
    1979: *Developmental Journey: A Guide to the Development of Logical and Moral Reasoning and Social Perspective*. Nashville: Abingdon Press.

Williamson, Clark M.
    1982: *Has God Rejected His People? Anti-Judaism in the Christian Church*. Nashville: Abingdon Press.

Wilmore, Gayraud S.
    1972: *Black Religion and Black Radicalism*. Garden City, N.Y.: Doubleday.

Wilson, Bryan R.
    1959: "An Analysis of Sect Development." *American Sociological Review* (February):3–15.
    1967: "The Pentecostal Minister: Role Conflicts and Contradictions of Status." Pp. 138–157 in *Patterns of Sectarianism*. Ed. by Bryan R. Wilson. London: Heinemann.
    1970: *Religious Sects*. New York: McGraw-Hill.

Wilson, John
    1978: *Religion in American Society*. Englewood Cliffs, N.J.: Prentice-Hall.

Wimberley, Ronald C.
    1976: "Testing the Civil Religion Hypothesis." *Sociological Analysis* (Winter):341–352.

Wimberley, Ronald C. and James A. Christianson
    1981: "Civil Religion and Other Religious Identities." *Sociological Analysis* (Summer):91–100.

Wimberley, Ronald C., Donald A. Clelland, and Thomas C. Hood
    1976: "The Civil Religious Dimension: Is It There?" *Social Forces* (June):890–900.

Wimberley, Ronald C., Thomas C. Hood, C. M. Lipsey, Donald Clelland, and Marguerite Hay
    1975: "Conversion in a Billy Graham Crusade: Spontaneous Event or Ritual Action?" *The Sociological Quarterly* (Spring):162–170.

Winter, J. Alan
   1977: *Continuities in the Sociology of Religion*. New York: Harper & Row.

Wood, James R.
   1970: "Authority and Controversial Policy: The Churches and Civil Rights."
      American Sociological Review (December):1057–1069.
   1972: "Personal Commitment and Organization Constraint: Church Officials
      and Racial Integration." *Sociological Analysis* (Fall):142–151.

Wood, Ralph W., Jr.
   1970: "Religious Orientation and the Report of Religious Experience." *Journal
      for the Scientific Study of Religion* (Winter):285–291.

Wuthnow, Robert
   1973: "New Forms of Religion in the Seminary." Pp. 187–203 in *Religion in
      Sociological Perspective*. Ed. by Charles Y. Glock. Belmont, Calif.: Wadsworth.
   1976a: "Astrology and Marginality." *Journal for the Scientific Study of Religion*
      (June):157–168.
   1976b: *The Consciousness Reformation*. Berkley: University of California Press.
   1976c: "Recent Pattern of Secularization: A Problem of Generations?" *American
      Sociological Review* (October):850–867.
   1981: "Two Traditions of Religious Studies." *Journal for the Scientific Study of
      Religion* (March):16–32.

Yeatts, John R., and William Asher
   1979: "Can We Afford Not to Do True Experiments in Psychology of Religion?
      A Reply to Batson." *Journal for the Scientific Study of Religion* (March):86–
      89.

Yinger, J. Milton.
   1957: *Religion, Society, and the Individual*. New York: Macmillan.
   1969: "A Structural Examination of Religion." *Journal for the Scientific Study of
      Religion* (Spring):88–100.
   1970: *The Scientific Study of Religion*. New York: Macmillan. Reprinted by
      permission of Macmillan Publishing Co., Inc. Copyright © 1970 by J. Milton
      Yinger.
   1977: "A Comparative Study of the Substructure of Religion." *Journal for the
      Scientific Study of Religion* (March):67–86.

Yinger, J. Milton, and Stephen J. Cutler
   1982: "The Moral Majority Viewed Sociologically." *Sociological Focus*
      (October):289–306.

Zablocki, Benjamin
   1971: *The Joyful Community: An Account of the Bruderhof*. Baltimore: Penguin
      Books.

Zaechner, R. C., ed.
   1967: *The Concise Encyclopedia of Living Faith*. Boston: Beacon Press.

Zald, Mayer N., and Roberta Ash
   1966: "Social Movement Organizations: Growth, Decay and Change." *Social
      Forces* (March):327–341.

Zald, Mayer N., and Michael A. Berger
 1978: "Social Movements in Organizations: Coup d'etat, Insurgency, and Mass Movements." *American Journal of Sociology* (January):823–861.

Zaretsky, Irving I., and Mark P. Leone
 1974: *Religious Movements in Contemporary America.* Princeton, N.J.: Princeton University Press.

Zygmunt, Joseph F.
 1970: "Prophetic Failure and Chiliastic Identity: The Case of the Jehovah's Witnesses." *American Journal of Sociology* (May):926–948.

Index

This book was set CAP in 10 and 9 point Garamond, leaded 2 points. Chapter numbers are 60 point Garamond Bold Condensed and chapter titles are 18 point Garamond Bold Condensed. The size of the type page is 27 by 47 picas.